People, Livelihoods, and Development in the Xekong River Basin, Laos

People, Livelihoods, and Development in the Xekong River Basin, Laos

Ian G. Baird
and
Bruce Shoemaker

White Lotus Press

White Lotus Co., Ltd
G.P.O. Box 1141
Bangkok 10501
Thailand

Tel.   (66) 0-38239-883-4
Fax   (66) 0-38239-885
E-mail   ande@loxinfo.co.th
Website   http://thailine.com/lotus

Printed in Thailand

Designed and typeset by COMSET Limited Partnership

ISBN   978-974-480-114-2   pbk.   White Lotus Co., Ltd., Bangkok

Table of Contents

List of Illustrations

List of Maps

List of Plates

2.1.   The Xekong River in Samakhixay District, Attapeu Province.
2.2.   The Xekong River in Kalum District, Xekong Province.
2.3.   One of the many rapids in the Xekong River in Kalum District, Xekong Province. Rapids provide important fish habitat and are popular fishing spots for local communities.
2.4.   Ethnic Ngkriang man and woman in Kalum District, Xekong Province.
2.5.   Ethnic Ye men in Dakchung District, Xekong Province.
2.6.   Three ethnic Katu Dak Kang elders in Dakchung District, Xekong Province.
2.7.   Ethnic Brao Hamong elder from Phouvong District, Attapeu Province.
2.8.   Two ethnic Katu men blow into either ends of a traditional variety of musical flute.
2.9.   Ethnic Brao Jree man plays traditional string instrument in Phouvong District, Attapeu Province.

List of Tables

List of Boxes

Abbreviations

ACF	Action contre la faim (INGO)
ADB	Asian Development Bank
ADP	Agriculture Development Project (World Bank)
ADRA	Adventist Development and Relief Agency International (INGO)
AIPP	Asian Indigenous People's Pact (INGO)
ALP	Austral-Lao Power Company
AMRC	Australian Mekong Resource Centre
APB	Agriculture Promotion Bank of Lao PDR
APSTEO	Attapeu Provincial Science, Technology and Environment Office
ASEAN	Association of Southeast Asian Nations
asl	above sea level
BOT	Build, Operate and Transfer Investment Project
BOOT	Build, Own, Operate and Transfer Investment Project (essentially the same as a BOT project)
CAOM	Centre des Archives d'Outre-mer (Centre for Archives from Overseas), Aix-en-Provence, France
CIA	Central Intelligence Agency of the United States of America
CITES	Convention on the International Trade in Endangered Species
ComFish	Community Fisheries: Supporting Food Security and Aquatic Biodiversity (WWF Project)
CMLN	Co-Management Learning Network
CPUE	Catch-Per-Unit-Effort
CUSO	Name of Canadian INGO (formerly an acronym: Canadian University Services Overseas)
DAFI	Development of Agriculture and Forestry Industry
dbh	Diameter at breast height (for tree measurements)

Abbreviations

DED	Deutscher Entwicklungsdienst (German volunteer agency)
EdL	Electricité du Lao
EGAT	Electricity-generating Authority of Thailand
EIA	Environmental Impact Assessment
EVN	Electricité du Vietnam
FAO	Food and Agriculture Organization of the United Nations
FCZ	Fish Conservation Zone
FMA	Forestry Management Area
FOMACOP	Forestry Management and Conservation Project
FRC	Forestry Research Centre (part of NAFRI)
GAPE	Global Association for People and the Environment (INGO)
GDP	Gross Domestic Product
GEF	Global Environmental Facility
GMS	Greater Mekong Subregion (ADB terminology for Cambodia, Vietnam, Laos, Thailand, Burma and southern China)
GoL	Government of Lao People's Democratic Republic; Government of Laos
GTZ	Deutsche Gesellschaft für Technische Zusammenarbeit (German government's aid agency)
HECEC	Hydroelectric Commission Enterprises Corporation (originally from Tasmania, Australia)
HHHP	Houay Ho Hydropower Project
HHPC	Houay Ho Power Company
HS1IP	Houay Samong 1 Irrigation Project
HS2IP	Houay Samong 2 Irrigation Project
ICC	International Christian Concern (INGO)
ICC	International Cooperation Committee (Geneva Accords)
ICP	Indochina Communist Party
IFAD	International Fund for Agriculture Development
INGO	International Non-Governmental Organization
IO	International Organization (i.e., UNDP, UNICEF, UNESCO, World Fish, etc.)
IRN	International Rivers Network (INGO)
IRRI	International Rice Research Institute
ITELCO	Information Technology Electricity Company of Japan
IUCN	The World Conservation Union
JBIC	Japan Bank for International Cooperation

JICA	Japanese International Cooperation Agency (Japanese government aid agency)
KPL	*Khaosan Pathet Lao* (news agency of the Government of Laos)
Kv	Kilovolt
LFNC	Lao Front for National Construction
LNMC	Lao National Mekong Committee
LNCE	Lao National Committee for Energy
LPRP	Lao People's Revolutionary Party
Lao PDR	Lao People's Democratic Republic
MACV-SOG	Military Assistance Command, Vietnam—Studies and Observation Group (secret division of US Army special forces)
MAF	Ministry of Agriculture and Forestry (Lao PDR)
MDB	Multilateral Development Bank (e.g., World Bank and ADB)
MIA	Missing in Action
MoU	Memorandum of Understanding
MRC	Mekong River Commission
MSG	Monosodium glutamate (a flavoring for food)
MWBP	Mekong Wetland Biodiversity Project (IUCN/MRC/UNDP/GEF project)
NAFES	National Agriculture and Forestry Extension Service
NAFRI	National Agriculture and Forestry Research Institute
NBCA	National Biodiversity Conservation Area (former name; now National Protected Area)
NCP	National Contact Point (in relation to the OECD)
NGO	Non-Government Organization
NPA	National Protected Area
NSC	National Statistical Centre
NVA	North Vietnamese Army
OECD	Overseas Economic Cooperation and Development Organization
PMO	Prime Minister's Office
PTOA	Power Trade Operating Agreement
PRF	Poverty Reduction Fund Project (World Bank project)
PS	Pakse site, a CIA designation for paramilitary sites in Military Region 4 in southern Laos
RLA	Royal Lao Army (up to 1975)
RLAF	Royal Lao Air Force (up to 1975)
RLG	Royal Lao Government

Abbreviations

RVN	Republic of Vietnam (South Vietnam up to 1975)
SC	Statistical Center
SGU	1st Special Guerilla Unit (US-financed and -advised unit on Bolaven Plateau during Second Indochina War)
SIDA	Swedish International Development Agency
SIP-Dev	Sekong Indigenous Peoples Development Programme (UNDP-supported development project in Xekong Province)
SK E&C	SK Engineering and Construction Company (South Korea Private Company)
SPC	State Planning Committee
STEA	Science, Technology and Environmental Agency of the GoL
SUFORD	Sustainable Forestry and Rural Development Project (World Bank project)
TFAP	Tropical Forestry Action Plan
TVIS	Thong Vay Irrigation Scheme
UNDP	United Nations Development Program
UNEP	United Nations Environment Program
USAF	United States Air force
UXO	Unexploded Ordnance
VIP	Village Investment for the Poor (a component of the World Bank's ADP)
VNA	Vietnam News Agency
VPFA	Village Protected Forest Area
WCS	Wildlife Conservation Society
WHO	World Health Organization of the United Nations
WWF	World Wide Fund for Nature
XEFOR	Xekong Sustainable Forestry Project (WWF Project)

Glossary of Lao Terms

Achan	Teacher, usually indicating that the person was once a Buddhist monk
Ban	Village
Ban Chat San	Resettlement site
Beung	Large natural pond
Chan	Short form for *Achan*
Chao	Title for members of the royal family
Chao Muang	District Chief (Chief of Principality in pre-colonial times)
Hin Lang	An area in southern Laos dominated by old volcanic rocks
Het	Mushroom
Houay	Stream
Keng	Rapids in river or stream
Kha	Literally, "slave"; very pejorative for Mon-Khmer language-speaking peoples *Khet* Sub-district or a particular area
Khet Chout Xoum	A focal site area (often associated with internal resettlement)
Khoum	Pit
Khoum Sang Pa	Pit in wetlands for catching fish
Khveng	Province
Kok	Tree
Kong	The equivalent to a district during the colonial period
Kout	Type of wetland with wetland forest
Lam	Intermediary between ethnic minorities and outsiders, often an ethnic Lao
Loum Pa	Pit in wetlands for catching fish
Mai	Tree or Wood
Meng	Insect

Mong	Gillnet
Muang	District or town (present) or principality (pre-colonial)
Nai Kong	Head of a *Kong* (see above)
Nam	River
Nam Keng	Seasonally inundated floodplain area
Nang	Ms
Noi	Small
Nok	Bird
Nong	Natural pond
Nyai	Large
Opharat	Deputy to *Chao Muang* during monarchy
Pa	Fish
Pa	Forest
Pa Dek	Fermented fish paste
Pa Sangouan	Protected forest area
Peuak	Bark
Phak	Edible vegetable / vegetation
Pha-nya	Dignitary
Pha Khou	Buddhist monk (*Phra Khru* in Thai)
Pho Thao	Grandfather / father-in-law / elder
Phou	Mountain or hill
Phou Phiang	Plateau
Phra	Designation for Buddhist monks
Phya	A person who represented the French in villages during colonial period
Prasat Hin	Stone stupa or "castle"
Tao	Turtle
Tat	Waterfalls
Thahan	Soldier
Thao	Mr
Thao	Type of filamentous algae
That	Stupa
Tavan Oke	East
Vang	Deep-water pool area
Vang Sangouan	Protected deep-water fish conservation area
Vat	Buddhist temple complex
Xe	River

Acknowledgements

We owe thanks to Richard Hackman, formerly of the Lao PDR/Canada Fund, Monty Sly from GAPE, and Martin Rathie for their assistance during field surveys, and for providing us with supplementary data about the Xekong River Basin. Thanks are also due to ACF for facilitating Ian G. Baird's trip to Kalum District in Xekong Province, including providing important logistical support. Peter Swift assisted by conducting supplemental field research, which has been incorporated into this book.

We are variously indebted to the following individuals: Phouvong Phetphaivanh, Bountiem Keophouvong, Somphong Bounphasy, Mark Dubois, Steeve Daviau, John L. Plaster, Jacqui Chagnon, Roger Rumpf, Joe Bennett, Eric Meusch, Constance Wilson, Alan Potkin, Monsiri Baird and Dot La-ounmuang for their assistance in providing important information; Rick Reece provided some general data regarding Salavan Province.

Various versions of this book were commented on in full or in part by Eric Meusch, Alan Potkin, Peter Swift, Richard Hackman, Martin Rathie and Joe Bennett. Thanks are owed to Laurent Jeanneau for translating French documents into English during archival research conducted at Aix-en-Provence.

Special thanks are due to Dave Hubbel for preparing the maps and for the important support he provided in editing a later version of the manuscript.

This book was prepared with funding from Oxfam America. Oxfam America promotes the generation of critical analysis and broader knowledge of key development and policy issues in the East Asia region. The views expressed in this volume do not necessarily represent those of Oxfam America. In addition, the views expressed in this book do not necessarily reflect the views of the Global Association for People and the Environment (GAPE) or any of GAPE's partners or funders.

Authors' Notes

I remember my first trip to the Xekong River Basin in Laos, arriving on a bumpy dirt road to Xekong town, dusty and treeless, but surrounded by impressive forest-covered mountains and situated adjacent to the Xekong River, which seemed so clear compared to the Mekong River, with which I was more familiar. The small market in Xekong was, as I remember it, full of large fish from the Xekong River. There were not as yet any hotels or guesthouses in town, so we were put up in a state-owned house next to the main road coming into town. A few days later I traveled from Xekong to Attapeu by army jeep (made in the USSR), which got stuck as we tried to cross the *Houay* Lamphan not far out of Xekong town. We had to push our vehicle out of the mud of the streambed. A little later, we bounced around inside the jeep as our driver skillfully negotiated us across the shallow but wide Xenamnoi River. Attapeu town was much more pleasant than Xekong, as there were many large trees growing along the sides of the town's main unpaved roads. It was a sleepy outpost with a slow pace, and it seemed like a much older place. In fact, it was, as Xekong town had only been carved out of the landscape by bulldozers a few years earlier, when Xekong Province was created out of parts of Salavan and Attapeu Provinces. The capital of Xekong had the feel of a "Wild West" frontier town.

From my very first trip to the Xekong basin in December 1991, I fell in love with it. I was fascinated by both the natural and cultural diversity that made the basin so special. I immediately wanted to spend more time there, and as it happened, I have spent quite a lot of time there. Things have changed a lot since my first trip. The main roads are now paved, and fifteen years has provided some time for at least some trees to grow along the roads. I still like the feel of Attapeu town more, but I learned long ago that it is the rural parts of both Xekong and Attapeu Provinces that are of particular interest to me. That is where most of the people live, and that is where the cultural and biological diversity is the greatest.

Ian G. Baird

I first visited the Xekong River Basin provinces of Attapeu and Xekong in 1990 while documenting the legacy of unexploded ordnance that heavily impacted the area. I remember the thick forests that lined the roads and the surprise of local officials that outside NGO staff were actually taking the considerable time required to visit the area. There was no running water or electricity in the Xekong provincial town and so we bathed in the Xekong River. While the Xekong basin region was not to be a central focus of my work in Laos, I ended up spending more time there in the late 1990s while documenting the impacts of hydropower projects recently constructed or under development. The region has always been of special interest and so, when Ian Baird approached me to assist in editing and providing some supplemental material for this study, I quickly agreed. The vast majority of the material presented here comes from his fieldwork and secondary research.

In March 2007, while engaged in finalizing my contribution to this study, I returned for a visit to the Xekong basin. It was my first time back in several years. While thick forests no longer line the roads of the region, the legacy of unexploded ordnance, alas, remains, and I heard new reports of UXO-related injuries and death. But what was most striking was the prospect of enormous and rapid change—unlike anything that has occurred in the past—that now appears likely to transform the people and the environment of the region in the near future. The prospect of that change provides new impetus for efforts to document the present-day situation and, to provide some insight for decision-makers so that those changes that do occur are in the best long-term interests of the region's people and environment.

Bruce Shoemaker

1

Introduction

The Xekong[1] River is one of the Mekong River's largest tributaries and is the only river apart from the mainstream Mekong that passes through parts of Vietnam,[2] Laos and Cambodia, the three countries whose territories once made up French Indochina. Together with the Sesan and Srepok Rivers, which both originate in the Central Highlands of Vietnam and flow through northeastern Cambodia, the Xekong contributes approximately 19% of the Mekong River's water volume (Halcrow 1999). The Srepok flows into the Sesan River, and the Sesan joins with the Xekong in Stung Treng Province, just a few kilometers before the Xekong River flows into the Mekong (Map 1).[3]

Despite the hydrological significance of the Xekong River Basin, there are no good summaries in any language of the livelihoods and rich cultures of the diverse peoples who inhabit the basin in Laos. This study is intended partly to fill the gap, although it will be impossible to cover everything of interest in this fascinating part of the world. The basin has mainly been referred to in the literature as a remote backwater and is frequently mentioned only in passing and in relation to more centralized places in the region like Champasak or Vientiane. Here, however, we hope to shift the focus, in order to make the margins of Laos the center of inquiry.

Originating in A loui District of Thua-Thien Hue Province in the Central Highlands of Vietnam, the Xekong River flows for only a short distance in that country before entering Laos, where it runs for approximately 320 km, and has a basin area of 22,960 km^2 (Map 2). It then enters Cambodia, where it flows for about 141 km to its confluence with the Mekong near Stung Treng town. The river has a watershed area of 5,105 km^2 in Cambodia, not including the Sesan and Srepok River basins.

The Xekong River Basin is endowed with considerable natural beauty, high biodiversity, and a large variety of ethnic identities. The basin has long been dominated by diverse Austroasiatic Mon-Khmer language-speaking groups, many

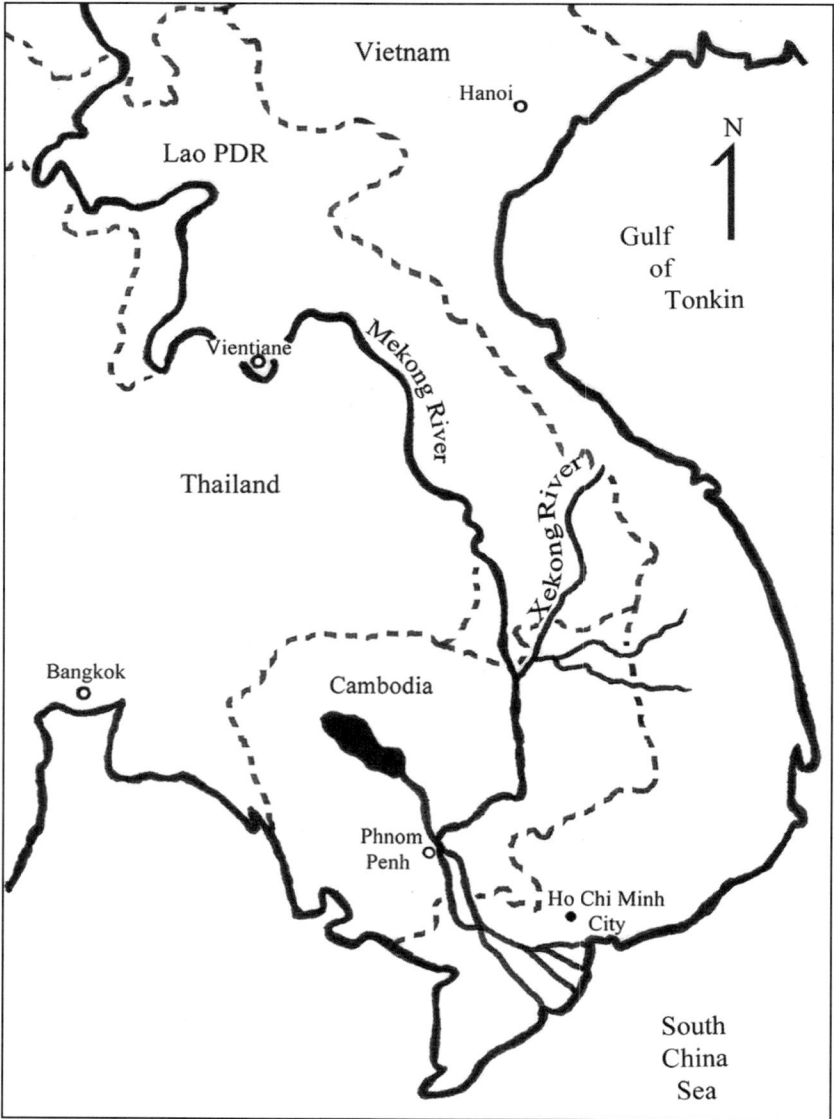

Map 1. The Xekong River

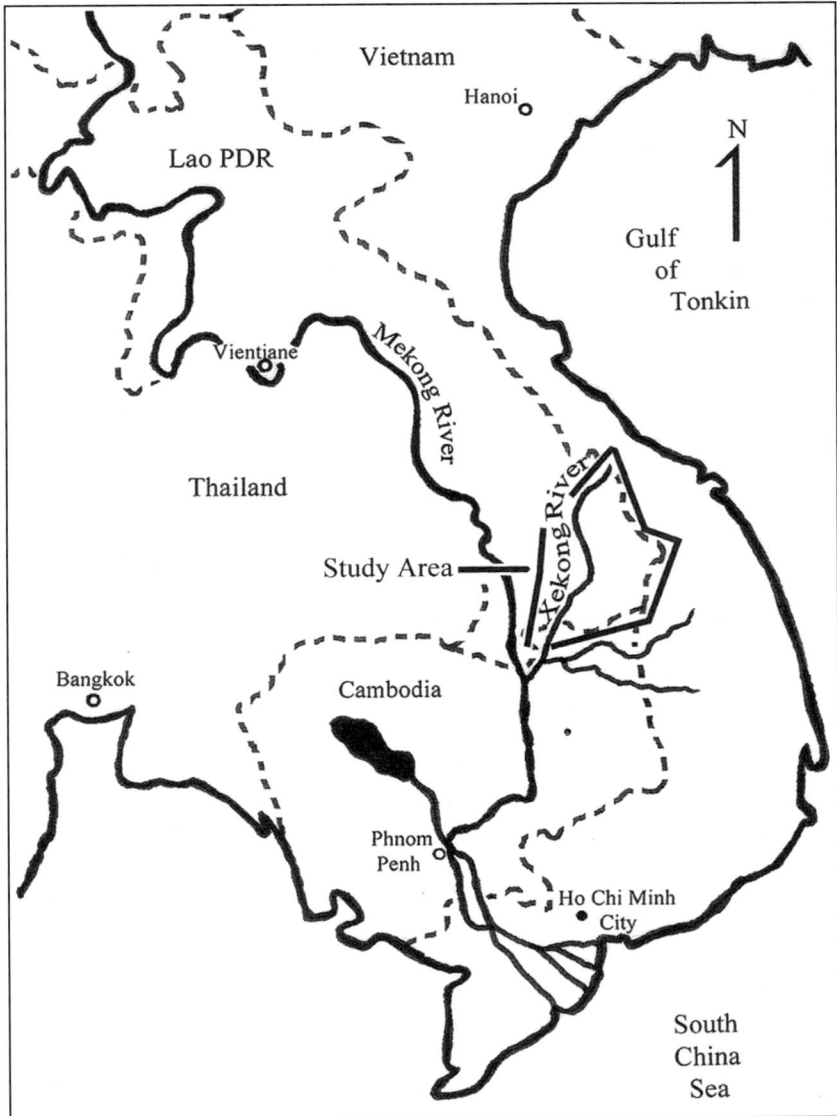

Map 2. The Xekong River Basin in Laos

of whom are believed to have resided in the area for over 5,000 years (Goudineau 2001; Xainyavong et al. 2003; LFNC 2005). Apart from the ethnic Lao people who have lived in the plains of Attapeu[4] Province for hundreds of years,[5] some ethnic Lao live in the Xekong basin in Pathoumphone District, Champasak Province, and some newcomers have relatively recently moved into the provincial capitals of Attapeu and Xekong.

There has been little ethnographic work done in the Xekong basin, especially considering the wide variety of ethnic groups found there, and there is certainly much to be learned about the people. Therefore, this book will only be able to scratch the surface of possibilities for future research.

The purpose of this study is to present a synopsis of the various factors related to the livelihoods of the diverse peoples who live in the Xekong River Basin in Laos. The study attempts to look at development and the environment as fundamentally interrelated issues. It considers a range of livelihood activities, including agriculture, forestry, fisheries, and other river-based livelihoods, as well as the different social, cultural, economic, political, ecological, and "development" issues affecting the people living in the basin. In other words, this study is essentially about the political ecology of development and livelihoods in the Xekong Basin in Laos, where political ecology is understood to represent a combination of political economy and ecology.

We have chosen to take a historical approach in presenting this story. The basin is changing rapidly as modernizing development becomes increasingly dominant at the same time as transportation and communication networks in the basin improve rapidly. While this study reports on the role of the Xekong River in livelihoods, the primary focus is not just to investigate the mainstream Xekong River, or river-based livelihoods, but to research its many tributaries and other areas of the Xekong basin, and issues of importance to people living in various parts of the basin. One of the main points of this study is to illustrate the necessity of considering a broad variety of livelihood activities in social, environmental, and development studies, rather than emphasizing just one or a few sectors, as is often the case. The value of this approach will, it is hoped, be evident by the end of the book.

Finally, while many of the historical events that have shaped the Xekong River Basin are presented in this study, and are critical for understanding many issues associated with livelihoods, the view of these events is ultimately dependent upon our perceptions during the period when this report was researched and written. This may appear obvious, but we think it is critical to acknowledge that our view of history, regardless how hard we try to be "neutral," is always flavored by the context and the times in which we find ourselves. There is never just one undeniable and straightforward history about anything. This study, then, should be seen as a snapshot of history; a look at the social, cultural, economic, ecological, and geographical landscape of an important watershed, in the context of the livelihoods, development and natural resource management issues facing the multi-ethnic people who inhabit it. In many ways, this study is a critique of modern development, created in a particular time and place.

Methodology

The field research that this study is based on was conducted periodically between December 2003 and February 2007, and the writing of the study was essentially finished in June 2007. Field investigations were conducted in all the districts in Attapeu and Xekong Provinces,[6] as well as parts of the Xekong River Basin in Champasak Province. A number of field methods were employed during investigations, including participant observation, individual and group interviews, and the interviewing of key actors like village chiefs, elders, and government officials. Sometimes specialists in particular livelihood activities, such as fisheries, were also consulted. Some interviews were short; others were long. Some people were interviewed once; others were interviewed on several occasions. Some interviews can be described as being generally participatory, while others were more extractive, depending upon the circumstances and the people being interviewed.

Apart from relying on "fieldwork" conducted specifically for this study, we have also drawn extensively on secondary data, including media articles and stories, academic research, and even archival research conducted by the first author at the Centre des Archives d'Outre-mer [Centre for Archives from Overseas (CAOM)], Aix-en-Provence, France in September 2005, mainly conducted as part of his PhD research in human geography.

This study has also relied on Ian G. Baird's previous research over the last fifteen years in Xekong, Attapeu, and Champasak Provinces. He has visited Attapeu and Xekong at least once a year since he first went there in December 1991 and has also gained experience through living and working in Champasak Province since 1993. These years of working in and near the Xekong basin have helped to provide substantial insights and historical context for the research. The study has also benefited from work done in Ratanakiri and Stung Treng Provinces in northeast Cambodia since 1995, helping to provide a sense of how things are viewed from "south of the border."

We have also gained information and important insights from a group of Lao videographers and development workers who have been researching similar issues and Lao colleagues working for the Global Association for People and the Environment (GAPE) in southern Laos.

This study is based largely on qualitative methods, although considerable quantitative data are included. A large number of villages were visited in various parts of the Xekong River Basin over the course of the study, but it would have been impossible to visit all of the hundreds of communities found in the basin in Laos, or to provide information on all the important factors affecting livelihoods in the basin. This book includes many stories and anecdotes that could be of interest to readers, but, undoubtedly, these represent only the proverbial drop in the bucket, and this limitation is inevitable in carrying out this sort of basin-wide study.

One important weakness of this study is gender. While we are conscious of the need to consider gender issues carefully and have tried to emphasize them as much as possible, we are certainly not capable of adequately reflecting the views of the diverse groups of women that populate the Xekong Basin. In any case, we have done our best to include what relevant information we have been able to acquire. It is hoped that someone will expand on this theme in the future.

We are also aware that one of the main strengths of this book—its inter-disciplinary approach—is also one of its weaknesses. That is, by trying to cover so many different issues and unravel important aspects of the complex issues with which we are dealing, we have invariably been unable to treat any one of them in as much detail as might have been possible with a more focused approach.

The linguistic diversity of the Xekong River Basin in Laos certainly presented an important challenge, and there are few, if any, people with the ability to speak all the languages used in the basin. Ian G. Baird largely conversed in Lao during interviews and discussions conducted during the study. All interviews with speakers of one of the more prominent Mon-Khmer languages used in the basin, the Western Bahnaric language of Brao, were conducted in that language. This research certainly would have benefited from our speaking other Mon-Khmer languages used in the basin, but at least one author was able to communicate directly with almost everyone he met during the study in either Lao or Brao. People from all ethnic groups in the basin are increasingly using the Lao language as the *lingua franca*, and Lao is also the main and only official language used for government affairs.

Organization

This book has been organized into a number of thematic chapters. Chapter 2 introduces the study area and the ethnic groups in the Xekong basin. Chapter 3 considers culture and religion. Chapter 4 provides a brief overview of the history of the Xekong Basin, including its role as a theatre for conflict and a battlefield during past wars and other violent conflicts. Chapter 5 assesses aspects of the agriculture situation in the basin, including swidden agriculture and internal resettlement of ethnic minorities from mountainous areas to the lowlands and along roads, and dry season irrigated rice cultivation in the basin, and Chapter 6 considers forests and livelihoods, and associated management issues. Chapter 7 examines living aquatic resources in the Xekong basin in the context of local livelihoods, with an emphasis on fish and fisheries, and Chapter 8 presents information regarding some of the multitude of other livelihood activities in the basin. Chapter 9 looks at protected areas and natural resource management issues in the basin. Chapter 10 reviews health and education issues, and Chapter 11 examines transportation and regional integration issues. Chapter 12 looks at large-scale mining. Chapter 13 considers electricity production and, particularly, large hydroelectric dams. The final conclusions of the study are presented in Chapter 14.

2

The Xekong River Basin in Laos

The Mekong River Basin covers more than 800,000 km^2 in China, Burma, Laos, Thailand, Cambodia, and Vietnam (Shoemaker et al. 2001). The Xekong River Basin is one of the 64 second-order river basins in Laos, of which 53, or 91% (about 204,000 km^2) of the country's land base, are within the Mekong River Basin and account for approximately 34% of the Mekong's total flow (Halcrow 1999, LNMC 2004). The Ou River Basin in northern Laos is the largest of the second-order basins with a catchment area of 24,500 km^2. The Xekong River Basin in southern Laos has the second largest catchment, with an area of approximately 22,960 km^2 (JICA 1999). If parts of the Xekong Basin in Vietnam (750 km^2) and Cambodia are included (5,105 km^2, excluding the Sesan and Srepok Rivers),[1] the Xekong Basin is among the most significant second-order river basins in the Mekong region, with an area of 28,815 km^2 (Rosales et al. 2003; WWF 2002b; 2005c; Thuan and Tep 2007) (see Map 3).

The rainy season in much of the Xekong River Basin in Laos occurs between May and October and is mainly influenced by the southwestern monsoon, but the mountainous eastern part of the basin, near the Vietnamese border, is also influenced by the northeastern monsoon (Van Staaveren 1993).

The headwaters of the Xekong River are in A loui District, Thua-Thien Hue Province, in the Central Highlands of Vietnam (WWF 2002a), at over 1,000 m above sea level. The headwaters are in a remote area best known internationally as the location of the intense military conflicts at "Hamburger Hill" and the "Battle of Khesanh," in which large numbers of Vietnamese troops and US marines were killed.

The Xesap River,[2] one of the major tributaries of the upper Xekong River, flows from Vietnam into southern Laos. The exact distance that the Xesap travels in Vietnam is not known, but it is probably about 40 km. Where it enters Laos, the

Xesap acts as the border between Kalum District, Xekong Province and Samouay District, Salavan Province. Soon after entering Laos, the Xesap is joined with the *Houay* Untrol[3] from the northeast, and then with the *Houay* Axam, slightly more downstream and just above Aleuk Village, from the east. It is only below where these three rivers join that local people know the river as the "Xekong."

The upper part of the Xekong River Basin is one of the least populated parts of Laos. Where it is very mountainous, there are few villages directly adjacent to the Xekong, as the surrounding geography is too steep. Instead, many villages, such as Laipo, Pom, Ape, Arong, and others in Kalum District, are situated in relatively flat areas on the tops of hills above the river. In Laipo, for example, it takes about half and hour to walk from the Xekong up the hill to the village, the nearest location of relatively flat land.

The Xekong Basin in southern Laos is conspicuously flanked to the west by a significant natural feature, the Bolaven Plateau (*Phou Phiang Bolaven* or *Phou Louang* in Lao), a steep-sloped mountain plateau of volcanic origin that reaches 1,426 m asl at its highest point near *Phou* Thevada,[4] an old cinder cone near Pakxong town in Champasak Province and the Annamite Mountain Range less conspicuously in the distance to the east. Some of the watersheds on the Bolaven Plateau also flow into the Xeset River Basin in Salavan Province, a tributary of the Xedon River, which runs into the Mekong River at Pakse, Champasak Province's present-day capital.

The eastern border of the Xekong catchment in Laos is easy to determine as it essentially coincides with the full extent of the international border between Laos and Vietnam in Xekong and Attapeu Provinces. As Kennon Breazeale points out, "The boundary between Laos and Vietnam follows or is close to watershed lines for most of its 2,100-km length" (2002: 315). Although much of the border between Laos and Vietnam does follow watershed boundaries, some sections of the border do not, with the headwaters of the Xekong River Basin within Vietnam's Thua-Thien Hue Province being but one example of this.

There is also limited documentation about how, in December 1904, the modern southern border between Laos and Cambodia was established by unilateral acts of the French administration of Indochina. The French colonial authorities decided to take Stung Treng Province (at the time including all of present-day Ratanakiri Province) from Laos and give it to Cambodia (Breazeale 2002; Ironside and Baird 2003) and to cede part of present-day Dak Lak Province, also part of Laos, to Vietnam. Unlike the establishment of other borders in the region, only one government was involved (Prescott 1975). As Prescott wrote: "The internal rather than international character of these boundaries makes its harder to establish their legal

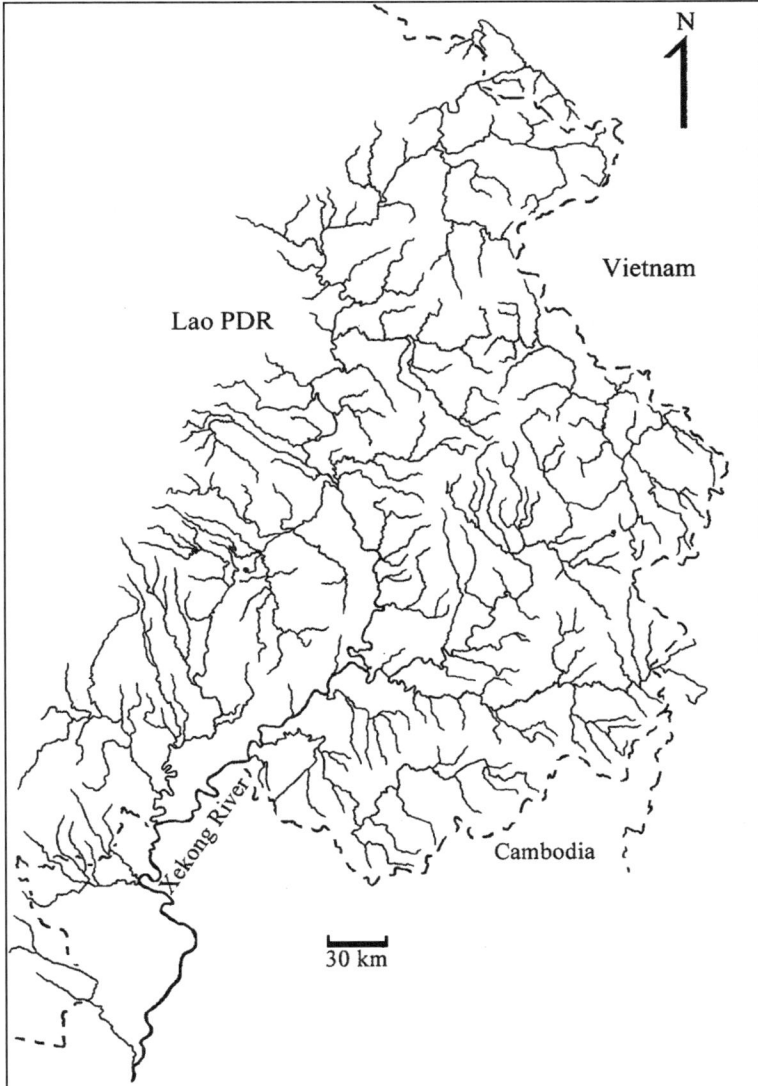

Map 3. Major Tributaries in the Xekong River Basin in Lao PDR (including tributaries flowing from Vietnam and into Cambodia)

basis and the reasons why the particular lines were selected" (1975: 457). However, it appears that for the most part the Laos-Cambodia border coincides with the northern boundaries of watersheds of the Sesan River Basin.

In Laos, the Xekong River Basin includes relatively small parts of Samouay, Ta-oi, and Salavan Districts in Salavan Province; most of Kalum, Dakchung, Lamam, and Thateng Districts in Xekong Province; parts of Pakxong, Pathoumphone, and Khong Districts in Champasak Province; and all of Samakhixay, Saysettha, Sanxay, Phouvong, and Sanamxay Districts in Attapeu Province (Map 4).

The Xekong River travels from Kalum District, where it flows from Vietnam south into Lamam District, before passing Xekong town, the capital of Xekong Province. This part of the riverbed is covered with large boulders and rock formations. The mountainous terrain flanking the river on both sides is largely covered with swidden fields and fallows in various stages of regeneration, as much of the population in this area is situated near the river. It then continues south, where the *Houay* Lamphan joins it from the west. Still flowing south, the Xekong is then joined from the west by the Xenamnoi River. At its confluence, the Xenamnoi acts as the administrative border between northern Attapeu Province and southern Xekong Province. From there, the Xekong continues south, where the Xekaman River, which is joined by the Xexou River not far upstream, meets it from the east. Continuing on in a southerly direction, the Xekong is then met by the Nam Kong River from the east. After the Xekong begins to act as the border between Cambodia and Laos, it is intersected from the west by the Xepian River, itself a recipient of the Xekhampho River and its tributaries in Attapeu and Champasak Provinces. The length of the Xekong River through these four provinces in southern Laos has been reported to be 320 km (Lao PDR Embassy, Washington, DC).

The Xekong then flows southwesterly into Siem Pang District, Stung Treng Province, northeastern Cambodia. There are officially 28,376 people in about 5,100 families and thirty-one villages, ten communes,[5] three districts in Stung Treng Province that are directly adjacent to the Xekong River in Cambodia, as well as a number of other villages not adjacent to the Xekong River but within the basin (Thuan and Tep 2007).

In Cambodia, the Xekong's tributaries, the Sesan and Srepok,[6] are very large rivers, and both originate in the Central Highlands of Vietnam, before flowing considerable distances westerly through northeastern Cambodia. The Srepok joins the Sesan, which then enters the Xekong about 10 km upstream of its confluence with the Mekong at the provincial capital of Stung Treng. The combined flow of the Xekong, Sesan, and Srepok Rivers, which together drain much of the Central Highlands of Vietnam,

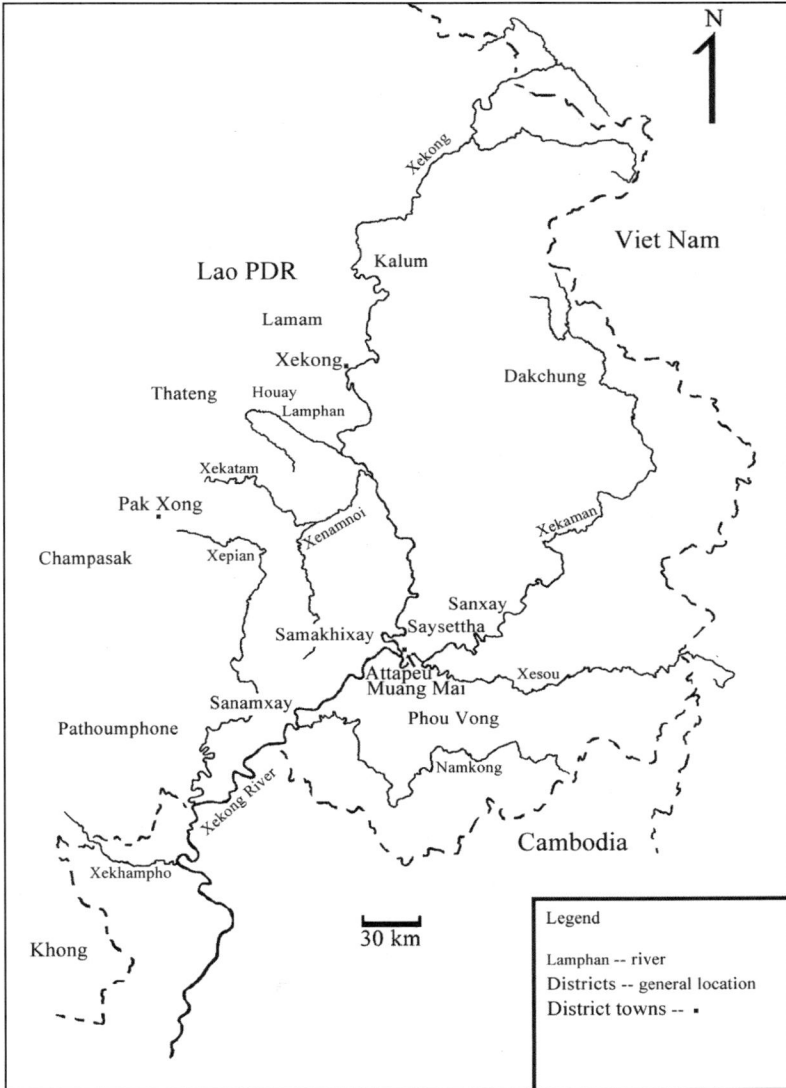

Map 4 The Provinces, Districts, and Major Rivers in the Xekong River Basin in Laos

southern Laos, and northeast Cambodia is approximately 19% of the flow of the Mekong at Kratie Province, just downstream from Stung Treng (Halcrow 1999), and Norconsult (2007a) has estimated that the Xekong itself contributes about 10% of the water in the Mekong. In Cambodia, near the provincial town of Stung Treng, the dry season Xekong flows at a speed of about 0.21 m/second, while in the rainy season it moves much more rapidly, at about 0.96m/second (Thuan and Tep 2007).

In Cambodia, the Xekong River flows over a distance of approximately 141 km. In the Central Highlands of Vietnam, the distance from the river's source to the Lao border is about 40 km. Therefore, when combined with the 320 km stretch in Laos; the length of the Xekong River is about 500 km.

Xekong Province

Xekong Province covers about 7,665 km^2, of which 60% consists of high moun-
tains, 35% of high mountain plateau, and 5% of lowland areas. There are four districts: Lamam, Thateng, Kalum, and Dakchung, which together encompass 44 sub-districts, 253 villages, and approximately 12,640 households (*Vientiane Times* 2006b) and 85,316 people (Pansivongsay 2006b). The average human population density of the province is one of the lowest in Laos, at just 11.1 people per km^2.[7] Most of Xekong Province is in the Xekong River Basin, except for about half of Thateng District, which is in the Xedon Basin.

Kalum and Lamam Districts receive significantly less rain than the other two districts in Xekong Province, Dakchung and Thateng. The first two receive an aver-
age of about 1,800 mm of precipitation per year, while the others get approximately 2,500 mm per annum. Dakchung and Thateng are relatively cool, with average temperatures of 24–26 C. as compared to 27–29 C. in Kalum and Lamam. For the whole province, the highest recorded temperatures are 33–38 C. and the lowest are approximately 3–5 C.

Xekong Province is adjacent to three Lao provinces: Attapeu to the south, Champasak to the southwest, and Salavan to the northwest. It is also adjacent to three Vietnamese provinces and four districts: A luoi District, Thua-Thien Hue Province to the north; Hyien and Dang Districts, Quangnam Province, to the north and east; and Dak Lai District, Kontum Province to the southeast. It shares a 280 km border with Vietnam (Xekong Province LFNC 2007). The provincial capital of Xekong, in Lamam District, is 49 km from Thateng by road, 74 km from Kalum, and 105 km from Dakchung.

Xekong Province has a diverse ethnic make-up, and 91.4% of the people are classified as coming from "ethnic groups"—8.6% are considered to be ethnic Lao (Xekong Province LFNC 2007). 83.5% of the province's population lives in rural areas (SC and SPC 2004; MAF and STEA 2004), and 177, or 70% of the villages in the province, are considered to be "in poverty" (*Vientiane Times* 2006b).

The number of poor families in the province has reportedly dropped from 8,000 in 2000 to just 2,644 in 2006; the government is expecting that poverty will be "eradicated" by 2010 (Pansivongsay 2006b). However, the criteria used to make this determination can be questioned, as it is not straightforward as to who is "poor" and who is not. Despite international efforts to define wealth and poverty quantitatively, these are socially constructed concepts that vary over time and space, and it is difficult to determine exactly what poverty is in rural Laos, as different people define it in different ways at different times. Some officials may well be distorting data in trying to gain credit for reducing poverty, an important national and LPRP objective. Once communities are made to limit shifting cultivation they are at times defined as having escaped poverty when, in fact, they may be worse off than before in terms of their economic and livelihood security, especially due to a reduction in subsistence fishing, hunting, and forest collecting.

Due partly to high levels of in-migration from other provinces in Laos and Vietnam, Xekong Province has the highest population growth rate in Laos, with a 3.2% average annual increase. The birth rate is 30 per 1,000, the highest rate for any province in Laos. Even though the death rate, 10 per 1,000, is the highest rate for any province in Laos as well, the birthrate far outstrips the death rate (SC and SPC 2004). Some of the population increase is associated with immigration from other parts of Laos and from neighboring Vietnam. According to SC and SPC (2004), 1,212 people immigrated into the province, while 891 moved out over the same one-year period (2003). Human demographic issues are becoming increasingly important in Xekong, although this is a relatively minor issue compared to other parts of Laos (Rosales et al. 2003). The capital of Xekong Province has a population of approximately 18,000 people and is the province's most populous town.

Rice is the major crop grown in Xekong Province. Officially, land cultivated with rice covers 7,130 ha of the total 12,000 ha of agricultural land in the province. Shifting cultivation reportedly accounts for about 1,500 ha (*Vientiane Times* 2004j) (compared to about 3,710 ha in 2003; Rosales et al. 2003). These figures may well be inaccurate, as district and provincial officials tend to underestimate the amount of swidden agriculture in order to be seen as following government policy to reduce or eradicate it. There are only about 200 ha of irrigated dry season wet-rice paddy land in the province.

In 2000, rice production for upland and lowland agriculture amounted to 17,310 tons, or an average of 2.43 tons per hectare. On a provincial basis, this is the lowest rice yield in the country, with rice shortages being frequent. On average, 78% of family income in Xekong Province is spent on food (Rosales et al. 2003).

In 2003, 90% of the people living in the province were not yet connected with the national electricity grid (Rosales et al. 2003), although there has been some expansion of services since then. For example, the district town of Kalum has recently been connected.

Xekong Province has undergone a number of administrative changes in recent decades, and many areas were referred to by different names in the past. Laos received official independence from French rule in 1954, after the French lost the decisive battle of Dien Bien Phu in Vietnam. The First Indochina War was over, and the French were forced to withdraw from Indochina. Not long after Laos received independence the Communist movement in eastern parts of the country began to grow. In 1954, present-day Xekong was part of Salavan Province, but in 1961 the growing Pathet Lao Communist movement established *Khveng Tavan Oke* ("the Eastern Province")(Xainyavong et al. 2003), which covered all of present-day Xekong Province, one sub-district now attached to Champasak Province, two that are currently part of Salavan Province, and Sanxay District,[8] which is now part of Attapeu Province. *Khveng Tavan Oke* overlapped with part of the area that the Royal Government recognized as Salavan Province. Xekong Neua District, an administrative area within *Khveng Tavan Oke*, is now the southern part of Kalum District and the northern part of Lamam District. Viengthong District was the center of present-day Lamam District. There was also Xekong Tai District, now the southern part of Lamam District, and Dakchung District. In the early 1960s, as Communist resistance grew, *Khveng Tavan Oke*, firmly in the hands of revolutionary Lao forces and their Vietnamese supporters, become an important stronghold where Pathet Lao officials were trained.

Districts, currently known as "*Muang*" in Lao, were called "*Kong*" during the 1950s and 1960s. In the east, these *Kong* were often named after ethnic leaders or ethnic groups favored by the government. For example, *Kong Senvan* covered the ethnic Ngkriang (Nye) area now encompassing part of Lamam and Kalum Districts in Xekong Province. Present-day Dakchung District was called *Kong Chavan*, after an important Triang (Talieng) leader from the area. *Kong Kalum* covered the northern part of present-day Kalum District.

In 1975, when the revolutionaries took power throughout Laos, *Khveng Tavan Oke* was dissolved and the area was administratively re-attached to Salavan Province. Sanxay District was transferred to Attapeu Province. It was not until 1984 that Xekong Province was established. Xainyavong et al. (2003) claim that this was due to the large area included in Salavan Province. However, Martin Stuart-Fox (2001) believes that Xekong Province was created to give "tribals" of the region more control over their affairs. In any case, the province's administrative borders have not changed since.

According to standard world economic indicators, Xekong is one of the most disadvantaged provinces in Laos, and the GoL has reportedly been trying to resolve the financial and management problems that are continuing to plague the province (Chagnon 2000; Keovichit 2004). In 2004, Xekong's GDP was reported to be 159.59 million kip,[9] and the average annual per capita income for the province a couple of years ago was the equivalent to US$176.24 (Keovichit 2004). Kalum District is considered to be one of the ten poorest districts in Laos. However, these statistics do not include all of the subsistence economy nor barter trade that continues to dominate many parts of the province.

In 2004, the province's revenue was reportedly 11 billion kip, an 11% increase from the previous year. The central government also contributed 20 billion kip to the province's coffers (Keovichit 2004). However, of the amount available to invest in 2004/2005 3 billion kip more was spent than the province's revenue (Phonpachith 2005a). Phonpachith (2005a) reported, in September 2005, that 2005/2006 provincial spending in Xekong would be reduced from the previous year to just over 9 billion kip, and that those funds would be used to support seventy-three projects related to the economy, socio-culture, education, and public health.

Attapeu Province

Attapeu Province is situated directly south of Xekong Province and covers 10,320 km² of which 7,350 km², or 71%, is reportedly still forested, at least to some degree. Only 155 km², or 15%, is under cultivation. Sixty percent of the province is mountainous, with the remaining area consisting of river valley bottoms and other lowland areas. Mountains in the eastern part of the province reach over 2,000 m asl, while some of the lowlands near the Xekong River are just 100 m asl. Virtually all of Attapeu Province is in the Xekong River Basin, except for the upper watershed of a few streams that flow from Phouvong District into the Sesan River in northeast Cambodia.

The province consists of five districts: Samakhixay, Sanamxay, Saysettha, Sanxay and Phouvong, and has a human population of about 104,465 (51.3% are female) in fourteen ethnic groups. The people of Attapeu are situated in 34 sub-districts with 211 villages, and include over 19,384 households (SC and SPC 2004; Meusch et al. 2003; MAF and STEA 2003; 2004). The human population density of Attapeu is somewhat higher than in Xekong Province, at 14.2 people per km^2, but is still much lower than the national average. Over a one-year period in 2003, 2,377 people immigrated into the province, while 2,552 people moved out. This contrasts with Xekong Province, where more people are moving into the province than are moving out (SC and SPC 2004). The provincial capital of Muang Mai in Samakhixay District has a population of about 19,200 people and is the province's largest town. There are estimated to be 9,000 families living in poverty in Attapeu Province (Meusch et al. 2003), mostly living in rural areas. Almost 88% of the province's people are in rural areas, a somewhat higher rate than for Xekong. In 2004, 51.3% of the families in Attapeu were considered poor. Attapeu has a birth rate of 24 people per 1,000, just slightly higher than the national average of 22 per 1,000. The death rate is 8 per 1,000 (SC and SPC 2004). Average life expectancy is 52 years for men and 55.5 for women (MAF and STEA 2003).

The most recent district to be added to Attapeu is Phouvong, created from parts of Saysettha and Sanamxay Districts in September 1991. Phouvong Tai existed prior to 1975, as a revolutionary district but was incorporated into Sanamxay District to the west in 1975, along with Kongmi in Lave District. Phouvong Neua also existed prior to 1975, but it was integrated into Saysettha District, along with *Khet* Somboun to the north, in 1975.

To the east, Attapeu borders Vietnam's Kontum Province and to the south it is adjacent to Cambodia's Ratanakiri and Stung Treng Provinces. Within Laos, Attapeu borders Xekong Province to the north and Champasak Province[10] to the west.

According to Jumsai (2000), the towns of Attapeu and Salavan were established in the early eighteenth century, during the time when the founder of the Kingdom of Champasak, the monk *Pha Khou* Phonsamek[11] resided in Champasak. Phonsamet appointed *Chao* Soisysamout (*Chao* Nokasat), the King of Champasak, who then appointed *Achan* Som as the first Governor of Attapeu (Jumsai 2000).

Nowadays, when asked the meaning of "Attapeu" in Lao, ethnic Lao people sometimes respond that it is a "local word." In fact, it was originally called "*Ik Kalpeu*," which means "buffalo excrement" in Brao. According to legend, upon discovering the location where the Mon-Khmer language speakers of the area raised their buffaloes on a beach on the banks of the Xekaman River, the Lao asked them the name of the location, pointing to the beach, but the tribal people did not understand Lao and said, "*Ik Kalpeu*," referring to the excrement on the beach they thought the Lao were pointing to. From then on, the name has been altered slightly. The Lao called it "*It Akapu*,"; the French corrupted it even more, calling it Attapeu.[12]

Seventy percent of the people in the province live in the lowlands, while the remaining 30% practice upland agriculture in mountainous areas. Meusch et al. (2003) concluded that these upland people "suffer from chronic food shortages," although they did not directly study the food security situation in upland areas (Meusch et al. 2003: 8). Upland people have long been viewed by most lowlanders and outsiders, including those working for development agencies in Laos, as being chronically poor and living in marginal areas. But this is not necessarily the case. The French historian Mathieu Guérin (2001) illustrated how, during the French colonial period of the early twentieth century, shifting cultivators in mountainous areas in Siem Pang District, Stung Treng Province, northeast Cambodia (near the border with Laos), were producing significant rice surpluses, and were, in fact, feeding many lowland rice producers during years of shortages. Yet even at that time French officials were under the impression that years when the uplanders sold rice to lowlanders were exceptional. However, Guérin found that this was the norm. In Attapeu, many elders have confirmed that the same was true, although documented evidence is limited. Oral histories tell us that the Brao Hamong in Phouvong District regularly used to sell upland swidden rice to ethnic Lao people in the lowlands in Attapeu before and during the French colonial period. This rice was mainly sold between the time that the highland rice became ripe and the time when the lowland rice was ready to be harvested—a difference often amounting to over a month.

Attapeu Province has 14,000 ha of "potential" lowland wet-rice paddy land, of which 3,500 ha are currently under rain-fed rice cultivation. Another 448 ha are irrigated paddy land (Meusch et al. 2003). Many GoL officials perceive that there remains a good deal of room for rice field expansion in the lowlands. In recent years this has led to significant efforts to relocate people from mountainous to lowland areas, with part of the justification being to encourage the intensification of rice production and to promote livestock raising as a secondary source of livelihood. Internal resettlement has often been associated with these efforts. Resettlement will be discussed later (see Chapter 5).

LNMC (2004) reported that neither Xekong nor Attapeu Provinces have any factories employing over a hundred workers. However, Attapeu is registered as having five factories with between 10 and 99 employees, and 239 factories with fewer than ten workers each. In Xekong, there are reportedly nine factories with between 10 and 99 employees, and 380 with fewer than 10 workers. In both provinces, the larger factories are all for wood processing.

Champasak Province

Champasak Province, one of Laos' largest and most populous provinces, had a population in 2002 of 600,905 in 93,689 families (MAF and STEA 2004), of whom about 85% were recorded as being ethnic Lao. The main ethnic groups in the Xekong River Basin in Champasak Province are the Jru and Heuny (Laven and Nya Heun, in Lao) in Pakxong, and the ethnic Lao in Pathoumphone.

Champasak Province borders Stung Treng and Prey Vihear Provinces in Cambodia to the south and southwest, and Thailand's Ubon Ratchathani Province to the west. Within Laos, Champasak Province borders Salavan Province to the north, and Xekong and Attapeu Provinces to the northeast and southeast.

As the largest of the four provinces in the Xekong River Basin in Laos, in terms of both total area and human population, Champasak has a total of ten districts, of which six are situated east of the Mekong. Parts of three (Pathoumphone, Pakxong, and Khong) are situated in the Xekong Basin, while Bachieng Chaleunsouk, Pakse, and Sanasomboun Districts are entirely included in other river basins, including the Xeset and Xedon. While quite large parts of Pathoumphone and Pakxong Districts are inside the Xekong Basin, only a small part of Khong District is within the basin—just the catchment area of the *Houay* Kaliang in the eastern part of the district. *Houay* Kaliang empties into the Xekong River after passing through northern Siem Pang District, Stung Treng Province, in Cambodia. Only the ethnic Lao villages of Napakiap, Sot, and Phon Vixay[13] are inside the Xekong Basin in Khong District, although other villages in Khong use land within the basin. In Pathoumphone District, of the 93 villages in the district, about 20 are in the Xekong Basin, and in Pakxong, of the 110 villages in the district, approximately 49 are in the Xekong Basin. Much of the area in Champasak Province within the Xekong Basin is relatively sparsely populated compared to other parts of the province. None of the district capitals or other urban towns in the province are in the Xekong Basin.

According to the *Vientiane Times*, Champasak Province has grown economically more than any of the other three most southerly-located provinces of Laos (Xekong, Attapeu, and Salavan) and the annual per capita income is reported to be about US$420. There are still reportedly 16,000 "poor" families in the province, a higher number than in either Attapeu or Xekong Provinces. However, poor people constitute a lower percentage of the total population of Champasak Province compared to Xekong and Attapeu. According to GoL sources, the number of poor families in Champasak declined 1.5% in 2005 compared to 2004. However, the people living in parts of the Xekong Basin in Champasak Province are generally poorer than those living in other less remote parts of the province. The provincial government claims that the province has completely eradicated shifting cultivation (*Vientiane Times* 2005b), but, in fact, swidden agriculture is still practiced in various forms throughout the province. However, lowland wet-rice agriculture is the main type of agriculture.

Salavan Province

There were 306,914 people in 50,614 families living in Salavan Province in 2002 (MAF and STEA 2004). Salavan borders Thua-Thien Hue Province in Vietnam to the east, and Ubon Ratchathani Province in Thailand to the west. Within Laos, Salavan borders Savannakhet Province to the north, and Champasak and Xekong Provinces to the southwest and southeast, respectively.

Although Salavan contains hundreds of villages and eight districts, only a few communities and very small parts of three districts are situated within the Xekong River Basin. Most of the province is in the Xepon, Xeset, and Xedon River basins. There are apparently no villages in the Xekong Basin in Samouay District, four in the Xekong Basin in Ta-oi District,[14] and only one in the Xekong Basin in Salavan District—situated along the road between Xekong town and Kalum District. Two other villages along the same road in Salavan District are apparently not in the Xekong Basin, according to maps prepared by UXO Laos. Considering the small part of the Xekong Basin in Salavan, the province is not considered in depth in this study.

The Ebb and Flow of the Xekong River

The entire Xekong River Basin is influenced by a tropical monsoon climate, including both the southwestern and northeastern monsoons, that affects different parts of the basin. There is a high variation of rainfall throughout the year and between different parts of the basin. The Xekong Basin is characterized by drastically varying hydrological cycles. Although there are no reliable quantitative data regarding how the discharge of the Xekong River varies in different seasons, the discharge of the mainstream Mekong in southern Laos varies about thirty-fold from its lowest levels in April to its highest water levels in August and September (Cunningham 1998). While the exact variations between dry and wet season hydrological levels are unknown, these differences are significant and the basin's ecology is closely adapted to these seasonal changes, as are the livelihoods of the people living in it. The importance of the ebb and flow of the Xekong River Basin and its significance to the ecology of basin and to the livelihoods of the people is discussed in later chapters.

The People of the Xekong River Basin in Laos

People with a high diversity of ethnic identities populate the Xekong River Basin in Laos. The vast majority are Austroasiatic Mon-Khmer language speakers. However, their exact origins are far from clear, and some researchers believe that they originated from Negroides[15] from Negropolenesien islands (Xainyavong et al. 2003). Lamb (1968) thought that some *"Kha"*[16] groups showed Negrito racial characteristics but that others appear to be members of the Mon-Khmer linguistic family. These early inhabitants of the region, collectively referred to as *"Khom"* in Lao, are believed by some researchers to have crossed with Mongoloids, or yellow skinned people, beginning in the first and second centuries of the Common Era; This is given as the reason why many of the region's present-day inhabitants have relatively dark skin, eyes, and hair, and why some have curly hair, wide faces, small noses, and prominent eyebrows and cheekbones (Xainyavong et al. 2003).

These people speak Mon-Khmer languages in the Bahnaric and Katuic branches, with Bahnaric language speakers inhabiting southern parts of the Xekong Basin in Laos and the latter inhabiting northern parts of the basin. Within the two groups there are a number of different languages and dialects. People speaking related languages can be found as far away as northern Laos, the Assam region of India (Munda family), and the southern Malay Peninsula (Aslian family) (Goudineau 2001).

It is not possible to say with any certainty when these people arrived in the Xekong Basin. Some historians have tried to explain the existence of Mon-Khmer language speaking people in mountainous areas in the basin as due to their having fled to the mountains in response to the arrival of ethnic Lao people to southern Laos around the thirteenth century. However, ancient Chinese chronicles document "fierce" populations of people living in the Annamitic Cordillera long before that period. These two hypotheses are not necessarily contradictory. Some groups of people have legends about migrations from west of the Mekong; other groups believe that they have always lived in the area (Goudineau 2001).

The Xekong LFNC (2007) has found that the Katu, Triang, and Ye peoples claim to originate from Vietnam but that the Ngkriang claim that they originated from Siem Pang District, in present-day Stung Treng Province, Cambodia. Even more surprising, ethnic Harak people claim that they migrated from the west side of the Mekong in present-day northeast Thailand. While this seems unlikely, it is impossible to refute these reports, as little information is available. In Vietnam, Cambodia, and Laos, these peoples have come into contact with Lao-Tai, Khmer, Vietnamese, and Cham peoples over the ages, having been involved in various tributary relationships. They have, however, always been considered to be "at the margins of civilization" by lowland people because of their different livelihood systems, languages, and cultures.

The Austroasiatics of the Xekong River Basin, including the Annamite Mountains and the Bolaven Plateau (*Phou Phiang Bolaven* or *Phou Louang* in Lao), have long been considered to be at the margins of civilization, whether in Lao, Siamese, Vietnamese, or Khmer history. Yet, throughout time they were able to retain their independence from the great state societies (Cham, Khmer, Vietnamese, Lao, Siamese/Thai) that successively emerged over the centuries. They also have played an important role by acting as a buffer between the Lao and Siamese/Thai and the Vietnamese. However, Austroasiatic language speakers have also long been respected by the lowlanders for their control over the "edge of the civilized world," and their power over the lands and the forests of the mountainous regions (Goudineau 2001). On the one hand, they have been seen as the original inhabitants of the land and the "older (albeit poorer) brother," but ethnic Lao people frequently look down on them, because of the perception that they are "backward" and, more recently, "undeveloped." Many ethnic Lao people believe that they have "evolved" more slowly than lowland groups (see, for example, LFNC 2005).

In Xekong Province, there are people from Katuic language branch groups who today refer to themselves as the Katu,[17] Ngkriang, Chatong, Dakkang, Brou, and Souay/Kui; and Bahnaric language branch speakers today called Triang, Jru, Heuny, Harak, Oy, Jru Dak, and Lavi[18] (Chamberlain et al. 1996; Chazee 1999; Engelbert 2001; Xekong LFNC 2007). There are also small numbers of people of other ethnic groups who have moved into the area more recently (see Table 1). Some tourism literature claims that there are villages of ethnic Katang people in Xekong Province, but this is not the case. However, there are many Katang in non-Xekong parts of Salavan Province.

The Dakchung District government recognizes three sub-groups of Ye in the district: Ye Kong, Ye Yeun, and Ye Dak. They also recognize five different Triang sub-groups: Triang Yam, Triang Kaseng, Triang Trong Meuang, Triang Kong, and Pa 'neng. There are also two Katu sub-groups in Dakchung: Dakkang and Trieu.

In Kalum, locals consider there to be two Ngkriang sub-groups, one in the mountains and one next to the Xekong River and five different varieties of Katu people: the Asan, Tang Peuvay, Arak Nye, Avang Sen, and the Peung da doich. There are also Chatong people, believed to be a sub-group of Katu. The Katu claim that they have originated from Vietnam.

In Lamam District, there are considered to be three "original" ethnic groups: the Harak, Lavi,[19] and Lao; and two more recent arrivals from Dakchung and Kalum, the Katu and Triang. In fact, the Lao are probably more recent arrivals than some admit.

In Thateng District, there are considered to be two types of Souay (Kui), one type of Jru, and four sub-groups of Harak. There are also Katu, Triang and Ta-oi (Brou) villages, which are more recent arrivals. The Global Association for People and the Environment (GAPE) has recently cooperated with the Xekong provincial Lao Front for National Construction (LFNC) to conduct locally managed ethnographic studies throughout the province and produce a Lao language book about all the ethnic groups in Xekong Province (Xekong Province LFNC 2007).

UNDP (1999a) reported two additional ethnic groups in Dakchung District not recognized in provincial statistics. There are three villages (Dak Pong, Dak Chang, and Tanpeuang) that are reportedly populated by ethnic "*Talou*" people (83 families in total in the district), and five villages (Konyong, Tangtalang, Tangyeuy, Tangnong, and Tangkalok) (208 families in total in the district) with "unclear" ethnic group status. The ethnic Ye are located in the most remote parts of Dakchung District, with more than half of the population being two to three days walk from its center. The Katu people in Kalum are located in even more remote areas; often-living two to three days walk from the district center (UNDP 1999c).

There are a number of different languages and dialects spoken in Xekong Province, and Chagnon (2000) reported that many people in Kalum and Dakchung speak more than one language or dialect. As a result, there have long been lingua franca in parts of the basin other than Lao to which people from two different ethnic groups tend to gravitate to when communicating. For example, in Kalum District the lingua franca near the district center is Ngkriang. In Lamam District, Harak is the lingua franca, and in Dakchung it is Triang language. However, everywhere in the Xekong Basin, even in remote areas, Lao language is becoming increasingly well-known and used between people from different ethnic groups.

Table 1. Ethnic Groups in Xekong Province[20]

Ethnic Group	Lao Name	Population	Percentage
Katu[21]	Katu	15,589	24.3
Triang[22]	Talieng	13,993	21.8
Harak[23]	Alak	9,953	15.5
Ngkriang[24]	Nye	7,038	11.0
Ye[25]	Ye	6,033	9.4
Lao	Lao	5,523	8.6
Souay (Kui)	Souay	2,237	3.5
Brou	Ta-oi	1,292	2.0
Jru	Laven	1,093	1.7
Lavi	Lavi	499	0.8
Others[26]		899	1.4
Totals		64,170	100.0

In Attapeu Province, the dominant ethnic group is the Lao, but the province has large numbers of Mon-Khmer language speakers from the Bahnaric branch, including significant populations of Brao, Oy, Cheng, Triang, Harak, Jru Dak, Sedang, and Halang people (see Table 2). In 1995, 36.9% of the population of Attapeu was recorded to be ethnic Lao. While the province's administrative boundaries have changed somewhat since 1954/1955, it is interesting that at that time only 29.7% of the population in Attapeu was recorded as being ethnic Lao (cited in Pholsena 2006). This may be because some Mon-Khmer language speakers are now identifying themselves as "Lao."

The Brao, Oy, Cheng, and Jru Dak languages are quite similar as they all belong to the Western Bahnaric language group (Sidwell and Jacq 2003). Illustrative of this, a Jru Dak man from Kase Village in Sanamxay District reported being able to understand Brao and Oy without having specifically to learn either; however, he said that he could not understand Ta-oi, a Katuic language.

In Phouvong District, there are considered to be four original Brao sub-groups, the Jree, Kavet, Hamong, and Ka-nying, although the Ka-nying largely migrated from Cambodia to Laos during the 1970s. There are also some people from the Umba sub-group living in the district, most having migrated from Cambodia during the war. The Brao call the Xekong River "*Dak Danai Tang Ong*" in their language. There are also a few Sedang villages near the Vietnamese border with Phouvong District. In Sanxay District, the main ethnic group is Triang, although there are also Ye Dak and Harak people living there. In Sanamxay District, there are a number of ethnic groups, including the Oy, Cheng, Brao, Jru Dak, and Lao. In Samakhixay District, there are Oy, Cheng, Brao, Harak, Heuny, and Lao people. There is one ethnic Sapouan[27] and one ethnic Soke village in Samakhixay District. In Saysettha District, there are ethnic Lao, Brao, Harak, Triang, and Cheng people.

Table 2. Ethnic Groups in Attapeu Province

Ethnic Group	Lao Name	Population	Percentage
Lao	Lao	32,159	36.9
Brao	Lave	15,191	17.4
Oy	Oy	14,337	16.4
Triang	Talieng	8,088	9.3
Cheng	Cheng	5,696	6.5
Laven-Sou[28]	Jru-Jru Dak	4,061	4.7
Harak	Alak	4,038	4.6
Ye	Ye	1,457	1.7
Heuny	Nya Heun	446	0.5
Sedang	Sedang	306	0.5
Others[29]		1,450	1.5
Totals		87,229	100.0

Ethnic Lao people largely populate Champasak Province (see Table 3), and the Lao are by far the most populous group in the lowlands of the Xekong River Basin in Pathoumphone District. Ethnic Jru and Heuny people historically inhabited upland parts of the basin, including the Bolaven Plateau in Pakxong District. There is also one ethnic Brao village in the Xekong Basin in Pathoumphone District, Champasak Province, and three other Brao villages in Pathoumphone and Khong that are situated outside of the basin but whose forests are inside it.

The parts of Salavan, Ta-oi, and Samouay Districts in Salavan Province that are in the Xekong River Basin are mainly populated by Mon-Khmer language speakers from the Brou (Ta-oi), Pako, and Katu ethnic groups.

There are also some long-time ethnic Lao inhabitants of mainly lowland parts of Attapeu Province and eastern Champasak Province. An increasing number of Lao language speakers are moving into the Xekong Basin to work as traders and government officials or to look for other livelihood opportunities, as the area is considered by outsiders to have large quantities of relatively untapped natural resources.

Table 3. Ethnic Groups in Champasak Province

Ethnic Group	Lao Name	Population	Percentage
Lao	Lao	424,993	84.8
Jru	Laven	24,584	4.9
Souay (Kui)	Souay	11,815	2.4
Brou	Ta-oi	8,106	1.6
Phou Thai	Phou Thai	6,383	1.3
Heuny	Nya Heun	4,506	0.9
Khmer	Khmer	3,769	0.8
Ngkriang	Nye	2,217	0.4
Brou	Katang	1,919	0.4
Brao	Lave	1,813	0.4
Harak	Alak	1,536	0.3
Others[30]		9,746	2.0
Total		501,387	100.0

Lao Government Policies and Ethnic Minorities

The Lao Front for National Construction (LFNC) is the section of the GoL responsible for ethnic issues in the country. In promoting the nation-building process of the Lao state, the LFNC states that:

> All ethnic groups of the Lao P.D.R. have contributed with their strength and forces to protect and develop the nation, and have a firm tradition of unity and concord. Especially since the country has been under the leadership of the Lao People's Revolutionary Party, the process of relationship and concord among the ethnic groups within the nation has been firm and rapid. (LFNC 2005: a)

According to Khampheuy Chanthasouk, the Vice-President of the National LFNC:

> [T]he mission of the LFNC is to guide people's minds in the right direction: it instructs them about the Party's policies as well as about the Government's laws and rules. It is the interface that links the Party-State and the "masses," defined as "people of all ethnic groups, social backgrounds and religions." (Pholsena 2006: 210)

The LFNC has, most recently, classified the people living in Laos into forty-nine different ethnic groups and over a hundred sub-groups. These are organized into four language groups: Lao-Tai, Mon-Khmer, Chinese-Tibetan, and Hmong-Ieu-Mien. The LFNC has stated that, "ethnic diversity is of great importance for development" (LFNC 2005: i).

The 1991 Constitution of Lao PDR (revised in 2003) states that Laos is officially a multi-ethnic country. It also proclaims that, "The State will carry out a policy of unity and equality between the various ethnic groups. All ethnic groups have the right to preserve and improve their own traditions and culture and those of the nation. Discrimination between ethnic groups is forbidden. The State will carry out every means to continue to improve and raise the economic and social level of all ethnic groups" (cited in Goudineau 2001). It also states that, "the right of a multi-ethnic people to be owners of the nation is exercised and guaranteed by the political system." Article 8 of the Constitution commits the state to promoting "unity and equality" among all ethnic groups, which have the right "to protect, preserve, and promote the fine customs and cultures of their own tribes and the nation." The state is also committed to developing the socio-economic conditions of all ethnic groups. However, as Vatthana Pholsena (2006) has pointed out, the GoL has never granted any special constitutional status to ethnic groups with regard to their parliamentary representation or in relation to creating autonomous areas, as is the case in China and as was temporarily done in North Vietnam in the early years of independence after 1954 (see Hardy 2003). The GoL prescribes that there should be no differentiation between ethnic groups, and, drawing on Marxist-Leninist ideas about ethnography, generally believes in an evolutionary process that will result in people from all different ethnicities ultimately seeing themselves as part of the "Lao Nation" (Pholsena 2006).

The written policies toward ethnic minorities appear quite admirable, especially when compared with neighboring countries like Thailand, which has long withheld recognition of much of its ethnic minority population as being citizens of the country. However, the GoL's shifting cultivation reduction and opium eradication policies and associated internal resettlement and village consolidation practices are negatively affecting ethnic minorities (Gonzales et al. 2005; Baird and Shoemaker 2005). The many problems associated with these issues are discussed later in this study.

Many ethnic minorities were able to ascend to positions in government and politics during and immediately after the revolution, often in recognition of their important contributions during the war years. Recently, however, it has become more and more difficult for ethnic minority people to establish themselves in high positions in government (Goudineau 2001). This is largely due to increased educational standards required for government officials, which has essentially excluded many ethnic minorities from becoming officials and resulted in their further marginalization. In fact, rhetoric regarding "poverty" and wealth is rapidly replacing the revolutionary rhetoric that dominated official discourse during the war and in the years immediately following 1975. As Vatthana Pholsena put it, "The discourse of struggle is being replaced by a discourse of lack" (2006: 218).

Ethnic Relations

This section deals with the relationships between people from different ethnic groups, an important issue in the Xekong River basin. In fact, ethnicity is but one of many identities that people have. Identities are also commonly created based on class, religion, gender, and nation-states, to name a few of the many possibilities. Social scientists generally see ethnicity and other identities as complex and fluid, shifting depending upon circumstances. Probably because of the many ethnic groups found in the Xekong Basin, ethnicity is of great significance to the people in the Xekong River Basin.[31]

The ethnic labels or ethnonyms used to refer to the different ethnic groups have changed over time and, not surprisingly, remain quite confused and in constant flux. It appears that in the past most people identified with particular small social groups (what might now be called villages) and had little sense of belonging to any larger socio-political systems or large ethnic groups. For example, in Kalum District there is a village called Tang Pril, which is named after a type of wild mango, called "*mak mouang khai*" in Lao. The plant grows plentifully in the wild near the village. As legend has it, French administrators once visited the community and asked the people to which ethnic group they belonged. The people insisted that they belonged to the "*Tang Pril*" ethnic group, but since they were the only village that claimed to belong to such a group, the French did not accept their explanation. Due to linguistic characteristics, the people were classified as Katu, and that is the group with which they currently identify. Although people were undoubtedly aware of the linguistic and cultural differences between themselves and other people long before the French arrived in Indochina (Engelbert 2004), changes to their administrative systems imposed by the French, as well as a desire to classify people according to previously relatively unimportant ethnic classification systems, resulted in the increasing importance of ethnic identity labels for Austroasiatic language speaking peoples during the colonial period.

It was certainly not only the French who sought to classify people on ethnic grounds. The Lao, like all other groups, have long used their own classification systems and labels for describing people seen as different from themselves. They were often satisfied to identify many groups under single labels, such as "*Kha*" and later "*Lao Theung*." Even when these groups were differentiated, they were often referred to by different ethnonyms, some with pejorative meanings. For example, the Lao called the Brao, *Lave*; the Jru became known as the *Laven*; the Jru Dak became the *Sou*; and the Heuny became known as the *Nya Heun*.

The Alak people refer to themselves as *Harak*, but since the Lao have difficulty pronouncing "*r*," and the initial "*H*" is soft, they started referring to them as Alak. The situation is similar for the Triang people, whom ethnic Lao normally call *Talieng*, due to linguistic problems pronouncing "*r*" and also because Lao cannot combine two consonants like "*Tr*" without putting a vowel in-between.

Sometimes people from other ethnic groups have contributed to the adoption of different ethnonyms. For example, the ethnic group Ngkriang was apparently named by neighboring Harak (Alak) people because, during a period of severe rice shortages, these people fled to the nearby forests and ate a type of fruit to survive. (This fruit is called *mak va* in Lao.) The people were initially called "those who eat the *Ngkriang* fruit,"[32] but over time the label was shortened to the "Ngkriang people," and it stuck. Later, the Lao started calling these same people the *Nye*, because when they asked them questions, they often replied, "No," which is pronounced "*Nye*" in their language. To this day, *Nye* is the most commonly used term to describe these people, with many from this group having accepted and internalized the label. In many cases, however, Ngkriang is preferred, both among most Ngkriang people and Lao officials who deal specifically with ethnicity issues.

The term Katu (or Kantu) is probably the most confusing, as it is now applied to a number of different groups of people with varying cultures and livelihoods and who sometimes speak mutually unintelligible languages. There have been a number of books written about the Katu in Laos, but almost all of this research has focused on a single sub-group, without mention of the other groups (Sulavan et al. 1994; 1995; 1996). This has upset some Katu from other sub-groups, who feel that their sub-groups have been ignored and suppressed. Some people believe that the "*Ka*" in Katu means uncle, and the "*tu*" means "the end of a stream." According to Viphone Chaoasan, the ethnic Katu Vice-President of the LFNC in Xekong Province and the former district chief of Kalum, nobody knows for sure what is the origin of the term "Katu" and many suspect that it is likely to be a relatively recent invention. One of the most plausible explanations is that the term was once used only to refer to forest-people without houses or a fixed location but that since then its original meaning has been lost and it has somehow come to describe a large group of different peoples, including some in Laos and an even larger population in neighboring parts of Vietnam.

Many ethnic Lao or other people from outside of Attapeu know little about the ethnic groups of the region. For example, Pongkeo wrote, in an article for the *Vientiane Times*, that "The Oye [Oy] people are one the most famous ethnic groups in the southern part of Laos, especially Attapeu Province, and they make up the majority of the Lao Theung ethnic group" (2003: 16). In fact, provincial statistics confirm (see Table 2 above) that there are more ethnic Brao people in Attapeu than Oy. The Oy, while an important ethnic group in Attapeu, only make up a small percentage of what might be considered the "Lao Theung" population of southern Laos.

Pongkeo also wrote that, "In the past, this group relied on slash and burn cultivation, but after the government's policy on poverty elimination was issued many families moved down from the mountain to live in the plain. They now earn their living with farming practice [*sic*], handicraft production and animal raising" (2003: 16). While ethnic Oy people have a history of doing swidden cultivation, and some have certainly been impacted by the GoL's shifting cultivation reduction program (see Chapter 5), the author seems to have missed the fact that some Oy people have been wet-rice cultivators for at least hundreds of years. Pongkeo presents them as being what he believes to be "typical" ethnic minorities. Engelbert (2004), however, reported that when the first Lao penetrated Attapeu in around the fifteenth century, the Oy had already long been producing wet rice. They had even developed systems on streams for irrigating terraced rice fields they had in the foothills. During the early French period, the Oy often produced more than enough rice to eat, and their rice fields were more productive and expansive than the rice fields of ethnic Lao people.

The Triang people are mainly found in Dakchung and Sanxay Districts. More recently, many have also been resettled to the lowlands in Lamam District. They often refer to themselves as ethnic Dakchung people rather than Triang or Talieng people. One ethnic Triang student studying at the ethnic minority school in the capital of Xekong Province said that Talieng people wear loin clothes and dress in traditional clothes, as compared to Dakchung people, who may not dress like that. Like most other ethnic groups in the region, the Triang have a complex identity/ ethnicity make-up. One group of people in Dakchung call themselves the Pa 'neng ethnic group, and refuse to be labeled Triang. There are currently three ethnic Pa 'neng villages, but they all originate from the same village. Other Triang people from the district claim that the Pa 'neng people speak almost the same dialect as members of other Triang sub-groups, and so should be classified as a sub-group of Triang. The word Pa 'neng apparently originates from the name of a river situated near where they live. When the Pa 'neng people heard this proposal, they were unhappy. One of their leaders was reported to have said, "We have over a thousand people now. That should be enough to establish a special ethnic group for us."

The Trieu are another group that speak a dialect close to, but different, from the Katu. Some feel that the Trieu should be classified as Katu,[33] but the Trieu object, as they do not want to be known as Katu. There are only six villages populated by Trieu people, and they all originate from the same village. The ethnic Dakkang people also speak a Katuic dialect similar to some Katu. There are only seven Dakkang villages.

There have been ethnic identity shifts in the Xekong Basin, often from belonging to a minority ethnic group toward becoming ethnic Lao. One example relates to Kasom Village in Samakhixay District. We have not visited the village, but people from neighboring villages reported that it is a "Lao village." Others who have worked in the village have reported that there are a few ethnic minorities in the village, but that the village is Lao in origin, and that ten ethnic Lao families from Phoxay Noi Village in Saysettha District originally established the community (Mark Dubois, pers comm. August 2006). However, back in 1894 Prosper Odend'hal visited the village, and later wrote that it consisted of "75% Laoized *Kha*."[34]

Another example is the village of Pha Pho in Pathoumphone District, on the western edge of the Xekong Basin. The village is currently considered to be "ethnic Lao," but Martin Rathie (2001) claims that it was an ethnic Kui (Souay) village where elephants were trained in 1897. The village is still well-known for its domestic elephants, but nobody admits to being ethnic Kui anymore. It seems that at that time the people were already well on their way to "becoming Lao,"[35] and that this process is now complete.

The village of Phon Vixay, in Khong District, Champasak Province, is another community whose population has changed ethnicity in recent years. The people now all identify themselves as ethnic Lao. But according to the nearby ethnic Brao villages of Phon Sa-at and *Ban* Na, the village was once considered to be Brao. It appears that the language disappeared from the village fifty to sixty years ago. Its Brao name was previously Touk Louk.

Ban Phon, in Lamam District, presents another example of the same sort of process. One of three "ethnic Lao" villages in Xekong Province, it is not really fully

"Lao" in origin, according to many elders in the province. Most of the people who live there and call themselves "Lao" have ancestors who were either fully or partly ethnic Harak or Kui. This indicates the long-term dominance of Lao culture through much of this region, as *Ban* Phon "became a Lao village quite a long time ago."

Another interesting example of identity conversion appears to lie with the ethnic Oy people in Attapeu Province. Most of the Oy believe that they have long inhabited the foothills of the Bolaven Plateau. However, there are four "ethnic Oy" villages populated by people who insist that they are Oy, but that they originated from far to the north, possibly present-day Xieng Khouang Province. The villages are Langao Neua, Langao Neua Mai, Langao Kang, and Langao Tai, and all appear to have originally come from the same village. It appears that the people from these villages were from another ethnic group in northern Laos and that they gradually converted to being ethnic Oy, adopting Oy culture and rituals. They speak Oy, but use a different dialect than other Oy villages. People from other ethnic Oy villages claim that the people from these villages did not really come from Xieng Khouang. But the people from the villages in question continue to insist that they did and claim that they settled for some time near Thong Vay Village, to the north, on their journey to their present location in Samakhixay District, Attapeu Province. The people from these villages also appear to have somewhat different facial structures, very dark complexions, and longer faces than people from other ethnic Oy villages.

The reason for this shift to being Lao is a result of the dominant position that the ethnic Lao have in the Xekong River Basin, and Laos more generally. The power of the ethnic Lao has privileged them in terms of other ethnic groups, leading to a devaluation of other ethnic groups, and associated discrimination. Some of the oppressed eventually decide that it would be advantageous for them to shift ethnic identities, and in the Lao context, this is seen as perfectly logical and acceptable by all, including the Lao. Ancestry is not considered the primary basis of ethnicity, as is typically the case in Western countries (see also Grabowsky 2004; Evans 1999; Jonsson 1997; Condominas 1990).

Apart from the fluidity of ethnic identities, other important elements in history relate to the ways in which people from different ethnic groups interact. It is not unusual for researchers to consider the relationships between dominant groups, like the Lao, and ethnic minorities; but it is less common to investigate how different minority groups, like the many Mon-Khmer language speaking peoples in the Xekong River Basin, interact. In the Xekong Basin these relationships are important and complex. One good example relates to past ethnic tensions between the Oy and the Brao people in Attapeu Province. In this case the importance of history continues to manifest itself in ethnic relationships and even in government decision-making processes. Engelbert (2004) reported that Brao people have a long history of raiding Oy villages, sometimes with the help of ethnic Cheng people, in order to steal valuables and take slaves, which they often sold to middlemen. The Brao were often the victims of the fierce Sedang and Jarai, and the Brao, in turn, attacked the more peaceful Oy people.

Another example relates to the Harak and Souay (Kui) people. The Harak historically inhabited the left bank of the Xekong and the southern foothills of the Bolaven Plateau. They identified the Souay as "*Youk*," a term that does not have a positive meaning. However, it is unclear to many Souay what the term *Youk* refers to. The French linguist Gerard Diffloth has found that some Harak vocabulary is closely linked to ancient Khmer. The Harak also tend to speak better Lao than many other Austroasiatic groups, due to their locations in the relative lowlands. In addition, one Harak man from Xekong Province explained that he did not like being called "*Alak*," because the origin of the word related to the Harak people being called thieves, or "*khi lak*" in Lao.

Many ethnic Brao people in Attapeu Province continue to dislike and fear the ethnic Sedang (*Hadang* in Brao) because, prior to the colonial period, the Sedang often attacked their Brao neighbors to the west. They developed a culture that required the sacrificial killing of humans and buffaloes. The human flesh was not consumed, but the buffalo flesh was. Since the Sedang did not want to sacrifice their own kith and kin, they often preyed on the Brao. Many people still know this story even though the Sedang stopped sacrificing people after the French took control of the area in the late nineteenth and early twentieth centuries. Yet, this history still impacts the ways in which Sedang and Brao people interact in real-life situations. There are also stories about the Oy once being the slaves of the Brao, before establishing their own communities on the west side of the Xekong in the foothills of the Bolaven Plateau.

These interactions are often based on history, which is critical for constructing and transforming ethnic and other identities. Ethnic identities are based both on self-identification and how people are identified by those who identify themselves as being different. There is no concrete formula for ethnic change, but it is always a complex issue contingent on the particular circumstances and local histories. More, these relations are critical in terms of local livelihoods. For example, when people from two different groups meet in the forest, the way they interact and recognize resource tenure is frequently influenced by their ethnicity. Ethnicity is also important in relation to government interactions with people from different ethnic groups. For example, most government officials are ethnic Lao, who have long dominated people from other ethnic groups. Therefore, previous relations play into present power relations and the way people interact with each other. Kinship exchanges between villages are also important in term of ethnic relations and have a long history in the Xekong River Basin (Goudineau 2001).

There is a history of complex barter trading between different ethnic groups in the region (Chagnon 2000). For example, between Kalum and Dakchung Districts, in Xekong Province, the Ngkriang and Katu peoples had a tradition of trading hand woven skirts to the Triang and Pakoh for buffalo. Buffalo were then used to trade for earthenware with the Brou Ta-oi people in Salavan. In Attapeu, the Brao sometimes traded rice to the Lao in the lowlands for salt, which was scarce in the uplands. Some Brao in the mountains, like those from Tra-oum Village, did not even raise buffaloes in the mountains. When they needed them for sacrifices, they would trade forest products and rice for buffaloes. The Brao would also grow cotton and trade it to the Triang and Harak, who would weave it and trade it back to the Brao. The Brao also hired out their labor to the Triang and the Harak to carry blankets and other clothes to ethnic Sedang areas to trade for gold. Some groups like the Katu have developed an identity based on their isolated locations and limited trade relations, whereas the Ngkriang have more of a trading orientation due to their position along the Xekong River, a historically important transportation route (Goudineau 2001).

Some GoL officials state they see the strong ethnic cohesion in Kalum and Dakchung Districts as an opportunity for development. However, Goudineau (2001) believes the Triang people in Dakchung are generally more accepting of outside development than people from Kalum. He hypothesizes that this may be due to the greater contact and trade relations between the Triang and neighboring Vietnam. However, in the early 1990s there were reports that back in the late 1970s some prominent people in Dakchung District had actually asked the GoL not to interfere in their affairs by imposing a development agenda on the district. The GoL intended to reward the people for their assistance during the revolution, but the people themselves, at least at that time, were not keen to accept the GoL's development model. Xainyavong et al. (2003) claim that the Triang people migrated from Vietnam to Laos about 125 years ago to escape French rule. Thus, they have a history of wanting to maintain their independence and isolated status.

There is still considerable racial prejudice by many ethnic Lao toward minorities. These feelings take various forms and often run deep. Chagnon (2000) reports that many ethnic Lao consider the people of Xekong Province to be generally "too independent minded" and that some have supposed that the socio-cultural characteristics of the minorities in Xekong mark them off from the dominant Lao-Tai society, presenting "a disadvantage for them in the process of development." Chagnon (2000) also writes that the social and cultural gap between the lowland Lao of other provinces and the indigenous mountain dwellers of Xekong is widening, although there is certainly a significant amount of acculturation of ethnic minorities into lowland Lao society occurring as well. There is still also a significant amount of ethnic bias in the Xekong River Basin, especially directed at the Mon-Khmer language speakers by ethnic Lao. For example, the ethnic GoL counterparts of a German volunteer agency working in Attapeu were frequently heard in 2005 referring to the minorities in Sanxay District as being "half human, half animal." Sometimes, these unjust biases are much less direct and are instead interjected more subtly into discourses surrounding ethnic minorities.

The first author overheard an interesting conversation between some young Lao men in Attapeu town one night in early 2006. They were sitting around talking and drinking Lao whisky. One of the men exclaimed that ethnic minorities are "*ladap tam*" ("low level"), but that there is one good thing about them. He explained that during the war all the national languages were known to Americans listening in on Pathet Lao telegraph messages, so "*Lave*" [Brao] was used for communications in order to ensure that the enemy could not intercept messages. This sort of indirectly biased discourse remains evident in many aspects of society, but it is notable that there have been some improvements. Most importantly, people tend to realize now that minorities have the same legal rights as others, and ethnic Lao people usually dare not intentionally make derogatory comments in front of minorities.

What Happened to the *Kaseng*?

The "*Kaseng*"[36] were long considered to be an ethnic groups inhabiting the area around Dakchung and Sanxay Districts, but when the Xekong provincial government surveyed Dakchung District in the late 1990s they could not find anyone who was self-identified as *Kaseng*. They assumed that all the *Kaseng* were living in Attapeu Province, but when they went to Attapeu, they were surprised to find that officials there were also unable to identify any villages populated by *Kaseng*. There are people living in the Xekong provincial capital who claim that they are *Kaseng*, but they are individuals, not groups of families or villages.

We later learned the origin of the term. It was first used during the time when the Siamese controlled Attapeu, probably during the nineteenth century, and was later used during the colonial period when groups of people, who now call themselves Harak and Triang, were violently opposed to French rule. Groups from present-day Dakchung and Sanxay Districts reportedly killed a number of French, and the French military then sent soldiers to the area to pacify the resistance. Tribal people, including their leaders, were forced by the French to conduct a ceremony that was believed to be successful in gaining some protection from tribal attacks. The tips of the blades of tribal swords were dipped into small containers of "special spiritual water" (*nam sep nam seng* in Lao), and the sword owners took an oath not to attack any French in the future. The tribals widely feared the consequences of breaking oaths made with "*nam sep nam seng.*" Failing to honor such oaths was believed to lead to negative retribution from the spirits.

LeBar et al. (1964) reported that the *Kaseng* were found on the higher parts of the Dakchung Plain, also known as *Phou Phiang Kaseng*, between Nam Touei and Nam Ang in *Muang* Chavan, Salavan Province. This is part of present-day Dakchung District, Xekong Province. They claimed that there were about 4,000 *Kaseng* people and that they spoke a language in the Mon-Khmer stock. The *Kaseng* were reported to be important weavers who traded with neighboring groups, particularly in the Chavan area. Chazee (1999) lists the *Kaseng* as inhabiting parts of Dakchung and provides a map to illustrate where they are found. Chamberlain et al. (1996) also lists the *Kaseng* as present in Laos, but acknowledges that it might be true that the *Kaseng* are a composite of Alak and Talieng peoples. They suggested that it might also be true that this term is an alternate one for those groups. However, they finally concluded that while the status of the *Kaseng* remained unclear, the language they spoke seemed to fall between Central and Northern branches of Bahnaric. In reality, *Kaseng* does not represent any ethnic group, although people in Dakchung call themselves *Triang Kaseng.*[37] Engelbert (2004) also reported that the *Kaseng* are now referred to as Triang.

Actually, the term "Triang" itself appears to have quite recent origins, and, according to Xainyavong et al. (2003), it was adopted during the colonial period. When the French went to their villages, elders would urge everyone to listen carefully to what the French had to say. "*tring, tring*" in their language means "listen, listen," and according to elders, the term was altered and adopted as the group's ethnonym.[38]

The *Phya* and *Lam* of the Brao

During the pre-colonial and colonial eras there were people in southern Laos known as "*Phya*" and "*Lam*" in Lao. *Phya* were appointed as representatives of the government in the villages, both during the Siamese and French eras. *Lam* were somewhat different. They were generally ethnic Lao men from well established villages who had developed special relationships with remote communities, especially ones populated by ethnic minorities with little other contact with the outside world. According to the French colonial administer of Attapeu, Antonin Baudenne (1913), these relationships originated during the Siamese period. Often, it was only possible to meet with people from these remote populations through the intermediaries, or *Lam*. If unknown people tried to contact them, the minorities would usually flee into the forest. As Baudenne commented, "The *Kha* seem to be very attached to their *Lam*" (our emphasis). The minorities trusted these individuals, and the *Lam* could persuade them to come to meetings, and so on. There was a sort of feudal patronage relationship between the *Lam* and the minorities. Baudenne explained that the *Lam* often exploited the weaknesses of the minorities and made good profits by exchanging things with them on favorable terms. They stayed months at a time in remote communities and spoke the local languages. This was probably quite important, as Baudenne wrote that local Brao people would often ignore the Lao language. The *Lam* collected taxes on all kinds of trade with these people, and paid some of those taxes to the Siamese and later the French. Baudenne recognized the exploitative nature of the *Lam*, but said that it was not yet possible to suppress them, as "the French need[ed] the *Lam* as much as the *Kha* needed them."

Lam continued to have influence, at least in some cases, into relatively recent times. In 1975, an ethnic Brao community was required to move from near the Cambodian border in the Xekong Basin to escape attacks by the Khmer Rouge. The *Lam* for the community, a man from the ethnic Lao village of Thapho, Khong District (located adjacent to the Mekong), convinced the Brao to resettle in Thapho. The Brao did so, living in Thapho for a brief time, before establishing the village of Phon Sa-at in Khong District, in which they live today. The *Lam* system is now rarely applied in Laos, and is strongly discouraged by the GoL, which regards it as a vestige of feudalism.

Plans to Resettle Ethnic Hmong People to Attapeu

In late 2000 and early 2001, the GoL, as part of its drive to eradicate swidden agriculture, devised an Agriculture Development Master Plan for the country that identified three provinces as still having substantial unused lowland areas suitable for wet-rice paddy conversion: Khammouane, Bolikhamxay, and Attapeu. Because of the unavailability of land for lowland rice cultivation in northern Laos, GoL officials decided that it would make sense to relocate people without paddy land in the north to places with land in central and southern Laos. As part of this plan, in early 2001 five ethnic Hmong leaders from northern Laos were asked to go to Attapeu to determine whether the land there would be suitable for their people. The Hmong leaders were apparently happy with what they found, but when senior Attapeu government officials realized that the Central government was hoping to relocate 100,000 people from the north (mainly Xieng Khouang and Houaphan Provinces) to Attapeu, they became concerned and found a way to stop the plan. Ethnic Hmong people had never lived in Attapeu, and provincial officials were concerned that conflicts would develop with the people already living there (Baird 2002; 2003a).

During the period in 2001 when this large-scale resettlement program was being considered, thirteen ethnic Hmong families were resettled from Bolikhamxay Province in central Laos to the ethnic-Brao dominated Phouvong District in Attapeu Province (Baird 2003a). The Brao found the Hmong to be industrious and were impressed by their ability successfully to farm areas dominated by *imperata* grasses. They were also impressed with the hunting skills of the Hmong, including their use of poisoned arrows.

However, the Hmong and the Brao did not get along well. For one, the Hmong were socially closed to the Brao, who were interested in making contact with the Hmong once they moved into a lowland area in the district. For example, Brao men were not allowed to talk to young unmarried Hmong women, and the Hmong refused to allow their unique varieties of chickens (which they had brought with them) to be raised by the Brao. They would not sell them live chickens. There were also conflicts when the Hmong claimed particular forest areas and streams near where they lived and refused to allow neighboring Brao people to fish, hunt, or gather forest products in those areas, even though the Brao had customarily used them. The Brao reported finding the Hmong to be quite aggressive toward them, generally not very friendly, and lacking in solidarity or "*samakhi*" with local Brao people, although the Hmong themselves were quite united.

The Phouvong District government, itself dominated by Brao, was shocked by the conflicts that developed between the Brao and Hmong, and soon concluded that the Hmong should return to Bolikhamxay Province. But the Hmong were not eager to return. It took considerable pressure from the government to get them to leave. Seven families left at the end of 2002 or early 2003 (Baird 2003a), but it took until early 2004 for the rest of the families to leave.

3

Culture and Livelihoods

One of this book's main objectives is to illustrate the importance of culture in relation to livelihoods systems. Many researchers have a tendency to consider either culture or livelihoods but rarely both as an integrated system. As the French anthropologist Yves Goudineau (2001) has pointed out, adapted intervention in remote ethnic minority communities requires specific cultural and social knowledge—knowledge that is often lacking among so-called "development specialists."

Religion

One important aspect of culture is religion, and, as Mole has put it, "Religion, whatever its name, has among its purposes, the integration of the individual's behavior with his society. It gives confidence for meeting crises which life inescapably brings. Moreover it introduces into the individual's existence, a stable core by which values may be assigned to ideas, events and proposed courses of action" (1970: 158). Broadly speaking, there are two main religions in the Xekong Basin in Laos: Animism[1] and Theravada Buddhism. In addition, there is a small population of Christians,[2] with many having been converted to Christianity during the French period.

People who write about Laos frequently describe its people, as Arthur Dommen (1985) did, as Theravada Buddhists in the lowlands and animists in the mountains. However, the situation is much more complicated, something that Dommen acknowledges later in this same book, *Laos Keystone of Indochina*. In reality, the lowland Lao have long retained many Animist beliefs. As Constance Wilson (1992: 9) put it, "Theravada Buddhism was accepted throughout Lao society while the Lao also retained the older cult of the spirits." At the beginning of the twentieth century, Baudenne (1913) went further, stating that in Attapeu the Buddhist temple was deserted, and that only the "*phi*" (spirits) were essential to the people. He also mentioned that frequent sacrifices were required to acknowledge the power of the *phi*, and that the Lao had picked up Animist taboos from the Austroasiatics.

Taking a contemporary example from the Xekong River Basin, the ethnic Lao village of Sompoy, in Sanamxay District, has a "*taho*" spirit house for the village, and an old woman in the village also acts as a medium, or "*nang thiem*" (literally, "false woman" in Lao). Typically, in such villages, every May all the families provide small offerings at the *taho*, and the *nang thiem* takes on the spirit of a male village leader from the past, donning unusual clothing to represent the character of the spirit that has entered her body. The *nang thiem*, usually an older woman, but occasionally a younger woman or man, typically drinks a good deal of homemade rice whisky (*lao khao* in Lao) directly from the bottle, as it is believed that she cannot get drunk. But the drink quickly affects her, and she takes advantage of her tipsy state to complain aggressively about any problems that exist in the village. This is the time of the year when she, as a representative of village women, is able to admonish the village headman (who is almost always a man) without fear of retribution (it's not her talking, it's the spirit). During this ritual, the village headman and others beg the medium to protect the community from illness or bad fortune, such as livestock epidemics, drought, or floods. The ritual often continues for a couple of hours or longer, with appropriate drumming and dancing. (The spirit wants everyone to be happy when the ritual takes place.) There is generally a small patch of protected forest around the *taho*. Apart from its spiritual role, it provides shade during these events.

There is a sacred seasonal pond called *Nong Kanan* on the border between Vat Louang and Vat That Villages, adjacent to the Xekaman River in Saysettha District. Near its edge is the "*lak meuang*," a stone in the ground that represents the center of the principality of Attapeu. There is a *nang thiem* in the villages, and she is the only one who ever enters the pond when there is water in it, but these rituals only occur once in many years. Elders in Vat Louang claim that the village's Buddhist temple was established about 400 years ago, but the exact date of its origin is uncertain.

The Mon-Khmer language speaking peoples, while predominantly Animist, also respect and practice many Buddhist rituals, or mix Buddhist and Animist rituals. For example, the Brao village of Halang Nyai in Samakhixay District performs various Buddhist rituals, such as the Lao New Year (*Boun pi mai Lao* in Lao) in April and "*Boun phravayt*" in May. Many minority villages also have lowland Lao Animist *taho* houses, but they rarely have *nang thiem*.

Clearly, Buddhist rituals are often interwoven with the Animist ceremonies of both Lao and other ethnic groups. It is probably true that there are almost no people in the Xekong River Basin who do not hold at least some nominally Animist ideas. The ethnic Brao village of Phya Keo in Sanxay District has replaced Brao annual village Animist rituals with Lao Animist rituals involving the use of a *taho*. Some follow Animist rituals of both the Lao and the minorities. As one old ethnic Brao man said, "If people say we are superstitious, then the Lao are equally superstitious."

Animism in the Xekong River Basin does not represent a single religion, but rather a wide variety of different belief systems and practices. Even within the same ethnic group, Animist practices differ widely from region to region, village to village, family to family, and even between individuals from the same family. There are too many differences to mention here, but it is interesting to note that this diversity of belief systems, and the lack of codification of the systems, are some of the main reasons why Animism does not have the same institutional status, both in Laos and internationally, as institutionalized religions such as Buddhism, Christianity, and Islam.

While religious freedoms are respected in the Lao Constitution, the Constitution does not recognize any forms of Animism as religion, and so officially the Lao Constitution does not protect it. In late 2005, senior officials in the LFNC in Vientiane told us that Animism is not considered an official religion in Laos because there are no specific written teachings (codification) for Animism; nor is there a specific church, temple, mosque, or other place of worship.

The first Christian missionary to visit Laos was probably the Jesuit Giovanni-Maria Leria in 1642. However, he did not travel to the Xekong River Basin. Despite several attempts over the years, it was not until 1878 that the next Catholic missionary set foot in Laos (Stuart-Fox 2001), and it was not until 1884 that the first French priest, Father Prudhomme, head of the Apostolic Mission of Laos, decided to travel to Attapeu—not so much to proselytize as to protest slavery in the town. There are no records of any missions ever being established in the Xekong Basin during the colonial period, although small numbers of people were converted to Christianity during and after it. The Kontum mission, located in the Central Highlands of present-day Vietnam, was the closest Christian presence to the Xekong Basin.

There have been some reports in recent years of Christians in Sanamxay District, Attapeu Province being persecuted by government officials. A Paris-based Lao exile group, "The Lao Movement for Human Rights," was the first organization to release reports about religious persecution against Christians in Attapeu. In early 2004, they claimed that eleven Christians had been arrested on 27–28 December

2003, for holding religious services on Christmas Day. However, a Lao Ministry of Foreign Affairs spokesman, Yong Chanthalangsy, made a public statement soon after, claiming that the accusations were false. He stated that the people were detained because they were found possessing poisons (Chang 2004). Government officials in Attapeu essentially repeated the same story, claiming that the poison was being illegally used for fishing. The credibility of the claims of the exile group making the accusation suffered because it stated that those arrested were ethnic Oy and Khmu (Chang 2004). While there are certainly many ethnic Oy people in Sanamxay District, there are no ethnic Khmu communities in southern Laos.

In early 2004, the US-based Christian human rights organization International Christian Concern (ICC 2004) reported that government officials had given an ultimatum to Christians living in Donthapat Village, Sanamxay District, to "leave their village or die." Furthermore, ICC (2004) implied that all the people of the village were Christians, but even Christians in Attapeu acknowledge that Christians are not in the majority in any villages. ICC claimed that "The government's goal is to eradicate Christianity" (2004: 1), a statement that does not appear to be supported by available evidence. However, in February 2004 the homes and livestock of some Christians were reportedly confiscated, and local government officials apparently made death threats against Christians during that period. Later the same year there were reports of improvements in the treatment of Christians in Sanamxay District. As of August 2004, Christians who were imprisoned and evicted from their homes in early 2004 were again allowed to gather and worship in the homes of their leaders in *Ban* Mai, and in the Sanamxay district town (Anonymous 2004a).

Illegal missionary-oriented activities by Western evangelicals appear to be the cause of at least some of the troubles experienced by local Christians in Attapeu. Foreign-based groups have at times conducted short-term "underground" religious activities in the region, which appear to have contributed to the government's suspicion of Christians and some of its repressive actions. For example, in 2001 two Caucasian foreigners posing as tourists distributed a large amount of Christian religious propaganda in the Attapeu town area, including Lao-language brochures and cassette tapes, leaving them behind in restaurants where they ate and scattering materials along the banks of the Xekong River, and wherever else they could. They only stayed in Attapeu a couple of days and were gone before the government could determine who they were. A Christian doctor living in Attapeu at the time acknowledged that this sort of behavior inflames suspicions and makes it more difficult for the small Christian community in the province.

According to Khampho Sochanthavong, the Vice-President of LFNC in Xekong Province, everyone is allowed the freedom of religious worship in Laos, provided that they do not aggressively attempt to convert people, cause community conflict, or advocate anti-government actions. He mentioned one example from Thateng District in which provincial authorities disrobed two Buddhist monks who were found to be aggressively trying to convert Animist villagers to Buddhism. He also mentioned that the GoL is against new Christians who do not agree to participate in communal work in their villages.

The 1991 Constitution of the Lao PDR states, "Lao citizens have the right and freedom to believe or not to believe in religions." Article 8 of the Constitution states:

> The state pursues the policy of promoting unity and equality among all ethnic groups. All ethnic groups have the rights to protect, preserve, and promote the fine customs and cultures of their own tribes and of the nation. All acts of creating division and discrimination among ethnic groups are prohibited. The state implements every measure gradually to develop and upgrade the levels of socio-economy of all ethnic groups.

Furthermore, Article 9 of the Lao PDR Constitution states:

> The state respects and protects all lawful activities of Buddhists and that other religious followers mobilize, and encourages Buddhist monks and novices, as well as priests of other religions, to participate in the activities that are beneficial to the country and people. All acts of creating division of religious and classes of people are prohibited.

Some international critics remain unhappy with Prime Minister's Decree No. 92, of July 2002, on the "Management and Protection of Religious Activities in the LPDR," publicized by the GoL as a measure in favor of religious freedom. They claim that the decree "regulates, in the least detail, the control of the ruling Party on all religious organizations and reinforces the official monitoring of activities and daily movements of Christian congregations in Laos" (Transnational Radical Party 2004: 1). The US State Department also includes Laos on "a worst offenders list of totalitarian states that view religions as a threat to their dominant ideology" (Chang 2004: 1).

The evangelical American Christian group, Joshua Project, is advocating radical measures to proselytize ethnic groups, like the Chatong people of Xekong Province, who they acknowledge have no known Christian "believers." On their website,[3] they made the following "Prayer Requests" in relation to the Chatong:

- Pray Christian health workers could gain access to the Chatong area and make a difference in their lives.
- Ask God to pierce the darkness of life in Xekong with his wonderful light.
- Pray the power of superstition and greed would be broken over people in Laos, and many would turn to God.

The Joshua Project also appealed to supporters to "Pray a strong evangelizing church would soon emerge among the demon-fearing Katu of Laos."

Spirits and Sacrifices

Animism is the dominant spiritual influence on people in most parts of the Xekong River Basin, although it may not always be the most visible religion, especially in urban and lowland areas. Sacrifices are often a part of Animist ceremonies devoted to appeasing spirits. A number of different ethnic groups in the Xekong River Basin in Laos have the tradition of sacrificing domestic animals to spirits, mainly chickens, pigs, and buffaloes, but also sometimes dogs, cats, and goats, depending upon the ritual and the context. Long ago the ancestors of the people now referred to as the Katu were involved in certain forms of human sacrifice (Condominas 1977; Mole 1970). At one point in the distant past, some Katu are believed to have decided to move beyond sacrificing buffaloes in order to demonstrate greater potency and maximize fertility (Condominas 1977).

According to ethnic Brao elders living in Phouvong District, the Sedang people from neighboring parts of Vietnam in Kontum Province used to attack and kill people from Brao villages to get the blood, hands, and livers of their victims. This is said to have happened whenever a young Sedang woman became pregnant out of wedlock. The young pregnant woman would be banished from her village and would not be allowed to return unless human body parts were obtained for use in ceremonies that included the sacrifice of buffaloes and pigs, and that would allow for the return of the woman to her village. Hoffet (1933) also confirmed that the Sedang conducted human sacrifices at least up until the middle of the twentieth century. As will be explained later, the Sedang were also known to eat some of the internal organs of their enemies after killing them in battle, indicating that certain forms of cannibalism also occurred. However, we are unaware of any recent cases of human sacrifice in the Xekong Basin, and there has generally been a reduction in animal sacrifices throughout the basin as well. This is due to economic factors, government efforts to discourage sacrifices, and general acculturation, often related to internal resettlement.

Although there has been a reduction in animal sacrifices in recent years, they remain important to many people in the basin, and these rituals certainly have an impact on livelihoods. As Robert Mole put it in referring to the Katu of Vietnam:

> The life of the average Katu is overshadowed by the fear of the many spirits believed to affect or control all parts of his life. His birth, childhood, marriage, economic life, death, and all other phases of existence are governed by taboos created to avoid offending the spirits. Broken taboos anger the spirits who may cause grievous sickness or death unless the offender quickly offers a satisfactory sacrifice.
>
> (1970: 159–160)

The Austroasiatic peoples of the Xekong River Basin have a huge variety of ritual expression. Rituals are performed as a part of annual ceremonies and in response to illness and misfortune, and there cyclic sacrifices are associated with the agricultural year (Mole 1970). Even within one ethnic group, there may be a number of quite different animal sacrifice ceremonies.

The Jru Dak people from Sanamxay District have their main village ritual (*het heet* in Lao) each year in March (the fourth Lao lunar month). This is apparently the only village-wide ritual performed by the Jru Dak, and each village reportedly performs their own ceremony. Apart from that ritual, other Animist ceremonies are reportedly performed periodically when people become ill. Other groups, like the Brao, tend to celebrate their New Year in January or February, whereas the ethnic Lao Buddhists celebrate the "Lao New Year" in April (the fifth Lao lunar month).

There are four main sub-groups of Brao people in Laos, all of whom are found in Attapeu Province. They are the Ka-nying, Hamong, Kavet, and Jree. The Ka-nying and the Hamong both sacrifice buffaloes when adult humans are seriously ill and if they have the resources to do so. Their buffalo sacrifices generally follow two stages. They may begin by sacrificing a buffalo via *bra bun*,[4] a certain type of ritual involving the planting of three short wild kapok trees. Days or months later, a second buffalo may be sacrificed via a *bra hanoi*,[5] a ritual that involves a single, long, wild kapok tree and elaborate decorations made of bamboo. The Kavet do not practice this type of ritual. They do sacrifice buffaloes, but via *bra kalophao*, a different type of ritual also involving the planting of three wild kapok trees. However, unlike *bra bun*, the middle kapok tree is shorter than the other two, and the head of the buffalo is tied in the middle after the animal is killed and all the meat from the head has been removed and consumed. Then there are the Jree, who claim not to have any tradition of buffalo sacrifice but do sacrifice pigs and chickens as part of certain rituals.

Sacrificial rituals can vary significantly, even between different sub-groups of the same ethnic group, but the situation is often even more complex, with differences occurring between villages within the same sub-group, or even differences between families and between individuals within the same families. It is not possible to provide more than a small sample of the ritual intricacies of the people of the Xekong Basin, but it is important to recognize that these spiritual issues are extremely important when considering livelihoods in the basin and the region's history.

Many ethnic minorities believe that spirits are the cause of illness and that sacrifices are needed to appease offended spirits. If a sacrifice is unsuccessful in curing the illness, it is generally assumed that the sacrifice was to the wrong spirit. Therefore, minorities place considerable importance on determining the right spirit to whom to devote a sacrifice. A number of methods are used to determine which spirits are involved, including examining egg yokes and measuring long sections of narrow lengths of bamboo.

The GoL has long tried to persuade local people to give up "superstitious" practices associated with various forms of Animism. Campaigns to suppress Animism were especially evident after 1975, up until the end of the 1980s, and in some areas into the 1990s. In recent years explicit efforts to suppress Animist practices have diminished greatly, and some practices have been slowly reappearing. Isolation after the war has sometimes resulted in the revival of religious traditions and artistic expression last practiced during the war years. In some cases this has been the result of minorities "turning in on themselves" after being neglected or persecuted in the post-1975 era (Goudineau 2001), but in other cases rituals seem to have been extinguished permanently or continue to decline. Sometimes villagers claim not to be practicing any Animist traditions, even when they are still doing so. This reluctance to admit involvement is sometimes linked to fears that, if they reveal their involvement in certain rituals, they might face admonishment from the government, including further attempts to abolish the practices. Sosonephit Phannouvong, an ethnologist and the deputy director of the Ethnic Groups Department of the LFNC, and Viphone Chaoasan of the Xekong LFNC confirmed that villagers are often fearful that outsiders will criticize their practices. There has been a generally greater decline in sacrifices, especially collective rituals, among villagers who have been resettled from the uplands to the lowlands and to near main roads, and when people from more than one ethnic group have been resettled into the same village. It appears that changes in location can have considerable impact on people's sense of identity, including ethnicity and use of traditional rituals.

While sacrifices remain an important part of the spiritual world of most minorities in the Xekong River Basin, it would be wrong to assume that their involvement in sacrifices precludes them from using modern or herbal medicines. In fact, most minorities are willing to use all measures to overcome illness. It is just that sacrifices are often the most familiar method and, for the generally cash-poor members of ethnic minorities, sacrifices can be performed without cash resources. Sacrificed animals certainly do have a market value, and government officials often criticize minorities for "wasting livestock resources on sacrifices." However, many people feel better about sacrificing a valuable animal they already own than they do having to spend a smaller amount of cash on modern medical treatment. Also, the people in the community consume the meat of sacrificed animals so, at a certain level, killing a chicken for dinner and killing one for sacrifice has the same practical result in terms of meat consumption.

There have been relatively few published studies from the Xekong Basin, but in 1967 Diane Alexander conducted a short but interesting one in Dak Trang Village, Pakxong District (Alexander 1978). Alexander's research was carried out in an ethnic Jru (Laven) village near the Royal Lao military base at Houay Kong. (It was one of the only villages on the Bolaven Plateau considered safe for her to work in at the time.) She considered peoples' beliefs about illnesses and medicines, and documented how people gradually, over her three-month stay in the village, became more willing to go to a hospital to treat illnesses instead of performing sacrifices. She acknowledged her own role in trying to convince villagers to adopt Western medicines over rituals and associated animal sacrifices. She reported that her efforts were at least somewhat successful although, ironically, she then became sick and had to leave the village prematurely. Because of security concerns, she was unable to return to the village to confirm her findings.

Local spirit-based belief systems can sometimes help protect some species of wildlife, forests, and other natural areas from negative environmental impacts. For example, few hunters would dare shoot a lone male gaur in the forest, as they believe that these animals have powerful spirits and that those who shoot them are prone to severe danger from those spirits. Many ethnic minority villagers also do not allow the eating of particular animals, like macaques, barking deer, or other species. There are a wide variety of beliefs; many are based on dreams, which are regarded as being important in the cosmology of the basin's Austroasiatic peoples (Xekong Province LFNC 2007).

Culture and Nature

Rivers, streams, deep-water pools, waterfalls, rapids, ponds, and other water bodies are often of considerable cultural importance to local people. In fact, liveli-hoods, culture, and water are intertwined in important and varied ways, as the following examples illustrate.

The Annual Boat Races in Attapeu Province

The annual boat racing festival celebrated in Attapeu Province illustrates the cultural importance of the rivers of the Xekong Basin. In 2004, the races in Attapeu took place on 30 October, the same day as in Vientiane. However, unlike Vientiane, where modern motorized boat racing is now allowed, in Attapeu it is prohibited, and most people say that they prefer traditional boat racing. The boat races in Attapeu take place along the Xekaman River in Samakhixay District, not far upriver from the river's confluence with the Xekong. In 2003, there were eighteen boats registered to race in Attapeu, but in 2004 interest in the races increased, with twenty-five boats registering. As it has over the past twenty years, the Attapeu Vietnamese (born) Association in the province participated in the race. Villagers from Xekong Village won the championship cup and the first prize of 1.5 million kip (Latsaphao 2004).

Although the annual boat races are organized as a lowland Lao event, people from other ethnic groups have long played important roles in the rituals associated with the races (Archaimbault 1964; 1972), although many of those rituals have been abolished or altered since 1975 (Evans 1998). One of the purposes of these races was for ethnic minorities to reaffirm their loyalty to the rulers of the lowlanders, while at the same time receiving the dignity of being recognized by the lowlanders as the first peoples, or the older brothers, of the land. In Champasak, for example, ethnic minorities[6] were always the first ones to ride in the longboats of the races. About twenty minority people would dress up in red and together take a longboat upstream from one end of Champasak town to the other, before floating the boat back downstream. Ethnic Lao people would paddle the boat, while the minorities played gongs and danced. The royal sovereign of Champasak would also give ethnic minorities the honor of sacrificing a buffalo as part of the rituals, and the ethnic minorities would drink jar beer with the sovereign and dance and play gongs as well (Archaimbault 1964; 1972). The minorities were given whatever they wanted to eat and drink by the ethnic Lao during the boat race period. Even today the ethnic Brao people from Phon Sa-at Village in Khong District, Champasak Province play a ritual role in the annual boat races in Khong District. Ethnic minorities used to play an important role in the boat races in Attapeu Province, but those rituals appear to have been suppressed since the revolution.

Spirits of the Water and the Forests

Many of the spirits and (mythical) creatures of most importance to the people of the Xekong River Basin are believed to occur in waters and forests. There are strong beliefs in the existence of serpent-like creatures known in Lao as *nyeuak* and in Brao as *nak*. For example, the Brao villagers from Halang Nyai, which is adjacent to the Xekong River in Samakhixay District, believe that a *nak* protects a sacred large boulder in the Xekong River, called "*Tamaw Tavao*" in Brao. Villagers reported that ten years ago the *nak* there ate a man from the village and that the blood of the person was sucked out and he then died. Villagers therefore often offer jar beer[7] and sacrifice pigs to the spirit of the boulder. It is fine for people to fish near the rock, they said, but it is taboo to eat on top of it. Apart from *Tamaw Tavao*, there are other special rocks in the Xekong River near Halang Nyai Village, such as "*Tamaw Humbrawk*" (fish trap rock), and "*Tamaw Jour*" (pig rock). Locals say that the mythical Brao leader known as "*Groong*" made these rocks.

At "*Keng Pha*," a sacred rapids area on the Xexou River, it is said that those who go there and are favored by the spirits are able to get one "*baht*" of gold, but if the spirits are unhappy, the gold will not be forthcoming. According to local ethnic Lao legend, there is a sacred Buddha image at the bottom of the deep pool just below these rapids.

There are believed to be other spirits in the water. For example, on the Nam Kong River, about 10 km upstream from Viangxai Village, there is a cave called "*Eup Kavang*" in Brao. The Brao believe that this is another place where the Brao mythical spirit hero, *Groong*, stopped on his way back from battle. There is a waterfall there, and the Brao say some of the rocks there are shaped like the chairs and tables where *Groong* rested. According to local legend, *Kavang* was a name of a person, and the spirit that stays there is called "*Arak Kavang*." (*Arak* means spirit in Brao.) Similarly, the Brao believe in the presence of *"Arak Brawng"* at large rapids on the Xexou River.

In the cosmology of the Brao, there are a number of powerful spirits that inhabit different areas, like unusual geological formations, forests, fields, houses, natural ponds, and rivers and streams. The Brao believe that many illnesses are the direct cause of angry spirits, and when water spirits (*Arak Dak* in Brao) are believed to be the cause of particular illnesses, the Brao sometimes choose to sacrifice a chicken as part of an offering ritual called *Bra Yang Dak*. If rituals are correctly conducted, and if the water spirits really are the cause of an illness, it is believed that such an offering can result in a cure. There are also various other geological formations in rivers and streams, such as deep-water pools and large boulders in the water that the Brao believe are the homes of powerful spirits worthy of respect.

The Brao people from Mai Na Koke Village, situated along the Xekaman River, believe in the power of one particular water spirit (*Arak Dak*) and every year they hold special Animist ritual ceremonies for it. They sacrifice a pig and a chicken and anoint a jar of rice beer in honour of the spirit. Villagers from many other communities along the Xekaman River also believe in water spirits, although *Ban* Mai Na Koke is apparently the only village that conducts unique ritual ceremonies for a particular water spirit.

In *Houay* Kase, a tributary of the Xepian River near Kase Village, in Sanamxay District, local ethnic Jru Dak people respect two large stones in the stream; one is believed to look like a man, the other like a woman. People believe that after Vat Phou temple was built west of the Mekong in Champasak Province, a man and a woman went from the temple to *Houay* Kase, died there, and were transformed into stones.

The ethnic Sok people from Sok Village in Samakhixay District say that there are three rapids in the mainstream Xekong inhabited by water spirits (*phi nam* in Lao). In the past, there were special ceremonies held for these spirits, but they are no longer conducted.

In Pak Thon Village in Lamam District, Xekong Province, the original ethnic Harak inhabitants of the village believe that a powerful spirit resides in a deep-water pool in the mainstream Xekong called *Vang Thamakan*. Villagers believe that the spirit will take vengeance on people from the village if it is disturbed.

On the mainstream Xekong, *Vang Tanoke* is a deep-pool area with a mysterious history. According to locals, during the war NVA soldiers were using a barge to transport soldiers and weapons across the Xekong, but half way across a large serpent came to the surface underneath the barge. Its back caused the barge to flip over, drowning a hundred soldiers in the deep-water pool. Local people believe that there are "sacred things" (*neo saksit* in Lao) in the area of deep-water, which is about a kilometer long.

There is also a sacred waterfall about 4 km from Dak Det Village in Saysettha District. Underneath the waterfall there is said to be an ancient Buddha image. Locals mix Lao and Brao languages when referring to the waterfall, calling it "*Dak Sai Nam Trang.*" "*Dak Sai*" means waterfall in Brao, and "*Nam*" is the Lao name for a stream.

Powerful spirits are also believed to reside in certain natural ponds, and in some cases small sacrifices are offered to these spirits before fishing takes place. This is not only the case for ethnic minorities but also for ethnic Lao. People from Kase Village reported that there is one deep natural pond where only fishhooks are used for fishing. Locals do not use gill nets or cast nets for fishing there; nobody prohibits people from using nets for fishing, but fishers are afraid to do so, because of the guardian spirit of the area. There are reportedly crocodiles in the area, and thousands of wild ducks (*nok pet* in Lao) use the wetland. In the dry season the wetland dries up, leaving mud, and the crocodiles move elsewhere.

Forests and individual trees are believed to be the homes of many powerful spirits. The Brao call forest spirits *Arak bree*, and spirits of trees *Arak lawng*. Sometimes, when a spirit in a particular tree is believed to be the cause of an illness, it is cut down to get rid of the spirit, but this does not occur frequently and probably does not have a significant impact on forest cover. *Arak bree* inhabit all forests, but some forests are thought to be home to more powerful and dangerous spirits. Areas believed to be the most dangerous are generally avoided. In other cases, trees cannot be cut down when they are expected to be the home for a particular spirit. For example, the ethnic Katu people from Don Village, Kalum District have a large tree adjacent to their village that cannot be cut down. When village sacrifices take place, animal blood is put on its trunk in order to appease the spirit.

Apart from spirits, the Brao, other Mon-Khmer peoples and even ethnic Lao believe in strange beings that lurk in the forest. One type of langur-like creature, called "*heung hang*" in Brao, is said to be fearsome. Another, called "*jok wok*" in Brao, is said to be a small but powerful primate-like creature that people fear. It is said to use one of its arms, which is shaped like a sharp sword, to kill people. Another being, called "*ya yai*" in Brao, is not believed to kill people but often calls people when in the forest, and may cause them to lose their way.

Many of the Austroasiatic peoples of the Xekong River Basin have strong beliefs about following signs in nature. For example, if someone is walking to another village and suddenly hears the sound of a *nok kathoua din* (in Lao) bird, the sighting is considered to be a bad omen for continuing on the path, resulting in the travelers returning home and making the trip the next day. Similarly, if a barking deer (*fan* in Lao) crosses in front a traveler's path, it is seen as a warning of danger ahead, and again, the traveler may decide to turn back for an hour or a day (Xekong province LFNC 2007). While these omens are not as important as they once were, many people know about them, and they are still practiced in many remote parts of the basin, especially by older people, but sometimes by younger ones as well.

Considering Culture in Development Work: Buffaloes in the Mountains

In 2004, the German volunteer agency, Deutscher Entwicklungsdienst (DED), received a small grant from the Lao PDR/Canada Fund to support livestock and agriculture training for ethnic Harak and Triang people in mountainous communities in Sanxay District. Agriculture extension workers helped train a large number of people on how to use buffaloes to till their smallholdings of wet-rice paddy fields in the mountains. Some tools for wet-rice agriculture were also provided. The training seemed to go well; however, in 2005 when they returned to the villages, the DED volunteers found that most of the people trained were not using buffaloes to plow their fields. After some investigation, it became evident that a cultural issue was involved. Since the Harak and Triang in this area mainly raise buffaloes for sacrifices, they believe that using buffaloes for agriculture work might tire them out and result in the buffaloes being less effective when sacrificed. People were fearful of tiring out or hurting the buffaloes, so many opted to prepare their small areas of paddy by hand.

It also became evident that the people did not want to pierce the noses of their buffaloes so that the animals could be used for plowing, both because they had no experience in doing so, and because they did not want to injure the buffaloes. Therefore, the agriculture extension workers agreed to help a small group of enthusiastic farmers pierce their buffaloes' noses.

Although the original training was not a total failure, understanding the cultural obstacles to using buffaloes for farming from the outset certainly would have made the project more successful. Culture is often more important in development than international aid agencies realize, acknowledge, or take into account when designing projects or interventions.

Plate 2.1. The Xekong River in Samakhixay District, Attapeu Province.

Plate 2.2. The Xekong River in Kalum District, Xekong Province.

Plate 2.3. One of the many rapids in the Xekong River in Kalum District, Xekong Province. Rapids provide important fish habitat and are popular fishing spots for local communities.

Plate 2.4. Ethnic Ngkriang man and woman in Kalum District, Xekong Province.

Plate 2.5. Ethnic Ye men in Dakchung District, Xekong Province.

Plate 2.6. Three ethnic Katu Dak Kang elders in Dakchung District, Xekong Province.

Plate 2.7. Ethnic Brao Hamong elder from Phouvong District, Attapeu Province.

Plate 2.8. Two ethnic Katu men blow into either ends of a traditional variety of musical flute.

Plates

Plate 2.9. Ethnic Brao Jree man plays traditional string instrument in Phouvong District, Attapeu Province.

Plate 2.10. Ethnic Brao Ka-nying women play bamboo instrument (*ding booh* in Brao) in Phouvong District, Attapeu Province. One woman hits the palm of her hand against the open top of one end of a bamboo section while another woman claps her hands rhythmically at the other end to make music.

Plate 2.11. Ethnic Brao Ka-nying play traditional Brao instruments in the mountains of Phouvong District, Attapeu Province.

Plate 2.12. Ethnic Brao Jree woman stands in front of hanging musical gongs in Phouvong District, Attapeu Province.

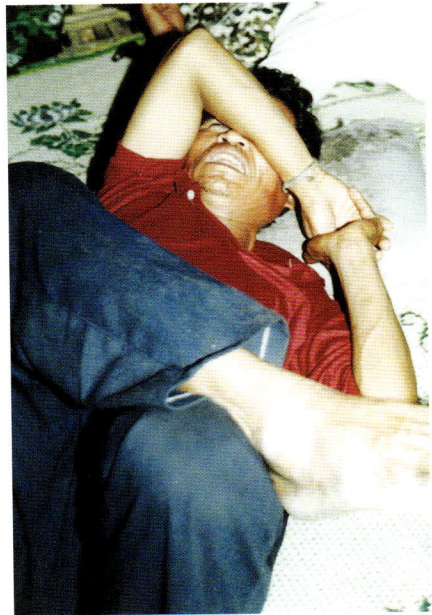

Plate 2.13. Ethnic Brao Hamong man lies down and sings a traditional epic story "*Meut Mooan Groong Yoong*" in Brao.

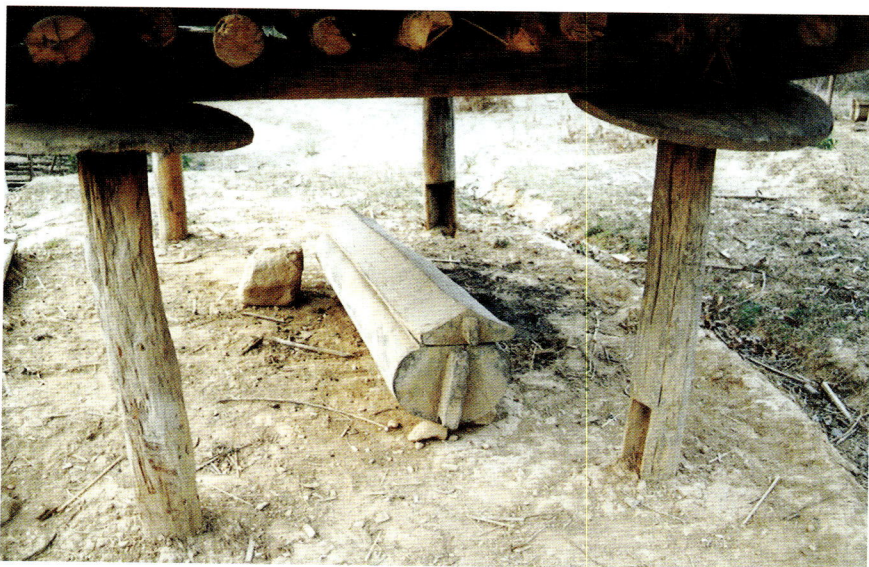

Plate 2.14. Ethnic Katu wooden coffin underneath a rice barn in Kalum District, Xekong Province. For the Katu, coffins are made and stored before someone dies. Making coffins in advance of death is taboo for other ethnic groups like the Brao.

Plate 2.15. Ethnic Brao Ka-nying grave with a zinc roof supported by bombie casings in Phouvong District, Attapeu Province.

Plate 2.16. Ethnic Ngkriang man carrying a baby while smoking a bong pipe filled with a dried mixture of local tobacco and sugarcane juice.

Plate 2.17. A wooden sculpture constructed as part of a communal house for an ethnic Ngkriang village in Kalum District, Xekong Province.

Plate 2.18. Ethnic Triang people drink rice beer in Dakchung District, Xekong Province.

Plate 2.19. Communal house in an ethnic Ngkriang village in Kalum District, Xekong Province.

Plate 2.20. Ethnic Brao Hamong house in Phouvong District, Attapeu Province.

Plate 2.21. Ethnic Brao Ka-nying house in Phouvong District, Attapeu Province.

Plate 3.1. Ethnic Brao Ka-nying performs an Animist ritual in the mountains of Phouvong District, Attapeu Province.

Plate 3.2. Ethnic Brao Ka-nying Animist ritual altar in the mountains of Phouvong District, Attapeu Province.

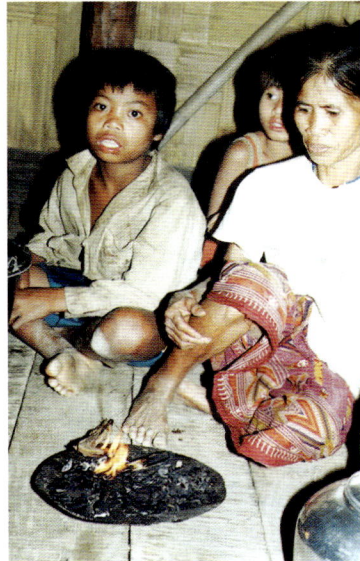

Plate 3.3. Ethnic Ngkriang woman peforms an Animist ceremony to cure an injured leg in Kalum District, Xekong Province.

Plate 4.1. Ethnic Brao men acting as Road-watchers for monitoring the Sihanouk Trail. They were based at Kong Mi in Attapeu Province in the late 1960s and early 1970s, where they were trained, supplied, and paid by the US Central Intelligence Agency (CIA). (Photograph taken by Doug Swanson.)

Plate 5.1. A small area of wet-rice paddy nestled between the mountains in Kalum District, Xekong Province.

Plate 5.2. A dry-season vegetable garden adjacent to the Xekong River in Attapeu Province.

Plate 5.3. Corn growing in a dry season upland garden in Kalum District, Xekong Province.

Plate 5.4. A school built in the Vieng Xay Focal Site and resettlement area by the ADB and Australian government funded "*Dek Nying*" Girls' Education Project in Phouvong District, Attapeu Province. The project has been criticized for building schools far from existing villages thus facilitating government initiated resettlement.

Plate 5.5. The market at the resettlement site and location of the new district center of Sanxay District, Attapeu Province. People have little to sell at the resettlement site and so the market is not functioning.

4

The History of the Xekong River Basin in Laos: A Story of Power, War, and Conflict

The Xekong River Basin in Laos is today arguably one of the more peaceful places in the world, with serious violent crime and conflict being rare. It is sometimes hard to imagine that the basin was once the scene of some of the most intense and prolonged violence in the history of the region, ranging from large-scale slave raiding in the 1800s to US Air Force aerial bombardment in the twentieth century. There have been numerous conflicts, acts of aggression, power struggles, and battles in and near the Xekong Basin throughout history. The violence that dominated many earlier periods continues to scar the landscape, both physically and emotionally, even during this more peaceful era. The following is a history of the Xekong Basin in Laos, including summaries of some of the key periods and the main actors involved in the various conflicts, assaults, and wars that have so profoundly affected the Xekong Basin.

The Pre-Colonial Period: Before the Lao

Archeological records tell us that the Khmer inhabited lowland parts of the Xekong River Basin during the Chenla era (CE 400–800). To this day, there are a number of stone Hindu Chenla ruins from this period in the basin, although detailed archeological research has not yet been carried out. *Vat Sipaket* or "*Ou Mong*" (tunnel)[1] is the name used by the Lao for one important ruin from this era (see box below). Another is found near the Nam Kong River, not far from Kong Mi (see box below), on top of *Phou Kang Hong* Mountain (*Jundoo Klang Rong* in Brao) in Phouvong District, where there is also an ancient stone archway (*Patou Khong* in Lao) reported by Lao villagers to have "*Khmer*" writing on it. Another ruins called *Sieng Kheng* in Lao is situated near the Xekaman River, Sanxay District. There are Chenla ruins near Haisok Village, Samakhixay District, near the Xekong River, and others near Sakhe Village in Samakhixay District, adjacent to the Xekong.

Despite the archaeological evidence, there is no mention of the Chenla era in Lao legend, as the Lao arrived much later. The Lao recognize the Cham and the *Khom* (Austroasiatic or Khmer) as the previous inhabitants. However, there is little known about the Cham presence in the Xekong Basin, and there is some dispute as to whether the Cham were ever in the area. Various Khmer kings probably had outposts in the Xekong Basin in present-day Laos over many centuries following the end of the Chenla era (Martin Rathie, pers. comm. August 2006).

Vat Sipaket or *Ou Mong*

Vat Sipaket (or what many local people simply call "*Ou Mong*," which means tunnel) is an important Chenla ruins situated adjacent to the Xexou River not far from its confluence with the Xekaman River, near Saisy Village, Saysettha District, Attapeu District. It covers about 1 hectare and includes sandstone structures and lintels, along with a laterite rock wall surrounding it. According to local ethnic Lao legend, the first inhabitant of *Vat Sipaket* was *Phao Thao* Lao Long. He had a beautiful daughter name *Nang* Sipaket. *Phao Thao* Lao Long said that whoever wanted to marry his daughter would have to be: 1) an ethnic Lao of royal decent, 2) an excellent soldier, and 3) able to build a large rock castle for her. *Pha-nya* Kammatha, whose mother was said to be Lao and his father Khmer, was able to fulfill all the criteria, including building *Vat Sipaket*. *Pha-nya* Kammatha married *Nang* Sipaket and they had one child, a son named *Thao* Khamkhat[2] (Bounthanh Chanthakhaly, pers. comm. 2006).

However, the Brao recognize a different history for the ruins, claiming that the great Brao epic hero "*Groong*" built the temple. From times past to the present day, Brao men lie down and sing the "*Groong Yoong*" epic story (*meut mouan Groong Yoong* in Brao) for up to three nights in a row. There are many characters in the stories, including "*Yoong*," *Groong*'s younger brother, and *Dao* Mam and *Nang* Lao, their parents. Some ethnic Lao from Saisy Village have incorporated part of this Brao legend into their own. The Lao elder who accompanied us to the ruins in early 2006 said that *Groong* built the temple.

An old man from Saisy Village claimed that various taboos are associated with the ruins. For example, singing "*Lam Salavan*" type of songs is prohibited, and anyone who does so will end up with "black marks between the corners of their mouths and the edges of their ears." In the past it was also taboo to make bricks from clay near the site, but that taboo is no longer followed, according to the elder. "There are other taboos," he continued. "Speaking English or French is prohibited. Speaking Lao is acceptable, but speaking Brao is even better." We were told that rituals were performed for the spirits at the ruins, including one that the elder called *vit phai* (*fai*) *kavai dak*, which is interesting, as "*vit fai*" is a Lao term for using cotton in a ritual, while "*kavai dak*" is the Brao equivalent. Here, Lao and Brao cultures and languages have become interwoven, and social barriers between ethnic groups have to some extent been blurred.

While historically the legend tended to protect the ruins, rumors of gold buried under the temple's main pillar (*beu sim* in Lao) led to the degradation of *Vat Sipaket*. Treasure hunters raided the area at least twice in the twentieth century, digging large pits in the ground searching for gold that they apparently never found. The first time, during the colonial period, the French hired people to dig under the structure in search of gold. The second time, in 1982/1983, a Lao treasure hunter named *Chan* Bouathong, who was believed to have "special powers" to find gold, gathered a group of people together to dig for gold there, without receiving official government permission. It was apparently during this round of digging that the main structure (*Prasat Hin* in Lao) fell down. *Chan* Bouathong was later arrested for illegally digging for gold at another location in Attapeu called "*Nong Sia*."

Neighboring Lao populations in *Muang Kao* (Saysettha district town) have also taken some stone lintels from the site, and two important lintels depicting Hanuman riding a Garuda, as well as a "*nak*" serpent, were transferred to the Buddhist temple *Vat Sili-a-vat* in Fang Deng Village, Saysettha District, decades ago. One of the lintels was completely encased by a cement stupa, while the other can still be seen and has been built into the base of the present temple. Other parts of the ruins have been used for making stairs up the banks of the Xekaman River, as well as for other purposes.

The Expansion of the Power of the Lao

According to Anonymous (1911), in the era of the "lost Lao" (*Lao Long* in Lao), during a time when "men and women all had pony tails," there was only one Austroasiatic couple, *Thao* Baulu and *Nang* Boulu,[3] and their nephews *Thao* Khine[4] and *Thao* Phum Sethi[5] living in Attapeu. In 1438, a hunter from Vientiane discovered the "lost Lao" in Attapeu and reported them to the king in Vientiane. The king ordered them to be brought to Vientiane. They were, and when they got there they agreed to pay the king tribute of 160 ticaux of gold per year (Anonymous 1911).

Chao Xetthathirath I (r. 1548–71) was one of the most powerful kings of Lan Xang. Originally from Luang Phrabang, he transferred his kingdom to Vientiane in 1560, partly as a defensive measure against Burmese invasion. Later he resisted Burmese occupation of Vientiane, after his Siamese allies at Ayutthaya were defeated in 1563 and again in 1567. He was responsible for building the *That Luang* stupa in Vientiane, an enduring symbol of the Lao nation.

In 1571, at the height of his power, Xetthathirath I disappeared somewhere in Attapeu or maybe Cambodia (Stuart-Fox 2001). Khmer chronicles tell of Lao invasions of Cambodia from the north in 1571 and 1572. Defeated by the Khmer and plagued by illness, the Lao apparently returned home (Wilson 1992). Some believe Xetthathirath I was killed during his military campaign in Cambodia near Angkor, due to the similarity between the names *Muang Ong Kan* and *Angkor* (Grabowsky 2004), or upon his return to Laos as a result of wounds sustained in battle. Others believe he was killed when his army was ambushed (Stuart-Fox 2001). It has also been suggested by some historians that he died in Attapeu (Simms and Simms 1999; Grabowsky 2004). A local historian in Attapeu is convinced that Xetthathirath I did indeed die in Attapeu, and in Vat That Village, Saysettha District a small *that* exists that was reportedly made for him. He believes that Xetthathirath I was tricked, ambushed, and killed by local lords on his way to Attapeu. It was actually his second trip, as Xetthathirath I had apparently visited previously. During that trip he took an Austroasiatic wife named *Nang* Samsy (Bounthanh Chanthakhaly, Attapeu historian, pers. comm. 2006).

According to legends documented by Anonymous (1911), Phaxay Xetthathirath, the son of Xetthathirath I and *Nang* Samsy, came to Attapeu from Vientiane in 1575, apparently looking for Xetthathirat I. He is said to have forced the local people to build him a house at *Muang Sok Muang Soum*, west of the Xekong, where he began to lead the Sapouan ethnic group. Phaxay was unmarried and did not have children. He also visited various other ethnic groups, including the "Salang, Lave and Kaseng." However, he was reportedly captured and taken as a slave by people from Oknia[6] Village, who had plans to sell him. Phaxay pretended to be mad, and only the people from Pak Nyeum Village were willing to buy him. He pretended to be unable to do most kinds of work, and so was left to look after the children in the village while his masters worked in their swidden fields. But when the parents of the children returned from their fields, they found that Phaxay had used magic to turn their children into pumpkins. Pumpkins were perhaps easier for him to look after than energetic young children. Once he turned the pumpkins back into children, the people were impressed and made Phaxay their chief. According to these legends, Phaxay then divided up the territories of the different ethnic groups in the area, including areas for the Kaseng, Salang, and Lave. At the time, Attapeu's influence appears to have extended to the mouth of the Sathai River, which flows into the Sesan River near the present-day Cambodia-Vietnam border. Phaxay put the people of Attapeu under the authority of *Thao* So and *Thao* Nyo, sons of *Thao* Phum Sethi.

Also according to Anonymous (1911), Phaxay organized a boat race in the Xekaman River at Vat Louang Village, present-day Saysettha District, in 1578. The Buddhist monks apparently lost the race to Phaxay's group of paddlers, and had to pay 1,000 coconuts to the winners. Phaxay sent the Cheng people to look after Vat Louang and collect the coconuts owed to them.

Palm leaf Lao language manuscripts from the nineteenth century record "*Muang Lao Long*" (the lost Lao principality) as being the first "Lao" village in the region of present-day Attapeu, settled after people migrated into the area from the north. According to the manuscripts, after *Pho Thao* Lao Long, the leader of the group, died, *Thao* Khamkhat, his son, renamed the principality *Muang Ong Kan*. It was located at the present site of *Vat Sipaket* along the Xexou near its confluence with the Xekaman (see box above). Later, *Muang Ong Kan* was moved north to *Muang Lamam*, near *Ban* Phon in present-day Xekong Province, and then to *Muang Sok Muang Soum*, near present-day Haisok Village in Samakhixay District, not far from the Xekong, north of Attapeu town. *Muang Ong Kan* was apparently based there for over two centuries, until the principality began being called "*Ik Kalpeu*" and finally "*Attapeu*" after it was moved to the present-day Saysettha district center, "*Muang Kao*" (old principality), established by the Kingdom of Champasak during the eighteenth century (Bounthanh Chanthakhaly, pers. comm. 2006).

The Early Slave Trade

It is usual for people from outside of the region to think of violence in Laos in relation to the conflicts that occurred in the latter half of the twentieth century, long after the French or Americans gained influence. However, in the consciousness of many people from the Xekong River Basin, the pre-colonial period represents one of the most violent periods in their history. It was certainly critical in shaping the historical landscape and the collective mindset of the region's peoples.

According to many Austroasiatic inhabitants of the basin, an intense period of violent conflict began during the Lao and Siamese periods. While they acknowledge some sporadic conflicts and violence between and within ethnic groups before then, including some slave trading, they claim that what came later was much more systematic and caused more serious disputes between ethnic groups. This generally fits with the conclusions drawn by Bourotte (1955) and Martin Rathie (2001). The slave trade in the Xekong River Basin was stimulated by increased Siamese demand for slaves (see below).

The Lao probably moved into the Xekong Valley at the end of the sixteenth century (Bourotte 1955), and were likely involved in some slave trade early on. In 1641, a merchant with the Dutch East India Company, Gerritt Van Wuysthoff, reported that the gold and slave trades were important in Champasak when he visited there (Stuart-Fox 2001). Seventeenth-century Attapeu was reputed to be the source of valuable exports including forest products, hides, skins, gold, and, possibly most importantly, slaves sold in Cambodia and Siam (Stuart-Fox 2001). During that time the King of Champasak, who controlled much of the Xekong Basin, traded mainly with Cambodia, using the Xekaman and Xekong Rivers, via Attapeu and Siem Pang, for transportation to the Mekong and then south to Phnom Penh. Smaller amounts of trade took place with Vientiane and Ayutthaya (Rathie 2001).

However, one of the most intensive periods of slave trade occurred in the Xekong Basin after 1778, when Siam took control of Champasak. Siam needed labor to recover from the devastation of Burmese invasions, and ordered various slave raids into the Xekong River Basin in Laos. The first official slave draft of people living in present-day Laos was in 1791. Large numbers of Austroasiatic people were enslaved during this period (Ngaosyvathn and Ngaosyvathn 1998).

In 1713, Champasak became independent from other parts of the Kingdom of Vientiane (Wilson 1992). Attapeu was under the nominal control of Champasak, but had not yet been elevated to the status of principality (*Muang*). It was, as Constance Wilson (1992) writes, the "golden age" of Champasak, a time of relative peace and prosperity. *Chao* Soysisamout, who ruled from 1713 to 1737, was followed by his son *Chao* Sayakouman, king of an independent Champasak from 1738 to 1778, and then a Siamese-dominated Champasak from 1778 to 1791 (Na Champasak 1995). Between 1713 and 1778 the independent *Chao* Soysisamout and *Chao* Sayakouman established many new principalities, including the *Muang* of Attapeu in 1777.

The Expansion of Siamese Power

The Xekong Valley came under Siamese control after 1778 when troops invaded Champasak and forced it to become a Siamese vassal state (Viravong 1964; Rathie 2001; Ngaosyvathn and Ngaosyvath 1998). In 1781, as Siam took increasing control over Champasak, the King of Siam appointed *Thao* Ngao as the new *Chao Muang* of Attapeu and *Chan* Thalangsi as the new *Oupharat* (Long 1890; Anonymous 1911). Attapeu began paying tribute directly to Siam in 1782, whereas it had previously paid tribute to Champasak. There was some initial resistance to Siamese dominance, but apparently none of the protests or uprisings represented serious problems for the Siamese. By 1784 Stung Treng was also paying taxes directly to Bangkok, and by 1798 Siem Pang was under Siamese suzerainty (Rathie 2001). Although Attapeu paid taxes to Siam for almost a century, up until the French took over in 1893, it was frequently in arrears with its payments (Wilson 1992).

Thao Ngao died in 1797 and was replaced by *Chan* Thalangsi a year later. He ruled for another sixteen years, until 1813. When *Thao* Ngao and *Chan* Thalangsi ruled Attapeu, they gradually convinced more independent Austroasiatic communities to become aligned with them (Long 1890; Wiphakphachokij 2004b). After *Chan* Thalangsi died in 1814, the King of Siam appointed *Thao* Phromabout (Phrom), the son of *Thao* Ngao (Long 1890; Wiphakphachokij 2004b). *Thao* Phromabout continued to work to gain control over more independent tribes (Wiphakphachokij 2004b).

In 1817, an especially well-known man (remembered by many of the Lao and Brao of today as "*Ay* Sa") arrived on the scene and was a cause of the subsequent momentous upheavals that occurred in the area. Stories differ widely regarding his role in these conflicts, but whatever the truth, he holds a prominent place in the memories of both the ethnic Brao and Lao inhabitants of Attapeu Province. Baird (2007c) has documented this contested history in detail, and thus we will not elaborate here.

For our purposes, it is important to understand that Ay Sa organized a large group of mainly Austroasiatic peoples from southern Laos and led them to attack and plunder Champasak, driving *Chao* Manoi, King of Champasak, from his seat of power. In that Champasak was a Siamese vassal, the King of Siam tried to suppress the rebellion, and his agents were able to drive Ay Sa and his army from Champasak to *Jandou Ya Kra*, or *Ya Pou* Mountain in Attapeu. The King of Siam called on *Chao* Anou of Vientiane to capture Ay Sa, and *Chao* Nyo, *Chao* Anou's son, was sent to the south. He was able to capture Ay Sa and send him to Bangkok.

Chao Manoi was executed in Siam for his failure to defend Champasak, and so, at *Chao* Anou's request and in gratitude for *Chao* Nyo's ability to end the rebellion, *Chao* Nyo was elevated, in 1821, to the position of King of Champasak (Viravong 1964) despite considerable opposition within the Siamese court. But Champasak was a frontier state with Annam, making the conflict important to the Siamese (Simms and Simms 1999), and they were grateful to *Chao* Anou for suppressing the *Ay* Sa rebellion. They felt obliged to grant *Chao* Anou's request to make his son King of Champasak.

Upon taking power, *Chao* Nyo immediately ordered a census to be undertaken to support the raising of taxes and the forced recruitment of *corvée* labor for constructing a protective perimeter around Champasak's new capital. Apparently *Chao* Nyo's rapid rise to power met with some resistance in Champasak. For one, he was said to be strict with local officials (Anonymous 2004b), and his attempts to impose Vientiane customs on Champasak also met with resistance (Stuart-Fox 1998). But before long, *Chao* Anou and his son *Chao* Nyo, upset with increasing Siamese influence in Lao affairs (Wyatt 1963; Ngaosyvathn and Ngaosyvathn 1998), began their famous rebellion against the Siamese, seeking an independent Laos in the vision of the Lan Xang era of *Chao* Fa Ngum during the thirteenth century.

After *Chao* Anou's defeat, the Siamese decided to destroy and depopulate Vientiane, moving tens of thousands of people to present-day Thailand (Turton 1998). The Kingdom of Vientiane ceased to exist, and Champasak was significantly weakened. While there may have been some depopulation of southern Laos by the Siamese after the war, Kennon Breazeale (pers. comm. 2006) found little documentation regarding the Siamese moving non-Tai peoples to the west side of Mekong between the 1820s and 1840s. Grabowsky also mentions that, "Although there were also Mon-Khmer ('*Kha*') speaking peoples among the deportees, the 'Kha' heartland in Northern and Southern Laos seems to have been relatively less affected by forced resettlement than the predominantly Lao areas around Vientiane and Central Laos" (1997: 151). Nevertheless, some people from relatively more accessible parts of the Xekong River Basin were probably moved during this period. For example, some ethnic Oy people were recorded in the 1930s as having stories about returning to the foothills of the Bolaven Plateau after escaping from the Siamese in the 1830s (Paul Sidwell, pers. comm. May 2005). However, some more distant groups, like the Brao Hamong, resisted Siamese attempts to control them and were apparently never moved away.

Thao Phromabout, the *Chao Muang* of Attapeu following the death of *Chan* Thalangsi, does not appear to have been punished by the Siamese after the defeat of

Chao Anou and *Chao* Nyo affair, and remained *Chao Muang* of Attapeu throughout this period. He died in 1830, after further expanding Attapeu's influence into the hinterlands. *Thao* Kam, the son of *Chan* Thalangsi, replaced *Thao* Phromabout as the *Chao Muang* of Attapeu in 1831, but was removed from office by the King of Siam in 1846 (Anonymous 1911; Wiphakphachokij 2004b). He ended up settling in Stung Treng (Anonymous 1911). In 1847, the King of Siam appointed *Thao* Houy as the new *Chao Muang* (Long 1890). At the time, according to *Thao* Long (1890), the borders of Attapeu were:

1) East to *Nong* Fa *Nong* Yot.
2) Northeast to Salavan at *Muang* Phim (Xekong River bank).
3) Southeast to *Muang* Siem Pang at the mouth of Sathai River (currently near the border between Vietnam and Cambodia)
4) West to Champasak at Khampho Village (Xekhampho River)
5) Northwest to *Muang* Salavan and *Muang* Khamthong at *Nong* Phong Thoung Louang
6) Southwest to *Muang* Siem Pang at Thom Ban Village, and to *Keng* Sak-at, along the Xekong River.

Wiphakphachokij (2004b) reported that, if starting out from the capital of the *Muang*, it took eight days to walk to *Nong* Fa *Nong* Yot, four days to walk to *Muang* Phim, three days to walk to Khampho, five days to walk to *Muang* Khamthong, five days to walk to Thom Ban Village, and three days to walk to *Keng* Sak-at. The southeast border at the mouth of the Sathai River was the farthest away.

Thao Houy died in 1863, and a year later *Thao* Phila was appointed to replace him. He only lived three years after becoming *Chao Muang* of Attapeu. *Thao* King was designated to replace him a year later. More and more minority villages agreed to pay tribute to Attapeu (Long 1890; Wiphakphachokij 2004b).

Pha Khou Niam: Another Holy Man in Attapeu

Ay Sa was not the last holy man to cause disruption in Attapeu. *Pha Khou* Niam (*Phra Khru* Niam in Thai) led a group of three other monks and two laymen followers to Stung Treng in the 1850s, after having traveled extensively in present-day northeastern Thailand, Cambodia, and northeastern Laos. *Pha Khou* Niam was born in Bangkok but his parents originally came from Vientiane. The group settled at a temple in a village under the jurisdiction of Attapeu and they soon gained a reputation for their supernatural powers. Not long after arriving in Attapeu, a fierce storm killed many locals. The monk took advantage of the incident and was able to draw many people to visit him and give him gifts. He claimed to be able to see both hell and paradise. *Pha Khou* Niam and his associates were boastful and vain, and were much feared. Some gave them gold and silver. Those who criticized *Pha Khou* Niam and his associates were dragged away and flogged by their followers (Wilson 1992; 1997).

When local officials found out what was going on, they tried to arrest *Pha Khou* Niam and his colleagues, but the group fled to the forests and lived there for a period. Later, in 1860, *Pha Khou* Niam claimed that he was an angel, a son of the King of Vientiane. He wanted to go to meet the King, and a party was held to send him off. Local people got him drunk, making it easy for officials with whom they were cooperating to finally arrest him and confiscate his possessions (Wilson 1992; 1997).

During the 1860s and 1870s, many villages in Attapeu, especially ones populated by Austroasiatic groups, paid their taxes using human slaves and bees' wax instead of the gold the King of Siam wanted. *Thao* King, the *Chao Muang* in Attapeu, took the slaves and bees' wax from the villages and traded them in Attapeu for gold, which was in turn sent to Siam each year (Long 1890). Thus, the slave trade was critical for providing tribute payments, or taxes, to Siam.

It is still common to hear stories about the Siamese era of control over the region and the slave trade that expanded during the time of their greatest influence. Since few wanted to give up their own friends and relatives to the slave trade, a preferable option was to attack other villages to capture slaves. While some groups, like the Brao, tended only irregularly to attack other villages, the Jarai and Sedang gained reputations as vicious attackers of communities in order to capture slaves to sell.

The Sedang frequently attacked neighboring Brao communities, capturing people for slaves and for sacrificing to their spirits. For example, in 1894 Prosper Odend'hal recorded a battle between ethnic Sedang and probably ethnic Brao people (called *"Kha Khat"* by Odend'hal) at a village near the Nam Kong River in present-day Attapeu. According to Odend'hal, the Sedang killed fifteen tribesmen and took three slaves, without sustaining many losses. Odend'hal reported that the Sedang ate the livers and lungs of those they killed, and burned the remaining parts of the bodies of their enemies in a bonfire.[7] During this difficult time many people were either killed or captured and sold as slaves (Bourotte 1955). People had to flee to remote mountains to avoid slave raids and most villages were heavily fortified.

In 1884, when *Thao* King was still *Chao Muang* of Attapeu, the King of Siam sent a letter to order every colonized town not to hunt "*Kha*" for slaves or to sell or exchange for them anymore. In the past, when it became time to collect taxes, Attapeu officials would take some gifts to give to the minorities and then ask for the tax to be paid in the form of human beings (Long 1890; Wiphakphachokij 2004b). When the minorities found that the King of Siam did not allow the Siamese or Lao people to hunt or trade for slaves among their communities, they became more assertive. They no longer obeyed or feared the authorities in Attapeu, and they stopped paying any taxes at all. Officers from Attapeu and other people who went to minority areas to do business or work were increasingly robbed, and the numbers of people captured to be sold as slaves even increased. *Chao Muang* King wanted to subdue the minorities, but he was afraid that doing so would anger the Siamese, so he dared not (Long 1890; Wiphakphachokij 2004b). In 1887, *Thao* King died (Long 1890), and was replaced by *Chao Muang* Mo, who was in power at the time that the French took control over Attapeu in 1893 (Long 1890; Wiphakphachokij 2004b).

In 1895, two years after the French took control of Attapeu and eleven years after the Siamese had banned slavery, there were still 1,000 slaves in the *Muang*, including 500 Vietnamese (Annamites), 300 tribals, and 200 Lao (Rathie 2001). Today, many people from Mon-Khmer language speaking groups blame the slave trade, which was active in the region for centuries, for the violence and many of the wars that took place between the original inhabitants of the area. With some justification, they believe that the slave trade turned these groups and communities against each other.

The French Colonial Period

The first French explorers to investigate the Xekong River in Cambodia were led by Doudart de Lagrée, a naval officer who was placed in charge of an expedition up the Mekong that also included the now better-known Lt. Francis Garnier. The expedition left Phnom Penh in 1866 (Stuart-Fox 1998; Osborne 2000), and after traveling up the Mekong, some members of the Lagrée-Garnier expedition (but not Garnier himself) explored the Xekong River and reached Attapeu in 1867. The area was known, then, to be a center for the gold and slave trades (Toye 1968). Garnier subsequently reported, after de Lagrée had died later during the trip, that tribal peoples captured in the mountains were being sold there for 150 francs, whereas the same slaves fetched 500 francs in Phnom Penh (Stuart-Fox 1998). The French gave glowing accounts of the wealth of Attapeu and adjoining areas, suggesting that lead, antimony, and gold could be mined and that timber, ivory, and spices were abundant (Prescott 1975). Lagrée estimated there were 6,000 ethnic Lao, 36,000 ethnic minorities, and no Chinese people in Attapeu (Wilson 1992). Rheinart d'Arfeuille also briefly visited Attapeu via the Xekong during this period (Harmand 1997). These early French explorers saw suppression of the slave trade as a key moral justification for colonialism.

The next French group to investigate the Xekong River Basin in Laos was led by Doctor François-Jules Harmand, a Christian evangelist prepared to aggressively spread French colonial "civilization." Harmand wrote about his visit to the area in 1877. He showed contempt for native peoples and was a great believer in French superiority and colonialism. He noticed that the slave trade integrated Attapeu, Champasak, and Stung Treng through the passage of convoys supervised by Malay, Chinese, and local slave merchants to the markets of Khorat, Bangkok, and Phnom Penh (Harmand 1997). He was later to become Governor-General of French Indochina.

The next French group to visit Attapeu, in 1882/1883, was led by Étienne Aymonier (Aymonier 1895). Like Garnier, Aymonier never actually made it to Attapeu, but he sent two Cambodian informants to gather information. Aymonier later wrote that the area was heavily forested; the towns and villages were small; and the variety of people considerable. He wrote that there was much intermingling between ethnic Lao and minority communities and that there were no taxes on trade in Attapeu. He also reported that the area was the center of the slave trade and that people became slaves due to wars and as a result of criminal activity, or even for not being able to pay their debts (Wilson 1992).

The famous Pavie Mission, which was represented in present-day northeast Cambodia and southeastern Laos by Captain P. Cupet, arrived in Attapeu in 1891. An entourage led by Captain J. de Malglaive traveled from the present-day Central Highlands of Vietnam to Attapeu in March of that year and spent a considerable amount of time in the region (de Malglaive 1893; Cupet 1997). During the same year, commandant Trumelet-Faber traveled overland from Tourane to the Xekong and back to Hue,[8] and, in early 1893, Monsieur Bonin tried to get to Attapeu from Tourane with fifteen militiamen. Ethnic minorities attacked his group, but he managed to escape.[9] He eventually reached the Xekong River and Attapeu, but even though he succeeded in reaching *Muang Kao* on the Xekaman River, the boats he was using then sank,[10] and he did not make it to the location where 300–400 Lao soldiers under Siamese command were reportedly waiting to cut him off. He reported that the population of Attapeu was constantly fighting and looting and that foreigners were unwelcome.[11]

Not until after the *"Pak Nam"* incident between the Siamese and the French in July 1893 did the Siamese reluctantly agree to sign over the east bank of the Mekong to the French on 3 October 1893 (Hall 1981; Savada 1995). However, the French had taken control of Stung Treng from the Siamese a few months earlier and had also, albeit unsuccessfully, tried to occupy Attapeu prior to the *Pak Nam* incident.

With France gaining official control of territories on the Mekong's east bank, Prosper Odend'hal, a French citizen of Irish origin, was ordered to depart from Hue and occupy Attapeu for France. Although it took him months of hard travel to finally reach Attapeu by December 1893, he did indeed take control of Attapeu for France from the Siamese and the Lao *Chao Muang* Mo.[12] Monsieur Ruthe followed him and became the first French Administrator of Attapeu in 1894. They initially set up their administration at *Muang Kao*, near the present-day center of Saysettha District and adjacent to the Xekaman River.[13] At this time, many parts of the province were still, in effect, unknown to the French.

Another famous explorer, Lt. Debay, spent a year in the Attapeu region between 1894 and 1895.[14] He learned much about the area but became notorious for his terrible treatment of the ethnic minorities and the others he hired and encountered in Attapeu and Annam.[15]

After the French took over Attapeu, *Chao Muang* Mo resigned and was replaced by *Thao* Seng, the former *Oupharat*. He worked under the French as *Chao Muang* initially, but was removed from his position seven years later for bad behavior (Anonymous 1911). At the time the French took control of Attapeu 600 men were paying taxes and, according to Anonymous (1911), only ethnic Laotians, Heuny (Nya Heun), Jru Dak (Sou), Sapouan, and Harak (Alak) people were "submitted" (that is, they had agreed not to resist French administration). There were also 170 Vietnamese slaves in Attapeu, with conditions varying considerably from person to person. Almost all had been captured in Quang Nam and Quang Ngai in Vietnam and then exchanged to Lao traders in Sedang communities in Kontum, Vietnam (Engelbert 2004).

In June 1901, not long after the beginning of the *Phou Mi Boun* revolt on the Bolaven Plateau, the ethnic Sedang peoples from the Annamite Mountains straddling Annam and Laos killed the French officer Robert, after the Administrator from Attapeu, Monsieur Castinier, set up a militia post near the confluence of the Psi and Peko Rivers, in present-day Kontum Province. The Sedang caught Robert and his men off guard when they attacked at about 9 a.m. Robert was speared multiple times, but the Sedang did not take any valuables. The next night they returned to burn down the post, which the French later rebuilt (Bourotte 1955).

In 1904, some rebellious ethnic Jarai, probably the King of Water and his followers, killed Odend'hal at *Palei Koueng*, in the Central Highlands of Vietnam near the border with Laos, even though Odend'hal thought that these Jarai had agreed to submit to the French.[16]

The Frenchman Henri Maître, who visited Attapeu in 1909/1910, after traveling overland from present-day Veun Say in western Ratanakiri Province to Attapeu, wrote a book about his trip called *Les Jungles Moi* (1912). In 1914, an ethnic Mnong or Bunong tribesman murdered him in present-day Mondulkiri Province, northeast Cambodia (Bourotte 1955; Hickey 1982).

Southern Laos was absorbed as a French colony (Savada 1995), while Annam, Cochinchina, and Cambodia were considered to Protectorates of France (Ngaosrivathana and Breazeale 2002) as was Luang Phrabang in northern Laos (Dommen 1985). Initially, Attapeu, Siem Pang, and Stung Treng were placed under the administration of Cochinchina, but on 1 June 1895 they were transferred to Lower Laos,[17] with the administrative center based on Khong Island in the Mekong. Then, on 19 April 1899 they were integrated into the unified territory of Laos, with its capital in Vientiane (Prescott 1975). Although Attapeu had once been a Khmer settlement, by the time of French occupation reportedly only ten Khmer were living there (Martin Rathie, pers. comm. 2006).

For the ethnic minorities, life under the French seemed relatively good, as the French were against the slave trade from their first visits to the Xekong River Basin. This is not to say that people were particularly happy with French rule, but for those threatened by the slave trade there was at least some relief. Various highlander groups also had some lesser known reasons for supporting French colonial ambitions. For example, the Sedang practice of capturing Brao people and others and then sacrificing them to the spirits was prohibited. The Oy, who had been frequently victimized by the Brao, were also happy to see a ban on the slave trade (Engelbert 2004). The French implementation of the ban on slave trading, which had actually been ordered by the Siamese before the arrival of the French but had not been seriously enforced by Siamese officials in Attapeu, helped significantly to improve relations between ethnic groups that had previously often attacked each other.

In 1904, Siem Pang and Stung Treng were transferred to Cambodia from Laos. Cambodia apparently did not have a serious claim on Attapeu (Prescott 1975), although Cambodians recognized Attapeu as an old Cambodian province (Chhak 1966). Then, in 1926, the center of Attapeu was moved to the site of the present capital of Attapeu Province, *Muang Mai*, Samakhixay District, on the west bank of the Xekong River and across from the confluence of the Xekaman River with the Xekong.

French control over remote ethnic minority areas was limited during the early colonial period and, for the most part, ethnic minorities living in remote areas were able to do as they pleased, except for requirements to pay taxes and provide *corvée* labor in support of French infrastructure development. Representatives of each village were selected to liaison with the French administration and their Lao and Vietnamese officials. The Kontum mission was the center of French activity in the highlands. Although the mission was not particularly far from where the ethnic groups lived in present-day Ratanakiri and Attapeu Provinces, Hickey (1982) makes no mention of any of the groups living outside of Vietnam in his book about the history of the ethnic minorities in the Central Highlands of Vietnam. It appears that these groups, including the Brao, had little contact with the French during the early colonial period.

Despite being freed from the slave trade, some stiff resistance was mounted against French rule in the Xekong Basin during the colonial period. Most importantly, many of the Mon-Khmer language speakers resisted paying taxes and providing *corvée* labor at the beginning of the twentieth century. There were also messianic reasons for the uprisings. The first and most important rebellion was launched in 1901 by the rebel highland leaders Ong Keo[18] and Ong Kommadam,[19] and the ethnic Lao messiah, Ong Thong.[20] From then on, they spent many years organizing resistance and revolution against the French while hiding from colonial troops. They were considered to be *"Phou Mi Boun"* (literally, persons with merit) or messiah figures, with special powers. Initially, they caused considerable trouble for the French, and at one point most of the Bolaven Plateau was in revolt.

After a lull in the movement there was a revival in November 1905; however, Ong Thong was captured and decapitated in Pakse in 1907, and in October of the same year, Ong Keo surrendered, leading to the apparent end of the *Phou Mi Boun* movement. Ong Keo died in November 1910 while trying to escape (Stuart-Fox 2001). In 1910, Ong Kommadam was also wounded, but he continued to organize against the French, spreading his influence east of the Xekong in the Annamite Mountains, to the south as far as present-day Ratanakiri and Stung Treng Provinces in northeastern Cambodia and to Dak Lak Province in the Central Highlands of Vietnam. This may have been one of the first appeals for "Pan-Highlander" unity and rebellion.

In 1924, Kommadam again became an important threat, and he began distributing propaganda written in his own script, which he called "*nang seu khom*." Then, in 1925, his followers circulated anti-French "calls-to-arms" on the Bolaven Plateau. A new outbreak of unrest broke out in 1934, eliciting strong French retaliation. Finally, after spending years hiding in the forests, and establishing a network of resistance, Kommadam was betrayed and a colonial militia commanded by a Vietnamese named Captain Nyo caught up with and killed him as he traveled with a small group of fellow rebels from the Bolaven Plateau to Attapeu. He died on 23 September 1936 (Stuart-Fox 2001; Engelbert 2004). Kommadam's two sons, Sithon and Khampanh, were arrested at the time of their father's death and interned in Phongsaly, northern Laos, until the Japanese takeover of the country in March 1945 (Engelbert 2004). Later, Sithon Kommadam would become a prominent ethnic leader in the south for the Pathet Lao Communists (Engelbert 2004; Burchett 1970).

Yves Goudineau (2001) believes that the most profound reason for the uprisings in southern Laos was colonial willingness to take control of Indochinese territory without any respect for the historical territories of the region's various ethnic groups. Martin Rathie believes that the reasons for the uprising were largely related to the French moving against Lao networks of control that had kept the area relatively harmonious under the Siamese (pers. comm. 2006). Gunn (1990) has argued that the imposition of taxes and *corvée* labor were the main causes behind the rebellion. Keyes (1977) has, however, pointed to religion as having a definite role in the revolt. There is also the strong possibility that, at least initially, much of the rebellion was indirectly instigated by members of the royal family in Champasak,[21] who were both eager to see the French out so that they could regain control over territories east of the Mekong and were also keen to free themselves from Siamese control. However, the Champasak royals may not have wanted to risk getting in trouble with the French by becoming directly involved in the rebellion.

Lesser known than Ong Keo and Ong Kommadam, but with similar ideas about ruling the minorities in the upper Xekong River Basin, was an ethnic Khmer named *Chao* Khoune, who was active in the upper Xekong Valley, and used propaganda similar to that of Kommadam to attempt to convince minorities to join him. He began his rebel movement in 1929, but the French arrested him in 1931, after which his movement died.

There were also other reported isolated acts of rebellion against the French by minorities up to 1939 and 1940, but none represented a serious threat to French control (Engelbert 2004).

In 1934, the colonial administration relegated Attapeu from being a province to being a district under the jurisdiction of Champasak, and not until after 1954, when Laos gained independence from France, was Attapeu again designated a province.

The Japanese Colonial Period

In June 1940, France fell to Germany, and in the same month Japan signed a Treaty of Friendship with the Phiboun Songkham government in what had recently become Thailand (formerly Siam). Poised to exert its influence on Thailand and French Indochina, in August 1940, the Japanese demanded special permission from France's Vichy government to use Indochina's ports, cities, and airports for troop movements. The Governor-General of Indochina at the time, Admiral Jean Decoux, saw resistance to the Japanese as foolhardy and chose instead to negotiate. By September, the Vichy government and Tokyo had signed a treaty allowing the Japanese to occupy the northern part of Indochina as far south as Hanoi. During the same month Japan formed a military alliance with the Axis, led by Germany. Then, in league with Thailand, the Japanese orchestrated a mock Thai offensive on Cambodia and Laos, and then stepped in and brokered the ceding of the west bank of the Mekong (including Champasak) and Siem Reap and Battambong to Thailand. Japan continued its infiltration of French Indochina, and, by July 1941, Japanese troops occupied all of its regions. On 7 December 1941, the day of Japan's surprise attack on Pearl Harbor, the Japanese invaded Thailand. The Thai government offered token resistance, but soon capitulated and declared war on the Allies (Hall 1981; Dommen 1985).

In the early 1940s, the Japanese dominated French Indochina, nominally under the control of France's Vichy government, and in March 1945, as de Gaulle's France prepared to liberate Indochina and the Allies bombed parts of Indochina and threatened to invade, the Japanese decided to take full control. On 9 March 1945, they initiated what was called the *"coup de force"*—taking full control of Indochina. On 10 March, they occupied Attapeu, and by 12 March Salavan was under Japanese control (Gunn 1988). There was a small amount of resistance against the Japanese by the Lao King in Luang Phrabang, but the Lao forces were no match for the Japanese. French officials were arrested and interned throughout Laos. Just six months later, the Japanese surrendered to Allied Forces (Dommen 1985).

Many remember the Japanese period of domination in Laos as one of the most oppressive periods in history. The Japanese were seen as being particularly brutal and intolerant. Their presence was not as heavily felt in many of the region's more remote areas, including many parts of the Xekong River Basin. There is, however, a story about rebels being killed by Japanese soldiers in the upper Xenamnoi River Basin that local people still remember. After the Second World War ended, the French would only remain in Laos for a few more years.

The Final Years of French Rule

The years immediately following the fall of the Japanese were complicated and confusing, as a result of the power vacuum created by the abrupt departure of the Japanese and emerging Lao nationalism (Dommen 1985). The French managed, by the end of 1945, to regain control of southern Laos (Engelbert 2004), but not without first overcoming resistance from Communist forces.

In the Xekong River Basin, it was between 1946 and 1948 that the Communist movement began to grow, albeit slowly at first. One of the most important boosts the Communists received during this period was recruiting Kommadam's son, Sithon, to their side in 1947 (Engelbert 2004). However, Vietnamese Viet Minh cadres made various mistakes in trying to gain influence over the population of the Xekong Basin during this period. By 1948 their high command acknowledged, in a resolution, that Laos and Cambodia still lacked a political basis to sustain a guerilla war (Engelbert 2004). However, Sithon Kommadam and Khamtay Siphandone helped influence a shift in tactics in 1949 in order to "Laoize" recruitment efforts. For example, Vietnamese cadres were required to make more efforts to learn Lao and understand local cultures and people from Laos were given more visible political roles (Engelbert 2004). From then on, Communist propaganda began spreading rapidly through the Xekong Basin and other parts of Laos, and the Indochina Communist Party (ICP) was able to field more recruits in the basin. However, by 1950 there were reportedly still only twenty Lao and minority members of the ICP in all of southern Laos (Engelbert 2004).

The first liberated area in southern Laos was officially founded in Dakchung on 1 March 1949. The next step involved military operations being launched from Vietnam on 10 October. These resulted in *Ban* Cheng and *Ban* Inthi, about 15 km southwest of Attapeu town, being "liberated," followed soon after by the take-over of *Ban* Mai and *Ban* Hin Lat near the Xepian River (Engelbert 2004). With these new bases under their control (at least during the nights) the Communists in Laos, with significant Vietnamese support, began putting increasing military and political pressure on the French (Vongsavanh 1978; Engelbert 2004). Vietnamese Communists, and their Lao and minority allies, worked to convince traditional leaders and elders of their cause. Some Vietnamese cadres went "native," learning local minority languages and dressing and acting like minorities in order to gain their support. Once that was achieved, they established and mobilized various groups and committees within the villages to support the revolution (Engelbert 2004). Despite counter operations by the French, the number of "liberated districts" continued to increase, and there were five by 1952: Dakchung, Lamam, Vienthong (Thateng), Sanxay, and Kalum (Engelbert 2004).

On 23 October 1953, the "French-Lao Treaty of Amity and Association" transferred all residual French powers to the Royal Lao Government (Stuart-Fox 2001). This did not satisfy the Communists, however, who continued their military campaign in southern Laos. Finally, on 30 and 31 December 1953, after a difficult struggle, Communist forces defeated a French battalion in Attapeu. They then advanced on Salavan and liberated all of the Bolaven Plateau (Gunn 1988). As Kaysone Phomvihane (1981: 18) wrote: "[I]n 1953 . . . . our armed forces, supported by Vietnamese volunteers, launched several successive attacks and liberated large areas in different parts of the country, including areas in the provinces of Sam Neua, Xieng Khouang, Kham Mouane, Attopeu, the Bolaven Plateau, and so on." Many Lao know the struggle against French colonialism as the "French War." Others know it as the First Indochina War.

The Post-Colonial Era

On 20 July 1954, despite US objections, the French and the Viet Minh signed the Geneva Agreement on Indochina (Burchett 1970). This allowed for Pathet Lao control of Sam Neua and Phongsaly Provinces in northern Laos (Dommen 1985). But there were no provisions for maintaining Pathet Lao control over the parts of the Xekong River Basin that they had previously controlled, so many Pathet Lao cadres traveled to Phongsaly and Sam Neua (Burchett 1970). Others secretly remained in Attapeu as Communist spies and observers.

In 1957, the Pathet Lao agreed to enter a coalition government with right wing and neutralist forces, and many Pathet Lao cadres returned from Phongsaly and Sam Neua to the Xekong Basin. During the first few years after Laos gained independence from the French the situation in the Xekong River Basin was relatively peaceful, although the Communists remained active in many parts of the basin.

Kaysone Phomvihane, later to become the President of the Lao PDR, participated in National Assembly elections for the Communists in Attapeu in 1958. Dommen (1985) claims that Kaysone was defeated at the polls because he was from the north of Laos and not well-known in the south. However, Communists in Attapeu were adamant that the rightist government stuffed the ballot boxes and robbed Kaysone of victory. Right-wing elements gained *de facto* control over the government of Vientiane, and, before long, many Pathet Lao cadres in Attapeu and Salavan had been assassinated. The heads of those murdered were publicly exposed to show that the Pathet Lao had ceased to exist (Burchett 1970), but it was far from their end, and the group soon took up arms again as part of its new "*han thit*" ("change direction") policy.

In 1959, North Vietnam decided firmly to support and strengthen the guerrilla war in South Vietnam (Vongsavanh 1978), and the Xekong Basin became increasingly important in this strategy. In the same year, the Pathet Lao and their Vietnamese mentors established three administrative districts in the eastern part of the province: Sanxay, Phouvong Tai and Phouvong Neua. The Xekong Basin was on the verge of becoming an area of intense conflict in the Indochina region.

On 23 March 1961 US President John F. Kennedy announced his support for the neutrality of Laos and, on 23 July 1962, the second Geneva Accords on the neutrality of Laos were signed (Stuart-Fox 2001). This was not much of a deterrent on North Vietnam's efforts to unite southern and northern Vietnam under Communist rule, but the agreement did deter the US and South Vietnam armies from placing large infantry formations to block the movement of North Vietnamese Army (NVA) supplies and troops. For this reason, the US decided to rely on aerial bombardment or interdiction in southern Laos as their main means of trying to shut down the movement of supplies to Communist forces in South Vietnam. During the war, southern Laos, below the 18th parallel, was often referred to as "the panhandle of Laos" (Vongsavanh 1978). Both the Vietnamese and the US chose to ignore Laos' neutrality, even though both claimed to be honoring it.

Beginning around 1960, routes through the Annamite Mountain Range served mainly as lines of communication for Communist couriers and small combat units but, by 1962, a network was being more fully used for transporting large quantities of supplies to their colleagues in southern Vietnam (Vongsavanh 1978). The routes used to move supplies and troops became known as the Ho Chi Minh Trail. In fact, the so-called "Trail" did not represent a single road, but rather a network of constantly changing routes, including roads, river ways, footpaths, and other transportation links. Traffic was highest during the dry season, between November and April or May, and lightest during the rainy season, when travel was difficult. The NVA moved supplies in stages and concealed supplies in storage depots. There were also rest and repair areas along the way. Most transportation was by truck, but boats and rafts, and even bicycles and foot porterage, were employed when need arose (Vongsavanh 1978; Van Staaveren 1993).

In 1962, the Royal Lao Air Force (RLAF) and the USAF began to bomb the mountainous part of the Xekong River Basin. By July 1964 events had propelled the US into deeper military involvement in both northern and southern Laos, including increased aerial bombing inside Laos. In October 1964, after receiving approval from the Lao Prime Minister Souvanna Phouma, USAF bombing of the Ho Chi Minh Trail increased considerably (Van Staaveren 1993). At first this bombing concentrated only on the Ho Chi Minh Trail, but by 1966 the "Sihanouk Trail," including parts of Route 110 (now Route 18a), which ran through Attapeu Province and then through a small part of Cambodia before entering Vietnam, was increasingly targeted (Van Staaveren 1993; Conboy 1995).

Considerable restrictions were placed on the USAF and RLAF in relation to the bombing campaign in southern Laos, although these were gradually relaxed over the years. Some rules were also secretly broken. The US and Lao governments were particularly concerned not to violate Laos' neutral status openly as defined by the 1954 and 1962 Geneva Accords. This meant that US ground troops were not officially supposed to be based in Laos, and that aerial bombing needed to be done as carefully and as discretely as possible. Nevertheless, many bombing missions took place in southern Laos over the years, with some of the best-known campaigns taking on the code names *Steel Tiger, Tiger Hound, SLAM*, and *Shock I* to *IV*. There were also large numbers of US citizens inside of Laos supporting the war effort. But things did not go as planned and many unauthorized targets were bombed over the years, some of which became of great concern to the Lao government and the US Ambassador in Vientiane (Van Staaveren 1993). The NVA provided strong security and good camouflage to avoid damage by air and ground attacks, as this network was crucial for continuing the war in South Vietnam.

The NVA increased their defenses along the Ho Chi Minh Trail over the years, and, by 1969, the RLAF had to stop its aerial attacks of the trail due to the effectiveness of NVA anti-aircraft artillery (Vongsavanh 1978). According to villagers who lived in bombed areas, as soon as they heard the planes coming, they would jump into bunkers or pits and take cover. As Wilfred Burchett wrote: "Through 1969, the tonnage of bombs dropped on Laotian villages exceeded that dropped in any year on North Vietnam, more than on Nazi-occupied Europe in any year of the Second

World War. The only way to escape the bombs was to accept concentration camp life behind barbed wire, living off US handouts" (1970: 169).

Seven large military bases were established in Laos by the NVA in the 1960s, of which five were particularly important for supporting NVA troops. Two were situated in the Xekong Basin; Base Area 614 was located east of Chavan, in present-day Dakchung District, and Base Area 609 was situated in eastern Attapeu Province in the tri-border area between Cambodia, Vietnam, and Laos. The most important logistical base was outside of the Xekong Basin near Xepon in Savannakhet Province. To provide some distraction from the arduous life of the NVA troops stationed along the trail, entertainment troupes sometimes passed through with presentations of patriotic plays and songs (Vongsavanh 1978).

On the Royalist side, Laos was divided into five military regions, of which Military Region IV, with its headquarters at Pakse, included the six provinces of southern Laos at the time: Salavan, Attapeu, Champasak, Xedon, Khong Xedon, and Sithandone (Khong Island). The entire Xekong Basin in Laos was included in this region, and the Na Champasak family, led by Prince Boun Oum Na Champasak, dominated this area. Major General Phasouk Rassaphak, a member of the Na Champasak family, commanded Military Region IV for almost fifteen years, from the late 1950s until Brigadier-General Soutchay Vongsavanh, originally from Luang Phrabang, took command in July 1971. Soutchay was in charge until early June 1975, when he was forced to flee the country due to Pathet Lao consolidation of control (Vongsavanh 1978).

The American military had started to organize the ethnic minorities in southern Laos against the Communists in the late 1950s under the "White Star" program, but the 1962 Geneva Accords forced the US military to end formal involvement in Laos and to shut down "White Star." But not long after 1962 the USA began to deploy Central Intelligence Agency (CIA) agents in Laos to organize paramilitary groups among the minorities to fight against the Communists.

In 1964, small groups of Laotian guerillas began to operate against the NVA and Pathet Lao operating near the Ho Chi Minh Trail. The first groups consisted mainly of ethnic minorities from the Bolaven Plateau. As the conflict increased, CIA efforts also increased, and in 1967 the 1st Special Guerilla Unit (SGU) was established on the Boloven Plateau (Eckhardt 1999). This army was financed and trained by the CIA. According to Eckhardt (1999), "These hardy warriors proved that indigenous forces could be as tough and disciplined as soldiers anywhere. The Bolaven Plateau was the tribesmen's home turf, and they did not like the idea of anyone messing around with their villages or way of life—neither the Pathet Lao nor the North Vietnamese." The 550-man unit was based at a place called PS-22 by the CIA and air operations people.

In 1965, the NVA began upgrading and increasing their use of the Sihanouk Trail as an extension of the Ho Chi Minh Trail. It branched off southeast of the Bolaven Plateau, south of Attapeu and *Muang Mai*. While the Sihanouk Trail was being built, the Royalist government, including Colonel Khong Vongnarath, then military commander of Attapeu Province, claimed to have no idea what was happening, even though explosions of dynamite could be heard day and night from along the new route (Vongsavanh 1978).

It was at this time that North Vietnam set up a special unit, Group 565, to secure the Ho Chi Minh Trail from ground attack (Dommen 1985). NVA security was strong, and Colonel Khong had a tacit understanding with the NVA to the effect that Royalist patrols would not range far from the limits of Attapeu town and the NVA would not shell or otherwise interfere with his garrison. Only occasional groups of spies, disguised as elephant hunters, would enter NVA-controlled areas to collect information about their strength and activities. Royalist forces dared not attack the NVA, as the danger of NVA retaliation was too great. The Lao leaders were also concerned not to lose control over lucrative commercial activities from which they were benefiting (Vongsavanh 1978). However, in December 1965, the USAF stepped up their bombardment of the southern-most part of Laos when it launched the bombing mission *Tiger Hound*, and by mid-1966 the anti-infiltration campaign in Laos further escalated, including the dropping of leaflets and defolia-tion operations (Van Staaveren 1993). Top Secret B-52 carpet-bombing in southern Laos also began in 1965.

By March 1966 Pathet Lao and NVA forces overrode Fang Deng and *Muang Kao* along the Xekaman River, intent on advancing on the capital of Attapeu Province. This was in order to consolidate their control of the Xekong and Xekaman River Basins and areas south of there so as to expand infiltration routes through northeastern Cambodia (Porter 1971). However, nighttime air strikes targeting the area between *Muang Kao* and the provincial capital resulted in heavy Pathet Lao and NVA casualties and kept them from reaching the provincial capital. This also allowed RLA troops to reoccupy *Muang Kao* and Fang Deng a few days later (Porter 1971; Van Staaveren 1993).

The NVA opened up the Sihanouk Trail for use in May 1966 and from that time onward large quantities of supplies began to flow through northeastern Cambodia. The NVA also used motorboats for shipping supplies down the Xekong River to the Cambodian border and floated bags of rice sealed in plastic down the

Xekong to Cambodia by day and night. However, NVA trucks did not move when threatened with air assault, and, when they did move, they were often camouflaged with branches tied to frames covering the truck bodies. They used floatable spans (hidden by day) or underwater bridges to cross rivers and streams. The drivers were experts at concealing their vehicles, either parking them under rock overhangs or in thickets of bushes.

Bridges became key air targets so underwater log and stone ramps were constructed for facilitating the crossing of narrow waterways. For crossing wide waterways bamboo rafts were kept moored on river banks, hidden by overhanging trees. Sometimes streambeds were used as roadways to avoid track signs. The roads, trails, and paths being used were linked with a stream and river transportation system (Vongsavanh 1978; Van Staaveren 1993). In 1966, the USAF could bomb boats and barges according to their rules but not long narrow-beam boats, which were presumably engaged in non-military traffic (Van Staaveren 1993). General Westmoreland, commander of US forces in Vietnam, complained about these and many other bombing restrictions in Laos (Van Staaveren 1993).

The conflict continued to accelerate, and by 1967 all the villages near the Ho Chi Minh and Sihanouk Trails, which had initially been spared being directly targeted in bombing raids, began to be hit. Most villagers were forced to flee into the forest (Vongsavanh 1978). By 1967 it was estimated that 1,200 tonnes of supplies were being transported per month along the Sihanouk Trail. The USAF set up a command post in Attapeu, and more B-52 bombing raids by USAF plane based at U Tapao in Thailand began (Van Staaveren 1993). With Vietnam, Laos, and Cambodia all involved in a conflict of increasing intensity, the Second Indochina War in Laos, often called the "American War," was well underway.

It was also in 1967 that the previously mentioned SGU at PS-22 began operating. Initially they were airlifted to the Chavan area in present-day Dakchung District, but their lack of fighting experience cost them dearly. NVA and Pathet Lao forces beat them badly, and the mission failed. Later, however, their harassment probes and other guerilla operations against the Ho Chi Minh Trail proved more successful. The SGU operated from 1967 to 1970, after which time some joined the rest of the Royalist troops and fought as line infantry (Eckhardt 1999); however, others continued to work under CIA's tutelage.

In 1970, the Pathet Lao suffered a temporary but serious setback after its military leader General Phouma Douangmala died while under Vietnamese care. His deputy, Boualien Vannaxay, blamed the Vietnamese for General Phouma's death and also felt that the Vietnamese were exerting too much control over the Pathet

Lao. Boualien led a group of about a hundred Pathet Lao soldiers to change sides and offer their services to the Royal Lao Government (RLG). Boualien and his colleagues proved useful to the RLG, which used surveillance information provided by them to launch a series of successful bombing raids.

On 15 March 1970, the Sihanouk government in Cambodia was brought down in a coup d'etat. A government led by General Lon Nol, who was supported by the US government and had gone to school with the Champasak rightist leader Prince Boun Oum, came to power. USAF assaults against the trail systems increased dramatically, as did the number of trail defenders and their response of anti-aircraft fire.

Despite the Boualien affair and the advent of the Lon Nol government, the Vietnamese and their Pathet Lao allies increased in strength and gained increasing control over the region. Before long, all sections of the Ho Chi Minh and Sihanouk Trails were protected with NVA anti-aircraft guns, sometimes supported by radar. Before 1970, the NVA hid their anti-aircraft guns and would often not fire at airplanes in order to remain concealed. After 1970 they fired at will at all planes (Vongsavanh 1978).

In 1970, the NVA lost access to the supply port of Sihanoukville in Cambodia and so the Ho Chi Minh and Sihanouk Trails became even more important for transporting supplies to South Vietnam (Dommen 1971; 1985). This explains why, in April 1970, the provincial capitals of Attapeu and Salavan were attacked and taken by NVA and Pathet Lao forces (Dommen 1971; 1985). The NVA wanted to use the Xekong for transportation downriver, and Attapeu town stood in the way. A few nights before the final attack on Attapeu, Pathet Lao agents posted notices in Attapeu, warning its inhabitants that the Pathet Lao would be taking control (Dommen 1971). Although Attapeu was, by some accounts, difficult to defend, the RLA made concerted efforts to do so on the first night of the attack on 28 April; however, by the second night it was clear that they could not sustain their defenses. When the Pathet Lao announced with a loud speaker from across the Xekong that everyone who put down his arms would be allowed to evacuate the town safely, the town's 400 defenders were quick to agree to the offer.

Once the NVA and Pathet Lao had taken the town, they burnt down all military installations but left civilian homes undamaged (Dommen 1971). Burchett (1970: 185) wrote that "Attopeu was an important base for the rightist forces and the main entry point for the clandestine Special Forces which the Americans were running into Laos from South Vietnam. Its loss was a severe blow against all American operations in that part of southern Laos." Fifteen thousand people were reported displaced in the Salavan and Attapeu areas around the time of the attacks (Whitaker et al. 1972). As Kaysone Phomvihane (1981: 34) later wrote about the 1970 offensive: "Soon we inflicted a blow on the enemy in the south, in the provinces of Saravane and Attopeu, both of which were almost completely liberated." One of the first acts after the takeover was to requisition approximately a hundred boats and send them down the Xekong to NVA transport units on the Cambodian border. The RLG lodged a protest with the International Cooperation Committee (ICC) over the capture of Attapeu (Dommen 1971) but with no result. In 1970, the Lon Nol government also abandoned Ratanakiri and Stung Treng Provinces, in northeast Cambodia just to the south of Attapeu, to Communist forces (Burchett 1970).

In December 1970, NVA troops began attacking irregular pro-government bases on the eastern part of the Bolaven Plateau. Despite having to contend with massive aerial bombardment, almost all of the Xekong River Basin was controlled by the Pathet Lao and their NVA allies by that time. In May 1971, the Pathet Lao and their Vietnamese allies continued moving west, attacking RLA positions near Pakxong town (Vongsavanh 1978).

Fierce fighting continued in southern Laos after 1970 and the USAF bombing of the south did not cease until 1973, when the Paris peace agreement was signed, supposedly to end the war in South Vietnam. A month later, a similar agreement was signed pertaining to Laos. The NVA, after 1973, was able to use the trails freely without fear of aerial bombardment (Vongsavanh 1978), although bombing continued for a time in adjacent parts of Cambodia. In fact, since the early 1960s there had been no serious ground attempts to impede use of the Ho Chi Minh Trail in the Xekong Basin. Only once did ground forces from the South Vietnam Army attempt to do so along the trail when they briefly attacked the Vietnamese at Xepon, Savannakhet Province, in February 1971 (Dommen 1985). After 1973, the RLA was reduced to less than a fourth of its size by the new neutralist government, and forward RLA and irregular units stopped offering even token harassment of the NVA. In the meantime, the Pathet Lao grew increasingly strong (Vongsavanh 1978).

According to Eckhardt (1999), between 1966 and 1971 630,000 troops, 100,000 tonnes of foodstuffs and 50,000 tonnes of ammunitions came down the Ho Chi Minh Trail. By 1970, 25,000 soldiers manned checkpoints and artillery positions along the trail and used 10,000 anti-aircraft pieces to defend the trail from US and Lao air power while 10,000 trucks moved along roads that were largely concealed from the air. Eckhardt (1999) acknowledges that Doan 559, the NVA unit from Hanoi charged with keeping the trail open, "did its job well."

The Communist revolution brought together ethnic minorities from various groups and parts of the region, many of whom previously had little contact with each other. The war opened the eyes of these people to the outside world, regardless of what side of the conflict they supported. However, the war also brought a great deal of pain and suffering to the region. Illustrative of the many changes that took place, prior to this period most ethnic minority males in the region grew their hair long, tying it up in a bun in the back of their heads. But once they joined the Communist movement, or the RLA, all males cut their hair short to conform to what was seen as appropriate for either the "revolution" or the fight against it.

Kong Mi: The Last Stronghold for Royalist Forces in Attapeu Province

Kong Mi was an important paramilitary base prior to 1975, when the Pathet Lao took over all of Laos. Most of the area in Attapeu Province east of the Xekong was "liberated" by Communist forces in the 1960s, with just one main exception: Kong Mi. Situated in the southeast mountains of Attapeu, the base, and the surrounding communities of mainly ethnic Brao people, was named after the Brao military leader *Ya* Mi, who came from the area. *Ya* Mi was appointed as a regional leader, or *"Nai Kong,"* by the French colonial government of Attapeu in 1917, after being a Buddhist monk[22] and then serving as a trumpeter for the French colonial indigenous guard.[23] He reputedly had seven wives.

Kong Mi was situated in what the Royalists knew as Lave District, 34 km southeast of Attapeu, and was strengthened in 1959 after being a smaller base during the colonial period. The Pathet Lao called the surrounding area Phouvong Tai District. The area became an important refuge for pro-Royalist Brao military and civilians in the 1960s, especially after 1966/1967 when CIA involvement there increased. It was during the 1960s that *Chao Muang* Tanh, son of the then ailing *Ya* Mi, took command of the area. He was in charge until the Ministry in Vientiane decided to install another Brao, Bong Beo, as his replacement in the early 1970s. He held his position until the fall of Kong Mi in 1975. *Ya* Tanh became the district chief of Khong District for a year, before resigning from political life after the Pathet Lao took control of the country in 1975. He died of old age in 2001.

The CIA was heavily involved at Kong Mi in the late 1960s and early 1970s and called Kong Mi "PS-7" (Conboy 1995). In 1967, the CIA assigned two "case officers" to Attapeu town, in order to specifically support Kong Mi. Doug Swanson, a former US Special Forces sergeant major who had previously spent time at PS-22 on the eastern Boloven Plateau, was put in charge. A younger man named Bob Parrot worked with him. They spent most of their time at Kong

Mi, which was already wholly reliant on aerial resupply. The CIA improved the runway at Kong Mi and installed extensive minefields surrounding the base. The CIA trained local Brao young men at Kong Mi to transform them into irregular warriors. Swanson and his partners divided up the hundreds of Brao[24] trained at Kong Mi into small groups and used them to attack the Sihanouk Trail (Conboy 1995).

The "Military Assistance Command, Vietnam—Studies and Observation Group" (MACV-SOG or simply SOG) mainly worked closer to the border with Vietnam and had other bases inside the Xekong Basin in Laos, but was not involved with Kong Mi. MACV-SOG was based in South Vietnam and conducted covert operations in Laos, Cambodia, and Vietnam (Harclerode 2001). All MACV-SOG members were volunteers, as working with the SOG was known to be dangerous. Half of those who entered MACV-SOG and operated in Laos were either wounded or killed during their service period. Their main job was to disrupt the Ho Chi Minh and Sihanouk Trails. MACV-SOG operated a radio relay station site located on a high tiny mountaintop codenamed the "Leghorn." The security detachment there was not Lao, but consisted of Montagnards from Vietnam. This site was in the Xekong Basin about 32 km northwest of the tri-border tip, where Laos, Cambodia, and Vietnam meet (John Plaster, pers. comm. 2006). It operated until the early 1970s, relaying messages between Laos, Cambodia, and South Vietnam. Another SOG base was located near the Xexou River and was called "The Bra."

Anti-Communist Brao were encouraged to congregate together in the same general area, and some were even transported to Kong Mi by Air America military helicopters. These included Kavet villagers from Vongvilai Tai, Kanteung, Lameuay, Phya, Phathainy, and Viangkham, all situated along the Laos-Cambodia border, and the Brao Umba communities of Phayang, Ke Kuang, Tambuan Reung, and Savanbao, also located in Cambodia. Other Brao villages were already in the area. Four sub-districts of ethnic Brao were established: Kong Mi, Kok Lak, Phya Vong, and Phya Vang. Each sub-district had between four and eight villages in them. Ethnic Brao people were always the main inhabitants of Kong Mi. Brao from Laos and Cambodia became involved on both sides of the conflict. In some areas they were joining the Communists, while others were coming together at Kong Mi with CIA support to fight against the Communists.

Khampho Sochanthavong remembers participating in an attack on Kong Mi in early 1964, following an unsuccessful assault a year earlier. This was the last Pathet Lao offensive against Kong Mi before the area was mined. He was a soldier in the Pathet Lao's 3rd company of the 1st division of southern forces. At that time, handmade bamboo *pungi* traps were mainly used around the perimeter of the base to defend it. According to Khampho, the attack was almost successful, but the Pathet Lao lost the element of surprise when the timing of their planned attack was revealed to Royalists. After that battle the surrounding areas were heavily land mined with CIA support. These mines resulted in many of the villagers' water buffaloes being killed, but they did successfully help defend the base. This was one of the few mined areas in the Xekong River Basin during the war, and some parts of this area remain mined.

Brao people now living in Tra-oum Village, Phouvong District, remember the first Americans arriving at Kong Mi in 1967, the same year that Conboy (1995) reported their arrival. However, the first American they recall was "Mr. Nyoke." (He got the nickname because he was prematurely graying.) His real name was Mike Deuel. He did not work there long before dying in an airplane crash in 1965. Then, "Mr. Doug" (Doug Swanson, mentioned in Conboy 1995) and "Mr. Bob" (Bob Parrot) were there for two years. Later "Mr. Mickie" (Mickie Kappes) and "Mr. John" (John Eckhardt) each visited, followed by "Mr. Gus," and others. These American CIA advisors often had Thai translators working with them. "Mr. Gus" was the last to leave Kong Mi when the US withdrew its personnel in 1973. The Brao road-watch teams at Kong Mi (who were all on the CIA payroll) were organized into "Teams." These Teams had around ten men each and were airlifted into different areas for behind the scenes surveillance and other military operations. There was a small airfield at the base. Kong Mi was considered to be quite rich in resources, and one old man from Tra-oum Village in Phouvong District commented that, "It is not possible to eat all the fish in the streams near Kong Mi."

Bernard Hours (1973) reported that the relocated ethnic Brao villages of Km 19 and Km 20 along the road between Pakxong and Pakse in Champasak Province largely relied on the US-paid salaries that Brao men from the villages generated through their military work at Kong Mi. He reported that much of this money was used to finance various Animist sacrifices of chickens, pigs, and water buffaloes.

In 1970, the USAF mistakenly carpet bombed their own soldiers and civilian supporters at Kong Mi. Even though nobody was attacking them, someone apparently incorrectly reported that the Pathet Lao had overrun the base. Between four and eight people were killed, according to different accounts.

Later the relatives of the people killed during this "mistake" were compensated with large amounts of money, as well as buffaloes and jars of rice beer for use in the funeral ceremonies.

Although the Pathet Lao would have been happy if Kong Mi had fallen, taking it was not a particularly high priority. The troops based there had become largely ineffective once the surrounding areas were mined, as the mines not only kept the enemy out, but also kept the inhabitants of Kong Mi boxed inside the base.

The military holdouts at Kong Mi finally surrendered to the Pathet Lao in mid-1975 at Ayak Stream, between Attapeu and Kong Mi. The leader of Kong Mi, Bong Beo, was sent to a re-education camp after 1976, but was released seven years later. He currently lives outside of Vientiane.

The Establishment of the Lao People's Democratic Republic (PDR)

In 1975, the Xekong River Basin underwent more changes. Following the Communist victories in Cambodia and South Vietnam in April 1975, the Pathet Lao moved to take control of Vientiane and important provincial capitals. On 18 May 1975, large numbers of Pathet Lao troops marched into Pakse without firing a shot. Brigadier-General Soutchay Vongsavanh fled soon after, realizing that the Pathet Lao was gradually taking control over the neutralist government that had governed since the ceasefire (Vongsavanh 1978).

The Pathet Lao officially established the Lao People's Democratic Republic (Lao PDR) on 2 December 1975. There were tremendous changes going on in all three of the countries that had once made up French Indochina. The Cold War continued to dominate the region's political landscape, with many believing that Thailand could be the next country to fall to the Communists. Rebel movements often attacked and disrupted the activities of the Government of Laos (GoL), making travel to rural areas in many parts of the country particularly difficult and dangerous.

Only in mid-1975, after Pakse had fallen, did the royalist forces stationed at their last stronghold in the Xekong River Basin, Kong Mi, in eastern Attapeu Province, surrender to the Pathet Lao. But before the surrender, some Brao people from Kong Mi, fearful of the Pathet Lao and their plan to resettle people from the uplands to the lowlands, decided to return to Cambodia. With limited access to outside information, they had no idea of the much more severe conditions they were to face once they came under the control of the Khmer Rouge.

In Cambodia, shortly before Kong Mi fell in Laos, the Khmer Rouge were becoming increasingly draconian and rigid in their ideology and methods. They became suspicious and paranoid about anyone with Vietnamese ties. A series of events during that period led to a number of ethnic Brao leaders facing escalating threats of harm due to allegations made by their Khmer Rouge superiors that they were "*Youan*" (a pejorative term for Vietnamese commonly used by the Khmer Rouge) sympathizers or collaborators. Despite various attempts to solve their problems without leaving Cambodia, and after making contact with the Vietnamese and Lao governments to inform them of the circumstances, over 5,000 people, mainly ethnic Brao from present-day Taveng District and the eastern part of Veun Say District, fled to Vietnam and Laos, half taking refuge in each country. Others soon followed. Mr. Khamteuang, Mr. Bun Mi, and Mr. Khun led the group that entered Laos, while the group that took refuge in Vietnam was led by Mr. Bu Thong and Mr. Souay Keo.

On 7 July 1976, many of the Brao who had taken refuge and settled in Vietnam joined Vietnamese forces to train and prepare for an invasion of Cambodia in order to oust the Khmer Rouge from power. Others from Laos would join them over the next couple of years. Finally, at the end of 1978, the Vietnamese invaded Cambodia, ousting the Khmer Rouge from power.

In that the ethnic Brao Cambodian exiles who invaded Cambodia together with the Vietnamese were some of the only people that the Vietnamese military could fully trust—since they were not in Cambodia during the main Khmer Rouge era—many were put into senior government positions after Vietnam took full control of the country. Most of the non-military Brao refugees from Attapeu Province were repatriated to Cambodia in 1982 and 1983. However, some of the ethnic minorities who remained in Cambodia throughout the Khmer Rouge period had developed close ties to the Khmer Rouge and many fled with the KR upon hearing of the Vietnamese invasion. They believed the Khmer Rouge warnings that the Vietnamese soldiers would kill them if they tried to surrender. Some fled and hid in the forest in fear for many years. Most surrendered to the Vietnamese-backed Hun Sen government in Cambodia by the end of the 1990s, although a small group only recently came out of the forest after spending years in hiding (see section below).

The post-1975 period in Laos allowed many of the ethnic minorities in the Xekong River Basin to return to their original territories, or at least other areas that were more suitable for them. Despite the cessation of large-scale armed conflict, on-going security problems, limited resources, and relative international isolation after 1975 still made "development," or long-term livelihood improvements for those living in upland areas, difficult.

Emerging from the Forest after 25 Years of Living in Fear

In November 2004, thirty-four people created a sensation when they emerged from the deep and remote forests that act as the border between Laos' Attapeu Province and Cambodia's Ratanakiri Province. Long thought by their relatives to have died in the war, and unaware of current events, they had been hiding in the forest, afraid that they still faced retribution from Vietnamese troops in Cambodia. The group had first lived with the Khmer Rouge in the jungles on the Cambodian side of the border, in Siem Pang District, Stung Treng Province, for ten years, starting at the time of the Vietnamese invasion in 1978. This continued until shortly before the end of the occupation, when Vietnamese troops raided their camp in 1989. The inhabitants scattered and fled deep into the forests, trying to escape. A small group of twelve people in four families ended up together. There were people from both the Kreung and Tampuon ethnic groups, but spoke Kreung together, as most were Kreung. The group traveled for five days and five nights and ended up taking refuge in a remote forest area most likely in southern Laos, in Attapeu's Phouvong District. The group had no idea whether they were in Cambodia or Laos. They were only able to prepare a few provisions before they fled, including one machete, one rice pot, a few plates, and a few handfuls of various seeds, such as rice, chilies, and some other vegetables and herbs. Their store-bought clothes eventually deteriorated, so they had to make clothing out of the bark of the tree called "*humbawk pray*" in Kreung. Fishhooks were crafted out of thorny vines, and other vines served as lines. Everything had to come from the forest. There was not even any salt or monosodium glutamate (MSG) available.[25] Chilies were used to flavor their food. Although constantly fearful that the Vietnamese might return to attack them, they managed to survive relatively well in the forest. They were always looking for food but never faced starvation (Phann and Purtill 2004).

After years of hiding without any contact with the outside world, the group finally decided to give themselves up. The psychological impact of constantly worrying about being attacked had finally got the best of them. First, they stole clothing that Brao villagers from Cheung Hiang Village in Phouvong District had hung out to dry, in order to cover their bodies. At that point, they discarded their bark clothing. However, a Brao villager saw them and called the local village militia. Soon after, the militia started pursing them, and the group gave up. The militia then turned the group over to the district authorities in Phouvong. The people from the forest were treated well by the ethnic Brao people who apprehended them. The group was well fed and given new clothing and other necessities. They continued to express fear about returning to Cambodia, in case the Vietnamese might kill them, and asked if they could settle in southern Laos. However, the GoL would not allow that. The Governor of Ratanakiri Province was contacted and soon after, he sent a delegation to Attapeu to escort the group back to Cambodia. Nine days after being apprehended, the group was back in Cambodia. They were surprised and happy to find that the Vietnamese troops had long since departed and that they did not face death or other punishment. They were given a few days of medical attention in the capital of Ratanakiri Province, Ban Lung, and were then sent back to their original villages, where they were allowed to settle peacefully. For the first time in many years they could live without the fear that they could be attacked and killed at any moment. The majority returned to Kroala Village in O Chum District, while other returned to villages in Bokeo District, also in Ratanakiri (Phann and Purtill 2004).

Over the fifteen years since they fled their KR camp and lived in the forest only one person had died, while twenty-three were born! However, almost immediately after leaving the forest, a 10-day old baby died at the provincial hospital of Ratanakiri Province (Phann and Purtill 2004; Baird 2008a). Not long after that, another child and one adult also died. It is not unusual for people who have been living in remote forested and mountainous areas to suffer serious illnesses after moving into heavily populated areas (see, for examples from Laos, Goudineau 1997; Baird and Shoemaker 2005). Three times as many people had perished in one month after leaving the forest than had died in the forest over the previous fifteen years! However, the ones that survived were still relieved and happy finally to be able to return to their homes and their long-lost families, all of whom had believed that they had died years earlier.

Enduring Legacies of the Last War

While the long period of the First and Second Indochina Wars are now receding into history, several legacies of that period still impact the Xekong River Basin. Unexploded ordnance and chemical contamination continue to affect people and the environment. War-related issues continue to impact relations between the United States and the countries of the region.

Unexploded Ordnance (UXO)

Laos has the dubious distinction of having been the heaviest bombed country per capita in history. Between 1964 and 1973 a minimum of two million tonnes of bombs, with a wide variety of designs and sizes, were dropped on Laos, a country with a population of about three million at the time. That is twice as many bombs as the Allies dropped on Germany during the Second World War. Laos also acted as a proving ground where various new models of ordnance under development could be tested. There were both large (250, 500, and 1,000 lb.) bombs and cluster bombs (large pods each containing hundreds of tennis-ball-sized bomblets, known in Lao as "*bombies*"). Some exploded on impact; others malfunctioned and did not explode right away.

One of the important aspects of the Xekong River Basin is that various parts of it served as "disputed areas" or "*Khet nyat nyeng*" during the Second Indochina War. As might be expected, the basin saw more than its share of battles and bombs during the 1960s and early 1970s. Although there are no exact statistics regarding the amount of ordnance that was dropped in the Xekong Basin, many areas are still heavily contaminated with a variety of unexploded ordnance (UXO)

While virtually the whole Xekong Basin was bombed at one time or another, bombing was especially intense in the eastern parts in Xekong and Attapeu Provinces, along the paths, roads, and rivers. The legacy of continuous bombing for so many years lives on, not only in the hearts and minds of those who were the direct or indirect targets of the bombing raids, but also among those who were born after the bombing had long since ceased. To this day, over thirty years later, they must still deal with the legacy of the UXO that litters the land. For example, in one location in Phouvong District, 150 live *bombies* were found in a 1-hectare area in 2005.

During the war there were many cases of aerial bombing killing large numbers of civilians, but, surprisingly, many villagers claim that most of the casualties of the bombing came long after it stopped and the war was over. As one villager from Phouvong said, "Very few people died when the bombs were dropped, but many died later when they were lighting their swidden fields on fire (causing bombs to explode), when taking bombies apart, or at other times."

In early 2005, in Phouvong District, one of the heaviest bombed areas during the war, three people from Houay Le Village died when a bomb exploded and two others died in Viangxai Village. In both cases, the people were out searching for scrap metal to sell and accidentally triggered bomb explosions when they tried to dig. In early 2006, two more people were killed in Phouvong and Sanxay Districts in Attapeu when bombs blew up people searching for scrap metal. Phonxay

Saykhounpor, of UXO Lao, the UNDP supported agency of the GoL charged with addressing the UXO legacy in Laos, was quoted by the *Vientiane Times* as saying, "We have prohibited people from hunting for scrap metal in areas with UXO, but some people still persist in this illegal activity" (Latsaphao 2006b: 2).

According to UXO Lao, in 2005 thirty-three people were killed and 112 injured as a result of UXO accidents in the nine-most UXO infested provinces in the country, which include Xekong and Attapeu. Males were involved in 89% of the incidents and children in 49%. This actually represents an increase in UXO accidents since 2002, and can largely be attributed to increased activity in the high-risk scrap metal trade (Latsaphao 2006b).

Herbicide "Agent Orange" Spraying

Apart from war ordnance, various chemical agents were used as part of the war effort. Between 1961 and 1971, herbicide mixtures, nicknamed by the colored identification band painted on their 208-l. storage barrels,[26] were used extensively by United States and Republic of Vietnam (RVN) forces to defoliate forests, clear perimeters around military installations, and to destroy crops as a means of decreasing enemy food supplies. Although between 1961 and 1965 the first agents used were Agent Purple and Pink, it was Agent Orange that became the best known of the various agents used, making up about 60% of all the chemical herbicides used during the war. These agents were used in smaller amounts than the herbicides used after 1965, but the herbicides used in the early 1960s may have accounted for much of the on-going dioxin contamination in Vietnam, as they were more toxic. 65% of the agents used throughout the war were highly contaminated with dioxins, and they have been widely implicated for causing serious negative environmental and human health impacts (Stellman et al. 2003). Applications were, on average, about twenty-seven times as high as for normal domestic uses of the same chemicals (Sutton 2002). Apart from dioxin contamination, Agent Blue was also recognized as dangerous due to its high concentrations of arsenic (Sutton 2002).

The USAF operations dispersed 95% of the herbicides used in Operation Trail Dust, which was the name of the overall herbicide program. Other branches of the US armed services, as well as RVN forces generally, used hand sprayers (backpacks), spray trucks, helicopters, airplanes, and boats to disperse herbicides (Sutton 2002; Stellman et al. 2003).

So far there have not been any scientific studies of dioxin levels in the Xekong River Basin in Laos, but Operation Ranch Hand (part of Operation Trail Dust) launched its first missions outside of southern Vietnam, on Lao sections of Ho Chi Minh Trail, in December 1965. Initial acknowledged spraying in Laos apparently only took place north of the 17th parallel (approximately adjacent to the present-day capital of Xekong Province and the northern border of the RVN). However, spraying also took place below the 17th parallel in Laos (southern Xekong Province and Attapeu Province), although documentation of spray activities in Laos remains incomplete (Stellman et al. 2003). In eastern Phouvong District, villagers remember large quantities of napalm being dropped on the forests in 1969 and 1970. They described it as a lot of gasoline being dropped and then burning everything up below. Roger Rumpf, an American who has investigated chemical spraying in Laos, believes that spraying took place in parts of Xekong and Attapeu Provinces between 1965 and 1971 or 1972, but there are few details regarding the exact amounts sprayed or where it took place. The Saigon military records that might have helped to clarify use are unavailable. Herbicide spraying undoubtedly occurred in many parts of the Xekong River Basin in Laos, but, overall, it was probably less severe than in adjacent parts of Vietnam (Stellman et al. 2003).

Most spraying was done in forested areas but some spraying was also done directly into the Xekong River to target transportation and gunboats on the river (Roger Rumpf, pers. comm. 2004). Khampho Sochanthavong, the present-day Vice President of the LFNC in Xekong Province, was a Pathet Lao soldier in Attapeu Province between 1962 and 1967 and recalls how the USAF sprayed large quantities of chemicals from planes all the way to the border with Cambodia, and maybe farther, in order to defoliate areas and expose roads that could then be more easily targeted in bombing raids. In present-day Phouvong District, the Ho Chi Minh Trail veered east to Vietnam, splitting from the Sihanouk Trail that continued south from Laos into Cambodia's Ratanakiri Province. According to Khampho, when the defoliants were first dropped, people were unaware of what they were or that they could affect their health. They noticed that the flowers of wild bananas (*youak kouay pa* in Lao), which are normally not sweet, became sweet after the herbicides were sprayed on them. They did not know why; they just ate them. Khampho said that fish did not die from the herbicides, which tended to float on top of the water "like a sheet of snow." Rice was apparently unharmed by the chemicals, which were especially effective in defoliating the large-leafed trees that provided cover to Vietnamese transport vehicles. When asked if the chemicals had adverse impacts on people's long-term health, he said that he thought that they had but admitted that no testing on this matter has ever been conducted in Laos.

Unlike in Laos, it was US policy not to spray adjacent parts of Cambodia, either directly or through drift spraying; however, at least one five-aircraft Ranch mission sprayed 19,000 l. of Agent Orange in Cambodia in April 1969 and another nine missions sprayed 136,000 l. partly over Cambodia. There may have also been additional unauthorized drift spraying in Cambodia. In May 1969, the Cambodian government started a diplomatic crisis when it charged the US government with spraying herbicides over large areas in northeast Cambodia. Visiting foreign scientists confirmed that defoliation had taken place due to chemical defoliants. The exact amount of defoliation remains a controversy, with the Cambodian government claiming that more occurred than some observers think is likely (Stellman et al. 2003).

In A luoi District, Thua-Thien Hue Province, in the headwaters of the Xekong Basin, a large amount of spraying took place (UNDP 1999f). The A luoi area was known as "D Resistance Zone" during the war (My 1999). My (1999) reports that even up to now vegetation has failed to return to many parts of A luoi, resulting in serious and continuing "war induced soil erosion" in sloped areas.

Chagnon (2000) reported that villagers told her that in Dakchung District Agent Orange was only used close to the Ho Chi Minh Trail. However, a gas station/store owner in Dakchung town told a Canadian volunteer in 2005 that during the war the waterways appeared to be targeted specifically and that the area around his village was sprayed extensively. He also claimed that after the spraying, which he said was yellow and done using relatively small planes, all the pregnant women in the village miscarried for about a year. It was emotionally difficult for the man to tell the story, but he clearly wanted to tell it (Joe Bennett, pers comm. July 2006). He also said that the planes shot the elephants in his area. Chagnon (2000) reported that the UNDP's SIP-Dev project in Xekong was going to seek special international assistance to 1) study soils, human fatty tissues, and mother's milk to detect dioxin levels and to pinpoint hotspot localities, 2) study health and birthing patterns in order to track the consequences and plan actions, and 3) organize a study tour for GoL officials to learn about Vietnam's long-term and on-going research on dioxin and birth defects. These plans were not implemented. Villagers also report that Agent Orange, or an associated defoliant, was used near the middle part of the Xekaman River in Sanxay District in areas between *Phou* Soi and Dak Bou Village.

Dioxin is a 50/50 mixture of 2,4,5-T and 2,4-D herbicide (UNDP 1999f; Sutton 2002; Stellman et al. 2003). It is the focus of health concerns because of its toxicity, even though many other dangerous chemicals with the potential to cause health problems were also used during the war. These chemicals are carcinogenic and teratogenic in laboratory animals. The most consistent associations have been with non-Hodgkin's lymphoma and soft tissue sarcomas (Sutton 2002), but some believe that diabetes, cancer, skin ailments, male sperm contamination, and birth defects in offspring are also a result of these chemicals (Roger Rumpf, pers. comm. 2004). US veterans groups believe that these chemicals are continuing to kill many Americans who participated in the war, either through direct contact or as a result of indirectly consuming contaminated food and drinking water. According to the *Encyclopedia Britannica*, "The toxicity of dioxin renders it capable of killing some species of newborn mammals and fish at levels of five parts per trillion (or one ounce in six million tons). Less than two millionths of an ounce will kill a mouse." Its toxic properties are enhanced by the fact that it can pass into the body through all major routes, including skin (by direct contact), lungs (by inhaling dust, fumes or vapors), or mouth (Sutton 2002).

Adding to the danger of these chemicals, the US military sprayed herbicides in Vietnam at six to twenty-five times the rate suggested by the manufacturer, even though the military was aware of the serious potential health impacts of being exposed to these herbicides (Sutton 2002). Mist drift of herbicides also resulted in chemicals traveling up to 10 km or more, thus affecting areas not targeted for spraying (Sutton 2002). Undoubtedly, the impacts on Vietnamese people have been even more severe as many were not only exposed to these dangerous substances during the war, but have also been exposed continually, for decades, since it ended. According to the UNDP (1999f) and Stellman et al. (2003), over 76 million liters of herbicides were sprayed during the war. Vietnamese sources sometimes put the amount at over 100 million l. (My 1999). The UNDP (1999f) estimates that over 10–14% of southern Vietnam's land area were sprayed, but Vietnamese researchers claim that 30,101 km^2 were affected in the RVN, representing 16.5% of the country.

The A luoi Valley, previously called the A Shau Valley, was an integral part of the Ho Chi Minh Trail during the war and was heavily sprayed from approximately 1965 to 1970, principally with Agent Orange, the most common agent used, and to a lesser extent, Agent Blue and Agent White (UNDP 1999f). Agent White, somewhat less toxic than some of the others, was mainly used against agricultural crops. Agent Purple and Pink were the most toxic, with the highest quantities of dioxin. Spraying took place at a nominal application rate of 4.78 kg/ha (Stellman et al. 2003). In the US, military herbicide operations in Vietnam were a matter of scientific controversy from their inception, especially after 2,4,5 T was banned from most US domestic uses in April 1970 (Stellman et al. 2003).

Considering the known negative health impacts of these chemicals, Hatfield Consultants, Ltd., of Vancouver, Canada, and the Government of Vietnam's 10–80

Committee (based in Hanoi) cooperated to conduct a preliminary assessment of the environmental and health impacts related to the spraying of Agent Orange and related herbicides in Vietnam (UNDP 1999f). After conducting dioxin tests between 1996 and 1999, Hatfield found that in A So Commune (formally named A Shau), in the headwaters of the Xekong Basin, fish fat (fish from ponds[27]), duck fat, soils, and pond sediment contained high levels of dioxins. Hatfield pointed out that if such high levels of dioxins had been found in countries like Canada, it "would probably result in the area being declared a contaminated site." Aquaculture pond fish dioxin levels were found to be high and would, in Canada, have triggered a consumption advisory process (i.e., recommendations on maximum human consumption levels) and possibly prohibitions against consumption (UNDP 1999f; Dwernychuk et al. 2002). Contamination was particularly high around the old A So US airbase, and two other bases (Dwernychuk et al. 2002). Wayne Dwernychuk and his colleagues also tested wild fish in the headwaters of the Xekong Basin in Vietnam for dioxin contamination, but, unlike the pond fish, the wild river fish were not found to be contaminated, probably due to the many years of seasonal flushing that occurs with monsoon rains (Wayne Dwernychuk, pers. comm. 2005).

Hatfield also found that human blood samples from A luoi were contaminated with Agent Orange dioxin. High levels were recorded in pooled blood from males and females older than twenty-five, and of both males and females from twelve to twenty-five. The detection of dioxin in the younger generation provided evidence that the valley environment remains contaminated and that dioxin is currently moving through the food chain into humans. Deformities, early cancers, and other medical conditions have been documented in the valley. Vietnamese health studies have also reported that birth defects are an order of magnitude higher in the A So area than in similar unsprayed areas in northern Vietnam (UNDP 1999f). My (1999) and Dwernychuk et al. (2002) reported that women's health has been particularly badly affected by dioxin contamination as it dissolves in maternal milk, even when found in small quantities. My (1999) has also reported that dioxin penetrating the ground soil via the surface water has caused delayed growth of vegetation, leading to the loss of the soil conservation capacity of forests.

In September 2004, a group of Vietnamese living in the USA filed a class action complaint in a New York court charging thirty-six chemical companies that produced herbicides used during the war with "product liability." The defendants include such well-known giants as Monsanto Chemical Company, Dow Chemical Company, Uniroyal Chemical, Inc., and Occidental Chemical Corp. The hope was that these companies, which financially benefited from producing and selling these dangerous chemicals, would finally be forced to pay at least something for the suffering caused by their products (Kokkoris 2004). However, on 10 March 2005 a Federal District Court judge in Brooklyn, New York, Jack B. Weinstein, ruled in favor of the companies and abruptly dismissed the case. In making his decision, the judge stated that the companies could not be held liable for the damage done by their products because "No treaty or agreement, express or implied, of the United States operated to make the use of herbicides in Vietnam a violation of . . . . international law until at the earliest April of 1975" (*Cambodia Daily* 2005: 2). But a lawyer for the victims' association said, in disgust: "The judge missed the point. He ruled as a matter of law that what these defendants manufactured was not a poison, whereas even these manufacturers recognized that it was at the time" (*Cambodia Daily* 2005: 2). Immediately after the decision, Vietnamese groups also expressed their anger (*Cambodia Daily* 2005). Nguyen Trong Nhan, Vice President of the Vietnamese Association for Victims of Agent Orange, said, "We just want justice." Ironically, about 10,000 US veterans receive disability benefits related to Agent Orange exposure, and even though the US chemical companies claim that there is no conclusive link to the health problems blamed on the defoliant, the same companies have settled similar court cases filed by US veterans for millions of dollars (*Cambodia Daily* 2005). Following the above setback, the group of US-resident Vietnamese decided to appeal the case to the Second District Court of Appeals, and as of May 2006 the case was still pending (*Vietnam News* 2006).

Thus far there have not been any similar cases brought to the courts on behalf of Lao victims, and nobody has even bothered to investigate the issue in detail. Oxfam America tried to support some efforts to learn more about the use of chemical defoliants in Laos and their health and environmental impacts there. They attempted to develop a partnership with the Science, Technology, and Environmental Agency (STEA), but the GoL stalled final approval of the project until it became clear that they had no intention of approving it. They were apparently concerned that such research might negatively affect their relations with the USA. Roger Rumpf, who was involved in the initiative, has firm data that 2,150,000 l. of herbicides were dropped on Laos during the war and the actual amount could be much higher. Most of what was dropped on Laos probably came from bases in Vietnam, but a small amount of super secret missions from Thailand may have been involved in herbicide spraying in Laos as well (Roger Rumpf, pers. comm. 2004).

Searching for Americans "Missing in Action"

Although the United States military withdrew from Vietnam, Laos, and Cambodia over thirty years ago, there has been a persistent, albeit declining, belief among a small but vocal number of Americans, including some veterans, that some of the US soldiers and military personnel from the war listed as "Missing in Action" (MIA) might still be alive, either imprisoned or living freely in Vietnam or remote eastern parts of Laos, including eastern parts of the Xekong River Basin in either Xekong or Attapeu. While the issue no longer attracts as much media or political interest as it once did (see, for example, *U.S. Veteran News and Report* 1991), 1,836 people were still officially classified as "Missing in Action" in 2005, 375 of them in Laos (Anonymous 2005). It has been a longstanding US political objective, and one of the highest US priorities in its relations with the Lao PDR, to try to provide a full accounting of these "missing" personnel.

At the end of US involvement in Laos, in 1973, the US government listed 569 people as MIAs associated with Laos, of which 194 have had their remains repatriated or identified in recent years. Of those still MIA, 41 are in a "no further pursuit" status, meaning that as a result of rigorous investigation, it has been concluded that the individuals died, and that their remains are unlikely to be recovered. In Laos, there were still 75 loss sites that have been located but awaited excavation in 2005. Of the original 81 individuals "Last Known Alive" in Laos (those who might have survived their loss incidents but did not return), the Department of Defense has determined the fate of 28, with 53 cases still remaining unresolved (Defense Prisoner of War/Missing Personnel Office 2005). It is unclear how many MIAs went missing inside or near the Xekong Basin in Laos, but undoubtedly some were lost there.

There have been many US missions to look for remains in the Xekong River Basin since the 1990s and in Xekong Province as recently as March and April 2005. For example, in 2003 a US team of investigators went to the old village site of Dak Kloung on the Xexou River in Attapeu Province, to dig for American remains. Villagers saw the group, but are unclear as to whether they actually found any American human remains. Villagers claim, however, that the Vietnamese government exhumed seven Vietnamese bodies from the Xexou area in 2003. The villagers who led the Vietnamese to the bodies were rewarded with 2 million kip. The Vietnamese also let it be known that they are interested in retrieving the body of a Vietnamese doctor named Lan, who is apparently famous in Vietnam, and they have offered a reward of 5 million kip for information leading to the recovery of her remains. There are reportedly 116 Vietnamese who remain unaccounted for in Attapeu.

In 2001, the US government, with Lao minders, went to *Khet* 8, one of the most remote parts of northern Kalum District, near the border with Vietnam, in order to look for the remains of dead American soldiers. A US helicopter came into land, and the ethnic Katu people on the ground thought that the Americans were reinvading Laos and prepared to shoot at the helicopter! Fortunately, the Lao soldiers flying with the Americans were able to yell out to the Katu to hold their fire, and a serious incident was narrowly averted.

In a separate incident, ethnic Ngkriang villagers from Talang Mai Village mentioned encountering US soldiers searching for the bones of dead American soldiers a few years ago. They were especially afraid of the African American soldiers, who they claimed were intimidating to children in the village. The soldiers would not sleep in the village, but instead set up camp outside. It was taboo for people to enter the village during this period, as bones of dead people were discovered on their territory.

Apart from the US government's work in partnership with the Lao authorities on this issue, other private American groups have tried to "take matters into their own hands" by engaging in a more activist-oriented approach to the issue. Some have raised funds to support private search efforts. As late as 2004, one private group, *Rolling Thunder*, a US veterans' motorcycle club, continued to support the costs of private MIA searches in the region, including efforts to search for MIAs in Sanxay District, Attapeu Province. In April 2004, the first author accidentally met one of these last few MIA investigators working with *Rolling Thunder* funding support. Larry Stark, aged 68, was riding a bus from Attapeu to Pakse, having come from mountainous areas in Sanxay District, Attapeu Province. The retired civilian employee of the US Navy (since 1998), who had himself been captured by North Vietnamese forces in the 1969 Tet offensive in Vietnam, spent a number of years as a Prisoner of War in and around Hanoi in what was then North Vietnam. He was traveling with his wife and an elderly Lao couple from Savannakhet Province. They were assisting with his research and translating for him. He claimed to have traveled to Laos six times over the past two years. This privately-funded MIA research effort did not have GoL permission to operate, but the group seemed to be able to get around the province without trouble. At the time they hoped they might finally be close to a major breakthrough, but apparently this did not materialize.

5

Agriculture, Livelihoods, and Resettlement

A wide variety of agricultural systems are practiced in the Xekong River Basin. They have developed based on local socio-cultural, economic, historical, and ecological circumstances, but also as a result of outside and even global influences. Many of the region's agricultural systems are reliant upon "local ecological knowledge," or "intimate knowledge" as Hugh Raffles (2002) likes to call it. This is knowledge held by farmers, and based on local experiences, sometimes developed over generations.

The goal of this chapter is to explain some of the main types of agriculture practiced in the Xekong River Basin and present issues related to internal resettlement. It will not be possible to describe all the varied agricultural systems practiced; however, the main ones are covered here. Since coffee cultivation will be described in the context of forests in Chapter 6, it will not be discussed here.

Mr. Khenthong Sisouvong, Deputy Governor of Attapeu Province, reported to the *Vientiane Times* in April 2006 that, "Agriculture production is an intrinsic component of the socio-economic development of the province because it is the livelihood of almost all Attapeu residents" (Syvongxay 2006: 3). The same can be said for other parts of the Xekong River Basin. There are many different livelihoods in the basin, but subsistence and semi-subsistence agriculture is the most important component of most of them. In Attapeu Province, 90% of households are involved mainly in agriculture for their livelihoods, and 97% of the agriculture conducted is primarily for subsistence. The statistics for Xekong Province are similar, with over 92% of households being involved primarily in agriculture, of which 95% is conducted mainly for subsistence (SPC 2000b and c).

In Attapeu, only 4% of farmers reportedly use chemical fertilizers while about 10% use pesticides. Just over 30% use organic compost. In remote districts, chemical fertilizer and pesticide use is even lower. In Phouvong, only 2% of the households reportedly use chemical fertilizers, and in Sanxay there is no reported usage. There is also little pesticide use reported from either district (SPC 2000b). In Xekong Province, 4% of farming families use chemical fertilizers and less than 5% use pesticides (SPC 2000c). In Attapeu, less than 5% of the rice seed used is improved varieties, with 15% of the rice seeds used in Samakhixay District being hybrids (SPC 2000b). In Attapeu, 98.8% of farmers reportedly own their own land for farming, while 99.4% claim to own their own land in Xekong Province (SPC 2000b and c).

Rainy Season Wet-Rice Agriculture

Wet-rice farming is one of the important agricultural activities in the Xekong River Basin, although it is largely limited to the lowland plains and some relatively small valleys tucked between mountains. There is only a small amount of wet-rice paddy cultivation in mountainous areas, including some terraced wet-rice fields in Dakchung District, and a bit of wet-rice paddy cultivation in mountainous parts of Sanxay District. Despite the geographical limitations, lowland wet-rice cultivation is becoming increasingly important in many parts of the basin, largely because officials have promoted this type of agriculture over upland swidden agriculture cultivation. Some officials hope that the excess harvests in the lowlands can be used to feed people in the uplands, using new and improved road networks to transport the rice. Indicative of changes over the last decade, in Xekong Province 37% of households reported developing new lowland wet-rice fields in 1998/1999, while 15.5% did so in Attapeu Province during the same year (SPC 2000b and c). Over the last decade or so there has been a big push for expanding lowland wet-rice cultivation in the Xekong Basin, as has been the case in other parts of Laos. There have also been increased efforts put into intensifying rice cultivation through the introduction of hybrid seeds and by promoting the use of chemical fertilizers and pesticides.

Historically, lowland wet-rice cultivation was mainly practiced by ethnic Lao communities living in the lowland plains of Saysettha, Samakhixay and Sanamxay Districts in Attapeu Province, and some neighboring parts of Pathoumphone and Khong Districts in Champasak Province. It also appears that many ethnic Oy people living in the Xekong plains, at the base of the Bolaven Plateau, adopted lowland rice cultivation hundreds of years ago. The Oy language includes some words related to lowland paddy cultivation that apparently originate from Khmer. Since ethnic Khmer have not inhabited the area for centuries, the Oy would seem to have been involved in—or at least in contact with—lowland wet-rice culture for a long time (Gerard Diffloth, pers. comm. 2000). However, for most ethnic groups in the Xekong River Basin, lowland rice cultivation has only been adopted relatively recently. Some Mon-Khmer language speakers still are not very familiar with this type of agriculture.

It was probably the Oy that Long (1890) was referring to in writing that when Phaxay first established Attapeu, he was able to convince the populations of fourteen villages west of the Xekong River on the foothills of *Phou Louang*, whom he called "*Kha na*" (the Austroasiatics who do lowland wet-rice cultivation), to submit themselves to being under the protection of Attapeu. Thus, the Oy were probably doing lowland wet-rice cultivation before the Lao arrived in Attapeu.

Some Jru Dak people also adopted lowland wet-rice cultivation relatively early, due to living in relatively low areas for a long period of time, in close proximity to ethnic Lao people who were practicing wet-rice agriculture. Apart from the Lao, the Oy, and the Jru Dak, the ethnic Trieu people in Dakchung District also claim to have a long history of wet-rice paddy cultivation, although they live in relatively mountainous areas.

There remain a number of problems in the Xekong River Basin with regard to being able to produce enough rice to feed the population. Although in some years it might be possible to do so, in 2004, which was a particularly bad year for rice crops due to drought, Xekong Province was reportedly able to produce only 12,983 tonnes of rice. This was far from the 26,496 tonnes needed to feed all the people in the province for a year. It was estimated that 82,713 people would not have enough rice to eat for the entire year in 2004/2005. Drought reportedly affected 3,727 ha of the 8,065 ha of land under rice production, resulting in a loss of about 10,032 tonnes of rice (*Vientiane Times* 2004i).

Dry Season Riverbank Vegetable Gardens

Wide seasonal variations in hydrology result in the occurrence of fertile soils in seasonally inundated areas and along the banks of the Xekong and its tributaries. The natural cycle of floods thus presents the best opportunity for conducting dry season vegetable gardening. This is one important way in which local people have long adapted their livelihoods to fit with the natural hydrological conditions.

In fact, there are various ways in which riverside gardens are managed (see Shoemaker et al. 2001). Some crops are planted when water levels are high, while others are sown only after they have already significantly receded. Different crops are planted to coincide with different seasons and parts of the hydrological cycle. For example, corn and tubers are often cultivated when water levels are relatively high and there is still some rain but, once water levels have declined to near their lowest levels, the dry sandy soils lower down riverbanks are suitable for different crops, like tobacco and watermelons. A large variety of edible plant species are grown in these gardens. Knowledge about the environmental conditions and how different crops react to different parts of the cycle help ensure success, provided that the hydrological cycle does not drastically change.

Both wet-rice cultivators and swidden farmers engage in riverside gardening in the dry season, as do those more relient on wet-rice lowland cultivation. Lowland ethnic Lao have a long tradition of planting dry season vegetable gardens on the alluvial soils of large rivers and streams in the Xekong Basin, taking advantage of the nutrients deposited during wet season flooding. Ethnic Lao villagers from Sompoi Village, Sanamxay District, adjacent to the Xekong, report planting an array of different crops along the edge of the river. They plant crops on the upper part of the riverbanks in May, when the rains first begin, and in October, when water levels first begin to decline. Some of the most important crops are chilies, long beans, and eggplants. Once water levels reach quite low levels, some farmers grow tobacco and watermelons, especially on seasonal islands in the river. In the ethnic Brao village of Hatxaisoung, Sanamxay District, tobacco is planted along the banks of the Xekong during the dry season, especially when water levels are quite low.

But swidden farmers also grow vegetables along the edges of streams and rivers in the dry season, although the floodplains in mountainous areas tend to be somewhat more restricted than in the lowlands. Nevertheless, dry season vegetable cultivation is often significant for the livelihoods of upland ethnic minorities. For example, Brao swidden cultivators in Phouvong District make quite large dry season vegetable and tobacco gardens along the Nam Kong River. In the uplands of *Khet* Somboun, near Vietnam, ethnic Brao villagers from Nam Souan (Dak Joor) Village make large dry season vegetable gardens adjacent to, and in the floodplain of the Ka-ol Stream. Swidden farmers frequently temporarily plant the stocks of cassava at the edges of rivers and streams during the dry season, to keep them moist and alive until the coming wet season when the stocks can be cut up and planted in swiddens.

While excess harvests from riverside gardens are sometimes sold at the local level or in markets, especially in lowland parts of the river in Attapeu Province, farmers, their families, friends, and neighbors generally consume most of what is produced.

Wild Wetland Dependent Vegetables

Apart from domesticated vegetable crops, many wild vegetables that local people eat are adapted to hydrological cycles. When water levels recede at the end of the rainy season, some of these vegetables begin to grow along the banks of rivers and streams as well as in other seasonally inundated areas. Although this is not technically "agriculture," this vegetation provides local people with important sources of food and nutrients. It is not only the vegetables that people plant in flood recession areas that are important for local livelihoods, but also the plants that grow naturally in these areas, both annuals and perennials, including large trees. Like those species cultivated by humans, these naturally growing plants rely on the rich soils found in these areas. One good example is a flowering riverine bush that both humans and fish eat: "*kok khai kin mak*" in Lao (*Telectadium edule* H. Baill. [Asclepiadaceae]). It is common to see fishers returning from checking their gillnets in the Xekong carrying fish that they have caught, along with a handful of the stems and flowers of *kok khai kin mak* to eat with the fish. There are many other wild plant species that are eaten as food.

In addition, fish and other aquatic animals rely heavily on naturally occurring plants found in the water, as habitat and sometimes as sources of food. Fish consume plants that grow at the edge of the water when it recedes. Baird (2007a) studied the relationship between riverine vegetation in the mainstream Mekong River just below the Khone Falls and fish consumption of these plants. Between 1993 and 1999, he identified at least 35 species of forest fruits, 13 species of fresh leaves, 3 species of flowers, and various barks and roots, in the stomachs of 1,617 fish specimens belonging to at least 73 species in 52 genera and 20 families. Eight fish species in the family *Pangasiidae* were found to be the most important consumers of fruits and other fresh vascular plant material. *Tor tambroides, Leptobarbus hoeveni, Hypsibarbus* spp., *Osphronemus exodon* and other fishes were also found to consume considerable amounts of plant matter. As part of the same study, fishers reported that fish consume 73 plant species, including 9 species suitable for baiting hooks to catch fish. Fish in the Xekong River Basin are equally relient on vegetation as food and habitat, and some species, like *Tor tambroides*, are much more common in the Xekong and its larger tributaries than in the Mekong.

Vegetation that grows on the fertile water recession soils is important as food for domestic animals, especially water buffaloes. Some plants are used as traditional plant-based medicines for people and livestock. Pigs, chickens, and, especially, ducks like to look for food along the edges of rivers and streams when water levels are declining. Recession soils and associated vegetation are often under-appreciated. They are actually important for various aspects of local livelihoods, while also serving other important ecological functions.

Domestic Livestock

As in Laos generally, raising domestic livestock is one of the most important components of livelihoods for people in the Xekong River Basin and selling livestock is one of the main sources of income for local people in the basin. The trade in livestock has a long history in the Xekong Basin and included elephants and buffaloes during pre-colonial times (Rathie 2001). While the populations of wild and domestic elephants have declined drastically, thus curtailing the trade in elephants, most families in the basin still raise domestic animals of one type or another, as is typical in subsistence and semi-subsistence agricultural-based economies. In Xekong Province, there are approximately 23,000 buffaloes, 14,700 cattle, 41,000 pigs (mainly indigenous varieties), 25,000 goats and 73,000 poultry (Goudineau 2001). Domestic livestock are the most important sources of income in the two most remote districts in Xekong, Kalum and Dakchung (UNDP 1999a and c). Much of the wealth of the Austroasiatic peoples living in mountainous areas is accumulated from raising livestock. In 1998/1999, 55.4% of households reported owning water buffaloes in Attapeu, as did 45.9% in Xekong Province (SPC 2000b and c). In Attapeu, 28% of the households reported owning pigs, while in Xekong 63.2% owned pigs (SPC 2000b and c). 44.5% of the households in Attapeu owned indigenous chickens, while 76.1% owned chickens in Xekong (SPC 2000b and c). The larger proportion of people raising chickens and pigs in Xekong compared to Attapeu probably reflects the high proportion of Austroasiatics in Xekong.

Historically, most Austroasiatics mainly raised water buffaloes, indigenous varieties of black pigs, native chickens, and dogs. All are important for ceremonial sacrificial purposes, with water buffaloes representing the highest form of sacrifice for many ethnic groups in the Xekong Basin (see section above on spirits and sacrifices). Dogs are also important for assisting in hunting and are typically eaten by uplanders, and lowlanders to a lesser extent. Traditionally, domestic chickens, pigs, and buffaloes were rarely if ever consumed without first being used in ritual sacrifices related to appeasing spirits, curing illnesses, or following the agricultural cycle. While ethnic Lao people and government officials often perceive the sacrifice of domestic animals as a waste of valuable meat, local people consume virtually all the meat from sacrifices, so in reality nothing is wasted through these practices. When large animals are sacrificed other family, village or neighboring communities are usually invited to participate in the rituals and partake in the feast that follows. Meat is divided up carefully between the guests, and it is expected that those receiving slabs of buffalo meat will some day repay the debt when they make a sacrifice. In almost all cases, alcohol consumption is associated with sacrifices. This includes distilled whisky for some groups and fermented jar beer for others. In the view of many, animal sacrifices represent both an important practical way of curing illnesses and preventing such things as animal epidemics and crop failure as well as being important for fulfilling social functions like sharing meat and drink with others. For example, ethnic Triang people in Dakchung District hold water buffalo sacrifices at various times of the year, and for different reasons, but annual sacrifices occur even when no problems are being experienced. They have more of a preventative purpose.

Every five, six, or seven years, depending upon circumstances, there is a major buffalo sacrifice in the vicinity of Dakchung District center. In April 2004, one of these important buffalo sacrifices took place in Dakchung Village. These major sacrifices alternate between different nearby villages. In April 2004, there were supposed to be eleven buffaloes sacrificed, but in the end the villagers claimed that they could only afford six.

Historically, and to a somewhat lesser extent now, some Austroasiatic peoples from particular villages in clusters of communities would sacrifice one or more buffaloes, and invite the other half-a-dozen or so neighboring villages in the cluster to the rituals and associated feasts. Then, the next year it would be the turn of another one of the group of villages to host a sacrifice of a similar size and to invite the rest of the cluster of villages to attend. In this way each village only had to host a large sacrifice of this kind once every seven years. Undoubtedly, the purposes of these sacrifices are two-fold. First, they are done to protect the interests of the village from unfriendly spirits that represent a threat to the community. Secondly, the sacrifices serve to create and maintain village alliances and personal friendships, which would have been important in the past when intertribal conflicts and wars were more common. They are still important today but for different reasons, such as for maintaining general solidarity between communities.

In many places in the Xekong Basin domestic livestock play an important role in the local economy. At times local people in remote parts of the Xekong River Basin, such as in Kalum and Dakchung Districts, use domestic animals for barter with traders and other villages and ethnic groups. For example, villagers in Kalum

District report that livestock is raised mainly for family use and that barter trade with domestic animals is more important than cash sales (UNDP 1999e). There are various networks of buffalo traders in the Xekong Basin. For example, in upper Kalum District locals report that ethnic Vietnamese traders from Salavan sometimes visit them to buy buffaloes. In 2004, they were generally paying about 3,500,000 kip per animal, and selling those same animals in Salavan for 5–6,000,000 kip each. They were paying 2 million kip each for cows and selling them for 3 million kip each.

Many families seldom sell livestock and consume all of the domestic animals that they raise during sacrifices over different seasons throughout the year. This sometimes leads to conflicts arising when lowland Lao people come to work for short periods in minority villages and want to purchase village chickens to consume. At times they may be lucky and find villagers with excess animals that they are willing to sell for consumption in the village.

More often they encounter locals unwilling to sell any of their few chickens, fearing that they might be needed for sacrificial purposes in case any health emergencies arise or to breed to increase the flock. Ethnic Lao people tend to think of domestic animals as an economic resource whereas the minorities often view them as a means for fighting off illnesses and other misfortunes. However, this is not to say that the economic factor is not becoming more important among the Austroasiatics.

Ethnic Lao people faced by a villager unwilling to part with one of his last chickens tend to perceive the villager as being stubborn and illogically disposed to blocking a potentially mutually beneficial economic exchange. Sometimes, they may accuse the local person of not being interested in making a profit, or of not knowing how to, or of being "lazy." However, the villagers may see things quite differently, and consider the outsider's request to buy one of his or her last chickens as unreasonable, and equivalent to asking someone to put himself and his families at risk by clearing out his medicine chest and leaving him to face serious illnesses without having recourse to animals that can be sacrificed to fend off the threat. These two different worldviews can lead to misunderstandings and even conflicts.

Sometimes villagers are coerced into selling a chicken even when they would rather not. This is especially the case when government officials visit, but the problem also occurs when international aid agencies work. Steeve Daviau mentioned this problem in an assessment he did on livestock raising in Kalum District (2003a), and a Canadian CUSO volunteer observed this same dynamic in Dakchung (Joe Bennett, pers. comm. July 2006) (see below).

Outside Development Efforts and Livestock Raising

It is particularly ironic when groups of lowland Lao health workers are dispatched by aid agencies to particular villages to promote increased nutrition, including protein-intake, but, during their time in the villages, they end up consuming a significant portion of the village's chickens—the exact type of animal protein that they have been encouraging the villagers to eat. In reality, the people then have even less to consume. Outsiders, mainly ethnic Lao, often want to eat chicken at almost every meal, something that is unknown among locals (see, for example, Daviau 2003a). While it may be true that these development workers usually pay the villagers a market rate for the chickens they eat, and that they often allow villagers to eat some of the chicken meat with them, the locals still end up consuming less chicken than they would have, had the development workers not been present in the first place. Furthermore, money received from selling chickens is rarely used to buy replacement meat for local consumption, but is instead frequently spent buying less nutritious food, like processed sweets, or clothing, or other items.

Domestic animal raising varies significantly based on ethnicity and geographical locations, depending on cultural and environmental factors. For example, in the past ethnic Triang people living on the high plateau of Dakchung District, called *Phou Phiang Kaseng* in Lao, found the plentiful flat grassland there highly amenable to buffalo-raising, and so many became specialists (Goudineau 2001). However, the number of buffaloes being raised in Dakchung has actually declined in recent years. There has also been a general reduction in the amounts of pigs being raised. The number of cattle and goats appears to be relatively stable (UNDP 1999b). In other steeper, more densely forested areas, like Kalum, raising large animals is much less appropriate but may still be important in some communities. There, 47% of households mentioned one of their main constraints to raising large livestock is lack of pasture (UNDP 1999d). Ethnic Brao people in Attapeu also report that in the past many villages did not raise any buffalo, due to inappropriate geographical conditions. When they needed buffaloes for sacrificing, they simply went to other communities that did raise buffaloes and traded for livestock.

Illustrative of the importance of good pasture for cattle raising, in around the late 1990s the Agriculture Promotion Bank (APB) in Kalum District provided loans to a number of farmers in Hatpe village to raise 104 cows, but many of the cows purchased for the villagers slipped and fell from steep areas and cliffs around the village. Others starved since there was not enough grass to feed them. There were only some *"mak bok"* seeds, which come from large trees in the forest, but not enough to keep the whole herd healthy. According to an INGO observer, 70 of the 104 cows died within about a year. They were not vaccinated, and there were problems with villagers not being able to choose the cows that they received from the APB. Some were too old, while others were too young. Interestingly, in 1999 none of the villages in Kalum reported raising cattle for personal use (UNDP 1999d), and cattle appear to be mainly seen as a cash crop, as they are not used in sacrifices. In this type of terrain, raising chickens probably makes more sense, and, over time, villagers have adapted to local cultural and environmental conditions.

In another case involving the APB, the availability of grass to eat was less of a problem, but ethnic Harak villagers from Nava Keng Luang Village, in Lamam District, complained about the cows that were provided by the APB, claiming that they were overpriced for their sizes, ages, and sex, with females being priced at 1,500,000 kip each, and males at 2,000,000 kip each. In addition, some were unhealthy, a few were too young, and many were too old (7–10 years old, instead of 3–4 years old, as expected). At first, when the villagers saw the thirty cows being offered to them, they did not want to accept them, as they were not receiving what they expected. However, the government officials said that they either had to accept the cows or lose the opportunity entirely. The villagers reluctantly accepted the cows, but later regretted their decision. They felt coerced into taking them. After three years, only twenty of the thirty cows were still alive, and villagers were complaining about not having been able to choose their own cows from the outset.

In another case, in Kalum District, the APB lent money to people from Pak Say Village so that they could buy cows. However, the villagers did not make proper use of the money. Half was used to buy cattle; the other half was spent buying clothes and other consumer goods. As a result, a lot of the funds were wasted. The APB in Kalum reportedly has little money to lend out, due to the many losses they have suffered with cattle raising loans, and the difficulties that they have had in collecting previous debts.

Pigs are an important domestic livestock species. In the lowlands crosses of Berkshire brown pigs are common. In ethnic Lao villages, pigs are often tethered and, since these pigs are not capable of finding their own food when tied up, they are mainly fed rice bran and human food scraps. Banana tree stems and other vegetation, depending upon how industrious the owner is, sometimes supplement this diet. However, most of the pigs raised in ethnic minority villages are indigenous black pigs, which are smaller than Lao pigs but, with their long snouts, more capable of finding their own food. Villagers can raise more pigs, as their pigs mainly roam free, where they find much of their own food, including forest food and human feces. They are also sometimes fed rice bran and food scraps, as well as the remnants of jar beer, but these pigs are much less reliant on being fed. However, pig epidemics are much more common in ethnic minority villages where pigs are allowed to run free. For example, in 2005 many pigs died in the remote mountain village of Lamong in Phouvong District. These sorts of epidemics also occur in ethnic Lao villages, but are generally less common.

Goats, ducks, and cattle are more recent additions to the kinds of domestic animals that villagers raise, but they are becoming increasingly popular and important in remote areas. Despite the types of problems raising cattle discussed above, 9.7% of households in Attapeu Province reported owning cows in 1998/1999, while 20.8% owned cows in Xekong Province during the same year (SPC 2000b and c). There do not appear to be any reliable statistics about goat and duck raising, but there has been a marked increase in goat raising in many parts of the Xekong River Basin in recent years. In 2004, the first author even saw a goat being sacrificed for spirits by Katu people in Don Village, Kalum District. One problem with free-range goat raising is, however, that the animals often damage agriculture crops, as they are skillful in getting through fences into gardens and accessing difficult places.

Xekong Province officials believe that there is a lot of cattle-raising potential in Dakchung District due to the abundance of grasses in natural fields year round. They have been targeting the area for cattle and buffalo raising for many years already (UNDP 1997). However, buffalo are the only type of livestock currently exported from Xekong Province in substantial quantities. Livestock diseases are endemic in the Xekong Basin and vaccination services are still weak (Goudineau 2001). During this study there were many reports of water buffaloes dying due to various illnesses. For example, in Kase Village, Sanamxay District, 200 buffaloes died in 2004, leaving only about ten in the village. This caused one farmer to comment that the villagers would have to hire tractors to plow their lowland wet-rice fields during the coming rice-growing season. He said that in the past families generally had twenty to thirty buffaloes each, but that in recent years many have died from illness. In a 2004 case, people from Dong Xay Village in Attapeu Province claimed that many buffaloes died of illnesses, and that the situation had been even worse in

2003, when some families lost more than ten buffaloes each. Epidemics can lead to major losses for farmers, since buffaloes are some of the most valuable things that they own. Significant percentages of family wealth are often tied up in large domestic animals, especially for ethnic minorities less inclined than lowland Lao to invest in expensive houses.

Livestock vaccination statistics for the basin are poor. There are reportedly no chickens or ducks vaccinated in Xekong or Attapeu, and only 3.7% of the pigs in Attapeu were vaccinated in 1998/1999, as compared to 1% of the pigs in Xekong Province. The situation is somewhat better when it comes to large animals. During the same year, 62.3% of the cows in Attapeu were vaccinated, compared to 23.1% for Xekong Province. Furthermore, 52.2% of the buffaloes in Attapeu were vaccinated during the same year, while 17.9% were vaccinated in Xekong (SPC 2000b; 2000c). Generally fewer animals in more remote areas are vaccinated and some farmers are hesitant to get their livestock immunized because they believe vaccinations will make their animals sick.

With the outbreak of Asian bird flu in Vietnam and the region, Laos has made an attempt to stop the spread of the disease by banning the import of chicken or chicken eggs. However, the smuggling of chickens, their meat, and eggs continues. On 26 April 2005, the *Vientiane Times* reported that 3,000 illegally imported chicken eggs from Vietnam had been confiscated and destroyed in the capital of Xekong Province. Authorities admitted that the illegal smuggling of chickens and their products was continuing in Xekong and other parts of the country (*Vientiane Times* 2005g).

Apart from disease and epidemics, UNDP (1999d) reported that 52% of villagers in Kalum District identified predation of domestic livestock by wildlife as a problem. In Dakchung, 79% identified predation as a significant problem (UNDP 1999b). Wildlife predation of domestic animals is found throughout the Xekong River Basin. There are various kinds of animal predation problems, ranging from tigers killing buffaloes (relatively rare except for the remotest areas) to birds of prey and snakes eating baby chickens.

Commercial Agriculture

Commercial agriculture in the Xekong River Basin is relatively insignificant to local livelihoods. Apart from coffee (discussed in Chapter 6), cardamom (*Amomum* spp.) is considered to be Xekong's most important agricultural export (Pansivongsay 2006a). Most of the cardamom is cultivated in Thateng District (312 ha of the district was covered in cardamom plantations in 1997, producing 52 tons of cardamom) (UNDP 1997). Villagers mainly collect cardamom in November, both from cultivated areas and from the wild. In fact, cardamom has a long history of being grown in the Xekong Basin. Rathie (2001) mentions that in the nineteenth century ethnic Lao people oppressed tribal peoples, including the Nya Heun. One of the main issues was the low prices that the Lao were paying for cardamom.

Cabbage is another crop commercially grown, mainly in Pakxong District. However, in 2004, cabbage prices plummeted to between 150 and 900 kip/kg from the normal price of between 1,500 and 2,500 kip/kg (*Vientiane Times* 2005a).

Apart from a small number of commodities, like coffee, cardamom, and cabbage there is a general lack of commercial agriculture in much of the Xekong Basin. The UNDP, in its socio-economic profile of Xekong Province, listed one of the main constraints of Thateng District as being that, "People do not want to give away their land to private companies even for concessions" (UNDP 1997: 61). There is particular interest by commercial agriculture investors to access lands with good quality soils, such as parts of Pakxong and Thateng Districts. However, local farmers most often want to retain their lands for their own use agricultural purposes. Therefore, agricultural concessions frequently represent a threat to the land rights of local people.

In 2001, some organic vegetable producers from Taiwan went to Attapeu to investigate possibilities for promoting organic vegetable growing for export to Taiwan. Prospects for the projects developing seemed hopeful, but in the end the deal fell through.

In 2004, a Vietnamese agricultural seed company teamed up with the Attapeu provincial Agriculture and Forestry Division to sell hybrid corn seed to villagers. All the corn seed packages had only Vietnamese labels. In Tra-oum Village, Phouvong District, local Brao people bought bags of seeds for 19,000 kip/kg at the end of the dry season. The government hoped that the corn produced by the villagers could be sold on the market, but villagers in Tra-oum ended up eating much of what they grew. People had no idea that the seeds were hybrids. A German agriculture advisor based in Attapeu complained that villagers were being told that they would be able to get 200–300 kg of corn per hectare, but she expected this was a significant overestimate, designed to encourage farmers to buy the seeds. Mr. Khaenthong Sisouvong, Deputy Governor of Attapeu Province said, "Successful marketing will play an important role in attracting international interest and investment" (Syvongxay 2006: 3). Considering the lack of agricultural export success to date in Attapeu, his comments appear justified.

In 2006, the Attapeu provincial government announced its hope that markets might be developed for exporting cash crops, particularly cassava and sweet corn, which could be used as animal feed. However, plans remain vague, with assistance being sought from Vietnam. One official told the *Vientiane Times* that "Presently farmers are only growing melon, green beans and vegetables to sell at the local market. However, we believe there is potential to expand cash crop farming in the province to export on a commercial basis" (Syvongxay 2006: 3). In Attapeu Province, cash crop expansion is being targeted in Sanxay and Phouvong Districts, due to the favorable climates there (Syvongxay 2006). In that there are large tracts of natural forests in these areas, it can be assumed that this expansion of cash cropping would come at a high cost in terms of natural forest destruction and biodiversity loss.

Despite the lack of commercial agriculture in the Xekong River Basin, the central government of Laos clearly sees agricultural growth as a key component of its development and poverty reduction strategies. Export-oriented commercial agriculture is being promoted, often without much consideration of the negative environmental and social consequences. It seems likely that commercial agriculture will expand in the future, especially now that road networks in the basin are improving. However, it is unclear whether local people will benefit from these changes, or if they will simply benefit outsiders and lead to a reduction of forests and other lands for local people. There is certainly much concern that agriculture concessions could jeopardize the livelihoods of local people.

Women and Agriculture

Women in Laos generally provide most agricultural labor and, according to the President of the Lao Women's Union, Ms. Onchanh Thammavong, women constitute 92% of the rural population engaged in agriculture (Latsaphao 2005a). The former Minister of Agriculture and Forestry, Mr. Sien Saphangthong, has also acknowledged that women make up the majority of the population engaged in swidden agriculture. However, they apparently do not have the same labor rights in agriculture as men (Latsaphao 2005a). The Xekong River Basin is certainly no exception. For example, in Sanxay District it has been observed that most of the hand digging for expanding wet-rice fields among the ethnic Triang people is done by women, not men. Women also do most of the weeding, which is labor intensive for swidden agriculture, especially when people have to work on short fallow rotations, as now promoted by the GoL.

There are important differences in gender roles between different ethnic groups. For example, ethnic Triang and Ngkriang women do most of the agricultural work in their societies, but for the Harak, men are responsible for conducting most of the agricultural work, while the women look after the children and take care of household activities (UNDP 1997). One Katu man in Kalum District said that Katu men and women work together on swidden agriculture but that, for the Ngkriang people, the men do most of the swidden agriculture while women spend more time fishing with scoop baskets (*sone* in Lao). Women reportedly catch more fish than men, but they generally catch smaller ones. Ethnic Ngkriang people from Tahieu Village also confirmed this to be true. Women from Tahieu emphasized, however, that they do not just go fishing but also collect wild vegetables to eat!

Commercial agriculture, including large agriculture concessions, represents a serious threat to women farmers, as they are frequently involved in small-scale subsistence agriculture on lands vulnerable to expropriation for commercial purposes.

Swidden Agriculture, Land and Internal Resettlement

The Food and Agriculture Organization of the United Nations (FAO) defines shifting cultivation, in the "humid tropics," as "a land use system based on a traditional, year-round, community-wide, largely self-contained and ritually sanctioned way of life that is still prevalent among tribal minorities in Southeast Asia and South America and a small, declining percentage of African farmers" (Warner 1991: v). Shifting cultivation is the most common term used when referring to this type of agriculture, but the term is applied to a wide variety of upland farming systems. While it will be impossible to explore all those systems here, they generally involve shifting from field to field; the use of fire to clear fields of debris and insects, and for fertilization; and the maintenance of long fallow periods, ranging from just a few years to decades. No plowing is involved. Slash-and-burn is another synonym for this type of farming, but it generally has more negative or pejorative connotations, as it emphasizes the impressive firing of new fields at the end of the dry season and implies a more primitive and haphazard form of cultivation. Swidden agriculture is the third term used, and it implies that the cultivated area is part of a larger agro-ecosystem. In this book the term slash-and-burn agriculture is not used, and shifting cultivation and swidden agriculture are applied interchangeably.

Historically, shifting cultivation has been the dominant form of agriculture practiced in the Xekong River Basin in Laos, and it remains an important source of livelihood in many parts of the basin. Most types of swidden agriculture involve identifying an area of forest in January (see box below), cutting down small trees and bushes in the understory of the area in the same month or in February, cutting down the large trees still standing in February or March, allowing the vegetation to dry out in the sun of the dry season, burning the swidden area in March or April, piling up and burning the remaining debris in March or April, planting multiple crops—often using wood dibble sticks—between April and June, and weeding from July to September. Harvesting crops is done over an extended period, usually beginning with corn in July or August. Rice harvest periods can vary significantly, depending on the duration of rains, planting times, and seed varieties, but these generally occur between September and November. Eastern areas of the basin affected by the southeast monsoon have quite different patterns. Weeding tends to be the most labor-intensive part of the production cycle. Depending upon soil and weed conditions, a swidden plot is sometimes used for just one year before being left for fallow so that the forest can then re-establish itself. In other cases, swidden agriculture may take place on the same plot for two or more years. Historically, this was generally only the case when soils were of exceptional quality. Swidden agriculture, like other local livelihood activities, requires considerable local ecological knowledge to improve the chances of success.

Using Rice Seeds to Determine a Good Place for Swidden

The ethnic Triang people have a particular method of choosing appropriate forest areas for swidden agriculture, apart from considering the quality of the forest and soils and its geographical location. Once a potentially suitable area has been identified, and before the forest there is cleared, a small area is cut and seven rice seeds are put inside a bamboo section. The section of bamboo is then sealed and buried at the future site of the swidden house for the field. The next morning the bamboo is dug up, and the rice seeds in it are removed and counted. If there are still seven seeds, the spirits are not believed to object to cultivating the area. If there are six or less, the area is abandoned and a new one is sought.

Some of the advantages of long-fallow swidden systems are that there is no tillage required and runoff of precipitation is limited. Sediment and carbon losses on sloping land are also reduced (Chaplot 2005). External inputs, including chemical or natural fertilizers, are only rarely used. Another important advantage is that swidden systems promote the intercropping of many different plant species. A large variety of crops are planted together with rice. These include different kinds of corn, chilies, taro, gourds, pumpkins, cassava, sorghum, beans, peas, watermelon, tobacco, sesame, cucumber, and various spices. In the ethnic Ngkriang village of Ta-neum, in Lamam District, villagers reported growing rice, corn, pumpkin, cassava, jam bean, taro, peanut, melon, watermelon, cucumber, Job's tears, sesame, banana, sugarcane, pineapple, tobacco, chili, gourd, wing bean, bottle gourd, green mustard, lemon grass, cotton, eggplant, and various condiments and spices in their swiddens. Often, a number of varieties of rice, eggplants, chilies, or other vegetables are cultivated.

Dibble sticks are generally used to make holes in cleared swidden fields and the rice seeds are deposited into these holes. Men generally do the dibble sticking with women following and depositing the seeds. Sometimes rice seeds are mixed together with other seeds, such as sesame. Other seeds are planted separately. For example, pumpkins are often planted in areas where a lot of ash has accumulated and cassava is frequently grown in the outskirts of swidden fields. Some plants are harvested before the rice, others at the same time, and some are only harvested afterwards. Some species, like bananas, can be harvested more than a year after being planted, but perennial crops are not commonly planted in swidden fields. However, selective weeding and the kinds of plants cultivated largely influences the nature of fallows. Baird et al. (1996) documented Brao swidden agricultural patterns in two villages in Ratanakiri Province, northeast Cambodia. They reported that the Brao plant 181 varieties of crops, including 36 varieties of upland rice and 145 other types of annual and perennial crops. The average family was found to cultivate between three and seven varieties of rice, and 60–100 types of crops per swidden plot. In our experience, farmers are always interested in obtaining new seeds and so it is not surprising to find that many swidden cultivators are often planting a wide variety of crops.

Rice is generally the main crop grown in swidden fields but in Kalum District it was reported that about 10% of the families in the district plant cassava as their main crop. As part of the same study, it was found that 94% of the rice production came from swidden agriculture. However, only 3% of the farmers surveyed reported being sufficient in rice for seven to twelve months a year (UNDP 1999d) and in Dakchung District no villages reported being sufficient in rice every year (UNDP 1999b). In Dakchung other grains are frequently planted apart from rice, including corn and sorghum.

Introducing Chemical Agriculture to Upland Farmers in Kalum

Most INGOs in Laos working in agriculture are promoting organic or sustainable systems. However, one INGO, Action contre le faim (ACF) working in the uplands of Kalum District decided, in 2003, to try to help improve upland agriculture for the farmers there through introducing chemical pesticides. The overall emphasis of ACF had been positive. In contrast to many development agencies in Laos, which often only support lowland rice production, they were trying to promote and improve upland agriculture, including looking at how to strengthen swidden agriculture. They introduced some different native varieties of upland rice from parts of northern Laos and, while trial and error was involved, some innovations were much appreciated by local farmers. There was a rice variety from Sayabouly Province known as "*khao phe deng*" that performed well in trials. Farmers reported that they were happy to get the seed.

However, ACF hired a French consultant who assessed the situation and found that farmers were facing various pest problems, ranging from the occasional elephant herd trampling their fields, to more common instances of macaques, wild boar, porcupines, and birds damaging crops, to even more frequent rodent and insect damage. The consultant recommended a number of chemical-based solutions. This apparently did not trigger sufficient debate within the agency, as a few years later, in 2004, a French woman working for ACF was not sure why chemical solutions had been recommended, but she felt obliged to implement them because "They were in the proposal." ACF introduced ant poison to villagers, along with two kinds of mouse poison. The first kind has the brand name Racumin, and comes in small round balls that, according to a villager in Kalum, "look like sugar balls." The manufacturer, Bayer, states on its website that, "Racumin Mouse and Rat Blocks are ready to use. It is an economical anti-coagulant product that requires repeated feeding over several days by the rodents to achieve control. In this way rodents do not become shy of the bait as may happen with acute baits. Pets and farm animals are at minimal risk as they are unlikely to gain repeated access to the bait." The Australian government defines this poison as "Very toxic in contact with skin and if swallowed."

Some villagers that we interviewed in Kalum said that they were afraid that their children might inadvertently eat the poison, believing that it was candy! There was also concern that the poison could have negative impacts on chickens, dogs, and cats should they ingest poisoned mice. Some villagers reported that the poison was only put in swidden fields, but that wild chickens from the nearby forests died after coming into contact with it.

Next, ACF decided to try Baraki, which is a trap-based poison for mice. It was not available in the market in Laos and had to be purchased in Thailand. Unfortunately, according to a villager in Bak Village, Kalum District, the mice did not eat the poison.

The ant poison, Sevin, was purchased by ACF for 12,000 kip/bag and sold to villagers in Kalum for the subsidized price of 5,000 kip/kg. There has been considerable controversy regarding this chemical in North America in recent years. It is highly toxic, and Lao workers from ACF acknowledged that farmers using these chemicals had little understanding about the potential negative health and environmental impacts and did not regularly follow their recommendations to use protective gear when using the chemicals. When asked, a villager in Bak Village appeared to be confused and lacked awareness about the potential negative health and environmental impacts associated with the poison, but thought using it was easier than destroying ant nests by hand, as was done in the past. In 2004, after 150 farmers from thirty villages (five farmers per village) had been given the chemicals to try out, ACF decided to expand access by helping to make the chemicals available in the local market in Kalum at a subsidized rate. ACF claimed this would make the use of these chemicals more "sustainable."

There are a number of potential problems with the approach adopted by this INGO. For one, the chemicals that they have introduced are potentially dangerous for human and animal health, especially when people are not fully aware of how or when to use them. The farmers were not involved in chemical agriculture before ACF started working in the area. The prevailing consensus among the vast majority of NGOs worldwide is that farmers are already overusing chemicals and that this is having negative impacts on human and animal health and the environment. Many development efforts are now focused on helping wean farmers off of such chemicals. Given the breadth of international experience in this regard, it is highly questionable for an INGO in Laos to be promoting chemical agriculture to people who are unfamiliar with its use.

These types of chemicals are expensive in comparison to local incomes, and their availability in remote areas such as the uplands of Kalum is sporadic at best. Providing them at a subsidized rate also risks creating dependency on these chemicals among farmers who will eventually be forced to pay their full cost, as ACF is not planning to work in the area indefinitely. To make matters worse, the chemicals they introduced did not turn out to be especially effective in reducing pests, even in the short term.

According to an ethnic Lao senior agriculture program staff person for ACF, the sale and/or distribution of these chemicals is illegal in Laos. He pointed out that mouse poison has had a devastating impact on domestic animals in northern Laos. He explained that in Luang Nam Tha Province, the use of mouse poison had wiped out the cat population to such an extent that the mouse population then increased due to the lack of predators. In the end, the people had more of a rodent problem than when they first started trying to get rid of the rodents! The German development agency, GTZ, actually bought cats for the villagers, in order to replace the ones killed by the poison. Even though he was working for ACF, this staff person was not sure why his INGO had received permission from the Ministry of Agriculture and Forestry to import the chemicals or why the lessons from the north were being ignored in Kalum.

According to a representative of ACF in Xekong at the time, ACF had not been able to do much research and had little information on other sustainable agriculture or organic solutions to village agriculture pest problems. They had only been in touch with the office of the International Rice Research Institute (IRRI) in Vientiane and had not been in contact with the Sustainable Agriculture Forum or its INGO members in order to learn more about such alternatives.

It could be argued that it is rather irresponsible of an international development agency to be promoting solutions for local villagers when they appear to have so little knowledge of the issue themselves. In this case, the ACF promoted chemical agriculture, despite all of its dangers, while ignoring inexpensive solutions that only rely on readily available local inputs. For instance, villagers in the area reported that if enough traps (*katam* in Lao) are used, mouse populations can be significantly reduced without having to use any poisons. One villager said, "If we used fifty *katam* per family we could catch twenty mice a night for five to six months a year. And we can eat them all. When poison is used, we can't eat the mice." Another farmer commented that using traps to catch mice was more effective and that he would not have used agricultural poisons if they had not been promoted by ACF.

Ecological Classifications of the Brao

Local knowledge developed over long periods is not only important for agriculture, but also for considering broader ecological issues. Baird (2000) documented 108 basic land-based categories recognized and named by ethnic Brao-Kavet people in their own language. Kavet descriptions of habitat types can range from the broad to the specific. This knowledge system is orally based and incorporates Brao experiences, culture and beliefs. It is essentially based on two general Brao-Kavet language ecological terms: *"Bree"* and *"Dak."*

Bree is often translated as "forest" in English, but in fact it means "the condition of the land" (Gerard Diffloth, pers. comm. 1999). A *"bree"* can be a forest, since forests often dominate the "condition of the land," but it can also describe areas that are not normally categorized as forests, such as grasslands, which the Brao call *bree treng*, and salt licks, which are called *bree graik*. Areas covered entirely by flat slabs of granite are known as *bree ta tar* or *bree ta maw ta tar*. *Bree* types are sometimes named after dominant species of plants or trees, but the term *bree* is not used to describe individual species. It is only applied to ecological areas, or biotopes (Baird 2000).

Dak localities are within river and streambeds and ponds, up to the top of the banks. *Dak* is "the condition of the water." Therefore, seasonally inundated forests in the riverbed are not called *bree* but *dak*, as these forests are seen by the Brao to be a "condition of the water" (Baird 2000; 2001a).

Of the 108 basic land classifications used by the Brao, 21 represent broad ecological classes, 12 are based on topology or landform features, six describe succession stages, seven are applied for soil characteristics, 57 are associated with dominant plant species, and five fall into the "miscellaneous" category. The Brao's creative combination of these various terms is not standardized, and there are a large number of possible combinations, depending on the meaning and emphasis (Baird 2000; 2001a).

This ecological classification system is critical for swidden agriculture, as it indicates to farmers different types of habitat and makes it clear to them whether the area has a good potential to be successfully farmed or not. Many ecological areas are considered generally unsuitable for swidden, while others are marginal, and still others are preferred. Although many outsiders believe that swidden farmers randomly choose their farming sites and haphazardly move from one place to another, research with the Brao indicates that the opposite is the case, and that considerable attention is paid by Brao farmers toward choosing suitable locations for swidden agriculture. However, government policies resulting in restrictions on shifting cultivation are making it increasingly difficult for the Brao to practice agriculture based on their local knowledge (Baird 2001a).

Swidden Agriculture and Government Policy

The GoL considers the fact that swidden agriculture is the dominant form of agriculture in the Xekong River Basin to be a serious constraint to development (Goudineau 2001). Since 1975, and especially since the late 1980s, the GoL has been promoting policies designed to reduce and eradicate swidden agriculture. The GoL's campaign to eradicate swidden agriculture is arguably, more than any other single factor, impacting the livelihood security of people living in the Xekong Basin.

In the late 1980s and early 1990s, the GoL, increasingly with the encouragement of large donors, expressed considerable concern over the shifting cultivation/ swidden agriculture practices of ethnic minority groups in the country. The 1990 Tropical Forestry Action Plan (TFAP) for Laos—supported by the FAO, UNDP, and World Bank—reported on and implicitly supported the resolution adopted at the First Lao National Conference on Forestry in May 1989 that by the year 2000 there would be a permanent change in the lifestyles of 60% of the 1.5 million people engaged in shifting cultivation. The plan was expected to affect 90,000 people a year over the next ten years (Evrard and Goudineau 2004). The idea was to promote agricultural intensification, land tenure reform, and industrial forms of forest exploitation, such as commercial logging and industrial fast-growing tree plantations. The TFAP provided key support to the GoL's policy, and encouraged them toward greatly intensified efforts to eradicate swidden cultivation (Goudineau 1997). In 1995, the Politburo of the Central Party Committee of Lao PDR adopted a policy to eradicate all shifting cultivation from the country by the year 2000. Several major donors moved to support the government in this endeavor, including in the Xekong River Basin (Baird and Shoemaker 2005).

Initially, few donors questioned the need to eliminate swidden agriculture. Many actively supported the policy, even though some donors seemed to be aware of the hardships being suffered by local people. The UNDP (1997: 56) reported in a profile about Lamam District, Xekong Province, that, "Farmers are still linked to nature, aware that slash-and-burn practices provide better income than lowland paddy fields." This UNDP report also quoted Dakchung District officials as claiming that the main constraint for local livelihoods has been that, "Slash-and-burn activities are very restricted" (UNDP 1997: 69).

Many donors saw the campaign against swidden agriculture as primarily a way to reduce deforestation and protect biodiversity. The human ecology element was rarely considered in much depth, let alone the political ecology of altering, reducing and, in some cases, eradicating swidden agriculture. However, as concerns grew over the impacts on food security of upland communities and associated resettlement, some reassessment began to quietly occur. While an important rationale for the initiative was to conserve upland forests, some observers have noted that there was simultaneously a large increase in commercial logging in these same forests, facilitated by the central government and the military and involving non-transparent revenue management (Anonymous 2000) (see also Chapter 6).

It is now clear that swidden agriculture has been unfairly blamed for forest destruction and portrayed as always being unsustainable. Outsiders often view this form of agriculture to be destructive and rarely recognize the benefits of these organic, mixed, and multi-cropping agricultural systems—including production of a wide range of grains, legumes, and vegetables and in protecting important native seed varieties.

Most researchers and academics working on upland agriculture recognize that swidden agriculture is neither always appropriate nor necessarily destructive (Warner 1991; Fox et al. 2000). In some cases, upland agriculture is being practiced sustainably in Laos and can be for many more decades due to low population densities and the occurrence of rapidly growing plant varieties, including many species of bamboo. This is particularly true for the Xekong Basin, where population densities in upland areas are still low. In other cases some assistance and technical support may be needed for upland agricultural adaptation. Some types of "pioneering" shifting cultivation, as practiced by particular ethnic groups, can be problematic, but even these problems are often exaggerated and, in any case, "rotational" forms of swidden agriculture are the norm for the Xekong Basin. However, rather than using a moderate approach that carefully considers all the factors, on a case-by-case basis, harsh broad-brush blanket restrictions against swidden cultivation have been applied in Laos, including the Xekong Basin, without adequately considering local conditions. The official Lao media often equates eliminating "slash-and-burn" agriculture with eliminating poverty—even when it may in reality be having the opposite effect (*Vientiane Times* 2003a; Vorakham 2002).

Anonymous (2000) has pointed out that the Lao term for swidden agriculture, "*het hai*" is now often replaced by local people and government officials with the term "*het souan*," which means, "to make gardens." This is prevalent in many parts of the Xekong River Basin, including Phoxay Village where ethnic Brao villagers tried to transform the image of their full-size swidden fields by calling them "*souan*." The term is much more politically acceptable. Some people even joke that nobody grows rice in "swiddens" (*hai* in Lao), but that they frequently grow rice in "gardens" (*souan* in Lao) (Anonymous 2000). Quite often swidden agriculture has been unfairly blamed for forest degradation in Laos, while the impact of commercial logging is rarely mentioned. Despite the serious social and environmental implications of the swidden agriculture eradication program, the UNDP helped the Xekong provincial government create a "Socio-Economic Profile of Sekong Province," in order to help attract international donors to support the province's development plans (UNDP 1997). The UNDP appears to have been supportive of plans for large-scale resettlement from the uplands to the lowlands, as they promoted the plan in their publication. Even though they appeared at some level to recognize that the land allocated for many resettled communities in Xekong Province was of poor quality and unsuitable for agriculture (UNDP 1997), the UNDP, nevertheless, uncritically endorsed the GoL policy, stating that:

> Development objectives of the government are: to ensure food security, reduce and progressively stabilize shifting agriculture, conserve natural forest resources, improve transport and communication infrastructures, improve the export-import balance, strengthen management and technical skills of staff. In this context, the provincial authorities of Sekong have set the following priority: to relocate 62 villages from Kalum to both Thateng and Lamam Districts. (UNDP 1997: 3)

While the GoL, backed by the UNDP, was stating that a main developmental priority was "food security," the lowland cultivation they were promoting was often actually resulting in reduced income and food security for those who had previously been engaged in swidden agriculture.

As efforts to reduce and eradicate swidden agriculture continued in the late 1990s, it became evident that it was not going to be possible to achieve the challenging goal of eradicating shifting cultivation by 2000, either in Xekong or the rest of Laos. In some areas there are few lowlands, as 80% of the country is considered to be mountainous or hilly. Thus, the deadline for eradicating swidden agriculture was extended in 2001 at the 7th Party Congress to 2005. More recently, most GoL accounts report that the deadline is now 2020, with significant progress toward that goal expected by 2010 (Baird and Shoemaker 2005; Gonzales et al. 2005).

Although the GoL remains committed to reducing and eradicating swidden agriculture (*Vientiane Times* 2004a, b and c), there has been, at least at some levels, recent reconsideration of the policy (Baird 2004; 2005). For example, the Deputy Governor of Savannakhet province told the first author that "pioneering" shifting cultivation (*hai leuan loi* in Lao) is banned, especially when large trees are cut down, but that rotational shifting cultivation (*hai moun vian* in Lao) is allowed, and is not being targeted for swidden agriculture eradication efforts (Baird 2004). In addition, Samanh Viyaket, a Politburo member and the Speaker in the National Assembly of Lao PDR, said—when addressing the National Assembly in May 2005—that, the government wanted to "*lout phone neua thi het hai*" (reduce the area used for swidden agriculture). The replacement of the word "eradicate" (*lop lang* in Lao) with "reduce" (*lout phone* in Lao) is significant. Some observers have cited a conference on uplands agriculture organized by the National Agriculture and Forestry Research Institute (NAFRI) in January 2004 in Luang Phrabang as a landmark in bringing the debate over swidden agriculture out into the open. There appears to be a reduction in the amount of strong anti-"slash-and-burn" agriculture rhetoric coming out of the state media recently, although critical articles about swidden agriculture continue to appear sporadically. There is some indication that the GoL may be softening its position regarding the eradication of swidden agriculture in areas with few other farming options. Some in the Ministry of Agriculture and Forestry in Vientiane have also stated unofficially that policy changes regarding shifting cultivation are in the works, although it may take years for them to become evident to local people (Baird 2004; 2005).

In April 2002, the Prime Minister's Office released a new Lao-language policy document that is significant for future resettlement from the uplands to the lowlands in Laos (PMO 2002). Apparently, this document was inadequately distributed when it was first made public, or perhaps those who received it did not initially take it seriously. In any case, it was re-released by the GoL in 2005, apparently to try to re-emphasize the document's importance at the local government level. The document reiterates that no pioneering swidden agriculture is allowed, but, significantly, it states that internal resettlement should not be promoted except under extreme circumstances when all other options to achieve "*asip khong thi*" (permanent occupations) have failed. In other words, the purpose of the document is to encourage local governments to avoid using internal resettlement as a means to reduce or eradicate shifting cultivation, except when absolutely necessary. It is unclear what impact this document is having in rural Laos, but it is noteworthy that government officials in Phouvong District were aware of it, so it is at least having an impact there. This policy document is apparently one of the reasons why Phouvong is reconsidering plans to resettle the ethnic Brao village of Lamong to the lowlands.

Nevertheless, in 2004, the Xekong provincial government announced that they were encouraging people in remote areas to find alternative sources of livelihood to swidden agriculture, with efforts to eradicate poverty high on the agenda. A provincial official was reported as stating that Xekong is focusing on wiping out the traditional shifting cultivation practices of local people. At the time, it was reported that there were still about 1,500 ha of land devoted to swidden cultivation in the province. However, authorities expected that the area would drastically decline—to 200 ha by 2005, a target that seems unlikely to have been met. One official was quoted by the *Vientiane Times* as saying, "We will encourage 60 families who now practice slash and burn cultivation to grow coffee, raise livestock and take up farming" (*Vientiane Times* 2004f: 1). The same official revealed that the province plans to promote the production of cash crops on 8,500 ha of land, and to allocate 700 ha of land for tree planting, in order to reach the province's targets. The province also wants to promote villager knowledge about what it terms "technology," in order to boost agricultural productivity (*Vientiane Times* 2004f). In 2004, ethnic Ngkriang people from Kloung Village, Kalum District, reported to the first author that the local government had told them that they would eventually have to phase out swidden agriculture and switch to cattle raising as their main occupation. However, the village headman stated that there were no farmers in his village with enough livestock to make a living from raising cattle without also engaging in swidden agriculture.

The main agriculture problems in Kalum District have been a lack of technical support, bird and rodent attacks, low yields due to unproductive soils and pest and crop diseases. The problems identified in Dakchung are similar, although there were more reports of drought and flood problems. The lack of technical support was hardly mentioned as an obstacle. Weeds were also more commonly mentioned as a problem in Dakchung, as was erosion and landslides, which was hardly mentioned in Kalum at all (UNDP 1999b and d). However, it is clear that the main problem for farmers in these areas is the restrictions that they face as a result of anti-swidden agriculture government policies.

In Dakchung and Kalum Districts, the government has been trying to support permanent upland fields (*hai khong thi* in Lao), but as of 1999 it was only reported to exist in the most remote part of Dakchung District, in Zone 6 (UNDP 1999b), and in Zone 1 in Kalum District (UNDP 1999d). UNDP (1999b and d) reported that almost half of the villages in Dakchung were experiencing declining rice production, probably due to restrictions applied by the GoL on swidden agriculture. None of the villages in either district, except for a few in Zone 3 of Kalum District, was reported to be self-sufficient in rice production. This statistic is deceiving, since almost no villages rely on rice as their only staple grain, as is generally the case in lowland parts of Laos. Maize, cassava, and other foods are important supplementary food sources. Just because a village does not produce "enough rice to eat," does not mean that it has a food security problem. In fact, they may have a surplus of food. In a UNDP Xekong project report, Jacqui Chagnon (2000: 2) wrote that "Swidden rice culture in the uplands is insufficient, forcing most families to plant cassava, maize, manioc and taro as subsidiary crops." A reasonable alternative explanation is that people grow several other crops apart from rice because they like variety in their diets and because their food security is improved through growing many starchy foods rather than just relying on rice. Too often outside "development" analysis, based on lowland Lao perspectives, overemphasizes the importance of growing enough rice rather than considering overall food security.

Land and Forest Allocation

Land and Forest Allocation (*beng din beng pa* in Lao) is a process designed to classify land uses and improve natural resource management. It was initiated in 1994 as part of a strategy to allocate land to farmers, intensify agricultural production, conserve forest areas, and clarify borders between villages (Watershed 2004), and was developed by the GoL with technical assistance from Vietnamese advisors. The World Bank and Australian bilateral assistance have supported land-titling work in lowland areas, which is quite a different program from Land and Forest Allocation, but the programs are nonetheless related. Land and Forest Allocation is often seen as useful for lowland communities not dependent upon swidden agriculture (MIDAS 1998), but when employed in upland areas it has severely restricted the land available for swidden cultivation. In fact, one of the program's main objectives is to reduce and eventually eradicate swidden agriculture. Fallow times are drastically reduced to just two or three years, making the proliferation of weeds a serious obstacle to good harvests, leading to the rapid deterioration of soil quality, and often resulting in increased agriculture pests and disease problems (SPC 2000a; ADB 2001; Chamberlain 2001).

While not explicitly associated with internal resettlement, the severe restrictions applied to swidden agricultural practices in upland communities, and the resulting impacts on their food security, have been a major "push" factor in inducing highlanders to resettle to the lowlands or elsewhere. Conditions for conducting uplands agriculture are often made so difficult that upland farmers feel obliged to follow government recommendations for them to resettle in the lowlands or next to major roads. They certainly cannot see a future for themselves in the uplands, considering all the restrictions.

Donors, including INGOs, are often asked to support Land and Forest Allocation as part of area development projects. In some cases, the requests are just for the per-diems and expenses that local officials need to undertake allocation work. Given the problems associated with poorly-implemented and conceived Land and Forest Allocation, this has the potential to put international aid agencies in the position of funding activities harmful to the livelihoods of the people they are supposedly assisting (Baird and Shoemaker 2005).

In recent years there have been efforts to review and correct flaws in the Land and Forest Allocation Policy (see, for example, Jones 2002). MIDAS (1998) tried, largely unsuccessfully, to adapt the Land and Forest Allocation Process for national protected areas. So far few substantial changes in the program's approach to swidden agriculture appear to have been implemented at the local level, leaving many critical obstacles neglected in practice. Some INGOs and other aid agencies are working on newer strategies that may resolve some of the problems seen in the past. However, these approaches require considerable research, analysis, community organizing, and technical expertise. It is not a matter of simply handing over per-diems to local counterparts. The head of the LFNC in Xekong Province pointed out, during a 2005 meeting on research of ethnic groups in the province, that it would be crucial to investigate land-use conflicts when doing field research on ethnicity issues, as he believes that conflicts over land have increased in many parts of the province since Land and Forest Allocation began being implemented in the 1990s.

Focal Sites

Focal Sites (*khet chout xoum* in Lao) have existed in Laos since the 1980s, and revolve around directing development resources to particular areas. These may include existing and long-established communities, but more commonly they are formed after people have been resettled.

In 1997, at the height of the GoL's promotion of the Focal Site concept, the two Focal Sites of Xekong Province were (1) Thong Vay, Donsa, Thongkong, and Thong-nyao—four ethnic Katu villages in Thateng District that were resettled from Kalum District many years ago, and (2) Thong Toklok, a large village of ethnic Katu people resettled from Kalum District in the mid-1990s (Kandone Village). In 1995/1996, when resettlement was at its peak in Xekong, the majority of the rural development budget for the province was spent on Focal Site development, including relocating people and clearing agricultural land for resettled people (UNDP 1997). There are still five "Focal Development Areas" in Kalum (*Vientiane Times* 2005f). In 1997, the UNDP wrote:

> Similar to other provinces in the country, the rural development institutions at the district level in Sekong are called Focal Zone Development Project Coordinators, since they are to undertake certain focal zones. The provincial authority designates the Focal Zone Coordinators. The RDC [Rural Development Committee] coordinators in each district are composed of 2–3 members, under the chairmanship of the district deputy governor (UNDP 1997: 6).

In Attapeu Province there are also a number of Focal Sites, including Viangxai, Phou Hom, and Houay Keo in Phouvong District, and in the Pa-am area of Sanxay District (formerly known as Nam Pa Focal Site). All these Focal Sites are heavily associated with internal resettlement of ethnic minorities from upland areas to the lowlands and along roads.

In the Xekong River Basin in Champasak Province, the Houay Ho dam resettlement area (called "*Ban Chat San*" in Lao) was once a Focal Site, but its Focal Site status was revoked in 2000. Many problems remain in the area (see Chapter 13).

Looking at Internal Resettlement

The idea to reorganize upland peoples through their internal resettlement is not a recent one. Its origins can, in fact, be found among French colonial officials of the early twentieth century. One of those was Antonin Baudenne, the French administrator of Attapeu from 1913 to 1919 and a long-time resident of French Indochina. In 1916, he wrote a report to the Résident supérieur of French Laos about the Brao people of Attapeu that clearly illustrates the view of many French civil servants at the time:[1]

> The Love [Brao] do not have villages as such. A locality is constituted by different groups of houses on a specific territory, usually distant from each other. That is a logical situation, considering their separatist tendencies. This situation is to the great despair of tax collectors. On that point, the *Nai Kong* [our emphasis] have applied my way of doing things. Every day habitations are being built closer to each other, forming more centers than before.

Later in the report he wrote:

> Those incorrigible nomads are totally against fixed settlement in one specific place. They abandon the soil every 2–3 years, pretending that it is expired. They immigrate for stupid reasons—the evil song of a bird, bad things seen in dreams, death, or serious disease of an inhabitant . . . . For those people to progress, they will have to settle down and radically change their way of life.

The French used local officials, including the *Nai Kong*, to reorganize the people of the Xekong River Basin in Laos spatially, especially the Brao and other ethnic minorities. While they were only partly successful in imposing their ideas, the local elite, including Communist leaders fighting to expel the French, came to internalize the discourses of the colonial power. Without recognizing it, they have, in essence, continued the work that the French began. In many ways, this resettlement concept is similar to French ideas about encouraging lowlanders living in overcrowded areas in Vietnam to resettle to less populated uplands. While the French wanted to promote this migration in Vietnam, it was not until the Communists took power in North Vietnam that the policy was actually implemented efficiently (Hardy 2003).

While not identified as an explicit policy objective at present, internal resettlement is an important and sometimes-Draconian tool used to achieve the objective of reducing shifting cultivation (Evrard and Goudineau 2004). Thus, the intensification of resettlement activities in the mid-1990s were often linked to the eradication of swidden agriculture, with a considerable burst of internal resettlement taking place during 1996 and 1997. Much of this resettlement was to lowland areas where wet-rice paddy production could supposedly occur, although some resettlement has also taken place along or near major roads in upland areas, especially when lowland paddy was unavailable.

Differing statistics float around regarding resettlement in Kalum District in the 1990s. One observer working for the UNDP reported that about 50% of the population was resettled from the district between 1996 and 1998, although about half of those were believed to have returned by 2004. Goudineau (2001) reported that approximately 40% of Kalum District's people were relocated between 1991 and 1997. This may be closer to the truth, as the population in Kalum was recorded as 13,562 in 1995 and 12,053 in 2002.

Illustrative of the importance put on internal resettlement in Xekong Province in the mid-1990s, officials from Dakchung District reported, in 1997, that in order to stop "slash-and-burn agriculture," the district would need to relocate 2,000 people to areas in Lamam and Thateng Districts where land for "permanent cultivation" was available (UNDP 1997). Since then, however, the level of internal resettlement in the province has declined. Most of the resettlement from Kalum went to Thateng District, a long with a small amount to Lamam, while the majority of the resettlement from Dakchung was to Lamam. In 2004, villagers in Kalum were telling a number of stories about people being resettled from Kalum to Thateng or Lamam. Villagers said that the situation for many of those resettled was quite bad, and that some decided to return to Kalum soon after being resettled. One ethnic Katu villager in Kalum District made the following remark:

> Some Katu people moved to Bachieng District during the war. But they don't have streams and rivers for fishing there or lots of forests like here for swidden agriculture. We don't want to move there. The government wants us to be in a stable village [*ban khong thi* in Lao], but this village has been here for a long time.

Internal resettlement has also been used in Laos as a tool for bringing peripheral ethnic minorities into the national-building project of the country, to provide them with more access to markets and government services such as health care and education, and for security and population control reasons (Baird and Shoemaker 2005).

Research on Resettlement in Laos

Recent studies from different parts of Laos, involving many ethnic groups, have clearly shown that the eradication and severe restriction of swidden agriculture, and associated internal resettlement, are often associated with chronic food shortages, increased and over-exploitation of forestry and fishery resources, decreased human and animal health, and increased soil degradation and other types of biodiversity degradation caused by adopting fallow cycles that are too short to allow for forest or soil regeneration. The end result is severe livelihood problems, increased poverty, and various socio-cultural and health problems (Gonzales et al. 2005; Baird and Shoemaker 2005; Evrard and Goudineau 2004; Ducourtieux 2004; Vandergeest 2003; Daviau 2001; 2003b; Chamberlain 2001; ADB 2001; SPC 2000a; Goudineau 1997). Hundreds of thousands of families are being affected by restrictive shifting cultivation policies throughout the country. In the late 1990s, 280,000 families, or 45% of the villages in the country, were dependent upon shifting cultivation for their subsistence (SPC and NSC 1999).

While there is not a province in Laos that has not been impacted by the GoL's swidden agriculture policy, it has been especially significant for mountainous northern and eastern parts of the country, including Attapeu and Xekong, as those provinces present relatively few good opportunities for developing large-scale wet-rice cultivation and include populations whose livelihoods are largely associated with upland environments. Thus, a large proportion of the population of the Xekong River Basin in Laos has been affected by internal resettlement.

Yves Goudineau (1997) and his colleagues prepared the first major study about internal resettlement in Laos, examining the situation in various parts of the country, including Attapeu and Xekong. He found that internal resettlement was having serious negative impacts on those being resettled. In particular, he discovered that large numbers of recently resettled peoples were dying of various illnesses, especially diarrhea and stomach-related problems (see also Evrard and Goudineau 2004).

Much of Goudineau's research took place in the Xekong River Basin. Then, in 2000, the SPC (2000a), funded by the ADB, studied poverty throughout Laos, focusing on the poorest parts of the country (also see Chamberlain 2001; ADB 2001). Again, the Xekong Basin was an important area for this survey, since much of Attapeu and Xekong Provinces are considered to be "poor." They found that many of the people considered by the government to be "the poorest in Laos" actually consider themselves to be newly poor, and that many attribute their poverty to government programs, including land and forest allocation and internal resettlement, often associated with efforts to reduce swidden agriculture. Alton and Ratanavong (2004) studied rural livelihoods in the context of internal resettlement in parts of Luang Nam Tha and Xekong Provinces. Their findings largely complemented the results of previous studies, indicating that the resettlement process is often accompanied by various livelihood problems. Baird and Shoemaker (2005) studied how international aid agencies, including NGOs, bilateral, international organizations (IOs), and multilateral development banks, like the ADB and the World Bank, are involved in supporting internal resettlement in Laos, either directly or indirectly, sometimes with their knowledge and sometimes without it.

Most recently, Gonzales et al. (2005) conducted an in-depth study of a number of upland districts situated in areas where the populations largely belong to ethnic minority groups and are deemed vulnerable to internal resettlement to lowland areas and along roads. They revealed that in the vast majority of these areas the upland populations are either slated for resettlement or have already been resettled. A number of other studies have also exposed various problems associated with internal resettlement in Laos, including Daviau (2001; 2003b), Vandergeest (2003), and Ducourtieux (2004). However, all of the latter studies were focused outside of the Xekong River Basin.

Village Consolidation

Village Consolidation (*tao hom ban* in Lao) is a GoL initiative for combining scattered smaller settlements by resettling people into larger permanent villages. The program is much like the Focal Zone program, albeit on a smaller scale. The idea is to create a smaller number of more densely populated communities. This is ostensibly to provide them with health, education, and other services more efficiently, but it also functions to integrate people into the dominant economic and cultural system.

Village Consolidation has been taking place in Laos since the 1970s; however, in recent years it has become increasingly central to the GoL's development strategy. The rhetoric used to justify consolidation equates it with "poverty alleviation," a priority for the international donor community. In 2004, the Politburo of the Central Party Committee of Lao PDR issued an order declaring that lowland villages should not have less than 500 people and upland villages not fewer than 200 (Lao Revolutionary Party Political Central Committee 2004). This has had a dramatic impact on a number of communities in the Xekong Basin.

Given the concerns over resettlement policy in Laos, the GoL has tried to distinguish village consolidation from resettlement. In a 1998 appeal to donors, orchestrated with UNDP support, the GoL stated:

> Village consolidation is our term for the establishment of permanent occupations. The promotion of permanent occupations encapsulates several national objectives such as rice production, commercial crops, stopping slash-and-burn agriculture and improving access to development services. This objective has often been wrongly identified with "resettlement," partly because the term "resettlement" has been used in some of our own documents, partly, because the problem that has to be attacked has not been clearly identified. (GoL 1998: 21)

Regardless of the rhetoric surrounding it, Village Consolidation involves moving or resettling people, and it is clearly a form of internal resettlement.

Since around 2002 there has been an increase in Village Consolidation in the Xekong River Basin in Laos. The policy has been heavily promoted throughout Xekong Province, especially in Dakchung and Kalum Districts, where there are many small villages. The push to consolidate small villages into large ones has advantages in terms of providing government services such as education and healthcare, but can often result in serious livelihoods problems due to crowding. This affects both agriculture and hunting and gathering activities in nearby forests and water bodies.

Dakchung is planning some of the most widespread village consolidation. In 2002, over a hundred unofficial villages were recognized as eighty-five official villages in the district, and by the end of 2005 village consolidation was expected to result in just seventy-five villages. Further decreases are planned by 2010, and by 2020 it is expected that there will only be thirty-five consolidated large villages. The district chief of Kalum reported that a minimum of a hundred people in twenty families are required to make a village in his district, this is actually less than the minimum of 200 people required by the central government.

Some international development agencies support Village Consolidation, as they believe it will be easier for them to implement their projects in a fewer number of large villages, compared to a large number of small villages (Baird and Shoemaker 2005). The UNDP SIP-Dev project in Xekong Province was until 2006 working in both Dakchung and Kalum Districts. They were not in favor of long distance resettlement from the mountains, but tolerated and even sometimes supported village consolidation. For example, they had a policy regarding the minimum number of families a village had to have before it could become a SIP-Dev project village. In 1999, soon after its inception, the project was actually keener about directly confronting resettlement issues, as the issue was prominent at that time. In fact, the Goudineau (1997) Lao resettlement study was actually credited for inspiring the creation of SIP-Dev. The project even stopped working in a village in 1999 due to government-sponsored village consolidation where they were working. In its later years, however, SIP-Dev appeared to make concerns about resettlement less of a priority and to conform more to the GoL's priorities regarding consolidation.

Village Consolidation has led to a number of unanticipated consequences for both villagers and outside development agencies. In 2003/2004, government officials convinced three smaller villages (Proi Neua, Proi Tai, and Loung Kong) to move into a single new location—Talang Mai, in Kalum District—using the pretext that an INGO working in the area would provide additional development support if they followed government policy. They were also told that if they did not agree to move to the proposed location, they would have to move to the lowlands in Salavan Province, a far worse option. Later, when the first author visited the village, the relocated people were disappointed, as the promised development support had not been forthcoming. Representatives of the INGO were unaware that the development assistance they were providing in the district was being presented to villagers in a way designed to convince them to consolidate.

One of the problems with the consolidated new village was that the area had been part of the Ho Chi Minh Trail during the war and was thus heavily bombed. It remains heavily contaminated with UXO. Two bombs blew up in the middle of the village during the first year after resettlement, after cooking fires were inadvertently built on top of them. Fortunately, nobody was hurt, but in one case the roof of a house was set on fire after a burning piece of shrapnel from a bomb fell on it and set the roof aflame. There are about 10 ha of relatively flat land near the village that could be developed into lowland wet-rice paddy, but the INGO decided not to provide support, as the area is too contaminated with UXO to make the development of the area economical or safe. Villagers were, nonetheless, trying to develop the paddy by hand in 2004, without INGO support. One farmer had developed just two sections (*hai* in Lao) of land and had already found three unexploded bombies.

Village Consolidation has also created considerable dissatisfaction among impacted communities and, in some cases, provoked various degrees of resistance. Kloung and Taseng, two ethnic Ngkriang villages adjacent to the Xekong upstream from the district center, were pressured by GoL authorities to consolidate in 2004. In fact, they only partly complied with the government's wishes. Instead of building one new village together, they created two separate villages quite close to each other. Initially, officials were not happy with their decision, but they eventually begrudgingly accepted the idea. There is now just one village head in charge of the two communities.

There were reports in 2004 that Chakeuy Village, in Kalum District, which has about fifty inhabitants, was resisting attempts by the district government to resettle them to either Rong Village or into the consolidated village of Taseng and Kloung. The Chakeuy villagers refused to comply, claiming that either of these options would put them too far away from their agricultural lands adjacent to the Xekong. They also did not want the name of their village to be lost, as it is historically significant to the people. But government officials continued to pressure the village, calling the people "stubborn."

While officials, including the district chief of Kalum, state that nobody is being forced to consolidate their villages, resistance to Village Consolidation can provoke strong government responses. Reportedly, when the village headman of Hanong Neua Village, in Kalum, did not agree to consolidate his village with Hanong Tai several years ago, he was arrested and jailed for fifteen days, where he was "educated" so that he would "understand the government's policy." A government official commented, "The headman did not understand the way of the Party." Since then, the two villages have consolidated into one. The GoL has used both the carrot and the stick to achieve its goal of Village Consolidation in Xekong and Attapeu. Apart from "educating" those opposed to Village Consolidation they have also offered 1,000 kg of milled rice for each community that agrees to consolidate.

In September 2005, the *Vientiane Times* (2005s) reported that the LFNC in Xekong Province had organized the relocation of three villages the week earlier and that, according to a press release from the LFNC, the villages had previously been situated in a remote region. A new village was established near the district center to accommodate the inhabitants of the three former villagers. The new village was expected to have about a hundred houses in it. The World Bank supported Poverty Reduction Fund was reportedly ready to provide money to the villagers once they had moved, as an incentive, and the LFNC in Xekong was hopeful that the people would be able to adapt to their new location.

In the best cases, these consolidations involve people all from the same ethnic group. But in a number of cases people from many different villages and ethnicities have been consolidated together. Frequently, this has contributed to acculturation and the loss of the use of minority languages. For example, Mitsamphan Village in Sanamxay District, Attapeu Province was originally an ethnic Oy village, but ethnic Brou, Brao, Cheng, and Lao people have moved in, resulting in Lao becoming the dominant language. These dynamics are not always as might be expected, however. For example, just five ethnic Harak families originally inhabited Pak Thon Village in Lamam District. However, in the late 1970s, well over fifty ethnic Triang and about twenty ethnic Ye families were moved in. It might have been expected that the customs and language of the Triang, the largest ethnic group in terms of numbers, would come to dominate the village's customs and culture. However, in many instances the Triang and Ye have adopted the customs of the original inhabitants, the Harak, and the Triang have not objected to Harak elders taking leading decision-making roles. Also, the Triang now follow the Harak taboos of only drinking jar rice beer when Animist ceremonies are being conducted and not at other times as they used to do.

Some officials do recognize the potential adverse affects of consolidating people from different ethnic groups into the same village. For example, in Kalum District, the *Chao Muang* stated that the district government realizes that it would be a bad idea, for cultural reasons, to consolidate Katu and Ngkriang villages into the same communities.

Internal Resettlement in Attapeu Province[2]

Some of the most extensive internal resettlement from the mountains to the lowlands in the Xekong River Basin, and more generally in southern Laos, occurred from 1996 until 1999 in Xekong Province. More recently, Attapeu Province has probably experienced the most severe government policy-induced internal resettlement in southern Laos, particularly in Phouvong and Sanxay Districts, in the eastern part of the province.

Internal Resettlement in Phouvong District

Phouvong District is ranked as the third poorest district in Laos. The population is predominantly ethnic Brao. The GoL has resettled all but one of the official twenty-three villages in the district since 1975 for various reasons. Since the mid-1990s over half have been moved from upland areas to the lowlands. Many smaller villages have been consolidated into larger ones, and some communities have been resettled in relative upland areas near the Vietnamese and Cambodian borders. There were even plans to resettle the district center from its present location to near the Nam Kong River, but local government officials appear to have successfully resisted the idea (see box below).

Phouvong District has experienced many of the same problems with internal resettlement that are typical of other parts of the country. Cheung Hiang Village, another ethnic Brao community in Phouvong, was initially resettled to the lowlands on the south side of the Nam Kong River, near the border with Cambodia, in 2003 and 2004 despite having generated large surpluses of rice doing swidden agriculture in the uplands before being resettled. The villagers did not want to move to the lowlands but were told that they had no choice but to follow the "Party-government plan" (*phen kan phak lat* in Lao). They were both pressured to move to the lowlands by government officials, and promised "development" once they arrived.

In the first year after being resettled, the people mainly survived on rice stock-piled in the mountains in previous years, even though they had to pay half of all the rice transported by truck from the uplands to the truck owners. The Cheung Hiang villagers were provided with thirteen buffaloes for sixty families (not enough for all the families), and some families received zinc-roofing sheets for their houses. But, most importantly, there has never been sufficient land available to develop lowland wet-rice cultivation in the area. Only some families have been able to develop small paddy areas near the village.

In 2005, the villagers from Cheung Hiang were told that they would have to resettle their village next to a new road on the north side of the Nam Kong River, in the lowlands. Once again, the people did not want to move, as they had already developed at least some lowland paddy on the other side of the river, and were planning to develop more. More importantly, the new resettlement site is in a dry dipterocarp forest area, and the closest source of drinking or bathing water is the Nam Kong River, 2 km away. A village leader stated, "We did not want to move near the road until a school had been built and a secure water source had been established. But, they [government officials] told us that we had to move before those things could be provided to us."

The people were then told that they had to relocate immediately, as the road was built for people to use, so they must live near it. They were told to organize their houses in single lines next to the road. Twenty of the village's sixty families followed these instructions and moved to the area in early 2005. But by mid-April 2005 the promised wells and school had still not materialized, despite the village headman requesting urgent help with clean water on three separate occasions. There was not a single year-round water source near the new village site until wells were finally drilled in 2006. Other problems remain. For example, there is a lack of forest resources in the area, and no nearby places to fish in the dry season. There are some areas that could be developed for paddy, but that would take many years. Three families from Cheung Hiang Village, and seven more from Vonglakhone, are still holding out in the uplands. As of 2005, they had not yet agreed to move to the lowlands.

The local government had waited for international aid agencies to come to work in Cheung Hiang Village to help solve the village's drinking water problems. During the rainy season, however, the people in the new resettlement village have no choice but to abandon it in order to farm lowland paddy south of the Nam Kong River, near the location of their previous village. At the height of the rainy season the water in the Nam Kong River is too strong to cross. The case of Cheung Hiang is a good example of one of the types of repeated resettlements in the lowlands that often occur after the initial failure of resettlement. Evrard and Goudineau (2004) provide examples of different reasons for successive movements in the lowlands after resettlement.

Tra-oum Village, another Brao community in Phouvong District, has also faced serious problems since being resettled into the lowlands in 2004. Shortly after the sixty families moved to their resettlement site near the district center, at least twelve people died of unidentified diseases. The resettled villagers did not have a clean source of water upon arriving in the area, whereas streams and springs run year round in the mountains. Despite being promised at least one hectare of lowland paddy fields per family upon resettling, most families have only received a fraction of what they need for subsistence. In April 2005, more than 50% of the sixty houses in the new village had been essentially abandoned, and many people have opted to live near their former lowland paddy and swidden fields. By 2006 only about 30% of the houses in the village remained occupied. There are few Non-Timber Forest Products (NTFPs) or other forest resources near where they live, as the area has already been heavily logged. Therefore, local people still travel back to the mountains on a regular basis to fish and collect NTFPs. The INGO ADRA has drilled three pump wells in the village, but people still have insufficient land for farming.

In one of the three Focal Sites in Phouvong District, *"Khet Chout Xoum Houay Keo,"* located near the Vietnamese and Cambodian borders in a relatively mountainous area, more than a hundred ethnic Brao families, mainly from Eetoum Village, were relocated in 2005. However, the lowland area where they were resettled was heavily bombed during the 1960s and early 1970s. Although it is supposed to be standard practice in the area before resettlement takes place, the village area has still not been checked for UXO left over from the war. While the plan is for those resettled to convert from being swidden cultivators to becoming lowland farmers, there is only a limited amount of land suitable for paddy in the area, and almost all of the available lowland areas are heavily contaminated with UXO.

In 2006, it was expected that it would only be possible for UXO Lao, the international donor-supported organization responsible for removing UXO, to clean up 8 ha of land. It was expected that this land would be given to sixteen families, but the vast majority of people resettled to the area may never get access to lowland paddy land. Even the 0.5 ha of paddy will not be enough for those families that do receive land to subsist on. For those continuing to do swidden, the government is requiring that after each year for the next five years the swiddens are planted with economic tree species, but some villagers are resisting, fearing that they will not be able to harvest the trees in the future. A private company is reportedly providing the tree seedlings.

Before establishing this new sub-district Focal Site, the plan had been to develop another nearby settlement, also called Houay Keo. However, more recently local authorities decided to promote the other new settlement area instead. There were several reasons for this. Much of the land surrounding the Houay Keo Focal Site area was owned or controlled by a Vietnamese agriculture development company called Chong Deo between 1999 and 2004. During this time the company failed in trying to develop cashew nut plantations on 500 ha of poor soils. Most of the cashew trees they planted either died or grew poorly, and they eventually had to abandon the few remaining trees after failing to fulfill their development contract with the GoL. There were rumors that cassava would be planted on the land once the cashew plantation failed, but this plan does not appear to be materializing.

In addition, the stream that runs by the old resettlement area of Houay Keo no longer flows year round, as it did when the area was first developed. This has resulted in acute dry season water supply problems for the people. Essentially, the government, by moving large numbers of people to a small area and then promoting inappropriate development there, has created what Jonathan Rigg has called, "a policy-induced Malthusian squeeze." In this case people have been cramped into a small area, resulting in overly intensive swidden agriculture in the watershed of their drinking water. At the same time, the government has allowed excessive commercial logging in the area, and much of the watershed has been degraded through the development of the failed cashew plantation, leaving only degraded and open grass and scrublands.

Around 10 a.m. on one morning in August 2005, the new Houay Keo resettlement village was devastated when a massive flash flood rolled down the Xexou River and flooded the village. Houses were inundated, and many were washed away. The water declined by 3 p.m. Since the flooding occurred during the daytime people were able to escape to high ground, and there were no casualties. "If it had happened at night, it could have been very different," commented a villager whose house was washed away. In total, fifty-four houses were lost in the flood.

Since the flooding, few families have wanted to construct new houses at this location. Two groups of ten and twenty families have moved to new settlements away from the Xexou River and near their new swidden fields. Those staying have built new houses on higher ground. In addition to being an area subject to a considerable risk of flash floods, the site is also still contaminated with UXO and lacks suitable land for either lowland paddy development or swiddens. It will be an uphill battle to convince people to move back to the area. The Houay Keo resettlement area is not off to an auspicious start, but it is all too typical of the poor planning and lack of resources that have characterized internal resettlement initiatives in southern Laos.

As in other areas, international donors have at times, knowingly or unknowingly, facilitated internal resettlement in Phouvong District. An example can be found in Vonglakhone Village where, in 2005, the local government enticed the ethnic Brao community to resettle from the south to the north side of the Nam Kong River, so as to be near a new school being funded by the ADB's *Dek Nying*" (girls) Education Project. Vonglakhone was relocated from upland areas a few years earlier, so this was their second government-promoted move in recent years (Baird and Shoemaker 2005).

Viangxai Village is a typical example of a resettled village subject to Village Consolidation. There was originally just Viangxai Village in the location, but the people from three other villages, Phya Viang, Vonglakhone and Houay Kiang, were moved there in 2002. Most people did not want to move together, but the local government insisted. Most of the Vonglakhone families moved a few kilometers down the Nam Kong River, but some still live in Viangxai. In 2004, there were officially 600 people in 160 families in Viangxai, although the village is spread out over a number of kilometers along the road from the Nam Kong River and the district center of Phouvong. Like Vonglakhone, a school has also been built in Viangxai by the ADB's *Dek Nying* education support project. The villagers originally wanted to create four separate villages, but the government insisted on establishing just one. Previously, when living in the mountains, most people grew enough rice to eat. But in 2003, after being moved to their new location, only two families were able to grow enough rice to subsist on. This was partly due to poor rains but, even if the rains had been sufficient, most would not have been able to grow enough food to eat, as they lack the appropriate skills or large enough lowland paddy fields to do so. Some also lack buffaloes and other tools.

Internal Resettlement in Sanxay District

In neighboring Sanxay District, internal resettlement has also been problematic. Ethnic Triang and Harak people have been relocated to the lowland Focal Site previously called "*Khet Chout Xoum Nam Pa*" but now referred to as "*Koum Ban Nam Pa*."[3] They have been facing serious health, food security, and livelihoods problems, as the majority of the people in approximately nineteen villages[4] were moved into the same general area between 2002 and 2004. One government official, one of the last people to resettle from the uplands after the district center of Sanxay was resettled to the Focal Site in January 2003, found that, by the time he had arrived, there was virtually no lowland farmland left for him or his colleagues. Even earlier arrivals have mainly only been provided with small areas of lowland paddy and, in 2004, people in the area were only able to produce enough rice for an average of three months consumption, leaving them with a shortage for nine months.

In 2004, rains were poor, leading to even more serious shortages in 2005. There was also a lack of buffaloes to plow what lowland fields are available. The soil in the resettlement area is poor compared to the soils near the upland villages where the people came from, resulting in difficulties in growing vegetables. Resettled people also report that there are more pests in the lowlands, including aphids. The government has built a covered building to serve as a market, but it is not being used, indicating that the market expansion that was expected after resettlement has not yet materialized.

In reality, there are few products for the resettled people to sell in the lowlands. There are few NTFPs, including fish and other forest products, to harvest in the area, leaving people short of food and money. There is a hospital, but staff are having problems collecting the large amount of money that recently resettled people owe them for treatments and medicine they have received. The local hospital reports that there has also been an increase in illnesses since the people were resettled, especially malaria, diarrhea, measles, and skin diseases.

In early 2004, fifteen people reportedly died over a short period of time due to diarrhea and malaria. There have also been increased instances of small-scale thievery, including stealing vegetables grown in family gardens, clothing, knives, rice, money, and other things. All in all, the situation is much more difficult than the relatively positive articles about the resettlement area that appeared in the Lao media in 2003 (Thammavongsa 2003a and b). One resettled ethnic Triang elderly man was quoted, in 2004, as saying:

It was convenient for us in many ways in our old village. For example, there was plenty of drinking water, land for swidden agriculture, and food to eat, including various kinds of vegetables. In the forests we were never without food. We were shifting cultivators, but that doesn't mean that we cut down large trees to make our swiddens. We had plenty of fallow areas for doing swidden agriculture. We didn't destroy large trees. But the government relocated us to the lowlands, and nothing is convenient for us here. For example, when we get sick we can easily go to the hospital if we have money, but if we don't have money we can't go to the hospital because they won't help us with medicine. You have to have money to get anything. In our old village, we had enough rice to eat every year because the soil was good quality. Apart from rice, we also had other kinds of vegetables, like cassava, taro, tubers, and papaya. However, we never took them to sell because the road wasn't good.

Indicative of the serious problems, one morning in early 2004 twenty families from Mai Thavan Village gathered up what things they could carry and, without telling anyone in advance, walked back up into the mountains to their original village. Considering the large concentration of people in the area and their poor circumstances, nobody could really blame them for returning.

Seven families from Dak Xang Village, seven from Dak Ngot and six from Dak Hiak also returned to the mountains in 2004. A number of other families are considering returning to the mountains. One villager who was contemplating moving back to the mountains stated in 2004:

> They moved us here like this, without providing adequate support. Before moving from our old village, we were promised everything if we moved. It is true that some things are more convenient here, but if things are still as they are, we will move back to our old village like the people from the other villages. People from many nearby villages are thinking the same as us. Regardless of the consequences, it will be better for us to die in our old villages.

A number of other people the government wants to resettle into the area do want to move, since they know that those who moved there are already facing various problems. One Triang government official admitted that if the people were allowed to decide where they wanted to live, the resettlement area would probably only have about 10% of the number of people in it as it did in 2004. However, the local government is trying to prohibit others from moving back to the mountains, in order to prevent the site's total collapse and failure. They are also eagerly looking for international funding assistance.

With all the problems that the resettlement area is facing, it might seem surprising that a ten km road to and from another resettlement area to the west, Dak Hiak, was funded using "emergency funds" provided by the German government bilateral funding agency, GTZ. In 2003, GTZ also provided the resettled people there with "food-for-work" rice (Thammavongsa 2003a), but by 2004, this program had ended. The INGO ADRA has installed pump wells in the resettlement area with AUSAID funding, and there are also plans for a large loan project sponsored by the IO International Fund for Agriculture Development (IFAD), which intends to work in resettlement villages to support agriculture, infrastructure, and income-generating activities. The ADB is also loaning the GoL money to upgrade the roads from Pa-am to Saysettha District center, in order to improve road access to the resettlement area, and they also plan to upgrade the road from Pa-am to Chaleunxay. In addition, IFAD plans to upgrade the road from Chaleunxay to Dak Bon Village in Nam Ngone Sub-district. The villages in Nam Ngone Sub-district remain as some of the last upland communities in Sanxay District. But after improvements have been completed, the

GoL wants to move more people from the uplands to live along these roads. All of the donors mentioned above appear to have accepted the resettlement plans of the government and their role in funding projects in support of resettlement.

Resettlement—Not Only a Village Affair

Resettlement is not only taking place at the village level, but also in some cases at the district level. A few years ago Sanxay District center was relocated, along with its government officials, from a mountainous area to its present location at Pa-am, in the lowlands.

In another case, a highly placed senior political leader suggested that the district center of Phouvong be moved to an area adjacent to the Nam Kong River at Viangxai, but local government officials resisted the idea, and the plan has now been quietly set aside. But for a few years the idea was taken seriously, and a brand new concrete district education office was built at Viangxai in anticipation of the district center's resettlement. It was used for just a few months before the officials abandoned the building and quietly moved back into the old Education office.

Lessons Unlearnt: The Story of the Resettlement of the Present Inhabitants of *Ban* Na

The ethnic Brao people who currently live in *Ban* Na Village in Pathoumphone District of Champasak Province were once members of four villages situated along the Lao-Cambodian border inside the present-day Xepian National Protected Area (NPA). They were named Tambiang, Ti, Cheung Hiang and Chano. During the war years, in the early 1970s, the RLG was worried that these people might supply food to Pathet Lao soldiers in the forest and so they relocated them to the lowlands near the Mekong River. Initially, they were moved near a Buddhist forest temple called "*Vat Pa.*" However, the people were struck down with an epidemic and forty-one died. The survivors abandoned the area and scattered, moving into various Lao villages in the lowlands. After a number of years, some of these people finally established *Ban* Na Village on the west side of Route 13 South, and were gradually joined by many of the other Brao people who had escaped the epidemic.

The human death toll and psychological impact of being relocated to the lowlands represented a terrible loss. However, over thirty years later, the GoL is still promoting relocation of a similar nature for ethnic minorities in the mountains. Little appears to have been learned about the problems associated with this kind of resettlement.

Looking for Alternatives to Internal Resettlement in Xekong Province

The French INGO, Action contre la faim (ACF) has been working in Kalum and Dakchung Districts in Xekong Province for many years and, like the UNDP's SIP-Dev Project, they were originally inspired by Yves Goudineau's work in the 1990s regarding problems with internal resettlement. Their involvement in Kalum District began in 1998. By 1999, ACF had decided to focus on providing assistance to people still living in remote mountainous areas so that they would not have to resettle.

The government in Xekong had decided on four criteria that villages should meet in order to stay in the mountains: 1) access to clean water; 2) 70,000 kip/family/month in income; 3) at least one child in each family finishes primary school; and 4) access to markets. ACF decided to focus its work on upland communities to help them meet these criteria and thereby avoid all the difficulties faced by resettled communities. At the time, ACF did not have the objective of influencing government policy regarding resettlement. They simply wanted to help people in the most effective way possible. More recently, however, ACF has become a leader in trying to address policy issues surrounding internal resettlement (see Gonzales et al. 2005).

By 2000 the amount of resettlement occurring in Kalum had decreased markedly and ACF began to put more of their attention toward addressing chronic food shortages. Since then, they have been implementing a service-delivery oriented development project in Kalum. ACF now takes the position that they will work in resettled communities for humanitarian reasons, in order to reduce the worst health-related problems associated with resettlement, but they will not support the resettlement process by providing broader development support beyond emergency needs in resettled villages. ACF also combines this limited support to resettled communities with attempts to open up dialogue with government officials in order to reduce the chances of inappropriate resettlement occurring in the future.

Irrigated Agriculture

Since the mid-1990s the GoL has invested a considerable amount of money in trying to increase the amount of irrigated farmland in the country. Increasing irrigated farmland has been key to the central government's rural development strategy and has been strongly supported by some of the country's largest foreign donors. The use of pumps for irrigated agriculture has also been promoted by advocates of hydropower dams in Laos, such as the "Panel of Experts" for the Nam Theun 2 Dam, as a promising compensatory source of alternative livelihoods for dam-impacted communities.

According to GoL statistics, in 2003, 2,538 ha of irrigated rainy season rice fields were farmed in Xekong and 1,493 ha of irrigated rice fields were cultivated during the same year's dry season. For Attapeu Province, 3,770 ha of rice fields were irrigated during the 2003 rainy season, and 2,293 ha were irrigated during the dry season (LNMC 2004). However, the actual quantity of dry season rice fields being irrigated in the two provinces is likely to have been, and still be, much less than official statistics indicate. Various provincial and district officials in the Xekong Basin privately acknowledge that they have been, and continue to be, under enormous pressure from central level authorities to report success in expanding dry season irrigation. This is widely believed to have led to exaggerated reports of the amount of land under irrigation each year. Even when a wide cross section of farmers report declines in irrigation, district and provincial figures invariably report increases. Shoemaker et al. (2001) also discussed the similar manipulation of dry season irrigated rice statistics in Savannakhet Province.

The GoL's Ministry of Agriculture and Forestry has implemented a number of small-, medium-, and large-scale gravity weir-based and pump-based irrigation projects in the Xekong River Basin in Laos. In the late 1990s, pump irrigation was heavily promoted not only in the basin, but also throughout the country (see also Shoemaker et al. 2001). However, many of these projects have either failed or resulted in significantly fewer benefits than initially expected. As the following examples demonstrate, pump irrigation, as implemented to date in the Xekong River Basin in Laos, has been a failed and ill-conceived development strategy that has had a generally negative impact on its intended beneficiaries.

The Ta-euang Gravity-Feed Irrigation Weir Project

The Ta-euang Irrigation Weir Project is located near Phalay Bok and Phalay Thong Villages in Pathoumphone District, Champasak Province. The Ta-euang Stream runs south to north through the Xepian NPA—one of Laos' most important parks (see Chapter 9)—before eventually flowing into the Xekhampho River, which runs into the Xepian River in Sanamxay District.

In 1998/1999, the Ta-euang Project was initiated near the northern border of Xepian NPA, reportedly at a cost to the GoL of 3 billion kip.[5] The INGO, World Vision, reportedly paid part of the costs (Sparkes 2000). The project was expected to turn Phalay Bok and Phalay Thong into villages able to produce two crops of lowland paddy rice per year, rather than the single wet season crop that they previously cultivated. A large amount of dry season irrigation was planned. Some villagers were upset about the large amount of rice field land that had to be given up to make way for the project's wide canal system, but they hoped that this sacrifice would at least be made up by increased production and the double-cropping potential that the project was expected to deliver. Although the project was completed as scheduled and was used for a few years to irrigate a small amount of dry season rice fields, by 2004 not a bit of water from the project was being used for irrigation. It has also had a number of unanticipated negative impacts.

A central flaw of the project is that those developing it assumed that the weir would be able to create a reservoir with enough water to irrigate a large area in the dry season. However, it appears that no surveys of the dry season discharge of the Ta-euang were undertaken as part of the project planning process. It was only after the project was completed, and people started to irrigate small areas of lowland rice fields, that it became obvious to the farmers that there was insufficient water for irrigating even relatively small areas of lowland rice paddy. Even though the weir causes the Ta-euang Stream to back up many kilometers, the actual dry season flow is far from sufficient. To make matters worse, severe insect infestations soon hit the dry season rice crop. Before long all dry season rice cultivation in the area ceased. The weir has not proved useful for improving wet season irrigation either.

One of the project's anticipated benefit was that increased water levels behind the weir would make boat transportation from Phalay Bok Village to Nong Ping Village easier. However, when the weir was planned few people questioned how the dam might negatively impact fisheries, including dry season fish migrations up the Ta-euang Stream. The stream, a perennial running water body, was blocked with a large cement weir. The village of Nong Ping is situated upstream from the project, inside the protected area, and has suffered from declines in fish catches directly attributable to decreased fish migrations upstream. Nong Ping villagers report that the weir has even affected the hydrology of the Ta-euang Stream upstream from their village, many kilometers from the weir. Since fish cannot get past the weir at Phalay, the dam has undoubtedly impacted fish populations, especially those upstream from the dam inside the Xepian NPA, near Nong Ping and Taong Villages. In southern Laos it has already been shown that even small irrigation weirs can block important fish migrations and negatively impact the environment and local livelihoods over quite long distances (Baird 2001c).

Apart from being incapable of irrigating dry season crops, reducing rice paddy land through canal building, and blocking fish migrations, the project was found to be detrimental to wet season rice agriculture, by causing heavy inundation of about 20 ha of paddy fields outside the project's original command area. This made cultivation of this previously productive land impossible. "It would have been better not to have built the project than to have built it," lamented one male villager. A village women said, "We would never have allowed the project to be built if we'd known the problems it would bring. We have more problems now than before the project was built!"

A newer development project has been initiated to attempt to address at least one of the serious problems that resulted from the original irrigation project. The GoL/World Bank supported Poverty Reduction Fund (PRF) has invested over 35 million kip to hire villagers from Phalay Bok Village to hand dig a new 5-m wide and 3-m deep canal to drain water from the reservoir to below the weir in the rainy season, in order to reduce the amount of wet season flooding caused by the project. There are technical challenges and it is as yet unclear whether this solution will be successful in reducing the negative impacts of the flooding caused by the original project. However, villagers are hopeful that the PRF's expenditure will reduce some of the poverty caused by the earlier attempt to reduce their poverty. Even if it is successful, that will not address the loss of villager rice fields due to the canal building, or the loss of fishery resources due to the blockage of fish migrations. If the mitigation plan does work, it may be a relatively good use of World Bank resources. However, it is rather ironic that this "success' would come through the partial dismantling of the same type of large irrigation project that the World Bank so-often promotes elsewhere in Laos.

The World Bank's "Agriculture Development Project"

In around 2003, the World Bank established the "Agriculture Development Project" (ADP), with one of its main objectives being to rehabilitate seventeen small- and medium-sized weir irrigation schemes and three electric pump schemes, and to convert two diesel pump schemes to electrical power. A large number of medium- to large-scale gravity weir-based and pump-based irrigation projects in the Xekong River Basin, first developed in the 1980s and 1990s, had either failed, not lived up to expectations, or were never completed due to corruption, unreliable contractors, or a lack of funding. The ADP, through investing the resources needed to complete or restore these projects, aimed to address this situation.

The irrigation component of the project was originally envisioned to cover a service area of 7,070 ha in Champasak, Attapeu, Salavan, and Khammouane Provinces. Three irrigation weir schemes and two pump schemes in the Xekong Basin have been considered for rehabilitation by the ADP. All but one of the weir systems are in Attapeu Province, with only the Thongvay Irrigation Scheme being situated in Champasak, on the Bolaven Plateau in Pakxong District (World Bank 2001).

The total value of the ADP loan to Laos was US$18.21 million,[6] including a number of other components apart from the irrigation work, such as the provision of small access roads, potable water and agriculture extension. Support for environmental management, adaptive research, and a "village investment for the poor" component[7] were also envisioned. However, the irrigation component, valued at US$8.55 million, along with US$440,000 in support of water users groups, was by far the largest part of the project. The next largest component was "implementation and project support." Costing US$2.12 million, it included the employment of a number of foreign consultants, mostly from Western countries (World Bank 2001). The Village Investment for the Poor (VIP) component was facilitated through a grant from the Japanese Social Development Fund, administered by the World Bank. The VIP program was supposed to focus on the poorest of the poor, with special attention being given to food security through support for income-generating activities, mainly in the agricultural sector.

The "Project Appraisal Document" for the ADP claimed that, "impacts on the environment are generally positive," that the few negative impacts would be easily mitigated, and that the project would have no negative impacts on ethnic minorities as those people are only in highland areas where irrigation is unsuitable (World Bank 2001). The Project Appraisal Document did not seem to recognize the amount of ethnic minority resettlement that has occurred to the lowlands in Laos, and also failed to consider that irrigation is sometimes quite suitable for the uplands. However, later in the same document, the World Bank (2001) proposes that an indicator for the VIP component of the project should be the number of ethnic minorities and women who receive loans. The reason for this apparent contradiction are unclear, and the implication is that, at least at some level, the project did intend to work in areas populated by indigenous peoples and impact their lives. It is possible that project staff wanted to be able to show that they would be assisting ethnic minorities while at the same time not wanting to have the infrastructure component of the project constrained by the Bank's "Indigenous People's Policy." The discourse appears to have been manipulated so that at places in the project document indigenous peoples are "visible," while in other parts they become conveniently "invisible." The following sections outline some of the irrigation projects the World Bank's ADP has been involved in since its initiation in the Xekong Basin.

The Thong Vay Irrigation Scheme

Thong Vay Village is located in Thateng District, and is within one of the district's two focal sites (the other being Xiang Mai, the site of the resettled ethnic Katu people from Kandone Village in Kalum District). The four villages in the area include the more than one thousand people who moved there in the late 1980s (UNDP 1997).

One of the projects considered for rehabilitation by the ADP was the Thong Vay Irrigation Scheme (TVIS), which the GoL had constructed along the Xekatam River near Thong Vay Village in Pakxong District, Champasak Province in the 1990s. The project, which included a less than meter-high weir situated about 10 km downstream from the source of the Xekatam River, was expected to provide dry and wet season wet-rice irrigation for a 130 ha command area. The project failed from the outset, and was never operational. The clay-deficient volcanic soils of the area used to construct the unlined main canal were too porous and could not hold enough water to make the project viable.

When ADP project staff investigated the planned project rehabilitation, which was budgeted at US$11,000 and expected to have a command area of 30 ha, they found that the soils were simply too permeable and determined that it would be necessary either to import more clay-based soils or cement line the canals in order to make the initiative viable. Furthermore, the off-take structure just above the weir was either incorrectly designed or constructed, as it was completely submerged and invisible under water during even moderate discharge conditions at the beginning of the rainy season. The costs of addressing all these flaws proved prohibitive, and the ADP abandoned the project in November 2004 (Alan Potkin, pers. comm. 2006).

While the project's failure was clearly based on its inappropriate and poor design, some provincial officials have taken to "blaming the victims" and have commented to me that the project failed due to there having been too much shifting cultivation in the area, resulting in less water than required for the irrigation system. By promoting this view, ethnic minority villagers can be portrayed as causing a well-conceived irrigation project to fail through their inappropriate swidden agriculture farming methods. In turn, the government can be seen as the victim of the villagers' poor natural resource management rather than the resettled villagers being seen as victims of poor government planning and implementation. Such conclusions are based on preconceived lowland ideas and official discourses about ethnic minorities being the cause of forest destruction, rather than an objective analysis of what happened. According to Alan Potkin, an environmental consultant employed by the project, there has been extensive commercial logging in the Xekatam watershed, but the officials who blamed the villagers failed to mention this.

The Houay Samong 1 and 2 Irrigation Schemes

While the World Bank has decided to scrap plans to rehabilitate the TVIS, it has committed to rehabilitating the *Houay* Samong 1 Irrigation Scheme (HS1IS), in Sanamxay District. The *Houay* Samong is a fourth-order tributary of the Mekong, first flowing into the Xepian and Xekong Rivers. The scheme was originally constructed in the 1990s by the GoL and was expected to provide wet and dry season irrigation for wet-rice cultivation in an approximately 150 ha command area near Hin Lat Village, adjacent to the Xepian River. However, it failed to live up to its potential when funding for the project dried up before it could be completed. While year round discharge levels have not been measured, World Bank consultants have made a rough estimate that the *Houay* Samong has a mean annual discharge of 10 m^3/second at its off-take. The ADP planned to reconstruct and line the main irrigation canal (1.22 km long), and main irrigation 1 canal (6.9 km long); construct a new drainage canal (0.85 km long) required for part of the command area currently unusable in the wet season; realign several secondary canals; upgrade several existing access tracks (5.06 km long); construct new minor water control structures; and improve existing major water control structures (Alan Potkin, pers. comm. 2006).

The project was originally constructed as the first phase of a two-phase initiative planned to irrigate 290 ha of wet-rice farmland. It was expected that the scheme would allow for significant population influx into the area, probably through resettling villagers from upland areas in other parts of Attapeu. It was also expected to absorb military veterans from a nearby army base. Because the project went way over budget and was never completed, the southern reaches of the larger command area had never received any water prior to the ADP's involvement in the project (Alan Potkin, pers. comm. 2006).

The *Houay* Samong 2 Irrigation Project (HS2IP) is the second phase of the original irrigation project. The southern diversion weir and diversion aqueduct for this scheme were built and installed at the time that the first phase of the project was initiated, but the second main canal was only partially excavated. Its distribution system was never completed. The World Bank reconfigured the latter components for the HS2IP and this project was due for rehabilitation in the second phase of the ADP. The command area for each phase of the project is 150 ha, while the first phase is budgeted at US$202,000, and the second at US$144,000 (World Bank 2001). It is unclear if this part of the ADP was ever initiated, as the project has experienced various problems (see below).

Farmers from the local area, who were not adequately consulted during the HS1IP project's original planning and construction, are now well aware that the original project design was poorly conceived and fundamentally flawed. That is why some of the key structures associated with the project never worked. For example, the off-take elevation for at least one large secondary canal was incompatible with gravity irrigation. The original plan also allowed for unintercepted upslope drainage to flow over the access trail and on into the main canal, resulting in serious erosion of the trail and the canal. In total, the HS1IP has come far from meeting its original expectations (Alan Potkin, pers. comm. 2006).

In the 2003/2004 dry season, World Bank consultants estimated that, despite the original project's major flaws, roughly 30–50% of the rice fields in the command area were in use. Of the many "white elephant" irrigation projects that the ADP was considering rehabilitating in Laos, this was deemed to be one with a relatively high potential. However, it appears the World Bank consultants failed to adequately consider a number of important factors that will determine the project's long-term impacts on the livelihoods of people in the area. One of these key factors regards fisheries.

The *Houay* Samong originates in the eastern escarpment of the Bolaven Plateau, before falling 100 m into the lowlands over a relatively short distance. It flows into the Xepian River about 3 km downstream from the village of Hin Lat. Roberts and Baird (1995b) collected fish in the *Houay* Samong and reported on fish biodiversity from the area. They found a wide variety of migratory fish present that are important to the livelihoods of local communities. If both the HS1IP and HS2IP are implemented, the World Bank consultants roughly estimated that 5 liters of water/ second / ha will be extracted, resulting in about 2 m^3 or 20% of the water in the stream being used for irrigation. They argue that this extraction by itself will cause little impact to the ecology of the *Houay* Samong basin (Alan Potkin, pers.

comm. 2006). While it may or may not be true that only 20% of the water will be removed for irrigation, the percentage removed for dry season rice production will likely be significantly higher, as dry season water levels are much less than wet season flows. The amount of water remaining in the lower Samong by the time it reaches the Xepian River in the dry season is likely to be significantly reduced, and this would have a serious negative impact on fish and fisheries of the *Houay* Samong and Xepian River. Despite the warnings raised by one of its consultants,[8] the World Bank's ADP has not expressed much concern over this issue.

Adding further to the potential project-related impact on fisheries was the July 2003 installation of a 160 kw hydroelectric generating facility by the Lao Army. Water diverted via a tunnel is reportedly able to generate 113 kilowatt-hours (Kwh) of electricity, supplying the local army base as well as six villages with electricity, including Tamayot, Samong Tai, Samong Neua, Hin Lat, Ban Mai, and Tha Hin Villages. A considerable amount of water is being used for generating electricity that was supposed to go to the World Bank-supported irrigation project.

The World Bank has estimated that 6–7 m^3/second of water is being used to generate power at the site. Below the powerhouse, some of the water is allowed to flow back into the main irrigation canal, while the rest is diverted back into the *Houay* Samong. It is unclear whether the additional diversion was originally envisioned as part of the project or not. The water used for producing electricity bypasses the main channel, where fish seasonally migrate upstream, resulting in potential problems of there not being enough water to accommodate the migrating fish. The irrigation and hydro projects will together require about 2.7 m^3/second of water, which may be close to the minimal annual discharge for the *Houay* Samong in some years. It may be that in most years the annual minimum discharge will be about 5 m^3/second but, even then, removing 2.7 m^3/second would constitute a significant downstream impact on the lower Samong Stream. At present about 1 m^3/second is being removed from the *Houay* Samong in the dry season in order to irrigate the part of the HS1IP that has been functional since the project was first constructed (Alan Potkin, pers. comm. 2006). The project is probably not, however, having a major impact on the discharge of the Xepian River, due to its much higher overall water volume.

The negative impact of this hydroelectric project—apart from some aesthetic impacts on the natural beauty of the area caused by the 11 Kv transmission lines leaving the project—is that the former cascade channel between the Bolaven Plateau escarpment and the valley below is dewatered for most of the year. World Bank project staff are unclear on whether or not this is having any impact on *Houay*

Samong fisheries. However, they do believe that the hydroelectric project's negative impacts are likely to eclipse those of the irrigation project. This point is debatable, as the water used to run the hydropower generator is largely returned to the *Houay* Samong and the dewatered part of the channel may well not be important for fish migrations, since the escarpment not far above there is certainly not passable by fish in any case. In contrast, however, water taken for the irrigation project is not returned to the *Houay* Samong, thus resulting in more significant impacts in the lower *Houay* Samong. The World Bank has reportedly been unsure whether or how to include impacts from the Army's hydropower scheme (even though it was facilitated by the irrigation project), within the planned subsequent mitigation activities of the project (Alan Potkin, pers. comm. 2006).

At the time of project planning, World Bank consultants reportedly acknowledged that these irrigation projects would inevitably have some localized impact on the hydrology of the *Houay* Samong, with ensuing negative impacts on human nutrition and livelihoods. However, they claimed that there was insufficient information about these types of impacts in Laos to make any predictions about the potential implications. They reportedly indicated that more information about how human livelihoods in Sanamxay District are linked to the aquatic ecology would have been useful and that an ADP commissioned study on this issue should have been undertaken (Alan Potkin, pers. comm. 2006). Such a study was never implemented. However, there are certainly several past studies on aquatic resources from Sanamxay District and other parts of lowland areas in Attapeu Province that already clearly indicate that aquatic resources are important for local livelihoods (Roberts and Baird 1995b; Mollot et al. 2005; Meusch et al. 2003). In 2006, work on the HS1IP was still underway, and it was expected that the project would be completed by late 2006. At the time of this writing it is unclear whether it was finished by that date.

Nakengkham Irrigation Project

The World Bank has also been attempted to rehabilitate the relatively large Nakengkham Irrigation Project in Samakhixay District of Attapeu through the ADP. The project is located near the provincial capital and adjacent to Route 16, just 6 km out of town, and was first constructed with GoL funding in the late 1990s. The project originally had a service area of about 200 ha (World Bank 2001). There are three villages with paddy fields in the service area of the project: Kengkham, Tha Hin, and Saphao.

Although rice crops were irrigated by the project for a few years after its original construction, the system fell into disuse due to the degradation of the unlined irrigation canals that were critical for the project. The rehabilitation was expected to return 200 ha to dry season rice production, at a cost of about US$250,000 (World Bank 2001). While the rehabilitation of this project was a high priority for the province, probably because of its "show piece" potential due to its location near to the provincial capital, local people who live in the project area were much less enthusiastic about the initiative when asked about the project in 2004 and 2005. There were several reasons for their skepticism. First, the project requires that water be pumped directly from the Xekong River into the irrigation system. The expected users were worried about the costs of electricity that this might entail.

Tha Hin, one of the villages in the command area of the project, is situated near the right bank of the Xekong, next to Route 16 running from Attapeu to Xekong Province. This provides many villagers with more lucrative potential income generation options than growing dry season rice. Farmers there are particularly concerned about the high costs of chemical fertilizers, pesticides, and electricity that dry season rice cultivation frequently requires. This has discouraged farmers throughout the country from growing dry season rice (see, for example, Shoemaker et al. 2001). They have also had severe problems with *"meng kheng"* infestations (see box below).

Meng Kheng Insects and Dry Season Irrigation

Growing swarms of *"meng kheng"* insects, which in large numbers can decimate rice crops, have discouraged many farmers from dry season rice cultivation throughout southern Laos. Pesticides, even if they were affordable, are not effective in eliminating these devastating swarms. Farmers report that they have tried to use pesticides but that the flying insects are largely able to escape pesticide applications, only to return to suck the life from rice kernels in a few days, once the effects of the pesticides decline. When they return the *meng kheng* are able to do more damage than ever before, as most of their natural predators, spiders and frogs, are less able to escape the pesticide applications, and so are decimated rapidly.

In some parts of Attapeu where *meng kheng* swarms have been particularly severe, desperate villagers have resorted to dragging mosquito nets over rice fields to catch them. Previously, nobody ate *meng kheng*, due to the putrid smell. While many still consider them inedible, some have recently begun consuming them. Before dry season rice cultivation arrived in southern Laos, *meng kheng* insects occasionally caused small amounts of crop damage, but they were rarely considered a significant threat to crops. This all changed with the arrival of dry season wet-rice irrigation. The reason relates to the insects' lifecycles, which are about four months long. In the past, they would do well during the wet season, when there were plenty of rice seeds to eat, but as soon as the dry season arrived and the food source ran dry, they could not survive in large numbers, and populations would drastically decline. Only small populations would be left to regroup the following wet season. However, with rice fields flooded with two crops per year, the *meng kheng* are able to survive in large and increasing numbers. Their populations have exploded, leading to serious problems for both dry season and wet season rice farmers. There were also reportedly other dry season rice insect infestation problems in Attapeu in 2005, caused by "*phya chan*" aphids and "*tak katen*" crickets. "Crickets have caused much damage to dry season rice crops in the area," said one farmer.

Other important problems relate to unpredictable water availability, villager conflicts over water, and the accumulation of debt by farmers from their attempts at dry season rice cultivation. While some farmers made money, many others lost considerable sums. Villagers have also lost confidence in the system by which their electricity consumption is measured, and there is a widespread belief that they have been charged for electricity they never used. In the past, villagers were also shocked at receiving single large bills for pump electricity consumption for the whole year. The bill was too large for farmers to pay at one time; however, in 2006 the system was changed so as to collect for pump electricity use every month.

Another problem mentioned by villagers is that in the past farmers noticed that if they did two crops of rice a year, the quality of the regular rainy season crop declined, probably due to soil degradation caused by overuse and increased pest problems. Rice landowners who did not want to do dry season rice cultivation were unwilling to let other farmers use their land for nothing and, even though it was against GoL policy, charged rents to other farmers who used their land. In 2006, after the irrigation system was repaired, government officials reportedly went to the villages and told farmers that collecting rents from other farmers who used their land for dry season production would no longer be tolerated. As one villager put it, the government officials "corrected the situation."

Another important issue is that many villagers already have a relatively lucrative dry season occupation. For generations, local people from Tha Hin Village have been collecting clay from areas near their village to do pottery, and currently they are the main producers of jars used for keeping fermented fish paste (*pa dek* in Lao) in southern Laos. This occupation is important for both the ethnic Lao people who founded the village and also for the approximately forty ethnic Brao families who were moved into the village about thirty years ago. They have learnt from ethnic Lao potters, and many have themselves become experts over the years. Many of these Brao people, who are generally the poorest people in the village, are involved in pottery for their primary livelihoods. There are even jar traders in the village who hire other people to make pottery for them. Not everyone has sufficient capital to make jars, as there is a time lag between when the jars are made and when they are sold.

Most Brao farmers are particularly unenthusiastic about the irrigation project. Some are resentful about the rehabilitation project, as their lowland rice fields, which they plant in the wet season, are largely outside the command area of the irrigation project. They are concerned that they will be forced to help maintain the rehabilitated irrigation project even though they are not benefiting from it. Moreover, they are worried that the insect infestations likely to result from dry season irrigation will adversely affect their wet season rice crops outside of the irrigation command area.

These negative impacts should arguably be considered as a cost to other farmers of doing dry season wet-rice agriculture. The World Bank/ADP does not appear to have seriously considered this, probably due to their overall lack of recognition of this issue and the difficulties in quantifying such impacts. The project seems mainly to be focused on the technical and water use aspects of the scheme rather than the broader ecological and livelihood issues associated with the promotion of dry season wet-rice irrigation. One World Bank consultant commented, anonymously, that he had heard that "villagers' arms were being twisted" to implement the irrigation and dry season rice-farming project. All the above explains why many villagers remain skeptical about irrigation rehabilitation, and why, in 2006, when the irrigation system started working again, many farmers reported that they planned to do just a little dry season rice production in the first year "to try it out first and see how things work out."

Other Projects

For a time the ADP was also considering rehabilitating the Naxaithong Pump Irrigation Scheme, about 20 km south of the provincial capital, in order to bring

60 ha of land under dry season production, at an estimated cost of US$84,000. This scheme was built in the 1990s, but fell into disuse due to its poor design and canal degradation (World Bank 2001). As explained below, pump irrigation has generally been quite problematic in Laos. Project officials have since decided that this project will be abandoned and that another dry season pump irrigation project at Na Phoke will replace it. The Na Phoke project is already operational but needed repairs. The work on that project was continuing in 2006. There are unconfirmed reports that many of the people who farm in the command area for this project live in the provincial capital, which is on the other side of the Xekong.

Reviewing the "Agriculture Development Project"

In May 2005, two-and-a-half years after the ADP began, a mid-term review of the project was initiated in Khammouane Province. One problem identified was keeping finances flowing, which was attributed to poor staff skills and management. Project analysis was also seen as being weak. The Project Coordination Office President, Khampheuy Bandasack, said that there did not appear to be clear target area selection criteria within the project. He added that the project had met with many difficulties, especially delays in documentation of environmental management plans, due to a poor understanding of World Bank requirements by the GoL. There had also been delays in developing a resettlement action plan for the project. The World Bank task manager for the ADP, Susan Shen, admitted that delays to many project components had caused a fall in the project's potential effectiveness (Mixab 2005). Others familiar with the project provide franker assessments concerning its problems. One observer claimed project managers were under considerable pressure because so little has been achieved over the first three years. In addition, there have been problems with project accounting. The accountant position in the project changed hands seven times over its first two years, resulting in considerable confusion. According to a consultant working with the World Bank, the Bank accused The National Agriculture and Forestry Extension Service (NAFES), which is responsible for the implementation of the project at the central level, of corruption. In 2005, efforts were made to transfer the project to another GoL executing agency, although in the end this could not be done.

In addition, the VIP part of the ADP ran into trouble. This component was implemented in nine villages in Samakhixay, Sanamxay, and Saysettha Districts in Attapeu. One problem was that the program stipulated that farmers were supposed to receive funds directly from the project so that they could purchase the inputs that they required. However, in reality, officials had different ideas. Some villagers believe these officials may have wanted to gain financially by being involved in the procurement process and so bought the inputs and provided them to the villagers instead. According to a consultant working with the project, all the small loans using Japanese grant money were dispersed to poor people but without much success in terms of the activities funded. The problems of the project may never be fully known, as the GoL no longer has funds available to pay for monitoring the effectiveness of the loans.

Pump-Based Irrigation Projects

During the late 1990s the GoL launched a massive program of investment in dry-season pump-based irrigation. For a limited time there was a development frenzy regarding these schemes in southern Laos. At the time, the GoL invested a large amount (an estimated US$30 million) of its meager foreign exchange reserves to purchase large numbers of diesel and electricity powered irrigation pumps from India (Shoemaker et al. 2001). Unfortunately, most of these investments were for poorly planned and ill-conceived projects that have shown poor results. There are still many on-going problems with these pump irrigation projects. No data related to how much farmers owe for pump irrigation electricity bills are available for the Xekong River Basin. However, recent reports indicate that there are serious repayment problems throughout Laos, including in the Xekong Basin. The central statistics indicate that 193 irrigation groups owe 19 billion kip to EdL for power provided to pump water into their irrigated fields (Latsaphao 2005c). The former Minister of the Ministry of Industry and Handicrafts, Oneneua Phommachanh, reported in 2005 that more than US$20 million in unpaid electricity bills needed to be recouped in order to allow for the expansion of the Lao electricity network. He said that without the payment of debts, expansion of electricity services would be difficult. He also pointed out that the outstanding debt was of concern to international organizations that might lend them money to expand rural electricity networks (Southivongnorath 2005).

Pump irrigation was developed more extensively in Attapeu Province than in Xekong, as there is much more potential for lowland wet-rice agriculture near the large rivers in Attapeu. Initially, a large number of farmers in many villages were enthusiastic about the prospects of growing two rice crops a year, as was the case in many other parts of the country. Some enthusiastic farmers—and especially government officials—even talked about achieving three harvests a year, as is sometimes done in the Mekong Delta in Vietnam. This enthusiasm, however, proved short lived. Farmers have already become disillusioned.

In addition to the previously discussed pest issues, the high costs of diesel fuel (even though the GoL tried to buffer these costs through subsidies) and, to a lesser extent, electricity (where available), became an important factor, as the costs quickly became higher than the benefits. This was especially true after the Lao currency was heavily devalued in the late 1990s, causing the costs of fuel to skyrocket. The increasing costs of imported chemical fertilizers and pesticides also discouraged dry season production. To make matters worse, large numbers of pump irrigation projects were implemented virtually simultaneously in the 1990s, which totally overwhelmed the small irrigation departments of the districts and provinces, resulting in many poorly designed and implemented projects. As mentioned above, farmers began to notice that, after growing dry season rice crops using chemical fertilizers in the dry season, their wet season rice crops declined due to losses in soil fertility. Previously, many farmers had not used any chemical fertilizers to grow rice in the rainy season but, all of a sudden, not using chemical fertilizers became less feasible. The final straw was the decline in rice prices at the end of the 1990s and the beginning of the twenty-first century. In just a couple of years, all the diesel-operated pumps in the Xekong Basin became idle. Not long afterward the electrical pumps, like the Nakengkham project (see above section) also ceased to function.

In recent years dry season wet-rice cultivation has continued to decline. For example, in Champasak Province, areas under dry season rice cultivation fell from 7,226 ha in 2004 to 2,700 ha in 2005. This was attributed partly to many farmers switching from rice to other market crops like soybeans, corn, long beans, and watermelons that require less water and labor. According to the Champasak Agriculture Office, another important reason for the decline was that the price of paddy rice declined from 1,200 kip/kg in 2004 to 1,100 kip/kg in 2005, even though the cost of production had increased over the same period, mainly due to increased fuel costs for tractors and pump irrigation (*Vientiane Times* 2005c).

In Xekong Province, dry season rice production also fell short of expectations in 2005, due to less rice being planted and declining yields. In 2005, 368 ha of dry season rice was planted, and the average yield was expected to be 3.8 tons/ha. Soukan Phanthalat, the head of the province's agriculture section, blamed inadequate water supply and insufficient use of fertilizers by farmers for these declines (*Vientiane Times* 2005l). In Lamam District, even though the total area under production actually increased to 241 ha, the harvest per hectare was expected to decline from

4.0 to 3.5 tons/ha, apparently due to the fact that many villagers were refusing to apply large amounts of expensive and soil-damaging chemical fertilizers. There was also an inadequate supply of irrigation water in some areas, leading to disputes over access to water for irrigating crops (Leukai 2005). However, in 2006, 408 ha of dry season rice paddy were planted, 40 more than in 2005 (*Vientiane Times* 2006a).

In Attapeu Province, dry season rice farmers had a hard time getting a reasonable price for their harvest in 2005 because rice traders complained that the quality of dry season rice was poor. In previous years, when dry season rice was first introduced, the difference in quality was not yet evident to traders, and prices were generally the same or similar. However, dry season rice, using hybrid varieties of seeds, is no longer as valued, and prices have declined. Harvests also declined to an average of 3.5 tons/ha, partly due to insect damage. The head of the provincial Agriculture Extension Center complained that farmers were refusing to use as much chemical fertilizer as recommended by the government. He acknowledged, however, that using large amounts of fertilizers was problematic because high costs contributed to high expenses and losses.

The brief experiment with pump-based irrigated dry season wet-rice cultivation has been costly. Many farmers remain indebted to the Agriculture Promotion Bank (APB), which extended credit to farmers for purchasing fuel, fertilizers, and pesticides. The APB has also been badly affected due its inability to collect on past debts to farmers, causing a significant cash-flow crunch. The GoL has not been able to generate a return on the large amount of money it invested to buy and import Indian irrigation pumps. Idle and now slowly rusting away, the pumps, which can be seen all along the edge of the Xekong, are a visible legacy of a failed and ill-conceived agriculture development strategy (see also Shoemaker et al. 2001).

Despite this legacy, government officials, particularly in Attapeu Province, are still promoting ambitious plans to expand the amount of irrigated agriculture and rice cultivation. By 2010, the area of irrigated rice fields nationally is targeted to reach 34,200 ha, and the amount of rain fed rice fields is expected to rise to 43,000 ha. Non-rice irrigated crops are expected to increase to 6,500 ha (LNMC 2004). Given the reality of the slow and problematic nature of efforts to increase rice production, these targets appear to represent wishful thinking rather than a realistic planning process. Whether international donors will continue to buy into this vision remains to be seen.

6

Forests and Livelihoods

Compared to other countries in mainland Southeast Asia, Laos still retains significant, albeit declining, forest resources. According to GoL statistics, as of 2002 41.5% of the country was forested, compared to 47% in 1992, 65% in the 1960s, and 70% in 1940 (VOA 2007; Anonymous 2000). Still, the forests of Laos support regionally and globally significant biodiversity, and provide essential subsistence for much of the 80% of the country's rural population (Anonymous 2000). In southern Laos, some of the most significant forest resources are in the Xekong River Basin, well known as one of the most forested parts of the country. In the Xekong Basin, forests have long been an important basis for local livelihoods.

There are an estimated 505,700 ha of forests in Xekong Province, of which 383,000 ha are classified as mixed deciduous (mainly located in Lamam and Dakchung Districts), 63,700 ha are semi-evergreen (mainly found in the Bolaven Plateau), 13,300 ha are dry dipterocarp, 11,200 ha are pine, and 30,400 ha are mixed pine. Included in these forests are some mixed hardwood conifer, montane conifer, and gallery semi-evergreen forests (Goudineau 2001). Xekong Province also supports many important populations of globally threatened wildlife (Rosales et al. 2003).

Attapeu also supports significant forest resources, and it is estimated that 71% of the province is forested. As in Xekong Province, there are a variety of forest types in the province, and these forests support many globally threatened and endangered species of wildlife, as well as local livelihoods.

Despite their importance to both the maintenance of global biodiversity and local livelihoods, forest resources are under severe threat throughout the Xekong Basin in Laos. These threats involve commercial logging, the establishment of industrial tree plantations, and other land use conflicts. International development assistance has so far had a limited impact in helping local people secure and better manage their forest resources. In some cases, such foreign assistance has had negative impacts. This chapter considers issues associated with forest resources in the Xekong River Basin.

Non-Timber Forest Products (NTFPs)

Non-Timber Forest Products (NTFPs) are generally considered to comprise all naturally occurring products in nature, apart from timber, that are collected and used by humans. Therefore, NTFPs include forest fruits, edible leaves, resins, and wildlife, such as mammals, birds, insects, and aquatic animals, like shrimp, shellfish, and fish. However, for the purposes of this study, aquatic NTFPs, including as fish, are dealt with in Chapter 7.

NTFPs are a significant source of livelihoods for people living in the Xekong Basin (Rosales et al. 2003). In fact, NTFPs have been important for the people in this part of the world since the beginning of recorded history. Early French explorers were impressed with the wealth of NTFPs coming from the region. The trade in NTFPs was also important to tributary relationships between upland tribal peoples and lowlanders. At the end of the nineteenth century, ethnic Jru (Laven in Lao), Jru Dak (Sou), Brao (Lave), Harak (Alak) and Heuny (Nya Heun) peoples sometimes sent tribute to the Kingdom of Champasak in the form of forest products (Rathie 2001).

The main marketable plant-based NTFPs collected and traded in the Xekong River Basin in Laos are hard or dry resin (*Shorea* and *Parashorea* spp.) (*khisi* in Lao),[1] wood resin (*Dipterocarpus alatus*/spp.) (*nam man nyang*), malva nuts (*Scaphium macropodium*) (*mak chong ban*), cardamom (*Amomum* spp., Zingiberaceae) (*mak neng*), fern roots (*Helminthostachys zeylanica*) (*phak tin houng*), yellow vine (*Coscinium usitatum*) (*kheua hem*), *Coscinium fenestratum* (*kheua hem khouay*), eaglewood (*Aguilaria crassna*) (*mai ketsana, bo heuang* or *mai dam*), *Persea kurzii* (*peuak bong*), rattan (*vai*), *Pentace burmanica* (*si-siet*), *Thysanolaena maxima* (*khem*), wild honey and beeswax (Superfamily Apoidea) (*nam pheung* and *khi pheung*), *Strychnos nux vomica* (*mak seng*), wild mushrooms (*het pho*), various species of bamboo, wild edible fruits and vegetables, and various medicinal plants (Mollot et al. 2005; Rosales et al. 2003; Xaidala and Ketphanh 2000; UNDP 1997; Baird 1995c). Many other NTFPs are mainly collected for local consumption and use, including wild vegetables, wild bamboo shoots, bamboo for housing, and so forth (Foppes and Saypaseuth 1996).

Forest fruits are important NTFPs in the Xekong Basin. Some are eaten; others are sold. One popular variety comes from a woody vine and is called "*mak nyang*" in Lao. They are often seen being sold by villagers at the height of the dry season. Along the road between Attapeu town and Sanamxay District, they sell for 1,000 kip per "*phout*" (bunch). There are too many species to mention here, but the most popular forest fruits are wild lychee (*mak kho len* in Lao), "*mak fai*" and "*mak neo*." Like *mak nyang*, these wild fruits become ripe at the end of the dry season in April and May. In Kalum District along the Xekong, villagers mentioned eating a lot of wild fruits and vegetables, including ferns (*phak kout* in Lao), *phak koum*, *mak deua* figs, *mak deua xang* figs, and *mak kheng*.

Different NTFPs are found in different habitats so it is critical to recognize the importance of habitat diversity when it comes to collection activities. Floodplains are important for many NTFPs (Mollot et al. 2005), while mountainous areas are critical for different ones. For example, the *peuak bong* bark harvested in Dakchung District mainly comes from relatively lower altitude parts of the district. People in higher altitude areas (such as near the district center) harvest more wild honey. In addition, people in high altitude areas of Dakchung and Kalum Districts harvest pinewood for night lighting, rather than the wood resin for torches more common in the lowlands. In these upland areas, there is little or no hard resin, even though it is plentiful in lowland areas.

Sometimes particular NTFPs appear in many habitats, but in some they are only found in small quantities, making their collection unviable to local people. For example, *peuak bong* (*Persea kurzii*) is common and widely collected in Pakxong and Dakchung Districts but is rare in many parts of Sanxay District.

Although Rosales et al. (2003) attempted to quantify the economic value of NTFPs to local livelihoods in Xekong Province (see box below), quantification exercises of this nature are difficult over large areas, as even nearby communities sometimes rely on quite difference NTFPs, based on local micro-habitat conditions and other factors. Extrapolating results from small numbers of villages is problematic. It is also sometimes difficult to apply economic values to NTFPs that are largely consumed in the villages, or traded within or between villages. While quantifying the economic value of NTFPs is difficult, there is no doubt that NTFPs represent some of the most important sources of livelihoods for local people and make up a significant source of local livelihoods in the Xekong Basin. It is important for people in the basin to have access to different types of habitats so that livelihoods can be supported with various products coming out of a variety of habitats at different times of the year.

The Importance of NTFPs in Xekong Province

Rosales et al. (2003) conducted a study in Xekong Province regarding the direct and indirect economic returns from conserving natural forests. The research considered the benefits and disadvantages associated with degrading forests through unsustainable logging operations, including establishing commercial tree plantations in place of natural forests. Although only three villages, one in Thateng District and two in Lamam District, were investigated to determine NTFP usage, the study produced some interesting findings. Estimates of direct use values show that NTFPs are worth the equivalent of between US$398–525 per household annually, a surprisingly high amount considering that the average income for Xekong Province is estimated to be just US$120/household.[2] The direct value of logging was, in contrast, just US$10.35/ha of forested land.

The study indicated that NTFPs are far more valuable than agriculture sources in subsistence economies, especially for the poor, and that NTFPs are an especially important source of non-cash income for local people (Rosales et al. 2003). The Xekong government only spends the equivalent of about US$1,887 a year on forest protection, which amounts to US$0.07/ha for the whole province. The study indicated that it would make much better sense, economically and socially, to invest more in protecting the forest and to allow less commercial logging (Rosales et al. 2003). However, it appears that the opposite is happening. This probably has much to do with who is making decisions about logging and forest protection in the province and who has the most to benefit from different natural resource management strategies. Senior government officials tend personally to benefit less from NTFPs than from logging.

One of the major problems identified by villagers in the Xekong River Basin and in other parts of Laos, including the remote districts of Dakchung, Kalum, and Pathoumphone, has been a lack of markets for many NTFPs (Baird and Bounphasy 2003; UNDP 1997). For example, *mak seng* (*Strychnos nux vomica*) are found in lowland parts of Sanxay District but are not sold there. However, they are commonly sold in parts of Sanamxay District (Mollot et al. 2005). Villagers in Sompoi Village, for example, reported selling them for 1,500 kip/kg, not a particularly high price. The prices for some NTFPs, like malva nuts, used to be high, but have declined a great deal in recent years (see box below). The prices of important NTFPs like malva nuts are critical for peoples' livelihoods. For example, 12 tons of malva nuts were harvested from forests near Kase Village in Sanamxay District in 2004 and were identified as one of the most important sources of income for local people. Even small changes in prices can have a significant impact on village income.

Sometimes marketing situations can be complicated. For example, villagers in Attapeu are only supposed to sell their malva nuts to traders with quotas from the Attapeu provincial government but, in reality, they often sell to middlemen from neighboring Pathoumphone District, Champasak Province, when those traders offer higher prices. Pathoumphone District is an extremely important area for malva nut harvesting and competition amongst buyers to attract village sellers has become heavy, resulting in better prices for collectors. For other NTFPs, like wood resin, the lack of government support for marketing has contributed to sharp declines in prices (see section below) (Baird and Bounphasy 2003). In Sanxay, villagers mentioned that there used to be a market for rattan, but that there does not appear to be one now, although people from Sok Village in Samakhixay District collect and sell rattan.

Traders from Champasak Province buy *het pho* (wild mushrooms) from villagers in Sanamxay District at the beginning of each rainy season and send the mushrooms by the sack to the Vang Tao/Chong Mek border crossing with Thailand for sale to traders there. Traders in Attapeu Province also gather *het pho* and send them by bus to Pakse and on to the Thai border. In 2005, traders were paying 5,000 kip/kg (US$0.50/kg) for them in Attapeu. They were selling them for 45 Thai baht[3]/kg (US$1.30/kg) at the Thai border.

There are also various other marketed plant-based NTFPs in the Xekong River Basin. For example, *khem* is sold in Kalum District for 500 kip/kg, and villagers in Sanxay District also sell *khem*. It is used to make brooms and is harvested in quite large quantities in some areas. Bamboo shoots are another important NTFP in the rainy season, and bamboo makes up an important part of local diets, especially in the rainy season. Sometimes bamboo shoots are dried in the sun and then preserved in bamboo tubes for consumption later in the year.

Resource Tenure and NTFPs

Resource tenure issues surrounding NTFP collection in the Xekong Basin are extremely important and complex. For example, villagers from dry and poor quality *hin lang* (a type of volcanic rock) forest areas in Pathoumphone District (where NTFPs are relatively difficult to find) often go hunting and fishing in parts of Sanamxay District, where resources are more abundant, especially near the villages collectively referred to as *"Ban Mouang Ban Ka."* Villagers there are unhappy that so many people from Pathoumphone come to the area, even though many have been doing so for as long as they remember. They were concerned that "outsiders" were harvesting too many resources when the headman from Keng Nam Ang Village in Pathoumphone was seen returning from swamp eel fishing in Sanamxay with 20 kg of eels. Other conflicts have occurred between local people in Sanamxay and Pathoumphone over the cutting of malva nut trees. This resource competition has been exacerbated by the general decline in many resources and seems to have resulted in some bad feelings between people in Sanamxay and Pathoumphone.

Some NTFP resources are managed privately, while other are managed as common property. The ownership of *ateum ta din* (in Katu) wild palm trees in the upper Xekong Basin in mountainous northern Kalum District presents an interesting example of a local private tenure system in place for a natural tree resource. Each tree has an owner, and some local families own thirty to a hundred trees. Three trees produce enough liquid to make about 30 l. of alcohol a year. In contrast, Malva nut trees are rarely managed as private property in the Xekong River Basin, but are instead recognized as common property. There are local rules (at the village or district levels) that regulate the harvesting of malva nuts, but everyone in the villages where the trees are found has an equal right to harvest the resource.

Hem Vine: An Economically Important Medicinal Plant

Prescription drug companies use yellow vine (*Coscinium usitatum*) (*kheua hem* in Lao) as an ingredient in medicines, and *hem* vine is currently in demand as a base ingredient for the modern medicine known as "berberine," which is highly effective against amoeba and various intestinal bacteria. The medicine is popular in Vietnam and Laos (Foppes et al. 1997), and the vine is also used as an ingredient in herbal Lao medicines. For example, it is used for curing stomach problems and diarrhea. A Lao pharmaceutical company, CBF, has developed a medicine it calls *"Hem-met 100."* It is mainly made of *hem* vine, and is advertised as a "natural" product. The Lao-Vietnam Company also buys yellow vine in Attapeu for export to Vietnam.

Hem is a thick woody vine that grows up trees and can reach 10–15 m long within two to three years. When a vine is cut, the plant does not die, but sprouts again from its base. If not over-harvested, the vine can be sourced sustainably on an on-going basis. Unfortunately, the rate of harvesting in many areas may well be occurring at an unsustainable rate (Baird and Bounphasy 2003).

Very low prices are presently being paid for *hem* vines. A Vietnamese company paid 5,000 kip/kg for one year a number of years ago, apparently in order to encourage people to collect and sell them the vine. It worked, and soon there was an oversupply. This glut resulted in a sharp decline in the price, which eventually bottomed out at just 50 kip/kg, according to Tavang villagers, in Pathoumphone District. Now, due to low prices, villagers in the Tavang area are no longer selling *hem* vines. People from the nearby villages of Phapho and Phalay, also in Pathoumphone District, still regularly sell *hem* vines. Villagers in Pathoumphone District are unsure what price others are receiving for the vines at present; however, wet vines are still purchased in some parts of the district for 150 kip/kg, and dried vines demand 1,000 kip/kg (Baird and Bounphasy 2003).

Dipterocarpus Wood Resin

Dipterocarpus wood resin is one of the most important NTFPs in the Xekong River Basin, especially in lowland parts of the basin. *Dipterocarpus alatus* (*kok nyang* in Lao) and *Dipterocarpus intricatus* (*kok tabeng* in Lao) are the main species used, although others, like *Dipterocarpus turbinatus*, *Dipterocarpus tuberculatus*, and *Dipterocarpus costatus*, are also tapped for resin. *Dipterocarpus alatus* is the most important species, both in terms of overall quantities of resin harvested per year and the harvest per tree. Although wood resin trees most commonly occur near rivers and streams, in parts of Sanamxay District where wetlands are abundant, at least some are found almost everywhere. Research done throughout mainland Southeast Asia has shown that wood resin extraction has a high potential for being sustainably managed by local people. Like any NTFP, villagers can potentially manage these resources poorly, but such cases appear to be the exception rather than the rule (Baird 2003b).

Wood resin tapping involves making inverted wedge shaped holes in the trunks of wood resin trees—ones with trunks that are larger than 45–50 cm diameter at breast height (dbh) (Baird 2003b). These holes are set aflame for a short period in order to stimulate resin production. Then from three to seven days are allowed for the resin to collect in the holes of the tree trunks. The tapper then returns to the tree and collects the resin in a container or a bamboo section. The tapper then lights the hole again, and lets it burn for less than a minute. Thus, the process is repeated. Large wood resin trees sometimes have two active tap holes in them, but single holes are the norm for smaller trees. This is fairly typical of the region (Baird 2003b).

Although most wood resin tapping in the Xekong River Basin takes place during the dry season, some also occurs when it rains. For example, in Kase Village, Sanamxay District, plastic or zinc pieces are used as "roofs" to keep rain from getting into the tap holes during the monsoon season.

Unlike most other forest tree species, *Dipterocarpus* wood resin trees are considered to be the inheritable private property of local people. If these trees grow up naturally, they are initially considered to be the community's common property, but if an individual invests labor in cutting a hole in the trunk of a tree for tapping, the tree becomes his exclusive property. Anyone else who wants to tap the tree must ask the owner's permission before doing so (Baird 2003b).

People from many villages in Attapeu Province use *Dipterocarpus* wood resin to make torches for night lighting, and villagers also sell torches in urban areas to use for starting cooking fires. Sanamxay is probably the most important district in the Xekong River Basin for wood resin collection. In Kase Village, where wetlands are common, wood resin is mixed with rotten wood (*khone doke* in Lao) and wrapped in *bai teuay* swamp reeds. In other areas, resin torches are wrapped in the large leaves of *Dipterocarpus tuberculatus* (*bai tong koung* in Lao) (Baird 2003b). People in Kase use the torches they make locally (there is no electricity in the village), and also sell them in the village for 2,500 kip each. People living nearer Sanamxay District center sell resin torches, but their torches are said to be smaller than those made at Kase Village. People from Kase used to sell torches in bulk to buyers who came to the village. Buyers from Champasak Province used to sometimes come by elephant to buy large quantities of torches to take back to sell in Champasak; however, after about 1988 people from Champasak stopped coming to Kase to buy wood resin.

Dongxai, Mai Na Koke and Tat Koum are three other villages along the Xekaman River in Attapeu where resin torches are commonly made for local use and sale. Near the Xekong in Samakhixay District, villagers from Kengsay, Kasom, Halang Nyai, Halang Noi, and Sakhe also collect wood resin to make torches to sell, as do villagers from Taong and Nong Ping Villages in Pathoumphone. Wood resin torches in these villages sell for 1,000 to 2,000 kip each. The resin torches from the ethnic Brao villages of Halang Nyai and Halang Noi are longer than those from Kasom and Kengsay. Villagers from Phoxay Village in Phouvong District also sell wood resin, including some in Saysettha District for caulking boats. Women from Sok Village buy resin torches from Halang Nyai Village to resell in their community.

Apart from torches, filtered and distilled wood resin can be used for various other purposes, including making varnishes and paints. It is also used as a base for perfumes, and *Dipterocarpus* tree wood is popular for construction, although it is not considered to be high quality wood (Baird 2003b).

Bulk liquid wood resin is not currently being sold in Sanamxay District, except in small quantities for local boat caulking. There is reportedly a private citizen living in Champasak Province who buys liquid wood resin. This trader apparently does not have an official quota to buy and sell wood resin, as there have been none issued in Laos since 1996, when officials decided that wood resin tapping was detrimental to the trees and that resin tapping contributed to increased forest fires (Baird and Bounphasy 2003; FRC and GAPE 2005). However, FRC and GAPE (2005) found that the lack of markets for wood resin has not only resulted in livelihood problems for villagers but has led to increased logging of wood resin trees. As one villager said, "If we can't sell the resin, we have to sell the trees." Rather than benefiting the forests, the prohibition on the trade in wood resin removed the incentives for protecting wood resin trees. Some observers have even speculated that the real reason for not issuing wood resin export permits was not to protect the trees, as claimed, but to make it easier for logging companies to convince villagers to allow their trees to be cut.

Local officials still recall when the Commerce Department of Sanamxay District came to buy wood resin from villagers in the early 1980s. At that time, wood resin was purchased by the metal barrel (300 l. each) and trucked to Pakse. The price was 20 kip/liter, but the value of the Lao currency was much more valuable than it is now. Wood resin was only purchased for one or two years. People from many villages in Sanamxay District claim that they could increase their wood resin tapping if there was a market for liquid wood resin, and the prices being offered were reasonable. Loggers have cut down some wood resin trees, but there are apparently still many trees near many villages that have not yet been cut. In Km 52 Village people tap a few wood resin trees per family. They could tap more trees if there were a more lucrative market for wood resin.

Villagers in Hatxaikhao Village in Saysettha District report that there used to be wood resin trees for tapping along the lower part of the Xekaman River and along the road between Hatxaikhao and Vietnam. These trees were mainly used for subsistence purposes but over the last twenty years commercial loggers have cut down almost all large wood resin trees. Nowadays, people living along the lower Xekaman must buy their resin torches from more remote villages.

Halang Nyai villagers reported that some people are selling their large wood resin trees for as much as 200,000 kip/tree, because they want to get lump sums of money. However, a village elder reported that people often received much less than that per tree, frequently only 40–50,000 kip each. "Vietnamese loggers paid for some trees," claimed the elder, "but they stole just as many without getting villager permission or paying for them." He said that the situation is bad and that many wood resin trees are being sold and stolen by loggers. He estimated that in the past there were fifty to sixty wood resin trees per family, but that now there are only a few left per family. The largest trees were the first to be cut. He feared that future generations would suffer as a result of a lack of wood resin trees. In Sompoi Village, locals said that there are at least a couple of thousand large wood resin trees in their village area, apparently in the eastern part of Xepian NPA (see Chapter 9). A logging company came to the village a few years ago and asked to buy them and cut them down; the villagers declined the offer.

One woman in an ethnic Heuny Village west of the Xekong River and east of the Bolaven Plateau reported that she has two wood resin trees in her swidden fallows that are tapped for subsistence purposes. She claimed that she has owned these trees for a long time and would not allow anyone to cut them down.

Hard Resin: An Important NTFP

The fragrant resin of *Shorea* and *Parashorea* trees is an important NTFP for local people in many parts of the Xekong Basin. Called "*khisi*" in Lao, it grows on large trees known as *mai bak* (or *mai xi dong* in Lao) (*Parashorea dussaudii*), *mai chik khok* (*Shorea obtusa*), and *mai tabeng khok*. It is often mixed with liquid resin of *Dipterocarpus* trees to create a substance suitable for caulking boats. Most of the trees that produce *khisi* are between 15–20 m high, and some are taller. Collection takes place year round; however, December to February is considered the best season. In the Xekong Basin most villagers collect *khisi* only after it has fallen naturally to the ground from the sides of trees. In some cases villagers find large pieces of dry resin partly buried in the ground, which they harvest by digging them out (Baird and Bounphasy 2003).

Hard resin production is not a threat to the resource, as the resin often falls out of the trees by itself. However, this resource and the livelihoods it supports are threatened by logging, since the large trees that produce hard resin are sometimes cut down for their timber, or are damaged when nearby trees are chopped down. Unlike *Dipterocarpus* wood resin trees, which are generally considered private property, the trees that produce hard resin are managed as common property where villagers have jurisdiction over the forests (Baird and Bounphasy 2003).

Davidson et al. (1997) reported that *khisi* is the most important NTFP collected in the Dong Ampham and Phou Kathong protected areas in Attapeu Province. In both January and May, they saw large numbers of 30 kg sacks next to the Xekaman River, waiting to be picked up and transported by boat downstream to market. In 2004, people in Sanxay District reported that a company comes to buy hard resin from villagers in bulk and in Kase Village in Sanamxay District local people said that there has been a market for hard resin for as long as they could remember. In Phouxay (Chalong) Village, Phouvong District, in early 2004 villagers were selling sacks of hard resin for 800 kip/kg (picked up by traders). During the same period villagers from Sompoi Village in Sanamxay District were selling hard resin for 1,500 kip/kg. People from Km 52 Village in northern Samakhixay District reported, in 2004, that they do not have much hard resin near their village, and that few come to buy it from them. If anyone does they offer low prices (400–500 kip/kg). Neighboring ethnic Heuny villages[4] situated on the eastern part of the Bolaven Plateau report that they cannot find enough hard resin to sell, as hard resin is not common in their areas.

One Lao trader in Attapeu Province said that he used to advance rice to villagers in eastern Phouvong and Saysettha Districts in lieu of getting hard resin in return the next dry season. He was paying 2,500 kip/kg for chunks of *khisi* from *mai bak or si* trees, and 3,500 kip for pieces of *khisi* from *mai chik*. Powdered *khisi* sold for 7,000 kip/kg. He did that for three years, but villagers still owed him 80 million kip in early 2004, so he stopped. Ethnic Brao people living along the Xexou River in Don Ngieu, Keng Makheua and Boung Vay Villages in Saysettha District reported that their most important source of income was selling hard resin. They also confirmed that traders sometimes give rice to villagers when supplies are low in the rainy season, and that the villagers repay those traders with hard resin the following year. However, locals also reported that logging in the forests near their villages is making it increasingly difficult to obtain hard resin.

A company owned by Mr. Oun, based in Attapeu, buys hard resin as well as strychnine nuts (*mak seng*), malva nuts (*mak chong*), and *peuak bong* bark. Locals from Kase Village reported that they were required to sell their NTFPs to this company. They believed they had to do this, or they might lose their quota in the future.

Eaglewood Resin: A Valuable NTFP

Eaglewood resin (*Aguilaria crassna*) (*mai ketsana*, *bo heuang* or *mai dam* in Lao) is probably the most valuable NTFP in the Xekong River Basin by weight. There are twelve grades of eaglewood resin, with widely varying prices ranging from as little as 3,000 kip per 100 grams to US$8,000 per 100 grams. Only about one in ten eaglewood trees contain marketable quantities of resin. While much of the collection in recent decades has been illegal, a legal harvest was allowed in Dakchung and Kalum Districts until it was cancelled in 2004. Reportedly, the provincial government wanted US$15,000 from Vietnamese collectors for the right to harvest eaglewood, but the Vietnamese said it was too expensive and refused to pay. In a separate arrangement, the village of Thamdeng, in Kalum District, received 10,000 kip for each eaglewood tree, regardless of its grade, that a Vietnamese company harvested near their village. This was considered to be a poor deal for the villagers.

In Attapeu it is reported that there has not been a legal harvest of eaglewood resin for many years, but this has not stopped Vietnamese from illegally harvesting eaglewood resin in the province. In general, villagers in Laos have not been very aware of the value of this NTFP and so have received few benefits from it. Vietnamese harvesters have been reticent about transferring their knowledge to Lao villagers. In some cases Lao people are employed by the Vietnamese to guide them to trees, but in other instances villagers have only learnt about the value of the eaglewood resources near their communities after the resource has already been overexploited and depleted by outsiders. Depletion of eaglewood trees is, in fact, a problem throughout much of the Xekong Basin. At Km 35 in Pakxong District there is a small factory for extracting eaglewood resin.

It is unclear exactly how the resin in eaglewood trees comes to be. In the past it was thought that insect infestation triggered resin production; however, Anders Jensen, who is studying eaglewood in Laos, reports that insect infestation may not be the only cause and that production may have something to do with tree wounds. Tree wasps are also believed to play a role in resin production. Fungus may also be a cause, but it has been found that even sterile wood creates the resin, so fungus is certainly not the sole cause. There is presently no clear conclusion to this mystery (Anders Jensen, pers. comm. 2004).

The Ups and Downs of the Malva Nut Trade

Malva nuts (*Scaphium macropodium*) (*mak chong ban* in Lao) are one of the most important NTFPs for local people in the Xekong River Basin. They are particularly ubiquitous in rich semi-evergreen forests at around 300–700 m asl, a habitat that is particularly abundant in Pathoumphone District. In years when there are a lot of fruits, every village in Pathoumphone has people involved in collecting and selling malva nuts to traders. Reaching 30–40 m or more in height at maturity, and well over 100 cm dbh,[5] these trees tend to begin fruiting at about ten to fifteen years, according to Pathoumphone villagers (Baird and Bounphasy 2003).

Malva nut trees are notorious for their odd and irregular fruiting patterns. They only fruit a maximum of once a year, and the fruits are generally collected over a short period, between the middle of March and the end of April. Baird (1995) reported that locals believe that malva nut trees experience mast (massive) fruiting once every seven years, with an intermediate lower peak during the third year. However, villagers in other areas have reported three-year, four-year, five-year, and seven-year mast cycle fruiting cycles (Baird and Bounphasy 2003).

Malva nuts are mainly sold to China and Vietnam, where they are considered to be a "cooling" medicine. They are also used extensively for curing stomach ailments, soothing the throat and curing dry coughs, including those of singers and orators (Baird and Bounphasy 2003). Malva nut prices were quite high during the first few years of the twenty-first century, but recently prices have declined significantly. Baird and Bounphasy (2003) reported that prices dropped from as high as 25,000 kip/kg in 2000 to about 10,000 kip/kg in 2002. In 2005, prices in Pathoumphone declined further to just 5,000 kip/kg, or even less. This is at least partly due to a glut of malva nut fruits already purchased by traders in Pakse. Some bought poor quality fruits that they could not easily sell. In 2004, for example, one trader in Pakse reportedly had 30 tons of malva nuts from the previous year in storage. This has had negative impacts on villager livelihoods and local government revenues, which have in part been generated, at least in Pathoumphone, from taxing the malva nut trade (Baird and Bounphasy 2003). Similar declines in prices have been reported from other parts of the Xekong Basin. People are still collecting malva nuts fruits, but there is less incentive to do so. There are also fewer incentives for protecting the malva nut tree forests from being cleared.

Many important management issues are associated with malva nut fruit harvesting. Some people only collect the fruits after they are ripe and fall naturally from the trees. Others, however, climb trees and shake the branches to get the fruits to fall. Provided that the fruits are ripe, villagers consider this method appropriate. However, it can be very dangerous to climb up and down malva nut trees, as there are no branches on their lower parts. For large trees, people often hammer small pieces of wood into the trunks to make ladders. This method is called "*fat pha ong*" in Lao. If a tree has a narrower trunk, it can be climbed like a coconut tree.

The most destructive harvesting method is to cut down trees to obtain their fruit. Another way of harvesting fruits, generally considered destructive, is the use of vines or metal wire that are tightened around the trunks of trees to induce the fruit to fall. It is also destructive to set fires under trees so as to induce fruit to fall.

Despite recent price fluctuations, there is increasing interest in growing plantations of malva nut trees in southern Laos. In Thateng District center an entrepreneur is selling malva nut tree seedlings for about 7,000 kip each. Villagers in Tamprin Village in Kalum District have already tried to plant malva nut seed, with district Forestry Department support, but the seedlings were not well cared for and most trees died. There are not yet any successful malva nut plantations in Laos, but there may be potential for these in the future. However, such trees require highly specific environmental conditions, and so care will need to be taken ensure that they are only planted in suitable habitats.

Honey Harvesting: Taboos and Tenure

Wild honey (from bees in the Superfamily Apoidea) is particularly abundant in the rich evergreen forests found in parts of Pathoumphone, Pakxong, and Sanamxay Districts. Some of the most important honey harvesting areas in Pathoumphone are in the Tomo River Basin, but others are inside the Xekong Basin. The Lao name for the main species of bee whose hives are harvested for honey and wax is *pheung phoum*. However, *pheung kon* and *pheung ton* honey is also important in parts of the basin. *Pheung kon* honey harvesting is particularly common in Dakchung District (see below). *Pheung phoum* make large and sometimes long nests, usually on tree branches, whereas *pheung kon* make their nests in the cavities of tree trunks.

Pheung phoum honey harvesting generally takes place in March and April. One person climbs up the tree with the bees' nest in it. Prior to ascending, one "*kheup*" (the length between one's thumb and stretched out middle finger) of wood is collected to smoke the bees out. This wood is wrapped in fresh "*bai tong kouang*" leaves that are quite durable (and are often used as roofing material). A small hole is made in the leaves. After the wood is lit, the honey harvester blows into the hole to get the wood inside to burn. Then the smoke that comes out is blown at the hive to chase the bees away from the nest. Once the bees have dispersed, the nest is cut off the tree branch and lowered to the ground.

Many people who harvest wild honey observe taboos that they believe are important for ensuring success in performing this sometimes dangerous job. Some do not use soap for a day or so before harvesting honey, for fear that the soap might somehow attract the bees. Garlic and the vegetable called *phak kha* in Lao are not consumed by some for fear of causing certain body odors that could potentially attract the bees. In addition, drinking alcohol prior to harvesting bee nests is not allowed. The leaves of galangal (*bai kha* in Lao) can also sometimes be used to ward bees off. No joking or fooling around is permitted when people are walking to where they plan to harvest honey. It is also important when a honey harvester is climbing a tree to carefully consider the mood of the bees. If they are observed to be in an angry mood, the mission must be temporarily abandoned.

Locals have a particular tenure system for *pheung phoum* bee nests in Pathoum-phone District. Each year the bees choose to make their nests on different trees. Villagers search for bees' nests in the forest early in the dry season. Whoever sees a tree hosting a nest has the right to use a knife to mark its trunk. It then becomes that person's property for the rest of the honey season. Nobody else is allowed to harvest honey from marked trees. This makes it possible for honey harvesters to wait until honey production is at its peak in March and April, rather than feeling forced to harvest earlier in the year, for fear that someone else will harvest before them. After the honey has been harvested, the tree reverts to being common property.

The wild honey harvested normally sells for 12–15,000-kip/kg, or 750 ml bottle, in the villages and then much more in urban centers. Once it arrives in towns it is usually diluted with water, sugarcane juice, or sugar.

Local Traditions for Harvesting Honey

The ethnic Dakkang people in Ayeun sub-district of Dakchung District have a long history of raising wild bees in their own special way. Villagers sometimes cut the hives of what the Lao call *pheung kon*, "tree burrow bees," and then transfer the intact hives back to their rice barns, where they raise them for a period before chasing the bees away and harvesting the honey. *Pheung kon* are small bees, and they produce only a liter or so of honey per nest, much less than what the larger *pheung phoum* bee produces.

More commonly, local people cut caverns in the sides of mainly softwood species of trees to create habitats that attract *pheung kon* bees, but without killing the host trees. The depth of the caverns varies depending upon the size of the tree, with larger trees having larger caverns. The height of the caverns is usually one "*soke*" (the length extending from one's elbow to the tips of one's fingers). The caverns tend to be narrower near the outer parts of the tree and wider on the inside. After the caverns are cut out with axes and knifes, doors are made from wood or bark and are fitted to the caverns. A small area is left for the bees to enter. Fire and smoke are used to dry out the caverns for the bees before they arrive. According to locals, about 50% of these human-made caverns attract queen bees that establish nests in them.

Once a year the doors of the caverns are opened, the bees are chased away with smoke, and the honey is harvested. Bees normally re-use caverns for many years. Villagers believe the same bees return to the same trees year after year. In some areas certain people may have large numbers of these bees' nests scattered throughout the forest. Unlike other parts of southern Laos, honey is harvested from these nests in September, while another type of thick, sugary honey is harvested from the same trees in April. It may be that the types of *pheung kon* bees in Dakchung are different from those found in lowland areas like Pathoumphone, since the altitude in Dakchung is significantly higher (Baird and Bounphasy 2003).

Rattan Collection and Processing

Rattan (*Calamus* spp.) (*vai* in Lao) is an important locally used and commercially traded NTFP in the Xekong River Basin. In the late 1990s, IUCN's NTFP Project attempted to train rattan collectors in Tavang Village, Pathoumphone District how to process rattan into food trays, chairs and other furniture. The hope was that they could switch from being primary rattan collectors, selling their rattan to outsiders from processing, toward becoming producers of rattan products that could generate better incomes for local people. Despite its initial promise, the project failed to convince Tavang villagers to make the transition. Rather than gaining any "value-added" income, they still only act as primary rattan collectors.

Rattan are slow-growing plants, and stocks have been overexploited and depleted in many parts of Laos (Evans et al. 2001), including parts of the Xekong River Basin. IUCN's NTFP Project tried to organize a rattan management system based on rotating blocks of forest so that rattan could be periodically harvested followed by intervals in which it would be allowed to regenerate. Unfortunately, this system is apparently no longer functioning.

There are at least seven well-known species of rattan collected by villagers in Pathoumphone District. They are known in Lao as:

1) *vai taleuk*
2) *vai xeuay*
3) *vai xavang*
4) *vai deng*
5) *vai hang nou*
6) *vai kam lao*
7) *vai vian*

Only *vai deng* and *vai hang nou* are commercially marketed in Pathoumphone. They are mainly sold for making cabinets, chairs, tables, basket handles, and parts of rice containers. Local villagers also use rattan for making various household items (Baird and Bounphasy 2003).

Marketed rattan pieces are generally at least 20 m long and, in 2003, they were generally being sold for 200 kip/piece (Baird and Bounphasy 2003). Rattan collecting was suspended in the Tavang Village area by authorities in 2005, but was allowed to continue in the nearby villages in Nong Ping and Taong. All these villages are inside Xepian NPA, and it is unclear why restrictions differ for rattan harvesters from village to village in the same general area.

Wildlife Trade

There is a considerable amount of wildlife trade in the Xekong River Basin of Laos, some of it open and some of it less visible (Singh et al. 2006; Nooren and Claridge 2001; Nash 1997). Wildlife trade regulations are not enforced consistently within the basin, and there are contradictions in government policies related to wildlife trade. In recent years there has been some confiscation of protected wildlife species in the main markets of Xekong and Attapeu, and some checkpoints have been established to attempt to regulate the trade (Singh et al. 2006). However, in early 2006 there was still plenty of small wildlife being sold in some places, such as at bus halting-places on the road between Xekong and Attapeu at Km 52 Village. Cooked squirrels and small birds are regularly sold there, and a rare live Asian Pied hornbill (*nok keng* in Lao) was seen for sale in 2006. However, threatened and endangered species are not sold as openly as they once were. Many of the most rare and highest valued species probably end up in markets in Vietnam and Thailand and never appear on the Lao market (Singh et al. 2006; Nooren and Claridge 2001; Nash 1997).

Wildlife trade remains an important economic activity for some local people in many parts of the Xekong Basin, despite the fact that many populations of wildlife, especially large and rare species, have declined in recent years. Nowadays, it is more common to see villagers searching for scrap metal in the forests than it is to see them looking for wildlife or other NTFPs (see Chapter 8). The importance of the wildlife trade to local livelihoods has declined due both to a lack of wildlife and an increased awareness about its illegality, particularly when involving endangered large mammals such as elephants, tigers, or bears.

Still, the trade in rare and endangered species is far from non-existent. In June 2004, a NGO worker in Xekong Province was offered what was probably an Asiatic black bear from a man in a nearby village. The worker did not buy it but later heard from an Agriculture and Forestry official in Lamam District that a Vietnamese man had purchased it for 1,200,000 kip, primarily for its gallbladder, which is believed to have medicinal qualities, especially for curing serious bruises and internal tissue damage. Singh et al. (2006) reported observing fourteen globally threatened and twenty-three CITES listed species in trade during field studies in Attapeu.

In the ethnic Brao village of Mak Kiang, Phouvong District, most families are involved in the trade. Reptiles, including snakes, monitor lizards, and turtles are some of the most important species in trade. One species that has been heavily impacted by the wildlife trade is the pangolin (*lin* in Lao), an anteater-type of mammal with valuable scales commonly used in Chinese traditional medicine (Baird 1995c). With a strong market in Vietnam, China, and Thailand, prices are currently very high (Singh et al. 2006), which has fueled the trade.

Another species commonly traded by villagers in the Xekong River Basin is the hill myna (*nok seng ka* in Lao). In Sompoi Village, Sanamxay District, villagers reported that young chicks were being sold for 80,000 kip each. The bird is popular as a pet. When trained, they can mimic human voice and "speak." However, hill mynas have been heavily impacted in many parts of the region due to habitat destruction and the wildlife trade and they are listed as an appendix three species with CITES in Thailand.

Parts of many wildlife species are used in Lao traditional medicines, but, with some notable exceptions (pangolins, bears, tigers, for example), most wildlife used as medicine in Laos are not specifically killed for medicinal reasons but are biproducts of hunting for food or acquired when wildlife is killed for other reasons (Baird 1995c). It can be expected that the new land routes being planned and built between Xekong and Attapeu Provinces and Vietnam will facilitate increased wildlife trade between the Xekong Basin and Vietnam and China (Singh et al. 2006; see also Chapter 11).

Commercial Logging

"There is mounting evidence that slash-and-burn activities may not be as destructive as has always been thought. Logging seems to be a much greater environmental threat to the country."

Roger Mollot (WWF 2005c: 16)

Commercial logging in the Xekong River Basin in Laos has not always been as heavy as at present. Up until the late 1990s, difficulties in accessing forest resources reduced the potential for logging. In Xekong Province, the UNDP (1997) reported, for example, that in 1997 there were no logging operations in Kalum District, due to the lack of road access and because the province had only three official places for logging: one 22 ha, another 754 ha, and a third 18 ha. When government quotas were provided, the timber was reportedly taken from these areas. In the early 1990s, annual logging quotas in Xekong Province were generally between 10–20,000 m³ of wood per year and, due to difficult extraction conditions and a lack of infrastructure and poor roads, these quotas were often underachieved. For example, the military-owned company, Development of Agriculture and Forestry Industries (DAFI) received an 8,000 m³ logging quota in Lamam District, Xekong Province in 1995 but was only actually able to log 1,000 m³ (UNDP 1997). In 1997, the UNDP stated that "It can be expected that with improved infrastructure Sekong will take a more active role in the marketing of its produce, and that commercial logging will increase" (1997: 39).

This was an accurate forecast. In recent years commercial logging in Xekong and Attapeu, and the parts of Champasak Province within the Xekong Basin, has increased dramatically, resulting in many natural forests becoming rapidly depleted. By 2002 provincial logging quotas for Xekong Province had increased to 23,000 m³, including 20,000 m³ of softwoods and 3,000 m³ of hardwoods, and in 2003 the provincial quota was 40,000 m³, including 5,000 m³ of hardwoods. For 2003, it was estimated that provincial revenues from this expansion would amount to US$520,000 as well as US$85,000 in taxes on timber, together accounting for a total of US$605,000 in revenue for the province (Rosales et al. 2003).

Similar increases in logging have been seen in other parts of the basin, and many communities have been adversely impacted by commercial logging activities near their villages. Wildlife and other biodiversity, along with the livelihoods of local people, are increasingly threatened by commercial logging operations, both legal and illegal.

Forestry practices in the Xekong Basin suffer from mismanagement and a lack of accountability. Although the logging quota for Xekong Province was expected to be 40,000 m³ in 2004, it was estimated to have reached only 8,000 m³, as logging companies were not able to cut all the wood for which they had quotas (Rosales et al. 2003). However, these calculations for legal logging operations seriously underestimate the actual number of trees cut. Many loggers are able to pay off forestry and customs officials to under-report the amount of timber that they are exporting, resulting in much more wood eventually being cut than has been officially approved. Anonymous (2000) also reported that the downgrading of logs by Lao forestry officials to less valuable species, and the recording of lower volumes of wood than are actually cut, are common practices. Officials who facilitate this are frequently paid high "allowances" for their assistance. The openness to which forestry officials discuss such practices suggests that they are the norm and that there is apparently little social stigma associated with these corrupt practices. There are various other tricks used by sawmill owners to access timber, including buying wood directly from villagers without having a quota and buying illegally cut timber from the government after it is confiscated, even when the same sawmill initially hired villagers to cut the confiscated trees (Anonymous 2000). An aid worker in Xekong Province said that, "Much of the money from logging is going into the pockets of government officials and companies; 1 m³ of quota often translates into 10 m³ of actual logging."

In 1999, in response to the Asian financial crisis, Laos increased its official national timber harvesting quota to 734,000 m³, in order to try to gain extra foreign exchange, but the quota dropped as the financial situation stabilized (Watershed 2004). Still, the national logging levels for Laos remained relatively high between 2000 and 2004. In 2000/2001 the official quota was 296,320 m³, but the planned and unplanned timber harvest was officially 438,194 m³. In 2001/2002 the official national quota was similar at 260,000 m³, and in 2002/2003 and 2003/2004 the official harvest rates were similar, when original quotas were combined with additional national quotas, additional provincial quotas, branch wood and unplanned quotas. In 2003/2004 the original national quota was 270,000 m³, but 15,010 m³ of additional national quota was added. Furthermore, the official "unplanned timber harvest," including additional quotas for provinces and districts, reached 93,452 m³, representing a large over-cut as compared with what was originally planned by the central GoL. In fact, 378,462 m³ was officially harvested for the year.

The *Vientiane Times* (2004j) reported that industrial processing in Xekong Province expanded 8% more than had been anticipated and that processing in the province was valued at 21 billion kip in the previous year. There were reported to be 389 processing factories in the province, with most production centered on the logging industry.

Indicative of increases in logging activities in Attapeu and Xekong Provinces, the Finance Office of Attapeu announced in November 2004 that it had earned more than 15 billion kip in revenue over the previous year, a significant increase.

More than half, over 8 billion kip, was generated through taxing the commercial logging sector (*Vientiane Times* 2004g). During the same year, Xekong Province generated less revenue, just over 10 billion kip. Again, most of this income came from commercial logging operations, and much of the 11 billion kip generated by Xekong Province in 2005 also came from logging (Keovichit 2004).

In 2005, the national logging quota declined to 150,000 m^{36} (GoL 2005), and the provincial logging quota for Xekong Province was reduced to 13,000 m^3 (Ben Hodgdon, WWF, pers. comm. May 2005). No additional quotas were expected over the year (GoL 2005). Logs remaining in log yards from 2004 were to be considered part of the 2005 quota for the provinces where they are being stored. If the amount exceeded the quota for a particular province, no more logging was to be allowed in natural forests for the year (GoL 2005). Only semi-finished wood products were permitted for export, including peeled or sliced veneer, chip and particleboards, and tree stumps from natural forests (GoL 2005). Statements indicated that, due to forest degradation and loss, the GoL "will reduce timber harvest from natural forests gradually and take steps to close natural forests officially" (GoL 2005: 4). A number of species of trees were banned from being harvested from natural forests, including *Dalbergia cochinchinensis* (*mai khanyoung* in Lao) and *Michelia champaca* (*mai champa pa* in Lao) (GoL 2005). Both species are found in the Xekong Basin. The provinces were expected to organize competitive bidding, following Ministry of Finance regulations, for logging contracts (GoL 2005), as previous experiences indicated that these processes have rarely been very competitive. At the same time, Prime Minister's Office (PMO) Order 25 prohibited the harvesting of all NTFPs from national protected areas (GoL 2005).

The reduction in official logging quotas appeared on the surface to be a positive development as, if implemented, it would lead to a decline in the 2005 timber harvest by more than 50%. One concern was that while stopping large-scale commercial extraction of some NTFPs would be a good step forward, blanket restrictions could potentially have negative impacts on many villagers' livelihoods. But in reality, neither reducing commercial logging nor stopping villagers from harvesting NTFPs is an easy task in Laos, no matter what central level plans or pronouncements are made.

It soon became apparent that these policy changes were no exception. Anyone who observed the amount of logs passing through Xekong Province in the dry season of 2005 would certainly not have suspected that there had been any reduction in logging in the province. Many logs were being exported to other provinces, and a number of new sawmills were operating. Every village visited in relatively inaccessible forest areas during this time was reporting increased logging activities by outside commercial logging companies. There was also continued heavy logging in parts of Attapeu and Champasak Provinces in the Xekong River Basin.

Parts of the Xekong Basin in Khong District have been heavily logged in recent years, and villagers from Phon Sa-at Village reported that most of the logging finished last year because there are hardly any large trees for cutting east of their village and outside the Xepian NPA. Government officials later confirmed that over 10,000 m³ of lumber was cut (in 2005), even though the original quota was supposed to be far less.

There have also been many exceptions and exemptions to the logging restrictions, even officially. For example, PMO Order 25 treats timber harvested from hydropower dams, electric transmission lines, and road right-of-ways separately from national logging quotas and has adopted a "special policy on harvest, bid and export" (GoL 2005: 3). While raw logs were still being exported to Vietnam from Phouvong District in April 2005, government officials claimed that in 2006 this would no longer be allowed. It is unclear whether the regulation has been enforced. For many years there has been almost universal recognition that a ban on the export of raw logs would be in the country's best interests. The export of these logs has nevertheless continued.

Nationwide, the reduction in logging mandated by the National Assembly in 2005 was completely ignored and, in fact, more was logged in 2005 than in 2004. In October 2005, Phouthonesy (2005b) reported that the nationwide logging quota approved by the National Assembly of 150,000 m³ was exceeded by about 500,000 m³ during the 2005 dry season! GoL officials have tried to provide various justifications for this situation. Speaking at the 8th session of the 5th Legislature of the National Assembly (in 2005), Deputy Prime Minister Dr. Thongloun Sisoulath admitted that in the past permission had been given to many private companies to take dead trees out of some of the nation's twenty National Protected Areas but that loggers had often taken advantage of the situation to cut down live trees. However, he said that this practice was about to end. He stated: "We will not give permission to remove dead wood, thus narrowing the opportunity for people to cut down trees" (Phouthonesy 2005b: 1). It is unclear how much of the extra cut wood came from the Xekong River Basin.

In March 2007, Somsavat Lengsavad, the Deputy Prime Minister, made some frank comments at a national forestry meeting about the forestry industry that indicates that there are still grave problems in Laos' forests. "I think the environment impacts can be seen in our age," he said, adding that the value of the wood sold would not equal the environmental destruction taking place. "The declining forest cover has resulted in changes of weather, drought and landslides," said Somsavat, "I think this is very dangerous. Our natural forests are destroyed, but the people we trust, whom our Party and government invested so much in building up, are also damaged. This pains us terribly," he said. "We should look back over the history of our past logging of the forests . . . .We should promote a culture of daring to propose problems for collective solutions. Don't fear reporting problems, we have to analyse the causes of logging and the gaps in our strategy" (*Vientiane Times* 2007).

Sawmill Investments Feed the Demand for Wood

The increasing number of sawmills being built in the basin has been a strong indicator of expanded logging activities. Overcapacity in timber processing encourages government agencies to find ways of getting additional logs to factories even when there are no official quotas for the quantities required to feed the expanded mills. This overcapacity is one of the most serious problems facing the forestry sector on a nationwide basis (Anonymous 2000; Jonsson 2006). The Xekong Basin is no exception.

New and expanded sawmills have popped up at many locations. In 2005, an investor from Pakse established a new medium-sized sawmill in Phouvong District, reportedly to saw wood for local demand. He claimed to have invested 400 million kip in the venture. There are other relatively new large sawmills located at Km 13 and Km 17, on the road between the Xekong provincial capital and Thateng District, and there are two sawmills in Thateng, one in Pakxong, one in *Ban* Phon, Lamam District, and a new one near Datkoum Village in Sanxay District. In Kalum District, there is a large new sawmill being built by the Xekong Phattana Company near the ethnic Katu village of Yaliang, 14 km from the district center. Villagers are unhappy that hundreds of hectares of forest, including part of their community protected forest area, are being cut and bulldozed to make way for the new sawmill, without any compensation being provided to them. Villagers have not been consulted about the company's actions and are unhappy about all the resources they are losing to the company, which now owns the land near the site of the future sawmill. A villager from Yaliang Village said, "We don't agree about the company establishing a sawmill on our land, because we are afraid that all the trees will be gone and that the company will confiscate our swidden and other farm land in the future."

There is also a large sawmill being built at km 17 in Saysettha District and an existing five-year old large sawmill at km 9 in Samakhixay District, adjacent to the main road leaving the province for Xekong Province. According to official statistics, there were seven sawmills and eleven furniture-making factories in Attapeu Province in 2005. The working conditions in these factories are reportedly poor.

At a sawmill in Phouvong recently established by Vietnamese investors, there have been on-going labor problems. Ethnic Brao laborers from neighboring villages report not receiving their full salaries each month. After two months of work, one month of salary is paid with a promise that the second month's salary will be paid after the third month. The idea is to provide an incentive for people not to quit, but this practice has made workers unhappy and has driven many away. There have also been reports of ethnic Brao workers being promised 300,000 kip per month but then only receiving 200,000 kip. This has caused many to quit. One Brao worker said, "We would rather use our own brains to find money than be cheated by the Vietnamese sawmill."

Vietnamese Logging Operations

Vietnamese logging companies and laborers are heavily involved in the commercial logging business in the Xekong River Basin in Laos. Many of those working for these logging operations are Vietnamese nationals. Most work seasonally, spending the dry season logging in Laos and the wet season back in Vietnam. In some cases Vietnamese companies have their own logging contracts but, quite often, Lao companies with logging quotas officially hire Vietnamese contractors to do the work. The Vietnamese have a reputation as hard workers. In 2005, there were officially two Lao logging companies operating in Phouvong District, but there were only a few Lao working with the companies to cut the trees down and haul the wood away. The vast majority of the laborers were Vietnamese. Many speak little Lao, but others, having worked in Laos for a number of years, speak quite a bit. The Vietnamese operations are often organized so that some groups do the logging, and others truck the timber over difficult mountain roads back to Vietnam. They are often particularly interested in high quality hard woods like rose wood (*mai dou* in Lao) and "*mai khen*" (in Lao).

Local villagers are suffering from the impacts of many of these operations. Sometimes loggers lie to local villagers, claiming that they have a quota when, in fact, they do not. Or they engage in cutting well beyond their quota. It is often difficult for villagers to know how much has actually been cut, and, thus, over-cutting is the norm. Local officials often appear unwilling or unable to adequately regulate these operations. Sometimes police or forestry officials go to inspect the logging operations. According to villager reports, these officials are often bribed to look the other way and even to help the loggers make sure that the villagers do not interfere with their operations. The officials then return to their superiors and claim that there are no problems or that they did not find any Vietnamese logging operations.

In an environment where salaries are low and irregular and there is little public accountability, corruption around logging has become the norm. There are reports of how some senior officials, noticing that relatively lower levels officials are getting rich after inspecting logging operations, end up going out and inspecting the operations themselves, so that they can get a piece of the action. This has at times resulted in multiple groups of people inspecting the same operations in unsystematic ways.

Some village headmen, villagers, and village militia, concerned about the rapid decline of their forests, have confiscated illegal chain saws being used by Vietnamese loggers in their village areas. For example, the ethnic Brao village chief of Houay Le Village, in eastern Phouvong District near the border with Vietnam, sent village militia under his control to arrest fifteen Vietnamese who were illegally logging inside Laos near their village. The loggers had a truck and a tractor, so the operation was cutting significant numbers of trees. In this case the villagers were successful in stopping the logging, at least temporarily.

While villagers have sometimes been successful at stopped illegal Vietnamese logging operations, they often become discouraged when, a few days after arresting illegal loggers and turning them over to authorities, officials have returned with the loggers to retrieve their confiscated logging equipment, including chainsaws. The officials will often then claim that the loggers had a quota for all the wood that they cut and that the loggers did not inform the villagers about the quota because the forests where they were logging are not under village jurisdiction. So they do not punish the loggers or even confiscate the wood they have cut. The loggers may then end up giving 5–600,000 kip to the village headman to get their chainsaws back. The money given to the headmen is often not distributed fairly among villagers. But even if it is distributed, or used for general community benefit, the value of the logs cut invariably exceeds the amount of money paid. This causes the villagers to become discouraged and cynical about assisting in ensuring the good management of their forests. They see that the system is working against them.

In one case, an official informed villagers that after all the *mai dou* and *mai khen* is cut down, the loggers were going to take other species, including *Dipterocarpus* resin trees situated along the edge of the Xekaman River, in order to fill their quota. The villagers responded that it would be difficult for them if their resin trees were cut down, because then they would have nowhere to get wood resin or hard resin to use and sell. The official was unsympathetic to their plight.

In another case, a Vietnamese company was provided with a fifteen-year concession agreement for logging in *Khet* Somboun, Phouvong District. An ethnic Lao trader familiar with these forests noted that logging was taking place at a much larger scale than expected. He commented that, "The trees will be all gone long before the fifteen-year concession expires."

In early 2004, an agitated ethnic Brao village headman and other villagers were observed trying to confront a Vietnamese logging company in Phouvong District. The company had previously received permission from the district government to log near the village, but, even though they had already exceeded their quota, they were still operating in the area. The villagers planned to confiscate the chainsaws being used and report the excess logging to the district chief, but they were not confident this would keep the loggers out of their forests for long. They claimed that over the previous three years the same Vietnamese company had depleted their forests, cutting down all the large resin trees in the area, regardless of whether they had private owners or not. For the trees that had local owners, the most villagers could get from the loggers was 10,000 kip for each large resin tree. In Tra-oum, Phouvong District, ethnic Brao villagers reported that Vietnamese loggers cut all of their resin trees down in recent years and that no compensation was provided for the losses. In areas of Sanamxay District outside of the Xepian NPA, it appears that a large proportion of the resin trees that villagers previously depended upon have been cut down in recent years.

The result has been extensive damage to the forests and to local livelihoods. Villagers report that this has also resulted in negative changes in the Xekaman River, including decreased water in the dry season. This has impacted boat transport along the Xekaman during the dry season, making it difficult for villagers to conduct various livelihood activities along the river.

Chopsticks or Swiddens: What's Best for the Bamboo?

Since the 1990s there has been a Vietnamese-owned chopstick factory located in Phouvong District along Route 18a,[7] on the southern boundary with Dong Ampham NPA, and near the Cambodian border. Davidson et al. (1997) reported that in the 1990s a MoU for the factory was signed between Vietnamese investors and the Governor of Attapeu Province. The factory is near the Vietnamese border and is staffed mainly by Vietnamese workers. It is reported to consume the same main type of bamboo (called *"bo mat"* in Brao and *"mai pa-o"* in Lao) that ethnic Brao people believe is the most suitable for swidden agriculture. Villagers claim that the factory cuts hundreds of truckloads of bamboo a year. In 2005, at the Houay Keo Focal Site, an ethnic Brao man, while sharing a jar of rice beer, pointed out how cutting bamboo for chopsticks is much more damaging to the bamboo than doing swidden agriculture in the same areas. He said, "These bamboo forests benefit from periodic burning, and quickly regrow after swidden agriculture takes place for one or two years. Within five years or more it is possible to do swidden agriculture in the bamboo forests again. But bamboo forests cut down for chopsticks take a much longer time to regrow, and they do not grow well." He was certain that investigations into this matter would help vindicate the views of local people, who are often blamed for destroying bamboo forests when conducting swidden agriculture (see Chapter 5).

Logging along the Lao/Cambodian Border: Harvesting No-Man's Land

In early 2005, unknown individuals and/or groups were taking advantage of the unclear international border between Attapeu Province in Laos and Ratanakiri Province in Cambodia to log the forests in the border area. Lao government officials in Phouvong District initially claimed that there were no raw logs being exported from Phouvong to Vietnam in 2005. But when they were informed that Cambodian border police had reported the presence of large numbers of Vietnamese logging trucks hauling raw logs along Route 18a from Laos to Vietnam—and passing through a 4 km-stretch of Cambodia—the Lao officials said that it was not Laos cutting the trees down, but that the Cambodians were cutting trees in Cambodia. The Lao officials then went on to claim that, in fact, the Cambodians were allowing Vietnamese loggers to cut trees along the border, with the Cambodians saying that the trees were in Laos. These conflicting reports make it difficult to know who is responsible for logging along the border, but it is clear that logging was occurring, and that either Lao or Cambodian officials, or both, were taking advantage of and profiting from the unclear international border.

It is difficult to know how much timber is being exploited in Laos, and in what ways. Logging in Laos is never conducted using proper management plans, although at times "sham" management plans are developed once rich forest areas are identified (Anonymous 2000). Criteria for giving out logging quotas are often unclear and non-transparent. Official timber quotas tend to be much less than the installed processing capacity in different provinces. For example, in the years 1997–1999 quotas in Champasak, Salavan, Xekong, and Attapeu Provinces were, at most, one-fifth of the installed capacity of those provinces. Wood harvested according to quotas is obviously only part of what is being harvested (Anonymous 2000).

There is also the matter of provincial and district logging quotas, approved by the central government, for building government offices, etc. These often include quotas provided to contractors not only for the materials, but also to pay for the cost of constructing the buildings. This encourages contractors to extract as much timber as possible through their quota and then to construct the building at the lowest possible cost. Communities receive only a small fee, if anything, for the logging that occurs in their village areas.

Considering the large amounts of money involved, it is not surprising that there are considerable conflicts between different levels of government officials, companies and locals over who benefits from logging, and to what extent. In 1997, Thateng District officials complained that the district was not receiving any benefits from logging, even though 5,600 m^3 of wood had been taken out of the district in the first six months of the year (UNDP 1997).

This situation has led to increasing dissatisfaction and disillusionment among impacted villagers. Some have complained about reduced supplies of NTFPs for villager use after logging has taken place (Anonymous 2000). Declines in wood resin from *Dipterocarpus* trees and hard resin from *Shorea* and *Parashorea* trees in the Xekong Basin are, for example, clearly attributable to increased logging.

Indicative of the view of many villagers relating to the logging situation in Attapeu, a man was overheard talking to a Buddhist monk as both crossed the Xekong by boat. The man told the monk that if the monastery has any plans to repair their temple, they should do so soon, because if the monks wait five or ten years, there will not be any large trees left in the forests. He commented, "The Vietnamese will have taken all the trees by then. There won't even be enough trees to build our houses. You know, it takes over a hundred years for a tree to grow before it can be logged. Not enough time is being given for the trees to grow."

International Aid for the Forestry Sector in Southern Laos

A number of international aid agencies have tried—so far with limited success—to promote more sustainable and equitable models of forest resource management in southern Laos. Following the collapse of its earlier "FOMACOP" project in central Laos, the World Bank initiated the Sustainable Forestry and Rural Development Project (SUFORD)—which is attempting to institute more sustainable forest management in Laos and to provide more logging revenues to communities for their development. Among its objectives, SUFORD is trying to institute is competitive bidding for logging contracts in the provinces. SUFORD is not yet active in the Xekong River Basin, outside of Pathoumphone District in Champasak. There is the possibility that this project may expand to Xekong and Attapeu Provinces at some point in the future. In preparation for moving into Attapeu and Xekong, as well as Bolikhamxay and Sanyabouly Provinces, SUFORD is mapping the forests throughout the country. Already, there have been reports of serious implementation problems for this project (Lang 2006; Jonsson 2006), and it is far from clear whether the project will be able to achieve its lofty goals.

WWF and Sustainable Forestry in Xekong Province

Large donors, such as the World Bank, have run into fundamental problems when trying to implement forestry programs in Laos that are supposedly meant to benefit local communities. This has, however, not dissuaded some INGOs from trying to institute participatory forestry projects aimed at both conservation and providing livelihood benefits to local villagers. In late 2004, after waiting well over a year for permission to begin implementation, WWF started the Sustainable Forestry Project (XEFOR) in Xekong Province. The project's initial objectives were to pilot sustainable forestry for livelihood improvement, integrated watershed management, and biodiversity conservation. XEFOR aimed to conserve forest resources and improve local livelihoods by implementing a production forestry system that would ensure local participation and equitable benefits sharing (WWF 2005a). The initial project partners were WWF, the Lao National Mekong Committee, and the Provincial Agriculture and Forestry Office of Xekong Province. The MAF's Department of Forestry was expected to be responsible for periodic monitoring.

One of XEFOR's main stated agendas was "to ensure the equitable use of the profits from timber sales, thus providing income for community development." The project also hoped to "establish a thorough forest management plan with an appropriate silvicultural regime, and engage in reduced-impact logging methods that minimize damage to soils and residual stands, thereby helping to maintain forest health and watershed function." XEFOR also planned to "recognize traditional areas of protection" (WWF 2005a: 1–2).

The XEFOR project recognized that, in Xekong Province as elsewhere in Laos, commercial forestry operations have rarely involved local communities in forestry planning, management, and revenue sharing—even though "most indigenous groups rely heavily on forests that are being logged and have managed such areas sustainably for generations. Unsustainable and unplanned logging by state companies (and other entities) often results in forest degradation that compromises indigenous livelihood systems like swidden agriculture and non-timber forest products collection, while leaving few if any of the profits from timber sales for local communities" (WWF 2005a: 2).

Despite its explicit commitment to the above objectives, WWF's XEFOR Project has run into considerable difficulty in implementing its vision, given the existing political reality in Laos. WWF initially wanted to institute the project in the more remote districts of Xekong where forest resources are greatest and potential conflicts over resource use are most acute. This was unacceptable to the GoL. XEFOR eventually ended up working in the *Houay* Pen Production Forest, which covers about 80,000 ha in Kalum and Lamam Districts, The area includes the previously designated provincial protected area of Phou Theung and two Forest Management Areas (FMAs), one in Kalum and one in Lamam. These FMAs were further divided into ten sub-FMAs, eight in Lamam covering about 60,000 ha, and two in Kalum covering about 20,000 ha.

The WWF project first focused on demonstrating sustainable forestry practices in two of the sub-FMAs in Lamam District on the west side of the Xekong River and north of the provincial capital. The two sub-FMAs where WWF began work are adjacent to the road from the provincial capital and Kalum District, and include the forest areas of the villages of Songkhone (including the sub-village Ta-neum),[8] Nang Yong, Nava Kang Mai, and Phon Kham, along with other villages. This area covers about 10,000 ha and is an area of considerably less importance for either biodiversity conservation or large-scale commercial logging than the other six sub-FMAs in Lamam District. Those FMAs are all on the eastern side of the Xekong and appear more prone to Vietnamese logging control than the areas on the west side of the river.

Participatory Rapid Assessments (PRAs) of the communities in the project area were conducted as planned. The project also planned to review the Land and Forest Allocation systems and practices in the villages where the project was working, together with the province. Land and Forest Allocation took place in all the villages, but implementation was reportedly "sub-optimal" due to limited financial and technical capabilities in the GoL. XEFOR planned to facilitate the creation of "village forestry committees" for organizing and managing villager involvement in production forestry activities, representing the villages in working with state agencies, and for managing the village development fund established using villages' shares of profits from timber sales. Forest inventory, ecological surveys, and forest management planning were envisioned (WWF 2005a).

In mid-2006, the project, after providing significant equipment, training, and other resources to local counterparts, ran into serious implementation problems, leading to the resignation of WWF's expatriate advisor. The full details have not been documented, but, according to reports, the main issue was that powerful interests, including those government officials benefiting from current logging practices, were uncomfortable with the prospect of sharing logging benefits with local villagers. According to one observer familiar with the project: "The government pulled the plug on it once it became apparent that they couldn't continue the same corrupt processes around logging and have the project as well . . . ." After this difficult period, WWF was able to renegotiate with the GoL and continue with the project. It is unclear what compromises or accommodations have had to be made in order to allow WWF to continue implementation of the XEFOR project, but it is believed that the GoL wants the project to fund development services for villagers and promote plantations rather than concentrate on forest management and revenue distribution issues.

Villager Forest Management and Logging

The GoL has affirmed its support for sustainable production forestry, at least in theory. Prime Minister Decree 59 (2002) and Ministry of Agriculture and Forestry Regulation 0204 (2003) both clearly re-confirm that villagers should participate in forest management, planning and revenue sharing (WWF 2005b). WWF noted that the "GoL is working to expand participatory sustainable forestry management throughout the country" (2005b: 2). Unfortunately, this optimistic statement contrasts greatly with the actual experience of the many rural communities that have lost or are losing customary control over their forest resources to outside commercial logging interests. This is true in Xekong Province, where WWF works, and in much of the rest of the country. Real commitment toward sustainable participatory forest management, at any level of the GoL, has not yet been proved.

Phouvong District officials stated, in 2005, that villagers are allowed to cut up to 5 m^3 of wood to build a house, but that most are "too lazy" to do so. Therefore, the officials argued that it was justifiable for Vietnamese logging companies to take the large trees, since villagers seemed unwilling to cut them. In fact, this is not a matter of people being "lazy." Many ethnic minorities place less importance on the sturdiness of houses than do the ethnic Lao. Not everyone is equally eager to adopt Lao-style houses, although many are certainly doing so. Also, in places like Phouvong and Sanxay, where there is considerable insecurity associated with internal resettlement, people are sometimes wary about investing in new houses, fearing that they might need to relocate again before long.

Village-level land-use planning, as well as Land and Forest Allocation, has been another major priority for Xekong Province. But due to a lack of funding and human resources, the province is behind most others in fulfilling targets set under the National Land and Forest Allocation Program. Out of a total land area of 7,665 km² of land, 66,000 ha had been allocated to 122 villages by 2003. However, most of this progress has been made in the more accessible districts of Thateng and Lamam, whereas only 5,056 ha belonging to 23 villages has been allocated in Kalum and Dakchung (Rosales et al. 2003).

Many villagers do cut down and hand saw wood, both for their own uses and to sell to other villagers or even people living in nearby towns. This is at times an important occupation for villagers, especially in the dry season. Sawing wood is most common among ethnic Lao. Many ethnic minorities have relatively little experience with sawing or processing wood as this has never been one of their cultural traditions.

Tree Plantations

The GoL, some private investors, and, notably, the Asia Development Bank (ADB), are promoting industrial tree plantations throughout Laos. Plans have been made for a dramatic expansion of plantations, although this has not occurred as rapidly as some interested parties had hoped. Nationwide, it was expected that 23,000 ha of land would be planted with trees in 2004, but only 17,600 ha were actually planted. The target for 2005 tree planting was 20,000 ha, but that target was also not met. It should be noted as well that the amount of land planted is not the amount of land where planted trees actually survive. Actual planting rates are probably much lower, as survival rates for trees planted in Laos are often poor for various reasons. In any case, the GoL plans to increase the area under 'forest cover' throughout the country to 500,000 ha by 2020 (Phengphachan 2005; Pansivongsay 2005).

There are many different types of tree plantations in the Xekong River Basin, with regards to the size of areas planted, the people who own the plantations, and the species of trees planted. Some are villager-owned tree plantations covering only small areas, up to a few hectares at most. These provide some livelihood benefits for local communities and are relatively benign from an environmental standpoint. Others are larger-scale industrial tree plantations operated on a commercial basis by outside interests. Those plantations have many more potentially negative impacts on local livelihoods, land tenure, and the natural environment.

Some ethnic Harak people in Pak Thon Village, Lamam District, have small teak plantations. Teak is a native species in northern Laos but not in the Xekong River Basin. It is generally not considered to have as many serious environmental impacts as some other species, especially eucalyptus, although recent research indicates that teak plantations do cause some soil erosion. Moreover, as teak is deciduous, it does not provide particularly good habitat for many wild animal and bird species when grown in monoculture plantations.

Attapeu Province is considering expanding teak plantations, due to their export potential (Syvongxay 2006). In Phouvong District, for example, the district chief has been actively promoting the idea of villagers establishing small teak plantations, and there are some medium-sized plantations being developed too.

The Economic Triangle Development Company, which has a large new sawmill in Saysettha District, is developing a 20 ha tree plantation (species uncertain) near Sok Village, in Samakhixay District, west of the Xekong. Ethnic Jru Dak villagers have found teak seeds and prepared their own seedlings for planting. In that teak has been grown in southern Laos since the time of the French, many local people are familiar with it.

People from Tamayot Village in Sanamxay District have planted about 10 ha of *nyang bong* trees for harvesting *peuak bong* bark (see NTFP section above). The villagers got the seedlings to plant from the district for free. The seedlings were reportedly purchased from outside of Laos. After three years they will be able to begin harvesting the bark (in strips so that the trees do not die) in cycles, and villagers will share the profits with the person in the district who provided the seedlings.

In Xekong, in apparent recognition of the depleting timber supplies in the province, the Forestry Office has encouraged people to establish tree plantations. In 2004, Mr. Bounlith Sakbouavong, chief of the provincial Forest Office, said that this was being done "in an attempt to replace destroyed trees." In 2004,

553 ha of plantations were planned for Xekong Province, compared to 539 ha in 2003. The target was not reached due to poor planning and coordination. In 2004/2005 the government planned to plant trees on 400 ha of land, using 200,000 saplings. It was expected that 200 ha in each Thateng and Lamam Districts would be planted on 1 June, Arbor Day in Laos. Companies were expected to plant a large portion of the area (*Vientiane Times* 2004h, 2004m). Most of these plantations consist of fast-growing trees like eucalyptus. Again, however, targets were not met.

Rhetoric within the GoL, echoed by corporate interests promoting plantations and their supporters, such as the ADB, often confuses plantations with natural forests and equates plantation development with forest protection or "reforestation." But plantations are not a substitute for forests. They are a form of industrialization that actually decreases the amount of natural forests in an area, and turns common property into privately controlled resources.

When large eucalyptus plantations are developed, the impacts go beyond simply removing any chance of natural forests regrowing as soils and water resources are frequently degraded. The manipulation of discourses for business purposes is clearly evident when it comes to the promotion of tree plantations in Laos. In most cases in the Xekong River Basin it is not unusual for mature or younger regenerating forests to be cut to make way for new plantations. These plantations are commonly portrayed as being the savior of the forests, but in reality they are what caused the forest destruction in the first place.

Mr. Sounthone Ketphanh, Deputy Director of the Forestry Research Center (FRC) in Vientiane, has pointed out that it is important to plant seeds and saplings that are compatible with the climate and other environmental circumstances relevant to target areas. If not, the plantations will prove ineffective, he said.

It has also been reported that in some places where trees have been planted, almost every sapling has died, resulting in a loss of investment and a waste of state funds. These problems have arisen due to planting trees in inappropriate places, planting inappropriate species, and, especially, due to a lack of care and watering after they have been planted.

Commercial tree plantations have not yet had a heavy impact on most of the Xekong River Basin in Laos. There were few tree plantations in Xekong Province up until recently. UNDP (1997) reported that there were just 26 ha of teak plantations in the province in 1997, of which most were planted in Thateng District. Two hectares were government-owned and the rest private.

Asia Tech

There is one part of the basin where tree plantations were already threatening local livelihoods in the 1990s: the Bolaven Plateau in Pakxong District. The 600,000-ha plateau, considered one of the most fertile regions in Laos, reaches over 1,200 m asl and has a varied ecosystem of savannah, natural grasslands, and rich forests, forming a watershed for the Xekong and six other tributary rivers of the Mekong in Laos (Watershed 1996).

In the 1990s, the Thai industrial agriculture and tree plantation company, Asia Tech International, obtained central GoL permission for a large tree plantation in Pakxong (Lang 2002). Initially, on 5 November 1990, the company wrote to the GoL to propose a project on 16,000 ha of land in Champasak Province. A year later, the central government provided a thirty-year concession agreement for the project, and took a 5% share in it. Asia Tech's plans fit well with Laos' Tropical Forestry Action Plan (TFAP), completed in 1990 with the support of the UNDP, the FAO and the World Bank (see Chapter 5). The TFAP called for increases in logging quotas, up to 280,000 m^3 annually, as well as more focus on promoting industrial tree plantations (Watershed 2004).

In 1992, Asia Tech began trials by planting 200 ha of eucalyptus, but most of the plantations failed or were abandoned (Lang 2002). The GoL shifted policies and decided to limit eucalyptus plantations to "degraded forest areas." The rich volcanic soils of the Plateau were considered unsuitable for eucalyptus. Therefore, in 1995 Asia Tech abandoned its eucalyptus plantation efforts and switched to planting pine (*Pinus caribia*) (*mai pek in* Lao).

Forenco, a New Zealand-based consulting firm, prepared a pre-feasibility report regarding the pine plantations for Asia Tech. They acknowledged that almost 5,000 people lived in the proposed plantation area on the Boloven Plateau, which is partially in the Xekong Basin, and partially in the Xeset Basin. The report stated, "Encouraging families to become settled in one area and to cease practicing shifting agriculture will eliminate many of the dangers to the plantation" (Watershed 1996: 15).

Asia Tech faced problems in the early 1990s, soon after its concession was granted, when district officials surveyed the district and could only find 12,404 ha of land to include in the concession. This land was handed over to Asia Tech by the Ministry of Agriculture and Forestry in order to avoid delays in the project, and the district was instructed by the Champasak governor to find more land for Asia Tech (Lang 2002). Asia Tech enraged locals when it started, in 1995, to fence off what had always been considered common lands (communal forests and grazing areas for livestock) by local people. It was the beginnings of what was to be a difficult relationship between local communities and Asia Tech. Prasan Singhonsai of Asia Tech stated in 1995: "The land conflict between the company and villagers living inside the company's area still exists because the allocated land contained nineteen villages" (Prasan 1995: 75, cited in Lang 2002).

Part of the problem was that local coffee growers have long been concerned about low temperatures, which sometimes dip below 0 C., and affect the highest points of the Bolaven Plateau, leading to large-scale die-offs of coffee plants. Farmers have observed that when their coffee plantations are surrounded by narrow strips (often about 50 m wide) of natural forest, the cold temperatures tend to do less damage to their coffee plants. As important as these forest strips are to local livelihoods, villagers had largely avoided registering them as their property, as they wanted to avoid paying land taxes. But when Asia Tech was granted the tree plantation concession, the government included essentially all lands not registered as villager property. When Asia Tech hired workers and brought in machinery to cut down the forests and clear the land, villagers became distraught. However, they could do little but watch the destruction, as Asia Tech had received permission to do the work from the highest levels of the GoL. Conflicts also developed in villages after Asia Tech paid some village headmen to identify the lands around their villages that were unregistered (Watershed 1996). Despite local resistance, Asia Tech was able to establish 900 ha of pine plantation (Lang 2002).

While Asia Tech invested a considerable amount to try to make its plantations a reality, they faced major problems. Forest fires swept through many of their plantations, causing considerable damage. It is unclear whether these were accidental, or if dissatisfied villagers trying to reclaim their land, or at least sabotage Asia Tech's efforts, set the fires. In any case, many pine plantations went up in smoke, although others survived. Conflicts with villagers continued. In 1996, the Ministry of Agriculture and Forestry inspected the concession, and in 1997 they removed 4,000 ha from the concession, leaving around 8,200 ha (Watershed 1996). The lands taken from Asia Tech were not, however, returned to the villagers. Instead, the government mainly turned them over to companies interested in growing coffee (Lang 2002).

By the end of the 1990s Asia Tech had run out of long-term funding to invest in the plantations or agriculture projects. Its once high-profile presence in Pakxong rapidly diminished. The Asian financial crisis played a significant role in the credit problems facing Asia Tech. In 1998, it sprayed insecticides on its plantations in Pakxong, but since then it has done little or no maintenance to its plantations. In

2000, 2 ha of maize was planted as a trial, along with 15 ha of sugar cane (Lang 2002), but not much has happened since then. Apart from causing serious ecological and socio-economic impacts to the Plateau and its people, the company also failed to make a profit for its investors, or benefit Laos significantly.

International Development Assistance and Eucalyptus Plantations

There have been cases of well-intentioned but uninformed or misinformed INGOs supporting the establishment of eucalyptus plantations in villages in the Xekong River Basin in Laos. In 2000, Xekong provincial officials informed all villages in the province that they should "reforest" at least one hectare of land each. The motivation behind this campaign was apparently to meet central government plantation development targets. The Canadian organization CUSO was working in the province and supporting agriculture and forestry activities in villages, and it was asked to help establish some of these plantations. CUSO agreed to include a plantation in each of the villages where they were active. For example, in Ta-neum Village, Lamam District, villagers replanted a swidden fallow near the village with eucalyptus trees provided by the province. The locals contributed labor, the province provided the saplings, and CUSO provided funds for the project, including support to transport the eucalyptus saplings to the villages. During a 2001 visit to Ta-neum, the first author found that neither the villagers nor the Canadian CUSO volunteer involved in the project had any knowledge of the well-documented negative social and environmental impacts of eucalyptus plantations. The villagers had no idea what they might do with the trees when they matured, and they were unaware of any potential markets for selling them. They were unclear why they had been asked to plant the trees in the first place, but indicated they had been told they needed to plant trees in order to "protect the environment." Instead of helping the villagers understand and address the actual situation they were faced with, CUSO was helping to facilitate a misguided and ill-conceived approach to forest management.

It should be noted, however, that CUSO does not have an organizational policy to support eucalyptus plantations and that the situation in Xekong represented an isolated incident. CUSO is no longer promoting eucalyptus plantations in the Xekong Basin.

Rubber Plantations

Dak Lak Province in the Central Highlands of Vietnam has expressed interest in cooperating with Xekong Province to establish rubber tree (*Hevea* sp.) plantations.

According to the *Vientiane Times* (2005n), Vietnam has successfully developed a rubber industry, and Vietnamese officials believe that Laos has similar potential to produce latex. Rubber is indigenous to Brazil, and there are no rubber plantations in the Xekong Basin at present. But the GoL has plans to develop them in Dakchung, Lamam and Thateng Districts in the near future. In 2005, Xekong provincial officials permitted some businessmen from Dak Lak Province to inspect the areas with potential for developing plantations and to assist Xekong provincial employees in establishing a viable rubber industry (*Vientiane Times* 2005n). The Deputy Governor of Xekong Province stated in 2006 that Vietnamese companies were interested in establishing commercial agriculture projects involving sugarcane, cassava, and rubber trees: "The provincial authorities [of Xekong Province] are submitting a proposal to the government for a Vietnamese owned rubber tree plantation in Lamam District and part of Thateng District." The plan is to expand rubber tree plantations to 50,000 ha between 2006 and 2010 (Pansivongsay 2006a). It is unclear where this land will come from, but it can be expected that natural forests will be converted to plantations. Fallow farmland of villagers will probably also be converted to plantations.

A Vietnamese rubber plantation project is being developed in Bachieng Chaleunsouk District, in Champasak Province, but not without causing serious problems for local people. Initially, 50 ha of land was confiscated from villagers for pilot projects, to test varieties of rubber trees while the investor conducted further survey work in the area (Pansivongsay 2006a). However, since then the project has expanded to cover thousands of hectares of productive agriculture and forest lands that the villagers once relied upon for their livelihoods.

Under the framework of promoting economic cooperation between Laos, Cambodia and Vietnam, the GoL also gave another Vietnamese company approval to exploit 10,000 ha of land in the provinces of Champasak, Salavan, Xekong, and Attapeu for cultivating rubber trees. This agreement is for a fifty-year concession period. It was expected that 2,000 ha of this concession would be developed in Champasak in 2005, and an additional 5,000 ha in the future. Initially, 1,000 ha were to be planted in Xekong, Attapeu, and Salavan Provinces in 2006. The details of where these plantations were to be located were unclear at the time of this writing (Xayasomroth 2005). There are also plans for a 300 ha rubber plantation in *Khet* Somboun, Phouvong District, near the border with Vietnam, and a Vietnamese company is planning this investment too. Villagers have many concerns regarding the potential loss of their agricultural and common lands and forests due to these rubber plantations.

Ban Na Village, Xepian National Protected Area, Swidden Agriculture, and Eucalyptus Plantations

An example of the confusion surrounding plantations and forestry issues can be found in the ethnic Brao village of *Ban* Na, in Pathoumphone District. The village is just outside the Xekong River Basin, but all of their traditional territories are within it. Most are now part of the Xepian National Protected Area (NPA). During the war, the RLG forcibly resettled the people of *Ban* Na into the lowlands due to fears that they were providing food to Pathet Lao resistance forces (see Chapter 5). A few years ago, four Brao families from *Ban* Na Village, facing food shortages and lacking agricultural land, decided to cut one swidden field each at the edge of the mountain that borders their village's official area, the Xekong Basin, and the Xepian NPA. Their attempt to re-establish their swidden agriculture system brought on a strong reaction from the district's Forestry Section. Not only were the villagers forced to abandon their newly cut swiddens, but they were also obliged to "reforest" the areas by planting them with eucalyptus saplings provided by the government. The Forestry officials' idea of "reforestation" (*pouk pa* in Lao) fits with government policy, but eucalyptus is a non-native species, originally from Australia, with almost no value as wildlife habitat or for protecting soil or water resources. In fact, the oils in the leaves damage the soil and prevent vegetation from growing in the understory. Eucalyptus can also negatively impact on the water table. Eucalyptus is strictly an industrial tree crop, used mainly for making pulp and paper. The planting of eucalyptus in swidden areas can be expected to cause much more damage to the forest and the biodiversity values of the NPA than the swiddens ever would have caused. Eucalyptus planted areas are no longer forests; they are industrial tree plantations. In contrast, swidden fields, after being used for a year or two, are left for fallow and allowed to re-grow into natural forests. Therefore, the swidden system keeps the land under various stages of forest regrowth, whereas planting eucalyptus takes land out of forest and turns it into industrial tree-crop land.

Hello Coffee, Goodbye Forests

Since the early twentieth century, Arabica and Robusta coffee has been grown in the suitably cool climate of the Bolaven Plateau. Originally introduced by the

French, the majority of the first coffee holdings were small. Most were owned and operated by the ethnic Jru people who have long inhabited the western part of the Plateau. Initially, this coffee was often grown in agro-forestry gardens, mixed with various other fruit trees and other domesticated plants. During the war the Bolaven Plateau was a major battleground between American-supported Lao Royalist forces and the Communist Pathet Lao forces and their North Vietnamese allies. This undoubtedly slowed the development of coffee plantations in the region. However, after the Lao People's Revolutionary Party took control of all of the country in 1975, the GoL turned to coffee as a potentially important source of foreign currency. In the late 1970s, many people from lowland parts of southern Laos, especially near the Mekong, were sent to upland areas in Pakxong and Bachieng Districts, and near the edge of the Bolaven Plateau in Pathoumphone District, to clear the natural forests and replace them with coffee plantations. Although many of the lowlanders did not want to go to the mountains to plant coffee, the authoritarian directives of the GoL left them few options but to participate in the program.

During this period the GoL vigorously restricted the private sale of coffee. Because the prices that the GoL paid were well below international market rates, illegal coffee smuggling became rampant. Considerable amounts of coffee were sold via Cambodia. During this time there was much money to be made through coffee smuggling, but considerable penalties were imposed on those caught, including jail time and heavy fines. Despite the vigorous promotion of coffee growing during this period, few lowlanders opted to stay in the highlands for longer than they were obliged to by government policy. Most became sick, and some even died in the mountains, due to being exposed to different climates and diseases than what they were used to. Just as people who move from the highlands to the lowlands often experience serious illnesses (see Chapter 5), so did the lowlanders adapt poorly to conditions in the uplands. As communal agriculture was discontinued in the late 1970s, the coffee promotion campaign was also abandoned. Most of the lowlanders who had toiled to plant coffee in communal plantations in the uplands gladly left their plantations to return to their lowland lifestyles. A smaller proportion decided to continue coffee farming privately in the mountains.

In the late 1980s, when the "New Economic Mechanism" policy was adopted by the GoL, signaling a decline in government controls over prices and commodity trading, coffee markets became more open. Prices were no longer fixed and private companies were allowed to trade in coffee. By the early 1990s, coffee prices were, in fact, rapidly increasing throughout the world. During this period, coffee growers prospered, and coffee plantations were expanded, both by uplanders and outsiders from the lowlands, who migrated into the mountains in Pakxong, attracted by the potential profits. Many farmers also switched from the old style of multi-crop agro-forestry coffee-growing systems to the cultivation of mono-crop coffee plantations, sometimes interspersed with *Thong* trees, which provide shade and improve soil quality. During this coffee boom, large areas of natural forests were chopped down to establish new coffee plantations, including parts of the Dong Houa Sao NPA in Pakxong and Pathoumphone Districts.

In the mid-1990s the French government, with the aim of improving coffee production on the Plateau, began promoting new hybrid varieties of coffee, known as *Cardimore* in Lao. Initially, farmers were attracted to these potentially high-yielding varieties, but many soon became disillusioned when they realized that the high yields were dependent upon high inputs of chemical fertilizers, which they had not applied in the past. Villagers often relied on cow manure from their farms to fertilize earlier varieties of coffee. While the older varieties are long lived, with some plantations dating back to colonial times, the new varieties are short lived. In addition, the older varieties are tall and better suited for agro-forestry systems, while the new short varieties perform best when exposed to high levels of sun in monoculture systems. While coffee agro-forestry systems are certainly not the same as natural forests, they nevertheless can act as important habitat for wild birds and other wildlife. *Cardimore* coffee is much less compatible with wild birds. Already, the conversion of large tracts of older coffee plantations in South America to new hybrid varieties of coffee has been correlated with declines in populations of migratory songbirds.

The coffee boom did not last long. As Brazilian coffee production came back on line and Vietnam greatly expanded its production, the small Lao farmers who had become highly dependent upon the international coffee market started to suffer. Large increases in coffee production in Vietnam, which became the third largest coffee exporter in the world, were blamed for drastic declines in coffee prices (*Vientiane Times* 2004e), but there were other factors as well. Whereas one bag of coffee could be traded for three bags of rice in the mid-1990s, by the end of the 1990s the situation had reversed, with farmers needing two to three bags of coffee to acquire a bag of rice. During this period the rapid expansion of coffee plantations stopped, as did the associated deforestation of the plateau. In many cases it was no longer profitable for farmers to harvest their coffee, as the costs of hiring laborers from the lowlands near the Mekong and the uplands of Xekong Province and elsewhere to collect the coffee cost more than what farmers could receive for their crops. Many farmers just collected what they could with their own labor, and left the rest of the harvest to rot. In 2002, when there was a glut in the international coffee market, Arabica was fetching just 800 kip/kg and Robusta demanded just 380 kip/kg at the farm gate.

Coffee prices remained low in the early part of this decade, but over the past couple of years there has been an increase in international market prices for coffee, resulting in it again becoming profitable to hire laborers to harvest coffee. In fact, 2005 saw the highest prices for coffee in five years at 9,000 kip/kg for Robusta (compared to 6,000 kip/kg in 2004) and 25,000 kip/kg for washed Arabica (compared to 12,000 kip/kg in 2004). There had been a reduction in coffee production in Laos, and in 2005 the country was only expected to export 10,000 tons as compared to 20,000 tons in 2004, with the largest export market being the European Union (*Vientiane Times* 2005e). The *Bangkok Post* (2005) reported that coffee prices reached fresh five-year highs in London, at US$1,204 per ton, in May 2005.

In recent years, there has been an increase in forest clearance in Dong Houa Sao NPA and other forested parts of the Bolaven Plateau to make way for new coffee plantations. In one case, a Vietnamese company cleared about 10,000 ha of the highly diverse natural forests on the plateau for coffee plantations. There are now reportedly 35,000 ha of coffee plantations in Pakxong District, and another 10,000 ha of other crops, including cabbages, potatoes, and vegetables (*Vientiane Times* 2005a). In 1997, there were also 1,472 ha of coffee plantations in Thateng District, although at the time only 1,046 ha were old enough to harvest.

During the period when coffee prices bottomed out in 2002, it became clear that many small farmers were extremely vulnerable to fluctuations in international coffee prices. This resulted in increased interest from INGOs in promoting fair trade organic coffee on the plateau. Oxfam Australia and the Jhai Foundation from the USA both took an interest in promoting fair trade coffee from the Plateau at the time. Jhai Foundation has been actively promoting international organic certification for coffee on the Plateau in order to improve the marketing of Lao coffee internationally, while promoting the use of more organic and traditional coffee farming methods. While these efforts are encouraging, they also involve downsides if the potential for facilitating further natural forest deforestation and local land tenure issues are not adequately considered and addressed. By 2001, coffee-based forest encroachment had already been identified by IUCN as the leading cause of deforestation inside the Dong Houa Sao NPA (Klaus Berkmueller, ex-senior advisor to Dong Houa Sao NPA, pers comm. 2001).

While the Bolaven Plateau remains the most suitable location for coffee growing in southern Laos, the GoL is also interested in promoting coffee production in other parts of the Xekong Basin, especially the relatively cool upland Dakchung Plateau region. So far coffee has only been grown there on a small scale. Following the planned improvements in roads from both the provincial capital and Vietnam, larger scale plantations of coffee may be coming to the area before long.

7

Living Aquatic Resources and Livelihoods

Fisheries

Fisheries are undoubtedly one of the most important and under-recognized sources of livelihood for people living in the Xekong River Basin, whether in the mountains, along large rivers in the lowlands, adjacent to small tributaries, or near wetland areas. Wild capture fisheries are probably more important for local livelihoods here than they are in most other river basins in Laos. A decade ago, the Xekong provincial government considered one of the advantages of the province in comparison to many others in Laos to be that, "the Xekong River provides plenty of fish for nutrition" (UNDP 1997). Even in mountainous areas like Dakchung District, far from the Xekong River, 99% of the villages in the district report harvesting fish for food, 12% report selling fish, and 14% report bartering fish for other goods (UNDP 1999b).

Rosales et al. (2003) attempted to calculate the amount of fish caught in Xekong Province annually. Using 2001 human population statistics, and assuming an annual per capita wild fish consumption rate of 28 kg/year, the official national average at the time, it was estimated that over 2,000 metric tons of fish are caught in the province per year, and that the value of this fish is almost US$1,360,000 (Rosales et al. 2003). UNDP (1999e) reported that river fish were some of the most important sources of income for people in Kalum District, Xekong Province.

Although no one has tried to quantify the value of fisheries in Attapeu Province in the way that Rosales et al. (2003) did for Xekong, it is undoubtedly true that the fisheries in Attapeu are also important and of high value. In fact, they are probably more important, especially in the lowland areas like Sanamxay District, where there are extensive natural wetlands.

Pathoumphone District in Champasak Province is another part of the Xekong River Basin that supports important wild capture fisheries. There, however, swamp wetland fisheries are especially critical for local livelihoods.

Although there have been no basin-wide studies regarding the importance of fisheries to subsistence and income generation, the studies that have been done indicate that aquatic resources, and especially wild capture fisheries, play a significant role in the livelihoods of much of the population (Mollot et al. 2005; Meusch et al. 2003). However, it is important to note that there are significant differences in the amount of fish consumed depending on geographical location. Villagers living in the Xekong Plains in Sanamxay District catch and consume much more fish than those living in lowland parts of Phouvong District (Mollot et al. 2005). This is partly due to cultural and associated livelihood differences between the ethnic Brao people in Phouvong and the largely ethnic Lao people in Sanamxay. But the main reason for the variations may well be differences in natural aquatic habitats. In the lowlands of Phouvong, there are few wetlands, and most streams dry out in the hot season. In Sanamxay, people are blessed with easy access to the Xekong and Xepian Rivers and extensive seasonal and perennial wetlands in the Xekong Plains. However, despite the importance of wild capture fisheries, a disproportionate level of emphasis has been put on aquaculture development, both among government officials and international development agencies (see box below).

Promoting Aquaculture, Ignoring Natural Fisheries

Foreign development assistance for fisheries in Laos has disproportionately emphasized aquaculture for at least a half a century, ever since the United States government started supporting agriculture development in Laos at the end of the 1950s (Bush 2004). For most development agencies, including NGOs, the term "fisheries" is mainly associated with "aquaculture" rather than "wild capture fisheries."

However, in Attapeu Province 84.7% of households report being involved in wild capture fisheries, whereas only 2.8% are involved in aquaculture (SPC 2000b). LNMC (2004) reports that the province has 100 hectares of irrigation canals, 9,600 ha of swamps or wetlands, 5,000 ha of rainfed rice fields, 8 ha of fish-cum-rice fields, 70 ha of fishponds, and 150 ha of dykes. The total area of wetlands is 14,928 ha. Aquaculture areas make up only a small percentage of this total.

In Xekong Province, 85.2% of households report being involved in wild capture fisheries, while 8.2% raise fish (SPC 2000c). In fact, wild fish are even more important than the above statistics suggest, as most of the fish raised in ponds are native species taken from the wild. LNMC (2004) reports that Xekong has 100 ha of irrigation canals, 4,470 ha of swamps or wetlands, 5,500 ha of rainfed rice fields, 10 ha of fish-cum-rice fields, 50 ha of fishponds, and 393 ha of dykes, amounting to a total wetland area of 10,523 ha.

While these statistics may well lack accuracy, they do indicate that aquaculture plays a relatively small role in the livelihoods of local people, as compared to other kinds of fisheries. Another more recent, and probably more accurate, report stated that there are 667 private ponds in Xekong Province, and fifteen government-owned ponds (*Vientiane Times* 2005p).

The above statistics clearly indicate that aquaculture is not particularly important to the livelihoods of people in the Xekong Basin. In contrast, wild capture fisheries are a key part of local livelihoods. However, they have received relatively little attention from the international development community.

There is a lack of hard evaluative data regarding the aquaculture initiatives that foreign development agencies have promoted. However, there is a great deal of anecdotal information indicating that they have not been very successful. For example, an ethnic Ngkriang villager from Kado Village, Kalum District, who had received support from an INGO to raise fish in an aquaculture pond, commented that "The fish are not large enough to justify the labor involved in raising them."

People from another village, Talang Mai, in Kalum District, who also received aquaculture support from the same INGO, reported that their attempt to raise fish in a pond had so far been unsuccessful. The farmer raised carp that he found in the Xekong. He fed the fish with termites and black and red ants on a daily basis, but he was discouraged by the time he was interviewed in 2004. He asked, "Why aren't the fish getting big?"

The Japanese government supported the establishment of an aquaculture center, including a fish hatchery, at *Nong* Bong in Xekong, and also funded some small-scale aquaculture there. However, according to government officials from Xekong Province, those efforts did not achieve as much as hoped. The grand expectations of aquaculture have not been realized.

International development consultants have tended to downplay the importance of wild capture fisheries and promote the development of aquaculture. For example, a UNDP-sponsored livelihoods study conducted by Alton and Ratanavong (2004) in Xekong and Luang Nam Tha Provinces recognized the need for interdisciplinary approaches to livelihoods studies but then still appeared to have greatly underestimated the importance of wild capture fisheries for local livelihoods. They refer to fisheries and aquaculture as essentially synonymous, and all their fisheries-related recommendations focus on the promotion of pond aquaculture. There is no mention of considering ways of enhancing the management of wild capture fisheries as a means of improving local livelihoods, despite the fact that recent aquaculture support projects in Xekong Province have not been successful.

On the positive side, recent livelihood studies conducted in Attapeu Province are notable exceptions to the general neglect of wild capture fisheries by outsiders (see Meusch et al. 2003; Mollot et al. 2005). Both move beyond considering only fish, with Meusch et al. (2003) providing an in-depth look at non-fish aquatic biodiversity, and Mollot et al. (2005) investigating wild capture fisheries in the context of other non-aquatic NTFPs. These studies demonstrate the importance of aquatic biodiversity in local livelihoods in the Xekong River Basin. In addition, Krahn (2003) emphasized the importance of wild fish for the ethnic Katu people she studied in Kalum District, in terms of food security and nutrition.

An important reason for the overemphasis on aquaculture, both by GoL officials and development agencies, are that educational systems are biased toward aquaculture. Both in Laos and internationally, educational systems tend to over-emphasize aquaculture at the expense of wild-capture fisheries. Indicative of the problem, the Southern Lao Agriculture College in Pakse, which covers all of southern Laos including the Xekong Basin, does provide training regarding "fisheries," but this "fisheries" curriculum only covers aquaculture. This is unsurprising, considering that the Lao teachers at the college who have studied fisheries overseas all only received training about aquaculture. Those who graduate from the agriculture college in Pakse often end up becoming district and provincial agriculture officials and so they emphasize what they learned: aquaculture.

The relative ease of quantifying production in a specific pond also favors aquaculture in the eyes of many aid agency and GoL planners. They are more comfortable with the quantifiable and measurable nature of aquaculture, versus the less predictable and more varied and complicated nature of many wild capture fisheries (see, for example, Bush 2004).

While outside agencies may promote aquaculture as one of their "poverty alleviation" strategies, the reality is that it is generally the financially better off who are able to invest in and take the risks associated with aquaculture. In most cases, aquaculture does not play an important role in alleviating the poverty of the poorest.

Despite its lack of importance to date, there is some evidence of increased interest in aquaculture in the Xekong River Basin among at least small numbers of ethnic Lao entrepreneurs from other parts of the country. For example, there are now some experimental cages for aquaculturally raising fish on the Attapeu side of the Xenamnoi River just upstream from the bridge across the river, and also along the edge of the Xekong in front of Attapeu town. It is unclear what species of fish are being raised in the cages, or whether there has been any consideration of potential negative impacts on wild fish stocks. In addition, farmers are becoming increasingly interested in raising fish in ponds.

General Characteristics of Fisheries in the Xekong River Basin

It would take a book to describe all the socio-cultural, livelihood, socio-economic, and environmental factors that differentiate the importance of different kinds of fisheries to various people in the Xekong Basin. The following represents an attempt to outline at least some of the main ones.

Beginning in the northern part of the Xekong River Basin in Laos, in northern Kalum District, people generally have a limited amount of modern fishing-gear, such as gillnets or castnets. Their financial means largely prevent them from investing in large quantities of fishing-gear and their remoteness also makes it difficult to access modern fishing-gear. Often their gill nets and cast nets are small, torn, or are in generally poor condition, reducing efficiency considerably. Local people, therefore, mainly rely more on more traditional fishing-gear like hooks and lines and various types of fish-traps. In Laipo Village, Kalum District, for example, locals reported that they rarely use gillnets for fishing, due to their high cost. Instead, they go cast netting for fish in the dry season, and use pole and lines for fishing in the wet season. In the upper Xekong, the water is too clear for effective hook-and-line fishing in the dry season. The village has only one canoe, shared among all the villagers.

Women and girls frequently use scoop baskets of various shapes to catch small fish important for subsistence. The type of scoop basket is often determined by ethnicity, with different ethnic groups using baskets of different shape and design. Villagers sometimes even catch fish with their hands when the fish hide in-between rocks and logs in small streams during the dry season.

As one moves southwards, the prevalence of nylon gillnets and castnets increases considerably. Some handmade traps are still used, but modern fishing-gear dominates, especially along the mainstream Xekong River in Lamam District. In this area, the Ngkriang people are well-known for their proficiency in fishing, and their knowledge of the river has helped them to become skillful boatmen. They are generally more involved in trading than many other groups, probably at least partly because of their ability to make use of the Xekong as a trade route (Goudineau 2001).

In eastern Xekong Province, including the areas near the Xekaman River in the southern part of Dakchung District, fishing is significant but, as in Kalum, modern fishing-gear is not as prevalent as in the lowlands. People here also use various types of tree barks and fruit to poison fish in small streams at the height of the dry season. This activity is not uncommon in the uplands and is nothing like the much more destructive fish poisoning taking place in some parts of the basin (see box below).

There are increasing amounts of modern fishing-gear used further south along the mainstream Xekong in Samakhixay and Sanamxay Districts, especially for ethnic Lao villagers. The ethnic Lao living in the lower reaches of the Xekaman River in Saysettha District are also heavily involved in fishing, not only near their own villages but also in more distant parts of the Xekaman and Xexou River Basins.

Villagers in Phouvong and Sanxay Districts have similar fishing patterns to people in Kalum and Dakchung. However, fishing has probably decreased in many villages in recent years due to internal resettlement to the lowlands, which often takes people away from important fisheries resources in the uplands. An example is the Kong Mi area in southeastern Phouvong District. Brao people who used to live there had plentiful fisheries resources, but now that they are living near the Phouvong District center in the lowlands, away from the Nam Kong River, they have much less access to fisheries resources. Ethnic Triang villagers from Sanxay District who have been resettled to the lowlands (see Chapter 5) have also reported being involved in much less fishing compared to what they once did when they lived in the uplands.

Wild Fish Diversity

The Xekong River Basin is home to a rich variety of aquatic life, including a high diversity of freshwater fish species. However, it is uncertain exactly how many fish species are in the Xekong Basin, and many remain undocumented by taxonomists.

At present 201 fish species, including 196 native species, are known from the mainstream Mekong just below the Khone Falls in Khong District, Champasak Province, on the Cambodian border (Baird 2001). It can be expected that a similar number are found in the mainstream Xekong River. When upland areas are considered, it seems likely that at least 300–350 fish species are found throughout the Xekong River Basin in Laos.

Indicative of how little is known about fish in the region, a number of species have been described from the Xekong River Basin in recent years (Kottelat 2000; Roberts 1994, 1995, 1997, 1998a and b). For example, the giant gorami (*Osphronemus exodon*) (Roberts 1994) was described from the Xekong Basin just over a decade ago, even though it is a large fish that reaches a maximum weight of over 5 kg. It makes nests out of small branches and roots of seasonally inundated plants and trees at the sides of large rivers in the dry season in order to facilitate nursing its young. The females coat their nests with a sticky substance that causes severe itching when touched. Another recently described species is the loach, *Botia splendida* (Roberts 1995). It is not nearly as large as *O. exodon*, but is certainly more brilliantly colored, with a deep blue body and a bright yellow tail with prominent black spots. So far, *B. Splendida* is only known from the Xekong Basin in Laos.

Three species in the carp genus *Poropuntius* were recently described from the Xekong River Basin on the Bolaven Plateau in Pakxong District, Champasak (Roberts 1998a; Kottelat 2000), and a number of other of loaches have been discovered from the Xekong Basin (Roberts 1997; 1998b; Kottelat 2000), including a new genus, *Serpenticobitis*, which was first described from the lower Xekaman River in Saysettha District (Roberts 1997). One of the species, *Serpenticobitis octozona* (Roberts 1997), is only known from the Xekong Basin in Laos (Kottelat 2001). Freyhof (2003) also recently described a new species of Balitoridae loach, *Sewellia albisera*, from the headwaters of the Xekong Basin in A luoi District of Hue, in the Central Highlands of Vietnam.

There are likely to be many undescribed fish species in the Xekong River Basin. For example, people from the mountainous areas of eastern Phouvong District report that there is a large fish species found only in the upper Xexou River and the upper Ka-ol Stream. Called "*treu geu-nyiang*" in Brao or "*pa wawm*" in Lao, locals claim that this species can get as large as a man's leg. It is not believed by local people to migrate. It could be an already known species, but it might be a previously undescribed species, as ichthyologists have never collected fish in the area.

Although the majority of fish species found in the Mekong mainstream below the Khone Falls in southern Laos are also found in the Xekong in Laos, there are a few species that are either not found in the Xekong River or are very rare. For example, *Boesemania microlepis* (*pa kouang* in Lao) is either non-existent or very rare in the Xekong River, and there have been no reports of any Ariidae catfish (*pa khat ok* in Lao) or *Polynemus* sp. (*pa chin* in Lao) from the Xekong Basin in Laos.

Non-Native Fish Species

Internationally, non-native fish species pose a well-documented danger to native species. To date, fortunately, no non-native fish species have been documented as having become established in the Xekong River Basin in Laos. Fishers from Done Chan Village, an ethnic Lao village situated adjacent to the Xekong River in Lamam District, state that they have never seen any common carp (*pa nai* in Lao; *Carpio carpio*) or tilapia (*pa nin* in Lao) (*Oreochromis mossabicus* and/or *Oreochromis niloticus*) in the Xekong River. This is in line with reports from many other villages along the Xekong. This is particularly significant, as most large rivers in the region contain many non-native fish species, some of which are destructive to native fish populations.

As already mentioned, the FAO and Japanese government have supported GoL initiatives to establish a fish hatchery and aquaculture promotion station at *Nong* Bong, not far from the provincial capital of Xekong Province. The production of fry and the raising of common carp and tilapia is being promoted, within the context of supporting pond aquaculture in the province. Xekong Province has only one aquaculture fish station, which produces about 800,000 common carp fingerlings a year (*Vientiane Times* 2005p; 2005q).

The international consensus among scientists and other fisheries experts is that common carp is a dangerous invasive species.[1] In some countries incentives are offered to those who are able to catch them. In other places it is illegal to release captured live carp back into the wild (see Fernando 1991; Costa-Pierce et al. 1993; de Moor 1996). However, in Laos the GoL and various international aquaculture promotion projects support the raising of common carp. Over the past few decades the species has become widely established in the wild in Laos. To date there has been little research or documentation of the potential negative impacts of non-native fish species in the Mekong River Basin (Welcomme and Vidthayanon 1999).

GoL planners and officials have so far failed to recognize and act on the threat posed by common carp and other non-native fish species to wild fish and their habitats. In many cases common carp have been deliberately released into wild rivers with the misguided intention of helping to revive declining wild fish populations. Exotic species have even been released into fish conservation areas (see below for details). In reality, there is no evidence to suggest that such releases have had any positive impact on wild fish populations. More likely, the opposite is the case. Even if these fish were never intentionally released into natural environments, past international experiences indicate that at least some are likely to escape from captivity and become established in the wild (Fernando 1991; Welcomme and Vidthayanon 1999).

Lao entrepreneurs are increasingly raising their own fish fry for sale, or going to Thailand to get fish fry that can then be sold to farmers. In addition, some INGOs are still transferring fish fry from Pakse using pumped oxygen inputs to the water, a method that is not easy for villagers to replicate due to a lack of appropriate technology. When the fish do not die, this may constitute a success in the eyes of some development organizations, but such "successes" are also long-term threats to native fish and fisheries in the region. While aquaculture is certainly at an early stage of development in the Xekong River Basin, it is likely to grow in the future. Thus, there is an urgent need for caution in introducing new and potentially destructive fish species through aquaculture.

Welcomme and Vidthayanon (1999) have pointed out that the greatest risks to native species from exotics relate to the uncontrolled movement of species and genetic strains into and within basins. They argue for the urgent rectification of the situation by developing policies related to this, as well as mechanisms for enforcing them. For specific regions, they believe that Codes of Conduct should be developed to reduce the impacts of future introductions of exotic species and that regional guidelines on quarantine and health certification, along with brood fish management, need to be developed as soon as possible. There is also the need for education activities for raising awareness in the government and the general public about the dangers posed by exotic species (Welcomme and Vidthayanon 1999).

Despite the urgency of this matter, there do not appear to be any efforts being made to ensure that non-native fish species do not become established in the Xekong River. In fact, the actions of government agencies and donors sometimes appear to be moving in the opposite direction. For example, on 13 July 2005, recognized as "National Fish Releasing and Wildlife and Aquatic Protection Day" in Laos, 68,000 fish fingerlings were released in eleven villages in Lamam District and three villages in Thateng District. Government agencies and the INGOs CUSO and Oxfam Australia contributed fish fingerlings to the cause. However, at least some of these were non-native species, including tilapia and common carp.

Similarly, in 2003 at least 10,000 of these fingerlings were released directly into the Xekong River in the Fish Conservation Area of Ta-neum Village in Lamam District. Some of these were tilapia, and others were two cf. *Hypsibarbus* spp. carps (*pa pak* in Lao) (Joe Bennett, CUSO, pers. comm. 2005) that may or may not be non-native species. That is, they might have been native species but one serious problem is that the genetic strains of these fish are likely to be different from the ones found in the Xekong River. They might come from the Chao Phraya River basin, in Thailand, or they might come from another part of the Mekong River Basin. They almost certainly do not come from the Xekong River Basin. Native species that contain genetic material not native to the basin should be considered as non-native. However, people rarely look beyond the species level when trying to determine whether a species is native or not. While scientific research on the genetics of Mekong fish is still in its infancy, we do know from other parts of the world that this is an important biodiversity issue. So far, however, the issue has received little attention within the development community in Laos.

If the non-native fingerlings had been released into enclosed ponds, the risk of them becoming established and negatively impacting native species would have been smaller. Releasing them directly into a natural water body—the river—was both irresponsible, due to the high risk they could become established, and waste-ful, as most fingerlings reared in captivity are unlikely to survive in the wild. In particular, tilapia prefer relatively stagnant habitats; the Xekong River flows too fast for them to do well. It is likely that they died soon after release, either because of their being released into inappropriate habitat or as a result of predation by native species.

In Attapeu, the situation is somewhat better, as the Mekong Wetlands Biodiver-sity Project (supported by IUCN, MRC, GEF, and UNDP) required, in 2006, that no non-native fish species be released into the Xekong Basin using their funding. Alternatively, the project has supported the release of "*pa pak*" (probably *Barbodes* or *Hypsibarbus* spp.). This may be a native species to the Xekong Basin but, as mentioned above, it is unlikely that the genetic material included in the released fish previously existed in the Xekong Basin. Therefore, these released fish could still be contributing to genetic pollution in the basin.

Non-Fish Aquatic Biodiversity

Little is known about the non-fish aquatic biodiversity of the Xekong River Basin and, so far, there have not been any systematic surveys of zooplankton, phytoplankton, crustaceans (shrimp and crabs), bivalve and gastropod mollusks, or aquatic insect biodiversity. At least two species of freshwater oysters (*ki* and *kouang* in Lao) have been identified in the Xekong, and there are many other bivalve and gastropod species in other parts of the basin. The large blue-green shrimp *Macrobracium* sp. (*koung nyai* in Lao) can occasionally be found in the Xekong River. It migrates all the way from the Mekong River Delta and South China Sea in Vietnam. For people in some areas crabs are not an important source of food but, in small streams in the upper Xekong Basin in Kalum District, locals catch significant amounts for consumption at the height of the rainy season in July and August.

The three rural lowland villages studied by Meusch et al. (2003) reported collecting and consuming four, six, and seven species of mollusks and four, six, and six species of crustaceans, respectively. Even in the uplands, like in Dakchung District, villagers harvest considerable amounts of aquatic snails. For example, people from Dak Vang and Dak Man Villages reported regularly collecting snails from the upper Xekaman River for subsistence. In Kalum town the first author also saw large amounts of edible bivalve shellfish from the Xekong being sold for 1,000 kip a bowl. Villagers in Kalum say that there are three kinds of edible snails in the Xekong (*graw-ap*, *graw-lo*, and *graw te* in Katu). People in Kalum reported that there is one type of snail harvested from the Xekong that needs to be pounded up before it can be eaten, whereas stream snails from the same area do not require the same pounding.

In the upper Xekong, in Kalum, people use a small type of basket trap (*ram* in Katu), which they place in shallow, moderately flowing rapids in the dry season. These traps are tied in place and shrimp are then attracted into them. No bait is used, but the traps are effective in catching shrimp. In Sanamxay District, a mosquito net-like fishing-gear called "*houan*" is dragged through the water. It is also primarily used to catch shrimp.

There are at least a couple of species of mole crickets (Gryllotalpidae) (*meng khi nai* and *meng chi lo* in Lao) found in the Xekong River Basin. They often burrow and nest in sandy riverbanks or sandbars. Children often cook mole crickets in the hot ashes of fires before eating them, and mole crickets are used as bait on hooks for catching *Bagarius yarrelli* (*pa khe* in Lao) fish during the cold season. In Attapeu, people from some lowland villages collect and consume up to seven species of aquatic insects (Meusch et al. 2003).

Wetland habitats in the Xekong River Basin are inhabited by a wide variety of snakes, turtles, frogs and toads. The tiger frog, *Hoplobatachus rugulosa* (*kop* in Lao), is one of the most commonly consumed amphibian species in the basin.

This species is listed in Appendix II of the Convention on the International Trade in Endangered Species (CITES), which means that its export across international borders is supposed to be monitored by signatories (Baird 2001). However, this species is actually sold in large quantities at markets in the Xekong Basin, as are *"eung"* frogs, a species not listed by CITES. Meusch et al. (2003) reported that the three lowland villages they studied in Attapeu Province harvested and consumed five, eight, and ten species of aquatic reptiles each, and six, eight, and fourteen species of aquatic amphibians, respectively.

There is also a large, green, crested species of semi-aquatic lizard or agamid, *Physignathus cocincinus* (family Agamidae; *Kathang* in Laos), which lives in trees near streams and rivers and lays its eggs in the sand in river and streambeds during the dry season. While the agamid try to make it look like they have buried their eggs in one location, they generally bury them in different but nearby locations. Villagers have figured this out and are not easily tricked. They often collect the eggs to eat.

There are at least two species of soft-shelled turtles in the Xekong River Basin, *Amyda cartilaginea* and *Pelochelys cantori*. The first is known in Lao as *pa fa ong*, and the latter is known as *pa pou lou*. Both are also known from the mainstream Mekong in southern Laos (Baird 2001) and from the Sesan River in Ratanakiri Province, northeastern Cambodia (Baird 1995a). Villagers catch soft-shelled turtles in various parts of the basin. For example, one was observed after being captured in the *Houay* Kase during the dry season of 2004. They are often sold to Vietnamese buyers who sell them to other Vietnamese involved in raising the species in Vietnam. Generally speaking, these buyers prefer smaller specimens (see Baird 1994b). Monitor lizards are also caught near the Xekong River, and are both locally consumed and traded.

Siamese Crocodiles

The largest reptile in the Xekong River Basin is the Siamese crocodile (*Crocodylus siamensis*; *khe* in Lao). In recent years, there have been a number of reports about the presence of Siamese crocodiles in Attapeu Province and eastern parts of Champasak Province (Thorbjarnarson 2003; Phothitay and Somphanith 2003; Phiapalath et al. 2001; Davenport et al. 1997). In Attapeu Province, the wetland area in Sanamxay District known as *Beung* Khe is the best-known crocodile habitat in the basin. It has been confirmed by villagers that a number of crocodiles are still found there. The area is 2–3 km north and northeast of the ethnic Jru Dak village of Pin Dong. The ethnic Lao village of Hin Lat, adjacent to the Xepian River, is located slightly farther away from these wetlands, as are Samong Neua and Samong Tai Villages (Thorbjarnarson 2003; Photitay and Somphanith 2003; Phiapalath et al. 2001). About 3,000 people live in the area surrounding the wetlands (Phiapalath et al. 2001) near the border with the Xepian NPA. The area includes about 700 ha of good crocodile habitat and seven separate wetland areas, the most important for crocodiles being *Beung* Khe and *Beung* Ke (Photitay and Somphanith 2003). Photitay and Somphanith (2003) reported that a villager gave a captive crocodile to a Buddhist temple in Sanamxay, but the monks did not know where the crocodile originated. They estimated that there are ten to fifteen adult crocodiles in the *Beung* Khe area, based on village reports. Crocodile eggs and young are seen in some years. Crocodiles are also reportedly found in the nearby *Houay* Kase.

During the 1990s, a Vietnamese company cut a road to *Beung* Khe in order to investigate the possibility of extracting peat from the wetland area to make natural fertilizer at its factory in Pathoumphone District. But they have reportedly abandoned plans to use the area, due to the low quality of peat there (Thorbjarnarson 2003).

The people in Pin Dong Village, the closest human settlement to the crocodile habitat, regularly fish and forage in the area and are familiar with the wetland and the crocodiles that live there. Locals are not fearful of the crocodiles; they even let their young children play near the swamp where crocodiles are found. They report that there has never been a crocodile attack on humans there. In the past villagers used to catch young crocodiles on fish hooks and sell them to wildlife traders. In recent years, however, the trade in young crocodiles is believed to have stopped. There is nonetheless some concern that fishing activities in the area could lead to accidental crocodile mortality or disturb them in other ways.

Although the crocodiles of Sanamxay District are certainly the best-known population in the Xekong River Basin, there are also reports of healthy populations of Siamese crocodiles in the upper Xekaman River Basin in Sanxay District and in the Xexou River in Attapeu (Davidson et al. 1997). In fact, crocodile populations there may well be larger and healthier than those in the Pin Dong area. Due to the remoteness of the area, there have not yet been any crocodile surveys conducted there. Davidson et al. (1997) reported that when they studied the area, crocodiles were still widely known along the

Xekaman River, but rare along the Xexou River. An unnavigable tributary of the Xexou River, the *Houay* Hintho, has also been reported by local people to support an important population of crocodiles. This area requires further study before the large dams planned for the Xekaman River alter the river's hydrology and ecology (see Chapter 13 for details about the impacts of dams on the Xekaman River). There are even some reports of crocodiles from the mainstream Xekong near Sakhe Village in Samakhixay District. Crocodiles are said to inhabit some deep-water pools over 10 m deep. Many local people believe in the existence of "spirit crocodiles" (*khe phi* in Lao), spirits that are believed to sometimes take the form of crocodiles. Spirit tigers and spirit serpents are also well-known to the people of the region.

Aquatic resources are clearly important to local livelihoods and human health. This is shown by formal studies and can be easily observed in the region. Meusch et al. (2003) reported that a broad diversity of aquatic plants and animals are frequently accessed and used by villagers from various ethnic groups in Attapeu Province. In fact, their study identified about two hundred species that are commonly used. In the three villages that Meusch and his colleagues studied in the Attapeu lowlands, local people reported collecting and consuming sixteen, nineteen, and thirty-one species of aquatic plants, respectively. For example, people living next to large rivers like the Xekong collect filamentous algae called "*thao*" in Lao and "*so*" in Sok. People use it in soups and also to make the famous Lao dish, "*lap*." Another type of algae (*pham* in Lao), is also eaten. It is not found in large rivers but in natural ponds. In the uplands, there are also different types of algae that people eat. The first author saw some in a stream near the ethnic Katu village of Don, in Kalum District. A young boy walking up the stream with us decided to snack on it. In Attapeu, better-off families ranked the collecting of non-fish aquatic animals low in importance but the opposite was the case for poorer families (Meusch et al. 2003). In the upper Xekong River Basin, a Katu boy was seen eating a type of algae that grows on rocks in a small stream.

Irrawaddy Dolphins

In Laos, dolphins are typically considered to be a type of fish (*pa* in Lao), but are, in fact, a cetacean, a mammal and not a fish. Irrawaddy dolphins (*Orcaella brevirostris*; *pa kha* in Lao) have long populated parts of the Xekong River

Basin in Cambodia and, in Laos, as far upriver as a little past the district center of Kalum District (Baird and Mounsouphom 1997). Central GoL officials first recognized evidence of the existence of dolphins in the Xekong in December 1991. Dolphins were also reported from the Xekaman River in eastern Attapeu Province and the Xepian River in southwestern Attapeu. They migrate up small tributaries of the Xekong River, such as the *Houay* Kaliang in Khong District, Champasak Province, especially during the height of the rainy season, probably to feed on spawning fish that are easy prey during that season (see below on fish migrations). The dolphins tend to spend only short periods in these small tributaries and, as soon as water levels begin to decline, they retreat to the mainstream Xekong River in Cambodia (Baird and Mounsouphom 1997).

In recent times, dolphins appear only occasionally to inhabit parts of the Xekong River Basin in Laos (Baird and Mounsouphom 1997). There are some deep-water pools in the Xekong River in Cambodia that Irrawaddy dolphins once stayed in year round. Nowadays, however, they are only inhabited seasonally at best (Baird and Beasley 2005). Over the past few decades the pattern has been for individual or small groups of dolphins to move up the Xekong and its major navigable tributaries, usually in the rainy season when water levels are high and some fish are moving into the tributaries from the Xekong and Mekong Rivers, including *Scaphognathops bandanensis*, *Hypsibarbus* spp., *Hemibagrus* spp., and many others (Baird and Mounsouphom 1997; Baird and Flaherty 2004; Baird and Beasley 2005). They sometimes follow schools of migrating small cyprinids, including *Henicorhynchus* spp. and *Paralaubuca typus*, up the Xekong during the dry season (Baird and Mounsouphom 1997; Baird et al. 2003). A number of years ago two dolphins were seen in the Xekong near Xekong town and, in March 2003, three were reported in the same general area. In November 2002, villagers from Done Chan Village reported seeing a dolphin in the Xekong.

Along the Xekaman River in Attapeu Province, ethnic Brao people have a fable about one of their leaders reincarnating as a dolphin. Generally, local people respect dolphins and do not have a tradition of hunting them or intentionally killing them. Even when they die by accident, people generally believe that their meat smells like human flesh, and so decline to eat it. However, there have been occasions in the 1980s and early 1990s when soldiers who did not know that the animals were dolphins and had never seen them before, shot and killed at least one or two dolphins (Baird and Mounsouphom 1997). In the Mekong, where the dolphins live most of the year, the major threat to their survival appears to be accidental entanglement in large-meshed gill nets. Populations are believed to be at critically low levels (Baird and Beasley 2005). There may be fewer than a hundred dolphins left in the Mekong River Basin, although the exact population size is disputed.

Aquatic Animals, Livelihoods, and Dietary Nutrition

Meusch et al. (2003) considered aquatic-based resource use in three rural lowland villages, one adjacent to the Xekaman River in Saysettha District, one in Sanamxay District, and one in Samakhixay District. The study was designed to assess the local availability and uses of aquatic resources, their importance to local livelihoods, and the overall health and nutritional status of the villagers in the study areas. The study found that local people use a wide variety of aquatic animals and plants, and that fish and other aquatic animals are the most important source of animal protein for local people. However, the research also concluded that, despite the importance of aquatic resources to local livelihoods and diets, there was still evidence of malnutrition and under nutrition among the local populations, indicating that typical diets are insufficient in the quantity and quality of food products consumed and are especially low in proteins and fats. Significantly, the study concluded that strategies for rural development, food security maintenance, and poverty alleviation should especially consider natural resource management issues in order to ensure the good health and well-being of local people.

Fish Migrations and Spawning Behavior

There is little published data about fish migrations in the Xekong River Basin, but they are important indeed. Roberts and Baird (1995b) provided some information about fish migrations in the Xekong Basin, as did Roberts and Warren (1994). Baird (1995a) reported that the majority of fish species in the Sesan River in northeast Cambodia migrate to and from the Sesan River and the Mekong at various times of the year to spawn and shelter in the shallows, streams, pools and rice fields. In that the Xekong River has many similar characteristics, it is likely that the situation there is similar. Baird and Flaherty (2004) hypothesized about important medium sized carps migrating between the Xekong, Sesan and Srepok rivers and the Mekong River in northeastern Cambodia and southern Laos. Baird et al. (1999) presents information about the migrations of many species of fishes in the Xekong

Basin in Laos. However, there is certainly much about the migrations of even the most important fish species that has yet to be documented. Some of the main fish migrations in the Xekong Basin are tentatively outlined below.

May to July

Every year during this period, when the monsoon rains arrive and the rivers and streams start to swell, many species of fish begin to migrate up the Xekong River from the Mekong, and from the Xekong into smaller tributaries. At this time fish also migrate up the Sesan and Srepok Rivers (Baird 1995a). Some of the most prominent species that migrate at this time of year are the medium-sized cyprinid carps ("white fish"), *Scaphognathops bandanensis* (*pa pian* in Lao),[2] *Mekongina erythrospila* (*pa sa-i*), *Labeo erythropterus* (*pa va souang*), *Bangana behri* (*pa va na no*), *Hypsibarbus malcolmi* (*pa pak kom*), *Cirrhinus molitorella* (*pa keng*), and possibly others. Most of these species enter tributaries to spawn during the monsoon season (Baird and Flaherty 2004).

At around the same time of year, a number of species of "black fish," including *Channa striata* (*pa kho*), *Clarias batratchus* (*pa douk*), *Systomus orphroides* (*pa pok*), *Trichogaster* spp. (*pa kadeut*), *Rasbora* spp. (*pa sieu ao*), and others, also enter streams and other wetlands, including lowland rice fields, where they reproduce (Baird et al. 1999).

Also in May, a number of Pangasid catfish enter the Xekong from the Mekong River. One large species is *Pangasius krempfi* (*pa souay hang leuang*), which migrates up the Mekong from the sea and brackish water areas in the Mekong Delta of Vietnam to spawn in freshwater during the rainy season (Roberts and Baird 1995a; Hogan et al. 2004; 2007). Other Pangasid catfishes migrate up the Xekong from the Mekong during this period, including *Pangasius larnaudei* (*pa peung*), *Pangasius hypophthalmus* (*pa souay kheo*), *Pangasius bocourti* (*pa nyang*), and *Pangasius macronema* (*pa nyone thamada*) (Baird et al. 1999; 2004).

In addition, other large catfishes, *Wallago attu* (*pa khao*) and *Wallago leeri* (*pa khoun*), migrate up the Xekong's tributaries at the beginning of the rainy season.

July to September

At the height of the rainy season, between July and September, *Labeo erythropterus* (*pa va souang*) and *Bangana behri* (*pa va na no*) migrate upriver and spawn near the surface of the water and in the middle of the channel of the Xekong. This happens both in the upper river in Kalum and in lower parts in Sanamxay. Local people call the spawning behavior of this species "*pa oke peo*," which means "the fish go out to the main part of the channel." Floating gill nets (*mong lai*) are used to catch large spawning individuals at this time of year. These fish are caught throughout the mainstream Xekong River, but also along the Xekaman River, where individuals reaching up to 20 kg have been reported. In the mainstream Xekong River, some of these large *L. erythropterus* reportedly reach 20–30 kg. Sakhe Village in Samakhixay District is one of the main communities involved in the fishery. Fishing takes place in July, August, or September, depending upon the particular location. (There is some variation from place to place.) However, in recent years there has been increasing concern about the impact to fish populations of catching these important brood fish during their spawning period. Therefore, the fishery has been banned at the district and provincial levels for a number of years. The ban appears to be only lightly and sporadically enforced, and the fishery continues in most areas. Sakhe villagers sell most of the fish that they catch in Attapeu town, but many of those fish end up being exported to Pakse or to Thailand via Ubon Ratchathani.

September to November

Wallago attu (*pa khao*) and *Wallago leeri* (*pa khoun*) migrate out of some medium-sized lowland streams, such as the Xekhampho and Xepian Rivers, and the Tangao and Khaliang streams, at the end of the rainy season, and there are important bag net (*chip*) fisheries associated with the movement of these very large fish.

At the end of the monsoon season, when water levels decline, many species of fish begin retreating from streams and wetlands, and moving into larger perennial water bodies, especially large rivers. At this time fence-filter traps (*tone*) and wing traps (*li*) are used to catch them. This is one of the most important fisheries for rural people in the Xekong River Basin. It is the time of year when the largest quantities of fish are caught; often enough to make fish paste (*pa dek*) for consumption throughout the year. People from many ethnic groups, and especially ethnic Lao people, also dry fish as "*pa katao*" or simply "*pa tao*" during this season, but it is especially common for dried fish to be prepared in the dry season.

At this time the *Pangasius krempfi* (*pa souay hang leuang*) that migrated upriver at the beginning of the rainy season all migrate downriver into Cambodia and later Vietnam (Hogan et al. 2004; 2007). However, there are no fisheries associated with these migrations, as they probably travel down the strongest part of the main channel, where fishing is not possible at this time of year. Other large pangasid catfish also move downriver, although some stay in deep-water areas for the duration of the dry season.

The medium-sized cyprinid carps, *Scaphognathops bandanensis* (*pa pian*), *Mekongina erythrospila* (*pa sa-i*), *Hypsibarbus malcolmi* (*pa pak kom*), *Labeo erythropterus* (*pa va souang*), *Bangana behri* (*pa van na no*), *Cirrhinus molitorella* (*pa keng*), and others also migrate out of the Xekong's tributaries, moving back into the Mekong at Stung Treng, northeast Cambodia. These fish then move down the Mekong, where they congregate near a place called *Tong Deng* in Khmer or *Thong Deng* in Lao (near the Stung Treng–Kratie provincial border). Strangely enough, they then turn around and begin migrating up the Mekong past Khone Falls, with some migrating upriver as far as Thailand (Baird and Flaherty 2004).

December to January

During this season, large *Probarbus jullieni* (*pa eun deng*) and *Probarbus labeamajor* (*pa eun khao*) cyprinid carps migrate short distances for spawning purposes (Baird 2006b). Villagers living along the lower Xekaman River claim that these species are mainly found in the mainstream Xekong River. There are various places along the Xekong where they are well-known, such as Ta-neum Village in Lamam District.

February to March

As water levels drop, large numbers of small cyprinids, including *Henicorhynchus lobatus* (*pa soi houa lem*), *H. siamensis* (*pa soi houa po*), *Paralaubuca typus* (*pa tep*), *Labiobarbus leptocheilus* (*pa lang khon*), *Lobocheilus melantaenia* (*pa khiang khang lai*), *Cirrhinus microlepis* (*pa phone mak koke*), *Botia* spp. (*pa mou man*), *Crossocheilus reticulatus* (*pa toke thoi*), *Thynnichthys thynnoides* (*pa koum*), and a number of others migrate from the Great Lake and Tonlesap River in the south up the Mekong and eventually into the Xekong River. Baird et al. (2003) estimated that at least thirty-two species migrate up to Khone Falls from the Great Lake in Cambodia each year, and the same species are believed to migrate from the Great Lake up the Mekong and then to the Xekong in southern Laos. Essentially, these fish all migrate up the Mekong with some continuing upriver past the Xekong confluence at Stung Treng town and others turning right into the Xekong. Local people believe that these fish migrate back downriver at the beginning of the rainy season, although some may remain in the Xekong Basin all year. Baird et al. (2003) have demonstrated that the timing of these fish migrations is closely linked to lunar phases, although hydrological factors are also a significant factor.

Historically, these migrating fish moved up the Xekong River and other tributaries as far as bio-geographical barriers,[3] such as large waterfalls. For example, on the Xekong, they migrate up as far as the 20–30 m high[4] *Tat Kalang* Waterfalls, in upper Kalum District. On the Xexou River, they are able to move upriver even farther, via the Xekong and Xekaman Rivers, to as far as the large rapids called "*Pha Phawng*" or "*Brawng*" in Brao. On both the Xekong and the Xexou Rivers, large dams are now envisioned to be built on these bio-geographical barriers for fish migrations. On 24 February 2004, the first author observed large schools of *Henicorhynchus lobatus* (*treu riel* in Brao and *pa soi*) moving up the Nam Kong River from the Xekong River near Viangxai Village, which is about 18 km upstream from the mouth of the Nam Kong. Ethnic Brao villagers said that, for the Nam Kong, fish are able to migrate upriver as far as the *Tat Heu Mam* Waterfalls, which is about 20 km upstream from Viangxai and reaches 50 m in height during the dry season.

During this season there are also important migrations of small loach fish *Nemacheilus* and/or *Schistura* spp. (*pa it*) up the Xekong River and other large rivers in the basin. These fish do not move together with *Henicorhynchus lobatus* (*pa soi*) but migrate along the edge of the Xekong during approximately the same season. In recent years, as *pa soi* runs have declined, *pa it* migrations have become relatively more important to local livelihoods. These species are much more important for Xekong River Basin livelihoods than they are for those living near the mainstream Mekong.

All the fish species mentioned above are consumed by humans, and are of importance to local people.

Pa soi Migrations: The Farther Up, The Fewer Fish

Henicorhynchus spp. (*pa soi* in Lao) migrations up the Xekong River have long been extremely important for the livelihoods of local people. *Henicorhynchus* spp. are the most numerous of the approximately thirty-two species of small cyprinid fishes that migrate up the Xekong from the Tonlesap in Cambodia, just as the same group of fishes migrates from the Tonlesap up the Mekong to southern Laos (Baird et al. 2003). However, in recent years the populations of these migrating species have become smaller and less frequent along the Xekong, especially in the upper parts of basin. For example, in Sompoi Village, Sanamxay

District, near the Cambodian border, there were reportedly three significant runs of *Henicorhynchus* up the mainstream Xekong River in 2004. However, upriver there were fewer migrations noticed by fishers. For example, in Done Chan Village, Lamam District, at the southern border with Attapeu, fishers reported two *pa soi* migrations up the Xekong River in 2004, but in the same year only one *pa soi* migration was observed in Nava Keng Luang and Ta-neum villages, in Lamam District, not far upriver from Xekong town. Further upriver, north of Kalum District center, in Kloung, Talang Mai, and Lai Po Villages, fishers reported that, historically, *pa soi* used to migrate past their villages every year, but that for the last three or four years they had not seen any!

These observations by fishers are significant in light of recent claims by the MRC and the Department of Fisheries in Cambodia that *Henicorhynchus* migrations from the Great Lake are not in decline, but that populations are instead fluctuating based on differences in annual flooding, with more flooding resulting in higher fish populations (see, for example, Hortle et al. 2005).

While hydrological factors are critical for Mekong fish production, including the species in question, the situation is likely to be much more complicated than annual fish production being based on hydrological factors alone. Other management factors certainly affect these fish stocks. Locals are claiming that the populations have steadily declined over a decade or so, with seasonal fluctuations based on hydrological patterns playing a role. Meusch et al. (2003) found that many of the households that they studied in Attapeu claim that they are no longer able to catch enough fish to preserve sufficient quantities of *pa dek* fermented fish to eat over the year. This is probably largely due to declines in *pa soi* migrations.

It appears likely that the main purpose of *pa soi* fish migrations during the dry season is to distribute the population over a wide area so as to optimize these algae eaters' feeding opportunities (see Roberts and Warren 1994; Roberts and Baird 1995; Baird et al. 2003). This means that *pa soi* migrate upriver until reaching a point where the density of their numbers is below a certain level. If the density remains below this level, the migration will go no further. If the density increases above that level, the *pa soi* migration will continue until another point of low density is reached and maintained, or the fish will migrate upriver as far as they physically can, before encountering bio-geographical barriers, in order to optimize their density within the maximum available habitat.

This is likely why *pa soi* migrations were observed every year in the past as far up the Xekong as Kalum District, but in recent years they have not been seen.

There are few, if any, fish reaching this part of the basin compared to previous years. This could either be because there are just as many fish as before, but they are being caught before they get far upriver, or because there are fewer fish overall than in the past.

The claims of the MRC and the Department of Fisheries, that *pa soi* migrations from the Great Lake are not in decline, overlook the problem that only fish catches from the Great Lake/Tonlesap River large-scale bag net (*dai* in Khmer) fishery are being monitored to gauge fish population sizes each year. It is possible that these *dai* catches are the same as in past years but that actual fish population sizes are smaller, resulting in real catch declines and associated negative impacts on livelihoods in the upper basin, where no data are being collected. Thus, *pa soi* populations, and those of many other fish species, may be declining in ways that cannot be indicated by looking only at the catches of the *dai* fishery.

Furthermore, fisheries management is not just about maintaining overall fish populations. It is also important to consider how fisheries resources are being distributed among people in different parts of the basin. This issue has received insufficient attention by analysts in the Mekong River Basin, even though some fish stocks migrate relatively long distances. To get a realistic impression of *Henicorhynchus* migrations and fish stocks, and how best to manage them, it will be necessary to look at fish stocks in the upper as well as the lower parts of the basin.

Special methods have been developed to access these fish every year from January to March, when cyprinid fish migrate up the Xekong from Cambodia. Locals in Sanamxay District rely on an ingenious way of catching these migrating species as they come upriver. First, in an area of rapidly moving water, a few meters-long wooden and bamboo barrier (called "*hok*" in Lao) is built running perpendicular to the flow of the water. Using their local knowledge, fishers have come to realize that many of these migrating fish are eager to get away from fast-flowing water when moving upstream. The barrier built by the fishers slows down the flow just downstream from it, and fish congregate behind the structure, seeking to rest there after moving up rapids downstream. This situation produces the perfect opportunity for fishers perched on top of the wooden structure to toss their castnets into the area behind the barriers. Large amounts of fish are caught this way. Fishers' knowledge can contribute to a better understanding of fish and fisheries (Haggan et al. 2007; Baird 2006c; 2007e).

Local people have long recognized that more fish generally migrate up the Srepok and Xekong Rivers in Cambodia than the Sesan River. There are a few reasons for this. First, the Xekong and Srepok are both generally deeper rivers than the Sesan, and so their habitats are more preferable for migrating fish. Secondly, most cyprinids migrate upriver along the edges of rivers. Therefore, if the fish leave the Mekong, enter the Xekong River and travel up along its southern bank, which the majority do, they will enter the Sesan River and will soon continue right into the Srepok, which flows into the Sesan from the southeast. On the other hand, if the fish leave the Mekong and move up the northern bank of the Xekong, they will mainly continue migrating right up the Xekong to Laos. Essentially, the Sesan is in the middle, between the Xekong and Srepok Rivers, so only fish that are "leftover" from those rivers end up migrating up the Sesan. There has to be a lot of fish migrating in the river before substantial numbers decide to go up the Sesan (Baird 1995a). Yet, every year some fish do migrate up the Sesan River. The Yali Falls Dam in the Central Highlands of Vietnam has altered the downstream hydrology of the Sesan River in Cambodia. This may well be affecting how many and when fish migrate up the Sesan (Baird et al. 2002).

Tat Fek: A Bio-geographical Obstacle to Fish Migrations?

The *Tat Fek* Waterfall is located on the Xenamnoi River not far upriver from its confluence with the mainstream Xekong River. In the dry season this waterfall is about 5 m high and, to anyone who sees it, it initially appears obvious that most fish cannot ascend it. It would be easy to assume that *Tat Fek* is a bio-geographical barrier to migrating fish; however, Roberts and Baird (1995b) found that in the rainy season, when the volume of water in the Xekong increases, the Xenamnoi River backs up and the waterfall disappears under the river, thus making it possible for fish to migrate up past the waterfall during that part of the year.

However, there is another waterfall upriver from *Tat Fek* called *Tat Xenoy*. It is 7 m high in the dry season, and 100 m wide. This waterfall is also known as *Tat Houa Khon*, due to an incident that took place there during the Japanese occupation of Laos. Japanese soldiers killed a number of resistance fighters, cut off their heads, and threw them into the waterfall (see Chapter 4). In that this waterfall is farther upstream, and at a higher elevation above the Xekong River than *Tat Fek*, it is not totally submerged during the rainy season, and is a bio-geographical barrier for fish year round.

There are many important links between migratory fish in the Xekong River Basin in Laos and those from the mainstream Mekong in Cambodia, Laos, and Thailand. Baird and Flaherty (2004) showed, for example, that some important medium-sized cyprinid fish species (including *Scaphognathops bandanensis*, *Mekongina erythrospila*, *Labeo erythropterus*, *Bangana behri*, and *Cirrhinus molitorella*) migrate between the Xekong, Sesan, and Srepok Rivers in northeastern Cambodia and southern Laos and the Mekong in northeastern Cambodia and southern Laos. Each year these fish move out of the Xekong, Sesan, and Srepok Rivers into the Mekong at the end of the rainy season. They then move back out of the Mekong into those rivers at the end of the dry season.

Due to the complexity of these migrations, interventions, such as dams, on one river have the potential significantly to impact fisheries on other rivers. For instance, the Don Sahong Dam, being considered for the mainstream Mekong River in the Khone Falls area of southern Laos (Vongsay 2006d), will negatively impact fisheries in the Xekong Basin in southern Laos, even though the dam will be on a different river and is quite far from the Xekong Basin. Dams being planned for the Xekong Basin in Laos could in turn negatively impact fishes and fisheries along the mainstream Mekong River in northeastern Cambodia and southern Laos. These types of linkages are not yet well understood or recognized among development planners and dam proponents within both government and donor agencies in the region.

Apart from lowland fish migrations, there are localized fish migrations in mountainous areas. For example, local people report that fish migrate up and down the Ka-ol Stream in eastern Phouvong District, although the number of migrating fish is believed to have decreased in recent years. There are also localized *Poropuntius* spp. (*pa chat* in Lao) fish migrations in the upper Xepian River on the Bolaven Plateau in Pakxong District. To date there have been no detailed studies regarding fisheries in upland areas of the Xekong River Basin. This should be a future research priority.

Very Large Fish

In general, women fish for smaller species of fish, while mainly men target larger species of which there are many in the Xekong River Basin. *Bagarius yarrelli* (*pa khe* in Lao) are often caught on hooks, but also sometimes in gill nets. They reach at least 40 kg, but still are not the largest fish found in the basin.

Another of the largest fish species is *Hemibagrus wyckioides* (*pa kheung*), which reaches 45–70 kg in the Mekong River. It is one of the most valuable and sought after fishes in the region (Baird et al. 1999), and most are exported to Thailand.

Two larger species of fish found in the Xekong River Basin are *Probarbus jullieni* (*pa eun deng*) and *Probarbus labeamajor* (*pa eun khao*), both of which occur in the mainstream Xekong and other large lowland rivers in the basin. They both reach about 70 kg in weight. These valuable fishes are often exported on ice to Thailand, even though *Probarbus jullieni* is a CITES Appendix 1 species, which means that international trade is prohibited except under special permission for scientific or research purposes (Baird 1994a; 2006b). *P. jullieni* and *P. labeamajor* are both listed in IUCN's Red data book, the first as "endangered" and the second as "insufficiently known" (Baird 1994a; 2006b).

One of the largest and most impressive fish species in the Xekong River Basin is the large carp *Luciocyprinus striolatus* (*pa sak*), which until recently was only known within the Mekong River Basin in Yunnan, China, where it was thought to reach only 45 cm in length. However, in the 1990s it was found in some of the large upland clear-water rivers in Laos, including the upper parts of the Nam Ou, Nam Ngum, and Nam Theun Rivers in northern and central Laos. In 1996, the first author found the species in the upper Xekaman River in Sanxay District and in the upper Xekong River in Kalum District. In the Xekaman River in Sanxay, they are especially well-known near Dak Bou Village. They do not occur in lower stretches of the rivers. For example, fishers in Done Chan Village, Lamam District only rarely catch any, and in Sanamxay District fishers do not know them at all. The species probably reaches a larger size than *Probarbus*, and is now known to be a much larger fish than once thought. *Pa Sak* reaches between 150–200 cm in length and between 70 and 100 kg in weight. The Xekaman is believed to represent the species' most southerly distribution. They tend to inhabit the upper part of the water column of deep-water pools. In the Nam Theun River, villagers reported to Tyson Roberts that the species eats long-tailed macaques feeding at the river edge, but we have never heard that story from fishers in the Xekong Basin.

Another large cyprinid fish found in the Xekong River Basin is *Catlocarpio siamensis* (*pa kaho*), which can reach between 2–3 m long when fully mature, and has been reported to occur in the Xekong, Xekhampho, and Xepian Rivers. However, like many other large fish species in the Mekong, it has become increasingly rare (Baird et al. 1999). It is the largest cyprinid fish in the Xekong River Basin.

Local fishers report that the largest catfish in the Mekong River Basin, *Pangasius gigas*[5] (*pa beuk*), and the "second" giant catfish, *Pangasius sanitwongsei* (*pa leum*) never occurred in the Xekong River Basin in Laos. Probably the largest "fish" in the Xekong River Basin is actually a giant stingray, *Himantura chaophraya* (*pa fa lai* or *pa fa hang*). This species has been reported to reach up to 500 kg in weight.

In the early 1990s, the first author saw a 400 kg individual that was caught in the Xekong in Cambodia.

There are also various reports of other large and mysterious fish in the Xekong, but it is difficult to confirm whether they really exist and, if so, what species they might be. However, the marine sawfish, *Pristis microdon* reportedly used to migrate at least as far up the Mekong as Khone Falls and could well have occasionally traveled up the Xekong as well. This species can apparently reach up the 6 m long (Baird et al. 1999).

Fishing Method Diversity

A large variety of fishing methods and gear are used in the Xekong River Basin in Laos. Differences are based on geography and other environmental conditions and also, at times, on ethnicity. For example, ethnic Lao people bait one type of basket-trap (*lan* in Lao), with bran to catch small cyprinids. The fish enter a small door in the basket to feed on the bran but once inside are unable to escape. Ethnic Brao people sometimes use a similar type of trap, although they call it "*tom*." Brao people consume large quantities of jar rice beer (*lao hai* in Lao), whereas the ethnic Lao are more likely to consume distilled whisky (*lao det* in Lao). Therefore, the Brao often have leftover rice and husks from jar beer that can be used for baiting fish-traps. Some ethnic Lao, on the other hand, may use the remains of alcohol distilling similarly. Thus, alcohol consumption patterns affect fishing methods.

The ethnic Katu people of Kalum District have a special type of scoop net that they call "*a neuk a ja hok*." It has a long wooden handle and a meshed net at the end. It is used in the rainy season to catch fish in relatively calm waters at the edges of larger streams, when the water is turbid and fish cannot see the net. Men mainly use this method. Katu women, in contrast, use bamboo funnels (*nook* in Katu) to scoop fish in streams. This sort of fishing is mainly done during the dry season in shallow streams.

Another method of fishing (*at khone* in Lao) involves finding an old underwater log with hollowed insides in streams, and blocking one end of it with sticks, rocks, and mud, before plunging one's arm into the other end and catching any fish that might remain inside. This is especially common in upland clear water streams, such as those in the upper Xekong Basin in Xekong Province. The first author observed another type of "fishing with bare hands" in the Saik Stream (a tributary of the Xekong) with ethnic Ngkriang men from Bak Village on a fishing trip during the dry season of 1996. The men observed skillfully maneuvered their hands under and in between the large boulders in the stream, pulling out medium-sized catfish, especially *Hemibagrus nemurus* (*pa kot* in Lao).

Some fishing-gear, such as castnets (*he* in Lao), are used in different ways. For example, in Sompoi Village in Sanamxay District fishers work as teams when fishing. One tosses a stone about 10 m in front of the boat, and then the second one tosses a castnet into the water. The idea is to scare fish with the stone so that they swim toward the place where the castnet will be tossed.

Along the major rivers, gillnets are mainly used in the dry season, when water levels are low enough to make their use easier. However, in the great wetlands, the *Khet Beung*, of Pathoumphone and Sanamxay Districts (see below), gillnets are mainly only used in the wet season in flooded areas with flowing water (*nam keng* in Lao), as they are not particularly effective or easy to use in small wetland areas during the dry season. Front funnel traps (*lope* in Lao) and castnets are also frequently used in the floodplains during the rainy season. In September and October, *tone* fence-filter traps are used to catch fish moving from seasonal wetland areas to perennial water bodies. For example, people from Sompoi Village in Sanamxay reported that much of the lowlands around their village become inundated *nam keng* wetlands for approximately three months a year.

Hooks and lines are used to catch fish in the dry season and *loum pa* and *sang pa* pit-fishing are important fishing methods at that time as well (see box below). One controversial dry season fishing method in *Khet Beung* involves burning matted grass floating on top of the water. The fish apparently become hot and attempt to surface to escape from the hot water by wriggling from it and crossing to other areas. However, skillful fishers are waiting to grab them with their bare hands.

Another method for catching fish in this sort of wetland in the dry season is called "*at hou pa*" in Lao (see box below).

In the rainy season, people in *Khet Beung* do not only use *lope pa* funnel traps to catch fish, but also *lope tao* funnel traps to catch hard-shell turtles, such as *tao kon* and *tao kap nyang*. These traps are put in swamp wetlands between September and November. No bait is used and some fish are also caught in *lope tao*.

During the rainy season, villagers from Kiet Ngong Village use hooks to catch fish but the bait differs, based on their ecological knowledge of changing local conditions. During May and June, earthworms are used as bait followed by crabs at the height of the rainy season from July to September. During September and October fish are used as bait.

While some different fishing methods have already been described above, it is not possible to treat this subject in any detail here. The main point is that there is a vast array of fishing-gear in use in the Xekong River Basin (see, for example, Claridge et al. 1997), which represents a significant aspect of the cultural heritage of the basin's people. This heritage is now threatened, as certain types of hand-made fishing-gear are being abandoned in favor of more modern fishing-gear, including monofilament gillnets and castnets.

Different Types of Fish Poisoning

There are two main categories of fish poisoning in the Xekong River Basin. The first can be called "natural fish poisoning," a long-practiced method applied mainly by Austroasiatic groups in the basin. It involves using various types of bark or fruits from forest species to poison a small side channel of a stream or a seasonal pond. This kind of fishing generally occurs at the height of the dry season. There is little environmental damage associated with it, as the natural poisons must be used in large quantities to cause fish to die, and are not strong enough to kill fish in flowing stream waters. This kind of fishing is generally conducted communally. Ethnic Katu villagers from Pom Village, Kalum District use the bark of a vine that they call "*a-yeum*" to poison fish, as well as the bark of two other trees that they call "*a-chak*" and "*a-kawh*." First, they divert the water of a small stream at the height of the dry season in order to isolate a small body of water and then they add the natural poison. All the fish killed are divided up equally.

The second type of fish poisoning is much more dangerous. It can be called "chemical fish poisoning" and generally involves the use of dangerous agricultural chemicals. When poured into rivers and streams these chemicals cause fish die-offs and other ecological damage over a large area. For example, in late 2004 some ethnic Lao villagers used the agricultural chemical methyl parathion (the Bayer Company brand name is Floridon) to poison the Cheung Hiang and Keua Streams inside the Xepian NPA in Pathoumphone District. In just three days the group was able to return with over 60 kg of fish, much more than would have been possible using conventional castnets, gillnets, and hooks and lines. Over the years there have been numerous reports of these types of illegal fishing activities in other parts of the Xepian NPA, including the Ta-euang Stream. Locals from Taong Village noticed the unusual catches and reported the incident to the district, the police, and the district Forestry Office in early 2005. In the Xexou River in Phouvong District, ethnic Lao people from the lowlands have been accused of using agricultural chemicals to poison fish. Local ethnic Brao people believe that this has resulted in reduced fish stocks in the river.

When concerns are raised about fish poisoning, it is important to distinguish between these two different methods. "Natural fish poisoning" as traditionally practiced, should be of relatively little concern. In contrast, "chemical fish poisoning" represents a serious threat to aquatic ecosystems and local livelihoods.

The Increasing Popularity of Modern Fishing-Gear

There have been many changes in fisheries in the Xekong River Basin in recent years. Fishers from Ta-neum Village, Lamam District, explained in 2004 that in the past bamboo was collected to make fish-traps. Bamboo side-hole funnel traps (*sai* in Lao), front funnel traps (*lope*) and drop-door traps (*chan*) are still commonly used in the Xekong Basin, as are wing trap barrages (*li*) and fence-filter barrage traps (*tone*). Now, however, only the lack of money prevents most people from getting as many modern nylon fishing nets as they can, as nets are plentiful in the provincial markets of Xekong, Attapeu, Pakse and Salavan as well as the district-level markets. There are no government-imposed restrictions regarding the use of these nylon nets.

In some cases, fishing-gear are made the same or similar to how they were decades ago, but their use and numbers has changed dramatically. For example, in the 1980s and 1990s the prevalence of nylon monofilament gillnets increased greatly, compared to multi-filament gillnets. The average mesh sizes of gillnets also generally declined in the 1990s and especially in recent years. It was only a few decades ago when natural fibers were used to make short and large mesh-sized gillnets. These locally made gillnets were soaked in animal blood to extend their lives. Sometimes a village only had a few of these nets and so they could only be used sparingly. However, gillnets made of natural fibers are no longer in use in the Xekong River Basin.

Hooks used for catching fish have also changed drastically in recent decades. Metal hooks used to be quite rare and, when they were used, were usually large and handmade. But now factory-made metal hooks of all sizes are readily available. Whereas vines and rope made of natural fibers were used as fishing-lines in the past, now everybody uses mass-manufactured nylon line. These changes have undoubtedly had an impact on the fish and fisheries of the Xekong Basin, although this has not yet been systematically studied.

There are also new fishing methods now being used. For example, the use of diving masks and spear guns for fishing has increased greatly in recent years. These techniques are now commonly being used in many parts of the basin. Younger men and teenagers are especially involved in these kinds of fishing. The older generation, in contrast, is not familiar with the gear. Done Chan villagers explained how fishers dive down in the water over 10 m to spear fish with their handmade wooden spear guns, using flashlights in sealed plastic bags to guide them. These fishers are often able to get 20–30 kg of fish in one night in this way. This method only began being widely used in 2001 and 2002. It is believed by many villagers to be having a negative impact on fish stocks.

Fishers from Done Chan also explained that fishers sometimes don masks and dive underwater with sealed batteries to shock fish. This method is illegal and is frowned upon by most villagers. In November 2004, a man from Done Chan died when he electrocuted himself by fishing this way. It is nevertheless still popular as large quantities of fish can be caught. For example, one fisher was able to catch 300,000 kip worth of *Bagarius yarrelli* (*pa khe* in Lao) catfish in a single night of fishing in February 2005. One ethnic Harak former revolutionary elder, dismayed about these types of destructive fishing activities said, "By the time the country achieves Socialism, there will be no fish left."

Electric shock fishing is an increasing problem in many parts of the Xekong River Basin and is widely perceived to be highly destructive to fish stocks. For those who want to harvest fish illegally, electric fishing is often preferable to explosives fishing, as nobody can hear the former. In eastern Phouvong District villagers reported that ethnic Vietnamese people use specially made machines to shock fish. In 2004, ethnic Brao village leaders in the area confiscated two of these machines. Many other communities report similar occurrences.

Another type of new fishing-gear used in the dry season involves stringing a large number of old condensed milk cans on a rope and dragging them along the riverbed in order to chase small loaches (*pa it* in Lao) (*Nemacheilus* and *Schistura* spp.) into specially adapted mosquito nets as they migrate up along the edge of the Xekong. This method is now widely used in the Xekong River Basin and is in use as far up as Kalum District center and as far downriver as Sanamxay District near the border with Cambodia. It has reportedly only been in use for a few years.

Another relatively new fishing technology is the use of rifles to shoot fish (*nying pa* in Lao). This method takes advantage of the behavior of some fish species that rise to the surface near shore in the dry season. *Channa micropeltes* (*pa meng phou*) and *Channa striata* (*pa kho*) are the main species targeted, as both are large, but others are also shot and caught this way. Most of the *Channa* are mothers protecting groups of newly born offspring, which are important brood stock. Therefore, many fishers believe that this fishing method is destructive.

Fishers Migrations

Not only do fish migrate seasonally but so do the people who are trying to catch them. Some fishers migrate with the fish, or to specific locations where fish are known to congregate during certain times of the year. There are also other factors, such as the end of agricultural activities and weather conditions. For example, the lower stretches of the Xekaman River are quite shallow, especially during the dry season, and there are few deep-water pools where large fish can retreat. Therefore, as reported by fishers in Saysettha District, in the dry season most large fish in the Xekaman are found in its upper stretches. This part of the river is not subject to as heavy fishing pressure as the lower stretches either. This explains why ethnic Lao from lower parts of the Xekaman have a long history of traveling up the river on long fishing trips during the dry season. Their trips last from a few to over ten days. They return with their catch, some of which is consumed at home and some of which is sold. Many use long-tailed motorboats to go up as far as *Tat Po* for fishing between December and May (first and sixth Lao months).

In the rainy season there is too much water and currents are too fast for fishers to travel long distances upriver by boat. People are also engaged in farming in that season, and have less time for fishing trips.

Most dry season fishing done by traveling fishers occurs in rapids using castnets at night. However, fish hooks, fixed gillnets (*mong kang*), and drift gillnets (*mong lai*) are also commonly used. There are lots of deep-water pools in the upper Xekaman, but these are often difficult to fish in because they are deep, except when explosives are used. While illegal, fishing with explosives is still sometimes done in remote areas.

People living along the Xekaman generally do not object to people from different villages fishing near other communities, especially when it is done for subsistence rather than commercial purposes. But there are exceptions. Some villagers report that a few communities collect a "village tax" of between 50,000–100,000 kip from each group of outside fishers during the season when *Hemibagrus wyckioides* (*pa kheung* in Lao) are abundant. This measure appears to be of recent origin and is undoubtedly based on the high value of this particular species. The village tax is then used for community activities. In addition, even villagers that allow subsistence fishing near their villages tend to discourage or prohibit fishing activities deemed to be out of step with local methods.

Fishers living along the river are not the only ones who fish the Xekaman. For example, some people resettled to Pa-am in Sanxay District (see Chapter 5) walk the 5 km to the river near Tat Koum Village in order to go fishing. This does not happen frequently, however, as the river is too far away, and many do not have money to buy fishing-gear anyway.

The village of Km 52 in the north part of Samakhixay District is not particularly near to either the Xenamnoi or the Xekong Rivers, but people there fish in both rivers. At times they travel to the mainstream Xekong for fishing trips. More often, however, they fish in the Xenamnoi, usually taking overnight trips.

Many people in villages along the Xekong make periodic migrations to other rivers for fishing. Many travel to fish in the Xenamnoi River, especially in the dry season between February and March. The ethnic Lao community of Sakhe, in Samakhixay District, is known as one of the main fishing villages along the Xekong, as most families there are involved in fishing. In the dry season fishers can often catch 10–20 kg/day of fish. However, in addition to fishing the Xekong, they also travel periodically to the Xenamnoi to fish.

In Sanamxay District people living in villages along the Xekong seasonally go fishing in the Xepian River, especially in the rainy season when many do lowland wet rice agriculture nearer to the Xepian than to the Xekong.

In Dakchung District people from all the villages fish, and many periodically travel long distances for fishing in the Xekaman River. For example, people from Dak Vang walk about an hour to reach the Xekaman. They often catch large *Wallago leeri* (*pa khao* in Lao) and *Hemibagrus wyckioides* (*pa kheung*) as well as featherback fish (Notopteridae).

In the dry season it is not unusual to see groups of fishers from various villages camping and fishing along the mainstream Xekong River. This occurs in the upper basin, in Kalum District, and also in lowland areas like Sanamxay District. Small fish are often caught and dried in the sun, whereas larger fish are frequently sold fresh or smoked. This has been taking place for longer than anyone can remember; although in the past these fishing trips were almost exclusively for subsistence purposes. The trade in fish has now become much more of a motivating factor.

Fish Marketing

Fishing in the Xekong Basin is still largely done for subsistence purposes and fish sharing within villages and between families remains common in many rural areas, especially in remote ethnic minority villages. However, market sales are an important aspect of fisheries in the basin as well, and the fish trade plays an important role in the rural economy. For example, in 2004 villagers from Ta-neum Village, Lamam District told a Canadian CUSO volunteer that, while more fish are consumed in the village than are sold, the seven households and ten families in the community still sell about 500 kg of fresh fish from the Xekong River to the market each year (50 kg per family). Traders come up the river to the village to buy fish, with four or five long-tailed boats and their drivers coming each day. They generally arrive at Ta-neum between 8 a.m. to 9 a.m. and buy medium and large fresh fish for 8,000 kip/kg (standard fish) and other more expensive species for higher prices. These buyers tend to sell the fish they buy at the Xekong town market for between 13,000 and 15,000 kip/kg. However, some special species, like *Hemibagrus wyckioides* (*pa kheung* in Lao) and other large catfishes, are much more expensive. Fish prices have remained relatively stable in recent years. The income generated from fishing may not seem like much, but for rural villagers in Xekong Province it is often one of their most important sources of cash income.

In the basin, most medium-sized fresh fish are marketed in the Attapeu and Xekong town markets, but some fish are sold in district centers and villages. For example, in Kalum District center market, one "*phout*" (a stringed bunch) of fish sold for 2,000 and 5,000 kip in February 2004, and one bowl of "*hoi lak tak*" (in Lao) shellfish was being sold for 1,000 kip. "*Khiat*" frogs were being sold for 1,000 kip, while "*pa kabang*" (in Lao) fish preserved in bamboo sections was priced at 2,000 kip per section.

A substantial proportion of the largest fish caught, especially expensive species like *Micronema* spp. (*pa nang* in Lao), *Probarbus* spp. (*pa eun*) and *Hemibagrus wyckioides* (*pa kheung*), are exported on ice to Thailand via Pakse and Ubon Ratchathani. Some undoubtedly end up being served in expensive Chinese restaurants in Bangkok (Baird 1994a; 2006b). Fishers generally believe that there has been a significant decline in the number of large fish in the Xekong River Basin in recent years.

While more fish are being exported from the basin than are being imported, in recent years fish from outside the basin have begun to be sold in the provincial markets of Xekong and Attapeu. This is partly because there is a demand for different types of fish that are not found in the Xekong Basin, but it is certainly also in response to there no longer being enough cheap fish from the Xekong to supply the market. Some large Xekong River fish are now too expensive for local people. This further reduces the quantity of fish available at local markets, thus making cheaper aquaculture and ocean fish imports attractive based on price. This includes aquaculturally raised *Pangasius hypophthalmus* catfish (*pa souay* in Lao) and ocean mackerel from Thailand (called *pa thou* in Lao). This all suggests that there are fewer fish reaching local markets than was the case a few years ago.

Attapeu Specialties: *"Mok bai mak houng"* and *"treu reeo"*

One of the famous local ethnic Lao Attapeu specialties is *mok bai mak houng* (in Lao), which is made of papaya leaves (*bai mak houng* in Lao), small bitter eggplants (*mak kheng*), and fermented fish (*pa dek*). *Mok bai mak houng* is unique. It is considered particularly delicious, because it is made with the famous fermented Attapeu fish paste (although it is now sometimes made with pig meat).

Mon-Khmer language-speaking groups make another specialty of Attapeu Province. Called *treu reeo* in Brao, this sun-dried fish is stored for extended periods in long bamboo sections.

Women in Fisheries

Women's participation in capture fisheries in Laos is important and well recognized among local populations. However, women mainly participate in fisheries in small water bodies using smaller fishing-gear than men. When women do fish on large rivers, it tends to be along the banks rather than in large open waters. For example, ethnic Katu men from Lai Po and Pom villages said that they tended to fish in the Xekong River in the dry season, while women tended to fish in streams. In addition, women often fish in small streams, ditches, rice fields, and other wetlands. Men frequently fish for large fish to sell, while women tend to fish more for subsistence. There are generally quite clear distinctions in the types of fishing operations in which men and women are involved (Garaway 1995; Liepvisay and Vongpanolom 1997).

Although women usually fish less than men, there are some exceptions, such as with ethnic Ngkriang women during the agriculture season. Furthermore, women are often more heavily involved in fish processing and marketing (Liepvisay and Vongpanolom 1997).

In upland areas, it is notable that women do much of the fishing. They do not catch particularly large fish, but they fish for food regularly, supplying their families with significant quantities of animal protein. The women often travel to small streams and other wetlands as groups in the dry season, where they fish mainly with basket scoop-traps. They mostly target fish hiding under or around rocky areas in rapids. They generally face upstream with their traps in shallow water against the ground and between their feet. Then they carefully disturb the rocks just upstream from where the mouth of the scoop trap is positioned. As the rocks are disturbed, the fish under and around them flee, often swimming with the current right into the waiting trap downstream, which is quickly and skillfully pulled out of the water with the catch. Based on personal experience, this fishing method may appear simple, but it is difficult to master. The local knowledge that women hold in terms of their use of scoop traps is important for maintaining their livelihoods.

Ethnicity affects the types of fishing activities that women engage in. For example, ethnic Ngkriang women from Ta-neum Village, Lamam District tend to fish for small fish using basket scoop-traps (*sone* in Lao) made of bamboo, used in flowing water in rocky habitat. However, ethnic Lao women tend to use "*swing*" scoop-nets to fish in the same areas.

Important Wetlands in the Xekong River Basin in Laos

There are many important wetland areas and varieties of wetlands in the Xekong River Basin in Laos. Some are perennial, and some are seasonal; some are flood-plains, and some are volcano-generated crater lakes; some are fast flowing streams, and some are slower-flowing large rivers.

Some of the most important, and probably the most expansive, wetlands in the basin are the 350 km² Xekong Plains in southern Sanamxay District, located partly inside Xepian NPA. The area supports important lowland aquatic and terrestrial biodiversity (Claridge 1996). The crocodile habitat of *Beung* Khe and *Beung* Ke near Pin Dong Village in Sanamxay District is included in the Xekong Plains (see above).

Associated wetlands in the eastern part of Pathoumphone District are sometimes referred to as "*Khet Beung*" because these wetlands include a large number of seasonal and perennial ponds. They are also interspersed with a combination of forest types broadly dominated by rich semi-evergreen forests (*pa dong* in Lao) and short, dry dipterocarp forests (*pa lang* in Lao) in areas with volcanic rock formations. This area is highly prone to rainy season flooding and is slow to dry out in the dry season. The people have developed their own patterns of fishing. Apart from being heavily involved in various river fisheries along the Xekong, Xepian, and Xekhampho Rivers in this region, villagers participate in particular types of seasonal and perennial wetland swamp fishing. This includes communal village wetland fishing called "*pha nong*" in Lao. In Pathoumphone District, villagers get much of their fish from hand-dug pits called "*loum pa*" or "*khoum sang pa*" (see below).

Another associated important wetland area in Pathoumphone is the *Beung Nong* Ngom wetland group, which covers an area of about 30 km^2 and includes a series of large, perennial, lowland swamp wetland areas, including *Nong* Ngom and *Beung Nyai* Kiet Ngong, along with freshwater marshes, lakes, ponds, rice paddies, and seasonally flooded grasslands, scrublands, and forestlands.

Beung Nyai Kiet Ngong retains water year round, and is still populated by Siamese crocodiles which sometimes, in the height of the wet season, move into the wetlands near Houay Ko Village. The wetland area is an extensive, shallow, saucer-shaped basin surrounded by forest and low, rounded hills with some rocky outcrops. During the height of the dry season the edges of the wetlands dry out and are heavily grazed by domestic elephants, water buffalo, and cows. At these times permanent wet sedge marshes and shrubby swamps occur as well as areas of persistent open water about 2 m deep. The habitat is important for various common and threatened birds, including Cattle Egrets, Harriers, Red-throated Pipits, Yellow Wagtails, and other passerines. Important water birds found in the area include Lesser Whistling ducks, Cotton pygmy geese, and Bronze-winged Jacanas. Some threatened and endangered birds are also found in the area, including Sarus Crane, Woolly-necked Stork, Lesser Adjutant, Red-headed Vulture, Long-billed Vulture, and White-rumped Vulture (Claridge 1996).

Beung Nong Ngom contributes to maintaining dry season flows in the Ta-euang Stream, which runs through the Xepian NPA. The wetland system as a whole probably helps to provide some flood height reductions in downstream areas during the wet season (Claridge 1996). The wetlands also help to recharge groundwater supplies. For example, Kiet Ngong Village gets its drinking supply from three to four wells dug at the edge of the *Beung Nyai* wetlands (Claridge 1996).

In addition to fish, eels, and other living creatures, villagers are able to harvest considerable amounts of vegetables in these wetlands. Edible vegetable varieties found around the Xekong Basin wetlands commonly collected, eaten, and sometimes sold by villagers include *phak kout*, *phak nam*, *phak ven*, and *phak top*.

"At Hou Pa"

Local people living near *Beung Nong* Ngom and other large wetlands in Pathoumphone and Sanamxay Districts have developed an innovative way of catching fish living in water underneath grassy areas. In Kiet Ngong Village local livelihoods are dependent upon knowledge of the resources and methods for harvesting fish from a large wetland swamp area, known as *Beung Nyai* in Lao. A method known as "*at hou pa*" literally translates as "stuffing shut the holes of fish," and is commonly practiced. In the dry season there is still plenty of water in the wetland but much of it is covered in thick matted grass. Local people have long observed that air-breathing fish species, particularly the snakehead *Channa striata* (*pa kho* in Lao), living under the matted grass find small holes in the grasses to rise up to surface for air. When these holes are found, fishers dig them out so that they are somewhat wider and then they stuff them full of grasses in order to block them. The fishers then wait and, when the snakehead fish try to swim through the grasses to reach the surface, they are partly demobilized by the grasses and are caught by hand. In the dry season, villagers living near *Beung Nyai* also sometimes remove lumps of grasses creating holes used for hook-and-line fishing.

One important wetland area in Samakhixay District is called *Nong* Long, near Somsanouk and Sysomphone Villages. It is a year-round natural wetland habitat located approximately a half-hour's drive from the provincial capital adjacent to the road to Sanamxay District. The wetland also borders Saysettha District. It is about 150 m wide and 1.5 km long, with water about 1.5 m deep in the dry season. It is believed to be an important spawning area for fish from the Xekong to which it is connected through seasonal stream channels.

The Attapeu provincial government has made the development of this area a priority. Unfortunately, earlier proposals for doing this essentially amounted to plans to turn the wetland into a large fish pond for raising exotic species! The recently terminated Mekong Wetlands Biodiversity Project subsequently tried to work with communities and the government to support a more community and environment friendly model. However, the situation remains challenging, particularly in light of the project's abrupt termination in late 2006. In 2005, the wetland dried up during the dry season for the first time. This may be linked to construction of a dam upstream and the extraction of water, but more information is required to determine this with certainty.

Swamp Eels

In the dry season swamp eels (*Monopterus albus*) (*ian* in Lao) make up a significant part of the catch in some of the lowland parts of the Xekong River Basin. Long narrow traps (*bang lan* in Lao) are used for catching swamp eels. Rotten mashed crab (*kapou* in Lao), frogs (*kop* or *khiat*) or fish are put in the traps to lure the eels in.

In Pathoumphone District, swamp eels are caught using a method called "*nye ian*," in which pounded worms or crabs are put on hooks as bait. The hooks are then lowered into holes where swamp eels are known to stay. In Pathoumphone, swamp eels sell for 17,000 kip/kg in the villages and up to 25,000 kip/kg in the Pakse market. These traps are also commonly used in Sanamxay District. In Phouvong District, along the lower parts of the Nam Kong River, ethnic Brao people use small frogs (*keet* in Brao) to bait hooks to catch swamp eels (*doong* in Brao).

Digging Pits in Wetlands to Catch Fish

In the *Khet Beung* area in the eastern part of Pathoumphone, there are many vast seasonal and perennial wetlands. Not surprisingly, the particular ecological conditions of these areas have resulted in the development of a number of specialized fishing methods, some of which have already been described. The best known is "*khout loum pa*"[6] or "*khout sang pa*."[7] This system involves individual families digging pits in seasonal wetland areas when water levels are down in the dry season. These pits, which are typically 1.5 m long, 1.5 m wide, and about 2 m deep, are filled up with branches and other pieces of wood. Fish enter them in the rainy season, when water levels rise and cover the pits with water. This particularly occurs at the end of the rainy season when water levels drop and some of the only remaining deep-water is in the pits.

During the dry season the owners of the pits remove the branches and debris, scoop out the remaining water and then harvest the fish. The main species caught are "black fish," including *Channa striata* (*pa kho* in Lao), *Clarias batrachus* (*pa douk*), *Trichogaster trichopterus* (*pa kadeut*), *Anabas testudineus* (*pa kheng*), *Ompok bimaculatus* (*pa seuam*), *Channa gachua* (*pa kang*), and *Rasbora* and *Esomus* spp. (*pa sieu*). Other species are also harvested, including swamp eels

(*Monopterus albus*) (*ian*), large tiger frogs (*Hoplobatrachus rugulosa*)[8] (*kop*) and snakes (*ngou pa*). Sometimes the harvesting process can take many hours and ends with many people feeling around in the mud at the bottom of the pits to find fish trying to escape capture. The number of pits per family is largely dependent on labor availability. Some families have just a few pits while others have fifteen or more. It takes considerable effort to empty water from these pits and some families with many pits are unable to harvest all of them before the end of the dry season. Although most villagers empty pits of water by hand, Phapho Village, which is relatively rich and is situated near *Beung Nyai*, sometimes use gasoline-powered pumps to drain their pits.

In places where wetlands are relatively small, like Thong Say, Toi, and Cheung Houay Villages, it is generally possible to harvest 5–8 kg of fish per pit. However, in Kiet Ngong and Phapho, where villagers have pits in much larger wetland areas, it is sometimes possible to harvest over 20 kg of fish. Since the fish sells for over 16,000–20,000 kip/kg, considerable amounts of income can be generated through this fishing system.

There does not appear to be any restrictions on where people can dig pits but, if someone's buffalo falls in and is injured or dies, the owner of the pit is responsible for damages. Therefore, pit owners put heavy fences around their pits to keep buffalo out. In Thong Say Village, if someone steals fish from someone else's pit and is caught, the thief is fined 500,000 kip per pit. Villagers from Kiet Ngong and Phapho have the largest number of pits in the area. In Kiet Ngong, there are five families in the village who do not farm but only fish for a living. The large size of the wetland near these villages makes fishing more attractive than in other areas. Other villages involved in this type of fishing in the Xekong Basin in eastern Pathoumphone are Keng Nam Ang, Kele Nyai, Kele Mai, Phalay Bok, Phalay Thong, Saming, and Kala.

Turning Wetlands into Natural Fertilizers

In a rather ironic turn of events, a Vietnamese company decided to invest in a natural fertilizer factory in an effort to practice more sustainable and organic agriculture. The business, called "Champa Biofer Factory," was located in Pathoumphone District, adjacent to Route 13 between Pakse and the border with Cambodia. During the first few years of its existence, the factory relied on the peat found in a wetland near the factory, but, beginning in early 2005, it received permission from local officials to harvest 300 trucks full of peat soil from the *Beung Nyai* wetlands near Kiet Ngong Village.

Although villagers from Kiet Ngong have not yet noticed any significant impacts on the *Beung Nyai* wetlands as a result of the extraction of peat, it is unclear what the impacts of continued peat extraction over a number of years might be on the wetlands system. Kiet Ngong villagers are not clear how many years peat extraction will occur as they have not been consulted about the extraction, and they have not received any compensation payments for extracting the peat. Only district and provincial authorities have received payments.

During the late 1990s and early 2000s, there was considerable concern that large-scale extraction of peat soil from the *Beung Nyai* Wetlands would adversely affect biodiversity values within Xepian NPA (see, for example, FOMACOP 2000).

The Upper Xenamnoi Wetlands cover an area of about 8 km² and includes about twenty wetlands on the Bolaven Plateau in Pakxong District, in the area surrounding the headwaters of the Xepian and Xenamnoi Rivers. In these upland wetlands, there are relatively few fish species (about twenty) compared to lowland wetlands (Claridge 1996; Roberts and Baird 1995b), but some of the species in the uplands are endemic (see Kottelat 2001; Roberts 1998a). The Xepian–Xenamnoi Dam threatens these wetlands (see Chapter 13). *Nong* Lom, one of the main wetlands in this area, was proposed as part of the reservoir for holding water diverted from the Xepian River, but a later proposal called for piping the water around *Nong* Lom (Claridge 1996).

Another important wetland in the Xekong River Basin is referred to by various names, including *Nong* Patomkeen, *Nong* Kai Ok and, most commonly, *Nong* Fa *Nong* Yot. The wetland is a 1-km² freshwater lake (a volcanic crater lake) and is believed to be the largest lake in the Annamite Mountain Chain. It is set on a high 1,100 m asl ridge top, which forms the boundary between Sanxay and Dakchung Districts and is approximately circular in shape (Claridge 1996). It resembles the volcanic lakes found in Ratanakiri Province, northeast Cambodia, the best known being Yak Loam Lake, near the provincial capital of Ban Lung. *Nong* Patomkeen drains into the *Nam* Palouat and then the Xekaman River.

The steep-sided banks of the wetland are largely forested, although local people have cleared some areas for swidden agriculture (Claridge 1996). The area was bombed during the war and defoliants were also dropped. It was designated as a provincial forest reserve in 1990 and became part of Dong Ampham NPA in 1993 (Davidson et al. 1997). *Nong* Fa *Nong* Yot is situated in a quiet area, and is flanked on all sides by mountains peaks. It was considered to be the eastern border of Attapeu during the pre-colonial period (Long 1890). The lake has clear blue water year round. Its depth has not been measured, but similar crater lakes in Ratanakiri Province, northeast Cambodia are over 70 m deep. Locals believe that the lake is sacred, and there are various mysteries and stories involving it. *Nong* Fa *Nong* Yot is not particularly known for its fisheries, but the Attapeu government believes that it has important tourism potential (see Chapter 8).

Finally, the Vang Tat wetlands cover a 1-km^2 area in Sanxay District, near the border with Dakchung District, and is just 2.5 km from the international border with Kontum Province, Vietnam. The Vang Tat Wetlands are just 8 km southeast of *Nong* Patomkeen and include at least five small freshwater lakes/ponds or freshwater marshes. The area is in the uplands at about 1,100 to 1,200 m asl. Like the *Nong* Fa *Nong* Yot wetlands, the Vang Tat wetlands were protected in 1990 by provincial decree and were later included in the eastern part of Dong Ampham NPA (Claridge 1996). The new road to Vietnam from Attapeu Province (Route 18B) has, for better or worse, made this wetland much more accessible to outsiders.

The Costs and Benefits of Turning Productive Wetlands into Wet-Rice Fields

Wetlands are an important and increasingly well-recognized source of livelihoods for many people in rural areas of Laos, particularly for poorer families without many other resources. However, a growing number of important wetlands, including ones in the Xekong River Basin, are being drained and converted into lowland wet-rice paddy. Such newly developed paddy tends disproportionately to benefit relatively well-off families. But, ironically, these conversions are frequently done in the name of "poverty alleviation" and with the support of international donors. Near Keng Nam Ang Village in Pathoumphone District, villagers drained an important perennial wetland in 2004 as part of a World Food Program (WFP) supported "Food for Work" project. The WFP paid 2.2 kg of uncooked husked rice per m^2 of wetland area converted, and villagers were given a month to establish the new rice fields. An approximate 1 ha area was drained for lowland rice production. Villagers report that the loss of fish from the area has had a significant negative impact on local livelihoods and that many of the edible plants that they used to collect for food from around the edges of the wetland have disappeared.

Villagers from Keng Nam Ang have become acutely aware of the loss of the drained wetland because their other main fishing area, the Xekhampho River, now has fewer fish in it than in the recent past. To make matters worse, the 2005 dry season saw some of the lowest water levels in the Xekhampho River in living memory, further impacting fish and other living aquatic resources.

The prospect of WFP soon funding more wetland conversion to rice paddy as part of a new initiative in Attapeu Province (see Phengphachan 2006) is of particular concern. The *Vientiane Times* quoted Christa Rader, the WFP Laos Country Representative, as saying: "These activities [in Attapeu] may include the construction of roads and bridges to make the village more accessible—especially to markets, the development of irrigation channels to increase the agricultural production of the village, the construction of fish ponds to create an alternative source of food." She was quoted as further stating that the WFP would be funding the "expansion of paddy fields to increase rice production" (Phengphachan 2006: 2). No mention was made of how these activities might negatively affect wetlands. While the goal of the project is to eradicate seasonal and chronic food insecurity, the likelihood that the project may actually contribute to destroying aquatic habitats critical to maintaining food security is of serious concern.

The World Bank-supported Poverty Reduction Fund Project (PRF) has already been involved in similar activities in Pathoumphone District. Its goal is to reduce poverty, and one of the activities was to support the development of new lowland paddy farms by local farmers, with the goal of increasing rice production and thus reducing poverty. The project paid 250,000 kip/ha to villagers to open up new paddy areas, but without considering where these new areas would be, what impact their development might have on other resources and the associated livelihoods of local people, or whom would gain and who would lose at the village level. Whether or not well intended, the PRF's efforts have sometimes resulted in serious negative impacts to the environment and local livelihoods. In one instance, in 2004, the PRF agreed to pay five relatively well-off families from Saming Village to develop a half-hectare of rice paddy each in a wetland area, locally known as *Kout Seuam*. Nobody in the PRF or the World Bank appears to have considered where the paddy fields be developed or what negative impacts would be associated with such development efforts. However, soon after the villagers had cut down the forest surrounding the wetland area in preparation for developing the paddy areas, forestry officials working for Dong Houa Sao NPA happened to pass by and noticed that the wetland was being destroyed. Since the area is inside the NPA, it was illegal to develop rice fields there and so they told the villagers to abandon their plans immediately. The PRF still paid for the work, but the rice fields could not be developed.

Apart from the obvious problem of the *Kout Seuam* being inside a NPA, another problem with the plan was that the people who wanted to convert the wetland into lowland paddy fields were not the same people who were already using the wetland to support their livelihoods through fishing and gathering wild vegetables from its edges. There were already some *"loum pa"* fishing pits in the wetlands, and these would have been unworkable and lost to their owners if the wetland had been converted for agricultural purposes. Ironically, the owners of the fish pits were generally poorer than those who wanted to develop the paddy land. The conversion of the area by the World Bank's "Poverty Reduction Fund" might well have actually contributed to increasing the gap between the rich and the poor and increasing poverty levels among the people who fish in the area.

Although *Kout Seuam* was saved from total destruction, it would not have been but for the presence of some quick-thinking and quick-reacting officials working for Dong Houa Sao NPA. It is likely that in areas outside of the NPA, where the PRF has also paid villagers to open up wetlands to make lowland paddy fields, other wetlands have already been lost to such activities. This may well have led to increases in poverty among those people who have had to sacrifice fisheries livelihoods to make way for expanded rice paddy fields. In 2005, after the environmental problems associated with wetlands destruction for paddy rice development were pointed out to the World Bank/PRF, it appears that the project ceased funding such conversions in Pathoumphone.

Gregory et al. (1996) found that, in Svay Rieng Province, Cambodia, the draining or otherwise destroying natural wetlands for agricultural purposes often has the potential to result in declining livelihood security for local people; the economic and subsistence value of aquatic products from wetlands often outweighs the potential rice-growing benefits of draining a wetland. It does not appear that any specific studies on the cost–benefits for local people and the environment have ever been conducted in advance of initiating these types of projects in Laos or elsewhere in the Mekong region. It would seem likely that, since only small areas of lowland rice paddy can be developed from much larger wetland areas, the costs of draining such wetlands may well be far more than the benefits received from developing them for agriculture.

There is now better recognition of the livelihoods importance of wetlands, especially for the poorest. Bringing this perspective into the mainstream of development thought, however, is still challenging. It runs strongly against dominant Southeast Asian lowland biases toward rice as the exclusive basis of food security. This has resulted in narrowly focused planning and decision-making and an unbalanced focus on lowland rice production to the exclusion of, or even at the expense of, other essential aspects of livelihood security.

Plate 5.6. An ethnic Triang man points out how poorly eggplants grow in the lowland resettlement area of Pa-am compared to where he previously lived in the uplands of Sanxay District, Attapeu Province.

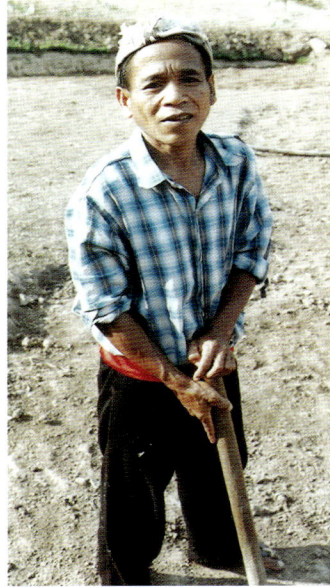

Plate 5.7. An ethnic Ngkriang man tries to open up new wet-rice paddy land near the Xekong River in Kalum District, Xekong Province. This is a dangerous activity as the area is still littered with unexploded ordnance. He had already found ten "bombies" while digging in 2004.

Plate 5.8. A resettled farmer and his child by his dry season wet-rice paddy field in Kalum District, Xekong Province. After resettlement the farmer was told to practice wet-rice agriculture but was not provided with training or support. He used native varieties of rice seed outside the normal rice-growing season. The results were poor. There is widespread evidence and a growing consensus that resettlement and land allocation initiatives have led to severe increases in poverty for many rural communities.

Plate 5.9. The Poverty Reduction Project of the World Bank funds the construction of a canal to drain water and decrease the negative flooding impacts of the Phalay Bok Irrigation system on wet-rice paddy land, Pathoumphone District, Champasak Province.

Plate 5.10. A man makes clay jars in Tha Hin Village, Samakhixay District, Attapeu Province.

Plate 6.1. *Dipterocarpus* wood resin trees at Ta-neum Village, Lamam District, Xekong Province.

Plate 6.2. Vietnamese logging truck operating in the mountains of eastern Phouvong District, Attapeu Province.

Plates

Plate 7.1. Women sell fish in Attapeu provincial market.

Plate 7.2. There are plenty of nylon gill nets for sale in Attapeu provincial market.

Plate 7.3. An ethnic Katu woman scoop-nets for small fish and shrimp in Kalum District, Xekong Province.

Plate 7.4. An ethnic Ngkriang girl and her younger brother prepare to go fishing with their handmade scoop net in the mountains of Kalum District, Xekong Province.

Plate 7.5. An ethnic Katu man demonstrates how long-handled scoop-netting is done in a mountain stream in Kalum District, Xekong Province.

Plate 7.6. An ethnic Katu man demonstrates how funnel traps are put out in small streams in the mountains of Kalum District, Xekong Province.

Plate 7.7. Young ethnic Lao boys with bran-baited fish attracting traps (*lan* in Lao) in Samakhixay District, Attapeu Province.

Plate 7.8. Fish being smoked above an ethnic Katu house fire in Kalum District, Xekong Province.

Plate 7.9. Ethnic Ngkriang women sell fish in the Kalum District market while smoking tobacco and sugarcane juice with a bong pipe.

Plates

Plate 7.10. Fish meat drying next to the Xekong River in Kalum District, Xekong Province.

Plate 7.11. An ethnic Brao man paddling a dugout canoe along the Nam Kong River in Phouvong District, Attapeu Province.

Plate 7.12. Ethnic Ngkriang boys preparing to put small nylon gill nets in the Xekong River in Kalum District, Xekong Province.

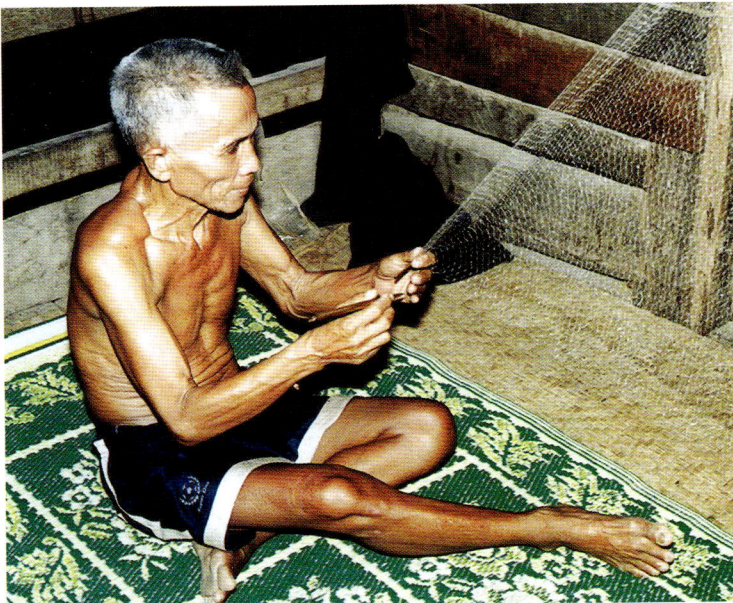

Plate 7.13. An ethnic Lao man weaves a nylon cast net in Sanamxay District, Attapeu Province.

Plates

Plate 7.14. An "*hok*" structure in the Xekong River, Sanamxay District, Attapeu Province. Ethnic Lao fishers cast-net off of it to catch migrating "*pa soi*" fish (*Henicoryhnchus lobatus*).

Plate 7.15. Ethnic Lao people scoop.net for small fish in the Xekaman River in Saysettha District, Attapeu Province.

Plate 7.16. Cans are dragged along the river to scare fish into nets in Samakhixay District, Attapeu Province.

Plate 7.17. Two men spear fishing with masks along the Xekong River in Samakhixay District, Attapeu Province. Mask-wearing spear fishers are now commonly seen along the Xekong River, whereas this method was not used a decade ago.

Plate 7.18. A bamboo and rattan funnel trap soaking in water before being completed in Attapeu Province.

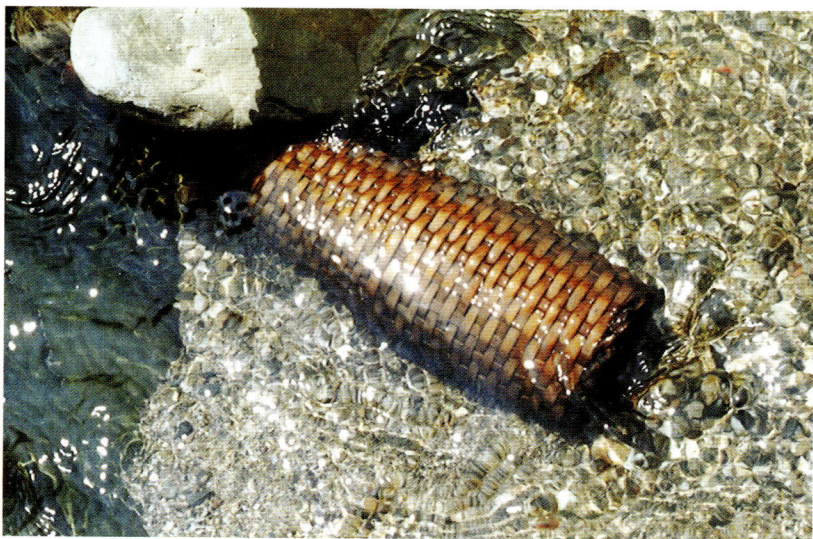

Plate 7.19. A shrimp funnel trap in the Xekong River in Kalum District, Xekong Province.

Plate 7.20. A woman carrying edible shellfish collected from Xekong River in Kalum District, Xekong Province.

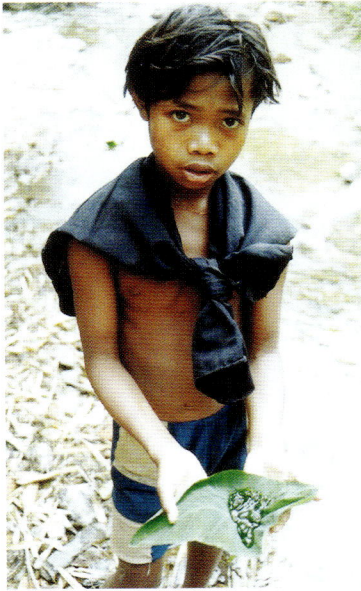

Plate 7.21. A young ethnic Katu man displaying edible algae collected from a stream near the Xekong River in Kalum District, Xekong Province.

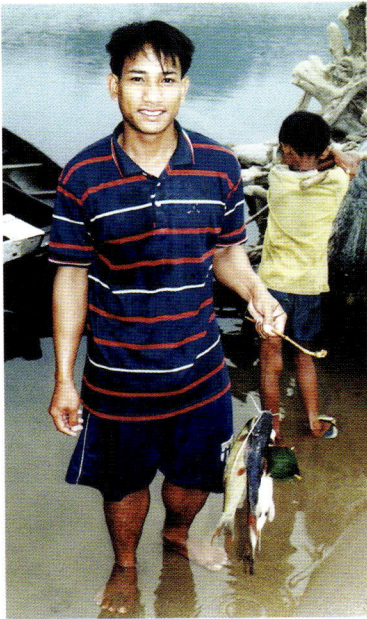

Plate 7.22. A government official working in Kalum District, Xekong Province relies on fish caught from the Xekong River to feed his family and supplement his meager government salary.

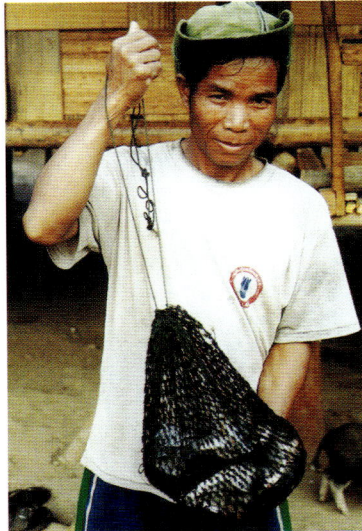

Plate 7.23. An ethnic Ngkriang man showing fish caught from the Xekong River in Kalum District, Xekong Province.

Plates

Plate 8.1. Bomb casings lined up near the Xekong River in Kalum District, Xekong Province. Nowadays scrap metal is an important source of income for local people, who collect metal from the forest to sell to traders.

Plate 8.2. Traditional equipment used by villagers in the Xekong River Basin for gold panning. Gold panning is an important source of income for many villagers in the region.

Plate 8.3. A traditional double-layered back basket (*ungeu* in Brao) in Phouvong District, Attapeu Province. Traditional back-baskets like this are becoming rarer, although standard back-baskets are still commonly used among the highlanders of the Xekong River Basin, with each ethnic group having their own particular designs.

Plate 8.4. Non-timber forest products (NTFPs), like these reeds, are an important source of livelihood for people in the Xekong River Basin in Laos.

Plate 8.5. Rattan tables made by ethnic Lao villagers in Sanamxay District, Attapeu Province.

Plate 8.6. A missile located at Pa-am in Sanxay District, Attapeu Province. Since this was taken, a fence has been built around the missile and tourists are being charged to see this relic of the Cold War.

Plate 8.7. An ethnic Vietnamese male trader in a remote area of Attapeu Province.

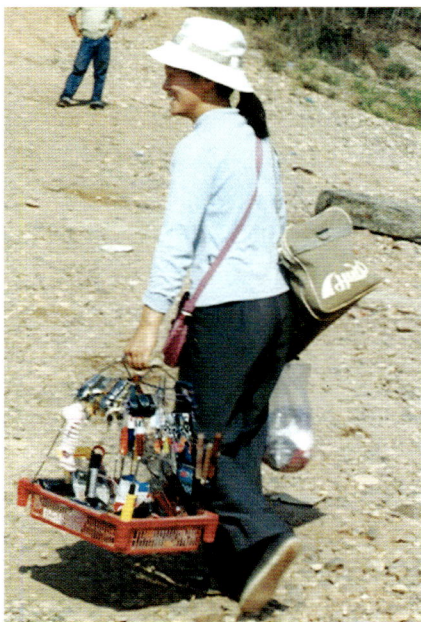

Plate 8.8. An ethnic Chinese female trader in Attapeu Province.

Plate 8.9. An ethnic Katu man makes a dugout canoe in Kalum District, Xekong Province.

Plate 8.10. An ethnic Ngkriang woman uses a traditional loom to weave in Kalum District, Xekong Province.

Plates

Plate 9.1. The *Keng* Chang deep-water fish conservation zone in Ta-neum Village, Lamam District, Xekong Province.

Plate 9.2. The CUSO-supported *Keng* Chang deep-water fish conservation zone sign of Ta-neum Village, Lamam District, Xekong Province.

Plate 10.1. Ethnic Ngkriang children study in a primary school in a village adjacent to the Xekong River in Kalum District, Xekong Province.

Plate 11.1. Dugout canoes remain an important means for traveling along the Xekong River in Kalum District, Xekong Province.

Plates

Plate 11.2. Long-tail boats are the main form of transportation up the Xekong River in Kalum District, but many rapids must be passed along the way.

Plate 11.3. A large ferry that regularly crosses the Xekong River near Attapeu town.

Plate 11.4. A small ferry that regularly crosses the Xekong River near Attapeu town.

Plate 11.5. A cement Laos-Cambodia border marker.

Plates

Plate 12.1. A gold dredging boat under repair in Samakhixay District, Attapeu Province. Local people have been heavily impacted by the damage done to the Xekong River through gold dredging.

Plate 12.2. A pile of rocks created by gold dredging along the Xekong River in Sanamxay District, Attapeu Province.

Plate 12.3. A waterwheel used for pounding rice in Dakchung District, Xekong Province.

Plate 12.4. A waterwheel used for pounding rice in an ethnic Ngkriang Village in Kalum District, Xekong Province.

Plates

Plate 13.1. Dugout logs used for funneling water into micro-hydropower generator.

Plate 13.2. A micro-hydropower generator operating on the Nam Kong River in Phouvong District, Attapeu Province.

8

Other Livelihoods in
the Xekong River Basin

In addition to agriculture and forest- and river-based livelihoods, dealt with in previous chapters, this chapter considers some other livelihood activities important for people in the Xekong River Basin in Laos.

Handicrafts

One important source of livelihood in parts of the Xekong River Basin is the making and selling of various kinds of handicrafts, often using bamboo and rattan (see box below). The different ethnic groups of Xekong Province make a wide variety of baskets, folk tools, and handicrafts (see Institute for Cultural Research 2005), and a wide variety of handicrafts are made in others parts of the basin as well. For example, the ethnic Ngkriang people in Kloung Village, Kalum District, make mats (*sat* in Lao), rice steamers (*houat* in Lao) and rice winnowers (*kadong* in Lao) to sell, as well as many other handicrafts for their own use. While some handicrafts are made for sale, the vast majority are not sold or traded. In many cases handicrafts are primarily made for local use, but small quantities of particular products are made to sell. These often provide just enough money to allow producers to buy enough salt and MSG to meet their family needs.

The three ethnic Brao villages of Houay Keua, *Ban* Na, and Phon Sa-at, in Pathoumphone and Khong Districts, are not technically within the Xekong River Basin, but the villagers access bamboo for making handicrafts from areas within the basin, inside the Xepian NPA. Most families in these villages make and sell bamboo handicrafts, especially rice steamers, rice baskets (*katip* in Lao), and rice winnowers. Men collect the bamboo from the forests, and both men and women, but especially women, make the handicrafts. They used to market their wares outside their villages themselves, walking from village to village carrying large quantities of bamboo handicrafts, but now buyers come directly to them and buy all they can produce. In 2006, the rice steamers wholesaled for 1,200 kip each, while rice winnowers sold for 1,500 to 2,000 kip each, and rice baskets sold for 3,000 kip each (depending upon size). On average, a woman can make about two rice winnowers per day, so this is clearly not a particularly profitable occupation. However, it is the most important source of income for the Brao people from these three villages.

People from Dakchung District are skillful in basketry and pottery (UNDP 1997) and, as discussed in Chapter 5, people from Tha Hin Village in Samakhixay District make and sell stoneware pottery (*hai* in Lao). A few ethnic Oy villages in Samakhixay District make earthenware, known as *maw din* in Lao (Leedom Lefferts, pers. comm. 2007). While there is considerable handicraft production going on in the villages for local use, and sometimes for sale, marketing is still limited. There is clearly much potential for expanding marketing possibilities for handicraft-making activities in the future. However, handicraft prices are often low, making other activities more attractive. So far handicraft production has not received much attention from development organizations working in the basin. The GoL is interested in possibilities, but has so far not been able to develop markets for many types of handicrafts.

Hand Dugout Boats and Coffins: Forms of Local Livelihood

A specialty item of the Xekong River Basin is handmade dugout canoes. Some ethnic Brao are well-known for making these boats. They are used within their own villages, but ethnic Lao also sometimes buy these well-crafted boats. In Attapeu, ethnic Brao living along the Nam Kong River in Phouvong District build some of the most beautiful single log canoes in the region. Lao people sometimes travel long distances to buy boats from the Brao. These boat builders rarely make more than a few boats a year, as they are made using hand tools.

Another dugout tree item that people make are coffins. While it is taboo for Brao people to make coffins before someone dies, this is not the case for some other ethnic groups. The Katu, for example, make their coffins in advance and store them just outside their villages, underneath their rice barns. Some people only make coffins for their families, but others sell or trade them within their communities. According to Katu people in Pom Village, Kalum District, such coffins are generally sold for about 200,000 kip. Coffins are also often bartered for rice, pigs, or chickens.

Textiles

Cloth weaving is an important livelihood activity for women in certain parts of the Xekong River Basin, especially among ethnic Triang and Katu women of Xekong Province, and among the Triang of Attapeu. Some ethnic Sapouan women from Samakhixay District also sell hand-woven clothes.

Weaving is popular in both Kalum and Dakchung, with 78% of villages in Kalum reportedly being involved in weaving and 63% in Dakchung (UNDP 1999b; 1999e). Dakchung District is well-known for traditional weaving, and all the ethnic groups in the district weave for their own use. Some near the district center sell a few woven items (UNDP 1997). Kalum District may be less famous for weaving than Dakchung, but there are some good weavers there as well. Only a few villages in Kalum were recorded as still predominantly making their own women's and men's clothes in 1999 (UNDP 1999c), but in Dakchung nine were recorded as still mostly making their own women's clothing. None still made their own men's clothing (UNDP 1999a). Ngkriang people in Kalum District reported that women living in the mountains have a history of weaving cloth for local use, but that those adjacent to the Xekong do not.

In Ta-neum Village, Lamam District, Ngkriang women used to weave, but only for their own use and in small quantities. However, with the support of the Canadian INGO, CUSO, they have expanded their weaving activities. As part of this initiative, some younger women who did not know how to weave have learned how to do so. They have set up a marketing group with CUSO's support. The long-term survival of the initiative depends upon marketing, but it is unclear if villagers will be able to maintain this on their own.

The method of weaving used by Austroasiatic peoples is historically quite different from that of ethnic Lao. The Lao have framed looms, but the Austroasiatics have unframed looms that are held at one end on the feet of women weavers. This results in the clothes made by Austroasiatic women often being slightly shorter than those made by ethnic Lao women.

In Xekong town, there is now a shop that sells hand-woven clothes made by women from Dakchung and, to a lesser extent, Kalum. In Attapeu Province the Lao Women's Union has set up a small shop to try to help women market their handmade clothes as well as other handicrafts made in rural areas. In Attapeu ethnic minority women also sometimes try to sell woven clothes in the market and even approach tourists on the streets to try to sell their wares. There may well be potential for increasing the amount of weaving done in the Xekong River Basin, but marketing remains a serious obstacle to expanding this livelihood activity.

Some development and government agencies have been promoting the natural dyeing of woven clothes in Laos, including parts of the Xekong River Basin, as it is recognized that natural dyes are popular with foreign markets.

UXO: Continuing Threat and Big Business

As outlined in Chapter 4, between 1964 and 1973 large quantities of bombs were dropped in the Xekong River Basin in Laos. Bombing was especially intensive along the Ho Chi Minh and Sihanouk Trails, and near military targets like Vietnamese army bases. Large quantities of live unexploded ordnance (UXO) remain in the area. This has left behind a paradoxical legacy. On the one hand, even decades after they were dropped, people continue to be killed and maimed by UXO throughout the Xekong Basin and, especially on the eastern side of the basin, where most of the bombing occurred. This UXO sometimes unexpectedly explode when farmers are breaking up the soil or when they are preparing land for lowland wet-rice or shifting cultivation.

Bombs also sometimes explode when people are trying to dismantle them. For example, in 2004 three youths were killed in a remote part of Attapeu Province when a cluster bomblet (known in Lao as a *bombie*) blew up while the group was trying to dismantle it to retrieve gunpowder. The group had apparently successfully dismantled two hundred bombies in a similar fashion before this one ended their lives. Similarly, in early 2006 two men were killed and a woman was seriously injured in Eetoum Village, Phouvong District, when a bombie that they were trying to dismantle blew up.

UXO are also increasingly being detonated by people searching for scrap metal. For example, in early 2005 five people were killed in Phouvong District when UXO exploded in separate incidents. People digging for scrap metal triggered the bombs. Two came from Houay Le Village, two were from Nam Souan Village, and two lived in Viangxai Village. In 2006, in a separate case in Phouvong, two villagers were injured when a bomb exploded while they were burning wood for cooking. As is often the case, the UXO was under the ground where they made their fire, and the heat from the fire caused the UXO underneath to detonate. The victims had recently relocated their house to a new location (Latsaphao 2006b).

UXO represents not only a significant human safety threat but a critical obstacle to development. Many areas potentially suitable for lowland wet-rice cultivation cannot be opened up and farmed due to the presence of large quantities of UXO.

In Kalum District, UXO Lao, the government agency responsible for addressing UXO issues in Laos, claims that there are so many affected areas, and that the UXO concentration is so high, that the clearance of agricultural land is not cost-effective. Instead, they are concentrating their limited resources on clearing schoolyards, places where road construction is occurring, and construction sites. For example, when development agencies like ACF and SIP-Dev want to put in a water system or build a school in a village, the first job is to get the area cleared of UXO. In such cases it is not unusual to uncover a number of unexploded bombies along even a few hundred-meter water line route. However, priorities in different areas vary. In Phouvong District UXO Lao is putting more efforts into clearing lowland agricultural land so that it can be cultivated. However, this is a slow and difficult process.

Despite the problems associated with UXO, the bombing legacy has ironically presented economic opportunities in the affected areas. Local people in bomb-strewn parts of the basin have been collecting and selling scrap metal from exploded bombs for many years to generate income. Recently, however, the price of scrap metal has increased substantially, leading to a boom in scrap metal collecting and large-scale scrap metal trading. Considering the relative declines in supplies and prices of naturally occurring NTFPs in the forests (see Chapter 6), scrap metal could be considered as the main "NTFP" that local people search for in many of the eastern parts of the Xekong Basin.

This, of course, is not a sustainable livelihood over the long term. Now that the scrap metal trade has increased, supplies of scrap are beginning to be depleted in areas closest to most settlements and main transportation routes. While UXO Lao is against people collecting scrap metal from bombs, and frequently advises villagers not to do so, the attraction of the income that can be raised by selling a bomb casing is too attractive to discourage many from searching for scrap metal in the forests. UXO Lao workers have even found UXO with live fuses in piles of scrap metal collected by villagers—ready to sell.

There are three main types of scrap bomb metal, and they demand different prices. The most abundant metal collected is iron (*lek* in Lao), which traders were buying in a relatively remote part of Phouvong District for 500 kip/kg in 2004 and 1,200 kip/kg in 2005, whereas the price was 400 kip/kg in the villages in Kalum in 2003. Aluminum (*ngom* in Lao) is the second most expensive, garnering about 4,000 kip/kg in 2004 at the village level and 6,000 kip/kg in Kalum District center. Although demand has recently increased substantially, people in Kalum have been selling scrap aluminum since 1981. The most expensive of the metals collected from bombs is copper (*thong* in Lao), and its price in Kalum District villages was 6,000 kip/kg in 2004, and 8,000 kip/kg at the district center. The high price of UXO metals has lead to frenzied searches by children and adults for metal to sell, and has prompted local governments to ban the selling of "new metal," as some children have, for example, been found stealing parts off of tractors and other working machinery to sell as scrap. It is a sort of giant garbage collection drive, or treasure hunt, in which villagers are benefiting. In some places, virtually every family is involved in collecting metal to generate income. Metal collecting has become such a lucrative livelihood activity in recent years that it is currently one of the leading sources of revenue for many families in the basin.

In early 2005, a number of ethnic Brao people in remote parts of Phouvong District started to buy metal detectors from Vietnamese traders to assist them in finding metal buried underground. Since then the number of metal detectors being used has rapidly increased in heavily contaminated UXO areas. The metal detectors cost between 300,000–500,000 kip each, a heavy investment for poor villagers. However, the metal detectors can quickly pay for themselves by identifying large caches of exploded bombs. While it has not yet been reported from the Xekong Basin, in Savannakhet Province scrap metal traders are actually providing metal detectors to villagers on credit, so that they can find metal to sell to them.

Some villagers in Kalum District claim that, apart from gaining income from collecting scrap metal from the forest, scrap metal collecting also helps clean up the forest and, in some cases, might even help open up areas for agriculture. They sometimes joke that they are doing more to rid the forest of UXO than UXO Lao will ever be able to do, and that they are doing it for free, whereas it costs a lot of money for UXO Lao to do the job.

Not all villagers receive a fair deal for the metal they sell. In one case it was reported that villagers in a remote part of Kalum District were receiving only 300 kip/kg for scrap metal but that traders were reselling it for 1,000 kip/kg. In less remote areas, such as in Sanamxay District, prices for scrap metal are higher, at 700–800 kip/kg. Often transportation difficulties necessitate that traders buy scrap metal at low prices.

Apart from selling UXO metal, a small number of people use it to make other products for sale. For example, in 2004 two people from Kloung Village in Kalum District were observed using aluminum from bombs to make metal storage boxes (sold for 300,000 kip each), buckets, and eating-trays (*pha khao* in Lao). The men involved in this craft said that they had been doing this for over ten years. However, this sort of activity is not common.

UXO Lao operates with significant donor assistance and employs many local people with attractive salaries. The result has been that in many remote areas of the Xekong Basin, where there is little commercial economic activity or few opportunities for well-paid employment, UXO Lao has become one of the most important sources of local employment, especially for ethnic minority males who do not have a high enough formal education to become government officials.

In sum, UXO represent both a continuing human safety threat and an economic development deterrent and, at the same time, one of the most important, albeit unsustainable, local sources of income through scrap metal collection and trade, value-added craftsmanship, and generating local employment. The legacy of UXO in southern Laos continuing to have a significant impact on the livelihoods of local people, well beyond what could have been anticipated at the time the bombs were dropped.

Tourism and Eco-Tourism

At present, tourism does not play an important role in the livelihoods of most local people in the Xekong River Basin in Laos. The area is still largely off of main tourist routes, and it could be said that tourism is in its infancy. Over the next decade this could change dramatically. In fact, it seems likely that tourism is going to be the new boom industry for at least some parts of the Xekong Basin.

Before 2002 neither Xekong nor Attapeu Provinces collected any statistics regarding the number of tourists visiting their provinces. However, in 2002 Attapeu reported receiving 6,831 tourists, and Xekong registered the lowest number of tourist arrivals of any province in the country: 574 visitors (LNMC 2004). This is undoubtedly an underestimate based on hotel and guesthouse stays. It might be expected that most foreign tourists arriving in Attapeu would have passed by Xekong, but many could have come from Cambodia or Vietnam via Route 18a.

In 2002, there were just four registered hotels and guesthouses in Attapeu, with a total of seventy-four rooms, while there was only one registered establishment in Xekong with fifteen rooms. However, there has been a significant increase in the number of establishments catering to foreign tourists. There are now a number of guesthouses and hotels in the capitals of both Attapeu and Xekong Provinces, and a small guesthouse has even been opened in the district capital of Saysettha. There are government-owned guesthouses in the capitals of Kalum and Dakchung Districts.

The Tourism Authority of Attapeu Province recently decided to try to develop eco-tourism and, in 2005, CUSO placed a Canadian co-operant (volunteer) in Attapeu to work with them full time on this. However, local ideas regarding the eco-tourism concept are not well developed, and she found the assignment to be challenging. During her stay, the Tourism Authority of Attapeu identified Dong Ampham NPA, the Xepian River area of Sanamxay District and, improbably, the Pa-am area in Sanxay District as potential eco-tourism sites. A home-stay eco-tourism system in *Ban* Mai, Sanamxay District, next to the Xepian River, was subsequently developed.

There is still much to be learned about tourism in Attapeu. For example, there is an old Soviet-era surface-to-air missile located at Pa-am, Sanxay District. When local officials observed that tourists found this war relic interesting and liked to take photos of it, they decided to put bamboo fencing around it and start charging 5,000 kip/person for tourists who want to see and photograph the missile. It is doubtful that this effort will go over well with most tourists.

There are a large number of beautiful natural locations in the Xekong River Basin, as well as interesting peoples and cultures. At least one eco-tourism company, Nature Discovery Tours, based in Phuket, Thailand, is now organizing custom kayaking tours down the Xekong in Xekong Province and is considering arranging them down the Xenamnoi River.[1] In addition, there are a small but increasing number of tourists traveling up the Xekaman River to *Tat Po* by hiring boats driven by local people.

One of the most notable potential tourist attractions in Xekong Province are the *Keng Luang* Rapids, situated on the mainstream Xekong River about 12 km north of the capital of Xekong Province. The area is currently only a local tourist spot, somewhere where government officials and their families come for picnics on weekends and holidays. There are many other beautiful rapids between Xekong town and Kalum District center, such as *Keng Teun*, *Keng Pan*, and *Keng Tapou*, where boats often tip over, and where villagers believe there are large amounts of gold at the bottom of the river. From Kalum District center up to *Vang Hai*, there are many other significant rapids, including *Keng Ya*, *Keng Ai*, *Keng Meun*, *Keng Yong*, *Keng Chouy*, *Keng Beup*, and *Keng Pro*. All contribute to the beauty of the Xekong and have potential as tourist spots. There are also rapids downstream from Xekong town, but they are generally "gentler" and less dramatic.

The provincial government of Xekong Province has expressed interest in expanding tourism. The Deputy Governor of Xekong Province, Phonephet Khiulavong, recently called for investors to develop tourism in the province (Pansivongsay

2006b). However, as in Attapeu, there is still only a limited understanding of tourism in the province. One serious limitation is that few people speak English or French.

At the same time as tourism is being promoted, the local governments in Attapeu and Xekong are continuing to tightly control access to many places, especially the remote districts situated adjacent to Vietnam. These outlying areas are not open to tourism, despite the rhetoric about the whole country being open to international travelers. Champasak Province is much more open to tourism of all types. However, this may change as road networks to the east continue to be improved and expanded and as local governments become more familiar with tourists. It is unclear what kinds of tourism are going to be promoted—small-scale people friendly tourism, eco-tourism, or larger-scale tourist resort models. For example, at *Nong Fa Nong Yot*, Sanxay District, there are plans for eco-tourism but also plans to develop a golf course around the crater-lake. The fundamental incompatibility of these two visions does not yet seem to be evident to local planners and officials. There is also concern that large tourist ventures controlled by outsiders will dominate tourism, resulting in fewer potential benefits for local people with less investment capital.

Gold Panning

Villagers have long panned for gold in the rivers and smaller tributaries of the Xekong Basin. The rich gold deposits there were recognized from the time that the first French explorers visited the area. In 1894, shortly after the French took over Attapeu from the Siamese, the French administrator Monsieur Ruthe wrote in his April report to the Governor General of Indochina in Saigon that gold panning was the main occupation for the people of Attapeu.[2] Constance Wilson, a historian of the region, has also reported that during the pre-colonial and colonial periods Mon-Khmer language-speaking "aborigines" did most of the gold panning in Attapeu (Wilson 1992). The French had great hopes that gold panning in the rivers and streams of the Xekong River Basin would be profitable, but initial results around Attapeu were apparently disappointing (Dommen 1985). Nevertheless, villagers in Xekong and Attapeu Provinces are still finding dry season gold panning to be a worthwhile livelihood activity. The UNDP (1999e) reported that 67% of the villages surveyed in Kalum District were involved in gold panning while 2% reported being involved in gold and silversmith work. In Dakchung, 21% of villages were reported to be gold panning, with about half of the families selling gold and the other half using it for barter trade (UNDP 1999b). Davidson et al. (1997) reported that gold panning along the Xekaman River only formed a minor supplement to local incomes. At present it appears that this activity generates a significant portion of income for many poor families along the Xekong, Xekaman, and Xexou Rivers, as well as along some small tributaries in the eastern part of the basin.

In the mountains of eastern Phouvong District, for example, ethnic Brao people living along the Ka-ol Stream sometimes pan for gold. Gold is measured as "rice pieces," and locals report that in 2004 one "rice piece" of gold was selling for 3,000 kip. There are 60 "pieces of rice" in one *kuk*, which was selling for 180,000 kip. There are said to be 6 *kuk* in a *bath*. Gold panning takes place exclusively during the dry season between January and June, and villagers report being able to get at least one or two "rice pieces" of gold per day of panning and sometimes as much as 1 *kuk*. The amount collected is more often on the lower end of the scale.

In Kalum District, the measurements used for panned gold from the Xekong River are different. Villagers there claimed that they get about 3–4 *houn* of gold per family from panning each year. One *houn* of gold sells for 30,000 kip. The money they get is often just enough for them to buy salt and MSG, two of the only products bought from the lowlands and which cannot be produced or found locally. Katu villagers from Laipo Village, Kalum District, told me that they make about 5,000–20,000 kip a day panning for gold in the upper Xekong near their village. The amount of gold collected seems to vary significantly from area to area.

Over the last few years there have been drastic changes in the way gold is extracted from the Xekong in Laos. Rather than using the small wooden or metal pans that villagers have long relied on, new extraction operations use large, metal, motorized gold-excavating boats. Operated by Chinese and Vietnamese workers, the boats moor themselves in the middle of the river and use aggregate excavating equipment and conveyor belts in the gold extraction process (see Chapter 12). Outsiders primarily do these excavations. Local villagers continue to be involved almost exclusively in gold panning. Gold excavating has, however, had a negative impact on gold panning, as it reduces the amount of gold available for local people.

External Labor

External labor is an important and growing aspect of many people's livelihoods in the Xekong River Basin. Kalum District has long been one of the main sources of seasonal agriculture workers, and 81% of villagers there reported being involved in external employment in 1999 (UNDP 1999e). They mainly hired out their labor during the dry season in Pakxong and Thateng Districts for collecting coffee, weeding and cutting trees and bushes in swidden fields. This compares to 47% involvement in external employment in Dakchung District (UNDP 1999b), which is still quite significant.

Participation in external labor is one of the main reasons why many of the ethnic minority males from Kalum and Dakchung can speak Lao reasonably well, even though there are no ethnic Lao villages near their communities. In 2004, however, villagers from Kalum reported that, over the past few years, the number of people migrating to work on other people's farms has declined significantly. This was said to be due to the influx of "development projects" into their villages, which were providing them with more incentives to stay home. They said that basic consumer goods are now available in the district center, whereas in the past they had to travel much farther to access them.

There are also seasonal labor migrations from Attapeu Province to the Bolaven Plateau for farming. Quite a few young ethnic minority people from Sanxay District go to Pakxong to pick coffee for a few months each year and to do weeding or clear new fields. People used to do this many years ago when they were living in mountainous areas, and those who have resettled to the lowlands are still doing it. People from other parts of Attapeu also seasonally travel to the Bolaven Plateau for work. This occurs mostly in the dry season when there is less agricultural work to do at home.

Apart from these kinds of intra-basin labor migrations, there are increasing numbers of people from the hinterlands of Attapeu, Xekong, Champasak, and Salavan traveling further afield to sell their labor. Some travel to work in construction or in garment factories in the Vientiane area. Many more are entering Thailand to work illegally. This sort of labor migration can be profitable, but it can also be risky and even dangerous. Many socio-cultural problems can occur after people have been away working in Thailand for many years (see, for example, Shoemaker et al. 2001). Many of the young men and women who travel to work in Thailand are naïve concerning how things are done there and the potential dangers they face. This "blind migration" makes them more vulnerable to human trafficking and other forms of exploitation. Some are not paid the salaries originally promised or have to endure long hours and difficult working and living conditions. Others are threatened and sent away without any salary. The workers have no legal recourse, as they are imprisoned and deported back to Laos if they are caught working illegally. Some end up being tricked or forced into participating in the commercial sex industry. An unknown number of such workers are likely to be returning to Laos carrying sexually transmitted diseases, including HIV/AIDS.

So far, most of the Lao nationals who have traveled to Thailand to work have come from areas near Thailand (see Shoemaker et al. 2001). However, as road transportation improves, and ethnic minorities become more aware of the world outside of their villages, the number of people from the Xekong Basin migrating seasonally or permanently to work in Thailand can be expected to increase substantially. Unfortunately, awareness levels about the risks involved remain low.

Other Activities

Apart from the various livelihood activities outlined above and in previous chapters, there are many others that have not been discussed, either because they are quite localized or since relatively few people are engaged in them. For example, in Kalum and Dakchung Districts, some other important livelihood activities include blacksmithing, producing alcohol, mat making, rice basket and rattan table making, sewing and weaving (UNDP 1999b and e). In Dakchung District, alcohol production was cited as a main source of livelihood (UNDP 1999b) with cassava alcohol often being made (Chagnon 2000). Jar beer (*Lao hai* in Lao) made from rice and sometimes "*ta nian*" grain (probably a type of millet) are the main sources of alcohol, and these are consumed on a regular basis for ritual and other reasons. In contrast, in Kalum District it is often taboo for people from the ethnic groups there to consume jar beer except as part of Animist rituals. So the consumption of jar beer is quite rare. Thus, in Kalum distilled rice whisky is more commonly made and consumed than in Dakchung. In Sanxay District, villagers also collect bamboo for making walls to sell to lowlanders.

Chinese and Vietnamese Traveling Traders in the Xekong River Basin

Large numbers of Vietnamese and Chinese traveling traders have poured into the Xekong Basin and other parts of Laos, and today they are frequently encountered throughout the basin, both in urban areas and in some of the most remote villages. Vietnamese men generally travel around with heavily loaded bicycles or older motorcycles. They are often seen selling cooking utensils, including pots and pans. The Chinese are more ubiquitous. They generally travel by foot, selling all kinds of cheap Chinese trinkets, from watches to small scissors to super-glue. Thousands of young Chinese men and women seem to be traveling to communities near and far in the basin to ply their wares.

Many speak little Lao, but they are quite capable of haggling with their Lao-speaking customers. In fact, they are much more oriented to bargaining for goods than are most Lao. In Lao culture it might be normal practice to barter the price of a shirt down from 10,000 kip to 9,000 kip. But items initially priced by the Chinese at 10,000 kip are often finally sold for as little as 2,000 kip! The gap between the asking price and the final price of the Chinese traders is high by Lao standards, but over time most Lao people have figured this out. Given Lao cultural traditions, few engage in the type of traveling commerce practiced by these Chinese and Vietnamese traders. However, some ethnic Lao traders take clothing to remote villages in the dry season, either to sell for cash or to trade for chickens and pigs.

9

Biodiversity and Natural Resources Management and Conservation

While some may view natural resource management as a narrow technical discipline, in the context of this book it has a much broader meaning and covers a wide range of social, cultural, economic, and even political practices associated with human livelihoods and ecological systems. The following are descriptions of some of the important natural resources in the Xekong River Basin in Laos and a number of mechanisms developed by people and different levels of government to manage them.

Wildlife Biodiversity

A number of field-based biodiversity studies have been conducted in the Xekong River Basin over the past decade or so, and their results have all indicated that the basin is globally significant for biodiversity conservation. Large mammals such as the Tiger (*Panthera tigris*) (*seua khong* in Lao),[1] Clouded Leopard (*Pardofelis nebulosa*), Asian Elephant (*Elephas maximus*) (*xang*), Douc Langur (*Pygathrix nemaeus*) (*kha deng*), Yellow-cheeked Crested Gibbon (*Hylobates gabriellae*) (*thani*), Dhole (*Cuon alpinus*) (*ma nai*), Asiatic Black Bear (*Ursus thibetanus*) (*mi*), and Sambar Deer (*Cervus unicolor*) (*kouang*), have, for example, been recorded in the Xekong Basin (Rosale et al. 2003; Duckworth et al. 1999).

In addition, a new species of deer, the large-antlered Muntjac (*Muntiacus vuquangensis*), is found only in Laos, Vietnam, and Cambodia. In Laos, it is only known from the Nam Theun River Basin, in the central part of the country, south to the border with Cambodia. Thus, some of the species' most important habitat is in the Xekong River Basin (Duckworth et al. 1999). There may also be populations of the once thought extinct but later rediscovered Indochinese Warty pig (Heude's Pig) (*Sus bucculentus*) in parts of the Annamite Mountain Range in the Xekong

Basin in Laos. However, so far there have been few documented reports of the species there (Duckworth et al. 1999).

Although Gaur (*Bos gaurus*) and Banteng (*Bos javanicus*) are still wild in parts of the Xekong Basin, there are no recent reports of either Wild Buffalo (*Bubalus arnee*) or Kouprey (*Bos sauveli*) in Laos although there were a number of reports of Kouprey in Attapeu Province in the 1990s. Feral populations of domestic buffaloes ran free on the Bolaven Plateau in the 1970s, but there is no evidence that these animals are present today. In some parts of the Xekong plains in the Xepian NPA, as well as the Dong Ampham NPA in Attapeu, domestic buffaloes continue to wander at will for weeks or months with little or no human contact, but these animals are not truly feral (Duckworth et al. 1999). They can, however, be dangerous if surprised or cornered in the forest. It is possible that the Saola (*Pseudoryx nghetinhensis*) may be found in the Xekong Basin, as there is an old report of its existence from Xekong Province, but Duckworth et al. (1999) discount this and believe that the species is not found there. Since there are no recent accounts of the species in the province, its southern range is believed to be the headwaters of the Xe Bang Fai River in Khammouane Province, central Laos.

It was once considered possible that the spiral horned Khting Vor (*Pseudonovibos spiralis*) occurred in the Xekong Basin (Duckworth et al.1999; Davidson et al.1997), but genetic studies conducted a few years ago in France revealed that the species probably never existed. All horns in collections appear to be of other bovine species, like cows, that have been skillfully altered to appear to be the spiral horned species. The existence of the Khting Vor appears to be a simple fraud (Hassanin et al. 2001). All local villagers interviewed in southern Laos deny knowing anything about the species.

Birds are abundant in the Xekong River Basin, and 178 species were recorded from Xekong Province in one study. These included such important birds for conservation as the Crested Argus (*Rheinardia ocellata*), Green Peafowl (*Pavo muticus*), Spot-bellied Eagle Owl (*Bubo nipalensis*), and Great Hornbill (*Buceros bicornis*) (Rosales et al. 2003). In another study of Dong Ampham NPA in Attapeu, 280 bird species were identified (Davidson et al. 1997).

Reptile and amphibian biodiversity in the Xekong River Basin is believed to be impressive, although many parts of the basin have not yet been properly surveyed. There may well be many species not yet known to science. Throughout Laos there are currently 166 recognized reptile and amphibian species. Although species occurrence has not been determined on a basin-by-basin basis, two new species of frogs have recently been described from the Xekong Basin in Kalum District, based on fieldwork conducted by Bryan Stuart in 1999 (Stuart and Chan-ard 2005; Stuart et al. 2005; see also section on Xesap NPA). Stuart only visited a limited part of the basin, so there may well be additional species that he did not observe.

Fish biodiversity studies in the Xekong River Basin in Laos have revealed a large number of species, including many new and endemic ones (Baird et al. 1999; Kottelat 2001) (see Chapter 7).

Protected Areas

Protected Areas covering both terrestrial and aquatic habits have, in recent decades, become the dominant management tool advocated in conservation biology. Protected areas can take many different forms and can have important socio-political and spatial implications beyond what is normally associated with biodiversity conservation (see, for example, Baird 2008b). There are, in fact, a wide variety of protected areas in the Xekong River Basin in Laos, including National Protected Areas (NPAs);[2] provincial, district, and village forest protected areas; government forest rehabilitation protected areas; village deep-water pool protected areas; and "spirit protected areas," including cemetery forests. There have even been attempts, albeit unsuccessful, to include parts of the Xekong River Basin in Laos within an "Indochina tri-state reserve for peace and nature," in cooperation with Vietnam and Cambodia (Westing 1993). The GoL formally recognizes some types of protected areas, but others are informally managed and only locally acknowledged.

Ling (1999) has argued that to ensure that globally important ecosystems and species are protected, "rational" planning and decision-making for managing Laos' biological diversity protection can only be done at the national level. In our view, it seems unrealistic to expect a centralized state such as Laos to be able to "rationally" manage areas without adequate local government and villager input. It is critical to recognize the many limitations associated with the centralized management of natural resources in Laos. These include the lack of human and other resources, a lack of knowledge about local circumstances at the central level, and a lack of real political or other power to enforce central control. Protected area management requires careful consideration of critical social, cultural, economic, and political factors that differ greatly between various locations. Local participation is not simply an option; it is a necessity. Baird and Dearden (2003) argue for a contextual approach to protected area management, in which different resources and circumstances require different levels of management. Communities can effectively manage some resources, while others may require joint efforts between governments and local people. Still others may require national action. Such an approach provides a balance between broad conservation goals and local realities, especially considering the considerable *de facto* power that local levels of government and even villages have in making natural resource management decisions in Laos.

National Protected Areas

There are a total of twenty National Protected Areas (NPAs) in Laos and four of those are either partially or fully located in the Xekong Basin. Those are the Xepian NPA, the Dong Ampham NPA, the Xesap NPA, and the Dong Houa Sao NPA. Prime Minister's Decree 164 established the first eighteen NPAs in Laos in 1993. Two more were added to the list in 1996.

The Xesap NPA, variously reported as 128,300, 133,500, or 149,000 ha in size, was one of the two new NPAs added in 1996 (Steinmetz et al. 1999; Robichaud et al. 2001). The other three NPAs in the basin are among the original eighteen established in 1993. The Xesap is partially in the Xekong River Basin in Kalum District and partly outside of it in Ta-oi and Samouay Districts of Salavan Province.

The size of the Xepian NPA is also unclear, with reports ranging from 217,300 to 341,800 ha. It is probably around 240,000 ha. It covers parts of Sanamxay District in Attapeu Province and Pathoumphone and Khong Districts in Champasak Province (Robichaud et al. 2001).

The Dong Ampham NPA is reported as covering either 197,500 or 200,000 ha in Phouvong and Sanxay Districts (Davidson et al. 1997; Robichaud et al. 2001).

The Dong Houa Sao NPA has been variously reported to cover 91,000, 94,700 or 110,000 ha. It is found in Pathoumphone and Pakxong Districts in Champasak Province (Robichaud et al. 2001).

There are also a number of proposed NPAs in the Xekong River Basin, including: Phou Theung[3] in Kalum District, the Xekhampho Corridor NPA in Sanamxay District; Phou Kathong in northwestern Attapeu Province; the northeastern Bolaven PA in northeastern Champasak Province and northwestern Attapeu Province; and the southwestern Bolaven PA in Champasak and Attapeu Provinces (Duckworth et al. 1999). These areas were proposed for protection in 1995 but do not appear to have been given serious consideration by the GoL recently. Given the lack of movement toward establishing any more NPAs in Laos, it seems highly unlikely that these areas will be protected anytime in the near future.

Although NPAs in Laos tend to have more prestige than provincial or district protected areas, the GoL has not been able to devote significant human or financial resources to ensuring that they are well managed for local livelihoods and biodiversity protection. During the 1990s, the World Bank's Forestry Management and Conservation Project (FOMACOP) supported the management of four NPAs, two of which are partly in the Xekong River Basin: the Xesap and Xepian NPAs. The Dong Houa Sao NPA also received support from a Dutch-funded IUCN project implemented in the 1990s. Xepian NPA was the recipient of a Denmark funded follow-up project in 2000/2001. But at present there are no large international projects in the Xekong Basin supporting protected area management.

Xepian NPA

Situated in the southwestern part of the Xekong River Basin in Laos, much of the Xepian NPA drains into the Xekong via the Xepian and Xekhampho Rivers. Some parts are also included in the *Houay* Kaliang Basin in Khong District. The Kaliang flows into the Xekong upstream from its confluence with the Mekong in Cambodia. Other parts in Pathoumphone District drain into the Xekong via the Khamphok and Khampha Streams in Siem Pang District, Stung Treng Province, Cambodia. There are twelve villages situated well inside the NPA, populated by ethnic Lao, Brao and Jru Dak people, as well as a large number of other villages in close proximity to the protected area (WWF 1997).

At least twenty-nine different habitats have been distinguished within the park, with most being relevant to wildlife. At least thirteen mineral licks have been identified. Some are earth licks, and others are situated next to streams (WWF 1997). Much of Xepian NPA is covered in increasingly rare lowland evergreen forest. This habitat is critical for many wildlife populations and so this NPA is believed to be one of the most important for biodiversity conservation in Laos (Robichaud et al. 2001).

Xepian NPA includes many rivers and streams that flow through lowland forests and wetlands, as well as some upland areas. There are believed to be thirty-nine species of large and medium sized mammals in the park, including thirteen globally threatened mammals and another twelve regionally at risk. Some of the most important are Asian Elephants (*Elephas maximus*), Gaur (*Bos gaurus*), Banteng (*Bos javanicus*), Tiger (*Panthera tigris*), Leopard (*Panthera pardus*), Clouded Leopard (*Paradofelis nebulosa*), Asiatic Black Bear (*Ursus thibetanus*), Malaysian Sun Bear (*Ursus malayanus*), Yellow-cheeked Crested Gibbon (*Hylobates gabriellae*), and Douc Langur (*Phgathrix nemaeus*) (WWF 1997).

There are a large number of globally threatened and regionally at risk birds in the NPA as well, including Lesser Adjutants (*Leptoptilos javanicus*), Woolly-necked

Storks (*Ciconia episcopus*), and Giant Ibis (*Pseudibis gigantea*) (WWF 1997; Baird 1997; Timmins et al. 1993). Forty-four species of reptiles, 21 species of amphibians, 176 fish species, 148 species of beetles, and 53 species of butterflies are known from the park. However, many more species from these groups are expected to occur (WWF 1997).

The Xepian NPA has received considerable research and management support over the years (Poulsen and Luanglath 2005), and it was one of the first NPAs in Laos to be the subject of extensive wildlife surveying (see, for example, Timmins et al. 1993). In the mid-1990s, the wildlife of the NPA was studied in considerable detail with the support of the World Bank and Global Environmental Facility (GEF) Protected Areas component of the FOMACOP Project (WWF 1997). However, the project lasted just five years. Later, a number of less extensive wildlife surveys were conducted through a DANIDA-supported project. In 2002, a planned extension of that initiative was suddenly cancelled after a new government came to power in Denmark. Since then, there has not been any structured international support provided for managing Xepian NPA, resulting in a considerable decline in government organized park management activities. Poulsen and Luanglath (2005) have documented the reduction in wildlife monitoring activities in the park since foreign funding ended in June 2002. Large numbers of people were working for the Xepian NPA when it was being directly funded, but, now that institutional support has been discontinued, only a couple of government officials are assigned to the park.

This experience suggests that PA monitoring activities heavily relient on large-scale foreign funding of limited duration may not be very sustainable. Effective PA projects in Laos would appear to need more modest amounts of funding, but over much more extended time-frames, even as long as twenty or more years. If co-management systems that meaningful involve PA staff and local people in management activities could be developed during periods when foreign funding is available, some level of management might still be possible once such funding ceases. This would be more realistic than expecting under-funded government agencies to continue effective management activities in the absence of outside inputs.

There is still some small-scale support being provided to the Xepian NPA. A French supported eco-tourism project has been operating in the park recently as has an ADB-supported eco-tourism loan project. In 2007, a new WWF eco-tourism project is beginning as well. The INGO Global Association for People and the Environment (GAPE) has been providing various forms of education assistance, including environmental education and NTFP management support, to communities situated in and near both Xepian and Dong Houa Sao NPAs (Baird and

Bounphasy 2003). Most recently, GAPE has begun working in Xepian NPA on a "Co-Management Learning Network Project" (CMLN), in collaboration with the Asian Indigenous People's Pact (AIPP), a regional INGO based in Chiang Mai, as part of a seven country regional program.[4] The project is promoting the regional exchange of experiences regarding indigenous peoples and PA management and is promoting the increased involvement and meaningful participation of indigenous peoples in co-managing resources inside Xepian NPA.

Dong Ampham NPA

Situated in the uplands and midlands of the southeastern part of the Xekong River Basin in Laos, the Dong Ampham NPA is drained by the Xekaman and Xexou Rivers, both of which flow into the Xekong. The name Dong Ampham refers to the core part of the park, but the NPA also covers areas referred to differently by local people. A small part of Dong Ampham NPA is adjacent to Virachey National Park in Ratanakiri Province, northeast Cambodia, and the NPA borders Kontum Province in the Central Highlands of Vietnam. The Mom Ray Nature Reserve in Vietnam is adjacent to Virachey National Park and is thus connected with Dong Ampham via Virachey (MoE, Cambodia 2003). Dong Ampham NPA is also connected to the northeast with the previously proposed 880 km² Phou Kathong PA (Davidson et al. 1997). Conservation studies envisioned that Phou Kathong would act as part of an interconnected corridor of PAs, linking Dong Ampham with Dong Houa Sao and Xepian NPAs via the Xekong plains and the Bolaven Plateau (Davidson et al. 1997), but this has not transpired. In fact, Phou Kathong is now considered a production forest.[5]

Dong Ampham NPA together with the previously proposed Phou Kathong PA, constitute important habitat for a number of globally threatened and endangered mammal and bird species. Part of the reason for the high levels of biodiversity in Dong Ampham is that the area covers a broad altitudinal range (100–2,052 m asl) and therefore supports a wide variety of vegetation types. In Dong Ampham, Davidson et al. (1997) confirmed the presence of eighty-four mammal species, of which there were thirty key species of conservation concern, including four rare large cats (Fishing Cat, Golden Cat, Clouded Leopard, and Tiger), at least six primate species, including two threatened taxa (Douc Langur and Yellow-cheeked Crested Gibbon), eight species of ungulates, including Gaur, Large-Antlered Muntjac, another smaller muntjac (probably Red Muntjac), Asian Elephant, and two bear species (Asiatic Black Bear and Malaysian Sun Bear). In addition, thirty-seven bird species found in Dong Ampham are considered to be key species of conservation concern, including two vultures, the Woolly-necked Stork, the Crested Argus, and large populations of Siamese Firebacks and Great Hornbills. There are also likely to be endemic and undescribed fish species in this largely upland NPA (Davidson et al. 1997; Robichaud et al. 2001).

Ethnic Brao people from Nam Souan Village, situated along the old road now known as Route 18a from Attapeu to Vietnam (via Cambodia) and near Dong Ampham NPA, said tigers were quite common near their village until recently. In 1991, one was killed after it entered the village. Another tiger entered the village in 1993/1994, but none have been seen since then. One Brao villager noted that "Over the last few years logging activities have frightened the tigers away."

Dong Ampham NPA is considered to be one of Laos' most important PAs, largely due to its geographical location on the high biodiversity Annamite Mountain Range (Robichaud et al. 2001). Davidson et al. (1997) suggested that Dong Ampham supports biodiversity of national significance, rivaled in Laos only by the Nakai-Nam Theun NPA and its proposed northern extension area in Khammouane Province, and the proposed Dong Kanthoung NPA on the west side of the Mekong in Champasak Province.

Arthur Westing (1993) considered whether Dong Ampham could be included within the "Indochina tri-state reserve for nature and security," envisioned by the United Nations Environment Program (UNEP) in the early 1990s. UNEP expected this tri-state reserve to contribute to biodiversity conservation of important natural habitats and to build cooperation between the three countries involved, so as to enhance human security. Westing was concerned, however, that fragmentation caused by Route 18a, which runs through the Dong Ampham near its border with Virachey National Park in Cambodia, would lessen the conservation effectiveness of this designation. The proposed 122,100 ha Nam Kong NPA—never designated at the national level—was, in fact, considered a better potential contribution to the expected 500,000 ha tri-state park. However, any plans or momentum to establish this tri-state park evaporated once the UNEP initiative to promote the idea ended. Despite subsequent expressions of interest from IUCN, WWF and the World Bank, no further progress has been made in developing the concept. Instead, the idea of tri-border economic development cooperation—through the "economic development triangle" concept—has eclipsed the tri-state park vision (see Chapter 11).

Davidson et al. (1997) recommended that a relatively small (approximately 240 km²) area southwest of the NPA be added to Dong Ampham, as it includes important dry dipterocarp and mixed deciduous forests, habitats poorly represented in Dong Ampham, and critical for a number of important large mammal species. There are apparently no permanent human settlements in this area. This addition, believed Davidson et al. (1997), would provide the opportunity to link Dong Ampham with the Nam Kong Provincial Protected Area to the southwest.[6]

Davidson et al. (1997) conducted the only detailed wildlife survey for Dong Ampham NPA, and there is no recent survey information about the status of wildlife within the park. Yet interviews with local people familiar with the area indicate that the NPA has recently experienced considerable logging and hunting pressures. It appears that the GoL has done little to ensure its protection.

Apart from wildlife, Dong Ampham has some interesting natural rock formations. There are reports of some rocks that look like "the chair of *Groong*," the epic mythical messiah of the Brao. There is also a natural *"patou khong,"* or archway of rocks, in the same area.

The Attapeu provincial tourism authority has expressed interest in developing Dong Ampham for eco-tourism in the future, but there are no clear plans for this.

Xesap NPA

Situated in the northern part of the Xekong River Basin, the Xesap NPA is included in both the Xe Bang Hiang watershed to the northwest and the Xekong watershed to the southeast. The Xesap River, which flows from the Xekong Basin's headwaters in Vietnam, divides the park into the eastern Xesap, bordering Vietnam to the north and east, and the western Xesap, bordering Vietnam to the north and contained mainly in Salavan Province. All of the eastern part of the NPA is in the Xekong River Basin, while the western part is not in the Xekong. There are no exact statistics available, but it appears that about 50% of the NPA is drained by the Xepon and Xelanong Rivers, which flow into the Xe Bang Hiang River. The southern watershed, which represents the other 50%, is wholly inside the Xekong Basin. Most of the NPA is mountainous and rugged—and 35% of the park is above 1,000 m asl—but gentler high elevation plateaus and valleys exist in central and southern Xesap. Xexap NPA is believed to be the home to important populations of a number of globally threatened and regionally at risk mammals and birds (Steinmetz et al. 1999; Robichaud et al. 2001). Although fish surveys have yet to be done within the NPA, it is highly likely that there are endemic fish species in the area that have not yet been described by taxonomists. Robichaud et al. (2001) prioritized Xexap NPA and others on the Annamite Range due to the high levels of biological diversity there.

Some wildlife surveys have been conducted in parts of the Xesap NPA but many parts are mountainous and difficult of access. Timmins and Vongkhamheng (1996) conducted the first preliminary study of the NPA but apparently never entered the eastern part of the park situated in Xekong Province. They did survey Phou Ahyon, which has been proposed as an extension to the NPA. Other surveys have focused on parts of the park in Ta-oi and Samouay Districts of Salavan Province (Stone 1999; Steinmetz et al. 1999). This was also the case for the study of large mammals conducted in the park by the Wildlife Conservation Society, which only covered parts of Samouay District (Schaller and Boonsou 1996). Schaller (1995) conducted a survey of large mammals outside the NPA boundaries (even before it was established) in Kalum and Dakchung Districts in Xekong Province.

Showler et al. (1998) were probably the first to investigate the part of the Xesap NPA in Xekong Province, as well as areas on the Dakchung Plateau south of there, concentrating on mammals, birds, and habitat. Bryan Stuart conducted a survey of reptiles and amphibians in the Xekong River Basin part of the NPA in June 1999, traveling eleven days each way from Kalum town! Even then, he just barely got into the NPA, demonstrating the remoteness of the area. He was rewarded for his efforts by finding a number of interesting reptiles and amphibians. Based on that survey, Stuart and Chanard (2005) described a new medium-sized species of ranid frog, *Huai absita*, from hill evergreen forests between 920–1,300 m asl. The species is known only from the Xesap NPA in the Xekong Basin as well as the Xelanong Basin in Samouay District of Salavan. Stuart et al. (2005) also described another new ranid cascade frog species, *Rana khalam*, based on Stuart's 1999 trip to Kalum. This species is not known in Salavan Province, but it has been found in Bach Ma and Ba Na National Parks in Vietnam.

Most recently, the INGO Village Focus International (VFI) has been working with communities near the NPA in Salavan Province to support and improve natural resource management. But there has been little focus by outside agencies on the part of the Xesap NPA in Kalum District of Xekong Province. The human population surrounding and living inside the NPA in Kalum District is low. In the late 1990s, it was determined that there were three villages inside the park in Kalum District and eleven nearby, with a total combined population of 1,693 people (Xesap NBCA summary 1999). Almost all the people are believed to be ethnic Katu.

Dong Houa Sao NPA

Dong Houa Sao NPA is partly situated in lowland areas but also includes a part of the western Bolaven Plateau. The NPA is largely situated in the Xedon and Tomo

River Basins, but a small part of the southeastern section of the NPA west of the Xekhampho River is located in the Xekong Basin. It supports many key mammal and bird species of conservation concern, but the area is not considered to be as important for biodiversity conservation as the Xepian, Dong Ampham or Xesap NPAs (Robichaud et al. 2001).

Dong Houa Sao has been subjected to substantial logging in Pathoumphone District in recent years, especially since the end of the IUCN supported project there. In 2005, the central Department of Forestry cracked down on logging in Pathoumphone, arresting and reprimanding a number of businesspeople and government officials and instituting a temporary ban on logging throughout the district. In Pakxong District, the expansion of coffee plantations has been the main threat to the habitat of the park, with large sections of the NPA having been converted to coffee plantations in recent years (see coffee section in Chapter 6). The GoL has done little to prevent the expansion of coffee plantations into the park.

Threats to Protected Areas

All four Xekong Basin NPAs are threatened by illegal logging, but Dong Ampham and Dong Houa Sao are being particularly degraded by on-going large-scale commercial logging activities.

Hunting for the wildlife trade has been identified as an important threat to biodiversity (Robichaud et al. 2001), particularly in areas near Vietnam, such as parts of the Dong Ampham NPA (Davidson et al. 1997). The GoL and foreign conservationists working in Laos have long identified the "encroachment" of NPAs by villagers as a serious problem. The *Vientiane Times* (2005j) quoted a Xekong Province official as saying that villagers still hunt wildlife illegally and engage in slash-and-burn cultivation. He suggested that officials should focus more on land allocation for villagers so that they would not need to enter protected areas, saying, "How do we identify poor people? If they wear ragged clothes and don't have enough to eat, they are considered poor. How can they possibly earn a living? They have no choice but to hunt in protected areas unless realistic management measures are implemented" (*Vientiane Times* 2005j).

Apart from logging, plantations, hunting, and other encroachment, the Xepian, Dong Ampham and Xesap NPAs are threatened by the construction of large dams. The Xepian–Xenamnoi Hydropower Scheme would divert the upper Xepian into the Xenamnoi River, leaving the lower Xepian de-watered and causing serious ecological and livelihood consequences within the Xepian NPA (Roberts and

Baird 1995b). The Xesap NPA is threatened by the Xekong 5 Dam, which would inundate the south border area of the park and make it more accessible to people (Steinmetz et al. 1999). The Dong Ampham NPA is threatened by dams on the Xekaman River, especially the Xekaman 1 Dam, which would inundate much of the old-growth lowland evergreen/semi-evergreen forest in the Xekaman River Basin, the area identified by Davidson et al. (1997) as of the highest biodiversity conservation value. In addition, the Xekaman 3 and 4 Dams would both affect downstream hydrology in the Xekaman River, thus negatively impacting Dong Ampham (see Chapter 13).

Guns Collected

Since the late 1990s the GoL has been attempting to collect privately owned guns (both rifles and hand guns) from villagers throughout the country, including in the Xekong Basin. For example, authorities confiscated all private rifles owned by people in Tavang Village, Pathoumphone District a few years ago. While Tavang is inside the Xepian NPA, even villagers living outside NPAs have had their guns collected. This has reduced the capacity of many villagers to hunt wildlife, and, in many areas, it has resulted in signs of increased populations of some wildlife species vulnerable to being hunted with guns. Despite these efforts, wildlife is still generally in decline throughout the basin.

Provincial and District Protected Forest Areas

Provincial and District "Protected Forest Areas" are another type of PA found in the Xekong Basin. These areas are often not clearly designated. They can be opened up to commercial logging and other "development activities" in a very short period of time.

There is no clear legislative structure surrounding this category of PA. They are usually established by decrees issued by district and provincial governors. The protected status of these areas can apparently be revoked at the whim of local officials, without following any particular process. Essentially, they serve as forest reserves until local government officials decide to allow access. For example, Phou Theung was a provincial PA in Kalum District but was then recategorized as a production forest (Ben Hodgdon, WWF, pers. comm. May 2005). Furthermore, no government officials are specifically assigned to provincial and district protected areas. Provincial and district forestry officials do sometimes intervene with regard to the management of these areas; however, their actions often appear to be sporadic, inconsistent, and of limited value.

In sum, most provincial and district PAs in Laos can be considered essentially "paper parks." This is also largely true for most NPAs, but at least with NPAs there is an established legal status, and in some cases there are management plans in place. One good example of a provincial or district PA in the Xekong Basin is the Nam Kong Provincial PA in Attapeu Province, adjacent to Virachey National Park in Cambodia. As mentioned above, it was considered the best option for being included in the proposed 500,000 ha Indochina tri-state reserve for nature and peace (Westing 1993). Despite its status, however, logging has been taking place in the area every year for the last number of years.

One district PA in Thateng District is called *Phouchouam*, but it only covers 3,300 ha (UNDP 1997) and its conservation status is unclear. Phou Katong, in Sanxay District, is another district PA (Davidson et al. 1997) with an unclear status. The very small 108 ha Dong Houa Xang PA, in Saysettha District and adjacent to the Xekaman River, is a good example of a provincial PA vulnerable to redesignation. Local government officials have indicated that they will move the ethnic Cheng village of Cheng Phoke to resettle directly adjacent to the PA. In early 2006, some families had already moved to the new village location. There has apparently been little consideration of how this move will affect the park.

In Attapeu Province, district and provincial governments have protected the escarpment forest between the road from Attapeu to Xekong and the Bolaven Plateau to the west. This was done with little or no consultation with villagers at the time the Houay Ho Dam was being planned (see Chapter 13). Local villagers used to practice swidden agriculture in the lower forests in this area, but for over a decade they have not been allowed to farm there. This has negatively affected the livelihoods of a number of communities.

Another category of provincial or district forest has recently emerged: "Rehabilitation (or Restoration) Forests." It is as of now unclear what exactly the term means in the local context. It appears to be a designation given to forests once logging has occurred and little valuable timber remains. The "Xenamnoi Rehabilitation Forest" in northern Samakhixay District, near the border with Xekong Province, covers 1,598 ha and is designed to promote the rehabilitation of degraded forest resources. The *Pa Houay La Ngiang Kao* rehabilitation forest area in Attapeu Province was established by the provincial government in Saysettha District near Hatxan Village along Route 18a (and 18b) to Vietnam, and covers 7,800 ha. For both of these areas, it is unclear how effective the government has been in promoting their rehabilitation, or what exactly encompasses the restoration vision. It is also unclear whether the aim is to restore diverse natural forests that could again support biodiversity. Some observers speculate that the end result could be the conversion of these areas to monocrop tree plantations rather than real reforestation.

Village Protected Forest Areas

There are a number of Village Protected Forest Areas (VPFAs) (*pa sa-ngouan ban* in Lao) in the Xekong Basin. Communities have established some of these in response to government pressure, in other cases local government and INGOs have supported the community initiatives to establish them. Some VPFAs have been developed informally by villagers to support the practical management of important natural resources; others have been created for spiritual reasons. Sometimes they are being protected for a combination of reasons.

Many rural villages, both Lao and ethnic minority, have forest areas surrounding them, and one of the most common types of VPFAs are "cemetery spirit forests" (*pa phi pasa* in Lao). Although generally not covering large areas (some are very restricted in size), they are a form of VPFA nonetheless. For example, a small *pa phi pasa* protected forest is located just outside of Hatsaikham Village in Sanamxay District. Villagers report that trees cannot be cut there. Another *pa phi pasa* PA with many large trees is in the territory of Saisy Village, adjacent to the Xekaman River in Saysettha District. The area extends to both sides of the Xekaman River. Vat Louang Village, also in Saysettha District, is another Lao village along the Xekaman that has a VPFA adjacent to the Xekaman. In the ethnic Katu village of Pom, in Kalum District, there is a *pa phi pasa* cemetery forest adjacent to the village in the mountains. All these areas appear to be well protected by the villagers. There are many more examples throughout the region. While not all well managed, village protected forest (and deep-water pool areas, see below) in the basin are associated with spirits, some of the best-protected areas are those being managed based on cultural beliefs regarding spirits. For example, the ethnic Harak village of Hin Dam in Sanxay District does not hunt or collect forest products, let alone do agriculture, in a spirit-protected mountain and forest near their village along the edge of the Xekaman, not far upriver from where the construction of the Xekaman 1 Dam is planned (see Chapter 13).

There are parts of NPAs, such as Xepian, officially under the authority of the GoL, but whose day-to-day monitoring responsibilities have, in fact, been turned over to villages inside or adjacent to the PAs. Generally, areas inside NPAs given to villagers to monitor and use in limited ways are small. But some villages are responsible for large areas. For example, the ethnic Lao village of Tavang, in Pathoumphone District, has been allocated a 3,440 ha village protected area inside Xepian NPA. The largest community managed forest area in an NPA is about 25,000 ha and is controlled by Taong Village, also inside the Xepian NPA.

A Fox Guarding the Henhouse? Government Involvement in a Village Protected Forest

Ta-neum is a small ethnic Ngkriang village located about 25 km north of the Xekong provincial capital on the west bank of the Xekong River. In 2004, there were seven households with fifty-one people in the community, including twenty-five women. The village is officially part of a larger village named Songkhone, another ethnic Ngkriang village situated a few kilometers down the Xekong. The Canadian INGO CUSO has been working in the village for a number of years, and part of their work has been focused on helping both Ta-neum and Songkhone set up village deep-water pool PAs. The area is rich in forest resources, with a reported 10,000 m^3 of wood in the village vicinity. Ta-neum has a protected community forest that covers an area of about 10 ha (a relatively small portion of the total village forest land), established with support from CUSO.

The rules for this area are: 1) no cutting trees, 2) no hunting wild animals, 3) no removing other natural resources (i.e., rocks, NTFPs, and so on), and 4) no removing plants useful as traditional medicines (as allowed in other forests). There are barking deer, Sambar deer, wild boar, and many species of small mammals, reptiles, amphibians, and birds found in the area, according to villagers. Elephants occasionally enter the area but are not seen often. There are reports of some large trees remaining in this VPFA. Interestingly, the sign for this protected area states that it is a "government protected forest" (*pa sa-ngouan khong lat* in Lao), not a community protected forest (*pa sa-ngouan khong ban*). In response to questions about the rationale for this, as it did not seem very empowering for the people to have their forest depicted as controlled by the government, villagers said that they supported the designation—arguing that outsiders would respect the rules more if they believed that the government was behind the protected forest.

Unfortunately, it appears that this area has not been as fully protected as originally envisioned. In 2004 and 2005, there was a considerable amount of commercial logging by Vietnamese companies inside the community forest, and a number of splinter roads were constructed near the village to facilitate log transfer. As the companies appeared to have government authorization, villagers were limited in how they could respond. They did try to limit the damage by insisting on accompanying loggers at all times. While the villagers originally hoped that having a government designation for their protected forest would help save it, it was, ironically, local government authorities who authorized these logging incursions. Despite efforts by the local community, forest resources appear to be in decline in the Ta-neum area.

Community Forests Run into Trouble in Xekong Province's Thateng District

In the early 1990s, the Australian INGO Community Aid Abroad (now Oxfam Australia), began working with Xekong provincial and Thateng District authorities to support local ethnic Katu villagers living in a relatively remote area to establish community protected forests. Initially, the process went relatively well, and the communities made agreements to protect the forests. However, in the late 1990s, without any notice or clear explanation, local authorities allowed a company to log inside these community forests. The villagers made some mild objections, but forestry officials said that the government needed to meet its quota of logs and so logging had to be allowed in the community forests, as there were no other easily accessible trees to be harvested in the area. The people believed there was little they could do to resist. This was unfortunate as good community management of natural resources is predicated on secure tenure over resources, so that long-term planning can take place with the confidence that foregoing the harvesting of resources today will lead to long-term benefits in the future. Oxfam Australia, while sympathetic to the villagers' plight, apparently did not view itself as in a position to advocate strongly for the community position, and it eventually withdrew entirely from supporting community forestry in Xekong Province.

Unfortunately, this is far from an isolated incident. There are reports from all over Laos of government-recognized community-protected forests being opened to commercial logging interests without meaningful consultation or the agreement of local communities. The situation has demoralized many INGOs working on community forestry in Laos, not to mention the local people who have made tremendous efforts to protect their forest resources, only to watch them being taken without notice by outside commercial logging ventures. For community forestry to be more successful, villages must gain firm tenure over resources. This will require much better recognition of the concept of villager control over local resources than is currently the case in Laos.

Community Fisheries Management

There are a variety of fisheries management strategies and practices in the Xekong River Basin in Laos. Most community fisheries management initiatives are based on villager perceptions that wild-capture fisheries are in decline. Others in the Mekong River Commission have, however, argued that fisheries are not necessarily in decline but that individual catches have declined because more people are chasing the same number of fish (see various issues of *Mekong Fisheries: Catch and Culture*). However, the framing of fisheries decline is not nearly as straightforward as that. The interests and positions of different players influence the direction and emphasis of studies. The results and observations can vary considerably, depending upon the positions and interests of those interacting with the fishery. Thus politics seems to have an important role to play in whether people believe fisheries are in decline or not (Bush and Hirsch 2005). In the Xekong Basin, villagers frequently believe that fisheries are indeed in decline.

Some organizations and projects advocate taking a technical approach to fisheries research and management, using catch-per-unit effort (CPUE) and other "hard science" methodologies. Others use more community-based approaches, or a mixture of the two. In the Mekong in Khong District, Champasak Province, there has been considerable controversy regarding the most appropriate approach to take. Hirsch (2004) described earlier tensions between measurement-based approaches (i.e., Warren et al. 1998) versus approaches based on gaining knowledge of the local fishery through the intimate study of community practices and familiarity with villagers (Baird 2001). This prompted what Hirsch calls "a syncretic approach whereby methods such as hydro-acoustic sampling of deep pools is being combined with CPUE measurements to assess the effectiveness of management through establishment of fish sanctuaries that are based on local knowledge and community-based processes" (2004: 94).

The World Wide Fund for Nature (WWF) and the Department of Livestock and Fisheries appear to be leaning toward a more community-based approach through two recently launched projects, "Community Fisheries: Supporting Food Security and Aquatic Biodiversity," (or ComFish), which began in May 2005, and "Participatory Management and Conservation in the Xe Kong River Basin" (the Xekong Project), which began in early 2006. ComFish is focused on empowering local villagers who live along the Mekong's tributaries and rely on fishing for their livelihoods. The project hopes to strengthen the livelihood systems and food security of rural communities and thus directly contribute to national poverty alleviation efforts. They are focused on enhancing the co-management of aquatic resources in the Xekong and Xepian River Basins in Laos, as well as the Xe Bang Hiang, Xe Bang Fai, Nam Ou, and Nam Kading River Basins in central and northern Laos.

In its project preparation document, WWF documents pointed out that, considering the high importance given to capture fisheries by rural communities, there is insufficient attention paid to the management and sustainable use of these resources. The project intends to promote an integrated approach to river basin management and support the sustainable use of fish and other aquatic animals and plants that are essential to food security and household income. This will include promoting the establishment of aquatic resource management plans using a co-management framework that involves local people and government in the planning and implementation process (WWF 2003). Roland Eve, the WWF Lao Country Director, stated, at the signing ceremony for the project: "[W]hat is most important is to ensure that the people living from aquatic resources could keep benefiting from this resource. Local people should be managing their resources for their benefit" (cited in Mendoza 2005a: 2). The Xekong and Xepian were two of the main rivers originally targeted by this three-year project (Mendoza 2005a). At present, however, WWF's Xekong project (see WWF 2005c) is the main initiative working on community fisheries in the Xekong Basin while ComFish is mainly concentrating its resources in other river basins in Laos (Roland Eve, pers. comm. March 2007).

Village Deep-water Pool Protected Areas

Many villages in the Xekong River Basin in Laos have established protected deep-water pools, either informally at their own initiative, at the direction of local government officials, or with government and INGO support. These areas are generally called "*vang sa-ngouan*" in Lao, and are common in many parts of Laos, although they take various forms in different places, depending on local circumstances (Baird 2006a).

No specific research has been done on deep-water PAs in the Xekong Basin; much more has been done in the Mekong in Khong District, Champasak Province. There, Baird and Flaherty (2005) found that local people largely believe that deep-water PAs have been successful in increasing the stocks of certain fish species and that different types of deep-water areas have benefited various fishes, probably because of the micro-habitat preferences of different species. Baird (2006a) and Baran et al. (2005) also found that just below the Khone Falls in Khong District, catch-per-unit effort (CPUE) deep-water gill net catches during the dry season were 132–206 g per net set, whereas CPUEs for the same nets used at the same time of the year, but placed in shallow or surface waters, were just 12–36 g per net set. Catches were three to twelve times higher in the deep-water areas, clearly indicating that fish do concentrate in deep-water areas in the dry season. Local ecological knowledge is critical for choosing the right deep-water areas to protect and in ensuring that the rules chosen for each area are suitable. Local ecological knowledge is critical for assessing and monitoring the effectiveness of deep-water protected areas. Villagers can take various approaches to this kind of work, depending on the circumstances (Baird and Flaherty 2005; Baird 2006a and 2006c).

According to the Director of the Livestock and Fisheries Division of Xekong province, two provincially recognized *vang sa-ngouan* were established in 2001. One was at *Vang Keng Chang*, near the sub-village of Ta-neum, Lamam District, and the second was established at *Vang Pak Houay Ko*, near Pak Poun Village, Lamam District. CUSO supported the establishment of both of these areas.

In 2003, Oxfam Australia began supporting the establishment of village wild-capture fisheries regulations, and the establishment of a *vang sa-ngouan* at *Vang* Houa Keng Luang, near Nava Keng Luang Village, in Lamam District. In 2004/2005, after a generally positive experience at this first site, Oxfam Australia decided to expand its support for village-based fisheries management regulations to other villages in Lamam District. Currently, Oxfam Australia is supporting the establishment of village-managed *vang sa-ngouan* in ten villages along the mainstream Xekong and one near the Xenamnoi River in Lamam District, just upstream from the bridge that crosses the river.

One of the ten communities along the Xekong where Oxfam Australia is supporting fisheries management is Pak Thon Village. The village has a deep-water 300 m x 300 m PA in the mainstream of the river called *Vang* Thamakan. The location has long been recognized as being inhabited by a powerful spirit (see section on gold mining in the Xekong in Chapter 12).

While the ethnic Harak founders of Pak Thon Village have long respected the spirit believed to be in the area, and do not fish there, they were glad to be able to cooperate with Oxfam Australia and local government officials to officially establish the area as a *vang sa-ngouan*. This ensures that the area has government-recognized rules associated with it that can be more easily enforced on outsiders. The villagers also prohibit agricultural activities near the edge of the deep-water pool. Historically, the area was not protected in this way, but people respected it anyway. More recently, however, some people began daring to break the traditional taboos, so villagers decided that more official regulations would be useful. Violators are fined 100,000 kip for first transgressions, 300,000 kip for second offenses, and 500,000 kip for third time violations. These fines have not yet been applied, as they are serving as a deterrent to those who might otherwise violate village regulations.

In Kalum District, a community protected deep-water area has been established at *Vang* Hai in the mainstream Xekong. The deep-water area has a legend surrounding it, in which it is said that some strong winds originated in the bottom of the deep pool, which is surrounded by two steep mountains. While an important reason for protecting the area is to conserve fish of all species and sizes, there is an especially large *Luciocyprinus striolatus* (*pa sak* in Lao) fish found in the area. In 2003, the villagers from Kado Village, Kalum District also established a *vang sa-ngouan* at *Vang* Pa Joor, a deep-water area just above some rapids on the Xekong. This was done in cooperation with the district Agriculture and Forestry Office and, according to village leaders, the community is generally supportive of the protected area. However, based on one night of first-hand observation, it is difficult to be sure about this. At Don Village, upriver from Kado, a *vang sa-ngouan* was established near the village in 2003, but the son of the village headman was observed fishing in the PA. He was clearly violating the rules painted onto the sign for the area. The villagers were embarrassed when asked about the *vang sa-ngouan*. A village leader said that locals were not deeply committed and needed to "have their awareness levels built up over time." He also said that the main reason they want the PA is to keep people from other villages from fishing in the area.

A Deep-Water Fish Protected Area on the Xekong River in Lamam District

Ta-neum Village in Lamam District not only has a community forest (see box above), but also a community fish protected area (*vang sa-ngouan* in Lao) at *Keng* Vang Chang in the Xekong River. The rules are, 1) no fishing in the area,

2) no taking any natural resources, such as sand and rocks, from the area, and 3) no cutting trees on the riverbanks adjacent to the area. According to the sign adjacent to Ta-neum's PA, the legal basis for establishing it are Articles 69 to 72 of the Forestry Law, numbered 01–96 and adopted on 11 October 1996.

In neighboring Songkhone Village a reported lack of solidarity among villagers led to a breakdown of the rules for managing their protected area. However, Ta-neum villagers have taken the task of protecting their deep-water area seriously. Their efforts to protect it from activities prohibited by the community became well-known and largely respected in Lamam District. The PA is one of the longest deep-water fish conservation areas in southern Laos; with dimensions of 50 m by 1,300 m, this conservation area spans the width of the Xekong.

The villagers monitor the area themselves and, if they find anyone violating the rules, they tell them to cease fishing there. If that does not work, they report violators to the district Agriculture and Forestry office and ask them to take action against the violating parties, including fining them and confiscating fishing-gear. In fact, the threat of district government involvement is often sufficient to scare off all but the most brazen violators.

Ta-neum villagers are convinced that, since protecting their deep-water pool, the populations of some fish species have increased, particularly non-migratory or locally migratory species, like *Micronema* spp. (*pa nang* in Lao) and *Belodontichys truncatus* (*pa khop* in Lao), both silurid catfishes being deep-water specialists. Large "*pa eun*" carp (*Probarbus jullieni*/spp.) weighing up to 30 kg each are also reported by villagers to be beneficiaries of the PA.

Many other species have also reportedly benefited. Villagers report that there are even Siamese crocodiles inhabiting the area. There are also otters. Villagers have especially noticed increases of fish during the dry season, when large species sometimes come to the surface and villagers see them (see also Baird 2007b, for details about how villagers living next to the Mekong sometimes rely on surfacing fish as a means for monitoring their deep-water PAs). According to villagers, there is also an oyster-like shellfish that is "larger than a jar used for drinking rice beer" that sometimes appears at the surface during the dry season. Villagers believe that this shellfish is associated with powerful spirits.

CUSO has provided extensive support to the initiative, including helping make attractive signs to delineate the area and donating a long-tail boat and engine to support village monitoring and enforcement activities. In 2004, a villager from Ta-neum used this boat to patrol the area during the dry season on a regular basis. He noticed few violations in the daytime, but suspected that some people from other villages were fishing the area at night.

Despite the interest and commitment of the Ta-neum villagers in managing their fishery PA, the community has experienced some management problems. There was one reported incident in which the village headman and his son fished in the PA using explosives, allowing them to get a lot of large fish to sell for their private benefit. Other villagers were upset when they learned of this, and a serious conflict between the village head and another village leader ensued. Social pressure put on the headman and his son by others in the community has reportedly been effective in preventing any more incidents of explosives fishing.

Now, however, Ta-neum villagers face even more serious outside threats to the integrity of their whole initiative. In March 2007, a Chinese river gold-mining operation was observed running right in the midst of the PA. These operations have had serious impacts on fisheries all along the Xekong and have been the source of considerable conflict and controversy (see Chapter 12).

The construction of the large Xekong 4 Dam (see Chapter 13) just upstream from *Vang* Keng Chang would undoubtedly result in even more serious and long-term impacts. Based on the experience of other such dams in Laos and the region, the project appears likely to destroy or seriously impair the whole fishery, resulting in serious negative impacts on the livelihoods of the Ta-neum villagers.

CUSO may well have been able to do little to prevent these developments, but, certainly, more engagement is needed by local governments and outside aid agencies in recognizing the importance of fisheries to local livelihoods, and in considering how the construction and operation of large dams, as well as mining operations in the river, will impact fish habitats and behaviors. These concerns need to be better communicated to those making the decisions regarding the implementation of these large-scale projects. At the most basic level, aid agencies working in such situations need to consider how they can best help villagers gain the critical analysis skills and awareness needed to understand the threats their communities face.

There are also *vang sa-ngouan* in Attapeu Province. For example, the ethnic Lao village of Saisy, in Saysettha District, established one on the Xekaman River about seven years ago. According to one elder from the village, the rules are not being violated. A well-known PA near the provincial capital is called Pak Khone Loung. It is situated in the Xekong between Xekaman and Muang Mai Villages, which are on opposite sides of the river. The *vang sa-ngouan* is 800 m long, and no fishing is allowed there. The area has been in existence for eight or nine years. There are concerns about some of their management practices, however, due to an annual release of exotic fish species into the area (see Chapter 7).

There is also a *vang sa-ngouan* on the Nam Kong River near Viangxai Village, Phouvong District and yet another one in *Houay* Treo near the district center of Phouvong.

In Pathoumphone District, a number of villages have deep-water fish conservation areas, including Phalay Bok and Nong Ping along the Ta-euang Stream. For Phalay Bok, the PA is in front of the Ta-euang weir (see Chapter 5) and Nong Hin, Houay Mak, and Khone Thout along the Xekhampho River. Tavang Village had a *vang sa-ngouan* along Keua Stream, near their village, but it has been disregarded in recent years.

Biodiversity Outside of Protected Areas

Although much of the Xekong Basin's remaining wildlife resources are situated in various types of PAs, there are important wildlife species and populations located outside of PAs. This was well documented by WCS (1995) in a wildlife survey of the area to be impacted by the Xepian–Xenamnoi Hydroelectric Dam (see Chapter 13). During their survey, they confirmed the existence of nine globally threatened birds, at least eleven globally threatened mammals and three globally threatened reptiles in the area to be affected by the dam. They also found eight globally near-threatened birds and seventeen species of birds, nine mammals and two reptiles that are considered "regionally at risk." For birds, the populations of Giant Ibis (*Pseudibis gigantea*), White-shouldered Ibis (*Pseudibis davisoni*), and White-winged Duck (*Cairina scutulata*) were judged to be of high importance for the global survival of the species. Populations of Tiger (*Panthera tigris*), Gaur (*Bos gaurus*), and Asian Elephant (*Elephas maximus*) were also deemed to be of great importance (WCS 1995). The areas studied were all outside of PAs.

In fact, at the time WCS conducted its study, substantial parts of the Xepian-Xenamnoi Dam project area and neighboring areas were being considered for inclusion in the country's network of PAs. These included the proposed Xekhampho NPA in western Attapeu Province and the proposed Bolaven Northeast NPA (WCS 1995; Duckworth et al. 1999); however, twelve years later, none of these areas has received protected area status.

Traditional Beliefs and Wildlife Protection

Apart from restrictions imposed by various types of protected areas, there are also traditional beliefs that affect the use and protection patterns of particular species. For example, the ethnic Ngkriang people from Ta-neum Village, Lamam District report that there is a herd of five to ten wild elephants that villagers sometimes see "during the season when the bamboo sprouts" (August to October). They apparently migrate from Samyot Mountain. According to villagers, spirits protect these animals and anyone who kills an elephant is obliged to sacrifice four or five buffaloes to appease the spirits. Despite their respect for the wild elephants these villagers are now faced with a major challenge. In the past two years some of the herd, probably facing a reduction in habitat due to the extensive logging in the area, has made serious incursions into the village, attacking rice storage facilities. Some families, already in a food-deficit situation, have lost significant amounts of their yearly rice supply. Villagers want to continue to respect the elephants but cannot afford to lose more rice. They are uncertain about what course of action to take.

People from Ta-neum also report that during the same season approximately ten gaur migrate from *Phou* Samyot. These animals are also believed to be associated with strong spirits, which helps to protect them. Villagers say that there are two sacred tigers in the same area that were responsible for saving the life of one of their ancestors. Sometime in the past the ancestor was very sick. The sick man dreamt about a tiger licking his body, and when he awoke he had fully recovered. Therefore, the ancestor instructed his descendents not to kill tigers.

Barking deer are not considered sacred animals, but villagers from Ta-neum believe that hearing the sound of a barking deer during negotiations, reconciliation, or judgment proceedings is inauspicious. If this happens, discussions must immediately stop and be postponed until the next day, or an unpredictable bad event will take place. Also, if a barking deer wanders into the village at anytime, four or five chickens must be sacrificed to prevent people in the village from dying in the near future. If a wild jungle fowl enters the village, people believe that it is a sign that there will be a fire in the village. Wild animals and spirits are closely associated in the minds of the people at Ta-neum. Many people from other Mon Khmer language-speaking groups in the Xekong Basin hold similar beliefs.

10

Health, Nutrition, and Education

This chapter addresses education, nutrition, and health, important "development" issues for the Xekong Basin and Laos generally. Only a brief summary of some of the key points related to these complex issues can be presented here.

Health

The human health statistics for the Xekong River Basin in Laos are not positive, even in comparison to other parts of Laos. In fact, they are notable for being among the worst in the country, with infant mortality and morbidity levels some of the highest in Laos. Dysentery, diarrhea, and malaria are common, as is tuberculosis. There are still periodic outbreaks of cholera, including in Sanamxay District in 1996, and Phouvong District in 2004.

Hygiene is generally poor throughout much of the Xekong Basin, particularly in the remote eastern parts of the basin, including Kalum, Dakchung, Sanxay, and Phouvong Districts. In Xekong Province, only 19% of people have access to "sanitation coverage," or toilets. The statistics are not much better for Attapeu, where 28% have access to toilets. Both provinces fall well below the national average of 42% (LNMC 2004).

Malaria is a serious health risk, with most parts of the Xekong Basin—outside of high altitude and urban areas—having high infection rates. Many people do not sleep under mosquito nets. *Falcipurum* malaria, a non-recurring but severe variety of malaria, is the main kind found in the basin. Vythilingam et al. (2003) investigated the occurrence of *Anopheles* mosquitoes and the occurrence of malarial parasites within these vectors in three villages in Xekong Province where malaria was known to be endemic. Sixteen species of *Anopheles* were identified, of which three were found to be malaria vectors. The presence of malarial mosquitoes was confirmed for both the rainy and the dry seasons, although parasite-carrying mosquitoes were somewhat more prevalent during the wet season. People in Ta-neum Village, Lamam District, like people from many other villages in the Xekong Basin, claimed that even though they all sleep under mosquito nets, malaria is their most serious health problem, followed by other fevers and stomach ailments.

There are three broad types of treatments for illnesses used by people in the basin: 1) modern medicines, 2) traditional plant or animal-based medicines, and 3) Animist rituals. These treatments are often combined in different and sometimes surprising ways.

While traditional medicines made of natural products (plants and animals) are popular in some parts of the basin, especially among ethnic Lao people, they are not widely used by most Austroasiatic peoples (see Baird 1995c). However, food taboos are common, and some basic traditional medicines are occasionally used. For the Austroasiatics, Animist rituals are often a more familiar way of dealing with illness. It would be wrong, however, to assume that people in these groups are not also willing to use traditional or modern medicines when provided the opportunity. In fact, they are generally opportunistic and receptive to a whole range of medical treatments. They are rarely attached only to Animist rituals (Goudineau 2001; Baird 1995c).

There are important nutrition problems among the people of the basin. For example, due to low levels of meat intake, fats are consumed in low quantities, resulting in deficits of fat-soluble vitamins such as vitamin A. This negatively affects the body's immune system and can lead to increased risk of infection (Meusch et al. 2003). Sometimes large fish that could constitute an important dietary source of protein and fats are sold or bartered away in order to acquire other things (Meusch et al. 2003). Meusch et al. (2003) found that culturally-based food taboos are commonly applied in Attapeu, especially for pregnant women and women who have recently given birth. They viewed these practices as having serious health implications for the local population. Miscarriages are common, and the rate of child stunting and wasting is high. Overall, they concluded that the health situation of the people studied was poor. Interestingly, the most remote ethnic minority village studied had the lowest rate of adult malnutrition, even though the village was being compared with a seemingly more prosperous lowland Lao community (Meusch et al. 2003).

Food and other taboos are important determinants of health practices. For example, ethnic Katu people must abandon their villages if a mother and her child die during childbirth. Therefore, women usually give birth in small birthing-houses built in the forests. Then, if the mother and her child die, other villagers do not have to face the hardship of abandoning their village and finding a new one. The situation is similar for the ethnic Ye people in Dakchung and Sanxay Districts. The mother and child must stay by themselves in the forest for a number of days before they can return to the village. Women give birth alone, without even the help of a midwife.

In both Xekong and Attapeu, there are provincial hospitals, and each district has a hospital, although the capacities of these facilities are limited. In Attapeu Province, there are twenty village health clinics present in as many villages (Meusch et al. 2003), just 9.2% of the province's villages (SC and SPC 2004). In Xekong Province healthcare facilities are even scarcer, with only 4.8% of the villages having health clinics (SC and SPC 2004). In Kalum and Dakchung Districts, there were no dispensaries, pharmacies or shops selling medicines in 1999 (UNDP 1999a and c). There are now some private traders in the district centers selling medicine. They generally lack formal medical training, yet they often end up being those who recommend what medicines people should take. There are few qualified health professionals, making the identification of appropriate medicines or other treatments problematic.

While the number of health facilities in the Xekong River Basin is gradually increasing, even when people have access to health facilities they are often unable to afford the medicines they need. For example, in 2006 an ethnic Brao man on the road between his village of Palai, in Phouvong District, and the district center, just a few kilometers away, reported that he had a bicycle and so could easily make it to the district hospital. After being examined and receiving a written prescription for medicine from a doctor, he was unable to buy the medicine, because he had insufficient funds and ended up returning home empty-handed. Some credit for medicines is given to patients in resettlement villages in Sanxay District, but hospital staff there said they were having a difficult time recuperating the money owed to them and that, in some cases, had to cut off patients from receiving further credit.

Consuming sufficient iodine for the prevention of goiter is problematic for many. Little seafood is consumed in the land-locked Xekong Basin. While iodinized salt is now being produced in Laos and sold in remote places like Attapeu, Meusch et al. (2003) found that 32% of the household salt samples they took during their study in rural Attapeu Province had insufficient iodine content (below 30 ppm[1]). Coarse salt, used for preserving fish, is the "poor man's salt" due to its lower price, but it was found to have the lowest levels of iodine, whereas fine salts showed varying levels of iodine content.

Monosodium glutamate (MSG) is a recent staple for most families in Laos, seemingly regardless of ethnicity. Ethnic Brao used to burn a type of bamboo (*eung le* in Brao) to make what they call "*Brao peng nyoua*" (Brao MSG). The ashes of the burnt bamboo were used to flavor food (*booh anghang* in Brao). A small amount of this was observed in Phouvong District, but most people now consume commercial MSG instead. There is considerable anecdotal evidence to suggest that MSG can have negative health impacts, but the scientific evidence against MSG is less conclusive.[2]

HIV/AIDS

Until recently, the Xekong Basin's relative remoteness helped protect it from exposure to HIV/AIDS. As late as 1997 there were no confirmed cases from Xekong Province (UNDP 1997), but there is now growing concern that HIV/AIDS is becoming a serious problem that is likely to become worse in the future, especially as new roads are built between Xekong and Attapeu and Vietnam (see Chapter 11) and as a result of large groups of laborers coming to work in sawmills and mines or to build large dams in the basin (see Chapters 6, 12, and 13).

In Xekong Province, an anti-AIDS committee is trying to prevent HIV/AIDS among young people, particularly women in or around the commercial sex industry, who are considered at high risk of being infected. The Chief of the Provincial Youth Training Center, Soukhanya Inthavong, in a 2004 interview with the *Vientiane Times*, acknowledged that in the past HIV/AIDS infection rates were relatively low in Xekong due to a lack of development projects. But as new projects have begun, the province has seen an influx of migrant workers and expects to see even more in the future. He stated: "This year Xekong Province has invested in many big projects such as the Xekaman 3 Dam and timber exploitation, so there are now many places receiving visitors." Out of 85 people "randomly" tested for HIV/AIDS in 2004, two were found to be HIV-positive. The government of Xekong Province is targeting the two most accessible districts, Lamam and Thateng, for education efforts. UNICEF has provided some awareness-raising support in Xekong, but the effort was not deemed sufficient. In 2004, Norway also provided 54 million kip to support anti-AIDS activities in the province (Vongmany 2004).

In May 2005, seventy people working for two sawmills were specifically targeted for an HIV/AIDS awareness-raising program (*Vientiane Times* 2005h), as the logging and wood processing industries are seen to be a major "hot spot" for potential infection. In December 2005, youth volunteers in Dakchung District also received basic training about HIV/AIDS. Villagers from ten villages surrounding the Xekaman 3 Dam site were also trained in order to try to stem the spread of the disease in that area. The influx of foreigners to work on the project is believed to represent a serious threat for spreading HIV/AIDS (*Vientiane Times* 2005t). Halcrow (1999) reported that sexually transmitted diseases, including HIV/AIDS, would be at a great risk of being transmitted during the construction phase of the Xekong 4 Dam.

Drinking Water

There has been considerable improvement in water delivery systems for villagers in recent years. According to the Xekong provincial government, about 60% of the population now has access to clean water. Since 1999, with the help of many international organizations, seventy-two villages around the province have received clean water systems (*Vientiane Times* 2004d), including artesian wells, ground water wells, and gravity-feed systems. The latter are particularly common and popular in mountainous areas like Kalum and Dakchung Districts. In contrast to these positive figures, the SC and SPC (2004) reported that only 55% of Xekong's villages have access to clean water. The LNMC (2004) claimed that just 48% of the population had access to clean water. In Attapeu, conditions are similar with between 49% and 60% of villages having access to clean water (SC and SPC 2004; LNMC 2004). Apart from wanting to expand basic water systems, the GoL provided piped water to 20% of the population in the country recently, and they hope to reach 50% by 2020 (LNMC 2004). However, most of those in the Xekong River Basin are unlikely to have piped water in the coming years.

It is interesting to consider what "clean water" actually means, both in international development terminology and in the Lao context. In normal "development lingo" a village located next to an uncontaminated mountain spring-fed stream is not considered to have access to "clean water." Such access is more often defined as access to clean water provided through external infrastructure, including gravity-feed systems, or wells. Thus, many people in remote mountainous areas are labeled as "not having clean water," even though they may actually have access to purer water than some lowland villages considered officially to have access to "clean water." In this spirit, UNDP reported that "None of the villages in Kalum has an improved, safe, water supply. The most common sources of water are rivers and streams" (1999e: 9). In Dakchung District, the main water source for 33% of the villages was reported to be rivers, streams, or lakes; 12% relied on shallow dug wells; 56% were dependent upon mountain springs for drinking water. Only 7% of the villages were reported to have serious water problems, and representatives of 78% of the communities reported having sufficient water resources, although many villages claimed that water supplies were declining (UNDP 1999a), probably due to increased logging activities.

In Kalum, people in 76% of villages reportedly access rivers and streams as their main water sources while the remaining villages use mountain spring water. Only 5% of the villages have serious water problems, and 77% reportedly have sufficient water resources.

The most serious problems associated with gaining access to drinking and other water can be found in some of the villages resettled at the initiation of the government (see Chapter 5). Cheung Hiang Village, in Phouvong District, is a good example of a community that has been moved to a very dry area without access to any dry season water sources. It is located 2 km from the Nam Kong River, where they get their water. People from Hatxan Village in Saysettha District have, in recent years, also been relocated from their former village sites along the Xexou River to very dry dipterocarp forest areas along the new Route 18b to Vietnam. They only have access to water from one stream, the *Houay* La Ngiang, a tributary of the Xekaman River. There is insufficient water in the stream to supply basic water needs during the dry season. The GoL has not provided pump wells for the people, and, while locals would certainly like to have drilled wells near their houses, the required 17 m or so of drilling to reach water and the cost of 2 million kip per well, is well beyond the financial means of any of the resettled people.

Unfiltered water from the Xekong River began being pumped into water tanks for domestic use in Attapeu town in 1982. In 1998, a filter system was added (MAF and STEA 2003). However, there are still sometimes problems accessing clean water during the dry season (MAF and STEA 2003). Shortages usually last for about two weeks a year, at which time people carry, cart, and truck water from the Xekong River to their houses. In 2004, the World Bank began funding the construction of a new water tower and water pumping system at Naxaithong Village, adjacent to the Xekong in order to increase the water supply to the piped water grid for the capitol of Attapeu. The project is also paying for expansion of the piped water grid into the suburbs, as far out as Tha Hin Village, Samakhixay District, 4 km from the town center.

Xekong town also relies on piped water from the Xekong, but the cost of water delivery in urban areas has increased considerably over the past few years. The price for water tripled a few years ago for Grade 1 commercial enterprises in

Xekong Province, like the Xekong Hotel. This has upset some business people in Xekong town.

In 2005, the Japanese aid agency JICA began supporting a promotional campaign designed to encourage people to use water wisely and sparingly, especially during shortages. This has included Lao signs put up in the provincial capitals of both Attapeu and Xekong Provinces.

Over the past couple of years, the INGO ADRA has been supporting the construction of pit toilets in the resettlement area at Pa-am in Sanxay District. They have also supported building toilets in many other villages in Attapeu Province, particularly for schools. There would seem to be at least some risk that toilet waste might contaminate the ground water, which is being pumped from wells that ADRA also funded. ADRA has, however, tried to ensure that well water is suitable for consumption, and so far there have not been any reports of problems.

The Controversy over Arsenic Poisoning and Clean Water Access

Over the past few years Attapeu Province has been at the center of a controversy in relation to the drilling of borehole wells and their potential for being poisoned with arsenic. A few years ago, the INGO ADRA received funding from AusAID, the Australian government's international development assistance agency, to provide clean water systems in lowland parts of the province and to build toilets. Some of the wells drilled were found to have quite high concentrations of arsenic contamination. Once AusAID learned of this situation in late 2002, it immediately insisted that the project be discontinued until the GoL approved a standard for minimum arsenic contamination in wells (Brendon Irvine, ADRA, pers comm. May 2005).

Since the first arsenic-contaminated wells were discovered in Attapeu, there has been considerable debate about establishing a national standard for arsenic contamination. The international standard set by the World Health Organization of the United Nations (WHO), is 10 mg/1., but some international development agencies and bilateral donors have suggested that the potential negative impact of not having access to clean water needs to be considered and that the levels set should depend upon the development context in different areas. They have argued that, considering Laos' present development status, 50 mg/liter would be a more reasonable maximum allowable concentration. Studies to date have shown that, at such a contamination rate, continual use for fifty to sixty years is required before unusual rates of skin cancer emerge. Since the average lifespan

291

of a person in Laos has not yet reached this level and in many areas there is a 3–5% mortality rate every year—largely due to a lack of access to clean water—it may save more peoples' lives to provide access to water even if it is moderately contaminated with arsenic.

AusAID decided that the arsenic testing process had to take place in Australia, even though this testing process requires about three months. This has caused some dismay over delays in allowing communities to use already drilled wells, which is especially troublesome during water shortages. Nevertheless, the Australian government, worried about the potential for future litigation and bad press, has taken a conservative approach. The adoption of this position was likely influenced by the situation in Bangladesh, where arsenic contamination occurred in wells drilled with outside development assistance. Donors who supported well-drilling there are being accused of causing about 2,000 deaths a year due to long-term arsenic poisoning.

At the beginning of 2003, ADRA decided to conduct a province-wide survey of bore hole wells and arsenic contamination in Attapeu Province. They found that 2%, or 12 of the 612 wells tested, had contamination levels of over 50 mg/l. Villagers reported one heavily contaminated well in Sompoi Village in Sanamxay District, adjacent to the Xekong. According to villagers, the water in that well was red and killed plants when used for watering. Not surprisingly, it is no longer in use. *Ban* Hatxaisoung in Sanamxay, near the Xekong, also had a well shut due to arsenic contamination. ADRA drilled about three quarters of the tested wells themselves, with most of the others having been drilled with UNICEF funding. All wells with over 50 mg/l. contamination rates have been shut. However, the 22–23% of the wells with contamination levels of 10–50 mg/l. continue to be used. A few wells with over 100 mg/l. of arsenic were identified. The severely contaminated wells were generally found in old riverbeds, often near the Xekong. This fits with a particular geological explanation for the problem (Brendon Irvine, ADRA, pers. comm. May 2005). Arsenic contamination of wells situated in alluvial areas adjacent to the Xekong, Sesan, and Mekong Rivers in Stung Treng and Kratie Provinces in northeast Cambodia have also been reported in recent years, as well as in other provinces in Cambodia (Chaeng 2006).

In early 2003, Laos set its maximum arsenic concentration standard at 50 mg/l. (Banphet 2005); however, there were still serious ethical and legal concerns raised by the international donor and NGO community. At the end of 2003, the Australian government changed its position again, hinting that it might not accept contamination levels exceeding the 10-mg/l. standard set by WHO, even if national standards in Laos are 50 mg/l. As of 2005, this issue was still being negotiated. At present, the national standard for Australia is 7 mg/l., while Europe and the USA have lower standards at 50 mg/l.. Europe is moving toward tightening its standards to 10 mg/l. (Brendon Irvine, ADRA pers. comm. May 2005).

There are also other potential health problems associated with well contamination in southern Laos, including those relating to iron, fluoride, and manganese contamination (Brendon Irvine, ADRA, pers. comm. May 2005).

Nutritional Changes and Livelihoods in the Xekong River Basin in Laos

While investigating dietary practices and changes among ethnic Katu people in Kalum and Thateng Districts, Jutta Krahn (2003) found that most upland cultures in Laos are undergoing rapid dietary change. "Development" policies and practices, such as relocating upland communities to lowland areas, are especially responsible for these changes due to the substantial livelihood shifts that accompany these initiatives. Government planners and international aid agency staff rarely consider these dietary factors. Krahn (2003) argues that development practitioners should "look into the cooking pot" and understand the nutritional impact of dietary change. She argues for the need to shift the focus on food security away from simply producing staples like rice toward considering other important food sources, such as wild fish and various forest and aquatic-derived NTFPs. She also points out that traditional food systems often provide essential nutrients within a holistic human ecological context and that many kinds of forest foods are more nutritious than domestic animals and garden vegetables. Swidden cultivators may not have impressive rice harvests, but it is critical to consider the other crops grown with upland rice in swidden fields. These include corn, millet, a variety of tubers and cassavas, beans, and dozens of other types of vegetables, as well as sugarcane, bananas, and papaya (see Chapter 5).

For upland peoples, it can be problematic, nutritionally, to switch from diets high in animal protein and low in carbohydrates (e.g., staples such as rice) to diets high in carbohydrates and low in animal protein. When resources are degraded, upland ethnic minority people often go from eating a variety of wild foods to eating meals comprising mostly, or only, glutinous rice, together with a basic "cheo" made of pounded chili, salt, and MSG. Food security is widely but incorrectly seen by many government and aid agency officials as being about rice sufficiency. To some degree this is unsurprising, as rice cultivation and trading is a key source of livelihood and income for many local people, yet this concept of food security is too limited and ignores the high nutritional potential of crops and NTFPs in the uplands. This is a difficult argument to make heard, however, at a time when the government is trying to reduce or eliminate shifting cultivation and is strongly focused on rice production (Krahn 2003).

There are other significant differences in diets in the uplands as compared to the lowlands and between ethnic groups. For example, ethnic Lao tend to use large amounts of fish paste (*pa dek* in Lao), whereas upland people tend to eat less fish paste and more vegetable paste (*nam phak* in Lao). *Nam phak* is often made with types of mountain cabbage that do not grow well in the lowlands or with cassava (*man ton* in Lao) leaves that are best cultivated in upland swidden fields. In Kalum District, ethnic Katu people often mix mountain cabbage-based *nam phak* with green onions (*phak boua* in Lao) and dried fish (*pa katao* in Lao). The Brao in Attapeu, however, frequently mix *nam phak* with buffalo skin or, more rarely, with the skin of douc langur (*hava* in Brao). There are also other varieties of *nam phak* in the Xekong Basin.

There has been little understanding or analysis of how the loss and reduced access to natural resources is affecting key nutritional factors, such as reduced intake rates of important trace elements found mainly in wild foods. Basic malnutrition issues still need to be investigated further (Krahn 2003). Krahn (2003) has also argued that because nutrition issues are rarely given sufficient emphasis to influence development planning and implementation, more cross-sectoral and organizational cooperation is needed in relation to analyzing nutritional issues.

Large development projects that severely impact local communities have often featured distorted food security planning. Ethnic Heuny people relocated to the Houay Ho Dam resettlement site (*Ban Chat San* in Lao) near Houay Kong Village in Pakxong District, were expected, for example, to be able to grow and sell coffee, and then use the money to buy rice. However, there was little consideration of what the people were supposed to eat with the rice. Insufficient land was provided for swidden agriculture or to grow sufficient amounts of other crops for local consumption. The resettled people were squeezed into a densely populated area near other already existing ethnic Jru communities. Not only did they have inadequate access to land for agriculture, but they lacked forests and streams for foraging, hunting, and fishing. The few streams near the resettlement area were quickly overused due to high human population densities (IRN 1999; Sparkes 2000; Khamin 2000;

Sayboualaven 2004). While the cash income levels of a few people at the resettlement site may well be higher than when they were still doing shifting cultivation in the forests, the money now being generated from hiring out their labor to coffee farmers in neighboring villages is often barely sufficient to buy enough rice to eat for that day. They still have insufficient access to meat, fish, and vegetables, as well as the various kinds of forest food that they once consumed. Even as cash incomes have increased, real wealth and nutritional levels have declined due to vast decreases in harvests of edible NTFPs (see Chapter 13).

Education

Attapeu Province

In Attapeu Province, there were 258 schools with a total of 21,653 students in 2002/2003, indicating that over the last decade the formal education system has been expanded considerably. Between 1996 and 2003 the GoL invested over 7,000 billion kip in education in Attapeu Province. Despite some successes, there remain many serious problems. For example, it has been estimated that only 61% of school-age children in the province attend school and that only 39% of students complete Grade 5, the supposed compulsory end of primary schooling in Laos. Instead, females and males average two and four years of schooling, respectively. About 69% of adults in Attapeu are considered illiterate, slightly higher than the national average (MAF and STEA 2003). In 1999, only 7% of the villages in the province were reported not to have any school; however, there are considerable discrepancies between some of the education statistics in Attapeu. According to MAF and STEA (2003), in 2002/2003 15% of the villages in the province did not have schools. But just one year later, SC and SPC (2004) reported that 49% of the villages did not have their own schools. This dramatic decline in schools seems highly unlikely, and the discrepancies in statistics might represent different ways of collecting data or setting the parameters for what is a village with a school. It is also possible that officials, for whatever reason, may have distorted some data.

There are also problems with finding suitable teachers and ensuring that teaching is consistent. For example, in 2004, there were reportedly forty teachers in Phouvong District. Even though there are no ethnic Lao villages in the district, fifteen of the teachers were ethnic Lao and unable to speak the local Brao language. As in many other places, teachers in Phouvong often do not teach regularly or even stop teaching for long periods. Sometimes they leave their school posts for various reasons and do not return for many weeks. This causes considerable disillusionment and disruption in many schools. The reasons relate both to the low salaries they receive and the fact that teachers come from outside areas and often feel isolated and dissatisfied with being posted in remote villages, especially those inhabited by ethnic minorities.

There is also the question of the quality of the school facilities that do exist. An estimated 60% of schools in Attapeu Province were "uncompleted" or "temporary" in 1999 (Engelbert 2004), and only 27% of the schools in the province have latrines. Many have leaky roofs and dirt floors, and most do not have lockable doors. There are often not enough desks and chairs for all students. However, the Director of the Education Division of Attapeu Province stated, in early 2007, that recently a lot of support has been provided by development agencies for upgrading school facilities in the province. According to him, the province's big problem now is not so much the quality of school buildings but rather the quality and quantity of education taking place in Attapeu, especially in rural areas; more emphasis needs to be placed on teacher training and improving the quality of teaching materials

While the ADB has spent a considerable amount of money in Attapeu building schools in the lowlands for recently resettled ethnic minorities from the uplands (see Chapter 5), the World Bank is planning to take a different approach by supporting the construction of fifty primary schools in upland areas. The project began in 2006, and local officials believe that its total budget is US$13 million. The ethnic Brao government officials in Phouvong were certainly aware of the implications of this approach to internal resettlement and recognized that this was an important symbolic gesture by international donors designed to show that they hoped to stop or reduce internal resettlement in Laos (see Chapter 5).

Another positive development occurred at the end of 2005 when Attapeu's first vocational school was opened with thirty-six instructors and 116 enrolled students. Courses on agriculture and livestock, food catering, and hotel services, and building construction are currently being offered (Sentho 2006). However, this is a small step when compared to the many obstacles to education in the province.

Xekong Province

The formal education system in Xekong Province is even less developed than in Attapeu. Only about 42% (30% for women) of the population is considered to be literate, while 28% are defined as "barely literate." Furthermore, only 26% of the adults have completed primary school, only 4% have finished junior high school, and a measly 0.6% have graduated from high school (Goudineau 2001; Chagnon 2000). Yet, despite many continuing problems, formal education has made considerable advances in recent years. As in Attapeu, it is difficult to know what education statistics (number of villages with schools, number of school-age children in school) to believe. It has been reported that only 37.8% of villages have schools in their own villages (SC and SPC 2004), but, as indicated above with respect to conditions in Attapeu, these statistics are far from certain.

In 1999, 81% of the schools in Xekong were considered "uncompleted" or "temporary" (Engelbert 2004). In some of the most remote areas, villages are a day's walk apart. Thus 4,000 children between 6–10 years old were reportedly without access to formal education in Kalum and Dakchung Districts in 2004, while 7,000 children from ages 6–10 were not attending school throughout the province (*Vientiane Times* 2004e). Generally, attendance rates for ethnic minorities and girls are lower than for other groups. There is a non-formal education program in Lamam District for promoting adult literacy (Goudineau 2001), but it is apparently not well developed or funded.

As indicated, education services in Kalum District are poor, and 17 villages, or 29% of those in the district, were reported to lack schools in 1999. 1,077 children between 6 and 14 years old were reported as not attending school, while 36 children were reported to be attending lower secondary school, and only four were attending upper secondary (UNDP 1999c). In May 2005, the *Vientiane Times* (2005i) reported that over 1,000 children in Kalum District between the ages of 6–10 years old were unable to attend school and that only 36 of the district's 63 villages had schools.

The Deputy Chief of the district Education Office reported that there was not enough funding to build many of the schools targeted for construction since 2000. More on-going support would also be required because, even if schools could be built, the district would still have inadequate funds for hiring teachers for the villages (*Vientiane Times* 2005i). There actually appears to be a reduction in the number of schools in the district, as UNDP (1999e) reported that there were 41 schools in Kalum, as compared to 36 in 2005. The number of children not attending school appears to be about the same (over 1,000 between 6–10 in 2005 as compared to 1,077 between 6 and 14 in 1999). This may relate to on-going government sponsored "village consolidation" efforts.

For Dakchung District, UNDP (1999a) reported that 53 villages, or 51% of the district's villages, did not have any schools, and that 1,492 children between 6 and 14 years old were not attending school. Only 224 children were attending lower secondary school, and only 29 were attending senior high school. A lack of schools, teachers, and teaching materials were cited as some of the main problems as well as parents not having the resources to buy basic school materials. As in Attapeu, teachers frequently stop teaching for extended periods.

In Xekong Province "ethnic diversity with different languages" is considered by many government officials to be a constraint on development (Goudineau 2001), rather than a valuable resource for people to use in their own human development. Many teenage children from the remote districts of Dakchung and Kalum attend the Ethnic Minority boarding school in the provincial capital. There is also a similar school in Attapeu. These types of schools have the advantage of being relatively well funded and being able to provide minorities with the type of formal education that they would be unable to obtain in their remote villages. However, they take children out of their villages, and many who leave end up never returning on a permanent basis. If they do return they often have a difficult time readjusting to "village life," as the skills learned in the towns are not always those required for rural survival. These ethnic minority schools place almost no emphasis on ensuring that these children have the skills to return and readjust to their original communities. In addition, since people from many ethnic groups are gathered together, there is often the erosion of indigenous language and culture among the students.

Champasak Province

The parts of the Xekong River Basin in Champasak include some of the most remote parts of the province. These areas have some of the worst attendance rates and quality of education in the province, although INGO support provided by the Remote Village Education Support Project in Pathoumphone District has helped to improve the quality and quantity of education available there in recent years (Hubbel and Phongphichit 2006).

There are still many obstacles to overcome. Many of the problems facing people in Pathoumphone are similar to those already described for Attapeu and Xekong. For example, it is often difficult to find qualified teachers in villages, as nowadays the completion of high school is required in most parts of the country before someone can study to be a teacher. In addition, teachers from less remote areas who are transferred to work in remote areas often find adjusting to the pace of remote village life difficult. Therefore, teacher turnover is high.

Formal vs. Non-Formal and Informal Education

Government officials and development aid agency staff often describe people, particularly ethnic minorities, in the Xekong Basin as uneducated or lacking education. Non-formal education is most commonly thought of as encompassing either adult literacy training or vocational training. These definitions fail to recognize the many other aspects of learning that are useful for people, and tend to undervalue non-formal forms of knowledge gained in family life. It is rarely recognized that children who are not at school may still be learning useful skills. Local ecological knowledge is important to local livelihoods but is almost exclusively acquired in everyday life outside of school. The conventional education system rarely acknowledges this and does little to support family or community learning processes, such as generation-to-generation knowledge transfers. Children who do go to school for many years may lose some opportunities for learning local ecological knowledge, indicating the need for a special emphasis within the formal education system to ensure that being a part of the standard education system does not have to mean losing out in terms of learning about nature and local livelihoods.

A study by Wester and Yongvanit (1995) found that people from farms and villages, and from remote provinces in northeast Thailand, generally know more about traditional food plants than urban dwellers. Those with vehicles know less than those without, and those with more education opportunities, who tend to migrate to urban areas, use and know less about traditional food plants compared to those from rural areas. Many of the people in the Xekong River Basin may not have much formal education, but they still have considerable practical local knowledge. It would be wrong to say, as is often the case with development discourses, that they are "uneducated."

11

Transportation and Regional Integration

Water Transportation

The rivers and streams of the Xekong River Basin have long been important arteries for transportation. The most important waterway is, of course, the mainstream Xekong River. It is navigable by motorized long-tailed canoe-like boats from well above the district center in Kalum in the north all the way down through Xekong and Attapeu Provinces into Cambodia and to its confluence with the Mekong River. There are no impassable rapids for hundreds of kilometers.

Villagers use the rivers to travel from village to village, from villages to agricultural areas, from villages to markets and administrative centers and also for going fishing, hunting, and collecting NTFPs. Non-motorized boats are often used for local travel and fishing near villages. If portaging is done, boats can travel upriver even farther, at least to Laipo Village in Kalum District. That is as far as the INGO ACF was transporting building materials by boat in 2004, in order to make gravity-feed water supply systems for ethnic Katu villages in that area. There are also a small number of long-tailed boats with 5–6 hp motors north of Kalum District town, but, according to villagers, only 11 or 13 hp engines are powerful enough for rainy season navigation along the Xekong above the district center to Kloung Village. In 2004, only ACF had engines powerful enough for their boats to make the trip.

Small boat transportation is also important for communities situated along the lower Xekaman, Xexou, Xepian, and Xekhampho Rivers in Attapeu Province. On the Xekaman River, if some portaging is done at various rapids along the way, motorboats can travel as far upriver as *Tat Po* in the dry season. The nearest village is Dak Kouk, a day's walk downstream of *Tat Po*. According to locals, there are twenty-seven major rapids between the mouth of the Xekaman River and *Tat Po*, a journey that villagers estimate to be about a hundred kilometers. From *Tat*

Po to Phiang Se Village (now relocated to Vang Tat, Sanxay District), the village that was farthest upstream, there are reportedly twenty-six more rapids along the Xekaman River. That means that there are a total of fifty-three rapids situated along the Xekaman from its confluence with the Xekong to Phiang Se, and still more upstream in Dakchung District.

Kalum has an advantage over Dakchung District in terms of river transportation, as long distance river transportation is not feasible anywhere in Dakchung due to the large number of rapids in the Xekaman River. In the largely ethnic Ngkriang populated *Khet* 1 and 2 of Kalum District and in the ethnic Katu populated *Khet* 5 many people have access to the Xekong for boat transportation.

Bamboo rafts are another important means of water transportation, especially for ethnic minorities living in remote mountainous areas. For example, the ethnic Ye people living near the Xekaman River in Dakchung District use bamboo rafts to cross the river. The ethnic Brao people from Phouvong District have long used bamboo rafts to transport themselves and goods from remote mountainous areas to market (see Baird 2000; Ironside and Baird 2003). Bamboo rafts are, however, now generally used less than in the past.

The only regular organized commercial public boat transportation (*heua doi san* in Lao) in the Xekong Basin in Laos today runs between the district center of Sanamxay south to Hat Nyai Village, near the Xekong River's confluence with the Xepian River at the border with Cambodia. It goes as far south as the military post near the border. The relatively large boats used on this route run a few times per day and generally take people from their villages along the Xekong to Sanamxay market in the morning and then from the district center back to their villages later in the morning, when the market slows down. In 2004, it cost 7,000 kip to travel from Sompoi Village to the district center by boat.

There used to be regular boat service along the Xekong River between Attapeu and Xekong towns, especially during the rainy season, but over the past few years, since the road between Xekong and Attapeu was paved and became passable year round, boat travel between Attapeu and Xekong has declined dramatically, and there is no longer a regular service. A few private boats still sometimes travel from Attapeu up to Xekong. The boat transportation system between Stung Treng and Siem Pang on the Xekong in Cambodia is important to villagers (Thuan and Tep 2007), undoubtedly more than any boat transportation systems in the Xekong Basin in Laos.

From the time that the French took control of Stung Treng and Attapeu in 1893 and 1894, the Xekong was the most important way of accessing and sending supplies to Attapeu. However, Lt. Debay reported in 1895 that many goods were being lost by boats traveling past rapids on the Xekong on their way up to Attapeu.[1]

He hoped that a good land route to Annam (Vietnam) could be established that would replace the Xekong River as the main artery of transport to Attapeu. But the Xekong River remained the transportation key to Attapeu up until the end of 1904, when Stung Treng and Siem Pang were severed from Laos and given to Cambodia by the French government. This change made it necessary for Attapeu to begin to consider improving land routes from Champasak to Attapeu.

At the beginning of the twentieth century, when the French attempted to establish new trade routes in the frontier region, the Xekong River was still of interest and was thus investigated, with the idea of using it for expanding boat transportation and commerce between Attapeu and Stung Treng (Rathie 2001). In 1907, the French administrator of Attapeu, Monsieur Sale, proposed that large steamboats be encouraged to travel up to Attapeu town from Stung Treng town for six months a year during the rainy season. Not much came of these efforts, but during this period water levels were measured at two important rapids on the Xekong in Attapeu, *Keng Louang*, and *Keng Phao* (also called *Chantaban*),[2] as these were considered the most important obstacles for boat transport along the Xekong. The first is situated about 12 km upriver from Xekong town, and the latter is located at the place where the Xekong enters Cambodia from Laos. It is unclear if steamboats ever traveled to Attapeu on a regular basis, as the separation of Siem Pang and Stung Treng from Laos increased Attapeu's relative remoteness. Large steamboats have certainly not been used on the Xekong since the French period. The US Naval Intelligence Division (1943) reported that only "small native craft" could reach Attapeu from the Mekong River and that, during the rainy season, the journey took eighteen days going upriver but only three days in the reverse direction.

Since independence, conflict and political differences, as well as remoteness, have contributed to reducing the importance of the Xekong as a trade and transportation route between Laos and Cambodia. There is currently no organized boat transportation system between Laos and Cambodia using the Xekong and few private boats travel between Cambodia and Laos. However, since there is no road between Attapeu and Stung Treng, the river is sometimes still used for transportation between the two countries. The border on the river is not officially open to international travelers but Cambodian and Lao nationals from the adjacent provinces can cross.

Road Development

The first Frenchman to survey the Xekong River Basin for potential road construction, especially to Annam (Central Vietnam), was the notorious Lt. Debay (see

Chapter 4) in 1894. His initial idea was to allow the indigenous people build and maintain a network of roads. He thought that they would be willing to do this, and he suggested that only some work, including dynamiting, should be done by the Vietnamese.[3] At that time there were few roads in the basin. Later, the French used annual *corvée* labor drawn from the local population to build and maintain roads. The road system was still rudimentary when the French left Indochina in 1954.

Rural infrastructure is, in fact, still quite limited in the Xekong River Basin, with Xekong Province considered to have the least developed communications and telecommunications infrastructure in Laos (Chagnon 2000).

Kalum District probably has the most difficult road transportation situation in the Xekong Basin, as there are few roads outside of that between the provincial capital of Xekong and the district center, and the new road to A luoi District in Thua-Thien Hue Province in Vietnam (see below).

Kalum is divided into eight sub-districts, or *Khet*, and it takes five days by foot to travel to the district center from *Khet* 7 and 8. These areas include Xesap NPA and are inhabited by a few small ethnic Katu villages (363 people or 4% of the district's population). UNDP (1999c) reported that 98% of the villages in the district chose road access as their main development problem. Only 2% mentioned agricultural problems as being more significant. It may well be that government interviewers who collected this data had a pro-road bias that was reflected in the survey process, as road building was seen from the start as a key aspect of the UNDP project. If questions had been framed differently, many villagers may well have seen land and agriculture as more important.

In 1999, the main means of transportation in Dakchung District, apart from walking, was reported to be bicycling (there were 120 bicycles in the district). There were also 88 horses (UNDP 1999a). 64% of the villages were reported to have no road access at any time of the year. None of the villages in *Khet* 6 had road access, and only 6% did in *Khet* 5. (Both *Khet* are mainly populated by ethnic Ye people.) Villagers also apparently mentioned lack of road access as their main development problem (UNDP 1999a).

Rural road transportation in eastern Phouvong and Sanxay Districts also remains quite difficult. In Sanxay, some villagers use small Asian horses for transportation, but horses are rare in Phouvong District to the south. Many parts of these two largely mountainous districts, as well as other parts of Attapeu, remain largely inaccessible by road during the rainy season. Heavy seasonal flooding in Sanamxay and Pathoumphone Districts makes road travel particularly difficult in these largely lowland districts.

Consultant Bias and Road Construction

A significant body of research in Laos demonstrates that, whatever its benefits, road construction also has significant negative impacts on local communities and the environment (see, for example, Lyttleton and Rattanavong 2004). Roads do not simply bring easy access for villagers and services but also provide easy access for loggers and others with interests in exploiting and extracting local resources. Unfortunately, consultants hired to perform EIAs for international aid-funded road construction projects in Laos consistently fail to provide balanced summaries of likely positive and negative impacts of new roads in remote rural areas.

In 2000, an international donor-initiated EIA was conducted regarding plans to upgrade the 102 km road to the capital of Xekong Province (Pacific Consultants International 2000). This study ignored or downplayed the potentially serious negative social and environmental repercussions of road construction. Rather than recognizing the role of logging in forest destruction, the consultants, without any justification, adopted the line that large areas of swidden fields were the main cause of environmental degradation near the villages.

The consultants collected some baseline data from a number of ethnic minority villages along the road, including information about the wildlife species found near them. However, these data were not used for any particular analysis and, while the potential negative impacts of road building on streams was mentioned, the issue was largely glossed over, as were issues associated with increased access to the villages by outsiders. The final summary of the report (Pacific Consultants International 2000: 90) includes some highly suspect conclusions that would seem to be divorced from reality to anyone with an informed understanding of present-day Laos. The report states:

> Throughout the road section no issues of significant environmental concern were identified other than those usual for a highway upgrading scheme which are addressed via suitable clauses in the contract specifications and by careful monitoring by the construction supervision consultants.
>
> As with most other Project road sections, the upgrading is highly unlikely to lead to any increase in logging, and although some impact on NTFP gathering and hunting by "outsiders" may result from the all weather access provided by the improvement works, it is anticipated that this potential will be adequately compensated by the increased facility of monitoring and control that can be exercised by the relevant

authorities. This may necessitate a degree of institutional strengthening, although this is considered to be of minor concern, and possibly more financial resources to pay, in particular for the direct expenses (notably fuel) of the increased monitoring/control activities.

The consultants did call for improved monitoring, but the project EIA did not include any provisions for supporting the costs of such monitoring. Only vague references were made to possible activities without committing the project to following up on any of the recommendations.

This sort of EIA "rubber stamping" of projects is all too common in Laos and the Mekong region generally. Companies are required by donor policies (or, in the case of large dams, by the GoL) to conduct EIAs on significant infrastructure projects. But the consultants hired to do these EIAs are generally not expected to provide any significant recommendations that would fundamentally argue against a project—or even significantly alter a project to the point where it would cost the developers more than a small amount of additional money. The consultants understand that the best way of ensuring that they will be hired again is to provide their customers (the developers) with what is required to move the project forward without causing too much trouble. Weak regulatory authorities, like the GoL's Science, Technology, and Environmental Agency (STEA), lack the capacity to provide appropriate oversight to these processes and are often subject to political pressures that favor projects. The result is a pro-project bias that often reduces the value of, or completely invalidates, the whole EIA process.

Over the past decade the road network in the Xekong Basin has rapidly expanded. For example, the road from Pakse to the Xekong provincial capital, via Pakxong and Thateng, was fully paved a few years ago and, in 2005, a paved road between Xekong and Attapeu was finally completed. The ADB provided a US$4 million loan for the improvement and paving of Route 16 from the Xenamnoi River—the border between Attapeu and Xekong Provinces—to the provincial capital of Attapeu. This project was expected to be completed by the beginning of the 2004 rainy season (*Vientiane Times* 2004b) but was not done until well into 2005. Various companies worked on this road prior to the ADB's involvement, but none was ever able to successfully complete their contracts. In Xekong, the bridge over the *Houay* Lamphan was the last part of the road to be completed; the ADB reportedly lent US$300,000 to the GoL to build it. In addition, the Xekaman and Xekong bridges, constructed with

Vietnamese support, were completed at the end of 2003. Most of the resources used to build these roads have come in the form of loans from foreign organizations and governments. While many of these loans have been made on preferential terms, it is still unclear how the funds to repay them will be generated. One might infer that these new roads are opening up access to the resources that can then be exploited and sold to pay off the loans.

New Roads to Vietnam from Xekong and Attapeu Provinces

The expansion of the road network is rapidly changing the spatial organization of the basin, especially its connections with neighboring Vietnam. There are at present three different international roads being developed between Xekong and Attapeu Provinces and neighboring Thua-Thien Hue, Quangnam, and Kontum Provinces in the Central Highlands of Vietnam. According to a Xekong Province official, these roads are being combined with province-to-province cooperation agreements with Vietnam, with the hope that Laos can attract more Vietnamese investment in natural resource extraction.

In August 2004, VNA (2004b) announced that a new Hong Van-Koutai "auxiliary border gate" for Vietnamese and Lao people had been opened between Kalum District and A luoi District in Thua-Thien Hue Province. According to the VNA, the new border crossing is located at Raba in Kalum, and is expected to contribute to socio-economic development, including facilitating trade between the two provinces and also contributing to improved border security. It appears likely, however, that this road will also greatly contribute to deforestation in Xekong Province, as Vietnam is increasingly looking to its neighbor to supply timber for its rapidly expanding economy.

As of 2006, the road connecting the Kalum District center and the border crossing was not passable, but in July 2004, VNA (2004c) reported that site clearance had been completed on 51 km of the 124 km from Kalum District center and the land border with A luoi District. The 9.22 billion kip contract to build this road was awarded to a Vietnamese company (KPL 2003a). At the same time, on the Vietnamese side of the border, 80 billion Vietnamese dong (US$5.3 million) has reportedly already been invested in building a 14-km road from the A luoi District center to the new border crossing with Laos in Hong Van Commune (VNA 2004c). The initial plan was to push the new road through from Xekong to the border, but those plans changed and the road is being built from the Vietnamese side south. It is unclear when the road will be completed.

In 2003, KPL (2003a) reported that a second road was being planned to Vietnam from Xekong Province. It was expected to cover 96 km between the provincial capital of Xekong and Dakchung District center. It was reported that the 33 km route to the border with Vietnam's Yang District in Quangnam Province would be upgraded for all-season use. The Lao side of the future border crossing is called Daktaoke and the Vietnamese side is called Dak Op, or Nam Giang (VNA 2003b). The Lao section of the road is notoriously difficult and mainly only passable during the dry season. Logging trucks with heavy loads have added to problems by badly damaging the road with their heavy loads. In 2005, Xekong Province officials report that the border was expected to become an international crossing by 2007, but the opening has not yet been announced.

The first UNDP-supported development project in Xekong Province was the upgrading of the road from the provincial capital to Dakchung, implemented between 1986 and 1991. Serious financial mismanagement occurred, and the road was not upgraded as planned. It was finally completed in 1999 but was then expected to be upgraded further to a Category 4 road over the five-year period between 2002 and 2006. The funding for this was initially planned to come from a US$35 million loan from the Lao Timber Company (Malaysia). Under the proposed terms of the deal, the GoL would have been expected to pay back the company in logs; however, the Malaysians subsequently withdrew. A Vietnamese company reportedly signed a new agreement in 2005 to build/repair the road, again in exchange for logging rights. These plans were then placed on hold due to new restrictions on the log trade in Laos. The current situation is unclear.

These types of agreements, in which logging rights are traded for road construction, have become increasingly common, especially with Vietnamese companies. There are concerns about forests being degraded as a result of overexploitation to pay for these roads. Moreover, there is increasing evidence that logging companies often take advantage of these arrangements to cut and export much higher volumes of timber than originally agreed upon, thus increasing their profit margins considerably and exploiting more of the forests than official statistics indicate (KPL 2003a). Xekong provincial officials want to build expensive new roads and other infrastructure, but they do not have the financial resources to do so. In some cases they have chosen, often using a non-transparent process, to barter away their people's natural resources to finance such road construction.

There will be an 18 km-long road built between the Xekaman 3 Dam site and the Vietnam border to facilitate construction of the dam. This crossing is apparently between Dak Pal in Dakchung District and Dak Pa Lo in Dak Lai District, Kontum Province, Vietnam.

The first bridge over the Xekong represents one of the biggest infrastructure changes in the basin. Built with Vietnamese support, the project has not been without problems. During construction a number of Vietnamese construction workers died due to accidents. The road crosses the Xekong from the middle of Attapeu town, in a densely populated area. The plan was originally to relocate twenty houses from areas adjacent to the bridge, but this idea has apparently been scrapped as the houses are mainly large and it would cost too much for the government to compensate the owners.

Associated with the above bridge, there is also a new road being built between Phouvong District and Kontum Province in Vietnam. The idea is to develop the east-west corridor connecting Thailand to deep-sea ports in Danang, Dung Quat, and Qui Nhon in central Vietnam via southern Laos (BBC 2001). In November 2001, a groundbreaking ceremony for the first phase of the project was held in Attapeu Province. It was expected that the whole project would take three years to complete and cost US$35 million, which would be provided to Laos by the Government of Vietnam through low-interest soft loans based on official development assistance. It was expected that the project would be completed by December 2004 (BBC 2001).

In July 2004, it was announced that the second phase of the construction of Road 18b from Km 37 to Km 113 in Attapeu Province to Bo Y, the border with Vietnam, was well underway. The second phase of the construction was 67 km long. From Attapeu town to the Vietnamese border, eighteen small bridges and three large ones were required. Two of the largest bridges, including the only bridge crossing the Xekong River and another one crossing the Xekaman River, were completed in 2003. All the bridges along the road were expected to be completed by the end of 2004 (*Vientiane Times* 2004c). After a series of delays, the road was finally finished on 15 April 2006, almost a year-and-a-half behind schedule. It was officially inaugurated in Attapeu town on 5 June 2006. By the time the road was completed, its price tag had risen from US$35 million to US$48 million (VOV 2006; *Vientiane Times* 2004c). During the inauguration, Deputy Prime Minister Khoan of Vietnam said that he believed that Road 18b would help develop the great potential of Laos' southern region as well as Vietnam's Central Highlands and central region, contributing to poverty reduction and improving the living conditions of the local people (VOV 2006). The road connects with Route 14 in Vietnam, providing the four southernmost provinces in Laos with access to seaports (*Vientiane Times* 2005d; VOV 2006). During construction, Attapeu vehicle owners liked to travel the road as Vietnamese construction workers were commonly selling gasoline from their trucks and other machinery for low prices.

The Demise of *Vang Tat*: A Natural Landmark

Vang Tat is a peculiar place. It is a natural landscape in Saysettha District, adjacent to the new Road 18b. The area almost looks as if humans created it. There are many large rocks standing up in strange positions, as if someone had placed them there. However, it seems likely that the rocks ended up where they are without human help. In any case, many people in Attapeu believe that the area had good potential for tourism development because of its unusual landscape. But when construction of Road 18b began, no plans were made to protect natural landmarks along the way. The Vietnamese road builders started to grind the large standing stones at *Vang Tat* into gravel for road construction. After a considerable amount of damage had already been done, provincial officials finally realized what was happening, and banned any further destruction of the standing rocks. A road-building camp and garage was allowed to remain at the edge of the area, with its associated garbage, used engine oil, and other pollutants from the many trucks that park there flowing into the area. The place is, quite simply, a mess.

Route 18a from Laos to Vietnam, via a small part of Cambodia, is the southern border of Dong Ampham NPA. Route 18b is situated north of route 18a. While in the past the exact routing of this new road was unclear, it eventually became clear that it cuts right through Dong Ampham NPA (see Chapter 9). Davidson et al. (1997) were concerned, even without knowing that the new road would cut through the NPA, about the potential negative impacts of the construction and upgrading of roads near Dong Ampham, but they possessed little information about specific road building plans for the area.

They apparently did not suspect that the new road would cut right through the park. They did, however, outline some of the potential negative impacts of road improvements in terms of nature conservation, even when roads only come near to protected areas. They mentioned increased hunting pressure, increased legal and illegal logging, in-migration, and the establishment of new settlements along roads, deforestation caused by agricultural expansion near roads and land erosion in steep areas. They pointed out that roads often represent significant barriers to certain species movements, such as those of some species of primates, preventing natural movements within, or the expansion of, their ranges (Davidson et al. 1997).

Other New Roads

At the time the Houay Ho Dam was built in the mid-1990s, the South Korean Daewoo Engineering Company built a new, but poorly planned, road from the Bolaven Plateau to Attapeu Province. Daewoo did such a poor job surveying for the road that it was initially routed down a steep part of the escarpment of the Boloven Plateau. Once the road building machinery had progressed to the edge of the escarpment, company workers realized that there was nowhere that a road could be built from there down to the Xekong Valley. Therefore, they had to backtrack and build the road down to the valley to the north.

When the road was completed, it was still built on an inappropriate route, making maintenance difficult (Khamin 2000). Only a short time after it was completed the road fell into disrepair and disuse. It has not been passable since a landslide closed it completely some years ago. There do not appear to be any plans to open it again. Most traffic to Attapeu now passes the Xekong provincial capital, as was the case before the new road was built. Most of this traffic now goes via Pakxong and Thateng before continuing on to Xekong, whereas in the past it passed through Lao Ngam District in Salavan Province. The road between Pakxong District and Thateng District was widened and paved in 2000, making this the preferred route for buses traveling to Xekong Province and then Attapeu.

Apart from the road that passes through Xekong town, there is another route to the basin from Champasak Province. That road goes from Km 49, south of Pakse, east across two important Xekong tributaries, the Xekhampho and Xepian Rivers. The Xekhampho flows into the Xepian, and the Xepian runs into the Xekong. After crossing the Xekhampho River, the road enters Sanamxay District. Buses sometimes travel this dirt road during the dry season, but the route is difficult. Both the Xekhampho and Xepian are moderate-sized perennial rivers without bridges, making crossing them quite difficult in the dry season—and impossible when water levels rise during the rainy season. The road itself is often flooded and impassable during the rainy season. In 2005, the GoL announced plans to upgrade this road, including paving it and installing eleven bridges between Pathoumphone and Sanamxay. Foreign funding is reportedly being provided in support of this project, but project details have not been released.

There is also a new road being built from Ban Mai Village in Sanamxay District, adjacent to the Xepian, up the Bolaven Plateau to Pakxong District in Champasak Province. The Sanamxay District government is reportedly financing this very basic road. This completely new route will pass through some important wildlife areas, opening them to legal and illegal hunting and logging by outsiders. The area that will be passed was once considered an important corridor between Xepian and Dong Houa Sao NPAs.

In 2001, a new road was built between Phouvong District center and the Nam Kong River in the south of the district. A Vietnamese company built it in exchange for logging rights in Phouvong. According to local officials, the deal was lucrative for the Vietnamese, but this was the only way Laos could afford the road. The road did not have to pass any mountains or large hills and was fairly straightforward to build.

There are rumors that a new road might be built to Cambodia from Phouvong District beginning in 2008. This route would cross the Nam Kong River 20–30 km upstream from Viangxai Village. These plan are far from certain as, even if a road was built to the border, it would be difficult to imagine it continuing on into Cambodia, across the Sesan River and on to the capital of Ratanakiri Province, Ban Lung. The proposed route is mountainous and a road would be difficult and expensive to build. It would pass through important wildlife areas within Virachey National Park, one of Cambodia's most important protected areas.

The ADB (2003b) reported that a project to upgrade a 54 km section of road between Saysettha and Sanxay Districts in Attapeu Province was being planned, but would require the resettlement of eighty-four households as well as the taking of some private and common lands, all adjacent to the road. This US$6.5 million project was originally expected to begin in 2005 and take three years to complete. The project has been delayed for unknown reasons. The ADB determined that the mainly ethnic minority communities along the road (there are fourteen villages with almost 7,000 people in them, 76% being ethnic minorities) would be vulnerable to road improvements, particularly because of their low literacy and numeracy levels. This triggered the need for an Ethnic Minority Development Plan as required by the ADB's "Policy on Indigenous People" (1999). The ADB's "Policy on Involuntary Resettlement" (1995) was also triggered. But because it was found that the ethnic minorities were often living amongst non-ethnic minorities, the ADB decided to call these plans "Community Development Plans" rather than "Ethnic Minority Development Plans" (ADB 2003b).

The ADB's plans appear poorly thought out. Apart from providing compensation for losses, the ADB decided that the poorest ethnic minorities would best be served by being provided with literacy and numeracy support as well as marketing and small business skills training. It seems likely that formal adult literacy and business training are far from the highest priorities for these small-scale farmers. This does, however, fit with the ADB's vision of using the roads they build to provide locals with more access to markets. The ADB agreed to support a number of recently resettled villagers living along the road by digging fish ponds for them and providing support for "food-for-work" to expand rice fields, since villagers along the road are not able to grow enough rice for subsistence. There does not appear to have been any consideration of the initiative's potential negative impacts on wetlands and the livelihoods of the poorest (see Chapter 7) (ADB 2003b).

The ADB road project has funded a "Social Action Plan" that includes HIV/AIDS awareness raising activities and "other measures against human trafficking" and for "traffic safety and land rights recognition." The ADB recognizes that one of the negative impacts of this project will be increased safety concerns, due to a higher volume of traffic and higher speeds. The ADB has claimed that it disseminated all the information about the project in the form of a written brochure in Lao, but, considering the low literacy rate of the people that will be affected (based on the ADB's own findings), using written brochures to disseminate information to mostly illiterate affected people seems inadequate at best. The ADB has also failed to consider how the upgrading of the road between Saysettha and Sanxay Districts might support the new Focal Site for resettlement being developed there, even though the Focal Site is mentioned in the ADB's "Community Resettlement Plan" (see Chapter 5). The ADB also seems to believe that the district government has the capacity and resources to officially deal with any grievances or complaints that locals might have about the resettlement process (ADB 2003b). The justification for this conclusion is unclear at best.

While ADB reports have recognized that the road project would result in cultural impacts, they have failed to consider how those types of impacts should be compensated for or mitigated. Given the ADB's narrow definition of compensation as "payments in cash or kind for an asset to be required or affected by a project at replacement cost" (ADB 2003b: ii), it is unsurprising that no compensation is suggested in lieu of the expected negative cultural impacts.

A dirt road runs between the Kalum District capital and Salavan District. It is mainly passable only in the dry season, as is the road between the capital of Xekong Province and Kalum District. This road has, however, been substantially improved in recent years. It is also possible to get to Kalum District center via a road from Ta-oi District in Salavan Province, but that route is only passable during the dry season. From there to the district capital of Kalum the road is not passable because of landslides.

Generally, efforts to improve roads and expand them in the Xekong Basin have been quite intensive in recent years and the trend is continuing. For example, the *Vientiane Times* (2006c) reported that between November 2005 and April 2006 the World Bank, the ADB, and the GoL all made significant investments in roads in Xekong Province, providing over 6 billion kip to construct and reconstruct eight roads that are together 175 km long. However, despite the fact that the road budget for the province by itself exceeds annual provincial revenues, the province's Communication, Transport, and Construction Department still considers the money available to be insufficient. It is seeking funding to improve other roads, including those to Kalum and Dakchung Districts.

Other Transportation Infrastructure

The vast majority of investment in transportation in the Xekong Basin is going toward road construction and improvement. Among the rare exceptions, the UNDP's SIP-Dev Project was planning, in 2005, to fund the construction of a suspension bridge across the Xekaman in Dakchung District, as local people in the area have a difficult time crossing the river, especially during the rainy season. The bridge was expected to be too small for cars but would meet an important need for villagers, who could walk, bike, or take carts or motorcycles across it.

No regular commercial air transportation services exist in the Xekong Basin in Laos, although in the 1990s Lao Aviation operated regular air flights from Pakse to Attapeu. However, demand was insufficient so flights were cancelled, and the airport in Attapeu has since been closed. Air transportation needs are met through the southern Lao transport hub of Pakse, in Champasak Province, where an international airport is located.

The Economic Triangle Development Initiative

In recent years, a new trans-boundary development initiative has gained momentum among many high-level government officials, politicians, international diplomats, and business interests. Called the "Economic Triangle Development Initiative," (*Sam Liam Phatthana Settakith* in Lao), the idea first emerged at a meeting in Vientiane in 1999 in which the Prime Ministers of Vietnam, Laos, and Cambodia agreed that "the consolidation and strengthening of solidarity, cooperation, and mutual assistance among the three countries would be a significant factor for the stability and development of each country." It was not until 25–26 January 2002, during the second meeting of the three prime ministers in Ho Chi Minh City, however, that the initiative was seriously discussed.

The leaders originally envisaged increased economic development cooperation between the seven provinces of Kontum, Gia Lai, and Dak Lak in Vietnam; Attapeu and Xekong in Laos; and Ratanakiri and Stung Treng in Cambodia. This encompasses a combined 85,648 km^2 of territory and a total population of over 3.7 million people (Thuan and Tep 2007; Shaw and Prak 2005; Engelbert 2004). Subsequently, Salavan Province in Laos was added to the initiative upon request (Deputy Provincial Governor, Xekong Province, pers. comm. February 2005). According to Engelbert, "The official goal of this most recent Southeast Asian development triangle is to increase trilateral co-operation in order to bridge the gap between the more highly developed Vietnam on the one side, and less-developed Laos and Cambodia on the other" (2004: 229).

The Prime Ministers of Cambodia, Lao PDR, and Vietnam officially signed the agreement for the Economic Triangle Development Initiative at an Association of Southeast Asian Nations (ASEAN) meeting in Ho Chi Minh City in November 2004 (Shaw and Prak 2005). The agreement is expected to bring increased agriculture support to the region and ease cross-border trade problems between the three neighboring countries (Shaw and Prak 2005).

Efforts to accelerate economic development cooperation have also received a boost from the agreement. The Government of Vietnam has produced a development triangle master plan, which indicates that the border areas between Vietnam, Laos, and Cambodia are to become a priority for development cooperation in the region (*Cambodian* Online 2004; Thuan and Tep 2007). The initiative focuses on developing a transport network, electricity, trade, tourism, human resources training, and health care (*Cambodian* Online 2004). For promoting tourism the slogan, "Three Nations–One Destination" has been developed (VOV 2004).

At a 2004 meeting of the leaders of the three countries held in Siam Reap, Cambodia, Vietnamese Prime Minister Phan was quoted as saying, "The three countries should coordinate closer to develop each country's potential to help the triangle escape from backwardness." He also proposed that priority should be given to infrastructure development, electricity networks, economic zone development at border crossings, human resources development, increasing investment capital for agreed projects, and the establishment of coordination mechanisms in the triangle (VOV 2004).

His Excellency Sok Siphana, Secretary of State for the Ministry of Commerce in Cambodia, speaking about the Economic Triangle Development Initiative, stated, "Work is underway to incorporate the northeastern provinces of Ratanakiri, Mondulkiri, and Stung Treng into economic partnership with bordering provinces in Laos and Vietnam" (Shaw and Prak 2005: 1). He also commented that roads will be built and more business promoted among the provinces. He added that each of the three countries has remote border provinces that are partly cut off from their own country's economy and can benefit from each other (Shaw and Prak 2005). Ly Quang Bich, Political Counselor at the Vietnamese Embassy, said, "[the agreement] will be a cooperation in planting trees and preserving the forests." He added that the three countries will also cooperate on combating "cross-border human trafficking" (Shaw and Prak 2005: 1). Formal documentation of exactly what kinds of development the agreement will bring has not yet been made available to the public (Shaw and Prak 2005).

In the spirit of this development initiative, one of the large new sawmills built in Attapeu Province near the new Route 18b to Vietnam has been named the "Economic Triangle Development Company."

While the Economic Triangle initiative has yet to have a strong direct impact on the region, there are numerous strategies and plans for developing the area in the works. The very idea that such an initiative is underway has given the business sector a boost, and land prices have risen in anticipation. According to the Deputy Governor of Xekong Province, Phonephet Khiulavong, the Government of Japan initially responded favorably to funding part of the US$1.5 billion plan. However, in early 2006 it appeared that the Japanese government had developed some serious reservations about taking the lead in supporting the plan. But in another turn of events, in early 2007 JICA announced that it would support the plan to at least some degree. One of the first projects will reportedly be the upgrading of Route 20 from Stung Treng east through Ratanakiri and into Vietnam. Construction is expected to start later in 2007. The ADB will also be involved in this project.

Other Initiatives

Apart from the Economic Triangle Development Initiative, there have been a number of other bilateral economic cooperation agreements between Xekong and Attapeu Provinces in Laos and neighboring provinces in Vietnam. For example, an agreement was signed in May 2005 between Xekong Province in Laos and Quangnam Province in Vietnam to cooperate in four areas: security, economy, agriculture, and investment. The two sides have agreed to work harder to end cross-border problems, including problems related to illegal cross border movements. Laos also wants Vietnam to invest more in developing Xekong's natural resources, such as mining (see Chapter 12). The border crossing between the two provinces will be upgraded to facilitate trade and tourism once the 21 km-road between the district capital of Dakchung and the border with Vietnam is completed (Phouthonesy 2005).

In March 2006, the Deputy Governor of Xekong Province announced plans to establish an integrated development area along the border between Xekong Province and Vietnam, in Kalum and Dakchung Districts. He claimed that the plan would lead to a number of projects to help improve the conditions of poor families in isolated rural areas. The projects were expected to cover areas such as health and education and help extend economic infrastructure to remote communities. The Deputy Governor stated that most development projects in the province were centered in the provincial capital and that this was a problem. He told a *Vientiane Times* reporter that "The most important thing is to invest in road construction, because roads can help to eradicate poverty and bring isolated people toward development" (Pansivongsay 2006b). However, despite the pro-rural rhetoric, in 2006, 5 billion kip of government funding was specifically allocated for renovating the main roads in the provincial capital of Xekong.

A Golf Course for Dakchung?

In 2004, a group of ethnic minority students from Dakchung District reported that plans have been drawn up to build an 18-hole golf course in Dakchung District near the Xekaman River downstream from the site of the future Xekaman 3 Dam (see Chapter 13). The plans are apparently on hold until the road between the capital of Xekong Province and the Dakchung is completed. At present, the journey is too long and difficult for golfers to make the trip!

Clarifying International Borders

In the late nineteenth century all of present-day Ratanakiri and Stung Treng Provinces, and parts of Mondulkiri, in northeast Cambodia as well as Dak Lak Province in Vietnam were part of Laos. In 1904, French authorities decided to transfer all of Stung Treng, including present-day Ratanakiri and Siem Pang, to Cambodia, apparently as compensation for the parts of Siem Reap and Battambang

Provinces in northwestern Cambodia that the French had ceded to Siam (present-day Thailand). Even though Cambodia was able to retrieve the lost parts of Siem Reap and Battambang just a few years later, in 1907, the parts of Laos given to Cambodia remained Cambodian territory (Ironside and Baird 2003). The overall process involved in establishing the new Lao/Cambodian border in 1904 was not transparent or well documented (Breazeale 2002). Since France controlled both sides of the border, it was not considered a matter of great importance and did not require the type of attention necessary with, for example, the border with Siam (Preston 1975). The Laos-Cambodia border was not demarcated on the ground at the time, and this has led to the unclear situation that still exists today.

Just over a century has passed since Stung Treng was removed from Laos, but the international border between Laos and Cambodia is still poorly defined. The demarcation of the border has become a controversial issue in the eastern and western parts of the Xekong River Basin in Laos. The Governments of Laos and Cambodia have jointly been attempting, in recent years, to clarify their borders. This is causing significant disruption and concern in some areas. In Sanamxay and Phouvong Districts, for example, there is concern among local people living near the border that they will lose large amounts of their land situated south of the Nam Kong River and east of the Xekong River to the border with Vietnam. One ethnic Lao villager from Sompoi Village, Sanamxay District said, "The area south of the Nam Kong River that the Cambodians want has always been part of Laos."

Similarly, the redefining and marking of the western section of the international border between Laos and Cambodia in Khong District has resulted in considerable dissatisfaction among the local population. Part of the Xepian NPA (it is unclear exactly how much) is now, apparently, in Cambodia. A place called "Din *Nam Kham Mouang*" has been designated as the new border between Cambodia and Laos in Khong District. Napakiap Village, in Khong District, is now considered to be inside Cambodia and much of the forests once thought to be in Laos, long used by villagers from Sot, Naveng, Naseuak, Phon Sa-at, and Nafang Villages, are now defined as in Cambodia. The remaining forest area available for local people is quite truncated. In April 2005, ethnic Brao villagers in Phon Sa-at Village complained about how they had lost much of the land that they once used for fishing, hunting, and NTFP gathering. Representatives of Phon Sa-at reported that Lao and Cambodian officials had put up new border markers and that they have been threatened with being fined 50,000 kip if caught on the Cambodian side of "the new border."

It appears that the GoL has agreed to at least some of the above changes. In March 2005, the *Phnom Penh Post* reported, that the Lao military promised to leave Cambodian territory after negotiations took place between the governors in Stung Treng Province, Cambodia and Champasak Province, Laos. An unnamed Cambodian Ministry of Defense official stated that a Lao military base was 2–4 km inside Cambodia, in Siem Pang District, Stung Treng Province. The Lao press has not reported any details about these negotiations or the demarcation of the border.

Most recently, however, it has become evident that other border problems remain. The spirit of cooperation in demarcating the border that existed a number of years ago has evaporated. At present, a stalemate exists, with three places along the border still contested. The first is along the Xelamphao River west of the Mekong, the second is near the only official international crossing between Laos and Cambodia, at Dong Kalo on the road between Pakse and Stung Treng, and the third is east of the Xekong south of the Nam Kong River. Mongkon Sasorith, a legal expert for the Lao Ministry of Foreign Affairs who specializes on Lao border issues with its neighbors, was unclear, as of March 2007, how long the border conflict with Cambodia would continue or the conflict could be resolved.

12

Large-Scale Mining

In Chapter 8 we described how people in the Xekong River Basin historically panned for gold in various rivers and streams during pre-colonial, colonial, and even present times. This chapter does not review local ways of acquiring and using mineral resources in the basin; instead it focuses on the increasing number of large-scale mining operations recently initiated or now being planned in the Xekong Basin and the likely impacts on local livelihoods of these projects.

When the French took control of Attapeu Province and the east bank of the Mekong River in 1893, one of their greatest hopes for commercial development in the region was mining. The area was already well-known for its gold deposits. Many mineral deposits of potentially great value were discovered in Laos during the French colonial period; however, little actual mineral extraction was done (Dommen 1985).

The Xekong River Basin has long been suspected of holding important mineral and gem deposits. In the early years of colonial rule, a number of French officials formed the Attapeu Mining Company and applied for a large gold mining concession in Attapeu. The concession was granted but, despite great hopes, the company was virtually inactive for a number of years. Finally, in 1911, the Governor-General of Indochina cancelled the concession, citing the company's inability to demarcate its boundaries within the time specified by the concession contract.[1] No mining occurred, and this was apparently the only mining concession ever attempted in the Xekong Basin during the French period.

Subsequent instability and the tense political situation in the region kept external mining interests out of the Xekong River Basin for many years; however, foreign investors have recently shown considerable interest in initiating mining operations there (Pansivongsay 2006a). A number of projects are being investigated at present.

The Vietnamese government is assisting the GoL in mapping the geology of southern Laos so as to promote investment in mining (Phonpachith 2006). In recent years the GoL's Ministry of Energy and Mines has conducted a number of surveys of mineral resources in the basin.

The past few years have led to an explosion of interest in the mining sector in southern Laos. It is difficult to keep track of the number of agreements and concessions that are being made between foreign mining concerns and the GoL. In January 2005, a survey team investigated mineral deposits inside Xepian NPA near Taong Village, Pathoumphone District. They found what they believed to be deposits of a mineral known in Lao as "*kalina*." The Ministry survey team took samples from the *Houay* Keua area, an important core zone of the park, for further analysis. Gems known as "*keo nang fan*" and "*keosi*" in Lao have also been found in the area, according to villagers from Taong Village. This type of mineral prospecting is not supposed to be legal within NPAs like Xepian, but, since it was approved by the central government, nobody seems willing to question the legality of operations.

There are also reputed to be "diamond"[2] deposits in the eastern mountains of Xekong and Attapeu Provinces, although the existence of these has not yet been confirmed.

There are reportedly plans to establish a gold mine in Sanxay District at *Nong* Fa *Nong* Yot and *Phou* Lek Fai near the Xekaman River. Davidson et al. (1997) reported that, at the time his group was studying Dong Ampham NPA, a team of Vientiane-based geologists visited the *Vang* Tat Noi area in order to explore the possibilities for mineral extraction in the region. This included collecting samples from near the *Nong* Fa *Nong* Yot Crater Lake, where there are supposedly "sapphires." At the time, it was unclear whether these deposits were significant. Davidson et al. (1997) expressed concern about mineral extraction within Dong Ampham NPA, and outlined some of the potential negative impacts on biodiversity that could result from such operations.

Xekong Province's supposedly abundant reserves of coal are being investigated for potential future exploitation (*Vientiane Times* 2005k). There is also reportedly some mineral prospecting occurring in Dakchung District. For example, deposits of onyx, a semi-precious gem, have been found there, and a mine site, reportedly adjacent to the road between Xekong town and Dakchung District, has been established. A Chinese company has surveyed for bauxite in Dakchung and has apparently found large deposits. Chinese companies are increasing their involvement in the mining sector in Laos. So far, thirteen Chinese companies have reportedly invested US$60 million in mining ventures throughout Laos (Phonpachith 2006). There have also been reports of mining possibilities for titanium and gold in Dakchung District.

In Kalum District, an Australian company is said to be planning a gold mine. In 2005, this company reported to the local government that they had not only found gold but a number of other valuable minerals. In addition, a Russian company began surveying for gold in Kalum in 2004 (Pansivongsay 2006a), and a Chinese company also went to investigate gold deposits at *Phou* Touang in Kalum District in 2004. Surveys for coal and steel in Kalum, and copper in Lamam, are also underway (Pansivongsay 2006a). Another foreign company is studying the mining potential in Kalum. How many of these surveys and proposed projects will result in the development of significant mining operations remains to be seen.

There is abundant international documentation of the negative social and environmental impacts and costs from the types of large-scale mining operations under consideration in the Xekong Basin in Laos. To date, however, there appears to have been little consideration or acknowledgement of how the impacts of these projects should be addressed.

Aluminum Production

One of the largest mines being proposed for the Xekong River Basin is a large bauxite mine on the eastern part of the Boloven Plateau. In February 2006, Vaughn (2006) reported that Ord River Resources, a large mining firm from Australia, entered into a deal with one of its major shareholders, China Nonferrous Metals, to explore and develop the Chinese company's proposed 100 million-ton bauxite project on the Boloven Plateau. Then, in November 2006, Riseborough (2006) reported that Ord had announced that the quality and the grade of the minerals of its claim in Laos were "greater than originally estimated." There are now plans to develop a "world class aluminum industry" on the Boloven Plateau. According to the Deputy Governor for Xekong Province, Phonephet Khiulavong, "The province is asking the government to seek investors to operate the bauxite project" (Pansivongsay 2006a).

It has not been officially announced, but Ord River Resources and its Chinese partner China Nonferrous Metals have apparently purchased the rights to build the Xepian-Xenamnoi Dam from its Korean investors in order to provide electricity for the aluminum production facility planned to go with the bauxite mining operation, since the production of aluminum requires a huge amount of electricity and is often associated with large dams (see Chapter 13). Thus far, however, there are no aluminum production facilities in Laos.

Some ethnic Heuny people in Pakxong District are upset about the proposed bauxite mine, as exploration has been taking place in the general area where they used to live before they were resettled as a result of the construction of the Houay Ho Dam. They were told that they had to leave in the late 1990s so that the area's forests could be protected, but the people now see that, instead of being protected, the area has been given over to a foreign mining corporations without any consultation with the area's original inhabitants.

Most recently, in August 2007, Latsaphao (2007) reported that the people from four villages in Dakchung District had agreed to allow the Lao Aluminum Industry Company to build an aluminum production factory on their land. Many villagers were reportedly "uncomfortable" with the idea of an aluminum factory being built on their land before a meeting between the headmen of the four villages and company representatives was organized on 31 July, which government officials also attended. However, officials reported after the meeting that the village headmen from Daklan, Dakpop, Dakseng, and Xieng Luang Villages "understood the point of this matter." According to the Head of the Energy and Mines Office in Xekong Province, Sida Souvannasay, villagers "did not agree to the idea of the factory, because no compensation for the use of their land had been mentioned. . . . However, the Lao Aluminum Industry Company eventually agreed to compensate them by exchanging their land for other land." The villages will be relocated, but the company has apparently agreed to provide new houses, schools, electricity, health centers, roads, and sanitation for the villages, among other things.

The company has been contracted to build an aluminum factory that will cover a 25 km^2 area and be licensed to operate for the next twenty-seven years. The value of the investment is reportedly US$329 million (Latsaphao 2007).

Gold Excavating

Although the idea for mining the Xekong riverbed for gold might seem relatively new, the idea has actually been around since the French period. On 12 May 1912, the Vientiane-based Résident supérieur of French Laos sent a message to the Governor-General of Indochina. He requested support for conducting a study of potential gold deposits in the sand of the riverbed of the Xekong, indicating that the French administration already suspected that the river held significant gold deposits.[3] However, the idea was apparently not implemented during the colonial period. In recent years, however, the situation has changed dramatically.

Gold Excavating in Xekong Province

The excavation, or dredging, of gold from the Xekong in Xekong Province using large boats and machinery began in 1999 or 2000. Local people quickly became opposed to it. For one, the damage done to the riverbed has been dramatic, and the riparian ecology has been seriously damaged, thus harming fishing in the river. Secondly, piles of debris generated from excavating obstructed boat travel and fishing operations. Finally, the Chinese gold dredgers became notorious in Lamam District for using electricity generated by the gold dredging boats to electrocute large quantities of fish, both for their consumption and to sell to fish traders in the provincial capital. For example, in 2001, two Chinese workers from a gold excavating boat were observed bringing two large sacks full of fish from Nava Keng Luang Village, Lamam District to the provincial market to sell.

Sitthisay Saysana Company, the owners of gold dredging operations in Xekong and Attapeu Provinces (see below) began dredging the Xekong in the northern part of Xekong Province, in Kalum District. They have gradually moved downriver. In 2005/2006 they became active downriver from Xekong town, in the southern part of the province.

In 2005, in Pak Thon Village, Lamam District, ethnic Harak village elders explained how a few years previously villagers were upset when a sacred 8 m-deep pool in the Xekong near their village (called *Vang* Thamakan) was dredged for gold by Chinese working for Sitthisay Saysana Company. The villagers had requested that the area not be dredged, as they believed that the water spirit from the area had been disturbed by the excavating and might take vengeance on them. A large black snake was seen near the deep-water pool after the dredging, indicating to villagers that the spirit of the area was unhappy. The villagers wanted to fine the Chinese the cost of a white buffalo, a white pig, and a white chicken in order to sacrifice the animals to the spirits, but the Chinese refused to pay anything, and provincial officials did not support the villagers.

People from a number of other villages along the Xekong in Kalum and Lamam Districts have also complained about the gold dredging. some villagers have complained about the gold dredgers electrocuting fish near their villages and lament that the Chinese have taught some villagers how to do so. Villagers have not received any compensation from the company for the impacts they have suffered because of the gold mining of the river.

One elder from Pak Thon said, in reference to the over-exploitation of river and forest resources by commercial interests: "My sons are away studying in school, but there is not enough time for them to learn. By the time they come back, there will be no resources left for them to use." Oxfam Australia has been working in Pak Thon to support improved fisheries management and conservation. It has, for example, helped to formalize the regulations for protecting *Vang* Thamakan. Directly addressing the impacts caused by the Chinese company is challenging; however, most recently the people of Pak Thon have at least managed to get the Chinese to stop dredging in the sacred area.

In Pakayom Village, Lamam District, villagers have found themselves in serious conflict with Chinese gold dredging operations, and in one instance villagers forced the Chinese to leave the area. One village leader said, "They did not contribute to the village, and I guess their activities were illegal too. So when we asked them to go away, they did" (WWF 2005c: 17).

Although gold excavating in the river stopped in some areas in Xekong Province in 2003, it has continued south of Xekong town and north of the border between Xekong and Attapeu Provinces in 2005. The gold dredgers are still operating in large numbers along parts of the Xekong in Xekong Province, and the provincial government apparently remains committed to exploiting gold deposits in the Xekong River (*Vientiane Times* 2005k), even though villagers are opposed to the operations. In mid-2006, there were reportedly sixteen gold dredging boats in the Xekong in Xekong Province, some operating and some not.

Keovichit (2004) reported that the Xekong provincial government had recently approved another "gold exploration project" in Kalum District; however, the report was unclear regarding whether this was for gold excavation in rivers or a land-based gold mining operation.

Gold Excavation in Attapeu Province

Dredging for gold in the Xekong River has expanded to Attapeu Province in recent years. Here too, gold excavating has become a very controversial issue, and local people appear to be widely opposed to it.

In 2004, the Sitthisay Saysana gold mining company, using mainly Chinese workers, began dredging for gold from the bottom of the Xekong in Sanamxay District, having already been operating in Xekong Province for several years.

Local people quickly realized that the operations were having serious negative environmental impacts on the Xekong by increasing downstream turbidity and causing the smothering of rapids with sand and silt. The miners only had a short-term contract that was scheduled to end in March 2004 but, despite local opposition, it was extended to June 2004.

The Mekong Wetlands Biodiversity Project and the Attapeu Provincial Science Technology and Environment Office (MWBP and APSTEO 2005) reported that a feasibility survey for gold excavation mining in the Xekong took place between August 2003 and June 2004 and that the mining operations in the Xekong in Attapeu were conducted under a joint venture arrangement involving the State Geological Exploration Unit of Laos (responsible for technical matters), and Sitthisay Saysana Company (responsible for funding and implementing the project). Gold mining in the Xekong in Attapeu moved from the exploratory phase to the production stage in October 2004. Annual renewable contracts for this mining were signed between the investors and the GoL. The concession arrangements are subject to annual review prior to extension.

The number of gold dredging boats in operation between the capital city of Attapeu Province, Muang Mai, and Sanamxay District increased dramatically, from just a few in 2003 and 2004 to twenty-five in 2005 (MWBP and APSTEO 2005). Even more were expected to be operating in 2006. Gold excavating in the Xekong was taking place almost all the way to the border with Cambodia. Two or three people generally operated one boat, with workers often working 18-hour days. Excavation operations frequently continued day and night. Approximately 5 m^3 of aggregate was excavated per hour per boat, providing a reported yield in gold of between 0.625–2.45 g, depending on the location (MWBP and APSTEO 2005).

Considering the potentially serious negative environmental and social impacts of commercial gold excavating in the Xekong, and the concern already generated about these operations at the village and local government levels (see below), it was timely for the MWBP[4] to cooperate with the APSTEO in April 2005 to assess the impacts of these operations. This took place as part of a hands-on training activity for government officials in conducting Environmental Impact Assessments (EIAs) (MWBP and APSTEO 2005). During the assessment of the area between the provincial capital and the district center of Sanamxay, it was found that gold excavating did indeed pose many serious environmental and social threats. Local people who were interviewed during the survey were critical of the operations.

In 2005, Sitthisay Saysana Company requested permission to expand its operations upstream from Muang Mai to the mouth of the Xenamnoi River, the border between Xekong and Attapeu Provinces. Regulations in Laos state that an EIA should be conducted and approved prior to the implementation of such projects; however, these regulations were not honored for the gold dredging operations in Attapeu or Xekong. The mining was underway long before any EIA reports were submitted. Later, the APSTEO submitted comments regarding the EIA, but as of 2005 the status of the amendments was unknown (MWBP and APSTEO 2005).

One serious problem related to gold mining in the Xekong is the use of mercury in the gold extraction process. It is mixed with gold derived from the sediment and is then heated with acid to purify the gold. Mercury is a dangerous element, even in small quantities. The mercury acid mix is released into the environment in three ways: 1) through evaporation from the heating process; 2) through the soil, since waste water is often poured onto the ground; and 3) directly into the water, including the Xekong, as waste water. This can cause fish kills downstream (MWBP and APSTEO 2005). A number of hydrological, biological, physical, and social impacts associated with this gold mining were identified during the EIA training. They related to mercury poisoning; the disruption of the riverbed, including benthic flora and fauna and erosion; habitat destruction associated with turbidity; water quantity associated with changes in river flow; access difficulties for boats and fishing-nets; and transportation and safety issues, especially at night. These data were collected over only a one-day period of fieldwork for the EIA-training exercise and so more information was required (MWBP and APSTEO 2005).

The results of the study were presented to the Deputy Governor of Attapeu Province, who said he would consider the results carefully and look into the issue in more depth. He requested a report from both the APSTEO and the Attapeu Provincial Industry and Handicrafts Office on the status and threats/impacts of gold mining activities on the Xekong. According to EIA regulations, such recommendations should help improve environmental management decision-making in the future (MWBP and APSTEO 2005).

Attapeu Province reportedly received 40 million kip in taxes from gold dredging operations in the Xekong in 2005, a relatively small return considering the problems these operations are causing to the environment and local livelihoods. That is one of the reasons why the government has been hesitant about extending the concession period since the mining concession expired at the end of 2005.

Rising Up against Gold Excavating in the Xekong River

Gold excavating concessions in the Xekong River has become unpopular with local people living in Sanamxay District. Villagers have become so upset about the damage being done to their river that they have been resisting in various ways. In early 2004, villagers in Nam Kong Village, Sanamxay District, became agitated when Chinese gold dredgers insisted on mining part of the river occupied by important spirits. The villagers could do little to stop them, but they did protest in their own way. A rumor, believed to have originated in their village, began circulating that the escalator on one gold excavating boat working in the sacred area had suddenly seized up. As the story went, five Chinese workers on the boat dove underwater to try to fix the problem, but the spirit of the water caused all of them to drown. This story was circulating in villages, including Sompoi, as if it were fact. A Lao employee of the company in the district center of Sanamxay was visibly annoyed when asked about the story. He denied that it was true and claimed that villagers were trying to make the gold dredgers look bad by fabricating stories and maliciously spreading rumors. Similarly, in order to make the Chinese workers look bad, locals living along the Xekong in Xekong Province often complain that those working on gold dredging boats defecate directly into the river—which they probably do.

By the end of 2004, when the number of gold dredgers increased dramatically, this type of passive resistance escalated into more violent and direct confrontation in the ethnic Lao village of Saphao, in Sanamxay District. Although the story is not entirely clear, the village headman is believed to have organized a large group of villagers to chase a number of the Chinese gold dredgers away by throwing rocks at them. The large mounds of rocks and debris the miners had created in the river particularly enraged the villagers, as they were blocking boat traffic and routes where villagers used to float gill nets (*lai mong* in Lao) for fishing. A number of Chinese were reportedly injured during the attack and the district police later put the village headman in jail for his involvement in the uprising. A local government official in Sanamxay District reported, in early 2006, that "Nobody in Sanamxay District is supportive of gold mining operations in the Xekong River. We want them to stop as soon as possible." This sort of vocal local opposition to a government-approved project is unusual for Laos, and especially in Attapeu.

Local people from Lavi Fang Deng Village in Lamam District are another community that has clashed with the Chinese gold dredgers. The ethnic Lavi villagers have a deep-water fish sanctuary in the Xekong near their village and, despite it being officially recognized by district and provincial government authorities, a gold excavating boat started dredging the area in 2005. Locals complained and attempted to fine the Chinese for violating village regulations. This was an important case, as it was initially unclear whether village regulations could be effectively applied to prevent the Chinese from damaging the fish sanctuary. However, the villagers were able to force the Chinese to move out of the area and were also able to force them to pay a fine of a pig and a case of Beer Lao as compensation. The fine was small, but it was significant in that it demonstrated that the government recognized village rules.

While the total amount of gold discovered through these excavations in the Xekong is unknown, the recent investment in new boats for gold mining in the river indicates that the operations have been profitable. But at the end of 2005 the gold dredging license for the Chinese companies working in Attapeu expired. Faced with significant local opposition, government authorities have thus far not issued new licenses for gold dredging operations. Apart from the local opposition to gold dredging, the Attapeu government was also reportedly unhappy with the Chinese dredgers, as they have evidently been violating one important condition of their agreement with the GoL. They were supposed to report all the gold that they acquired from their operations so that appropriate taxes could be calculated. However, in late 2005 Champasak police intercepted Chinese miners attempting to smuggle gold from Attapeu into Thailand, and 40 kg of gold was confiscated. This indicated that more gold was being extracted from the river than the Chinese were reporting.

The Chinese clearly expect to continue dredging for gold, and, in early 2006, a number of new gold dredging boats were trucked to Attapeu (apparently from China) and assembled in the water near the bridge over the Xekong at Muang Mai town. There have also been efforts to expand gold mining operations in the Xekong to Cambodian parts of the river, in Siem Pang District, Stung Treng Province. According to NGO reports from Cambodia, local government officials have stated that there are no plans to allow gold dredging operations in Siem Pang. However, in early 2006 the Chinese still seemed hopeful that they would be able to start dredging for gold in Siem Pang, and they also hoped to continue working in Attapeu. In mid-2006, there were sixty-two gold dredging boats in the Xekong in Attapeu Province. Of these, thirty-six were apparently situated near the Cambodian border waiting for permission to proceed, and the others were parked near the provincial capital. Some appeared to be in the process of being dismantled.

After waiting for permission to dredge for many months, miners were disappointed when the expected permission to expand their fleet was not received, and so gold dredging in Attapeu stopped in 2006, and apparently was only continuing in Xekong Province in 2007.

Thus far, gold excavating has only been allowed in the Xekong, but authorities have also considered allowing gold excavating along the Xekaman and Xexou Rivers in Attapeu Province. But with the present local opposition to gold dredging operations, it is unclear whether this expansion will be allowed.

Regional experience suggests that Lao decision-makers should take the concerns over the environmental and livelihood impacts of these types of gold dredging operations seriously. Gold mining in Kachin State, Burma, has, for example, resulted in severe environmental impacts, including those related to releasing mining chemicals like mercury and other waste directly into rivers and fundamentally changing the structures of riverbeds, causing severe impacts to aquatic life and negatively affecting local livelihoods (Images Asia Environment Desk and Pan Kachin Development Society 2004). Oxfam America (2004) has also reported on some of the serious negative human health, livelihoods, and environmental impacts of small-scale gold mining in Cambodia, including the use of dangerous chemicals like mercury for extracting gold. However, none of the case studies presented in their report addressed the type of riverbed gold mining that has been taking place in the mainstream Xekong River in Attapeu Province. Further research on mining issues in the basin is urgently needed.

13

Electricity, Hydropower, and Rivers

Laos is frequently identified regionally and internationally as a country with considerable "unutilized potential" for hydropower.[1] The Xekong River Basin forms an important part of this potential. As has been detailed in Chapters 5, 6, 7, and 8, rivers are a key element in the livelihoods of many thousands of people in the Xekong Basin in Laos. There is probably no other single issue with the potential to affect dramatic change in the basin in the next few years than the planned production of electricity through the development of large hydroelectric dams using the region's rivers. These developments are likely to have a profound effect on the landscape and the people of the basin.

At present, only a small proportion of households in the Xekong River Basin in Laos are connected to the electricity grid. But the vast majority of the proposed electrical generation from the area's rivers will not be for local use but rather for export to neighboring countries. The vision is to transfer the power using a high voltage regional power grid and an electricity trading system (IRN 2004a; 2006). Various international donors and multilateral banks are expected to provide most of the funding for the power grid. Local communities in the Xekong Basin are likely to pay considerable costs for these projects in terms of lost livelihoods, and it seems likely that they will receive few, if any, benefits. The initiation of large-scale hydropower projects and associated roads and transmission lines has already had a serious impact on the livelihoods of some communities in the basin.

This chapter provides an overview of the main issues associated with hydropower development in Laos, with specific attention to the details of projects in the Xekong River Basin. Issues such as local power needs, the export of power, and the proposed regional grid are considered, and then descriptions are provided of some of the main hydropower projects currently in operation, under construction, or being considered for development in the basin. In recent years the pace of hydropower development in the region has accelerated dramatically. Changes are happening so quickly that it is challenging to keep track of recent developments. It is likely that whatever is written here will soon need updating, but there is already a great deal of information available that should be considered in understanding issues related to hydropower in the region.

Local Power Needs and Generation

The *Vientiane Times* (2004j) reported in 2004 that 2 million Kwh of electricity were used in Xekong Province annually to serve 3,669 families in 34 villages, representing 29% of the population. This, however, only includes villages connected to the national electric grid and does not consider the many off-grid micro-hydro or solar systems in use in the province (see section below). In Attapeu Province, there are even fewer villages connected; in 2004, it was reported that only 11.9% of the villages were connected to the national electricity grid (SC and SPC 2004).

Until recently Attapeu Province was receiving just 1.5 million Kwh of electricity for domestic use annually, despite the large size of the province's Houay Ho Dam (see below). However, due to problems with being unable to provide electricity to all the irrigation and other industrial projects that need power, the provincial government now plans to begin receiving 20 MW of power from Champasak Province. The *Vientiane Times* reported that "Electrical power in many industrial factories is completely cut off in the province when the dry season arrives from December to May. This is also true for irrigation projects in the province" (cited in Latsaphao 2006a: 3).

Electricité du Lao (EdL) has been raising the costs to Lao consumers of electricity in recent years in order to make investments in large dam construction and other electrical services for the domestic market more viable. In recent history, electricity in Laos has been priced well below international market rates. International donors like the World Bank and the ADB have been insisting that the GoL raise its domestic prices for electricity, both to facilitate investment in the sector and to reduce the debt burden of EdL. But as prices have risen, the amount of accumulated debt by consumers has also increased, and EdL has been having a difficult time collecting this debt. In 2006, the Minister in charge of EdL threatened to cut off electricity to consumers who had not paid their electricity bills (Southivongnorath 2006).

The GoL has plans to significantly expand the electricity distribution system in the country in the coming years and projects that 90% of the population will have access to electricity by 2020 (EdL 2003), compared to 37% in 2004. Both the capital cities of Xekong and Attapeu Provinces received access to grid electricity as well as regular telephone services in the mid- to late-1990s. In 2003, Sanamxay district center was connected to the electricity grid, and in 2006 the grid was further extended to the district center of Kalum.

Access to electricity in southern Laos and the region is certainly expanding rapidly, and, while there are plans to rely on solar power and small dams to meet much of the local electrical needs of remote communities (Phouthonesy 2004; World Bank 2004), it is still expected that the vast majority of electricity to be produced in the Xekong Basin will be from large dams and for export.

Micro Hydropower: A Different Approach to Meeting Local Power Needs

Although there are no large dams, transmission lines, or, in some cases, even roads to many of the rural villages in Kalum and Dakchung, the mountainous terrain in both districts is highly amenable for micro hydropower generation. Even though these are some of the poorest parts of Laos, and no government or international support is being provided, most villages now have at least partial access to electricity generated by small dynamos that the villagers have installed on their own in streams. Recent years have seen a dramatic increase in the number of villages with dynamos. In 1997, there were reportedly just 33 in Xekong Province, with a total of 17.7 Kw of electricity generating power. However, according to the Xekong provincial Office of Industry and Handicrafts, just six years later the number had expanded to about 300 (Rosales et al. 2003). The UNDP (1999a) reported that in Dakchung District 363 households in 58 villages were using electricity produced by dynamos (10.7% of all households) and that 56% of all the villages in the district had at least some access to electricity. UNDP (1999c) also reported that in Kalum District 235 households in 41 villages were using electricity produced by dynamos (12.6% of total households) and that 71% of the villages had at least some access to electricity. Since then, the number of villages using dynamos has increased further.

Rosales et al. (2003) reported that each dynamo requires regular maintenance amounting to about US$5–10 per year, and has an average life expectancy of five to ten years. The average micro-hydro generator runs for about six to ten months a year, with some operating year round. Each generator produces power for approximately 1,333 hours a year, with a capacity of between 200–300 watts each. Therefore, for 300 generators the total amount of electricity generated is about 99,975 Kwh. Rosales et al. (2003) argue that the water used to produce this energy is an indirect benefit of the forests of the Xekong Basin. The value of this electricity ranges from 84 to 569 kip/Kwh, which translates into US$792 to US$5,367 of total value per year.

Although the electricity generated from dynamos is generally only enough for lighting, this is the main reason local people want electricity, so they see these systems as meeting their basic needs. There are generally two kinds of dynamos: 1) the "standing" variety that is installed in a roughly vertical position, and 2) the "laying-down" variety installed horizontally on the streambed. They generate the same amounts of power, but the standing variety is cheaper and requires more water to operate. In Kloung Village people said that 300 Kw laying-down dynamos cost 700,000 kip, while the 500 Kw laying-down varieties were priced at 900,000 kip. For 300-Kw standing dynamos, the price was just 430,000 kip, while 500 Kw standing dynamos were priced at 500,000 kip.

The micro-hydropower dynamos come from Vietnam and are either purchased by local people or are acquired through labor exchanges with ethnic Pako villagers from adjacent parts of Vietnam. The ethnic Katu and Ngkriang villages of Laipo, Don, Pom, Kado, Talang Mai, and Tahieu in Kalum District are good examples of remote communities with access to electricity from dynamos. In around 2000 or 2001, these villages got their first dynamos from Vietnam. In 2000, villagers from Laipo installed their dynamo on a small mountain stream near their village. They found that there was not enough water at the height of the dry season to run the dynamo but that it worked fine for up to ten months per year. There are now three to nine dynamos in use per village. Each one serves two to three families with enough electricity for nighttime lighting. Dynamo users are mainly the better off members of the community, but they would hardly be considered rich outside of their society.

In Pom Village, there are three 300 kw dynamos on Troung Stream, next to the village. While the dynamos in Laipo are simply placed in a high gradient stream, in Pom an ingenious small wooden barrage has been made in the stream. Water is funneled from there into hollowed logs that are open at one end. At the other ends dynamos are placed. Water swirls around at the ends of the hollowed logs and then flows into the dynamos. During the dry season, between November and April, the dynamos are placed in the middle of the stream, but during the rainy season, when water levels rise, they are located at the edges, higher up on its banks.

Rather than purchasing dynamos with cash, which is often in short supply, many of these villagers have acquired them through entering into cooperative labor exchanges with ethnic Pako peoples (who speak languages similar enough to the Katu for the two groups to communicate) living on the other side of the border in Vietnam. Young men from the villages walk about three days through the forest to villages along the border in Vietnam. There, they hire out their labor to transport dynamos to other villages in the south of Laos where Vietnamese traders are able to sell them, as people in those villages are closer to markets and generally have more money to spend. Some villagers reported that each man must carry four dynamos to sell, but at the end he gets to keep one as his payment. In *Ban* Don villagers reported getting the dynamos in the same way, but that they only had to carry three dynamos to get one. It usually takes three days to carry the dynamos to the villages along the Xekong River in Kalum where they are stored in preparation for being sold. The traders also provide the laborers with rice to eat during the trip.

The Pako purchase the dynamos in Vietnam for between 150–200,000 kip each and sell them for 6–700,000 kip each, thus giving them enough profit to pay for the labor required to transport the dynamos and still make a good profit. The Pako who sell the dynamos generally do not carry them when they travel to sell them; they leave this difficult work to the hired Katu. One Katu said, "The Pako from Vietnam do not carry any dynamos. They have money. They do not need to do that."

The spread of dynamos has occurred not as a result of any outside aid or with the encouragement of government officials. Instead it has come about through the efforts of entrepreneurial ethnic minorities in Vietnam and an interested population of ethnic minorities in Laos. This represents a local solution to the lack of electricity in remote areas, a simple and inexpensive solution that villagers can afford through their own labor or with relatively small amounts of money.

Micro-Hydropower as a Micro-Enterprise

In 2005, an ethnic Brao villager from Viangxai Village in Phouvong District, purchased a laying-down variety of dynamo and the wiring required to produce electricity at a small rapids on the Nam Kong River near his house. His total investment was about 1 million kip, not including light bulbs. He is now able to produce enough electricity year-round to light his own and four nearby houses. He is also able to charge six small batteries every day. Since he receives 2,000 kip for recharging each battery, he is able to generate 12,000 kip in revenue a day, or about 360,000 kip a month. Not including the lighting, he and his neighbors are getting, he was able to recover his cash investment in just three months. Since the generator is just sitting in the river and is not altering water flow, the negative environmental and social impacts of such systems are insignificant.

Using Water Power to Save Labor

Large wooden waterwheels could, until well into the 1990s, be seen along rivers in the Xekong Basin. They were used both for pounding rice and for raising water for irrigating gardens. An illustration of a large set of waterwheels from the region was included in de Malglaive (1893), indicating that these devices have a long history of use in the basin. In many areas of the basin such large waterwheels are apparently no longer in use because of the introduction of electricity.

In Kalum District, local people still use smaller waterwheel devices to save labor. For example, in Tahieu Village mountain spring water is used to operate rice-pounding devices (*khok mong nam* in Lao) rather than using human labor. There are twelve families with these devices, one for each family. The rice is placed in pestles, and then water is used to make the mortars go up and down until the rice is dehusked. Generally, one device can dehusk one full pestle of rice every twelve hours during the dry season. In the rainy season it takes about eight hours to complete the dehusking of one full pestle of rice, more than enough to feed most families. According to villagers, the main benefit of this indigenous technology is that it saves on women's labor. Villagers from Tahieu would like to improve on their system by exchanging the bamboo sections currently used for piping the water to using plastic PVC pipe. They would also like to exchange the wooden pounding-pieces with more durable ones made of cement.

Solar Power

Solar power is increasingly being used in villages not connected to the national power grid in the Xekong Basin, and the GoL considers solar power to be a viable alternative for electrifying remote villages, especially those too far away to be connected to the main electricity grid. However, unlike the case of micro-hydropower, local people have not yet taken the initiative to invest in solar projects because capital investment costs are generally high. Instead, most solar power projects in southern Laos have been supported by international donor aid.

For example, the World Bank has been working with the Ministry of Industry and Handicrafts to support the piloting of small solar power electricity generation projects in remote villages in Champasak and Xekong Provinces. In these cases, individual families have been given the option to participate in the project. All participating families have received solar panels and the associated battery technology for lighting and are required to pay the GoL 10,000 kip a month over many years to pay off the cost of the hardware. This money can then theoretically be transferred to another village in need. One village in Pathoumphone District that has participated in this project is the Brao village of Houay Ko located in the Tomo River Basin but directly adjacent to the Xekong Basin. There, villagers seem happy with the system. There appears to be considerable potential to expand solar power usage in the Xekong River Basin, especially in its more remote areas.

Private companies are also involved in providing access to solar power. During a March 2007 visit to the Ta-neum area in Xekong Province, the second author observed a settlement in which almost every house had a small solar panel. The panels charged up 12-volt batteries that could be used in the evening for lighting and small accessories such as radios. Villagers reported that they did not own the systems; a private company, Sunlabob, owns and maintains the panels and associated equipment, and villagers pay a monthly fee to rent the equipment. In this way, they do not have to make a large initial investment in the solar systems. The use of such systems appears to be increasing in remote parts of the province.

Exporting Electricity

The GoL plans to produce at least 6,000 MW of electrical power by 2020, a substantial increase from the 615 MW of electricity currently being produced from nine dams (LNCE 2003). Most of this planned new electricity would be for export to Thailand and Vietnam (Phouthonesy 2004). The GoL has signed an agreement to export 3,000 MW of power to Thailand, including power from the controversial World Bank- and ADB-supported Nam Theun 2 Dam, now under construction in central Laos. In 2002, the Vietnamese and Lao governments also signed an agreement for Laos to export 1,000 MW of power to Vietnam each year between 2006 and 2010 (Lang 2003). More recently, Laos and Vietnam have agreed that 2,000 MW of Lao power will be sold to Vietnam by 2010 (Sakdavong 2004a; Thammavongsa 2004).

Damming the Tributaries, Not the Mainstream

While the mainstream Mekong River has been identified as having a high potential for the production of electricity, hydropower development in Laos has, until recently, been concentrated on Mekong tributaries that, cumulatively, also have a high hydropower potential (Phouthonesy 2004). This was in large part due to the potential for controversy if a project in one country on the Mekong would impact other countries. Laos is a member, and host, of the Mekong River Commission, which has attempted to set up decision-making processes of consensus between MRC members for such trans-boundary projects. The Director-General of the Department of Electricity of Laos, Houmphone Bulayaphol, was quoted by the *Vientiane Times* as stating: "The Mekong is a huge river flowing through several countries and there should be more surveys on how the construction of power plants would impact the environment and livelihoods of people living in the vicinity of the river" (Phouthonesy 2004: 1). Mr. Houmphone acknowledged that there is a need for a more transparent investment policy when it comes to electricity production, stating, "We have to consider the mechanism and investment laws and environmental impact studies, because Laos is not the only country with potential for electricity production" (Phouthonesy 2004: 2). However, more recently, preparatory studies for the Don Sahong and Xayaburi Dams on the mainstream Mekong in Laos have been approved by the GoL, indicating that they appear to be moving toward supporting mainstream Mekong River dam development, despite the grave environmental and social impacts that those projects would cause.

While the Xekong Basin is still being strongly promoted as a place to invest in dam development, there has been little discussion about the trans-national consequences of damming one of the large tributaries of the Mekong: the Xekong River. It is rarely mentioned that the Xekong flows through three countries: Vietnam, Laos, and Cambodia.

At least seventeen large dams have been seriously considered for construction in the Xekong Basin in Laos (OA and OA 2005) (Fig. 5). Not all of these proposals will proceed, at least in the near term. But, as Map 6 illustrates, the Xekong Basin landscape would change drastically, becoming fragmented if a significant number of these dam projects go ahead.

Little research has been conducted on the likely negative impacts of these proposed projects on the Xekong and its tributaries. The potential for downstream impacts, not only on Lao villages but also in Cambodia, has received almost no official attention or recognition. Many observers believe that, before these projects proceed, there is an urgent need for further study and awareness raising, so that the real costs of these projects are better understood by decision-makers.

With this in mind, the Mekong Wetlands Biodiversity Project (MWBP) conducted some training activities for government officials in Attapeu Province, including one about EIAs and hydroelectric dams, in December 2005 (*Vientiane*

Times 2005o). They also supported some other environmental awareness-raising activities in Attapeu (see, for example, Mendoza 2005a). However, there is still a general lack of awareness over the implications of the simultaneous development of these large-scale projects, both within the government and in the villages that would be impacted.

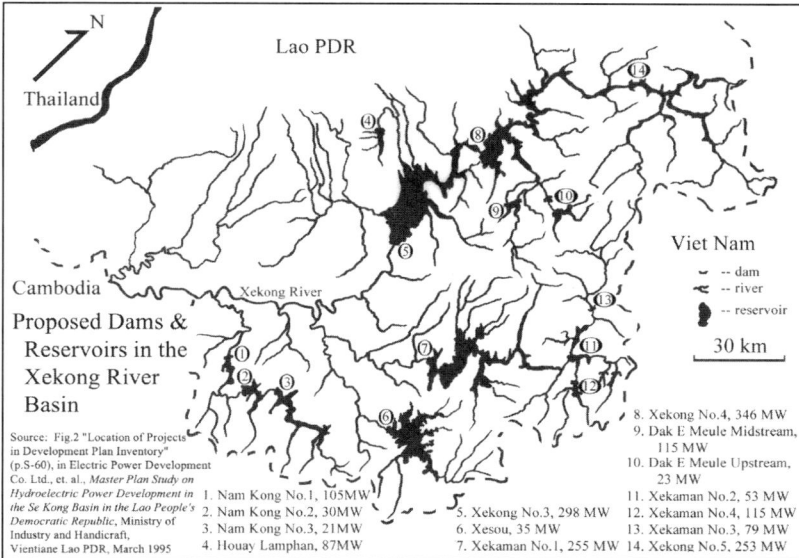

Map 5. Proposed Dams and Reservoirs in the Xekong River Basin

The Vietnamese government has reported that Electricité du Vietnam (EVN) and the power plant construction company Song Da Construction Corporation[2] have been granted permission by the GoL to build five dams in Laos.[3] This is in addition to the Xekaman 3 Dam, already under construction (see sections below). The total investment would be about US$1.3 billion. The Vietnamese consortium also plans to build a 500-Kv transmission line to bring the power to Vietnam (Reuters 2003a and b). The line has not yet been built, and, in July 2005, the *Vientiane Times* quoted the Chief of the Bureau of the Secretariat for the Lao National Committee for Energy (LNCE), Xaypaseuth Phomsoupha, as stating, "We don't yet have any projects to sell electricity to Vietnam. Projects planned for

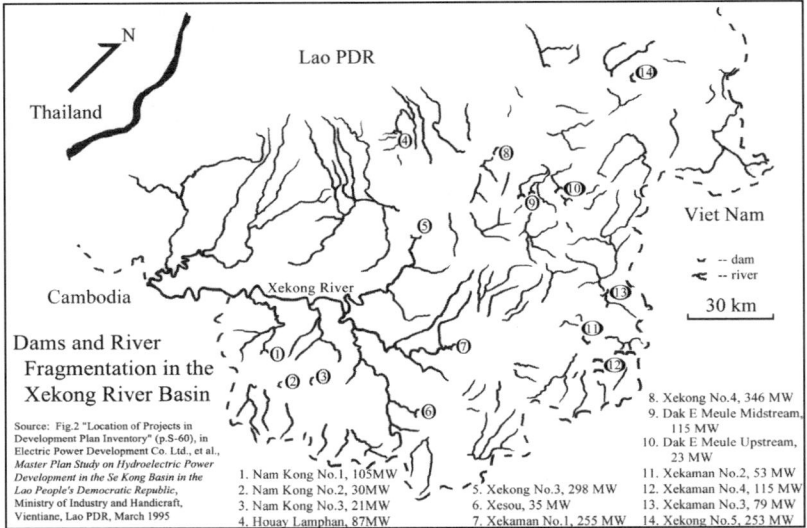

Map related labels:

N

Lao PDR

Thailand

Viet Nam

Cambodia

Xekong River

-- dam
-- river

30 km

Dams and River
Fragmentation in the
Xekong River Basin

Source: Fig.2 "Location of Projects in
Development Plan Inventory" (p.S-60), in
Electric Power Development Co. Ltd., et al.,
*Master Plan Study on Hydroelectric Power
Development in the Se Kong Basin in the
Lao People's Democratic Republic,*
Ministry of Industry and Handicraft,
Vientiane, Lao PDR, March 1995

1. Nam Kong No.1, 105MW
2. Nam Kong No.2, 30MW
3. Nam Kong No.3, 21MW
4. Houay Lamphan, 87MW
5. Xekong No.3, 298 MW
6. Xesou, 35 MW
7. Xekaman No.1, 255 MW

8. Xekong No.4, 346 MW
9. Dak E Meule Midstream, 115 MW
10. Dak E Meule Upstream, 23 MW
11. Xekaman No.2, 53 MW
12. Xekaman No.4, 115 MW
13. Xekaman No.3, 79 MW
14. Xekong No.5, 253 MW

Map 6. Dams and River Fragmentation in the Xekong River Basin

hydropower development to send electricity to Vietnam, such as the Xekaman 3 [in Xekong Province] and Nam Mo projects in Xieng Khouang Province, are still under negotiation" (Thammavongsa 2005: 2). However, with the construction of the Xekaman 3 Dam now proceeding, it may not be long before Laos is exporting power to Vietnam.

Phouthonesy (2005) reported that Vietnam had agreed to increase the purchase of power from Xekaman River dams by the end of 2005; however, none of the dams planned for the Xekaman was ready to produce power by the end of 2005, so the implementation of the agreement has been delayed.

A Regional Electricity Grid

A number of international donors in the region, including the World Bank, the Japan Bank for International Cooperation (JBIC), Agence Français de Developpement, the Swedish International Development Agency (SIDA), and the Association of Southeast Asian Nations (ASEAN) have been promoting a regional Mekong power grid and electricity trading system (IRN 2003; 2004a; 2006). However, the most prominent backer of the system known formally as "Power Interconnection and

Trade in the Greater Mekong Subregion" is the Asian Development Bank (ADB) (IRN 2004a; 2006).

The Mekong power grid was first envisioned during an ADB-sponsored energy sector study for the region conducted by Norconsult, one of Norway's largest hydropower consulting firms. Subsequently, the ADB financed a number of studies to guide the system's development. In 2002, the ADB facilitated the signing of an Inter-Governmental Agreement on Regional Power Trade at a summit of GMS leaders, in order to facilitate the establishment of the "Mekong power grid" (IRN 2004a; 2006). This agreement committed the six Mekong governments to establishing a regional power market. It also created a high-level leadership body to coordinate implementation of regional power trade (IRN 2006). This was followed, in July 2005, with regional leaders signing a MoU on the Regional Power Trade Operating Agreement, the first step in creating rules for regional electricity trading (IRN 2006).

The ADB envisions that China's Yunnan Province, Burma, and Laos will generate cheap, reliable, and sustainable power for the growing electricity markets in Thailand and Vietnam (IRN 2004a). There are also plans to export electricity to Cambodia. Many of the dams that would fuel the grid are planned for the Xekong River Basin in Laos. According to the ADB, the initiative will enable countries to reduce national investments and power reserves, provide a more reliable supply of electricity, reduce operational costs, reduce greenhouse gas emissions, and increase consumer access to the cheapest and most environmentally friendly sustainable source of electricity in the sub-region (ADB 2003).

Because the system will be largely fueled by hydropower generated by new large dams, it has been criticized by the International Rivers Network, which views these dams as largely destructive to the environment and local livelihoods (IRN, 2004a; 2006). IRN is conducting on-going research and analysis on the grid project and has stated that "This initiative threatens to undermine the fragile Mekong River ecosystem that millions depend on for their livelihoods and survival" (IRN 2004a: 1). In a 2004 report, IRN expressed a number of initial concerns over the grid project, including accusing the ADB of not consulting affected people, including ethnic minorities, and of systematically ignoring social and environmental impacts.

Fisheries resources have not been well assessed, and the ADB has failed to seriously consider the cumulative impacts of the grid or the large dams that will feed into it. The ADB has not followed its own policies in promoting the Mekong grid nor the recommendations of the World Commission on Dams (WCD) in relation to the grid (IRN 2004a). IRN has also expressed concern that transmission lines will open up remote areas to new large dam development and negatively impact on people living near them (IRN 2006). According to analysis by IRN (2004a; 2006), the initiative's economic benefits are marginal at best and have not been verified, and a full range of available options to meet energy demands needs to be more seriously assessed.

In November 2004, the ADB commissioned report, "The PTOA-General Design, Final Report: Study for a Regional Power Trade Operating Agreement in the Greater Mekong Sub-Region" was completed. The report presents a design for the "Power Trade Operating Agreement" (PTOA) for the regional electricity grid and describes an organizational structure and operational procedures that promote electricity trading among the GMS countries. The report calls for a four-stage implementation strategy designed to harmonize the capabilities and procedures of member nations (Garrett 2005).

The authors of the PTOA report envision that the system will eventually evolve in a uniform manner to a market-based system, but they do not include a timetable for implementing the four-stage plan. Details are provided only for the first two stages. The Thai NGO Palang Thai, concerned about the GMS electricity grid, commissioned an independent review of the report by Canadian electrical engineer Dr. Bretton Garrett. Dr. Garrett was highly critical of the initiative, his most serious concern relating to the wisdom of committing to an expensive, long-term electricity trade arrangement without any certainty of economic benefits. While he acknowledged that, from an engineering standpoint, interconnecting power systems can bring operating benefits, he stated that "the costs may not always justify the benefits" (Garrett 2005: 1). Like IRN, he believes that the costs and benefits of the grid have so far not been adequately considered (Garrett 2005).

Dr. Chris Greacen (2005) from Palang Thai has also argued that the proposed transmission system is risky for electricity consumers and is likely to mainly benefit investors. Even the ADB's own consultants have estimated that an investment of US$43 billion in transmission lines would yield savings of just over 2% compared to a limited power trading scenario (IRN 2006). However, despite the criticisms and the uncertain economic feasibility of the plans, the ADB and other donors are continuing to support the implementation of the Mekong grid system. The momentum for the grid seems to propelling the plan forward, despite the serious concerns raised.

Some of the Mekong power grid transmission lines are already under construction, including a 112 km 115-Kv transmission line running from Ban Na sub-station, in Pathoumphone District, to Sanamxay District, linking the Xekong Basin and its electricity supply with the rest of the region. Lao language reports indicate the World Bank and Indian government are jointly funding this line (US$11.3 million and US$8 million, respectively). Alternatively, VNA (2004a) reported that the whole project would cost US$24 million, and include contributions of US$12 million from the GoL and US$10 million from the Government of India.

The construction has led to the cutting of an approximately 4 km long 100 m wide swath through part of Xepian NPA, from Napho Village to Kiet Ngong Village. Interestingly, the Xepian NPA master plan, prepared by FOMACOP—a project funded by the World Bank and the GEF—did not include provisions for such a transmission line.

From Ban Na sub-station, there is a separate 115-Kv transmission line running parallel to Route 13 to Hatxaikhoun Village in Khong District and then past Dong Kalo, along the border between Laos and Cambodia, south to Hang Kho and Stung Treng town. This line is apparently being funded by the Chinese government and is being managed by CERIECO, a Thai company.

This second high voltage transmission line was 70% finished to the Cambodia border in April 2005 and at last report was close to being completed. In June 2006, the *Vientiane Times* (2006e) reported that electricity would be exported from Laos to Stung Treng, Cambodia, in 2008, after the necessary pylons and grid were installed. However, in November 2006 it was reported that while it had been agreed to export power from Laos to Cambodia, the price still needed to be negotiated and that it was not expected that power would be sent to Cambodia until 2009. Construction on the grid on the Cambodian side was expected to begin in mid-2007 (Vaenkeo 2006).

A third 115-Kv high voltage transmission line is being built from Ban Na sub-station to Thailand via Soukama District, Champasak Province, and Bounthalik District, Ubon Ratchathani Province, Thailand. There was a regional transmission line envisioned from Thailand to Vietnam, passing through Laos, but, in June 2006, ADB staff told representatives of IRN that the idea was being abandoned, apparently because of problems with securing an agreement to extend the Nam Theun 2 Dam transmission line. Therefore, the ADB is proposing a new transmission line between Ubon Ratchathani (Thailand), *Ban* Sok (in the Xekong River Basin in Khong District, Champasak Province, Laos), and Pleiku (Vietnam). In June 2006, the best route for the line was still being considered. It is expected that this new transmission line would initially have five dams linked to it: Xekaman 1, Xekong 4, Xekong 5, Xepian-Xenamnoi (all in the Xekong Basin) and another dam that was not disclosed (Carl Middleton, IRN, pers. comm. August 2006). This transmission line would also pass through Xepian NPA, where it is likely to cause considerable environmental damage.

The ADB and the World Bank, through a series of loan projects, have funded most of the GoL's ambitious rural electrification expansion program over the past decade. The World Bank, working together with its related environmental lending mechanism, the GEF, is continuing this trend by expanding transmission lines for supplying electricity to rural communities through the provision of a US$20 million loan and a US$3.75 million GEF grant (World Bank 2004). This project, called the "Second Southern Provincial Rural Electrification Project: Phase I," was scheduled to begin in early 2005 and to be completed by the end of 2007.

This project's first phase aimed to provide 52,000 rural households with access to electricity (including 10,000 to off-grid households). The project's main environmental benefits were expected to be the promotion of renewable energy use in rural areas and increased energy efficiency, so that more energy can be exported to Thailand to replace fossil fuel electricity. Although some off-grid renewable energy expansion, including institutional development, was to be paid for by the GEF as part of the project, the GEF would mainly be supporting large-scale hydropower. Large dams would generate the vast majority of the power used for this project.

Although these dam projects can be expected to cause serious negative environmental and social impacts, they go unmentioned in the project document (World Bank 2004). Instead, the benefits of "renewable" energy are heralded. The World Bank's funding is to pay for rural electrification, while "GEF will provide the financing for technical assistance activities central to both successful physical implementation of Phase 1 and preparing a more sustainable and economical approach to meeting the GoL's long-term goals for electrification" (World Bank 2004: 10). While the GEF is intended as a funding mechanism for sustainable energy and climate protection, this GEF grant will, paradoxically and in a serious distortion of stated GEF objectives, support efforts to alter free-flowing rivers.

Villagers Unhappy with New Transmission Lines from Ban Na to Attapeu

Villagers living near the path of the new 112-km high voltage transmission lines being built from Ban Na substation, in Pathoumphone District, Champasak Province to Sanamxay District, Attapeu Province have expressed dissatisfaction with the process of negotiations and the amounts of compensation that they have been offered for their lost land. Villagers have been compensated for the land that has been used to install the transmission line posts, which are situated every 100 m along the route. They state that they have not received a fair rate of compensation, nor have they been compensated for the land adjacent to the posts, which has been damaged and covered up with excavation spoil and dirt during construction. For example, in Kele Nyai Village, locals received 200,000 kip in compensation for the one piece of lowland paddy land lost to the project, but they received nothing for the adjacent land that was damaged and covered with spoil. Villagers were unhappy, but most were afraid to speak out directly to officials. Villagers from Kiet Ngong Village also complained that they did not receive any compensation even though their land has been taken. Villagers feel uninformed and uncertain about when and how much compensation they should have received.

In addition, the Ban Na substation has been situated directly adjacent to the ethnic Brao village of *Ban* Na. Apart from having 4 ha of village communal land expropriated to build the substation—with only limited compensation being provided—there are the potential risks of electro-magnetic radiation on local people living near the high-voltage lines. So far, no warnings have been provided to villagers, who are totally unaware of the potential risks to their long-term health.

Large Dams in the Xekong River Basin

The Houay Ho Dam is currently the only operating large dam in the Xekong River Basin in Laos, Vietnam, and Cambodia; however, there are plans for a number of other large dams in the basin, and one of those—the Xekaman 3—is currently under construction in Dakchung District. Apart from the above two projects, there are at least nine other large dam projects currently envisioned for the Xekong Basin in Laos (Department of Electricity 2004), and a number of other dams have been investigated (JICA 1995; Halcrow 1999). OA and OA (2005) list a total of seventeen large dams that have been considered for construction in the Xekong River Basin in Laos in recent years.

The Japanese International Development Agency (JICA) was the first international donor to promote large dam building in the Xekong Basin in Laos. Between November 1990 and March 1992, JICA hired the Japanese company EPDC to prepare detailed engineering plans for the Xekatam Dam (see also section below).

This initial feasibility study was for a relatively small dam, with an expected 2 MW capacity during its first stage and an eventual capacity of 6 MW. The goal was to generate power for the provincial capitals of Attapeu and Xekong and, eventually, to contribute power to Laos' part of the southern regional power grid (EPDC 2005). This project was not implemented, however, and instead, in 1995, JICA funded "The Master Plan Study on Hydroelectric Power Development in the Se Kong Basin in the Lao People's Democratic Republic" (JICA 1995). Through this research, JICA identified a number of sites for developing large dams in Laos and recommended many dams for future construction. Their goal was clearly to promote the development of much larger dams than what was originally envisioned for the Xekatam Dam. The Xekaman 1, Xekong 4, and Xenamnoi Dams were given priority status. JICA did not consider any of the potential social or environmental impacts of these projects in Laos, and there was almost no mention of downstream impacts on Cambodia. Engineering and technical aspects of dam developments were the focus of JICA's study.

In the late 1990s, the ADB sustained interest in dam-building efforts in the Xekong River Basin by hiring Sir William Halcrow Consulting to conduct the US$2.5 million "Se Kong, Se San and Nam Theun River Basins' Hydropower Study" (Halcrow 1999). One of the study's significant findings was that there is little baseline information about these rivers, their fisheries, watersheds, or peoples (Lang 2003; Halcrow 1999). While still oriented toward recommending large dam projects for possible ADB funding in Laos, Vietnam, and Cambodia, the report was, at least in comparison to the earlier JICA study, much more conscious of the potential social and environmental impacts of the dams. There was some consideration of downstream trans-boundary environmental and social impacts. Based on a ranking system, in which social and environmental factors were taken into account, a different set of large dam projects became optimal under Halcrow's calculations; however, neither the JICA nor the Halcrow studies included any serious options or alternatives to large dams.

Most recently, the Lao National Committee for Energy (LNCE) conducted a "Power Sector Strategy Study" for the whole country in which a number of dams in the Xekong River Basin were recommended. They included the Xepian-Xenamnoi Dam, the Xekaman 1 and 3 Dams, the Houay Lamphan Nyai Dam, and the Nam Kong 1 Dam (LNCE 2003).

The following sections present detailed information about the large dams either built, under construction, or envisioned by the GoL (planned at various stages) for the Xekong River Basin in Laos, including all the projects mentioned briefly above.

The Houay Ho Hydropower Project

The Houay Ho Hydropower Project (HHHP) is located on the eastern part of the Bolaven Plateau. Situated 160 km east of Pakse and 30 km northwest of the capital of Attapeu Province, the dam is a concrete-faced, rock-filled structure 76.5 m high. The reservoir is on the Bolaven Plateau in Pakxong District of Champasak and the powerhouse is below the plateau, in Samakhixay District of Attapeu. The dam was constructed across the small *Houay* Ho, a tributary of the Xekong. The HHHP is an inter-basin transfer project that diverts water between rivers in the same sub-basin. The catchment area of the dam is 191.7 km². A concrete-lined waterway (980 m long) starts at an open cut intake before running into a vertical pressure shaft (104 m) that leads to a lower headrace tunnel connected to a powerhouse by a short penstock, both situated at the bottom of the Bolaven Plateau (Sparkes 2000).

This was the first large dam in Laos to be built following a fully Build-Own-Operate-Transfer (BOOT) or Build-Operate-Transfer (BOT) development model (Wyatt 2004). A MoU was signed in March 1993 (Wyatt 2004), and, in July 1993, HECEC was awarded a contract by Daewoo Engineering Corporation, Ltd. of South Korea to conduct a feasibility study for the dam (IRN 1999). Just two months later a thirty-year concession agreement to build the project was negotiated between the GoL and Daewoo (Wyatt 2004). Daewoo financed the bulk of the construction and commissioning costs for the 150 MW dam, which includes a 32–37.5 km² reservoir with a gross storage capacity of 596 million m³ of water. The total project cost has been estimated at US$220 million,[4] with US$50 million being financed through equity and the remainder coming from a variety of international banks and institutions (Sparkes 2000).

The Houay Ho Power Company (HHPC) was created specifically for the HHHP, with Daewoo holding 60% of the shares and the Thai trading company Loxley Public Company, Ltd. and the GoL each owning 20% each (Wyatt 2004; IRN 1999). In October 1995, a power purchase agreement was signed with the Electricity Generating Authority of Thailand (EGAT) to sell 126 MW of electricity from the project to Thailand, at 4.22 cents/Kwh, beginning on 1 September 1999 (IRN 1999). Construction started in November 1994; the main dam and headrace tunnel shaft were done by April 1997; and the project was ready to produce power by the end of 1998 (Wyatt 2004; IRN 1999).

The HHHP has long been a controversial project, both because of the way in which the original concession agreement was structured and with regard to the significant social and environmental problems it has generated, in particular serious unresolved resettlement problems (Wyatt 2004; Sayboualaven 2004; Sparkes 2000; Khamin 2000; IRN 1999; 2004b). The project was rapidly developed despite the fact that the Korean and Thai firms had little experience in developing BOOT projects. But they were anxious to gain rights to what was believed to be one of the most profitable large dam projects in Laos (Wyatt 2004). According to one GoL observer from the Ministry of Industry and Handicrafts, "It [Houay Ho] had a bad smell. We never got to see any studies for the project. I don't think any were done" (cited in Wyatt 2004: 144). Many government officials were opposed to the original agreement regarding Houay Ho. The Deputy Prime Minister at the time, Khamphouy Keoboualapha, signed off on it with little consultation with Ministry of Industry and Handicrafts or EdL. He reportedly had close links to Thai business interests, including Loxley. Daewoo financed the equity share of the GoL with a US$10 million loan. The terms involved an average commercial interest rate of 9% for a twelve-year period with a four-year grace period (Wyatt 2004).

Critics both inside and outside of Laos have noted that the project was developed with inadequate transparency and that the GoL received a poor deal. This was reportedly due in part to the GoL's not having adequate legal representation during negotiations with Daewoo. According to international consultants familiar with the project, the GoL is receiving almost no dividends and will not get any until the concession period is almost over. Worse, EdL will not receive any project dividends for the first twelve years of the dam's operation. That means that, beginning in 2000, EdL had to find US$1.8 million a year to cover interest payments on the US$10 million equity loan it took from Daewoo but is not yet eligible to receive any dividends from the dam (Wyatt 2004). There are also few taxes or royalties being paid to the GoL from the project (IRN 1999). The concession agreement for the project did not stipulate responsibility for resettlement or other social and environmental impacts, thus making it possible for Daewoo to relinquish all responsibility for resettlement with a single payment of US$230,000 (Wyatt 2004; Sparkes 2000). This left the GoL with the task of dealing with these issues by itself.

A draft preliminary EIA was prepared for the project by the Swiss consulting firm Electrowatt[5] in cooperation with Daewoo, but it was of poor quality and not even completed until after project construction was well underway (Wyatt 2004; IRN 1999). The draft may never have been finalized; once the concession agreement was signed the need for such a study became redundant in Daewoo's view. Not until 1999 did the GoL pass its Environment Law, making EIAs for large dam projects compulsory. Construction of the project also began before the project's pre-feasibility study was completed and before a power purchase agreement had been signed with EGAT. Essentially, construction began without knowing the project's potential return, risks, or costs (Wyatt 2004).

Another serious problem was the logging contracts associated with the project, which were given out to a Thai company but later widely criticized in Champasak Province, as log-deficient sawmills in Pakse were not given access to any of the timber. Instead, the raw wood was sent straight to Thailand (IRN 1999; Khamin 2000; Sayboualaven 2004).

Road building associated with the project was poorly planned and implemented (see Chapter 11). In fact, the road that was built from the project area to Attapeu Province has since been abandoned due to the difficulty and high costs of maintaining the road. As well, serious cost overruns associated with the dam resulted in much lower than expected revenues (IRN 1999; Khamin 2000; Sayboualaven 2004).

In the power purchase agreement for the dam, EGAT agreed to pay 50% of the cost of the electricity in US dollars and the other half in Thai baht. But after the Asian Financial Crisis reduced the baht's value, EGAT agreed, in August 1998, to pay 55% of the cost of power in US dollars. Daewoo also had to cover the costs of waiting eight months to sell power to Thailand as the dam was completed ahead of schedule, but Thailand, by then in the grips of financial crisis, insisted on not buying any power from the project until the specified contract date of September 1999 (IRN 1999).

The project has had serious environmental and social impacts and has led to great suffering for the resettled ethnic minority villagers associated with the dam. Only one village was situated in the reservoir inundation area (Nam Han Village, comprising 99 people in eighteen families), and one other was recommended for relocation due to the loss of river flow below the dam and the elimination of fishing (Thang Ngao Village, twenty-five families) (Wyatt 2004; Sparkes, 2000). However, a scheme was developed to relocate thirteen villages from the Houay Ho and Xepian-Xenamnoi Dam areas. These included Nam Han and Thang Ngo Villages, and Latxaxin Village, the site designated for project dirt extraction. There were three options tabled for relocating Nam Han and Thang Ngao Villages and other villages in the area: 1) relocation in the reservoir catchment area; 2) relocation to another hill area of comparable altitude; and, 3) relocation to a lowland area close to irrigation-fed lowland rice fields.

The third option would have involved the most dramatic changes in local livelihoods but the second would have required significant livelihood changes.

The first option would have been the most preferable to local people, but, despite recommendations from some consultants that there was inadequate land at the "*Ban Chat San*" resettlement sites covered under the second option, the GoL chose it and relocated approximately 2,500 people from eleven villages. They went mostly to a resettlement site known as *Ban Chat San*, near *Houay* Kong in Pakxong District. Two other large villages are still threatened with resettlement (one ethnic Jru and one ethnic Heuny village) (Sparkes 2000; Sayboualaven 2004).

The relocated people came from the villages of Nam Han, Thong Ngao, Xenoi, Nam Leng, Keo Khoun Muang, Done Khong, Latxaxin, and Nam Tiang. The vast majority of the people were from a small Mon-Khmer language-speaking ethnic group, the Heuny (Nya Heun). A few from Don Khong were ethnic Jru (Laven). In 2003, there were 475 households in these eight villages, including 1,752 people, of which 849 are females (Sayboualaven 2004).

Apart from the main *Ban Chat San* resettlement area, there are two other nearby resettlement areas located near the ethnic Jru villages of Houay Kong and Nam Tang. One is for the ethnic Heuny population of Ta Yeuk Seua Village that, in 2003, included forty-seven families and 247 people. The resettled Heuny people from Houay Soi and Nam Kong Villages populate the other nearby resettlement area. Relocated in 1999, Nam Kong had eighty-two households and 287 people in 2003, while Houay Soi had 101 households and a population of 308 people (Sayboualaven 2004).

There have been a large number of serious and on-going problems associated with the resettlement of the eleven villages to these three resettlement sites. First, the resettled people received insufficient food compensation during the resettlement adjustment period. They never received substantial portions of the promised three years of food aid; it somehow "disappeared" before being distributed at the resettlement sites (IRN 1999). Water supply was poor. Forced resettlement is a traumatic experience in the best of cases and can lead to severe health and related problems, but health services at the site were inadequate.

The most fundamental and intractable problems, however, have revolved around land. Those resettled were not provided with sufficient land or access to natural resources (forests and streams for NTFP collection, hunting, and fishing) to allow them to rebuild their livelihoods. This has resulted in a severe and on-going food security crisis and the impoverishment of those resettled (IRN 1999; Khamin 2000; Sayboualaven 2004).

Initially, the GoL guaranteed the resettled people a considerable amount of land. The resettlement areas were together classified as a provincial Focal Site for development (see Chapter 5), but when the resettled people tried to farm the land allocated to them, many found that the land they were supposedly given was customarily used by neighboring villages. The ethnic Jru people from communities continued to lay claim to their fallow swiddens and would not allow the resettled people to use the land. This has resulted in serious land shortage problems for the resettled people. Only about 20% of the original land supposedly allocated to the resettled people turned out to actually be available for them to use. The resettlement plan depended upon a strategy to convert subsistence-oriented swidden cultivators to cash-crop coffee growers over a short period of time. This would be a difficult task in the best of circumstances, but, in addition to receiving inadequate land, training, or other support, coffee prices fell dramatically soon after the people were resettled. It was not feasible for farmers to rely on coffee bean sales as their only source of income. The Focal Site designation was dissolved in 2000, but many problems remained.

Not surprisingly, many of the resettled people have unofficially abandoned the resettlement site, choosing to return to their former agricultural and village areas, where some have cut new swidden fields. In 2006, it was estimated that up to 70% of the families had fled the resettlement area. Officially, the government does not allow people to return to live near their old villages so the people have been forced either to secretly go there or to request permission to return "temporarily." Sometimes these "temporary" trips last for months, followed by short trips back to the resettlement area, and then back to their old village areas again for another extended period. Often, villagers end up spending most of their time away from the resettlement site, even though they are officially still resident in the *Ban Chat San* (Sayboualaven 2004). This has caused a severe and on-going disruption to the lives of those who were resettled. In that a large percentage of the 5,552 ethnic Heuny people in Laos in 1995 have been relocated as part of the scheme, the movement represents a critical threat to the cultural survival of the whole Heuny ethnic group (Khamin 2000).

Houay Ho has also resulted in various negative downstream impacts, including near the Xekong River and the project's powerhouse at the bottom of the Bolaven Plateau in Samakhixay District. Ethnic Heuny people from Khoum Kham Village have been impacted by flood damage caused by water releases downstream from the powerhouse and before the water enters the Xekong. Riverbanks have been eroded, livestock drowned, and much of the village's lowland rice fields have been affected by flooding attributed to the dam. No compensation has apparently been provided to those impacted.

The ethnic Sok people, a sub-group of the Oy ethnic group who inhabit Sok Village, have also been indirectly impacted by the project. Much of their land was confiscated to create a protected area surrounding the project. No compensation was provided to villagers for their losses. The ethnic minorities in Khoum Kham, Mixay, Km 52 and Nam Han Villages have lost much of their agriculture land to the dam-associated protected area. Farming is now restricted near the powerhouse, and, again, no compensation was given (Sayboualaven 2004). Villagers from Sok Village do not believe that releases of water from the dam's powerhouse have adversely impacted fish or fisheries downstream, but no specific studies have been conducted on this.

Should NGOs be Subsidizing the Social Costs of Private Sector Dams?

World Vision, one of the largest INGOs in the world, played a significant role in the early years of Houay Ho Dam-associated resettlement, contributing US$112,000 to the resettlement work over a four-year period lasting from 1994/1997 (Wyatt 2004; Sparkes 2000).

The agency reportedly supported a Food-for-Work program for the clearing of land for coffee production (more than 100 ha); provided school furniture and upgrading; assisted with coffee seedlings and training for farmers; and initiated septic tank installation and health awareness activities. World Vision categorized this work as a "food security" program and insisted it was not involved in actual relocation, but it was clearly working with recently relocated villages (Sparkes 2000) and assisting in providing inputs to address problems directly related to the forced resettlement of the communities.

In 1997, the World Vision manager in charge of southern Lao programs told the first author that the agency had been "following the provincial lead" in responding to a GoL request to support the project. World Vision staff also said that they had a mandate to help all people in need.

The involvement of an INGO in a project such as this raises serious questions. It is widely accepted that, as a basic matter of economic principle, private developers should pay for the social and environmental costs, or externalities, of their projects. When an NGO or other donor supports such costs they are, in effect, subsidizing the developers and making it easier for them to implement projects such as this. In the case of Houay Ho, there was no overriding public benefit to the project that justified the resettlement in the first place.

World Vision was also unable to address in any substantive way the fundamental problems with the site. The danger is that INGO involvement in such a situation may just improve the project's external image and make it look as if problems are being addressed. The reality in this case, however, is that the assistance had little or no long-term impact, other than to make it easier for the government to avoid paying the real costs of the whole project. Those resettled remain severely impoverished and disempowered. In separate interviews with both authors in 1997/1998, World Vision staff were unable to provide any clear justification or analysis of their position on these issues. It appeared, in fact, that they had not really thought about it much.

From Daewoo and Loxley to Tractebel

When the Asian Financial Crisis began in 1997, Daewoo was greatly affected. Needing to liquidate assets in order to deal with a crippling debt, in 2001 Daewoo and Loxley sold all their holdings in the HHPC to the Belgium-based multinational Tractebel S. A.[6] and its Thai partner MCL (Tractebel's Thai unit). The 80% share in the company was sold for US$140 million (Financial Times 2001; Tractebel 2001). Tractebel became the largest shareholder in the HHPC. The GoL maintained a 20% holding in the dam, as per the original agreement with Daewoo and Loxley (Dow Jones 2001). Upon purchase of the dam, Tractebel's CEO, Dirk Beeuwsaert was quoted as stating, "Houay Ho is a low-cost producer, able to generate energy when demand is highest, and therefore plays a significant role in Thailand's energy supply" (*Financial Times* 2001: 1).

In February 2002, not long after Tractebel purchased the HHPC, it was reported that the project experienced technical problems. Erosion at the powerhouse was blamed for incapacitating the electricity generators, and the power lines were threatened with collapse. US$50,000 had already been spent to buy new equipment to repair the power lines, but more work was still required (*Pathet Lao* 2002). Local government officials reported that electricity production from the dam was much less than originally anticipated, at least partly because the dam was leaking. Concerns grew that the dam's life might be much shorter than anticipated—perhaps just thirty-five years (only five years longer than the BOT agreement with Tractebel).

Following its purchase, Tractebel apparently made little or no effort to address unresolved problems related to the impacts of the dam on local people and the environment, nor did it take constructive steps to attempt to ease problems facing the resettled communities. It took a series of international reports about the continuing problems facing the resettled people to put dams in the Bolaven Plateau back in the spotlight (see Sayboualaven 2004).

Tractebel purchased Houay Ho with financing through export credits provided by the Government of Belgium. This subjected the company to the environmental and social impact guidelines of the Overseas Economic Cooperation and Development (OECD) Organization. In 2004, concerned groups in Belgium learned of the severe problems facing the relocated people and realized that Tractebel was violating OECD guidelines. The Belgium-based INGO Proyecto Gato subsequently filed a formal complaint with the OECD against Tractebel in relation to Houay Ho.

Tractebel had a difficult time defending its actions, as the issue of environmental and social impacts did not appear to have been seriously considered prior to its purchase of the dam. These issues continued to be ignored after the purchase. The OECD National Contact Point (NCP) in Belgium has an established committee responsible for reviewing complaints. Proyecto Gato argued to the NCP that Tractebel should be held responsible for problems facing local people in the resettlement area. Tractebel, and its powerful owner, Suez, responded that the INGO should sue Daewoo and the GoL—not them—for the problems facing the people. In an effort to improve its image and show it was doing something, Tractebel hired a contractor to fix and maintain fifteen wells in the resettlement area. Some of these, however, still have insufficient water, and the total number of wells is insufficient for all the people without enough access to water.

Most recently, Tractebel has supported the building of a new school and the repairing of a road to the resettlement area. While Proyecto Gato's actions appear to have resulted in increased attention being paid to the resettled communities by both Tractebel and the provincial government, little has been done to address the most fundamental issue: lack of access to land and natural resources for those who were resettled.

This case marked the first time that a private company (albeit with government export credit support) involved in a Lao dam has been forced by environmental and social guidelines in their own country to follow international investment standards set out by the OECD. In early 2005, the Belgian Ambassador to Laos, at Tractebel's request, visited the Houay Ho Dam resettlement area, indicating the interest that the case has received. After many months, the OECD committee in Belgium ruled that Tractebel was not responsible for the impacts of the project before it purchased the HHPC in 2001, even though it now owns the same company that built the dam. Remarkably, while Proyecto Gato argued that Tractebel bought both the company's assets and liabilities, the OECD did not accept the argument.

Future Plans

It has been proposed that some of the water from the Houay Ho Dam might be diverted into the Xeset River Basin in order to support electricity generation at the already operational Xeset 1 Dam in Salavan and the planned Xeset 2 and 3 Dams in the upper basin in Pakxong District (Maunsell and Lahmeyer 2004). This is quite tentative, however, and may be unrealistic.

More recently, Tractebel has reportedly been investigating possibilities for diverting water from either the Xepian or Xenamnoi Rivers in order to allow the Houay Ho Dam to run twenty-four hours a day, instead of between 7 pm and 4 am, as is the case at present. That investment would require over US$20 million (Latsaphao 2005b). There was no mention of whether any of these funds would be used to compensate the large number of people that the diversion is expected to negatively impact. It may well be that the impacted people have again been forgotten in the planning process.

The Xepian–Xenamnoi Dam

The proposed Xepian–Xenamnoi Dam, to be located in Champasak and Attapeu Provinces in the Xekong Basin, has been in the planning stages for many years. At one point it was envisioned to have a capacity of 438 MW (IRN 1999), but later estimates have pegged its expected installed capacity at between 390 MW (LNCE 2003) and 235 MW (Maunsell and Lahmeyer 2004). Cost estimates have also declined, based on a smaller proposed project size.

The South Korean company Dong Ah signed the first concession agreement with the GoL for this dam on 17 August 1994 (LNCE 2003). This agreement came less than a year after Daewoo and Loxley had signed a similar agreement with the GoL to build the Houay Ho Dam. It involved a similar type of "BOT" agreement, negotiated in a similarly non-transparent manner with little or no input from local government officials or villagers (IRN 1999).

Dong Ah's plan for the project specified the damming of two major rivers on the Bolaven Plateau, the Xenamnoi and the Xepian. Both are large, forested, mountain rivers with permanent year-round flow. A single wide, low saddle dam some 900 m across and up to 35 m high was to block the Xepian River and an adjacent smaller nearby tributary, the *Houay* Nam Liang. A small reservoir would be created and the water diverted via a canal into a relatively large reservoir created by a 78-m high dam on the Xenamnoi River (IRN 1999). Another stream, the *Houay* Mak Chan, was also to be dammed and diverted into the Xenamnoi reservoir. The combined water in the Xenamnoi reservoir would then flow some 630 m through a tunnel to the base of the Bolaven Plateau. The power station for the project was expected to be located next to the tunnel opening near the village of Lagnao Kang, 8 km northwest of Attapeu town. Outflow from the power project was supposed to flow about 4 km down the streambed of the *Houay* Phok into the mainstream Xekong River (Roberts and Baird 1995b).

The building of access roads and camps for the dam began in 1996, and the project seemed certain to move ahead. A revised concession agreement for the project gave Dong Ah a 55% share, with the GoL taking 25%. An unspecified Thai partner held 20% equity. The main dam on the Xenamnoi River was expected to create a 38-km^2 reservoir (IRN 1999).

Like Daewoo, Dong Ah was badly affected by the Asian Financial Crisis in the late 1990s. Its debt load increased rapidly and, because of a decline in the demand for electricity in Thailand, EGAT first offered a low price and then announced it was not interested in signing a power purchase agreement for the project during the timeframe Dong Ah had anticipated (IRN 1999). The company withdrew from the project in 1998/1999, closing its Lao office and removing the heavy equipment used to build roads and prepare project sites. Dong Ah collapsed completely at the end of 2000. Before leaving southern Laos, however, Dong Ah managed to scar the landscape considerably by building a new road and substantially damaging a forest being protected by the provincial hospital as a place to collect medicinal plants.

After several years of inactivity, the GoL made several attempts to negotiate a new agreement with outside firms for the project's development. The LNCE (2003) recommended that, because of past transmission line negotiation problems, the GoL should step in and coordinate negotiations so that the project could become connected to the ADB-envisioned regional electrical grid. Maunsell and Lahmeyer (2004) expected that the project could be hooked up to the proposed Ban Sok 500 Kv transmission line in Attapeu, making it possible to export electricity either to Thailand or Vietnam. The KPL (2006) reported that a MoU for conducting an 18-month feasibility study for the dam was signed in early August 2006 between the GoL and SK E and C and Korea Western Power Company. The MoU estimated that the project would have a capacity of 400 MW.

While not officially announced, it has recently been rumored that Ord River Resources Company of Australia, together with its Chinese partner, China Nonferrous Metals, have purchased the rights from the Koreans to build the Xepian-Xenamnoi Dam in order to provide electricity for the aluminum production facility planned as part of a bauxite mining operation the companies are developing on the Boloven Plateau (Vaughn 2006; Riseborough 2006). Aluminum refining requires large amounts of power (see Chapter 12).

Projected Social and Environmental Impacts

Regardless of whatever final configuration and ownership arrangement is agreed upon, it is clear that the Xepian-Xenamnoi project, if built, would have serious social and environmental impacts. These impacts have consistently been downplayed or ignored by project proponents as well as the consulting firms supposedly tasked with providing unbiased project analysis. In 1995, the Swiss consulting firm Electrowatt prepared an EIA for Dong Ah with input from an INGO, the Wildlife Conservation Society (WCS). The fisheries portion of the study (Roberts and Baird 1995b: 14) stated: "Considering its important and relatively intact natural resources in fishes as well as in forests, mammals, birds and other organisms, we recommend that plans to dam and divert the upper Xepian be dropped from the Xenamnoi-Xepian project. Only in this way can the fisheries, wildlife, and village resources of the area be protected and preserved for future generations."

It was evident that the dam would virtually dry up downstream parts of the Xepian River, causing serious impacts to fisheries and local river-based livelihoods. The lack of water in downstream parts of the Xepian would also have serious implications for the Xepian NPA. Roberts and Baird (1995b: 14) stated: "We further recommend that the Xepian be officially recognized as a National Protected River by the GoL. This would complement and reinforce National Protected Areas already established in the lower Xepian basin." However, as Bush and Hirsch (2005) have pointed out, it is villager perspectives and interpretations of fisheries, like those included by Roberts and Baird, that are the most frequently omitted when it comes to studies and EIAs of large-scale projects such as large dams or mining operations. Thus, it should be of no surprise that Electrowatt excluded any mention of the above recommendation in its final report to Dong Ah. The wildlife section of WCS's report also made various recommendations related to wildlife issues in the area; however, none, including proposed follow-up wildlife surveys, was ever implemented (Lang 2003). Even after having been one of the consultants hired for the survey, the first author was never provided with a copy of the final version of the EIA.

Roberts and Baird (1995b) expected that Hin Lat, Mai, Samong Tai, Phon Sa-at, and Hat Nyai Villages[7] would be especially impacted by drastic reductions of water in the Xepian River. It was also expected that Don Khong Village would be negatively impacted; however, the community was resettled to a *Ban Chat San* near *Houay* Kong after the study took place (Sayboualaven 2004). In 1995, there were over 300 families in these five villages, including Don Khong (Roberts and Baird 1995b).

Many other communities that use the river seasonally would be seriously impacted. For example, many people from Sompoi Village, Sanamxay District, adjacent to the Xekong, have lowland paddy rice fields many kilometers away near the Xepian River. The families that own paddy land there spend a considerable part of the year adjacent to the Xepian. Roberts and Baird (1995b) recommended that fishers living along the Xekong, but who fish in the Xepian, should be eligible for compensation due to losses in fisheries.

The Xepian-Xenamnoi Hydropower Project is also expected to have negative impacts on fisheries in the Xekong River Basin downstream from the dam—in the Xepian, Xenamnoi, and Xekong Rivers. The impacts are difficult to predict but are expected to be significant (Halcrow 1999; Roberts and Baird 1995b).

The dam would cause serious negative hydrological impacts in the lower Xenamnoi River, even if environmental compensation flows are provided. The villages along the Xenamnoi River that would be particularly impacted are Houa Muang, Dan, and Khoum Kham. It was expected that Xenoi Village would be impacted; but the village has since been relocated into the *Ban Chat San* resettlement area near *Houay* Kong. There were about 180 families in these villages, including Xenoi, in 1995 (Roberts and Baird 1995b). Severe reductions of water in the lower Xenamnoi River are expected to have major negative impacts on fisheries-based livelihoods. In 1995, people from Dan Village reported that fish constituted 80% of the animal protein they consumed. At Xenoi, villagers reported that fish made up 60% of their animal protein. Generally, fisheries made up 60–90% of the animal protein in peoples' diets in the project impact area (Roberts and Baird 1995b).

A number of villages situated along the Phok Stream would also be heavily impacted by the increased volume of water deposited into the stream from the project's powerhouse. These include Lagnao Tai, Champhao, Lagnao Kang, Khem Sang, Langao and La Leuee Villages (at the mouth of the *Houay* Phok). There were close to 450 families in these villages in 1995. Roberts and Baird (1995b) noted that the fisheries resources of the people were at risk, including substantial paddy field fisheries based largely on *Channa striata* (*pa kho* in Lao) and *Clarias* spp. (*pa douk* in Lao).

Although some of the villages in the project area were relocated at the time that the Houay Ho Dam was being built (Sayboualaven 2004), two villages on the

Bolaven Plateau are still threatened with resettlement if the dam is built: the ethnic Jru village of Nong Phanouan and the ethnic Heuny village of Houay Chote. In 2003, there were 122 households and 591 people in Nong Phanouan, and 125 families and 599 people in Houay Chote. The forests and water bodies near these villages are relatively rich in natural resources, including various important NTFPs. People hunt and fish, and there are some small coffee plantations for generating supplementary income. Most locals are self-sufficient in rice, and many generate 2–4 million kip (US$200–400) a year from selling coffee (Sayboualaven 2004).

The people from these villages are opposed to being resettled. They have seen the problems that others have faced after resettlement and do not want to experience a similar fate (Sayboualaven 2004). After years of uncertainty, in May 2005, Champasak provincial officials gave the first strong indication that the villages would not have to be relocated, even though about a hundred houses have been built for villagers at a resettlement site near Ta Yeuk Seua Village.

Despite the potential negative impacts of the project, the LNCE (2003) described the Xepian-Xenamnoi Dam as, "attractive and viable," although it also added that, "careful management of environmental impacts is needed." The project's final design has yet to be determined. Some possible configurations would be more environmentally and socially destructive than others, but, in any case, it is clear that the Xepian–Xenamnoi Dam would cause serious and widespread negative environmental and social impacts. Local livelihoods would either be destroyed or severely disrupted in many areas and in many ways. The experiences at the nearby Houay Ho Dam do not bode well for the prospect of local communities receiving adequate compensation for their expected losses.

The Xekaman 3 Dam

The Xekaman 3 Dam, currently under construction in southern Dakchung District, will be the first dam built in Xekong Province (International Water Power and Dam Construction 2005). The project is located near the border with Vietnam on the Nam Poag-O River, a tributary of the Xekaman, and a fourth-order tributary of the Mekong. The dam site is surrounded by high-altitude pine forests on a part of the river surrounded on both sides by large mountains between 850 and 950 m asl.

There have been conflicting reports about the project's scope, ownership, and status. It was originally conceived to have a capacity of 79 MW, and cost US$118.5 million to build (Ministry of Industry and Handicrafts 1994). Since then there have been reports that the project would have various installed capacities, including 126

MW (EdL 2003), 210 MW (VNA 2003b and 2003c; Reuters 2003a; Lang 2003), and 300 MW (Maunsell and Lahmeyer 2004; VNA 2003a). Most recently, however, International Water Power and Dam Construction (2005) reported that the project will have a capacity of 250 MW, and generate 1,000 GWh of electricity per annum (Phonpachit 2005b; Thammavongsa 2006).

The current design, according to Vietnamese workers at the site, calls for a tall dam 100 m high and 800 m wide and a narrow reservoir only 700 m wide at places. The reservoir is expected to have a capacity of 110 million m^3. A Vietnamese geologist working on the project reported that the reservoir for the project will be 5.2 km^2, and a Vietnamese driller said that it would be about 32 km long. In contrast, Maunsell and Lahmeyer (2004) estimated that the dam would be 128 m high, with a crest length of 430 m, and have a 12-km^2 reservoir. The firm also estimated that the project would require 90 km of road to be rehabilitated and 40 km of new road to be built.

It is currently expected that 90% of the electricity produced by the dam will be exported to Vietnam, with about 10% retained for domestic use (Phonpachit 2005b). Project construction was initially projected to begin in 2004 (VNA 2003a and 2003c), but Vietnamese workers at the dam site said that some preparatory construction began a year earlier. However, in November 2005, EdL reported that negotiations regarding the concession agreement for the project were still continuing and that full-scale construction had not begun. At the end of 2005 the safeguard documents for the project were reported to still be under review by the GoL, with the Science, Technology, and Environment Agency (STEA) of the GoL having already issued a conditional certificate for the project. A Power Purchase Agreement (PPA) for the dam still needed to be signed with EVN, but, again, negotiations regarding this were apparently well under way at the end of 2005. EdL acknowledged at the time that roads to the project site had been built to facilitate drilling for geotechnical studies. In March 2006, the project had still not officially started, although construction was expected to begin by the end of the second quarter of the year (Vietnam News Agency 2006).

In December 2005, International Water Power and Dam Construction (2005) reported that Vietnam had invested US$273 million in the project, via the Vietnam-Laos Joint Stock Electricity Investment and Development Company, a consortium comprising six Vietnamese businesses, including EVN and the Song Da Corporation, which together hold 60% of the equity in the new company. International Water Power and Dam Construction (2005) also reported that US$203 million is being provided for the project via the "Development Assistance Fund" and commercial banks.

In March 2006, VNA (2006) reported that Song Da owned 60% equity in the dam. Whatever the stake of different players in the project, it will be Vietnam's largest-ever investment in a foreign country, and will be a 25-year BOT project (International Water Power and Dam Construction 2005). In August 2007, International Water Power and Dam Construction (2007) reported that two Vietnamese banks, Vietcombank and the Bank for Investment Development of Viet Nam, have agreed to provide US$66 million in financing for the Xekaman 3 Dam, which is expected to cost a total of US$331 million. While the GoL has apparently been allocated an ownership share in the dam, the size of its share is unclear. The dam is scheduled to be operational by 2008 (International Water Power and Dam Construction 2005; VNA 2003a and 2003c) or by 2009 (Phonpachit 2005b).

The dam site is located 25 km from the district center of Dakchung, and is accessible from it by truck via a poor quality road only usable during the dry season. Otherwise it is a six-hour walk. In late 2004, Vietnamese working at the dam site would walk to Dakchung town once every two to three months. Efforts have been made to open the Daktaook-Nam Giang border between Xekong and Quangnam, to facilitate construction of the dam (VNA 2003c), and a new 18-km road has been built from the dam site to Vietnam (Route 14d). This new road goes through lowland paddy and swidden agriculture fields belonging to people from Dak Man Village.

Projected Social and Environmental Impacts

There is a lack of data on the possible impacts on local communities and the environment from the Xekaman 3 project. No comprehensive EIA is publicly available. Given the project's size and location, however, large-scale impacts can be expected. The dam will certainly alter the downstream hydrology of the Xekaman River, and these changes should be expected to be largely negative, as has been the case for other dams in the region (see Fisheries Office and NTFP 2000; Shoemaker et al. 2001; IRN 1999).

There are reportedly seven ethnic Dak Ye populated villages (Dak Charang Noi, Dak Charang Nyai, Dak Moung, Dak Kay, Vang Ly, Blong Noi, and Blong Nyai) situated downstream from the dam site in Dakchung District. The people from these villages depend heavily on the Xekaman River for fishing, vegetable collection, and other purposes. While these villages are considered by the Dakchung District government to be in danger if the Xekaman 3 Dam breaks, there has been little consideration of other potential hydrological impacts, such as irregular water releases like those that have occurred with other dams in the region, such as Vietnam's Yali Falls dam on the Sesan River in northeast Cambodia (Fisheries Office and NTFP 2000; Baird et al. 2002). Many more communities live further downstream along the Xekaman River in Sanxay and Saysettha Districts.

According to Dakchung District officials, central level authorities responsible for the project approached the Dak Charang villagers to ask them to relocate from the area. However, villagers have strongly resisted moving from their present location due to their stable food security situation that is based on access to land and natural resources. They also expect easier access to electricity at their current location once the dam is built. There is little awareness of potential negative impacts from the dam.

The UNDP (1997: 68) confirmed the generally stable food security situation for ethnic minority communities in the area, stating that the ethnic Ye people "live in the remote mountainous areas, have sufficient rice, and produce tobacco, mangoes, oranges, and other related fruit crops." The ethnic Dak Ye people largely practice swidden agriculture. Rice is grown, but it is not the most important carbohydrate in their diet. The rice they eat is non-glutinous upland rice and, unlike other parts of the Xekong Basin, rice here is often harvested between July and September, when there is a dry period before the rains resume. The people in this area eat more tubers and corn than rice, sometimes mixed with rice.[8] They also have a history of raising livestock, especially native pigs, buffaloes, and, more recently, cattle.

Dakchung District officials report that over forty villages situated upstream from the Xekaman 3 Dam will be negatively impacted by the project. Most of the people in these villages are ethnic Triang, although some are Dak Ye. The GoL plans to reduce the number of villages in the area through village consolidation (see Chapter 5) and to relocate many of the people to more accessible areas. The dam project may well provide the GoL with further justification for carrying out its objectives for stopping swidden agriculture and consolidating ethnic minority villages in the area.

The reservoir will, at most, only inundate one village, Mang Ha Noi. The people from the village fish in the Xekaman River on a daily basis, and their livelihoods are highly linked to the river. There were reported to be 172 people in thirty-two families and twenty-eight households in Mang Ha Noi Village in 1999. River fish was cited as one of the village's main sources of income at the time (UNDP 1999a). Halcrow (1999) reported that the limits of upstream migrations of floodplain fish were unknown, but that most fish in this region were expected to be highland species, with some probably endemic.

Halcrow (1999) also reported that the Xekaman 3 Dam would be extremely damaging to the interests of the Dong Ampham NPA. Construction of road access to the Xekaman 2 and 3 dam sites was expected to "provide an almost uncontrollable route to the most sensitive sites on the northern boundary" of the park. The access road for Xekaman 3 will be about 131 km in length. Long transmission lines will also cross large expanses and provide easier access to these remote areas.

The Xekaman 1 Dam

The Xekaman 1 Dam has been in the planning stages since the early 1990s (Coleman 1995; Baird 1995b; IRN 1999) but, so far, construction of what would be one of the region's largest and tallest dams has yet to begin. While it remains a high priority project for the GoL, there do not appear to be concrete plans for building the dam. The LNMC (2004) listed the project as "postponed," but recent announcements suggest that there is still active interest in the dam.

The Xekaman 1 Dam would be located in Sanxay District, in the Annamite Cordillera, about 85 km upstream of the Xekaman's confluence with the Xekong (Maunsell and Lahmeyer 2004). The dam was originally expected to have a capacity of 250–300 MW (GHD 1994; Coleman 1995; IRN 1999), but, more recently Vietnamese planners have estimated that the dam could be developed with a capacity of at least 300 MW (Reuters 2003b). Others have estimated that capacity could climb to as high as 468 MW (Sakdavong 2004a; LNCE 2003; Maunsell and Lahmeyer 2004). The dam is now expected to be 184 m tall (Maunsell and Lahmeyer 2004), and, if built to that size, it would constitute the second highest concrete-faced rock fill dam in the world. The dam's reservoir area is expected to be 224 km^2 (Maunsell and Lahmeyer 2004). It has been estimated that 35 km of road would need to be rehabilitated for the project, and 23 km of new roads built. A 820 m tunnel would also be required (Maunsell and Lahmeyer 2004).

The first concession agreement to build the Xekaman 1 Dam was signed by HECEC, a semi-autonomous company established by the Government of Tasmania.[9] Initially, HECEC planned to begin constructing the dam in November 1995, together with the John Holland Construction Company of Australia and the Brazilian company, Companhia Brasileira de Projectos e Obras (CBPO). However, the deal collapsed. Later, rights to build the dam were transferred to the newly formed Austral Lao Power (ALP) Company, established by leading people within HECEC (IRN 1999).

ALP signed a concession agreement to build the dam and the southern transmission line on 15 November 1997 (LNCE 2003), but in 2001, after years of little progress and a financial scandal, ALP pulled out of the project (Lang 2003). In 2004, there were reports of a US-based company, New England Power, operating as Ascan International, signing a new MOU for development of the project (Thammavongsa 2004; Sakdavong 2004a); however, that MOU was reportedly later cancelled as well.

While Thailand was originally seen as the main market for power from Xekaman 1, Vietnam has now emerged as the more likely buyer, particularly as a transmission line from the dam to Vietnam would be shorter than one to Thailand (Thammavongsa 2004). In March 2006, the *Vientiane Times* reported that the Viet-Lao Power Investment and Development Joint-Stock Company, also responsible for building the Xekaman 3 Dam, had signed a MoU with the GoL to conduct an 18-month feasibility study for the project (Vongsay 2006b). The company's chairman, Le Van Ton, was quoted as saying, "The survey will be completed next year, and the construction is expected to be complete by 2010" (Vongsay 2006b). It was reported that the 465-MW capacity dam would cost US$535 million and that Laos would have a 30% share in the 30-year concession project.

In November 2006, International Water Power and Dam Construction (2006) reported that the GoL and the Lao-Viet Electrics Investment and Development Company had signed a MoU for the construction of a 465-MW capacity Xekaman 1 hydroelectric power plant in Laos, at the cost of US$550 million, and in August 2007, VNA (2007) also reported that The Viet Nam-Laos Power Joint Stock Company (presumably the same company as above) had signed a MoU for the construction of the Xekaman 1 Dam, priced at US$380 million. Song Da Corporation apparently owns 49% of the capital of the company, compared to 11% each for the Bank for Investment and Development of Viet Nam and the PetroVietnam Financial Company, and 10% for the Viet Nam Oil and Gas Company.

Projected Social and Environmental Impacts

Regardless of who builds the Xekaman 1 Dam, its construction and operation is expected to result in severe negative environmental and social impacts. The dam would flood 158 km^2 of river valley bottom, as well as part of Dong Ampham NPA (Halcrow 1999).

There are significant resettlement-related issues with the Xekaman 1 Dam. Halcrow (1999) reported that in 1993, many communities were relocated out of the reservoir area. It recommended that, if the dam were to be built, all communities relocated from the area after 1993 should be considered as being relocated in preparation for the Xekaman 1 Dam and that the dam's developers should therefore compensate them. Halcrow was clearly concerned about the GoL moving people out of potentially dam-affected areas in anticipation of projects in order to increase the dam's attractiveness to investors.

All the people moved out of the Xekaman 1 reservoir area were officially resettled as part of the GoL's swidden agriculture eradication program. The GoL maintains that they were not moved because of the Xekaman 1 Dam (Lang 2003; see, also, Baird and Shoemaker 2005; Gonzales et al. 2005; and section in Chapter 5 on resettlement in Sanxay District). As of 2004, the villages of Dak Kleup, Done Khen, Vang Khen, Vang Hin Dam, Phieng Se, and Ton Chouy had been relocated from the future reservoir area of the dam and villagers from Dak Bou Nyai (52 households and 300 people), Dak Bou Noi (thirteen households and 87 people) and Dak Kouk Noi (forty-two families and 230 people) had been told to prepare to relocate. The people there do not want to move but feel that they may have little choice but to do so. GHD (1994) estimated that 2,000 people in 400 families would need to be relocated during project development, although many of those have probably already been resettled. ADB and GoL (2004) estimated that more than 800 people would need to be relocated if the project were to proceed. If people who have already been moved from the area are included, this number would obviously be much higher.

Dak Bou Nyai Village: An Uncertain Future

Dak Bou Nyai (fifty-two households and 300 people) is an ethnic Triang village in Sanxay District situated on the top of a mountain overlooking the Xekaman River. While construction of the Xekaman 1 Dam would not result in the village being flooded, the community is still scheduled for relocation, as it would become an island surrounded by the reservoir. Villagers report that they currently have enough rice to eat every year. They also have lots of taro, tubers, and other edible vegetables. They do not want to relocate, because they have noticed that other villages relocated to resettlement sites such as Pa-am, Vang Tat, and other places have not received the support promised and have suffered greatly. But if the dam is built, much of the land they use for agriculture and resource collection would be flooded. The uncertain future of the village has affected the villagers psychologically. Many state that they dare not try to "develop" their village, or build new, bigger houses, for fear that they might be forced to move. The village does not have a school, and villagers would like one built. But government authorities have told them that, since the village is going to be relocated anyway, there is no sense in building one at the old village location. The people feel like they are in limbo.

The Xekaman 1 Dam would have serious negative downstream impacts. More than 10,000 people live along the Xekaman River downstream from where the dam would be built (IRN 1999). The hydrological changes caused by the project threaten to disrupt the Xekong plains (Halcrow 1999), one of Laos' most important wetland areas (Claridge 1996). Maunsell and Lahmeyer (2004) considered that, while the economic performance of the 438-MW version of the project would be good, its environmental impacts would add to the difficulty of securing financing for the project. The large and deep reservoir the dam would create makes the project particularly problematic. Earlier projections were that the reservoir would take seven years to fill-up, causing "permanent damage" to the downstream ecology and wiping out fisheries and the livelihoods of communities dependent upon them (IRN 1999). More recent estimates are 39.5 months (Maunsell and Lahmeyer 2004), which is still over three years.

Once operational, downstream dam releases would undoubtedly be quite different than natural flows, especially if the operation of the dam does not attempt to simulate the natural flow of the river (an environmental flow regime). This seems likely based on past experiences in Laos and the region. Overall, this project would severely impact downstream hydrology, not only in the lower Xekaman River but also in the Xekong below its confluence with the Xekaman. Downstream users, including those in some quite densely populated areas near the district center of Saysettha, would suffer dramatic changes (Halcrow 1999). Fisheries would certainly be heavily impacted, as would the downstream ecology of the whole riverbed.

The riverbank morphology in the lower part of the Xekaman is of special concern. There is the riverbed proper, largely inundated with water year-round. Then, there is a second level of land a few meters up that is inundated only during the rainy season. This wide area is covered in rich alluvial soils and are used extensively for dry-season vegetable gardening. Tobacco, long beans, lettuce, chilies, eggplants, and green onions are among the predominant crops, and many others are grown as well. The next level up is the natural levee, where most houses are located. Farther from the river there is a dip in land elevation where lowland rice fields are generally located. Changes in hydrology could badly impact the seasonal cycles of riverbank vegetable gardening and also cause the area used for vegetable growing to erode.

Downstream erosion would damage important natural habitats along the Xekaman River. Vegetation along the river acts as important fish habitat, and it is crucial for fishers. For example, bundle-basket traps (*kha* in Lao) are filled with sticks to attract fish. The sticks are removed when fishing takes place, and the traps are pulled onto the shore, trapping the fish inside. During the dry season women and children frequently use scoop nets (*sving* in Lao) to catch small fish and shrimps in the Xekaman. The loss of riverside vegetation and associated impacts on fisheries and people's fishing methods, as experienced on the Sesan River in northeastern Cambodia following the construction of the Yali Falls dam in Vietnam (Baird et al. 2002; Fisheries Office and NTFP 2000), would result in negative consequences to local livelihoods along the lower Xekaman River.

GHD (1994) played down the project's potential downstream impacts and failed to recognize that these impacts were inevitable. Instead, they stated that the impacts were uncertain and required more study. They did, however, acknowledge that "The damming of the Xekaman River will create a large artificial lake and result in a substantially altered flow regime for the river, and its living dependents, below the dam" (GHD 1994: 17). They then went on to state: "The chemical nature of the modified river flow will change as processes occur at depth within the reservoir and sediments collect behind the dam wall. Changes to the river's turbidity (possibly also temperature), dissolved oxygen, acidity and alkalinity, and flow regimes will combine to have effects on the habitat value for fisheries in the lower part of the watercourse" (GHD 1994: 17).

When the Xekaman 1 Dam was first being considered in the early 1990s, few people living downstream were aware of the project's potential negative downstream impacts (Baird 1995b). Downstream residents are now much more aware of the project and its potential impacts. Many local people are opposed to the dam, although most dare not speak openly about their concerns. The people in the area first became widely aware of the downstream impacts they would be faced with when the government surveyed a number of villages along the Xekaman River downstream from the planned dam-site, in order to determine how many wells would need to be installed once the dam's reservoir started to fill. One young man from Fang Deng Village, Saysettha District, said, "We are concerned about the dam, but we can't say anything. We don't want our river destroyed, but what can we do? This is a government project."

During the time that HECEC and ALP were involved in developing the Xekaman 1 Dam, there was considerable interest in determining the commercial value of the forested portions of reservoir, roads, and transmission line corridors (GHD 1994). The opportunity to log the reservoir area may well have been a prime motivation for the involvement of private companies in the project, particularly ALP. When ALP was involved, logging the reservoir was expected to be one of the project's most profitable aspects (Lang 2003), since the dam area was estimated to have 2.2

million m³ of standing timber in it, with a value of US$190 per m³. Of this, the dam's inundation area was estimated to have 420,000 m³ of logs (IRN 1999). Over the past few years, there has been a large amount of logging in the reservoir, even though it is far from certain whether the dam will be built.

Although the "Initial Environment Examination of the Xekaman #1 Southern Transmission Line Project" (GHD 1994) claimed that Dong Ampham NPA was outside of the hydro project development area, Halcrow (1999) disagreed, as did Davidson et al. (1997). Halcrow (1999) stated that the dam would cause serious negative impacts to Dong Ampham NPA, by flooding all low-lying habitats along the park's northwest border, as well as all the tributaries draining into the protected area. Wildlife and fish migrations would also be seriously impeded. A 158-km stretch of valley bottom, and possibly as much as 99% of the low slope land suitable for lowland agriculture, would be lost to the project's large reservoir (Halcrow 1999).

The Xekaman 4 Dam

In the early 1990s, the Xekaman 4 Dam was proposed for the Xekaman River in the headwaters in Dakchung District, upriver from where the Xekaman 3 Dam is being constructed. The project would be situated near the border with Vietnam's Quangnam Province. It was initially expected to have a capacity of 115 MW and cost US$450 million (Ministry of Industry and Handicrafts 1994). In 2003, the Vietnamese government announced its interest in taking on this project, with a projected size to 55 MW in capacity, if it receives permission from the GoL (Reuters 2003b; VNA 2003b). VNA (2007) reported in August 2007 that an MoU had been signed for the Viet Nam-Laos Power Joint Stock Company to construct the dam, estimated to cost US$94 million.

Halcrow (1999) reported that approximately 80 km of valley bottom would be flooded in five separate valleys in the upper Xekaman catchment if the dam were to be built and that access roads close to the Vietnam border would promote considerable encroachment into the area. A 179-km long access road would also be required for this project (Halcrow 1999). Furthermore, around 30 km of upland-river and their fish stocks, including some possible endemic species, would be destroyed by the project's reservoir (Halcrow 1999). Finally, Halcrow (1999) reported that logging the reservoir area would probably not be economical and, as a result, construction could result in inadequate vegetation removal, causing high biomass loadings after reservoir flooding.

The Xekatam Dam

The Xekatam River, in Pakxong District, is a fourth-order tributary of the Mekong, flowing into the Xenamnoi and then the Xekong River. The "Xekatam Small-scale Hydroelectric Power Development Project" was first conceived through a study supported by JICA in 1992 (JICA 1995). Japanese aid and private sector interests have, for years, strongly influenced this project's development. An MoU to build a dam on the Xekatam was signed by the "Hydropower Company" of Japan and the GoL on 15 October 1994, but nothing ever came of that agreement (LNCE 2003). While JICA has supported studies designed to facilitate dam development in the Xekong Basin, the agency has not yet financially supported the actual construction of any large dams in the area.

While the design of the Xekatam Dam is still unclear, the information currently available indicates that the dam is likely to have a small reservoir and be built at the bottom of a steep valley. It will inundate significant stretches of the Xekatam Noi and Xekatam Nyai Rivers. Apparently two different locations have been seriously considered for the dam. The first is along the Xekatam River between Houng and Thong Houng villages (ethnic Heuny). This location is flanked by Thong Vay Mountain. There are about 370 ha of lowland paddy farmland located upstream of this proposed dam site, much of which could be flooded by the project's reservoir. The second option is to build the dam right at the Xekatam Waterfalls (*Nam Katam Tok* in Lao)[10]. This option would require tunneling through a large mountain. There is a large depression there, and about 30 ha of village agricultural land nearby would be impacted. This option is apparently more expensive because of the drilling required. For either scenario, a section of the Xekatam River would be virtually dewatered. The diverted water would flow into the Nam Houng River and then back into the Xekatam further downstream.

Maunsell and Lahmeyer (2004) estimated that the project's installed capacity could be 12–100 MW. They looked at the 12 MW option, which did not maximize economic benefits but did preserve the natural beauty of the Xekatam Waterfalls. Those falls, along with Phanong Waterfalls, are considered an important "eco-tourism and cultural tourism site" (Syvongxay 2006: 3). Maunsell and Lahmeyer (2004) estimated that, under the first scenario, the dam would be 18 m high and cost US$19.4 million to build. An estimated 18 km of roads would need to be rehabilitated as well as 6 km of new roads built.

Although the LNMC (2004) listed the Xekatam dam as having been postponed, in the same year Kansai Electric Power Company of Japan signed an MoU for the project. The two parties agreed to study the potential for building a 57 MW dam at the cost of about US$100 million. Power from the dam would be partly exported to Thailand and partly consumed in Laos. On 1 October 2004, the Lao press announced that the project had initiated an 18-month feasibility study of environmental and economic impacts. The dam's exact size, cost, and power-generating capacity was to be determined as part of the survey (Sakdavong 2004b). However, in June 2005, less than nine months later, half the period of time allocated for the environmental and economic impact assessment, the *Kyoto News* (2005) reported that Kansai had already decided to build the dam and that the project was expected to be completed by 2011. It was reported that the dam would have a 50–60 MW capacity and cost 10–14 billion JPY (Japanese yen). Kansai expected to lead a joint venture with the GoL and reported that an unnamed Thai company would assist in managing the project.

Projected Social and Environmental Impacts

Ethnic Heuny people from Thong Houng, Nam Houng, and Nam Touat rely heavily on the proposed dam's reservoir area for their livelihoods. People conduct swidden agriculture and plant various other crops year round. In all, there are seven ethnic Heuny populated villages in the project area, all in Pakxong District, near the borders with Lamam and Samakhixay Districts (see Table 4).

Table 4. People Living in the Direct Vicinity of the Planned Xekatam Dam

#	Name of Village	Households	No. of People	Female/ Male	Year Village Established in Present Location
1	Nong Theuam Nyai	7	38	17/21	1953
2	Nong Hin	27	140	71/69	1963
3	Nam Houng	36	225	122/123	1950
4	Nong Mek	86	480	260/220	1961
5	Nam Touat Neua	29	162	81/81	1952
6	Nam Touat Tai	24	127	61/66	Recently relocated to Attapeu, reportedly due to remoteness
7	Thong Houng	8	41	20/21	1968
	Totals	217	1,213	618/601	N/A

In that much of the Heuny ethnic group has already been badly impacted by the construction of the Houay Ho Dam, the area affected by the proposed Xekatam Dam represents one of the last strongholds for Heuny culture. Buffalo, pig, and chicken sacrifices for spirits are still commonly performed, and there is still substantial wildlife in the area. The area is generally considered rich in natural resources, including valuable large tree species such as red wood (*mai deng* in Lao),[11] rosewood (*mai dou*), *Dipterocarpus* wood (*mai nyang*), *mai kha-nyoung*, and *mai champa pa*.

The Xekatam River is rich in aquatic resources. Some of the species of fish in the river include *Hypsibarbus* or *Barbodes* spp. (*pa pak*), *Hemibagrus wyckioides* (*pa kheung*), *Poropuntius* sp. or spp. (*pa chat*), *Acantopsis* and/or *Acanthopsoides* sp. or spp.) (*pa hak kouay*), *Channa* sp. (*pa kado*). There are also many other smaller species. Villagers generally use small-scale fishing-gear such as castnets (*he*), gill nets (*mong*), hooks (*bet*), side-funnel traps (*sai*), swing traps (*sadoung*), and standing-up traps (*toum*).

From the dam site down to the confluence of the Nam Houng River the Xekatam River will be almost completely dewatered. Villagers from Nong Theuam Nyai, Nong Mek, Nong Hin, and Nam Houng all use this part of the river for drinking, domestic, and livelihood purposes. Local people in the area have expressed great concern over their future. Further impacts can also be expected downstream from the confluence of the Nam Houng with the Xekatam. It is unclear what compensation, if any, will be provided to impacted communities located downstream of the dam.

Villagers were initially provided with almost no information about the project or how it might affect them. They had little awareness about the potential downstream impacts of irregular water releases from the project or the implications of releasing low quality water into the Xenamnoi and Xekong Rivers. Villagers were told that Nam Houng Village would need to be relocated, as the dam would be built just above the village. Once they gained more information about the project, villagers reportedly told local officials that they would not move if they were forced to endure similar conditions to those experienced by people relocated to a *Ban Chat San* as a result of the construction of the Houay Ho Dam (see above).

Later, villagers from Nam Houng became dismayed that a large area of lowland rice paddy fields owned by the community would be destroyed and otherwise impacted by the project. Those living in the immediate project area have requested, via an outside observer, that if any dams are built on the Xekatam River, the foreign investors should be responsible for ensuring that people are appropriately compensated for all impacts. They do not want the GoL to be held responsible for providing this compensation because of its limited resources. A villager from Nam Touat Neua stated, in February 2005: "If the Japanese Company is going to build the dam, we will not prohibit them from doing so. It is for the development of the country. But we ask that no impacts are allowed to affect us, and that we receive assistance so that we have enough to eat and live."

The Xekong 4 Dam

The Xekong 4 Dam is one of the largest dams planned for the basin. It would be built on the mainstream Xekong River in southern Kalum District, just above the *Keng* Chang rapids near Ta-neum Village, Lamam District (see Chapter 9). The proposed location is 13 km downstream from the confluence of the *Houay* Axam, in Lamam District (Norconsult 2007a). In the early 1990s, a South Korean company, Hyundai Engineering, signed a MoU with the GoL to investigate possibilities for constructing a 346-MW capacity dam costing US$755 million (Ministry of Industry and Handicrafts 1994); however, Hyundai later withdrew from the project.

A second MoU for the project was signed between the GoL and Modular Company on 21 January 1994, but that MoU was also cancelled (LNCE 2003; Maunsell and Lahmeyer 2004). Lahmeyer International conducted a pre-feasibility report for the project in 1997 (Maunsell and Lahmeyer 2004), and in 2003 the Vietnamese government announced its intention to support building of the dam. Various estimates of the installed capacity have been made including 310 MW (VNA 2003a and b; Lang 2003; Reuters 2003b), 443 MW (EdL 2003), 450 MW (LNCE 2003), and 485 MW (Maunsell and Lahmeyer 2004). Maunsell and Lahmeyer (2004) also recommended that the project should supply the Vietnamese market via the Ban Sok sub-station, 120 km from the dam and that a 170 m high dam be built creating a 160 km² reservoir extending 65 km upstream. It would take an estimated 14.5 months to fill the reservoir after construction. 18 km of new roads would be required, along with the upgrading of 14 km of existing roads. The estimated cost of the project was US$592 million.

In 2004, the LNMC listed the project as cancelled, but, in March 2006, the *Vientiane Times* reported that a Russian firm, Regional Oil Company, had signed an MoU to conduct an 18-month feasibility study of Xekong 4 (Vongsay 2006a). The project was expected to have an installed capacity of 470 MW and cost US$600 million. The same company, in December 2005, had also signed MoUs to investigate the feasibility of building the Xekong 5 and the Nam Kong 1 and 3 Dams. The

Vientiane Times quoted the Managing Director of Regional Oil, Oley Kabardin, as saying, "If the results of the study are good for the investment, we will sign another MOU for the next phase of the project."

Soon after the Xekong 4 MoU was signed, the *Vientiane Times* quoted the Deputy Governor of Xekong Province, Phonephet Khiulavong, as saying, "Xekong will become a huge power hub in Laos" (Pansivongsay 2006a). "If the project feasibility study is favorable and an agreement to build the dam is signed, the Russian company Vostokhydro Energostroy will undertake the construction phase of the Xekong 4 project. Construction is expected to take about three years to complete" (Vongsay 2006a). It has been reported that Russia is currently increasing its investment in Laos, especially in hydroelectric dam development, food processing, and mining (*Vientiane Times* 2006d). Then, more recently, in October 2006, the *Vientiane Times* (2006f) reported that the Regional Oil Company of Russia had signed an agreement with the GoL to complete the construction of the Xekong 4 (460 MW), Xekong 5 (400 MW), and Nam Kong 1 Dams (240 MW) in 2012, 2014, and 2013, respectively, at a combined cost of US$1.5 billion. Construction was expected to begin in mid-2007.

The agreement stated that the GoL would not own more than 20% of the shares in the projects and that the projects would be operated on thirty-year BOT terms. It was also reported that the Nam Kong 3 Dam was not agreed upon, as an appropriate dam site could not be found. The Director-General of the Regional Oil Company of Russia, Eleg Kabardin said, "We are studying and drafting particular plans to maintain the environment near the construction areas." He also stated that "Once construction was completed, the company would increase fish numbers in the dams, which would also provide water for agricultural activities. Destroyed trees would be replanted."

According to EdL, construction of the Xekong 4 and 5 Dams, as well as the Xekaman 1 and Xepian-Xenamnoi Dams, is being hindered by a lack of firm commitment from Vietnam to buy power from these dams and also because Thailand has recently said that it would only buy power from new dams if the energy is channeled through one of three transmission lines located in Savannakhet, Vientiane, or northern Laos. The southern Lao dams are hindered because power would need to be sent over 300 km to Savannakhet in order to be exported to Thailand. The costs of building transmission lines to do that would significantly increase overall costs. In early 2007, a team of Russian and Vietnamese engineers were conducting detailed engineering studies at the dam site. A 4 km-access road had also been constructed.

In June 2007, Norconsult (2007a) completed an "Initial Environmental Examination" of the project. According to this report, the dam is expected to consist of a concrete-faced rockfill dam with a crest length of 860 m and a height of 155 m. It would create a long narrow and deep 147.5-km² reservoir, with a length of 95 km. 150 km² of largely forested land would be inundated, including some important wildlife habitat. The dam is also expected to be substantially larger than previously envisioned, with an installed capacity of 600 MW.

Projected Social and Environmental Impacts

Halcrow (1999) had earlier reported that the construction of the Xekong 4 Dam would require that 3,439 people be relocated from the project's reservoir area and that half of the project's reservoir would be inside the proposed Phou Theung NPA. 157 km² of valley bottom would be flooded, as well as 110 km² of dense forest and a number of villager swidden areas. Halcrow (1999) also reported that some endangered large mammal species in the area might be negatively impacted by the project.

Norconsult's (2007a) more recent Initial Environmental Examination confirms that impacts from the project would be even more severe than envisioned by Halcrow's earlier study. The dam would necessitate the resettlement of over 5,000 people located in twenty villages located along the Xekong. 98% of those who would be resettled are ethnic minorities, most being ethnic Ngkriang, Harak, and Katu. The Norconsult report acknowledges that the district center of Kalum would need to be resettled, a point of past ambiguity, and states that it has been proposed that all the resettled population be relocated to the same place, where a new district centre is to be established. So far, however, the site has not been determined. However, Norconsult stated that "The proposed resettlement sites are not suited to permanent subsistence type agriculture because of the management and fertilizer requirements of the soil for intensive use" (2007: 13). Regarding those to be resettled, the report notes that "Under Lao law they have to be fully compensated for any losses so that they have an equivalent or higher standard of living" (Norconsult 2007: 12). The reality in Laos, however, is that people impacted by large dams are never properly compensated for their losses.

Some "anticipatory resettlement" actually began several years ago. The ethnic Harak village of Pakayom was moved 30 km downstream to its present location in 2002. While the village is in the proposed project area, villagers were only told that they needed to move in order to stop "slash-and-burn agriculture." The resettlement has not been successful. One community leader was quoted by WWF as saying:

"I don't want to criticize the government, but we do have problems. Our production of rice is very low here. We have a lot of land, but it is not suitable for rice cultivation. I proposed to the government to help us with livestock, but they do not have any funds. We do have a school now, which is good. But many times when we are hungry, the children have to go to the forest instead of going to school."

(WWF 2005c: 13)

As has been the case elsewhere in Laos, resettlement for the Xekong 4 Dam appears likely to lead to the impoverishment of local communities and to exacerbate environmental problems. One Lao WWF staff member recently stated that

"Most of the time resettlement is not accompanied by any effective training and education on adapting to lowland environments. As a result, it tends to exacerbate the poverty and suffering of many communities and can also easily worsen the degradation of natural resources, instead of preventing it. The resettled communities convert riverine and forest lands to suit lowland agriculture systems, without having any idea of the impact of the loss of critical habitat for wildlife and capture fisheries."

(WWF 2005c: 15)

Norconsult (2007a) reports that the Xekong River would, all the way to its confluence with the Mekong 150 km downstream from the dam, be impacted by the Xekong 4 project. No direct mention is made of negative impacts in Cambodia, although many can be expected. At Attapeu, dry season flows are expected to be 84% more than at present, with rainy season water levels being reduced on average. Since the dam would produce electricity from eight to sixteen hours per day, "the daily flows and downstream river levels will change significantly" (Norconsult 2007a: 10). The project would also cause considerable downstream hydrological disruption during the time the reservoir is being filled. There is a 90% chance that it would take about three years to fill the project's reservoir Halcrow (1999). Norconsult (2007a) projects that, because sediment would be trapped in the reservoir and due to the deficiency of sediment below the dam, downstream erosion would occur. Water quality in the reservoir is expected to be stratified and quite poor, with deep areas being anoxic and uninhabitable by fish. Water releases may result in fish kills downstream because of the poor quality of the water. The release of cold water is expected to lead to changes in aquatic fauna downstream. Ultimately, biodiversity and fish populations are projected to decline considerably, and fish migrating up the Xekong would certainly be unable to pass the dam: "Fish that undertake long distance migrations up the Se Kong from the Mekong will be blocked by the dam and may lack the necessary triggers for migration such as the early wet season flood" Norconsult (2007a: 12). Riverbanks would tend to become less productive, and deep-water pools would gradually be filled up. The mitigation of some of these impacts would require a more natural flow management to be developed (Norconsult 2007a); however, it is not at all certain that the dam operator would be required to do this as part of its concession agreement.

Given the scale of these projected impacts and the importance of fish and other aquatic resources to local communities already described in Chapter 7, it is clear that local livelihoods would be severely impacted by the Xekong 4 Dam.

There would also be severe impacts on wildlife. The dry season sandbars in the Xekong are important habitat for a number of species of river birds, such as River Tern (*Sterna aurantia*), River Lapwing (*Vanellus duvaucelii*), Small Pratincole (*Glareola lactea*), Great Thick-knee (*Esacus recurvirostris*), Little-ringed Plover (*Charadrius dubius*) and Mekong Wagtail (*Motacillo samveasnae*). Changes in downstream hydrological patterns in the Xekong River caused by the construction of Xekong 4 and other large upstream dams could have negative impacts on river bird populations, through causing sandbar nesting habitat to be flooded and through increasing young bird mortality in the dry season. Available sandbar habitat for nesting birds would be reduced, due to the projected higher water levels in the dry season.

Similar problems have already occurred along the Sesan River in northeast Cambodia as a result of the construction of the 720 MW Yali Falls dam in the Central Highlands of Vietnam (Claassen 2004; Fisheries Office and NTFP 2000). To reduce the negative impacts on downstream bird populations, Claassen (2004) recommended that the flow regime of the Yali Falls dam be operated to replicate the natural daily seasonal flow cycle of the Sesan River. To date, there has been little consideration given to managing dams in the Mekong River Basin with such an "environmental flows" perspective.

The Xekong 5 Dam

Few details are available about the Xekong 5 Dam, but it is earmarked for the mainstream Xekong in Kalum District, upriver from Don Village, at the 20–30 m high *Tat Kalang* Waterfalls. This is quite a remote area, and there are no villages near the dam site, although the small Katu settlement of Ape is located slightly upriver. The area is apparently rich in fish. At times villagers from Don Village go to the area on fishing trips.

Maunsell and Lahmeyer (2004) reported that the Xekong 5 Dam is expected to consist of a 250-m concrete arch dam and include two 200-MW Francis units in a cavern powerhouse located downstream of the dam. They estimated that the dam's reservoir would cover an area of about 70 km² and be 30 km in length. They also estimated that the dam's construction would involve building 40 km of new roads to the project site, which is not currently accessible by road. They also estimated that a 250-km transmission line would be required to connect to the proposed 500-kV system at *Ban* Sok in Attapeu, enabling the project's electricity to be marketed in Thailand or Vietnam.

Like the Xekong 4 Dam, the South Korean company, Hyundai Engineering, was the first to sign an MoU with the GoL to investigate the potential for building the Xekong 5 Dam. The GoL initially envisioned the dam as having a capacity of 253 MW at a cost of US$574.6 million (Ministry of Industry and Handicrafts 1994). Hyundai eventually withdrew from the project, as they did with the Xekong 4 Dam. In April 2000, the Italian company, Sondel, signed a MoU with the GoL, giving it the exclusive mandate to investigate the site (LNCE 2003; Maunsell and Lahmeyer 2004); however, Sondel has apparently not been actively working to develop the project for years (Maunsell and Lahmeyer 2004). During the time they were involved, the estimated installed capacity of the dam was increased to 250 MW (LNCE 2003).

In 2003, the Vietnamese government expressed its desire to build the Xekong 5 Dam, but with a reduced capacity of 200 MW (VNA 2003a and 2003b; Lang 2003; Reuters 2003b). Other foreign investors have looked into the project. More recently, in December 2005, the Russian Regional Oil Co., Ltd. signed a MoU with the GoL to conduct an 18-month feasibility study on the Xekong 5 (300 MW) (see above). The company plans to sell some of the power produced domestically but wants to export most to Vietnam (*Vientiane Times* 2005s). The Russian ambassador to Laos, Yuri Andreevich Raikov, was quoted by the *Vientiane Times* (2005s: 1) as saying "These projects will contribute to socio-economic development and will help improve transport infrastructure and living conditions for the people of Laos." The agreement to investigate these dams was signed during the visit of the Russian Deputy Foreign Minister Alexander Alekseev to Laos in April 2006. He said that his country is interested in investing in the electricity, mining, food processing, and other sectors in Laos (Associated Press 2006). Since then, as outlined above, the Russia Regional Oil Co., Ltd. has completed its study of the project and signed an agreement with the GoL to build the project on a BOT basis. It is unclear when construction might begin.

Projected Social and Environmental Impacts

At a time when there remained considerable uncertainty surrounding plans for the Xekong 5 Dam, the GoL nevertheless decided to relocate one village from the project's reservoir area. About one-third of the people evicted from the village as a result of the move died within a year because of malaria (Lang 2003).

Halcrow (1999) had a difficult time accessing population statistics for the inundation area of the Xekong 5—the company's numbers varied from 789 to 1,728. However, the ADB and GoL (2004) have estimated that 5,870 people would need to be relocated if the project proceeds. Halcrow (1999) determined that approximately 135 km² of valley bottom habitat would be lost, representing a considerable threat to biodiversity. Part of the Xesap NPA would be inundated by the project's reservoir. In 1995, Xesap NPA was ranked third in terms of conservation importance in all of Laos. Halcrow (1999) recommended that plans for building Xekong 5 Dam should include providing management support for protecting Xesap NPA. Steinmetz et al. (1999) also mention the Xekong 5 Dam as a threat to Xesap, both in terms of flooding the southern border area of the park and by causing the relocation of people living near the park. Concerns were also raised that the dam might facilitate increased outside access to the protected area. The dam's potential impacts on the NPA were considered serious enough that, in 1997, Xesap NPA staff suggested a significant change in the southern border of the park in order to avoid having parts of the NPA flooded. However, it does not appear that the park's borders were ever altered.

According to Halcrow, there is a 90% chance that it would take over three years to fill the reservoir of the Xekong 5 Dam. This would certainly lead to serious downstream impacts, not to mention significant impacts in the reservoir area. The impacts would occur during both the construction and operation periods. The re-regulation of dam releases would be required in order to reduce the most serious downstream risks, including those presented by water releases into the narrow downstream passages below the dam. The people impacted by the Xekong 5 Dam would also require special consideration, since most come from vulnerable ethnic minority groups (Halcrow 1999).

LNCE (2003) reported that because of the serious potential impacts of the Xekong 4 and Xekong 5 Dams on the mainstream Xekong River, the Nam Kong

1 and the Xekaman 3 Dams were being considered as alternatives. Based on the recent agreements with the Russians, however, both projects now appear to be back on the development agenda.

Houay Lamphan Dam

The Houay Lamphan Nyai Dam is considered to be one of four priority dams for domestic electricity production and would be located on the Xekong River in Lamam District. GoL long-term projections are for it to be in operation by 2010 or 2012. Its capacity is expected to be 59–70 MW[12] (Department of Electricity 2004; EdL 2003). Maunsell and Lahmeyer (2004) reported that the project has good year-round generation characteristics and is well positioned to reduce dependence upon dry season imports from Thailand via the southern grid. They found that it had good promise and should be pursued. There is relatively little information available about this proposed project, although it has been reported that it would be constructed in the general vicinity of three ethnic Lavi villages (LNCE 2003).

In the early 1990s, the South Korean company, Sambu Construction, signed a MoU with the GoL to investigate the potential for building the Houay Lamphan Nyai Dam. At that time, it was estimated that the dam's capacity would be 103 MW and that it would cost US$233.8 million to construct (Ministry of Industry and Handicrafts 1994). They have apparently withdrawn from the project, as did other South Korean companies interested in hydropower in Laos in the early 1990s.

Since then, it has been estimated that a 77-m high dam with an installed capacity of 56 MW would create a 9 km² reservoir on the *Houay* Lamphan, cost US$66.51 million, and require 36 km of new roads to be built (Maunsell and Lahmeyer 2004). Maunsell and Lahmeyer (2004) reported that JICA has been approached for funding to conduct a feasibility study on the project; however, there have been no recent reports of plans to develop the dam.

The Xexou Dam

The Xexou Dam is another project on the books, but it does not appear to be in development at present. This dam would be built at a large and locally sacred rapids area of the Xexou River called "*Brawng*" in Brao, or "*Pha Phawng*" in Lao. Brao people claim that a powerful spirit, "*Arak Brawng*," stays there and removes fishing long lines put out at night in the area. Therefore, nobody dares to fish there. The GoL does not consider this to be a priority project (LNCE 2003), but villagers report that people looking at hydro development still visit the dam site almost every year. The GoL first estimated that the dam, if built, would have a capacity of 35 MW and cost US$142 million to construct (Ministry of Industry and Handicrafts 1994). The Department of Electricity (2004) estimated its capacity at 59 MW. ADB and GoL (2004) estimated that 500 people would need to be relocated if the dam were built.

The Nam Kong 1 and 3 Dams

Hyundai Engineering signed MoUs with the GoL to investigate possibilities for building the Nam Kong 1 and 3 Dams on the Nam Kong River in Phouvong District in the early 1990s. Both the Nam Kong 1 and 3 Dams would be in areas historically inhabited by ethnic Brao people. The Nam Kong 1 Dam would be located about 20 km from the Lao-Cambodian border (Maunsell and Lahmeyer 2004). It was initially estimated to have a capacity of 105 MW and cost US$233 million to build (Ministry of Industry and Handicrafts 1994); however, it is now expected to be larger, either with an installed capacity of 150 MW (Maunsell and Lahmeyer) or 238 MW (EdL 2003; Department of Electricity 2004). The principal market for power from this project is expected to be Cambodia or Vietnam (EdL 2003; Maunsell and Lahmeyer 2004). EdL (2003) has listed the expected completion date as 2015. The LNCE (2003) reported that the Nam Kong 1 Dam was only marginally viable, but the project was considered attractive because no human resettlement was expected to occur and because the project would be strategically located in terms of the ADB-envisioned regional electricity grid. Under the scenario examined by Maunsell and Lahmeyer (2004), a 32-m high concrete dam with a 12.1 km² reservoir would be built at a cost of US$202 million. It would require 32 km of new roads.

The Nam Kong 3 Dam was earlier estimated to have a capacity of 21 MW and to cost US$100 million to construct (Ministry of Industry and Handicrafts 1994). ADB and GoL (2004) estimated that 1,550 people would need to be relocated if the dam were built.

In December 2005, the Russian Regional Oil Co., Ltd. signed a MoU with the GoL to conduct 18-month feasibility studies on both Nam Kong 1 and Nam Kong 3 Dams. The planned capacity of Nam Kong 3 was increased to 35 MW (*Vientiane Times* 2005s). Subsequently, in October 2006, the company signed a MOU with the GoL to proceed with construction of Nam Kong 1. At that time, the project was expected to have a capacity of 240 MW and be completed in 2013. No construction MoU has yet been agreed upon for Nam Kong 2. Surveyors from Russian Regional

Oil could not find the proposed location of the dam, thus delaying the process (*Vientiane Times* 2006f).

In June 2007, Norconsult (2007b) completed an "Initial Environmental Examination" for the project. It is now expected to be an 80-m concrete-faced rockfill dam with a 150 MW capacity. Dire negative environmental impacts are predicted for the Nam Kong River. Although the reservoir is only expected to cover 18.4 km², the Nam Kong River would be flooded 30 km above the dam site, creating a deep and anoxic reservoir in which few fish would be able to survive. Although no resettlement is expected to occur in the project area—since almost all of the Brao villagers who historically lived in the area have already been moved to the lowlands—a 30 km stretch of the Nam Kong River downstream to its confluence with the Xekong would be badly impacted. The report stated that "The daily flows and downstream river levels will change significantly and such changes will be appreciated down to the junction with the Se Kong" (Norconsult 2007b: 11). Furthermore, poisonous waters released from the reservoir may kill fish and other organisms downriver. Norconsult (2007b: 12) wrote, "The release of poor quality water from the reservoir will have an effect upon the aquatic flora and fauna in the first stretches of the river below the dam, tending to reduce both diversity and populations." The report concluded that "There is potential for a loss of aquatic biodiversity and productivity in the Nam Kong River and its associated wetlands downstream due to these changes in flow" (Norconsult 2007b: 14). Riverbank agriculture and fishing in the Nam Kong River would be badly impacted, thus having negative impacts on the livelihoods of the ethnic Brao people living downstream from the project. As of July 2007, a full EIA had not yet been prepared for the project.

Other Large Dams

Halcrow (1999) considered all of the above projects in its study, along with the Xekaman 2[13] and Nam Kong 2[14] Dams in Attapeu Province and the Xekong 3 and Dak E Meule[15] (upper and middle) Dams in Xekong Province. The 298 MW Xekong 3 Dam on the mainstream Xekong was considered particularly unlikely to proceed, as it would require a large human resettlement scheme, including the relocation of 6,492 people and the associated re-establishment of infrastructure for the provincial capital of Xekong Province, which would be inundated. Fish migrations and river-based livelihoods would be severely impacted by this dam (Halcrow 1999; Ministry of Industry and Handicrafts 1994). The other dams are no longer listed as priorities by the GoL (Department of Electricity 2004).

383

In May 2006, the *Vientiane Times* reported that the GoL and a foreign investor, the Information Technology Electricity Company (ITELCO) of Japan, signed a MoU in Vientiane to conduct a hydropower project survey on the *"Houay* Kadan" in Pakxong District, Champasak Province. This project, if constructed, is expected to have an installed capacity of about 30 MW and to cost US$45 million. An 18-month survey began in May 2006, and, if the results are economically positive, the investor is expected to agree to build the dam. The *Vientiane Times* made no mention of potential negative social or environmental impacts. There is little more known, although the *Vientiane Times* did mention that the power generated would be used locally (Vongsay 2006d).

Summary

So many large dams are being built, or are in various stages of planning, that one can expect the Xekong River Basin to change drastically in the future, even if only some of the largest projects go ahead as planned. Many of these are proceeding despite a large number of unanswered questions and concerns about their potential negative impacts. There has been little consideration of the long-term costs and benefits of such large dam projects. Given the "pro-project bias" of consulting firms, developers, and international financial institutions such as the ADB, key policymakers in the country do not appear to have been provided with sufficient high quality information upon which to base their decisions. The people and communities in proposed project areas also lack basic information about expected impacts. As plans for these projects proceed, the views and interests of these local people, those most at risk of negative impacts, are, for the most part, being completely ignored. Some agencies, such as WWF are attempting to open up dialogue on the important issues of the environment, biodiversity, and social impacts (WWF 2005c). Appeals for a more careful and reasoned approach do not, however, appear to be having an affect on the rapid pace at which hydropower dam development is occurring in the Xekong River Basin in Laos.

14

Conclusions

This study of the Xekong River Basin in Laos has, it is hoped, illustrated the complex nature of this unique region, an area with a rich history, diverse cultures, and tremendous natural resource assets. While the Xekong Basin has faced many periods of dramatic change over history, the present period is bringing on rapid changes unlike any that the basin and its people have ever before experienced. The advent of large-scale, mostly externally initiated, infrastructure development—roads, plantations, mining, and dams—have the potential to transform the geographical face of the basin on an unprecedented scale. In particular, the massive scale of proposed large dams and diversion schemes appear likely to have severe negative impacts on local people and the environment through the altering of longstanding hydrological cycles upon which local cultures and livelihoods are based.

Apart from these physical changes, sweeping demographic and cultural transformations also occurring, especially as a result of the large-scale internal resettlement of ethnic minorities from the remote uplands and their integration into lowland ethnic Lao culture. The many related agricultural, forestry, and fishery-oriented changes taking place in the basin have large socio-cultural and environmental implications and are leading to significant changes in traditional livelihoods over a short time.

While some of these changes can be considered positive, many have potentially negative implications, both for humans and the environment. Unfortunately, as is often the case, the vulnerable and disadvantaged are most frequently at risk, and these people are commonly the least prepared for dealing with rapid change. So far, there is little evidence that the long-term interests of the people or the environment of the basin are being adequately considered by those decision-makers behind many of the changes now taking place.

While there will never be consensus regarding which sorts of changes are desirable and which are not, or even what constitutes "good" development, we hope that this study has helped to provide some insight into who can be expected to gain and lose from the changes now occurring in the Xekong River Basin. Our concern has been to identify some of the most vulnerable people and the groups that appear most likely to suffer from these changes, and to provide some insight and analysis regarding why this is likely to be the case.

We do not expect everyone to share all of the perspectives presented or to give priority to the same issues of concern highlighted here. But whatever one's point of view, we hope that this book can serve as a useful reference, both for helping to document the situation in a poorly understood part of the world and to provide insights into issues that need to be taken into account during this period of rapid change.

The idea for this book has its origins in our long-term fascination with the landscapes and peoples of the Xekong River Basin, but it also emerged out of our deep concern over the challenges faced by the peoples and environment of the basin. We hope that the approach taken will help readers gain insight into why the Xekong River Basin is so special and why its development represents a great opportunity but also a considerable challenge and threat. Finally, we hope that this volume helps readers consider how the livelihoods of the people of the Xekong River Basin in Laos, and other river basins in Laos and the region, are invariably linked with history, the environment, culture, politics, and the social systems that bring people together and push them apart. Outside researchers and decision-makers are likely to continue to have a significant influence on the future direction of development in the region. It is essential that they understand how these many factors are intricately connected with one another in a geographical area that is unique but so often misunderstood.

Notes

1
Introduction

[1] Although Xekong is often spelt Sekong (including in Cambodia), we prefer to follow Lao spelling conventions, since this report mainly deals with the Xekong River Basin in Laos.

[2] The correct way to spell it is "Viet Nam" (as the Vietnamese do), but following English language conventions we use the spelling Vietnam here.

[3] Technically, the Sesan and Srepok Rivers could be considered part of the Xekong River Basin, as the water from both rivers flows into the Xekong before it reaches the Mekong in Stung Treng Province, Cambodia. However, for the purposes of this study, the Srepok and Sesan River Basins are considered to encompass separate basins, and not parts of the Xekong Basin, and the statistics presented here are based on the premise that they are separate.

[4] The name of this province is often spelt Attopeu in French literature, but we prefer the spelling Attapeu.

[5] An Information and Culture official, Bounthanh Chanthakhaly, from Samakhixay District, Attapeu Province believes that ethnic Lao people first came to the Attapeu plain 888 years ago. The area was apparently called *"Muang Lao Long"* after the Lao established themselves there. They came from a place to the north known as *"Muang Theng Kalong."* Ethnic Khmer people apparently controlled much of the lowlands when the Lao arrived. Following Briggs (1949), however, it seems highly likely that the Lao arrived in Attapeu much later.

[6] Fieldwork was conducted in Kalum, Dakchung, Lamam, and Thateng Districts in Xekong Province and Samakhixay, Sanxay, Saysettha, Phouvong, and Sanamxay Districts in Attapeu Province.

2
The Xekong River Basin in Laos

[1] "Second-order" river/river basin is a tributary that flows directly into the Mekong River. Using this definition, the Xekong River is a second-order river, while its large tributaries and their basins, the Sesan and Srepok rivers in northeast Cambodia and the Central Highlands of Vietnam are third- and fourth-order rivers/river basins, respectively. As noted in Chapter 1, as this study is mainly focused on the Lao part of the Xekong River Basin, we are excluding the Sesan and Srepok River basins from the Xekong River Basin.

[2] The Xesap River is called "*Axap*" in the language of the Katu people living in the vicinity of the river.

[3] The river is also called *Xe Lan* in Lao.

[4] *Phou* Set (1,569 m asl) and *Phou* Thong Vay (1,716 m asl) are also features of the emergent sandstone basement stratigraphy that includes the Bolaven Plateau.

[5] A commune is the equivalent to a sub-district in Cambodia.

[6] Ethnic Lao refer to the Srepok River as the *Sepawk*, where Khmer speakers refer to the river as the *Srepok*.

[7] Kalum District has an especially low population density at 3.4 people/km^2.

[8] At the time, Sanxay District was larger, and included part of present-day Phouvong District. Sanxay extended to the Vietnamese border parallel to *Vang* Tat.

[9] At the time of this study, the exchange rate was approximately US$1 = 10,400 kip.

[10] Champasak was known as Bassac in pre-colonial times, but for the sake of consistency, we have chosen to use Champasak throughout.

[11] He was also known as *Phra khou khi home*, because he was believed to be so venerable that even his "excrement smelt good" (*khi home*).

[12] The French spelled it Attopeu.

[13] Phon Vixay is rumored by neighboring villagers to have once been an ethnic Brao (*Lave*) village that changed its identity to Lao a number of years ago. This claim has not been confirmed.

[14] Namely, Tungkarai, San Ya Yone, Leuk Dong, and Thong Katai Villages.

[15] Called *khon dam* in Lao.

[16] A pejorative in Lao for Austroasiatic people, meaning "slave."

[17] The Katu can be referred to correctly as both the Katu and the Kantu. The name Katu apparently originated in Vietnam (Viphone Chaoasan, LFNC Xekong Province, pers. comm. May 2005). According to Katu people in Kalum District, in adjacent parts of Vietnam people similar to Katu are often referred to as *Peuang*. There are some dialectal differences, but they can generally understand each other.

[18] Lavi is considered to be one of the most archaic Bahnaric languages in existence (Paul Sidwell, pers. comm. May 2005).

[19] However, the Lavi believe that they migrated into the area from either Thailand or Dakchung District long ago.

[20] These statistics come from 1995. A new nationwide census was conducted in March 2005, but the figures were not available for this study.

[21] This category apparently includes the Dakkung, Chatong, and Trieu ethnic groups, and various sub-groups within the Katu ethnic group. In Laos the Katu are generally referred to as Katu, the Pako, In, Katang, Ta-oi, and Chalong. According to Jutta Krahn, in the distant past at least some of the people now called Katu called themselves *Monui*.

[22] This category apparently includes the Triang Kong, Triang Yam, Triang Kaseng, Triang Trong Meuang, and Pa 'neng sub-groups.

[23] There are a number of variations in Harak dialects, indicating that more research on the existence of sub-groups is required.

[24] Local people consider there to be two sub-groups of Ngkriang.

[25] The Ye are often classified into three separate sub-groups, the Ye Kong, Ye Yeun, and Ye Dak.

[26] These people come from a variety of ethnic groups, and originally come from outside the province. There were only ten Vietnamese reported in the province, certainly many fewer than are present.

[27] Sapouan is considered by many to be a sub-group of Oy.

[28] The 1995 statistics record Jru (Laven) people, but Jru Dak (Sou) people are not listed. Therefore, since Jru Dak people are more abundant than Jru in Attapeu, the statistics for the two groups are probably mixed together into a single category known as "Laven." Engelbert (2004) reported, however, that the Sou and Sapuan groups are being recorded as Oy.

[29] There are no ethnic Halang (Keuyawng) people listed as living in Attapeu Province, but there are at least two ethnic Halang populated villages near the Vietnamese border in Phouvong District.

[30] There were only 167 Vietnamese listed as living in Champasak Province in 1995. The number of ethnic Vietnamese is certainly many times higher than that, and it appears that many ethnic Vietnamese have reported themselves as being ethnic "Lao."

[31] Ethnicity is not, however, the only aspect of identity important to people in the Xekong River basin. The nation-building process in the Xekong River Basin is also critical, as are attachments to revolutionary identities, as indicated by Pholsena (2006).

[32] In Harak.

[33] Clearly, the Katu are a confusing ethnic group to classify, with at least the following ethnonyms being applied to them: Teu, Attout, Kao, Khat, Thap, Nguon Ta, Ta River Van

Kieu, Phuong, Katu, Kato, and Ka-ta, just to name some applied in Vietnam (Mole 1970).

[34] *Kha* is a pejorative for Mon-Khmer language speaking groups that is now widely frowned upon in Laos, but was previously used by the Lao and later the French, following the Lao. It is still used by some Lao, but it is considered very insulting to the people who are called *Kha*.

[35] P. Odend'hal, 1894. Report to the Governor-General of Indochine, Hue, 24 February 1894, CAOM Indochine 9030.

[36] Often written *Kasseng* by the French.

[37] Including Dak Treup and Dak Koy Villages in Dakchung District and Dak Nong, Dak Hro, Dak Bras, and Dak Heun Villages in Sanxay District.

[38] Engelbert (2004) has pointed out that while some changes in ethnic names have taken place over history, ethnic group names existed among the people themselves before the colonial period. He wrote, "It is not as if the French 'invented' these words or they are responsible for the division of the Mon-Khmer peoples into different groups" (236). Instead, he blames the Lao and Siamese for not using the correct names of the people, and just calling them "*Kha*."

3
Culture and Livelihoods

[1] In English, animist is normally not capitalized, but we prefer to give it the same status as institutionalized religions, and therefore spell it Animist.

[2] There are at least eight villages in Sanamxay District, Attapeu Province in which parts of the populations are Christian: Ban Mai (ethnic Lao), Mitsamphan (ethnic Oy mixed with other groups), Tha Hin Tai (Oy), Tha (Oy), Kok Ong (Oy), Khang Theung (Oy), Oudomxay (Cheng), and Don Phai (Cheng). According to the Lao Front for National Construction in Xekong Province, there are only two families and eight individual Christians in the whole province. Most reportedly live in Ban Phon, Lamam District. However, it is unclear how accurate the province's statistics are in this regard.

[3] <www.joshuaproject.net/peopctry.php?rop3=1020428&rog3=LA>

[4] Also known as *bra dap* by Brao people (the short *bra*). This term is considered inoffensive to the spirits, while *bra bun* is used more cautiously.

[5] Also known as *bra jroung* by Brao people (the tall *bra*). It is an inoffensive synonym for *bra hanoi*.

[6] In the past the Lao essentially considered the "*Kha*" to be a single ethnic group, regardless of their various languages or customs, although people from various language groups certainly participated in the ceremonies of the boat races.

[7] There are various recipes for making jar beer. Sometimes people use yeast from the market, and sometimes they make their own yeast. In Phon Sa-at Village, Khong District, ethnic Brao people use ginger, chilies, galangal root, sticky rice, sugarcane, a vine called "*pra-em*" in Brao, and a rhizome called "*chan drook*" in Brao. Once all the ingredients are mixed together, the yeast is ready to use five to six days after drying in the sun. After a jar of beer is made, using the homemade yeast above and rice and rice husks, the jar is sealed, and can be drank within about three days minimum, but preferably ten days or more. There is also a variety of rice, "*jeh booh*" in Brao, which can be used to create yeast for making jar beer.

4
The History of the Xekong River Basin in Laos:
A Story of Power, War, and Conflict

[1] There is not actually any "tunnel" at the *Ou Mong* or *Vat Sipaket* ruin, but the entrance gate, before it collapsed due to treasure hunting, resembled a tunnel to local Lao people; thus the name.

[2] *Pha-nya* Kammatha apparently pre-dated the founding of the Kingdom of Champasak by *Nang* Phao, *Nang* Pheng, and *Achan* Phonsamek.

[3] These names could well be Lao derivatives of "Brao."

[4] Possibly Vietnamese.

[5] *Sethi* means a rich person in Lao.

[6] Probably referring to Khmer.

[7] P. Odend'hal, 1894. Report to the Governor General of Indochine, Hue, 24 February 1894, CAOM Indochine 9030.

[8] Lt. Debay, 1895. Exploration de la chaine d'Annam entre Tourane et Moung Lao–Attopeu. CAOM Indochine 6614.

[9] Debay 1895 (as above).

[10] Bonin 1893. Message to Résident supérieur of Annam in Hue, 1 May 1893, CAOM Indochine 22213.

[11] Debay 1895 (as above).

[12] Odend'hal 1894 (as above).

[13] Ruthe 1894. Installation du Poste d'Attopeu, 24 May 1894, Attopeu, CAOM Indochine 23557.

[14] Debay 1895 (as above).

[15] Judge of Tourane, 1901. Message to Procureur général, Chef du service judiciaire en Indo-Chine, Tourane, 6 December 1901, CAOM Indochine 50960.

Notes

[16] Directeur de l'École Française d'Extreme-Orient, 1904. Assassination of Prosper Odend'hal. Message to Governor General of Indochina, Hanoi, 21 June 1904, CAOM Indochine 7992.

[17] When the French first established Laos, they set up Upper Laos, based in Luang Phrabang, and Lower Laos based on Khong Island. In 1899, Upper and Lower Laos were combined, and the capital established in Vientiane (Dommen 1985).

[18] He was probably ethnic Harak (Rathie 2001; Pholsena 2006). The French often referred to him as "Bac Mi." *Ong Keo* translates into English as "Lord Gem."

[19] Some claim that he was ethnic Heuny (Nya Heun) from Nong Mek Village (Rathie 2001; Stuart-Fox 2001), which still exists in Pakxong District. However, Engelbert (2004) claims that he was ethnic Jru from Ban Long Lao, at the time located in Thateng District, Salavan. His mother was apparently ethnic Ta-oi.

[20] He was ethnic Lao, claiming to be a descendent of *Chao* Anou.

[21] Tournier, 1901. Rapport sur les évenements des Bolovens, 17 August 2001, Khong, Bas-Laos, CAOM Indochine 20756.

[22] A. Baudenne 1917. Rapport de tournée chez les Khas Kong Mun de la province d'Attopeu du janvier au 1 février 1917. CAOM, Résident supérieur du Laos.

[23] Résident supérieur of Laos, 1924. Notes on the State of Attopeu Province, Vientiane, 1 January 1924, CAOM Résident supérieur du Laos, E5.

[24] It is difficult to know exactly how many Brao paramilitary soldiers there were, as creative accounting resulted in large numbers of "ghost soldiers" being on the payroll.

[25] MSG has become an important ingredient in food for the Brao and most other people in the region in recent years, even for people living in remote villages with little contact with the market economy.

[26] Colors included Pink, Green, Purple, Orange, Modified Orange, White, and Blue (liquid and powder form) (Stellman et al. 2003).

[27] Unfortunately, wild fish from the Xekong River Basin in Laos were apparently not tested for dioxin contamination, and it is unknown whether they are contaminated.

5
Agriculture, Livelihoods, and Resettlement

[1] Baudenne, A. 1916. Rapport de tournée chez les Khas Lovés de la province d'Attopeu du 2 au 16 decembre 1916, 23 decembre 1916, CAOM, Résident supérieur du Laos.

[2] Parts of this section are based on information originally included in Baird and Shoemaker (2005).

[3] This area was previously called Pa-am, and is still commonly referred to as Pa-am by local people.

[4] The number of villages and people in the resettlement area is unclear, as some people have returned to the mountains, and others that are supposed to move there are still in the mountains. Before the resettlement program began, there were sixty villages in the district.

[5] This statistic came from villagers in the project area, and may well be inaccurate. The exchange rate at the time is unclear, as the project was built during the general period of the Asian Financial Crisis.

[6] In 2004, advertisements for the ADP in the *Vientiane Times* reported that the value of the loan for the project is US$16.6 million.

[7] This component is funded by the Japanese Social Development Fund, which is administered by the World Bank.

[8] The consultant, Alan Potkin, reported that the original diversion weir was designed to divert much more than 20% of the water from the *Houay* Samong. He also recognized that fish migrate right up to the headwaters of the *Houay* Samong, and that the stream is well known for supporting rich fish stocks and soft-shelled turtles (*pa fa ong* in Lao) (Alan Potkin, pers. comm. 2006). Despite his conclusions, or perhaps because of them, the World Bank rejected Potkin's work, including the interactive CD that he created to explain the various components of the project.

6
Forests and Livelihoods

[1] Unless otherwise noted, all local names of NTFPs are in Lao.

[2] Rosales et al. (2003) reported that the average annual income in Laos is estimated to be US$420/household, much higher than the Xekong provincial average.

[3] The exchange rate is about 35 baht per US$1.

[4] These were not amongst the communities resettled as a result of the Houay Ho dam (see Chapter 13).

[5] Berkmueller and Vilavong (2000) reported the largest malva nut tree, near Lao Nya Village, Pathoumphone District (outside the Xekong River Basin), as being of 293 cm in circumference.

[6] 120,000 m³ to be exported, and 30,000 m³ for local construction (GoL 2005).

[7] This road was previously called Route 18; the Americans referred to it as Route 110 (Van Staaveren 1993) (see also Chapter 11).

[8] The people from Ta-neum are officially registered as living in Salavan Province, but the village is, in fact, situated in Lamam District. The people are presently applying to be officially recognized as residing in Xekong Province.

7
Living Aquatic Resources and Livelihoods

[1] South Africa, Australia, and Switzerland are among the many countries that see common carp as a serious threat.

[2] Unless otherwise noted, all local names of fish, or '*pa*', and fishing-gears, are in Lao language.

[3] Bio-geographical barriers are places where fish cannot naturally pass.

[4] Some sources said the waterfall was as tall as 70 m high, but we were unable to confirm this.

[5] Also frequently referred to as *Pangasianodon gigas*.

[6] Villagers in Kiet Ngong, Phapho, Phalay Bok, Houay Mak, Toy, Cheung Houay, and other villages use this term.

[7] Villagers in Thong Say use this term.

[8] This species is not listed on Appendix II of CITES, as the species has declined throughout much of its range, and is internationally traded in large quantities.

8
Other Livelihoods in the Xekong River Basin

[1] <http://seakayaking-thailand.com/destinations/laos.htm>.

[2] Monsieur Ruhle, April 1894, Attopeu Report. Attopeu, 14, May 1894, CAOM Indochine 20941.

9
Biodiversity and Natural Resources
Management and Conservation

[1] Unless otherwise noted, all local names are in Lao.

[2] "National Protected Areas" (NPAs) were previously called "National Biodiversity Conservation Areas" (NBCAs). In Lao, they are called *pa sa-ngouan heng xat*.

[3] Phou Theung was previously a provincial protected area, as well as a proposed National Protected Area; however, it is now considered a Production Forest area (Ben Hodgdon, WWF, pers. comm. May 2005).

[4] Thailand, Laos, Cambodia, Malaysia, Indonesia, Vietnam, and the Philippines.

[5] In Laos, a "Production Forest" is officially considered to be a forest open to commercial logging operations.

⁶ This provincial protected area has recently been heavily logged with at least the tacit approval of government officials at some level in Laos and/or Cambodia.

10
Health, Nutrition, and Education

¹ Part per million.
² Monosodium Glutamate, *Wikipedia* 2007.

11
Transportation and Regional Integration

¹ Lt. Debay 1895. Exploration de la chaine d'Annam entre Tourane et Moung Lao–Attopeu. CAOM Indochine 6614.
² Sale, 1907. Message to Résident supérieur du Laos, 7 September 1907, Attopeu, CAOM Indochine 23831.
³ Debay 1895: 1.

12
Large-Scale Mining

¹ J. Morel 1913. Message regarding Attopeu gold concession, 16 June 1913, CAOM Indochine 2910.
² It is unclear if they are actually diamonds.
³ Résident supérieur du Laos. 1912. Message to Governor-General of Indochina, Vientiane, 12 May 1912, CAOM Indochine 2914.
⁴ The MWBP, terminated in late 2006, was a joint initiative of the IUCN, the UNDP, the MRC, the GEF, the Royal Netherlands Government, and the Water and Nature Initiative.

13
Electricity, Hydropower, and Rivers

¹ Laos is frequently cited as having the potential to generate 8,000 MW of hydro-electricity from just the mainstream Mekong River in Laos, and another 13,000 MW from its tributaries.
² Song Da Construction Corporation is well known in Vietnam for its lead role in constructing the Hoa Binh dam on the Red River in the north and the Yali Falls dam in Galai

Notes

Province on the Sesan River in the central highlands. It is Vietnam's largest hydroelectric company.

[3] The Xekaman 1,3 and 4 Dams, the Xekong 4 and 5 Dams, and the Xepian–Xenamnoi Dam.

[4] IRN (1999) estimated the cost of the project as being higher, at US$250 million.

[5] Electrowatt is now fully owned by the Finnish company, Jaakko Poyry.

[6] On 31 October 2003, Tractebel S. A. merged with Societe Generale de Belgique S. A. The name of the company created as a result of the merger is Suez-Tractebel S. A., a wholly owned subsidiary of Suez. It includes Suez International Energy and Tractebel Engineering.

[7] Hat Nyai Village is on the Xekong near the mouth of the Xepian.

[8] Rice and tubers mixed together is called "*khao meuat*" in Lao. Some groups of Katu people in Kalum District sometimes mix rice with sesame seeds.

[9] Hydroelectric Commission Enterprises Corporation (HECEC) was created by the Hydroelectric Corporation (HEC) of Tasmania, Australia, in 1987, and was designed to operate on a commercial basis overseas, especially targeting Asia and the Pacific Islands.

[10] There are two 100-m high waterfalls at *Nam Katam Tok*.

[11] Unless otherwise noted, all local names in this section are in Lao.

[12] LNCE (2003) states that the size of the dam is 70 MW, not 59 MW.

[13] This dam would be built in Sanxay district, Attapeu Province on the Xekaman River and is expected to have a capacity of 53 MW and to cost US$308 million to build (Ministry of Industry and Handicrafts 1994).

[14] This dam would be built on the Kong River in Phouvong District, Attapeu Province, and is expected to have a 30 MW capacity and to cost US$124 million to build (Ministry of Industry and Handicrafts 1994).

[15] This dam would be built on the Emun River in Xekong Province (JICA 1995) and was earlier expected to have a capacity of 23 MW and to cost US$122 million to build (Ministry of Industry and Handicrafts 1994).

References

Alexander, D. 1978. The introduction of modern medicine into a tribal village: The Loven of Dak Trang, Laos. Pp. 209-233. In Moser, R. R., and M. K. Gautam (eds.), *Aspects of Tribal Life in South Asia: Strategy and Survival*. Proceedings of an international seminar held in Berne, 1977.

Alton, C., and H. Ratannavong. 2004. Service delivery and resettlement: Options for development planning. Final report. Livelihoods study. Lao/03/A01, UNDP/ECHO, Vientiane.

Anonymous. 1911. *Historique de la province d'Attapeu*. Attapeu, 11 June 1911. 61 pp. +

Anonymous. 2000. Aspects of forestry management in the Lao PDR. *Watershed* 5(3): 57-64.

Anonymous. 2004a. Religious freedom in Laos: Persecution alongside progress. CSW USA reports.

Anonymous. 2004b. *Phongsavadan Nakhone Champasak*, 21 pp.

Anonymous. 2005. Newsletter/Review of 2004. National league of families of American prisoners and missing in Southeast Asia, 22 March.

Archaimbault, C. 1961. L'Histoire de Campasak, *Journal Asiatique* 294(4): 519-595.

Archaimbault, C. 1964. Religious structures in Laos. *J. of the Siam Soc*. 52(1): 57-74.

Archaimbault, C. 1972. *A Course de pirogues au Laos: Un Complexe culturel*. Ritbus Asiae Publishers, Ascona, Switzerland.

Asia Pulse. 2005. Korea's SK EandC in talks with Laos govt on hydroelectric plant. *Asia Pulse*, 20 July.

Asian Development Bank. 2001. *Participatory Poverty Assessment, Lao People's Democratic Republic*, Manila, 108 pp.

Asian Development Bank. 2003a. Technical assistance for the study for a regional power trade operating agreement in the Greater Mekong Subregion. Technical assistance report, ADB, Manila, 2 pp.

Asian Development Bank. 2003b. Resettlement and community development plan. Xaisetha-Sanxai road (Attapeu). Roads for rural development project (ADB TA-3756-Lao). ADB and Ministry of Communication, Transport, Post, and Construction, Vientiane, 131 pp.

Asian Development Bank and Government of Lao. 2004. Nam Theun 2. Cumulative impact analysis. Manila and Vientiane.

Australian Mekong Resource Center [AMRC]. 1998. Inventory of existing and planned hydropower dams on the Mekong River systems. AMRC, University of Sydney.

Aymonier, E. 1895. *Voyage dans le Laos*. Ernest Leroux, Paris, 2 vols.

Baird, I. G. 1994a. Freshwater fisheries, with special reference to *Probarbus jullieni* and *Probarbus labeamajor* in southern Lao PDR and northeastern Cambodia and the Fish trade between northeastern Cambodia, southern Lao PDR, and Thailand. TRAFFIC Southeast Asia, Kuala Lumpur, 30 pp.

Baird, I. G. 1994b. The trade in soft-shelled turtles (*Trionychididae*) between southern Lao PDR and Vietnam. TRAFFIC Southeast Asia, Kuala Lumpur.

Baird, I. G. 1995a. A rapid study of fish and fisheries; and livelihoods and natural resources along the Sesan River, Ratanakiri, Cambodia. Unpublished Livelihoods and Natural Resources Study report, Oxfam (UK and Ireland) and Novib, Ban Lung, Ratanakiri, Cambodia, 54 pp.

Baird, I. G. 1995b. Investigations of the Xekaman and Xexou Rivers, with special reference to freshwater fish and river ecology; and a review of the potential social and environmental impacts of large dam projects being considered for these two rivers in Attapeu Province, southern Lao PDR. Report prepared for the Protected Areas Division of the Dept. of Forestry, Vientiane.

Baird, I. G. 1995c. Lao PDR: An overview of traditional medicines derived from wild animals and plants. TRAFFIC Southeast Asia, Kuala Lumpur, 52 pp.

Baird, I. G. 2000. The ethnoecology, land-use, and livelihoods of the Brao-Kavet indigenous peoples in Kok Lak Commune, Voen Say District, Ratanakiri Province, northeast Cambodia. NTFP Project, Ban Lung, Ratanakiri, Cambodia.

Baird, I. G. 2001a. The ethnoecology and swidden agriculture system of the Brao-Kavet indigenous peoples of Ratanakiri Province, northeast Cambodia. Pp. 182-190. In *Shifting Cultivation: Towards Sustainability and Resource Conservation in Asia*. IFAD, IDRC, CIIFAD, ICRAF and IIRR, Cavite, Philippines.

Baird, I. G. 2001b. Aquatic biodiversity in the Siphandone Wetlands. Pp. 61-74. In Daconto, G. (ed.), *Siphandone Wetlands*. Environmental Protection and Community Development in Siphandone Wetland Project, CESVI, Pakse.

Baird, I. 2001c. A catchment approach to small-scale irrigation schemes in Lao PDR. *Watershed* 6(3): 36-41.

Baird, I. G. 2002. Laos. Pp. 291-299. In *The Indigenous World 2001-2002*. International Work Group for Indigenous Affairs, Copenhagen.

Baird, I. G. 2003a. Laos. Pp. 276-283. In *The Indigenous World 2002-2003*. International Work Group for Indigenous Affairs, Copenhagen.

Baird, I. G. 2003b. *Dipterocarpus* wood resin tenure, management and trade: Practices of the Brao in northeast Cambodia. MA thesis, Dept. of Geography, University of Victoria, Canada, 245 pp.+.

Baird, I. G. 2004. Laos. Pp. 269-275. In *The Indigenous World 2004*. International Work Group for Indigenous Affairs, Copenhagen.

Baird, I. G. 2005. Laos. Pp. 352-359. In *The Indigenous World 2005*. International Work Group for Indigenous Affairs, Copenhagen.

Baird, I. G. 2006a. Strength in diversity: Fish sanctuaries and deep-water pools in Laos. *Fisheries Management and Ecology* 13(1): 1-8.

Baird, I. G. 2006b. *Probarbus jullieni* and *Probarbus labeamajor*: The management and conservation of two of the largest fish species in the Mekong River in southern Laos. *Aquatic Conservation: Freshwater and Marine Ecosystems* 16(5): 517-532.

Baird, I. G. 2006c. Conducting rapid biology-based assessments using local ecological knowledge. *Nat. Hist. Bull. Siam Soc.* 54(2): 167-175.

Baird, I. G. 2006d. Laos. Pp. 338-346. In *The Indigenous World 2006*. International Work Group for Indigenous Affairs, Copenhagen.

Baird, I. G. 2007a. Fishes and forests: The importance of seasonally flooded riverine habitat for Mekong River fish species. *Nat. Hist. Bull. Siam Soc.* 55(1): 121-148.

Baird, I. G. 2007b. Local ecological knowledge and small-scale freshwater fisheries management in the Mekong River in southern Laos. Pp 247-266. In Haggan, N., B. Neis, and I. G. Baird (eds.), *Fishers' Knowledge in Fisheries Science and Management*. UNESCO, Paris.

Baird, I. G. 2007c. Contested history, ethnicity, and remembering the past: The case of the Ay Sa Rebellion in southern Laos. *Crossroads* 18(2): 119-159.

Baird, I. G. 2008a. The case of the Brao: Revisiting physical borders, ethnic identities, and spatial and social organization in the hinterlands of southern Laos and northeastern Cambodia. Pp. 595-620. In Goudineau, Y., and M. Lorrillard (eds.), *Recherches nouvelles sur le Laos*, Études thématiques No. 18, EFEO, Paris and Vientiane.

Baird, I. G. 2008b (In press). Controlling the margins: Nature conservation and state power in northeastern Cambodia. In Bourdier, F. (ed.). *Facing Development: From Interference to Survival among the Indigenous Populations in Cambodia, Laos, and Vietnam*. Silkworm Books, Chiang Mai.

References

Baird, I. G., K. Tubtim, and M. Baird. 1996. The Kavet and the Kreung: Observations of livelihoods and natural resources in two highlander villages in the districts of Veun Say and Ta Veng Ratanakiri Province, Cambodia, August 1996, Unpublished Livelihoods and Natural Resources Study report, Oxfam (UK and Ireland) and Novib, Ban Lung, Ratanakiri, Cambodia.

Baird, I. G., and B. Mounsouphom. 1997. Distribution, mortality, diet, and conservation of Irrawaddy dolphins (*Orcaella brevirostris* Gray) in Lao PDR. *Asian Marine Biology* 14: 41-48.

Baird, I. G., V. Inthaphaisy, P. Kisouvannalat, B. Phylaivanh, and B. Mounsouphom. 1999. *The Fishes of Southern Lao* [In Lao]. Lao Community Fisheries and Dolphin Protection Project, Ministry of Agriculture and Forestry, Pakse, 162 pp.

Baird, I. G., M. Baird, Chum Moni Cheath, Kim Sangha, Nuon Mekradee, Phat Sounith, Phouy Bun Nyok, Prom Sarim, Ros Savdee (Phiap), H. Rushton, and Sia Phen. 2002. A community-based study of the downstream impacts of the Yali Falls dam along the Se San, Sre Pok, and Sekong Rivers in Stung Treng Province, northeast Cambodia, Se San Protection Network Project, Partners for Development (PFD), Non Timber Forest Products Project (NTFP), Se San District Agriculture, Fisheries and Forestry Office, and Stung Treng District Office, Stung Treng, Cambodia.

Baird, I. G., M. S. Flaherty, and B. Phylavanh. 2003. Rhythms of the river: Lunar phases and migrations of small carps (Cyprinidae) in the Mekong River. *Nat. Hist. Bull. Siam Soc.* 51(1): 5-36.

Baird, I. G., and P. Dearden. 2003. Biodiversity conservation and resource tenure regimes—A case study from northeast Cambodia. *Environmental Management* 32(5): 541-550.

Baird, I. G., and S. Bounphasy. 2003. Non-timber forest product use, management, and tenure in Pathoumphone District, Champasak Province, Southern Laos. Remote Village Education Support Project, Global Association for People and the Environment, Pakse, 35 pp.

Baird, I. G., and M. S. Flaherty. 2004. Beyond national borders: important Mekong River medium-sized migratory carps (Cyprinidae) and fisheries in Laos and Cambodia. *Asian Fisheries Science* 17(3-4): 279-298.

Baird, I. G., M. S. Flaherty, and B. Phylavanh. 2004. Mekong River Pangasiidae catfish migrations and the Khone Falls wing trap fishery in southern Laos. *Nat. Hist. Bull. Siam Soc.* 52(1): 81-109.

Baird, I. G., and M. S. Flaherty. 2005. Mekong River fish conservation zones in southern Laos: Assessing effectiveness using local ecological knowledge. *Environmental Management* 36(3): 439-454.

Baird, I. G., and I. L. Beasley. 2005. Irrawaddy dolphin (*Orcaella brevirostris*) in the Mekong River in Cambodia: An initial survey. *Oryx* 39(3): 301-310.

Baird, I. G., and B. Shoemaker. 2005. *Aiding or Abetting? Internal Resettlement and International Aid Agencies in the Lao PDR*. Probe International, Toronto, 44 pp.

Bangkok Post. 2005. Oil spikes, coffee hits new highs. 30 May.

Banphet, T. 2005. Plans to reduce arsenic levels. *Vientiane Times*, 15 July 2005.

Baran, E., I. G. Baird, and G. Cans. 2005. *Fisheries Bioecology at the Khone Falls (Mekong River, Southern Laos)*. World Fish Center, Penang, 84 pp.

Baudenne, A. 1913. Les Khas de la region d'Attopeu. *Revue Indochinoise* 19(8): 260-274.

Baudenne, A. 1914. Les Khas de la region d'Attopeu. *Revue Indochinoise* 19(9): 421-443.

Berkmueller, K., and V. Vilavong. 2000. Laogna malva-nut survey trial. 28/2/00-1/2/00. Dong Houa Sao and Phou Xieng Thong NBCA Project. IUCN and the Forestry Section, Champasak Province, Pakse, 3 pp.

Bourotte, B. 1955. Essai d'historie des populations montagnards du Sud-Indochinois jusqu'au 1945. *Bull. de la Société des Études Indochinoises* 30(1), 116 pp.

Breazeale, K. 2002. Laos mapped by treaty and decree, 1895-1907. Pp. 297-336. In Ngaosrivathana, M., and K. Breazeale (eds.), *Breaking New Ground in Lao History: Essays on the Seventh to Twentieth Centuries*. Silkworm Books, Chiang Mai.

Briggs, L. P. 1949. The appearance and historical usage of the terms Tai, Thai, Siamese, and Lao. *J. of the American Oriental Society* 69(2): 60-73.

British Broadcasting Corporation. 2001. Work begins on Vietnam-Laos highway. 29 November.

Burchett, W. 1970. *The Second Indochina War: Cambodia and Laos*. International Publishers, New York, 204 pp.

Bush, S. R. 2004. A political ecology of living aquatic resources in Lao PDR. PhD thesis, School of Geosciences, University of Sydney, 359 pp.

Bush, S. 2005. Fish decline in the Sekong/Se San/Sre Pok River Basin: An introduction to its causes and remedies. Oxfam Australia, Victoria, Australia, 15 pp.

Bush, S. H., and P. Hirsch. 2005. Framing fishery decline. *Water Resources, Culture, and Development* 1(2): 79-90.

Cambodia Daily. 2005. US judge dismisses VN Agent Orange suit. *The Cambodia Daily*, Phnom Penh, 12-13 March: 2.

Cambodian Online. 2004. Vietnam, Laos, and Cambodia mull economic triangle, Phnom Penh, 23 July.

Chagnon, J. 2000. Xekong Indigenous People's Development Program. Inception report and extended program strategy. SIP-Dev, UNDP, Xekong.

Chamberlain, J., C. Alton, and A. Crisfield. 1996. Indigenous peoples profile, Lao PDR. Part 1 and 2, CARE International for the World Bank, Vientiane.

References

Chamberlain, J. 2001. Participatory poverty assessment, Lao PDR. ADB, SPC, National Statistics Center, Vientiane.

Chang, P. J. 2004. Laos denies charges of denying religious freedom. *The Christian Post*, San Francisco, 13 January.

Chaplot, V. 2005. How shifting cultivation limits runoff, sediment, and carbon losses on sloping land. *Juth Pakai* 3: 16-27.

Chazée, L. 1999. *The People of Laos: Rural and Ethnic Diversities*. White Lotus Press, Bangkok, 187 pp.

Chaeng Sokha. 2006. Well-water users show signs of arsenic poisoning. *Phnom Penh Post*, 21 September–5 October: 4.

Chhak, S. 1966. *Les Frontiers du Cambodge*. Dalloz, Paris, Tome 1, 179 pp.

Claridge, G. (comp.). 1996. *An Inventory of Wetlands of the Lao PDR*. Wetlands Program, IUCN—The World Conservation Union, Vientiane.

Claridge, G.F., T. Sorangkhoun, and I. G. Baird. 1997. *Community Fisheries in Lao PDR: A Survey of Techniques and Issues*. IUCN—The World Conservation Union, Vientiane, 70 pp.

Claassen, A. H. 2004. *Abundance, Distribution, and Reproduction Success of Sandbar Nesting Birds below the Yali Falls Hydropower Dam on the Sesan River, Northeastern Cambodia*. WWF/Danida/WCS/Birdlife International, Phnom Penh, Cambodia, 43 pp.

Coleman, M. 1995. Money and the Mekong: Australian hydro-electricity in Laos: A report prepared as an academic requirement for the B.Soc.Sc. in Socio-Environmental Assessment and Planning (SEAP), RMIT, Melbourne.

Conboy, K. (with James Morrison) 1995. *Shadow War: The CIA's Secret War in Laos*. Paladin Press, Boulder, CO, 454 pp.

Condominas, G. 1977. *We have Eaten the Forest: The Story of a Montagnard Village in the Central Highlands of Vietnam*. Hill and Wang, New York, 423 pp.

Condominas, G. 1990. *From Lawa to Mon from Saa' to Thai: Historical and Anthropological Aspects of Southeast Asia Social Spaces*. An Occasional Paper of the Dept. of Anthropology, RSPS, Australian National University, Canberra.

Costa-Pierce, B. A., J. Moreau, and R. S. V. Pullin. 1993. New introductions of common carp (*Cyprinus carpio*) and their impacts on indigenous species in Sub-Sahara Africa. *Discovery and Innovation* 5(3): 211-221.

Cunningham, P. 1998. Extending a co-management network to save the Mekong's giants. *Mekong River Catch and Culture*, Mekong River Commission, 3(3): 6-7.

Cupet, P. 1898. *The Pavie Mission Indochina Papers, 1879-1895. Vol. 6: Travels in Laos and among the Tribes of Southeast Indochina*. Trans. Walter E. J. Tips. 2000. White Lotus, Bangkok.

Daconto, G. (ed.). 2001. *Siphandone Wetlands*. CESVI, Bergamo, 192 pp.

Davenport, D., R. Tizard, and V. Phommavongsa. 1997. *Trip report: Ban Mai*. Wildlife Conservation Society, Vientiane.

Daviau, S. 2001. *Resettlement in Long District, Louang Namtha Province*, Action contre la faim, Lao PDR.

Daviau, S. 2003a. *Cultural and Technical Study of Traditional Animal Husbandry, Kalum District, Xekong Province, Lao PDR*. Action contre la faim, Vientiane, 46 pp.

Daviau, S. 2003b. *Resettlement in Long District, Louang Namtha Province. Update 2003*. Action contre la faim, Vientiane, 36 pp.

Davidson, P., W. G. Robichaud, R. J. Tizard, C. Vongkhamheng, and J. Wolstencroft. 1997. *A Wildlife and Habitat Survey of Dong Ampham NBCA and Phou Kathong Proposed NBCA, Attapeu Province, Lao PDR*, CPAWM/WCS, Vientiane.

De Malglaive, J. 1893. Six mois au pays des Khas. *Le Tour du Monde* 25: 385-411.

De Moor, I. J. 1996. Case studies of the invasion of four alien fish species (*Cyprinus carpio, Micropterus salmoides, Oreochromis macrochirus* and *O. mossambicus*) of freshwater ecosystems in southern Africa. *Trans. Roy. S. Afr.* 51: 233-255.

Defense Prisoner of War/Missing Personal Office. 2005. *Progress in Laos as of February 7, 2005*. Office of the Assistant Secretary of Defense/International Security Affairs, Washington, DC.

Dept. of Electricity. 2004. List of hydropower projects in the Sekong Basin. Power System Division, Dept. of Electricity, Ministry of Industry and Handicrafts, Vientiane.

Dommen, Arthur J. 1971. *Conflict in Laos: The Politics of Neutralization* (revised edn.). Praeger Publishers, New York and London, 454 pp.

Dommen, Arthur J. 1985. *Laos: Keystone of Indochina*. Westview Press, Boulder, CO, 182 pp.

Dow Jones. 2001. S Korea Daewoo Eng sells Laos pwr plant stake to Dutch co., 13 September.

Duckworth, J. W., R. E. Salter, and K. Khounboline (comps.). 1999. *Wildlife in Lao PDR: 1999 Status Report*. IUCN — The World Conservation Union/ Wildlife Conservation Society/Center for Protected Areas and Watershed Management, Vientiane, 275 pp.

Ducourtieux, O. 2004. Shifting cultivation and poverty eradication: a complex issue. Paper presented at the Conference on Poverty Reduction and Shifting Cultivation Stabilization in the Uplands of Lao PDR: Technologies, approaches, and methods for improving upland livelihoods, NAFRI and Lao-Swedish Uplands Agriculture and Forestry Research Program, Luang Prabang, 27-30 January 2004.

Dwernychuk, L. W., H. D. Cau, C. T. Hatfield, T. G. Boivin, T. M. Hung, P. T. Dung, and N. D. Thai. 2002. Dioxin reservoirs in southern Viet Nam—A legacy of Agent Orange. *Chemosphere* 47: 117-137.

References

Eckhardt, J.G. 1999. Ground interdiction of the Ho Chi Minh Trail was the 1st special guerilla unit's reason for being. *Vietnam* 12(1): 18-21.

Electricité du Laos. 2003. Country report: Current developments of power sector in the Lao PDR. Paper presented at Group Training Course in Hydropower Resources Development and Management, Trondheim, Norway, 2-19 June 2003. <www.ich.no/kurs/hdiwrm2003/Laos_Presentation.pdf>.

Emerson, B. (ed.) 1997. The natural resources and livelihood study, Ratanakiri Province, northeast Cambodia. The Non-Timber Forest Products (NTFP) Project, Ban Lung, Ratanakiri, Cambodia.

Engelbert, T. 2001. Sudlaos. Historisch-ethnographische Regionalstudie. Teil 1. Die provinz Attapeu. Laos Projekt Publikationen Nr. 4, Berlin University, 85 pp.

Engelbert, T. 2004. From hunters to revolutionaries: The mobilization of ethnic minorities in Southern Laos and northeastern Cambodia during the First Indochina War (1945-54). Pp. 225-270. In Engelbert, T., and H. Dieter Kubitscheck, *Ethnic Minorities and Politics in Southeast Asia*, Peter Lang, Frankfurt am Main.

EPDC. 2005. Se Katam, Lao PDR. <www.jpower.co.jp/english/international/consultation/detail/se_as_laos01.pdf.>.

Evans, G. 1998. *The Politics of Ritual and Remembrance: Laos since 1975*. Silkworm Books, Chiang Mai.

Evans, G. 1999. Ethnic change in highlands Lao. Pp. 124-147 in Grant Evans (eds.), *Laos: Culture and Society*. Silkworm Books, Chiang Mai.

Evans, T. D., K. Sengdala, O. V. Viengkham, and B. Thammavong. 2001. *A Field Guide of the Rattans of Lao PDR*. Royal Botanic Gardens, Kew, 96 pp.

Evrard, O., and Y. Goudineau. 2004. Planned resettlement, unexpected migrations, and cultural trauma in Laos. *Development and Change* 35(5): 937-962.

Fernando, C. H. 1991. Impacts of fish introductions in tropical Asia and America. *Can. J. Fish. Aquat. Sci.* 48 (Suppl. 1): 24-32.

Financial Times. 2001. Tractebel, Thai partner acquire 80 pct stake in hydro project for 140 mln usd. AFX Europe, 14 September.

Fisheries Office, Ratanakiri Province and NTFP Project. 2000. A study of the downstream impacts of the Yali Falls dam in the Se San River Basin in Ratanakiri Province, northeast Cambodia. Ban Lung, Ratanakiri Province, Cambodia, 66 pp.

FOMACOP. 2000. Xe Pian National Biodiversity Conservation Area Management Plan. Forest Management and Conservation Program, Vientiane.

Foppes, J., and T. Saypaseuth. 1996. Field report No. 1: On trip to Soukhouma and Pathoumphon Districts, 30-1 to 2-2, 1996. Champasak Field Team. Unpublished report prepared for the Non-Timber Forest Products (NTFP) Project, Pakse, Lao PDR, IUCN—The World Conservation Union and the Dept. of Forestry, Pakse.

Foppes, J., T. Saypaseuth, K. Sengkeo, and S. Chantilat. 1997. The use of non-timber forest products on the Nakai Plateau: Report on a short mission from 26/2 to 30/3 1997 prepared for NTEC, Thakek, Khammouan Province, Lao PDR.

Forestry Research Center and the Global Association for People and the Environment. 2005. Report on the study of positive and negative aspects of harvesting nyang oil [In Lao]. Vientiane, 16 pp.

Fox, J., D. M. Truong, A. T. Rambo, N. P. Tuyen, L. T. Cuc, and S. Leisz. 2000. Shifting cultivation: A new old paradigm for managing tropical forests. *BioScience* 50(6): 521-528.

Freyhof, J. 2003. S*ewellia albisera*, a new balitorid loach from Central Vietnam (Cypriniformes: Balitoridae). *Ichthyol. Explor. Freshwaters* 14(3): 225-230.

Garaway, C. 1995. Women in fisheries and aquaculture development in Lao PDR. Renewable Resource Assessment Group, Imperial College, London.

Garrett, B. 2005. Executive summary of the report, Power trade operating agreement scheme in the Greater Mekong Sub-region creates consumer risks. Report Commissioned for Palang Thai (Thailand), Bangkok, 2 pp.

Gonzales, G,. E. Diaz-Boreal, and P. Cottavoz. 2005. Lao PDR: Is resettlement a solution for human development? Action contre la faim, Vientiane, 33 pp.

Goudineau, Y. (ed). 1997. Resettlement and social characteristics of new villages. Basic needs for resettled communities in the Lao PDR. An Ostrom survey. Vols. 1-2, Supported by UNDP and UNESCO, Vientiane.

Goudineau, Y. 2001. A brief note on ethnicity in Sekong. Consultant report. ORSTOM/ UNDP. Sip-Dev, Sekong.

Government of Lao PDR. 1998. *The Rural Development Program 1998-2002 The Focal Site Strategy. Outline of an Approach. Program Support and Investment Requirements.* 6th Round Table Follow-Up Meeting, Vientiane, 13 May 1998.

Government of Lao PDR. 2005. Order of Prime Minister on forest management and forest business. PM Order 25, Vientiane.

Grabowsky, V. 1997. Lao and Khmer perceptions of national survival: The legacy of the early nineteenth century. Pp. 145-165. In Kuhnt-Saptodewo, S., V. Grabowsky, and M. Grobheim (eds.), *Nationalism and Cultural Revival in Southeast Asia: Perspectives from the Center and the Region*, Harrassowitz Verlag, Wiesbaden.

Grabowsky, V. 2004. The Thai and Lao ethnic minorities in Cambodia: Their history and their fate after decades of warfare and genocide. Pp. 197-224. In Engelbert, T., and

References

H. Dieter Kubitscheck, *Ethnic Minorities and Politics in Southeast Asia*, Peter Lang, Frankfurt am Main.

Greacen, C. 2005. A gamble that leaves us holding the bill. *Bangkok Post*, 30 June.

Gregory R., H. Guttman, and T. Kekputherith. 1996. Poor in all but fish: A study of the collection of ricefield foods from three villages in Svay Theap District, Svay Rieng. *Working Paper*, No. 5. AIT Aquaculture Outreach (Cambodia), Phnom Penh.

Guérin, M. 2001. Essartage et riziculture humide. Complementarité des ecosystems agraires à Stung Treng au début du XX siècle. *Aseanie* 8: 35-56.

Gunn, G. C. 1988. *Political Struggles in Laos (1930-1954): Vietnamese Communist Power and the Lao Struggle for National Independence*. Duang Kamol, Bangkok, 325 pp.

Gunn, G. C. 1990. *Rebellion in Laos: Peasant and Politics in a Colonial Backwater*. Westview Press, Boulder, 224 pp.

Gutteridge, Haskins, and Davey Pte, Ltd.. 1994 (Draft). Initial environmental examination of the Xekaman No.1 and Southern transmission project. Hydroelectric Commission Enterprises Corp., Australian-Lao Hydro and Transmission Projects, Vientiane.

Haggan, N., B. Neis, and I. G. Baird (eds.), *Fishers' Knowledge in Fisheries Science and Management*. UNESCO, Paris, 437 pp.

Halcrow, Sir William, and Partners [Halcrow]. 1999. Se Kong, Se San and Nam Theun River Basins' hydropower study. Final report. ADB, Manila.

Hall, D. G. E. 1981 (4th edn). *A History of South-East Asia*. St. Martin's Press, New York, 1070 pp.

Harclerode, P. 2001. *Fighting Dirty: The Inside Story of Covert Operations from Ho Chi Minh to Osama Bin Laden*. Cassell and Co., London, 625 pp.

Hardy, Andrew. 2003. *Red Hills: Migrants and the State in the Highlands of Vietnam*. Nordic Institute of Asian Studies, Copenhagen, 359 pp.

Harmand, F. J. 1997. *Laos and the Hilltribes of Indochina: Journeys to the Boloven Plateau, From Bassac to Hue through Laos, and to the Origins of the Thai*. Translation of *Le Laos et les populations sauvages de L'Indochine* in *Le Tour du Monde*, 1878-79, Paris, by. Walter E. J. Tips, White Lotus Press, Bangkok.

Hassanin, A., A. Seveau, H. Thomas, H. Bocherens, D. Billiou, and Bui Xan Nguyen. 2001. Evidence from DNA that the mysterious "*linh duong*" (*Pseudonovibos spiralis*) is not a new bovid. *Comptes-Rendus de l'Académie des Sciences*, série III, Sciences de la vie, 324: 71-80.

Hickey, G. 1982. *Sons of the Mountains: Ethnohistory of the Vietnamese Central Highlands to 1954*. Yale University Press, New Haven, CT.

Hirsch, P. 2004. The politics of fisheries knowledge in the Mekong River Basin. Pp. 93-102.

In Welcomme, R. L., and T. Petr (eds.), *Proceedings of the Second International Symposium on the Management of Large Rivers for Fisheries, Vol. II.* FAO Regional Office for Asia and the Pacific, Bangkok. RAP Publication 2004/17.

Hirsch, P., and A. Wyatt. 2004. Negotiating local livelihoods: Scales of conflict in the Se San River Basin. *Asia Pacific Viewpoint* 45(1): 51-68.

Hoffet, J. F. 1933.Les Mois de la chaine annamitique entre Tourane et les Boloven. *Terre Air Mer La Géographie* 59(1): 1-43.

Hogan, Z. S., P. B. Moyle, B. May, M. J. Vander Zanden, and I. G. Baird. 2004. The imperiled giants of the Mekong. Ecologists struggle to understand—and protect—Southeast Asia's large migratory catfish. *American Scientist* 92 (May-June): 228-237.

Hogan, Z., I. G. Baird, R. Radtke, and J. Vander Zanden. 2007. Long distance migration and marine habitation in the Asian Catfish, *Pangasius krempfi. J. of Fish Biology* 71: 818-832.

Hortle, K., P. Ngor, R. Hem, and S. Lieng. 2005. Tonle Sap yields record haul. *Catch and Culture*, Mekong River Commission, 11(1): 3-7.

Hubbel, D., and B. Phongphichit. 2006. Evaluation of the Global Association for People and the Environment. GAPE, Pakse.

Hours, B. 1973. Les rites de defense chez les Lave du Sud Laos. *Asie du Sud-est et Monde Insulindien* 4(3): 31-60.

Images Asia Environment Desk and Pan Kachin Development Society. 2004. At what price? Gold mining in Kachin State, Burma. Images Asia, Chiang Mai, 63 pp.

Institute for Cultural Research. 2005. *Folk Tools of Ethnic Groups of Sekong.* Japan Foundation Asia Center and the Ministry of Information and Culture, Vientiane, 225 pp.

International Christian Concern. 2004. Prayer point, 17 March 2004, Washington, DC.

International Fund for Agricultural Development [IFAD]. 2005. Executive board—84th session, agenda item 9, EB 2005/84/R.9/Add.1, Rome, 18-20 April 2005, 3 pp.

International Rivers Network. 1999. *Power Struggle: The Impacts of Hydro-Development in Laos.* IRN, Berkeley, CA.

International Rivers Network. 2003. Trading away the future. The Mekong power grid. IRN, Berkeley, CA, 4 pp.

International Rivers Network. 2004a. Sizing up the grid: How the Mekong power grid compares against policies of the Asian Development Bank. IRN, Berkeley, CA, 14 pp.

International Rivers Network. 2004b. The legacy of hydro in Laos. IRN, Berkeley, CA, 4 pp.

International Rivers Network. 2006. Trading away the future: The Mekong power grid. IRN, Berkeley, CA, 4 pp.

References

International Water Power and Dam Construction. 2005. Vietnam to invest in Laos. *International Water Power and Dam Construction*, 8 December.

International Water Power and Dam Construction. 2006. Xekaman 1 agreement signed. *International Water Power and Dam Construction*, 2 November.

International Water Power and Dam Construction. 2007. Asia banks agree finance deal for Sekaman, *International Water Power and Dam Construction*, 2 August.

Ironside, J., and I. G. Baird. 2003. Wilderness and cultural landscape: Settlement, agriculture, and land and resource tenure in and adjacent to Virachey National Park, northeast Cambodia. Biodiversity and Protection Area Management Project, Ministry of Environment, Ban Lung, Ratanakiri, Cambodia.

Japan International Cooperation Agency. 1995. Master plan study on hydroelectric power development in the Se Kong Basin in the Lao People's Democratic Republic. Final report. Summary. Electric Power Development Co., Ltd., New Jec, Inc., and Pasco International, Inc., Tokyo and Osaka.

Japan International Cooperation Agency. 1999. Hydrological data book. Interim report. Vientiane.

Jones, P. (coordinator) 2002. Existing land tenure and forest lands study, by Lao Consulting Group, for Ministry of Finance, Dept. of Lands, Land Titling Project IDA Loan CR 2832 LA, May 2002, Vientiane, 77 pp.

Jonsson, H. 1997. Cultural priorities and projects: health and social dynamics in northeast Cambodia. Pp. 536-567. In McCaskill, D., and K. Kampe (eds.), *Development or Domestication? Indigenous Peoples of Southeast Asia*. Silkworm Books, Chiang Mai.

Jonsson, T. 2006. Control of timber production. Sustainable Forestry and Rural Development Project—Lao PDR, Vientiane.

Jumsai, M. L. M. 2000 (4th edn). *History of Laos* (including history of Lannathai and Chiangmai). Chalermnit, Bangkok, 288 pp.

Keovichit, L. 2004. Xekong Province facing a difficult year, *Vientiane Times*, 24 December.

Keyes, C. F. 1977. Millennialism, Theravada Buddhism, and Thai society. *J. of Asian Studies* 36(2): 283-302.

Khamin, Nok. 2000. More trouble for the Heuny. *Indigenous Affairs* 4: 22-29.

Khao San Pathet Lao. 2003a. Sekong to be linked to Vietnam by two roads. Vientiane, 22 January.

Khao San Pathet Lao. 2003b. Tractebel invests in Houay Ho dam, Vientiane.

Khao San Pathet Lao. 2003c. Production of electricity for export to Vietnam is on plan. Vientiane, 24 October.

Khao San Pathet Lao. 2006. Korean investor invests in hydro power development. Vientiane, 7 August.

Kokkoris, C. P. 2004. "Agent Orange" product liability litigation. Amended class action complaint filed in the United States District Court, Eastern District of New York by the plaintiffs, "The Vietnamese Association for the Victims of Agent Orange/Dioxin" against the defendants, 36 companies that produced herbicides used during the Vietnam War, 10 September 2004, New York, NY.

Kottelat, M. 2000. Diagnoses of a new genus and 64 new species of fishes of Laos (Teleostei: Cyprinidae, Balitoridae, Bagridae, Syngnathidae, Chaudhuriidae and Tetraodontidae). *J. South Asian Nat. Hist.* 5: 37-82.

Kottelat, M. 2001. *The Fishes of Laos.* WHT Publications (Pte), Ltd., Colombo.

Krahn, J. 2003. Dietary change in Lao upland kitchen. *Juth Pakai, New Thought*, UNDP, 1: 4-14.

Kyoto News. 2005. Kansai electric to build hydroelectric power plant in Laos. 10 June.

Lamb, A. 1968. *Asian Frontiers: Studies in a Continuing Problem.* Pall Mall Press, London, 245 pp.

Lang, C. 2002. *The Pulp Invasion: The International Pulp and Paper Industry in the Mekong Region.* World Rainforest Movement, Montevideo, 220 pp.

Lang, C. 2003. Laos: Vietnamese consortium plans to build six dams in Laos. *World Rainforest Bulletin*, No. 74.

Lang, C. 2006. Laos: FSC certified timber is illegal. *World Rainforest Bulletin*, No. 110.

Lao Consulting Group. 2003. Food security for Xekong Province: Market survey. Action contre la faim, European Union, and Lao Consulting Group, Vientiane.

Lao Front for National Construction. 2005. The ethnic groups in Lao PDR. Dept. of Ethnics, Lao Front for National Construction, Vientiane, 271 pp.

Lao Nation Committee for Energy. 2003. Power sector strategy study. Ministry of Industry and Handicrafts, Vientiane.

Lao National Mekong Committee. 2004. Report on the outcomes of studies and analysis carried out in sub-area 7L. In MRC Basin Development Plan (BDP). <www.mekong-info.org/mrc_en/home.nsf/0/DEB6A96EB78BD437472566BA003EB130/$FILE/BDP_DOCLIST.htm>.

Lao Revolutionary Party, Political Central Committee. 2004. Instruction order on creation of village and group of village development, 09/PCC, 8 June, Vientiane.

Latsaphao, K. 2004. Boat races in Attapeu. *Vientiane Times*, 2 November.

References

Latsaphao, K. 2005a. Women's rights in agriculture. *Vientiane Times*, 27 April: 2.

Latsaphao, K. 2005b. Houay Ho Hydropower may upgrade to 24-hour production. *Vientiane Times*, 24 October.

Latsaphao, K. 2005c. Farmers owe 19 billion kip to EdL. *Vientiane Times*, 2 November.

Latsaphao, K. 2006a. More electricity for Attapeu. *Vientiane Times*, 13 April.

Latsaphao, K. 2006b. UXO kills two in Attapeu. *Vientiane Times*, 26 April.

Latsaphao, K. 2007. Villagers agree to aluminum factory in Xekong. *Vientiane Times*, 3 August.

LeBar, F. M, G. C. Hickey, and J. K. Musgrave. 1964. *Ethnic Groups of Mainland Southeast Asia*. Human Relations Area Files Press, New Haven, CT, 288 pp.

Leukai, X. 2005. Xekong rice below target. *Vientiane Times*, 21 April: 2.

Liepvisay, N., and K. Vongpanolom. 1997. The role of women in capture fisheries and aquaculture in Lao PDR. Paper presented at the Workshop on National Fisheries Institute and Aquatic Resource Research in Lao PDR, 19-21/03/97, Vientiane.

Ling, S. 1999. A biological system of prioritization for protected areas in Laos. Wildlife Conservation Society, Vientiane, 35 pp.

Long, T. 1890. *Kham hai kan reuang Muang Attapeu* [In Thai]. Bangkok.

Lyttleton, C., and H. Rattanavong. 2004. Watermelons, bars, and trucks: Dangerous intersections in northwest Lao PDR. Institute for Cultural Research and Macquarie University, Vientiane, 118 pp.

Maître, H. 1912. *Mission Henri Maître (1909-1911) Indochine Sud-Centrale: Les Jungles Moi*. Émile Larose, Libraire-Editeur, Paris, 575 pp.

Maunsell and Lahmeyer. 2004. Power system development plan for Lao PDR: A report prepared for the Ministry of Industry and Handicrafts and the World Bank. Maunsell, Ltd., Auckland, New Zealand. <www.poweringprogress.org/energy_sector/power_system_dev_vol_a.htm>.

Mekong Wetland Biodiversity Project, Attapeu Provincial Science Technology and Environmental Office. 2005. Gold mining in Attapeu. Attapeu, 2 pp.

Mendoza, V. S. 2005a. A fisheries project by the people. *Vientiane Times*, 18 May: 2.

Mendoza, V. S. 2005b. Attapeu celebrates Wildlife Conservation Day. *Vientiane Times*, 14 July.

Meusch, E., J. Yhoung-Aree, R. Friend, and S. J. Funge-Smith. 2003. The role and nutritional value of aquatic resources in the livelihoods of rural people: A participatory assessment in Attapeu Province, Lao PDR. FAO Regional Office Asia and the Pacific, Bangkok, Publication No. 2003/11, 37 pp.

MIDAS Agronomics Co., Ltd. 1998. Land-forest allocation in protected areas in the Lao

PDR: Issues and options. Unpublished report prepared for the Forest Management and Conservation Project Conservation Sub-Program. MIDAS Agronomics Co., Ltd, Vientiane, 36 pp.

Ministry of Agriculture and Forestry and Science, Technology, and Environment Agency. 2003. *Biodiversity Profile for Attapeu Province.* Vientiane, 66 pp.

Ministry of Agriculture and Forestry and Science, Technology, and Environment Agency. 2004. *Biodiversity Country Report.* Vientiane, 151 pp.

Ministry of Industry and Handicrafts, Lao PDR. 1994. Lao PDR planned hydroelectric dam projects, Ministry of Industry and Handicrafts, Vientiane.

Ministry of Environment, Cambodia. 2003. Virachey National Park management plan 2003-07. Phnom Penh.

Mixab, P. 2005. ADP reviews its Khammuan work. *Vientiane Times,* 5 May.

Mole, R. L. 1970. *The Montagnards of South Vietnam: A Study of Nine Tribes.* Charles E. Tuttle Co., Rutland, Vermont and Tokyo, 277 pp.

Mollot, R., C. Photitay, and S. Kosy. 2005. Hydrology, habitat and livelihoods on the floodplains of southern Lao PDR. Pp. 155-176. In Burnhill, T. J., and M. M. Hewitt (eds.), *Proceedings of the 6th Technical Symposium on Mekong Fisheries,* 26-28 November 2003, Mekong River Commission, Vientiane.

My, Nguyen Quang. 1999. The on-going environmental and health impacts of war. National University of Hanoi, 5 pp.

Na Champasak, S. 1995. *Pavat Nakhonekalachampak Nakhabouri Sisattanakhanahout (Nakhone Champasak)* [In Lao]. Paris, 144 pp. +

Nash, S. V. (ed.) 1997. *Fin, Feather, Scale, and Skin: Observations on the Wildlife in Lao PDR and Vietnam.* TRAFFIC Southeast Asia, Petaling Jaya, Selangor, Malaysia.

Naval Intelligence Division. 1943. *Indo-China: Geographical Handbook.* Series for Official Use Only, US Government Printing Office, Washington, DC, 535 pp.

Nooren, H., and G. Claridge. 2001. *Wildlife Trade in Laos: The End of the Game.* Netherlands Committee for IUCN, Amsterdam.

Norconsult 2007a. Environmental impact assessment (EIA) of the reservoir impoundment for the Se Kong-4 HEP. Synopsis of the initial environmental examination. Vientiane, 17 pp.

Norconsult 2007b. Environmental impact assessment (EIA) of the reservoir impoundment for the Nam Kong-1 HEP. Synopsis of the initial environmental examination. Vientiane, 18 pp.

Ngaosrivathana, M., and K. Breazeale (eds). 2002. *Breaking New Ground in Lao History: Essays on the Seventh to Twentieth Centuries.* Silkworm Books, Chiang Mai, 383 pp.

References

Ngaosyvathn, M., and P. Ngaosyvathn. 1998. *Paths to Conflagration: Fifty Years of Diplomacy and Warfare in Laos, Thailand, and Vietnam, 1778-1828*. Southeast Asia Program Publications, Cornell University, Ithaca, NY, 270 pp.

Osborne, M. 2000. *The Mekong: Turbulent Past, Uncertain Future*. Atlantic Monthly Press, New York, 295 pp.

Oxfam America. 2004. Small-scale gold mining in Cambodia: A situation assessment. Oxfam America, Phnom Penh.

Oxfam America and Oxfam Australia [OA and OA]. 2005. Inventory and GIS resource of river based developments in the Sekong, Sesan, and Srepok River Basins. Phnom Penh.

Pacific Consultations International (in association with Burapha and CDRI). 2000. Rural access roads improvement project. Pp. 85-90. In Environmental Impact Assessment Report, Dept. of Roads, Ministry of Communication, Transport, Post, and Construction, Vientiane.

Pansivongsay, M. 2005a. Revenue collection down. *Vientiane Times*, 16 May.

Pansivongsay, M. 2005b. Forests crucial for life. *Vientiane Times*, 25 May: 6.

Pansivongsay, M. 2006a. FDI pours into Xekong. *Vientiane Times*, 14 March.

Pansivongsay, M. 2006b. Xekong plans integrated development zone. *Vientiane Times*, 20 March.

Pathet Lao. 2002. Houay Ho hydropower station runs into problems. *Pathet Lao Daily newspaper*, Vientiane, 20 February.

Phengphachan, V. 2005. Trees planting drive on Arbor Day. *Vientiane Times*, 19 May: 2.

Phengphachan, V. 2006. Attapeu poor given food for work. *Vientiane Times*, 14 February.

Phnom Penh Post. 2005. Lao military agrees to leave Cambodian soil. 11-24 March.

Phann, A., and C. Purtill. 2004. Wanderers emerge from life of constant fear. *Cambodia Daily*, Phnom Penh, 10 December: 1, 16.

Phiapalath, P., M. K. Poulsen, and K. Luanglath. 2001. Siamese crocodile in Bung Khe, Attapeu Province in Lao PDR. Report to Xepian NBCA Project, Pakse.

Pholsena, V. 2006. *Post-War Laos: The Politics of Culture, History, and Identity*. Cornell University Press, Ithaca, NY, 255 pp.

Phonpachit, S. 2005a. Govt to inject almost 10 billion kip in Xekong. *Vientiane Times*, 29 September.

Phonpachit, S. 2005b. Laos targets electricity export to Vietnam. *Vientiane Times*, 30 December.

Phonpachit, S. 2006. China assists mining sector in Laos. *Vientiane Times*, 21 April: 7.

Phothitay, C., and Somphanith. 2003. Crocodile survey report of wetland areas in Savannakhet and Attapeu Provinces. Living Aquatic Resources Research Center, National Agriculture and Forestry Research Institute, Ministry of Agriculture and Forestry. Vientiane, 18 pp.

Phouthonesy, E. 2004. Dam construction to power export plans. *Vientiane Times*, 27 February.

Phouthonesy, E. 2005a. Xekong-Quang relations enhanced. *Vientiane Times*, 17 May: 2.

Phouthonesy, E. 2005b. Govt moves to conserve forests. *Vientiane Times*, 12 October: 1.

Phommvihane, K. 1981. *Revolution in Laos.* Progressive Publishers, Moscow, 255 pp.

Pongkhao, S. 2003. Oye people keep tradition alive with music. *Vientiane Times*, 4-6 March.

Porter, M. F. 1971. The defense of Attopeu. HQ PACAF, Tactical Evaluation Center. Project Checo Report. Project Contemporary Historical Examination of Current Operation Report. Washington, DC.

Poulsen, M. K., and K. Luanglath. 2005. Projects come, projects go: Lessons from participatory monitoring in southern Laos. *Biodiversity and Conservation* 14: 2591-2610.

Prescott, J. R. V. 1975. *Map of Mainland Asia by Treaty.* Melbourne University Press, 518 pp.

Prime Minister's Office. 2002. Order of the Prime Minister regarding occupations and determining permanent settlements for the people. 04/NY, 12 April, Vientiane.

Raffles, H. 2002. Intimate knowledge. *International J. of Soc. Sci.* 173: 325-335.

Rathie, M. 2001 (draft). Siamese domination of the Lao-Cambodian frontier region. Paper presented at Australian National Thai Studies Conference, RMIT, Melbourne, 12-13 July.

Reuters. 2003a. Vietnam signs hydro deal in Laos. Hanoi, 28 July.

Reuters. 2003b. Vietnam eyes five hydropower plants in Laos. Hanoi, 4 August.

Riseborough, J. 2006. Ord river flags Lao bauxite project potential. *Mining News*, 16 November 2006.<www.miningnews.net/storyView.asp?StoryID=68947>.

Roberts, T. R. 1993. Artisinal [*sic*] fisheries and fish ecology below the great waterfalls of the Mekong River in southern Laos. *Nat. Hist. Bull. Siam Soc.* 41: 31-62.

Roberts, T. R. 1994. *Osphronemus exodon*, a new species of giant gouramy with extraordinary dentition from the Mekong. *Nat. Hist. Bull. Siam Soc.* 42: 67-77.

Roberts, T. R. 1995 *Botia splendida*, a new species of loach (Pisces: Cobitidae) from the Mekong Basin in Laos. *Raffles Bull. Zool.* 43: 463-467.

Roberts, T. R. 1997. *Serpenticobitis*, a new genus of cobitid fishes from the Mekong Basin, with two new species. *Nat. Hist. Bull. Siam Soc.* 45: 107-115.

References

Roberts, T. R. 1998a. Review of the tropical Asian cyprinid fish genus *Poropuntius*, with descriptions of new species and trophic morphs. *Nat. Hist. Bull. Siam Soc.* 46: 105-135.

Roberts, T. R. 1998b. Systematic revision of the balitorid loach genus *Sewellia* of Vietnam and Laos, with diagnoses of four new species. *Raffles Bull. Zool.* 46: 271-288.

Roberts, T. R., and I. G. Baird. 1995a. Traditional fisheries and fish ecology on the Mekong River at Khone Waterfalls in southern Laos. *Nat. Hist. Bull. Siam Soc.* 43: 219-262.

Roberts, T. R., and I. G. Baird. 1995b. Rapid assessment of fish and fisheries for the Xenamnoi-Xepian hydroscheme in southern Lao PDR. Unpublished report for the Wildlife Conservation Society, Vientiane.

Roberts T. R., and T. J. Warren. 1994. Observations on fishes and fisheries in southern Laos and northeastern Cambodia, October 1993-February 1994. *Nat. Hist. Bull. Siam Soc.* 42: 87-115.

Robichaud, W, C. W. Marsh, S. Southamakoth, and S. Khounthikoummane. 2001. Review of national protected areas system in Lao PDR. Lao–Swedish Forestry Program, Division of Forest Resource Conservation, Vientiane, 136 pp.

Rosales, R. M. P., M. F. Kallesoe, P. Gerrard, P. Muangchanh, S. Phomtavong, and S. Khamsomphou. 2003. The economic returns from conserving natural forests in Xekong, Lao PDR. Lower Mekong Eco-regions Technical Paper Series, No. 1, Lao National Mekong Committee, MAF, NERI, Belgium Embassy, IUCN, DFID and WWF, Vientiane, 92 pp.

Sakdavong, K. 2004a. Hydropower bringing in the investors. *Vientiane Times*, 30 July.

Sakdavong, K. 2004b. Japan to invest in southern Xekatam dam. *Vientiane Times*, 1 October.

Savada, A. M. 1995. *Laos: A Country Study*. Federal Research Division, Library of Congress, Bernan, Lanham, Maryland, 336 pp.

Sayboualaven, P. 2004. Hydroelectric dams and the forgotten people of the Boloven Plateau. *Watershed* 10(1): 52-59.

Schaller, G. 1995. A wildlife survey in the Annamite Mountains of Laos. Unpublished Field Report, Wildlife Conservation Society, Vientiane.

Schaller, G. and Bounsou. 1996. A preliminary survey of the northern Xe Sap region, Salavan Province, 25 April-11 May, Wildlife Conservation Society, Vientiane.

Scott, J. C. 1985. *Weapons of the Weak: Everyday Forms of Peasant Resistance*. Yale University Press, New Haven, CT, 389 pp.

Sentho, V. 2006. Vocational school open in Attapeu. *Vientiane Times*, 11 January.

Shaw, W., and Prak Chan Thul. 2005. Remote provinces to hook up with Laos, Vietnam. *Cambodia Daily*, 14 July.

Shoemaker, B., I. G. Baird, and M. Baird. 2001. *The People and their River: A Survey of River-Based Livelihoods in the Xe Bang Fai River Basin in Central Lao PDR*. Lao PDR-Canada Fund for Local Initiatives, Vientiane, 79 pp.

Sidwell, P., and P. Jacq. 2003. *A Handbook of Comparative Bahnaric, Vol. 1: West Bahnaric*. Pacific Linguistics, Australian National University, Canberra, 225 pp.

Singh, S., R. Boonratana, M. Bezuijen, and A. Phonvisay 2006. Trade in natural resources in Attapeu Province, Lao PDR: An assessment of the wildlife trade. TRAFFIC, MWBP, Vientiane, 92 pp.

Southivongnorath, S. 2005. Electricity expansion needs foreign funds. *Vientiane Times*, 17 August.

Showler, D. A., P. Davidson, K. Salivong, and C. Vongkhamheng. 1998. A wildlife and habitat survey of the southern border area of Xe Sap National Biodiversity Conservation Area and Dakchung Plateau, Xekong Province, Lao PDR. Wildlife Conservation Society, Vientiane.

Simms, P., and S. Simms. 1999. *The Kingdom of Laos: Six Hundred Years of History*. Curzon, Richmond, Surrey, UK, 240 pp.

Southivongnorath, S. 2006. EDL demands prompt payment. *Vientiane Times*, 12 January.

Sparkes, S. 2000. TA for capacity-building for environment and social management in energy and transport. Case study 2: Houay Ho Hydropower Project (TAR Lao 3501), ADB, Vientiane, 21 pp.

State Planning Committee. 2000a. Poverty in the Lao PDR. Participatory Poverty Assessment (PPA), Vientiane, 26 pp.

State Planning Committee. 2000b. Agriculture statistics study 1998/99: Attapeu Province. Vientiane.

State Planning Committee. 2000c. Agriculture statistics study 1998/99: Xekong Province. Vientiane.

State Planning Committee and National Statistical Center. 1999. The households of Lao PDR (socio and economic indicators 1997-98). SPC and NSC, Vientiane.

Statistics Center and State Planning and Cooperation. 2004. 2003 Population census. Vientiane.

Stellman, J. M., S. D. Stellman, R. Christian, T. Weber, and C. Tomasallo. 2003. The extent and patterns of usage of Agent Orange and other herbicides in Vietnam. *Nature* 433: 681-687.

Steinmetz, R., T. Stones, and T. Chan-ard. 1999. An ecological survey of habitats, wildlife, and people in Xe Sap National Biodiversity Conservation Area, Saravan Province, Lao PDR. World Wide Fund for Nature—Thailand Program Office, Bangkok.

Stone, T. 1999. A bird survey of Xe Sap National Biodiversity Conservation Area, Saravan

Province, Lao PDR. World Wide Fund for Nature—Thailand Program Office, Bangkok.

Stuart, B. L., and T. Chan-ard. 2005. Two new *Huia* (Amphibia: Ranidae) from Laos and Thailand. *Copeia* (2): 279-289.

Stuart, B. L., N. L. Orlov, and T. Chan-ard. 2005. A new cascade frog (Amphibia: Ranidae) from Laos and Vietnam. *Raffles Bull. Zool.* 53(1): 125-131.

Stuart-Fox, M. 1998. *The Lao Kingdom of Lan Xang: Rise and Decline.* White Lotus Press, Bangkok, 234 pp.

Stuart-Fox, M. 2001. *Historical Dictionary of Laos* (2nd edn). Asian / Oceanian Historical Dictionaries Series, No. 35, Scarecrow Press, Lanham, Maryland and London, 527 pp.

Sulavan, K., T. Kingsada, and N. A. Costello. 1996. *Katu Traditional Education for Daily Life in Ancient Times.* Institute for Cultural Research, Vientiane, 21 October.

Sulavan, K., T. Kingsada, and N. A. Costello. 1995. *Aspects of Traditional Medicine.* Institute for Cultural Research, Vientiane, 11 August.

Sulavan, K., T. Kingsada, and N. A. Costello. 1994. *Belief and Practice in Katu Agriculture.* Institute for Cultural Research, Vientiane, 8 August.

Sutton, P. L. 2002. The history of Agent Orange use in Viet Nam: An historical overview from a veteran's perspective. Agent Orange/Dioxin Committee, Vietnam Veterans of America, Inc., Silver Spring, Maryland, SummDIOX2002-16. Paper presented at the US–Viet Nam Scientific Conference on Human Health and Environmental Effects of Agent Orange/Dioxins, Hanoi, 3-6 March.

Syvongxay, K. 2006. Attapeu plans to export cash crops. *Vientiane Times*, 6 April: 3.

Thammavongsa, P. 2003a. GTZ says Attapeu project a success. *Vientiane Times*, 8-10 July.

Thammavongsa, P. 2003b. Highlanders happy with lowland lifestyle. *Vientiane Times*, 18-21 July: 15.

Thammavongsa, P. 2004. Xekaman 1 waits on US backing. *Vientiane Times*, 26 July.

Thammavongsa, P. 2006. Hydropower project to benefit Laos, Vietnam. *Vientiane Times*, 9 January.

Thorbjarnarson, J. 2003. Conservation of Siamese crocodiles in Lao PDR: Report of a trip to review the situation concerning the critically endangered Siamese crocodile and make recommendations. Wildlife Conservation Society, Vientiane, 18 pp.

Tractebel. 2001. Tractebel buys into Laos hydro project. Tractebel Press Release, Brussels, 13 September.

Thuan, Try, and Tep Bunnarith. 2007 (In preparation). Sekong river-based livelihoods study in northeast Cambodia, CEPA, Phnom Penh, 65 pp.

Timmins, R. J., W. Duckworth and T. Evans. 1993. A wildlife and habitat survey of the Xe Piane National Biodiversity Conservation Area. LSFCP, Vientiane.

Timmins, R. J. and C. Vongkhamheng. 1996. A preliminary wildlife and habitat survey of Xe Sap National Biodiversity Conservation Area and mountains to the south, Saravan Province, Lao PDR. CPAWM/WCS, Vientiane.

Toye, H. 1968. *Laos: Buffer State or Battleground.* Oxford University Press, London, 245 pp.

Transnational Radical Party. 2004. Civil and political rights. Written statement submitted to the Commission on Human Rights of the United Nations Economic and Social Council, Sixth Session, Item 11 of the provisional agenda, 10 March 2004, Office of the UN High Commissioner for Human Rights, Geneva.

Turton, A. 1998. Thai institutions of slavery. Pp. 411-457. In G. Condominas (ed.), *Formes extrêmes de dépendence: Contributions à l'étude de l'esclavage en Asie du Sud-Est,* EHESS, Paris.

UN Development Program. 1997. Socio-economic profile of Xekong Province. Rural Development Program Formulation, UNDP Lao PDR, Vientiane, 86 pp.

UN Development Program. 1999a. Database. Dakchung. General characteristics. IRAP with Rural Development Committee MCTPC/UNDP Project LAO/95/001, Xekong, 152 pp.

UN Development Program. 1999b. Database. Dakchung. Agriculture. IRAP with Rural Development Committee MCTPC/UNDP Project LAO/95/001, Xekong, 171 pp.

UN Development Program. 1999c. Database. Kalum. General characteristics. IRAP with Rural Development Committee MCTPC/UNDP Project LAO/95/001, Xekong, 117 pp.

UN Development Program. 1999d. Database. Kalum. Agriculture. IRAP with Rural Development Committee MCTPC/UNDP Project LAO/95/001, Xekong, 118 pp.

UN Development Program. 1999e. Socio-economic and access profile. Kalum IRAP with Rural Development Committee MCTPC/UNDP Project LAO/95/001, Xekong, 24 pp.

UN Development Program. 1999f. Preliminary assessment related to spraying of Agent Orange herbicide in A loui District. HHP Newsletter, UNDP, 4(1): Feb-Apr.

US Veteran News and Report. 1991. And yet another photo appears. . . . Kingston, NC, July 1991.

Vaenkeo, S. 2006. Cambodia agrees to purchase electricity from Laos. *Vientiane Times,* 3 November.

References

Van Staaveren, J. 1993. *Interdiction in Southern Laos, 1960-1968*. Center for Air Force History, Washington, DC.

Vandergeest, P. 2003. Land to some tillers: Development-induced displacements in Laos. *International Soc.l Sci. J.* 55(1): 47-56.

Vaughan, M. 2006. Ord River awash with Lao bauxite. *Mining News*, 28 February 2006 <www.miningnews.net/storyView.asp?StoryID=66067>.

Vientiane Times. 2004a. Province focuses on water, sanitation needs. 2 March.

Vientiane Times. 2004b. Attapeu highway to finish construction soon. 16 March.

Vientiane Times. 2004c. Second phase of road 18 underway in Attapeu. 6 July.

Vientiane Times. 2004d. Xekong people secure water use. 7 July.

Vientiane Times. 2004e. More than 30 villages in Xekong lack schools. 15 September.

Vientiane Times. 2004f. Slash and burn cut in Xekong. 14 October.

Vientiane Times. 2004g. Revenue increases in Attapeu. 4 November.

Vientiane Times. 2004h. Xekong to replant trees lost to felling. 28 November.

Vientiane Times. 2004i. Xekong warns of looming rice shortage. 13 December.

Vientiane Times. 2004j. Industry expanding in Xekong. 21 December.

Vientiane Times. 2005a. Champasak coffee down. 18 March: 2.

Vientiane Times. 2005b. Champasak races ahead. 25 March: 12.

Vientiane Times. 2005c. Champasak dry rice harvest down. 28 March: 2.

Vientiane Times. 2005d. Road heading to sea. 28 March: 2.

Vientiane Times. 2005e. Coffee prices up, production down. 19 April: 7.

Vientiane Times. 2005f. Xekong farming. 13 April: 2.

Vientiane Times. 2005g. Smuggling chickens discovered. 26 April: 2.

Vientiane Times. 2005h. Xekong HIV/Aids campaign. 5 May: 2.

Vientiane Times. 2005i. Kalum children unable to study. 6 May: 2.

Vientiane Times. 2005j. Villagers encroach on conservation areas. 13 May: 3.

Vientiane Times. 2005k. Xekong's opportunities for development. 19 May: 2.

Vientiane Times. 2005l. Xekong rice harvest underway. 23 May: 2.

Vientiane Times. 2005m. Preparing for Arbour Day in Xekong. 24 May: 2.

Vientiane Times. 2005n. Xekong rubber tree plantation. 24 May: 2.

Vientiane Times. 2005o. World Environment Day celebrated in Attapeu. 7 June.

Vientiane Times. 2005p. Over 68,000 fingerlings to be released. 12 July.

Vientiane Times. 2005q. Protective umbrella for wildlife, aquatic species. 13 July.

Vientiane Times. 2005r. New village in Kaleum District. 8 September.

Vientiane Times. 2005s. Russia to develop Lao hydropower. 23 December.

Vientiane Times. 2005t. Xekong teaches AIDS prevention. 29 December.

Vientiane Times. 2006a. Xekong grows dry season rice. 17 February.

Vientiane Times. 2006b. Xekong still living in poverty. 29 March.

Vientiane Times. 2006c. Xekong Province needs funding for road works. 3 April: 3.

Vientiane Times. 2006d. Russia to increase industrial investment in Laos. 26 April: 1.

Vientiane Times. 2006e. Laos to export electricity to Cambodia. 12 June.

Vientiane Times. 2006f. Power stations surge forward. 24 October.

Vientiane Times. 2007. Deputy PM raises alarm on declining forests. 1 March: 1.

Vietnam News. 2006. Hearing delayed in Agent Orange case. Hanoi, 11 May: 3.

Vietnam News Agency. 2003a. Viet Nam to join Laos in building hydropower plant. Hanoi, 30 June.

Vietnam News Agency. 2003b. Vietnamese company invests in building power plant in Laos. Hanoi, 26 July.

Vietnam News Agency. 2003c. Viet Nam, Laos to build hydro-electric power plants. Hanoi, 12 September.

Vietnam News Agency. 2004a. Laos' power transmission line to be finished next year. Hanoi, 8 June .

Vietnam News Agency. 2004b. Laos and Viet Nam have agreed to build more roads linking the two countries. Hanoi, 10 July.

Vietnam News Agency. 2004c. Vietnam-Laos border gate opens. Hanoi, 3 August.

Vietnam News Agency. 2006. Song Da Corp. to build hydropower project in Laos. Hanoi, 4 March.

Vietnam News Agency. 2007. Business join hands for electricity production in Laos. Hanoi, 6 August.

Viravong, Mala Sila. 1964 (rpt. from 1959). *History of Laos.* Paragon Book Rpt. Corp., New York, 147 pp.

Voice of America News 2007. Laos concerned about dwindling forest areas, 15 March. <www.voanews.com/lao/archive/2007-03/2007-03-15-voa4.cfm>.

Voice of Vietnam. 2004. Tripartite meeting charts development course for the triangle. 21 July 2004, Hanoi. <www.vov.org.vn/2004_07_21/english/chinhtri1.htm>.

Voice of Vietnam. 2006. Vietnamese government funds road projects in Laos. Hanoi, 6 June. <www.tnvn.gov.vn/?page=126andnid=14449>,

Vongmany, S. 2004. Xekong needs funds to fight AIDS. *Vientiane Times,* 21 December.

Vongsavanh, S. 1978. *RLG Military Operations and Activities in the Laotian Panhandle.* Indochina Monographs, US Army Center of Military History, Washington, DC, 120 pp.

Vongsay, P. 2006a. Russian investors ink Xekong agreement. *Vientiane Times,* 13 March.

Vongsay, P. 2006b. Xekhaman 1 hydroelectric power project for Attapeu. *Vientiane Times,* 20 March.

References

Vongsay, P. 2006c. Hydroelectric plant to benefit local community. *Vientiane Times*, 8 May: 7.

Vongsay, P. 2006d. Hydroelectric power project's economic benefits considered. *Vientiane Times*, 28 March.

Vythilingam, I., R. Phetsouvanh, K. Keokenchanh, V. Yengmala, V. Vanisaveth, S. Phompida, and S. L. Hakim. 2003. The prevalence of Anopheles (Diptera: Culicidae) mosquitoes in Sekong Province, Lao PDR in relation to malaria transmission. *Tropical Medicine and International Health* 8(6): 525.

Warner, K. 1991. *Shifting Cultivators: Local Technical Knowledge and Natural Resource Management in Humid Tropics*. Community Forestry Note 8, FAO of the UN, Rome, 80 pp.

Watershed. 1996. "Promoting the plantation of economic trees": Asia Tech in Laos. *Watershed* 2(1): 15-16.

Watershed. 2004. Making money from trees? Commercial tree plantations in Lao PDR. *Watershed* 9(3): 19-29.

Welcomme, R., and C. Vidthayanon. 1999. Report on the impacts of introductions and stocking in the Mekong Basin and policies for their control. Mekong River Commission, Phnom Penh.

Wester, L., and S. Vongvanit. 1995. Biological diversity and community lore in northeastern Thailand. *J. of Ethnobiology* 15(1): 71-87.

Westing, A. H. (ed.) 1993. *Transfrontier Reserves for Peace and Nature: A Contribution to Human Security*. UN Environment Program, Nairobi, 127 pp.

Whitaker, D. P., H. A. Barth, S. M. Berman, J. M. Heimann, J. E. MacDonald, K. W. Martindale, and R. Shinn. 1972. *Area Handbook for Laos*. US Government Printing Office, Washington, DC, 337 pp.

Wildlife Conservation Society. 1995. Results of a survey of terrestrial wildlife in the area to be affected by the proposed Xenamnoi–Xepian hydroelectric project. Wildlife Conservation Society, Vientiane.

Wilson, C. M. 1992. Champassak in the nineteenth century: The survival of southern Lao culture. Paper presented at the Cultural Crossroads of Asia Seminar, 24-26 July, Southeast Asian Studies Summer Institute, University of Washington, Seattle, 124 pp.

Wilson, C. M. 1997. The holy man in the history of Thailand and Laos. *J. of Southeast Asian Studies* 28(2): 345-364.

Wiphakphachonkij, Toem. 1987. *Prawattisat Isan* [In Thai]. Rpt. from 1970 (*Song Fang Khong*). *Munnitthi Khrongkan Tamrasangkhomsat lae Manutsat*, Bangkok.

World Bank. 2001. Project Appraisal document on a proposed credit in the amount of

(US$16.70 M equivalent) to the Lao People's Democratic Republic for an agricultural development project. Rural Development and Natural Resources Sector Unit, East Asia and Pacific Region, World Bank, Washington DC, 79 pp.

World Bank. 2004. GEF project brief on a proposed credit in the amount of USD20 million equivalent and proposed grant from the Global Environment Facility Trust Fund in the amount of USD3.75 million to the Lao People's Democratic Republic for a second southern provincial rural electrification project, Phase 1. Energy Sector Unit, Infrastructure Dept., East Asia and Pacific Region, World Bank, Washington, DC, 151 pp.

Worldwide Fund for Nature. 1997. Rapid and participatory biodiversity assessments (BIO-RAP) in Xe Piane NBCA. WWF-Thailand Project Office and Burapha Development Consultants, Global Environmental Trust Fund, National Biodiversity Conservation Areas Program in Lao PDR, Vientiane, 182 pp. +

Worldwide Fund for Nature. 2001. Attapeu forest management project. Lao PDR. Draft project document submitted to the Danish Ministry of Foreign Affairs, DANIDA, Vientiane, 67 pp.

Worldwide Fund for Nature. 2002a. Field study: Thua Thien Hue Province, Hanoi.

Worldwide Fund for Nature. 2002b. Assessment of the special-use forest system and its management in Thua Thien-Hue Province. Strengthening Protected Area Management in Viet Nam—SPAM Project. WWF Indochina Program, Hanoi and the Forest Protection Dept., Ministry of Agriculture and Rural Development, Hanoi.

Worldwide Fund for Nature. 2003. Community fisheries: Supporting food security and aquatic biodiversity. WWF Indochina Program—Lao Program Office, Vientiane.

Worldwide Fund for Nature. 2005a. The Xekong sustainable forestry project (XEFOR). Project Fact Sheet. WWF Indochina Program—Lao Program Office, Vientiane.

Worldwide Fund for Nature. 2005b. The Xekong sustainable forestry project (XEFOR). Project brief—February 2005. WWF Indochina Program—Lao Program Office, Vientiane.

Worldwide Fund for Nature. 2005c. Development comes at a cost: Conserving the Xe Kong River basin in Lao PDR in the face of rapid modernization. Living Documents, DGIS-TMF Program, Gland, Switzerland, 23 pp.

Wyatt, A. B. 2004. Infrastructure development and BOOT in Laos and Vietnam: A case study of collective action and risk in transitional developing economies. PhD diss., Division of Geography, School of Geosciences, University of Sydney, 316 pp.

Wyatt, D. K. 1963. Siam and Laos, 1767–1827. *J. of Southeast Asia History* 4(2): 13-32.

Xainyavong, S., K. Nyounnalath, H. Soichi, and N. Futoshi. 2003. *The Life and House of the*

References

Tariang People. Institute for Culture Research, Ministry of Information and Culture, Vientiane, 206 pp.

Xaydala, K. and S. Ketphanh. 2000. Non-timber forest products with commercial potential in Lao PDR. Forestry Research Center, NAFRI/IUCN and NAFRI/CARE, FRC/NTFP/Technical Paper #1, Vientiane.

Xayasomroth, K. 2005. Plantation du hévéas. *Le Renovateur* (Vientiane). <www.lerenovateur.org.la/Contents/2005-347/Plantation.htm>.

Xekong Province Lao Front for National Construction. 2007. *The Ethnic Groups of Xekong Province, Lao PDR* [In Lao]. Vientiane, 89 pp.

Index

Note: Because of frequent usage, the Xekong River as well as the main provinces (Champassak, Sekong, Attapeu) and main districts within those provinces are not listed here.

Index